2000

Guidebook To

CALIFORNIA

TAXES

Includes Personal

Income Tax Return

Preparation Guide

CCH Editorial Staff Publication
Russell S. Bock, Consultant

Certified Public Accountant,
Consultant to Ernst & Young;
Former Lecturer in Tax
Accounting, University of
Southern California and
University of California,
Los Angeles

CCH INCORPORATED
Chicago

This publication is designed to provide accurate and authoritative information in regard to the subject matter covered. It is sold with the understanding that the publisher is not engaged in rendering legal, accounting, or other professional service. If legal advice or other expert assistance is required, the services of a competent professional person should be sought.

ISBN 0-8080-0401-8

No claim is made to original government works; however, the gathering, compilation, magnetic translation, digital conversion, and arrangement of such materials, the historical, statutory and other notes and references, as well as commentary and materials in the Product or Publication, are subject to CCH's copyright.

PREFACE

This *Guidebook* gives a general picture of the taxes imposed by the state of California and the general property tax levied by the local governments. All 1999 legislative amendments received as of press time are reflected, and references to California and federal laws are to the laws as of the date of publication of this book.

The emphasis is on the law applicable to the filing of income tax returns in 2000 for the 1999 tax year. However, if legislation has made changes effective after 1999, we have tried to note this also, with an indication of the effective date to avoid confusion.

The taxes of major interest—income and sales and use—are discussed in detail. Other California taxes, including estate taxes, are summarized, with particular emphasis on application, exemptions, returns, and payment.

Throughout the *Guidebook,* tax tips are highlighted to help practitioners avoid pitfalls and use the tax laws to their best advantage.

The *Guidebook* is designed as a quick reference work, describing the general provisions of the various tax laws, regulations, and administrative practices. It is useful to tax practitioners, businesspersons, and others who prepare or file California returns or who are required to deal with California taxes.

The *Guidebook* is not designed to eliminate the necessity of referring to the law and regulations for answers to complicated problems, nor is it intended to take the place of detailed reference works such as the CCH CALIFORNIA TAX REPORTS. With this in mind, specific references to the publisher's California and federal tax products are inserted in most paragraphs. By assuming some knowledge of federal taxes, the *Guidebook* is able to provide a concise, readable treatment of California taxes that will supply a complete answer to most questions and will serve as a time-saving aid where it does not provide the complete answer.

With the 1987 edition, Mr. Russell S. Bock relinquished his role as primary author of the *Guidebook To California Taxes,* but continues in close association as a valued consultant. For almost 40 years, Mr. Bock set the standard for accuracy and clarity in explaining California taxes, and with his continuing guidance, we are confident in our dedication to maintaining the *Guidebook* as the premier professional handbook that it had been throughout his tenure.

SCOPE OF THE BOOK

This *Guidebook* is designed to do four things:

1. Provide a quick step-by-step guide to the preparation of individual resident, nonresident, and part-year resident income tax returns.

2. Give a general picture of the impact and pattern of all taxes levied by the state of California and the general property tax levied by local governmental units.

3. Provide a readable quick-reference work for the personal income tax and the tax on corporate income. As such, it explains briefly what the California law provides and indicates whether the California provision is the same as federal law.

4. Analyze and explain the differences, in most cases, between California and federal law.

HOW TO USE THE BOOK

1. If you know the section number of the comparable federal law on the point in which you are interested, consult the Federal-California Cross-Reference Table and Index at the beginning of the portion of the book devoted to the tax involved.

2. If you know the section number of the California law, consult the California-Federal Cross-Reference Table and Index.

HOW TO USE THE RETURN PREPARATION GUIDE

1. Information can easily be found by consulting the Table of Contents to the *Guidebook* for residents' returns at page 41, or for nonresidents' and part-year residents' returns at page 63.

2. Explanations relating to specific lines on the residents' return can be found by consulting the cross-reference chart at page 43.

HIGHLIGHTS OF 1999 CALIFORNIA TAX CHANGES

The most important 1999 California tax changes received by press time are noted in the "Highlights of 1999 California Tax Changes" section of the *Guidebook,* beginning on page 5. This useful reference gives the practitioner up-to-the-minute information on changes in tax legislation.

FINDERS

The practitioner may find the information wanted by consulting the general Table of Contents at the beginning of the *Guidebook,* the Table of Contents at the beginning of each chapter, the Topical Index, the Table of Cases Cited, the Table of Franchise Tax Board Legal Rulings, or the Summary of Principal Items of 1999 Legislation.

The Topical Index is a useful tool. Specific taxes and information on rates, allocations, credits, exemptions, returns, payments, collection, penalties, and remedies are thoroughly indexed and cross-referenced to paragraph numbers in the *Guidebook.*

December 1999

HIGHLIGHTS OF 1999 CALIFORNIA TAX CHANGES

California conformed in 1999 to some of the federal income tax amendments made by the IRS Restructuring and Reform Act of 1998. Highlights of these amendments and other 1999 California tax changes are noted below.

Taxpayers and Rates

● *Personal income tax filing thresholds increased*

For taxable years beginning after 1998, the personal income tax filing thresholds are increased to reflect any dependency credit or credit for old age that may be claimed (see ¶ 104).

● *Minimum tax reduced for new, small corporations*

For income years beginning after 1998, the minimum franchise tax payable by new, small corporations for their first two years of business is reduced to $300 and $500, respectively, and is completely eliminated for corporations that incorporate or qualify to do business after 1999. Also, the prepayment requirement is eliminated for all corporations, except credit unions, after 2000 (see ¶ 809).

● *State-chartered credit unions exemption enacted*

State-chartered credit unions are exempt from corporation franchise (income) tax beginning with the 1999 income year (see ¶ 804).

● *LLC qualifications expanded*

Effective January 1, 2000, limited liability company (LLC) membership of one or more is valid and adequate (see ¶ 618).

● *LLC fees increased*

For 1999, LLC fees are increased (see ¶ 618).

Credits

● *Dependent exemption credit decreased*

The dependent exemption credit is decreased from $253 to $227 for the 1999 taxable year and is thereafter indexed for inflation (see ¶ 109).

● *Exemption credits may reduce regular tax below tentative minimum tax*

For taxable years beginning after 1998, personal, dependent, blind, and senior exemption credits may reduce a taxpayer's regular tax below the tentative minimum tax, after the allowance of the minimum tax credit (see ¶ 112a).

● *Research and development credit increased*

For taxable and income years beginning after 1998, the credit for qualified research expenses is increased from 11% to 12% (see ¶ 139, ¶ 810a).

● *Eligibility for dependent parent credit clarified*

Taxpayers are ineligible to claim the dependent parent credit if they qualify to file as a head of household or as a surviving spouse, effective for taxable years beginning after 1998 (see ¶ 125a).

Gains and Losses

● *Small business stock exclusion expanded*

For taxable years beginning after 1998, the personal income tax exclusion of gain on the sale or exchange of qualified small business stock is no longer limited to stock that was originally issued before January 1, 1999 (see ¶ 513).

Conformity to Federal Law

For taxable and income years beginning after 1998 (except as noted below), California conforms to federal amendments relating to:

—the treatment of Roth individual retirement account (IRA) rollovers, effective for taxable years beginning after 1997 (see ¶ 318);

—the amount of assets that may be currently expensed under IRC Sec. 179 (see ¶ 310a);

—the amount that may be deducted for health insurance payments made by self-employed individuals (see ¶ 301);

—the definition of a "principal place of business" for purposes of home office expense deductions (see ¶ 301);

—use of the same recovery periods for depreciating tangible personal property and pollution control facilities for alternative minimum tax (AMT) purposes as for regular tax purposes (see ¶ 112a, ¶ 810);

—the *de minimis* threshold for imposition of penalties for underpayment of personal income tax (see ¶ 107a);

—the gross income exclusion for distributions from Medicare Plus Choice medical savings accounts (see ¶ 246);

—applicable to liabilities remaining unpaid as of October 10, 1999, the requirements for obtaining innocent spouse relief or electing separate liability (see ¶ 104a, ¶ 710);

—the waiver of early withdrawal penalties on a post-1999 distribution from a qualified retirement plan or IRA when the distribution is due to a notice to withhold from the plan (see ¶ 206);

—generally applicable after October 10, 1999, prohibited disclosures of software trade secrets (see ¶ 717);

—applicable to taxable years ending after October 10, 1999, the suspension of interest and penalties upon failure to provide notice of an individual's tax liability within an 18-month period (see ¶ 709, ¶ 710);

—effective October 10, 1999, the guaranteed availability of installment agreements for individuals under certain circumstances (see ¶ 107); and

—effective for costs, fees, and expenses incurred and services performed after April 7, 2000, expanded authority to award costs and fees (see ¶ 701, ¶ 701a, ¶ 1401, ¶ 1401a).

Additional Deductions and Exclusions

● *Special carryovers provided for losses from winter freeze*

For taxable and income years beginning after 1998, taxpayers who suffered losses as a result of the freeze that occurred in 1998-99 in designated disaster areas may claim extended carryovers of those losses (see ¶ 307, ¶ 1004).

● *Holocaust and internment victim compensation exclusion expanded*

For taxable years beginning after 1998, an exclusion from gross income is available to (1) holocaust victims, or their heirs or beneficiaries, for any settlements received for claims against an entity or individual for any recovered asset and (2) people that received payments from the Canadian government in reparation for interning people of Japanese ancestry during World War II (see ¶ 247).

Special Tax Incentives

● *Tax incentives for LAMBRA businesses revised*

For taxable and income years beginning after 1998, the sunset date for the special tax incentives provided to local agency military base recovery area (LAMBRA) businesses is repealed, the employer's credit for LAMBRA wages and the LAMBRA sales and use tax credit are modified, and the expense deduction for LAMBRA property is revised (see ¶ 133, ¶ 136, ¶ 309, ¶ 310f, ¶ 810a, ¶ 1008, ¶ 1018).

Returns and Payment

● *Estimated tax safe harbor thresholds increased*

For taxable years beginning after 1998, the estimated tax safe harbor threshold for high-income individuals is increased (see ¶ 107a).

● *Requirements for reporting federal changes clarified and expanded*

Effective for federal determinations that become final after 1999, the "date of a final federal determination" from which a California personal income or corporation franchise (income) taxpayer must report changes to the Franchise Tax Board (FTB) or file for a refund or credit is defined, and corporation franchise (income) taxpayers must report all federal changes to the FTB (see ¶ 104, ¶ 805).

● *Corporation, partnership, and LLC filing and payment deadlines revised*

Beginning January 1, 1999, corporations must file returns and pay taxes by the 15th day of the third month after the close of their income year, and partnerships, limited partnerships, and LLCs not treated as corporations must file returns and pay taxes and fees by the 15th day of the fourth month following the close of their taxable year (see ¶ 616, ¶ 618, ¶ 805).

● *Information statement filing requirements eased*

Effective January 1, 2000, the information statement required to be filed by corporations and LLCs need only be filed biennially (see ¶ 618, ¶ 805).

● *Filing status may be revised*

Effective January 1, 2000, the FTB may revise a taxpayer's California filing status if it is based on an incorrect federal filing status (see ¶ 110).

● *Credit card payments allowed*

Personal income taxpayers may use credit cards to pay their 1999 taxes and taxes owed for prior years (see ¶ 107).

● *Treatment of deposits outlined*

Effective January 1, 2000, a cash bond deposited to stop the running of interest on a proposed personal income or corporation franchise (income) tax deficiency assessment generally is not treated as a payment of tax for purposes of the statute of limitations for refunds (see ¶ 715, ¶ 716, ¶ 1415, ¶ 1416).

Taxpayer Remedies

● *Interest abatement provisions expanded*

Applicable to disasters declared after 1997 with respect to taxable years beginning after 1997, the FTB must abate interest for certain individuals who incurred losses in areas declared by the Governor to be disaster areas (see ¶ 709). Also, the FTB may abate interest accruing on a deficiency based on a final federal determination of tax if interest was abated on the related federal deficiency (see ¶ 709, ¶ 1409).

● *FTB allowed to compromise tax liabilities*

Effective October 10, 1999, the FTB may administratively compromise final personal income and corporation franchise (income) tax liabilities (see ¶ 720, ¶ 1419).

● *Period for filing credit or refund claim modified*

Applicable to all claims for which the statute of limitations has not expired as of January 1, 2000, the prescribed period for filing a credit or refund claim is modified (see ¶ 715, ¶ 1415).

● *Employee relief from liability for unremitted withholdings*

Beginning October 10, 1999, an employee's tax account may be credited for withheld earnings that were not remitted to the FTB by the employee's employer (see ¶ 712).

SUMMARY OF PRINCIPAL ITEMS OF 1999
LEGISLATION
AFFECTING CALIFORNIA PERSONAL INCOME TAX
AND TAXES ON CORPORATE INCOME

Law Section	Comparable Federal	Summary of Change
PERSONAL INCOME TAX:		
17039	None	Allows exemption credits to reduce regular tax below tentative minimum tax
17052.12	41	Increases research and development credit
17053.45	None	Revises LAMBRA sales and use tax credit
17054.5	None	Revises dependent parent credit
17085.7	72	Waives penalties for early withdrawal from plan or account subject to levy
17156.5	None	Provides exclusion for internment compensation
17207	165	Allows deductions for losses from 1998-99 freeze
17268	None	Repeals LAMBRA expense deduction sunset date
17273	162(*l*)	Increases self-employed health insurance deduction
17276.5	172	Repeals LAMBRA NOL deduction sunset date
17507.6	408A	Conforms Roth IRA provisions to federal law
18152.5	1202	Expands small business stock gain exclusion
ADMINISTRATION:		
18501	6012(a)	Revises return filing thresholds
18521	6013	Filing status provisions revised
18533-34	6015	Innocent spouse relief expanded
18601	6072(d)	Corporate return due date modified
18622	None	Corporate reporting of federal return changes modified
18673	None	Employee relief from liability for unremitted withholdings provided
19005	None	Credit card payments authorized
19008	6159	Availability of installment agreements expanded
19041.5	None	Specifies treatment of deposits
19059	6213	Reporting of federal return changes modified
19064	7609	Suspends running of limitations period
19104	6601	Interest abatement allowed
19109	6404	Expands abatement of interest for disaster victims
19116	6404	Suspends interest and penalties
19306	6511	Due date for credit or refund revised
19443	None	Administrative compromises of tax liability authorized
19504.5	7612	Improper disclosure of software trade secrets prohibited
19542.3	7213	Imposes penalty for improper disclosure of software trade secrets
19705	None	Imposes penalty related to tax liability compromises
19717	7430	Revises criteria for awarding costs and fees
21013	7430	Expands authority to award costs and fees
TAXES ON CORPORATE INCOME:		
23153	None	Revises minimum tax requirements
23221	None	Revises minimum tax requirements
23609	41	Increases research and development credit
23622.8	None	Revises manufacturing enchancement area credit
23645	None	Revises LAMBRA sales and use tax credit
23701y	501(c)	Exempts state-chartered credit unions
24347.5	165	Allows deductions for losses from 1998-99 freeze
24416.5	172	Repeals LAMRA NOL deduction sunset date

CONTENTS

CONTENTS

PART VI—DEATH TAXES

PART VII—MISCELLANEOUS TAXES

PART VIII—DIRECTORY/RESOURCES

PART IX—DOING BUSINESS IN CALIFORNIA

FOCUS ON ELECTRONIC COMMERCE

INTRODUCTION TO INTERNET/ELECTRONIC COMMERCE

⋙→CAUTION: Paragraph references are to the CCH California Tax Reports.

WHAT IS ELECTRONIC COMMERCE?

For purposes of taxation, the term "electronic commerce" can be understood to mean the sale of tangible or intangible goods or services by electronic means. In most cases, this means sales transactions in which the seller and the buyer communicate over the Internet or a private network such as America Online. The object of the sale is frequently a product in electronic form or a service that is also delivered over the Internet, but it may also be tangible personal property or an electronic product in tangible form, such as a prepaid phone card, delivered by conventional means. Activities that are related to a sale, such as advertising, shopping, ordering, and payment, are also considered to be electronic commerce when they occur over the Internet or a private network.

Sales/use tax may apply to a variety of transactions in an electronic commerce environment. This may include taxes on charges for tangible personal property or taxable services purchased via the Internet, or intangible personal property that may or may not be comparable to tangible personal property otherwise available in a traditional "Main Street" environment. Sales tax on Internet access services is also imposed by some states.

● *Federal Internet Tax Freedom Act*

The Federal Internet Tax Freedom Act (P.L.105-277, 112 Stat. 2681) bars state and local governments from imposing multiple or discriminatory taxes on electronic commerce, including taxes on Internet access, for a period of three years from its enactment date of October 21, 1998. The moratorium does not apply to taxes that were imposed and enforced prior to October 1, 1998 (see ¶ 60-445).

Prohibited multiple taxes are taxes imposed by a state or local government on the same, or essentially the same, transactions in electronic commerce that are also subject to a tax imposed by another state or local government without a corresponding credit or resale exemption certificate for taxes paid in other jurisdictions. The moratorium against multiple taxes does not include taxes imposed within a state by the state or by one or more local governments within the state on the same electronic commerce, nor does it prohibit other taxes from being imposed on persons who are engaged in electronic commerce even though that commerce has already been subject to a sales/use tax.

Prohibited discriminatory taxes are: (1) taxes imposed on electronic commerce transactions that are not generally imposed and legally collectible on other transactions that involve similar property, goods, services, or information; (2) taxes imposed on electronic commerce transactions at a different rate

⋙→*CAUTION: Paragraph references are to the CCH California Tax Reports.*

from that imposed on other transactions involving similar property, goods, services, or information, unless the rate is lower as part of a phase-out of the tax over a five-year or lesser period; (3) collection or payment obligations imposed upon a different person or entity than would apply if the transaction were not transacted via electronic commerce; (4) classification of Internet access service providers or online service providers for purposes of imposing on such providers a higher rate of tax than is imposed on providers of similar information delivered through other means; (5) collection obligations imposed on a remote seller on the basis of the in-state accessibility of the seller's out-of-state computer server, except for taxes on Internet access that were imposed and enforced prior to October 1, 1998; and (6) collection obligations imposed on a remote seller solely because the Internet access service or online service provider is deemed to be the remote seller's agent on the basis of the remote seller's display of information or content on the out-of-state server or because orders are processed through the out-of-state server.

● *Sales subject to tax*

Tangible personal property: The California sales tax is imposed on sales of tangible personal property at retail. The California use tax is imposed on the storage, use, or other consumption in California of tangible personal property purchased from any retailer for storage, use, or other consumption in California. Charges for producing, fabricating, processing, printing, imprinting, or otherwise physically altering, modifying, or treating consumer-furnished tangible personal property (cards, tapes, disks, etc.), including charges for recording or otherwise incorporating information on or into such tangible personal property, are generally subject to sales/use tax (see ¶ 60-210).

Prewritten programs transferred to the customer in the form of storage media or by listing the program instructions on coding sheets are subject to California sales/use tax, whether they are usable as written or whether they must be modified, adapted, and tested to meet the customer's particular needs. However, charges for custom modifications to prewritten programs are notaxable if the charges for the modifications are separately stated. The tax applies to the sale or lease of the storage media or coding sheets on which or into which such prewritten (canned) programs have been recorded, coded, or punched. The sale or lease of a prewritten program is not subject to California sales/use tax if the program is transferred by remote telecommunications from the seller's place of business, to or through the purchaser's computer and the purchaser does not obtain possession of any tangible personal property, such as storage media, in the transaction. Likewise, the sale of a prewritten program is not a taxable transaction if the program is installed by the seller on the customer's computer except when the seller transfers title to or possession of storage media or the installation of the program is a part of the sale of the computer (see ¶ 60-310).

The California sales/use tax does not apply to the sale or lease of a custom computer program, other than a basic operational program, regardless of the form in which the program is transferred. Nor does the tax apply to the transfer of a custom program, or custom programming services performed, in connection with the sale or lease of computer equipment, whether or not the charges for the custom program or programming are separately stated. However, charges for custom modifications to prewritten programs are nontaxable only if the charges for the modifications are separately stated. Otherwise, the charges are taxable as services as part of the sale of the prewritten program. When the charges for modification of a prewritten program are not separately stated, tax applies to the entire charge made to the customer for the modified program unless the modification is so significant that the new program qualifies as a custom program. Written documentation or manuals designed to facilitate the use of a custom computer program by the customer are nontaxable, whether or not a separate charge is made for the documentation or manuals (see ¶ 60-310).

California sales/use tax does not apply to separately stated charges for transportation of property from the point from which shipment is made "directly to the purchaser," provided the transportation is by other than facilities of the retailer. Transportation charges are regarded as "separately stated" only if they are separately set forth in the contract for sale or in a document reflecting that contract, issued contemporaneously with the sale, such as the retailer's invoice. If a separately stated charge is made designated "postage and handling" or "shipping and handling" only that portion of the charge that represents actual postage or actual shipment may be excluded from the measure of tax. A separately stated charge designated "handling" or "handling charge" is not a separate statement of transportation charges. Tax applies to such charges, notwithstanding the fact that postage or shipment charges may or may not be affixed to or noted on the package (see ¶ 61-150).

Dial-up access: Charges made for the use of a computer, on a time-sharing basis, where access to the computer is by means of remote telecommunication are not subject to California sales/use tax (see ¶ 60-310).

California does not impose a sales/use tax or telecommunications tax on Internet access and would be prohibited from doing so under the moratorium imposed by the federal Internet Tax Freedom Act. "Internet access" includes offering or provision of storage, computer processing, and transmission of information that allows a customer to use resources that can be found on the Internet (see ¶ 60-310).

Digitized products: While most states impose sales tax only on tangible goods, whether or not the sale is made on the Internet, the treatment of sales of digitized products transacted via download varies among the states. The transfers may be treated as either tangible or intangible goods or the provision of taxable services.

California considers the sale of digitized products via download as a nontaxable sale of intangible goods. For example, the legal department of the California State Board of Equalization (SBE) has determined that digitized color photographs were not subject to tax, provided that they were furnished via modem or other remote telecommunication, rather than on a storage medium, such as a tape or disk; however, the SBE has also held that digitized satellite images were subject to tax as tangible personal property, because these sales were not transacted via modem or other remote telecommunication (SBE (Sales Tax Counsel) Rulings, 120.0660 (9/19/55), 120.0663 (3/12/96), 120.1200 (7/14/94); ¶ 60-310.71) (see ¶ 60-310, ¶ 60-445).

⇻→*CAUTION: Paragraph references are to the CCH California Tax Reports.*

Services: The taxability of services varies among the states. California does not tax personal or professional services. If in addition to rendering service the service provider regularly sells tangible personal property to consumers, such sales are taxable. If the true object of the contract is the service per se, the transaction is not subject to tax even though some tangible personal property is transferred. For example, a firm that performs business advisory, record keeping, payroll, and tax services for small businesses and furnishes forms, binders, and other property to its clients as an incident to the rendition of its services is the consumer and not the retailer of such tangible personal property. The true object of the contract between the firm and its client is the performance of a service and not the furnishing of tangible personal property (see ¶ 60-665).

California sales/use tax applies to the conversion of customer-furnished data from one physical form of recordation to another physical form of recordation. However, the tax does not apply to developing original information from customer-furnished data. In that case, the tangible personal property used to transmit the original information is merely incidental to the service. Charges for producing, fabricating, processing, printing, imprinting or otherwise physically altering, modifying or treating consumer-furnished tangible personal property (cards, tapes, disks, etc.), including charges for recording or otherwise incorporating information on or into such tangible personal property, are generally subject to tax. A transfer for a consideration of the title or possession of tangible personal property which has been produced, fabricated, or printed to the special order of the customer, including property on which or into which information has been recorded or incorporated, is generally a sale subject to tax. However, if the contract is for the service of researching and developing original information for a customer, tax does not apply, because the tangible personal property used to transmit the original information is merely incidental to the service. Charges for the transfer of computer-generated output are subject to tax where the true object of the contract is the output and not the services rendered in producing the output. Examples include artwork, graphics, and designs (see ¶ 60-310, ¶ 60-665).

Electronic transmissions of information that do not involve the transfer of tangible personal property are not taxable (SBE (Sales Tax Counsel) Ruling 120.1175 (4/29/94); ¶ 60-310.71). Thus, charges for the same data processing activities may be taxable or nontaxable depending on the means of transferring the finished product to the customer. If the customer receives the data on storage media such as tape or disk, the charges are subject to tax. If the data is transferred electronically (modem to modem) and no tangible personal property is transferred, there has been no sale and the tax does not apply (see ¶ 60-310).

Where a data processing firm has entered into a contract that is regarded as a service contract and the data processing firm, pursuant to the contract, transfers to its customer tangible property other than property containing the original information, such as: duplicate copies of storage media; inventory control cards for use by the customer; membership cards for distribution by the customer; labels (other than address labels); microfiche duplicates; or similar items for use, tax applies to the charges made for such items. If no separate charge is made, tax applies to that portion of the charge made by the

⋙➔*CAUTION: Paragraph references are to the CCH California Tax Reports.*

data processing firm that the cost of the additional computer time (if any), cost of materials, and labor cost to produce the items bear to the total job cost (see ¶ 60-310).

● *Nexus and collection responsibility*

Once it is determined that a taxable transaction is involved, it must be determined whether nexus (connection to the state) is sufficient to trigger tax liability and on whom tax collection responsibility rests. Unless a vendor has substantial nexus with the purchaser's state, the state has no constitutional basis for the imposition of income tax or sales/use tax collection responsibility.

Differences between sales tax and income tax nexus: The presence in the state required for sales/use tax nexus is greater than for income tax nexus. The nexus rules for the sales/use tax and the corporate income tax are generally the same: the physical presence of the taxpayers' employees, agents, or property usually creates a taxable connection with the state. However, The U.S. Supreme Court has ruled that some form of physical presence is needed to establish nexus with regard to sales/use taxes (*Quill Corp. v. North Dakota,* 504 US 298 (1992)). There is no such rule with respect to corporate income tax; therefore, intangible property and economic presence could be sufficient to create a filing responsibility for income tax but not for sales/use tax (see ¶ 12-420, ¶ 60-445).

Public Law 86-272 protects a foreign corporation from state income tax if its only business activities in the state are the solicitation of orders for sales of tangible personal property. Solicitation activity related to the sale of services or intangible property, including electronic commerce, is not protected. Consequently, a software company may lose the protection of Public Law 86-272 if it solicits sales in the state, and it distributes some of its products electronically. Mere "solicitation" is not protected if sales involve both tangible and intangible property (see ¶ 12-420).

Sales/use tax: Out-of-state retailers are required by California statute to collect and remit use tax on their retail sales if they are engaged in business in the state. "Engaged in business in the state" includes, in addition to the actual retail sales, various activities that constitute sufficient minimum contacts with the state, including advertising in the state, mail-order solicitation, and solicitation through certain telecommunications methods (see ¶ 60-210).

Sellers are not subject to California sales/use tax when: (1) the buyer orders directly from the out-of-state seller or from the seller's California agent; (2) the goods are shipped from a point outside the state, and (3) there is no participation in the sale by any in-state place of business of the seller or by an agent connected to an in-state place of business (see ¶ 60-210).

A retailer who takes orders from customers in California through a computer telecommunications network located in the state is not "engaged in business" in California, provided that (1) the telecommunications network is not owned by the retailer when orders are taken, (2) the orders result from the electronic display of products on the network, and (3) the network consists substantially of on-line communications services other than the displaying and taking of orders for products (see ¶ 60-210).

≫→*CAUTION: Paragraph references are to the CCH California Tax Reports.*

The extent to which California can in fact compel a person outside its borders to collect its use tax is limited by federal constitutional provisions, notably the Commerce Clause, as construed in the National Bellas Hess and Quill cases (see ¶ 60-210).

An out-of-state retailer's use of a computer server on the Internet to create or maintain a World Wide Web page or site is not considered a factor in determining whether the retailer has a substantial nexus with California. No Internet access provider, or World Wide Web hosting services is deemed the agent or representative of an out-of-state retailer as a result of the service provider maintaining or taking orders via a Web page or site on a computer server that is physically located in California (see ¶ 60-210).

Income tax: The following activities, conducted within California, go beyond mere solicitation; therefore, they are not immune under Public Law 86-272 and subject out-of-state sellers to nexus for California income tax purposes: (1) making repairs or providing maintenance, (2) collecting delinquent accounts; (3) investigating credit worthiness; (4) installation or supervision of installation; (5) conducting training courses, seminars, or lectures; (6) providing engineering functions; (7) handling customer complaints; (8) approving or accepting orders; (9) repossessing property; (10) securing deposits on sales; (11) picking up or replacing damaged or returned property; (12) hiring, training, or supervising personnel; (13) providing shipping information and coordinating deliveries; (14) maintaining a sample or display room in excess of two weeks (14 days) during the tax year; (15) carrying samples for sale, exchange or distribution in any manner for consideration or other value; (16) owning, leasing, maintaining, or otherwise using any of the following facilities or property in-state; (a) repair shop, (b) parts department, (c) purchasing office, (d) employment office, (e) warehouse, (f) meeting place for directors, officers, or employees, (g) stock of goods, (h) telephone answering service, (i) mobile stores, *i.e.,* trucks with driver salesmen, or (j) real property or fixtures of any kind; (17) consigning tangible personal property to any person, including an independent contractor; (18) maintaining, by either an in-state or an out-of-state resident employee, of an office or place of business (in-home or otherwise); and (19) conducting any activity in addition to those described as immune in the following list if it is not an integral part of the solicitation of orders (see ¶ 12-420).

The following activities are immune under Public Law 86-272: (1) advertising campaigns incidental to missionary activities; (2) carrying samples only for display or for distribution without charge or other consideration; (3) owning or furnishing autos to salesmen; (4) passing inquiries and complaints on to home office; (5) incidental and minor advertising, *i.e.,* notice in newspaper that a salesman will be in town at a certain time; (6) missionary sales activities; (7) checking of customers' inventories (for reorder, but not for other purposes); (8) maintaining sample or display room for two weeks (14 days) or less during the tax year; and (9) soliciting of sales by an in-state resident employee of the taxpayer, provided the employee maintains no in-state sales office or place of business (see ¶ 12-420).

P.L. 86-272 provides immunity to certain in-state activities if conducted by an independent contractor that would not be afforded if performed by the

⋙➜*CAUTION: Paragraph references are to the CCH California Tax Reports.*

taxpayer directly. Independent contractors may engage in the following limited activities in the state without the taxpayer's loss of immunity: (1) soliciting sales; (2) making sales; and (3) maintaining a sales office (see ¶ 12-420).

● *Sourcing of sales*

The sourcing to most states of the sale of downloadable digitized products over the Internet depends on whether the state classifies the sale as a sale of tangible personal property, a sale of intangible personal property, or a sale of a service. Generally, a sale of tangible personal property is sourced to its delivery destination and a sale of a service or an intangible is sourced to the state where the income-producing activity took place.

For purposes of the California income tax, foreign corporations allocate income based on a three-factor apportionment formula: property, payroll, and sales. The sales factor is double weighted. Sales of tangible personal property are attributed to California if (1) the property is delivered or shipped to a purchaser in California, and (2) the property shipped from an office, store, warehouse, factory, or other storage place in California, provided that the taxpayer is not taxable in the purchaser's state. Receipts from sales other than sales of tangible personal property are attributed to California if the income producing activity that gave rise to the receipts is performed wholly within California, or the income producing activity is performed within and without California but the greater proportion of the income producing activity is performed in California based on costs of performance (see ¶ 12-585).

FREQUENTLY ASKED QUESTIONS

⇛→CAUTION: Paragraph references are to the CCH California Tax Reports.

Taxability And Nexus

1. QUESTION: Is an out-of-state vendor required to collect sales/use tax on all Internet sales subject to tax?

→ *ANSWER:* No, an out-of-state vendor is not required to collect sales/use tax on Internet sales unless the sales are subject to the tax (see "Taxable Sales," below) and unless the vendor has a sufficient connection (nexus) to the state (see "Connection to the State," below).

2. QUESTION: Is an out-of-state vendor required to pay income tax on income from all Internet sales attributable to the state?

→ *ANSWER:* An out-of-state vendor may make Internet sales into the state without incurring liability for income tax by avoiding nexus (see "Connection to the State," below) even if the vendor has sales attributable to the state (see "Where Sales Occur," below).

Taxable Sales

3. QUESTION: Are services, performed and delivered over the Internet, subject to sales/use tax?

Background: Most states impose a sales tax on some types of services. Some states tax a much larger number of services than others. (Hawaii taxes over 150 and Illinois taxes less than 20). A minority of states impose sales/use tax on on-line content transferred by means of electronic commerce. Some states tax all on-line sales as sales of tangible personal property. Some states tax them as a separate category of taxable services. Some states tax certain "content-related" electronic services, but exempt other similar services.

→ *ANSWER:* Most services in California are not subject to sales/use tax, although tangible personal property furnished in connection with the performance of a service may make the entire transaction taxable. If the service is not otherwise subject to the tax, it is not taxable if performed and delivered electronically. See ¶ 60-445, ¶ 60-665.

4. QUESTION: Are Internet sales of digitized products, manufactured for general retail sale (software, electronic greeting cards, etc.), subject to sales/use tax?

Background: Sales made over the Internet may include tangible goods that are delivered by mail or common carrier, as well as software or other digitized products, services, or information that are transmitted electronically. While sales taxation in most states applies only to tangible goods, the treatment of digitized product transactions via download varies among the states, as either tangible or intangible goods transactions.

≫→*CAUTION: Paragraph references are to the CCH California Tax Reports.*

→ *ANSWER:* In California, digitized products, delivered electronically, are considered intangibles and as such are not subject to tax. They are considered tangible and subject to tax if delivered in hard copy or on a storage medium, such as tape or disk. See ¶ 60-665, ¶ 61-310.

5. QUESTION: Are Internet sales of custom-made software subject to sales/use tax?

Background: Although most states tax canned software sold on a tangible medium as tangible property, most states treat custom software as nontaxable intangible property. A minority of states tax custom software sales as taxable services or as sales of taxable tangible personal property.

→ *ANSWER:* California exempts sales and leases of computer programs (other than programs that are fundamental and necessary to the functioning of a computer) that are prepared to the customer's special order. See ¶ 60-665, ¶ 61-310.

6. QUESTION: Are charges for dial-up access to a computer database, information or other on-line content subject to sales/use tax?

Background: A minority of states impose a sales/use tax on all on-line content transferred by means of electronic commerce. Some states tax specific types of content such as data processing, E-mail, news and weather reports, airline reservations, games, data bases, and software downloads. Some states tax on-line sales as sales of tangible personal property, and some as a separate category of taxable services. Other states classify on-line sales of downloadable content as nontaxable sales of intangible property, not taxable tangible property.

→ *ANSWER:* In California, charges for dial-up access to a computer content are sales of intangible personal property not taxable sales, provided all of the content received by the subscribers is sent over the telephone lines and any hard copies generated are printed by the subscribers themselves. Electronic transmissions of information that do not involve the transfer of tangible personal property are not taxable. See ¶ 60-310.

7. QUESTION: Are Internet sales of on-line or downloadable entertainment and news services subject to sales/use tax?

Background: See Question 6.

→ *ANSWER:* Internet sales of on-line or downloadable entertainment and news services are not subject to California sales/use tax. Neither entertainment nor news services are on the list of enumerated taxable services; therefore, they are not taxable services, and their Internet delivery does not make them taxable (see Answer 3).

8. QUESTION: Are on-line or downloadable newspapers and magazines subject to sales/use tax?

Background: See Question 6.

→ *ANSWER:* On-line or downloadable newspapers and magazines are not subject to California sales/use tax. Although the sale of newspapers and

>>→*CAUTION: Paragraph references are to the CCH California Tax Reports.*

periodicals is generally subject to tax, California would classify these sales as nontaxable sales of intangibles (see Answers 4 and 6).

9. QUESTION: Does California impose a sales/use tax on Internet access?

Background: The federal Internet Tax Freedom Act (P.L.105-277, 112 Stat. 2681) bars state and local governments from imposing multiple or discriminatory taxes on electronic commerce, including taxes on Internet access, for a period of three years from its enactment date of October 21, 1998. The moratorium does not apply to taxes that were imposed and enforced prior to October 1, 1998.

→ *ANSWER:* California does not impose a sales/use tax or telecommunications tax on Internet access. The state would be prohibited from doing so under the moratorium imposed by the federal Internet Tax Freedom Act. See ¶ 60-445.

10. QUESTION: Are charges made for the time-share use of a computer in the state subject to sales/use tax?

Background: Some states that treat the electronic transmission of information content as a taxable computer service impose a sales tax on data processing services, which is defined to include providing computer time. Other states would characterize computer time-share as the lease of tangible personal property.

→ *ANSWER:* Charges made for the use of a computer on a time-sharing basis, where access to the computer is by means of remote telecommunication are not subject to California tax. However, a contract for use of an off-site computer is taxable as a lease if the person or the person's employees direct and control its operation while on the premises where the computer is located. See ¶ 60-310.

11. QUESTION: Are services rendered in connection with the creation, development, or maintenance of a web site, subject to sales/use tax?

Background: The creation, development, or maintenance of a web site could be classified and taxed by various states as a graphic design service, an information service, a data processing service, a computer service, or some other type of service.

→ *ANSWER:* Services rendered in connection with the creation, development, or maintenance of all or part of a web site are not subject to California sales/use tax. Designing and implementing computer systems, consulting services, providing technical help, maintenance of equipment, and consultation as to use of equipment are all nontaxable services unless performed as a part of the sale of tangible personal property. See ¶ 60-310.

12. QUESTION: Is shipping and handling, charged in connection with the delivery of tangible personal property sold over the Internet, included in the basis for the sales/use tax?

Background: Most states do not include the actual costs of shipping goods to the purchaser in the tax base if such costs are separately stated.

≫→*CAUTION: Paragraph references are to the CCH California Tax Reports.*

→ *ANSWER:* The California tax does not apply to separately stated charges for postage or shipping by common carrier, but only to the extent of actual postage or shipping fees. Handling charges are taxable. See ¶ 61-150.

Connection to the State

13. QUESTION: Can the state require an out-of-state retailer, maintaining a Web page on a computer server in the state, to collect sales/use tax on mail order sales into the state?

Background: Web sites could be classified by some states as electronic advertising or intangible property. However, some states hold that Web sites located on a third-party computer server in the state and for which a monthly or annual fee is paid, are leases of tangible personal property, which create a physical presence in the state sufficient to constitute nexus for sales/use tax.

→ *ANSWER:* An out-of-state retailer's use of a computer server on the Internet to create or maintain a World Wide Web page or site is not considered a factor in determining whether the retailer has a substantial nexus with California for sales/use tax purposes. No Internet service provider, online service provider, internetwork communication service provider, or other Internet access provider, or World Wide Web hosting services are deemed the agent or representative of an out-of-state retailer as a result of the service provider maintaining or taking orders via a web page or site on a computer server that is physically located in California. See ¶ 60-445.

14. QUESTION: Is an out-of-state retailer's use of an in-state server on the Internet to create or maintain a World Wide Web page or site considered a factor in determining whether the retailer has a substantial nexus with California for income tax purposes?

Background: In some states, Web sites could be classed as electronic advertising or intangible property and taxed, or exempted, as such. However, other states would take the position that contracts in which a monthly or annual fee is paid for sites located on a third-party server in the state are leases of tangible personal property (*e.g.,* the computer), which create a physical presence in the state, or that such a site constitutes intangible property presence. However, even if this is the case, the sites are likely to be considered a *de minimis* presence.

→ *ANSWER:* There is no direct California law on this point; however, the rule stated in ANSWER 13 follows the general trend toward liberalism in Internet taxation and declares that maintaining a Web page on an in-state server is not a factor in determining nexus, at least for sales/use tax purposes. See ¶ 60-445.

15. QUESTION: Can the state require an out-of-state retailer, without sufficient nexus to be subject to the income tax, to collect sales/use tax on sales made over the Internet?

Background: The U.S. Supreme Court has preempted the rules in this area (see the Answer to this Question).

⇶→*CAUTION: Paragraph references are to the CCH California Tax Reports.*

→ *ANSWER:* No, the presence in the state required for sales/use tax nexus is greater than for income tax nexus. The nexus rules for the sales/use tax and the corporate income tax are generally the same: the physical presence of the taxpayers' employees, agents, or property usually create a taxable connection with the state. However, The U.S. Supreme Court has ruled that some form of physical presence is needed to establish nexus with regard to sales and use taxes (*Quill Corp. v. North Dakota,* 504 U.S. 298 (1992)). There is no such rule with respect to corporate income tax; therefore, intangible property and economic presence could be sufficient to create a filing responsibility for income tax but not for sales/use tax. See ¶ 12-420, ¶ 60-445.

16. QUESTION: Can an out-of-state retailer, without sufficient nexus to be subject to the sales/use tax, have nexus for income tax purposes?

Background: Under federal law, an out-of-state retailer, without sufficient nexus to be subject to the sales/use tax, could have sufficient nexus for income tax. The U.S. Supreme Court has ruled that some form of physical presence is needed to establish nexus with regard to sales/use taxes (*Quill Corp. v. North Dakota,* 504 U.S. 298 (1992)). There is no such rule with respect to corporate income tax; therefore, intangible property and economic presence would be sufficient to create a filing responsibility for income tax on sales but not for the sales/use tax.

Public Law 86-272 protects a foreign corporation from a tax on or measured by net income derived within the state from interstate commerce if its only business activities in the state are the solicitation of orders for sales of tangible personal property. Solicitation activity related to the sale of services or intangible property, including electronic commerce, is not protected. Consequently, a software company may lose the protection of Public Law 86-272 if it has salespersons who solicit sales on its behalf in the state, and it distributes some of its products electronically. Mere solicitation is not protected if sales involve both tangible and intangible property.

→ *ANSWER:* California has no specific rule in this are, but the general principals outlined in the Background for this Question are applicable. See ¶ 12-420, ¶ 60-445.

17. QUESTION: Does the use of a computer server in the state give rise to sales/use or income tax nexus for an Internet Service Provider (ISP) that uses it?

Background: Some states hold that the location of a computer server gives rise to tax nexus for an ISP that uses it (but may not own it), typically by classifying the use as a lease of tangible personal property (the computer) that creates a physical presence in the state. However, as a practical matter, ISPs who do not own their own server do not know where the server they are using is located. Also, in most cases, multiple servers in different locations are used.

→ *ANSWER:* There is no direct California law on this point with respect to ISPs; however, charges made for the use of a computer, on a time-sharing basis, where access to the computer is by means of remote telecommunication are not subject to tax (see Answer 10). See ¶ 60-310.

⋙➔*CAUTION: Paragraph references are to the CCH California Tax Reports.*

18. QUESTION: Can advertising on the Internet, on a third-party Web page, give rise to nexus for sales/use tax or income tax?

Background: Public Law 86-272 protects a foreign corporation from a tax on or measured by net income derived within the state from interstate commerce if its only business activities in the state are the solicitation of orders for sales of tangible personal property. Solicitation activity related to the sale of services or intangible property, including electronic commerce is not protected. Consequently, a software company may lose the protection of Public Law 86-272 if it has agents who solicit sales on its behalf in the state, and it distributes some of its products electronically. Mere "solicitation" is not protected if sales involve both tangible and intangible property.

➔ *ANSWER:* There has been no direct ruling as to whether advertising on the Internet can give rise to nexus. However, in an analogous situation, the California State Board of Equalization (SBE) was constitutionally prohibited from assessing use tax against an out-of-state mail order company whose contacts with California consisted only of (1) entering into advertising contracts with California broadcast and cable television companies, (2) soliciting sales by direct mail order through a single catalog and periodic direct mailings, and (3) shipping orders to California customers by U.P.S. and occasionally by parcel post. Such minimal contacts did not constitute the "physical presence" within California as required by the U.S. Supreme Court in *Quill Corp. v. North Dakota,* 504 U.S. 298 (1992). See ¶ 60-075.

Where Sales Occur

19. QUESTION: Is the sale of downloadable digitized products over the Internet by an out-of-state vendor sourced the same for income tax sales factor purposes as the sale of the same products delivered on a storage medium, such as tape or disk?

Background: The sourcing to a state of the sale of downloadable digitized products over the Internet depends on whether the state classifies the sale as a sale of tangible personal property, a sale of intangible personal property, or a sale of a service. Generally, a sale of tangible personal property is sourced to its delivery destination, a sale of a service or an intangible is sourced to the state where the income-producing activity took place.

➔ *ANSWER:* When software, information databases, and other digitized products are sold in tangible form, the sales are considered sales of tangible personal property, sourced, for sales factor purposes to California if the property is delivered or shipped to a recipient located in California (except sales to the United States Government).

If the product is delivered electronically (*e.g.,* via modem), it is considered a sale of intangible personal property, and it is attributed under the income-producing activity rule. If the income-producing activity can be readily identified, the income is included in computing the sales factor, and if the income producing activity occurs in California, the sale is attributed to California. If the income-producing activity is performed both within and outside of the state, then the sale is attributed to California if a greater

≫→*CAUTION: Paragraph references are to the CCH California Tax Reports.*

proportion of the income-producing activity is performed in the state than in any other state, based on the costs of performance. See ¶ 12-585, ¶ 60-310.

20. QUESTION: Under what circumstances for income tax sales factor purposes, are an in-state vendor's Internet sales of software, information databases, electronic greeting cards, and other digitized products sourced to the state?

→ *ANSWER:* Software, information databases, and other digitized products sold in tangible form are considered sales of tangible personal property, sourced, for sales factor purposes (except sales to the United States Government), to California if the property is delivered or shipped to a recipient located in California, or if the property is shipped from a place of storage in California and the taxpayer is not taxable in the state of the purchaser.

If the product is delivered electronically (*e.g.,* via modem), it is considered a sale of intangible personal property, and it is attributed under the income producing activity rule (see Answer 19). See ¶ 12-585, ¶ 60-310.

Specific Transactions

21. QUESTION: Are sales of prepaid telephone debit cards subject to sales/use tax?

→ *ANSWER:* Sales of prepaid telephone cards are not taxable in California, because the true object of the transaction is the sale of a nontaxable service (future telephone service). See ¶ 60-720.

TAX CALENDAR

The following table lists significant dates of interest to California taxpayers and tax practitioners.

February
1—Annual oil spill fee information return due
28—Personal income tax information returns due

March
1—Oil and gas production tax report due

Surplus line brokers' return and payment due
15—Corporation franchise and income tax return and payment due[1,2]

April
1—Insurance companies' gross premiums tax reports and payments due[3]

Last day to file property tax return
10—Last day to pay semi-annual installment of real property tax[4]
15—Personal income tax returns and payment due[1,5]

Returns and payment by partnerships, limited partnerships, and limited liability companies classified as partnerships due[1]
30—Private car tax reports due

May
1—Insurance companies' retaliatory tax information return due

June
15—Ocean marine insurance tax reports and payments due

July
First Monday—Oil and gas severance tax payments due
Six weeks after first Monday in July—Last day to pay first installment of oil and gas production tax

August
15—Oil and gas production charge due[6]
31—Unsecured personal property taxes delinquent at 5 p.m.

---

[1] Corresponding dates apply to fiscal year taxpayers.
[2] Estimated tax payments due on the 15th days of the 4th, 6th, 9th, and 12th months (due on the 15th day of the 4th month if estimated tax does not exceed minimum tax amount).
[3] Insurers, except ocean marine, whose tax for the preceding year was $5,000 or more prepay their current tax on or before April 1, June 15, September 15, and December 15. Surplus line brokers whose tax for the preceding year was $5,000 or more must make monthly installments on or before the first day of the third calendar month following the end of the accounting month in which the business was done.
[4] Due date for city taxes fixed locally.
[5] Estimated tax payments due on the 15th days of April, June, September, and January.
[6] If assessment is $500 or more, one-half of the charge is due on August 15 and one-half on the following February 1.

December

1—Insurance companies' retaliatory taxes due

10—Last day to pay tax on personal property secured by real estate and semi-annual installment of real property tax

   Private car tax due

Monthly Requirements

1st—Carriers' alcoholic beverage tax reports and payments due

10th—Oil and gas producers' reports due

15th—Alcoholic beverage tax reports and payments due

25th—Gasoline tax reports and payments due

   Oil spill fees due

   Cigarette and tobacco products tax reports and payments due

   Diesel fuel tax reports and payments due[7]

Last day—Intrastate telephone service supplier surcharge report and payment due for second preceding month

Quarterly (Jan., Apr., July and Oct.) Requirements

20th—Manufacturers lubricating oil tax and reports due

Last day—Use fuel tax reports and payments due

   Sales and use tax returns and payments due[8]

   Electric utility surcharge returns and payments due

Quarterly (Apr., June, Sept. and Dec.) Requirements

15th—Estimated financial institutions' income tax and corporate franchise and income tax payments due[9]

Quarterly (Apr., June, Sept. and Jan.) Requirements

15th—Estimated personal income tax payments due[9]

---

[7] Interstate truckers report and pay quarterly.

[8] Prepayments required of persons whose average monthly estimated measure of tax liability is $17,000 or more.

[9] Corresponding dates apply to fiscal year taxpayers.

PART I
Tax Rate Schedules and Tables

PERSONAL INCOME TAX RATE SCHEDULES FOR 1999

These are the official rate schedules on which the tax tables that follow are based. These schedules *must* be used if taxable income is more than $100,000. For taxable income of $100,000 or less, the tax must be figured from the tax tables.

Schedule X

Use if your filing status is **Single, Married Filing Separate and Fiduciary**

If the taxable income is:

over—	But not over—	Computed tax is:	of the amount over—
$ 0	$ 5,264	$ 0.00 + 1.0%	$ 0
5,264	12,477	52.64 + 2.0%	5,264
12,477	19,692	196.90 + 4.0%	12,477
19,692	27,337	485.50 + 6.0%	19,692
27,337	34,548	944.20 + 8.0%	27,337
34,548	and over	1,521.08 + 9.3%	34,548

Schedule Y

Use if your filing status is **Married Filing Joint and Qualifying Widow(er)**

If the taxable income is:

over—	But not over—	Computed tax is:	of the amount over—
$ 0	$ 10,528	$ 0.00 + 1.0%	$ 0
10,528	24,954	105.28 + 2.0%	10,528
24,954	39,384	393.80 + 4.0%	24,954
39,384	54,674	971.00 + 6.0%	39,384
54,674	69,096	1,888.40 + 8.0%	54,674
69,096	and over	3,042.16 + 9.3%	69,096

Schedule Z
Use if your filing status is **Head of Household**

If the taxable income is:

over—	But not over—	Computed tax is			of the amount over—
$ 0	$ 10,531	$ 0.00	+	1.0%	$ 0
10,531	24,955	105.31	+	2.0%	10,531
24,955	32,168	393.79	+	4.0%	24,955
32,168	39,812	682.31	+	6.0%	32,168
39,812	47,025	1,140.95	+	8.0%	39,812
47,025	and over	1,717.99	+	9.3%	47,025

ALTERNATIVE MINIMUM TAX

The tenative minimum tax rate is 7% (see ¶ 112a).

PERSONAL INCOME TAX TABLES FOR 1999

1999 California Tax Table

To Find Your Tax:
- Read down the column labeled "If Your Taxable Income Is . . ." to find the range that includes your taxable income from Form 540A, line 16 or Form 540EZ, line 16.
- Read across the columns labeled "The Tax For Filing Status" until you find the tax that applies for your taxable income and filing status.

Filing status: **1 or 3** (Single; Married filing Separate)   **2 or 5** (Married filing Joint; Qualifying Widow(er))   **4** (Head of Household)

If Your Taxable Income Is... At Least	But Not Over	The Tax For Filing Status 1 Or 3 Is	2 Or 5 Is	4 Is	If Your Taxable Income Is... At Least	But Not Over	The Tax For Filing Status 1 Or 3 Is	2 Or 5 Is	4 Is	If Your Taxable Income Is... At Least	But Not Over	The Tax For Filing Status 1 Or 3 Is	2 Or 5 Is	4 Is
1	50	0	0	0	6,451	6,550	77	65	65	12,951	13,050	218	155	155
51	150	1	1	1	6,551	6,650	79	66	66	13,051	13,150	222	157	157
151	250	2	2	2	6,651	6,750	81	67	67	13,151	13,250	226	159	159
251	350	3	3	3	6,751	6,850	83	68	68	13,251	13,350	230	161	161
351	450	4	4	4	6,851	6,950	85	69	69	13,351	13,450	234	163	163
451	550	5	5	5	6,951	7,050	87	70	70	13,451	13,550	238	165	165
551	650	6	6	6	7,051	7,150	89	71	71	13,551	13,650	242	167	167
651	750	7	7	7	7,151	7,250	91	72	72	13,651	13,750	246	169	169
751	850	8	8	8	7,251	7,350	93	73	73	13,751	13,850	250	171	171
851	950	9	9	9	7,351	7,450	95	74	74	13,851	13,950	254	173	173
951	1,050	10	10	10	7,451	7,550	97	75	75	13,951	14,050	258	175	175
1,051	1,150	11	11	11	7,551	7,650	99	76	76	14,051	14,150	262	177	177
1,151	1,250	12	12	12	7,651	7,750	101	77	77	14,151	14,250	266	179	179
1,251	1,350	13	13	13	7,751	7,850	103	78	78	14,251	14,350	270	181	181
1,351	1,450	14	14	14	7,851	7,950	105	79	79	14,351	14,450	274	183	183
1,451	1,550	15	15	15	7,951	8,050	107	80	80	14,451	14,550	278	185	185
1,551	1,650	16	16	16	8,051	8,150	109	81	81	14,551	14,650	282	187	187
1,651	1,750	17	17	17	8,151	8,250	111	82	82	14,651	14,750	286	189	189
1,751	1,850	18	18	18	8,251	8,350	113	83	83	14,751	14,850	290	191	191
1,851	1,950	19	19	19	8,351	8,450	115	84	84	14,851	14,950	294	193	193
1,951	2,050	20	20	20	8,451	8,550	117	85	85	14,951	15,050	298	195	195
2,051	2,150	21	21	21	8,551	8,650	119	86	86	15,051	15,150	302	197	197
2,151	2,250	22	22	22	8,651	8,750	121	87	87	15,151	15,250	306	199	199
2,251	2,350	23	23	23	8,751	8,850	123	88	88	15,251	15,350	310	201	201
2,351	2,450	24	24	24	8,851	8,950	125	89	89	15,351	15,450	314	203	203
2,451	2,550	25	25	25	8,951	9,050	127	90	90	15,451	15,550	318	205	205
2,551	2,650	26	26	26	9,051	9,150	129	91	91	15,551	15,650	322	207	207
2,651	2,750	27	27	27	9,151	9,250	131	92	92	15,651	15,750	326	209	209
2,751	2,850	28	28	28	9,251	9,350	133	93	93	15,751	15,850	330	211	211
2,851	2,950	29	29	29	9,351	9,450	135	94	94	15,851	15,950	334	213	213
2,951	3,050	30	30	30	9,451	9,550	137	95	95	15,951	16,050	338	215	215
3,051	3,150	31	31	31	9,551	9,650	139	96	96	16,051	16,150	342	217	217
3,151	3,250	32	32	32	9,651	9,750	141	97	97	16,151	16,250	346	219	219
3,251	3,350	33	33	33	9,751	9,850	143	98	98	16,251	16,350	350	221	221
3,351	3,450	34	34	34	9,851	9,950	145	99	99	16,351	16,450	354	223	223
3,451	3,550	35	35	35	9,951	10,050	147	100	100	16,451	16,550	358	225	225
3,551	3,650	36	36	36	10,051	10,150	149	101	101	16,551	16,650	362	227	227
3,651	3,750	37	37	37	10,151	10,250	151	102	102	16,651	16,750	366	229	229
3,751	3,850	38	38	38	10,251	10,350	153	103	103	16,751	16,850	370	231	231
3,851	3,950	39	39	39	10,351	10,450	155	104	104	16,851	16,950	374	233	233
3,951	4,050	40	40	40	10,451	10,550	157	105	105	16,951	17,050	378	235	235
4,051	4,150	41	41	41	10,551	10,650	159	107	107	17,051	17,150	382	237	237
4,151	4,250	42	42	42	10,651	10,750	161	109	109	17,151	17,250	386	239	239
4,251	4,350	43	43	43	10,751	10,850	163	111	111	17,251	17,350	390	241	241
4,351	4,450	44	44	44	10,851	10,950	165	113	113	17,351	17,450	394	243	243
4,451	4,550	45	45	45	10,951	11,050	167	115	115	17,451	17,550	398	245	245
4,551	4,650	46	46	46	11,051	11,150	169	117	117	17,551	17,650	402	247	247
4,651	4,750	47	47	47	11,151	11,250	171	119	119	17,651	17,750	406	249	249
4,751	4,850	48	48	48	11,251	11,350	173	121	121	17,751	17,850	410	251	251
4,851	4,950	49	49	49	11,351	11,450	175	123	123	17,851	17,950	414	253	253
4,951	5,050	50	50	50	11,451	11,550	177	125	125	17,951	18,050	418	255	255
5,051	5,150	51	51	51	11,551	11,650	179	127	127	18,051	18,150	422	257	257
5,151	5,250	52	52	52	11,651	11,750	181	129	129	18,151	18,250	426	259	259
5,251	5,350	53	53	53	11,751	11,850	183	131	131	18,251	18,350	430	261	261
5,351	5,450	55	54	54	11,851	11,950	185	133	133	18,351	18,450	434	263	263
5,451	5,550	57	55	55	11,951	12,050	187	135	135	18,451	18,550	438	265	265
5,551	5,650	59	56	56	12,051	12,150	189	137	137	18,551	18,650	442	267	267
5,651	5,750	61	57	57	12,151	12,250	191	139	139	18,651	18,750	446	269	269
5,751	5,850	63	58	58	12,251	12,350	193	141	141	18,751	18,850	450	271	271
5,851	5,950	65	59	59	12,351	12,450	195	143	143	18,851	18,950	454	273	273
5,951	6,050	67	60	60	12,451	12,550	198	145	145	18,951	19,050	458	275	275
6,051	6,150	69	61	61	12,551	12,650	202	147	147	19,051	19,150	462	277	277
6,151	6,250	71	62	62	12,651	12,750	206	149	149	19,151	19,250	466	279	279
6,251	6,350	73	63	63	12,751	12,850	210	151	151	19,251	19,350	470	281	281
6,351	6,450	75	64	64	12,851	12,950	214	153	153	19,351	19,450	474	283	283

Continued on next page.

1999 California Tax Table – Continued

Filing status: 1 or 3 (Single; Married filing Separate)   2 or 5 (Married filing Joint; Qualifying Widow(er))   4 (Head of Household)

If Your Taxable Income is... At Least	But Not Over	1 Or 3 Is	2 Or 5 Is	4 Is
19,451	19,550	478	285	285
19,551	19,650	482	287	287
19,651	19,750	486	289	289
19,751	19,850	492	291	291
19,851	19,950	498	293	293
19,951	20,050	504	295	295
20,051	20,150	510	297	297
20,151	20,250	516	299	299
20,251	20,350	522	301	301
20,351	20,450	528	303	303
20,451	20,550	534	305	305
20,551	20,650	540	307	307
20,651	20,750	546	309	309
20,751	20,850	552	311	311
20,851	20,950	558	313	313
20,951	21,050	564	315	315
21,051	21,150	570	317	317
21,151	21,250	576	319	319
21,251	21,350	582	321	321
21,351	21,450	588	323	323
21,451	21,550	594	325	325
21,551	21,650	600	327	327
21,651	21,750	606	329	329
21,751	21,850	612	331	331
21,851	21,950	618	333	333
21,951	22,050	624	335	335
22,051	22,150	630	337	337
22,151	22,250	636	339	339
22,251	22,350	642	341	341
22,351	22,450	648	343	343
22,451	22,550	654	345	345
22,551	22,650	660	347	347
22,651	22,750	666	349	349
22,751	22,850	672	351	351
22,851	22,950	678	353	353
22,951	23,050	684	355	355
23,051	23,150	690	357	357
23,151	23,250	696	359	359
23,251	23,350	702	361	361
23,351	23,450	708	363	363
23,451	23,550	714	365	365
23,551	23,650	720	367	367
23,651	23,750	726	369	369
23,751	23,850	732	371	371
23,851	23,950	738	373	373
23,951	24,050	744	375	375
24,051	24,150	750	377	377
24,151	24,250	756	379	379
24,251	24,350	762	381	381
24,351	24,450	768	383	383
24,451	24,550	774	385	385
24,551	24,650	780	387	387
24,651	24,750	786	389	389
24,751	24,850	792	391	391
24,851	24,950	798	393	393
24,951	25,050	804	396	396
25,051	25,150	810	400	400
25,151	25,250	816	404	404
25,251	25,350	822	408	408
25,351	25,450	828	412	412
25,451	25,550	834	416	416
25,551	25,650	840	420	420
25,651	25,750	846	424	424
25,751	25,850	852	428	428
25,851	25,950	858	432	432
25,951	26,050	864	436	436
26,051	26,150	870	440	440
26,151	26,250	876	444	444
26,251	26,350	882	448	448
26,351	26,450	888	452	452

If Your Taxable Income is... At Least	But Not Over	1 Or 3 Is	2 Or 5 Is	4 Is
26,451	26,550	894	456	456
26,551	26,650	900	460	460
26,651	26,750	906	464	464
26,751	26,850	912	468	468
26,851	26,950	918	472	472
26,951	27,050	924	476	476
27,051	27,150	930	480	480
27,151	27,250	936	484	484
27,251	27,350	942	488	488
27,351	27,450	949	492	492
27,451	27,550	957	496	496
27,551	27,650	965	500	500
27,651	27,750	973	504	504
27,751	27,850	981	508	508
27,851	27,950	989	512	512
27,951	28,050	997	516	516
28,051	28,150	1,005	520	520
28,151	28,250	1,013	524	524
28,251	28,350	1,021	528	528
28,351	28,450	1,029	532	532
28,451	28,550	1,037	536	536
28,551	28,650	1,045	540	540
28,651	28,750	1,053	544	544
28,751	28,850	1,061	548	548
28,851	28,950	1,069	552	552
28,951	29,050	1,077	556	556
29,051	29,150	1,085	560	560
29,151	29,250	1,093	564	564
29,251	29,350	1,101	568	568
29,351	29,450	1,109	572	572
29,451	29,550	1,117	576	576
29,551	29,650	1,125	580	580
29,651	29,750	1,133	584	584
29,751	29,850	1,141	588	588
29,851	29,950	1,149	592	592
29,951	30,050	1,157	596	596
30,051	30,150	1,165	600	600
30,151	30,250	1,173	604	604
30,251	30,350	1,181	608	608
30,351	30,450	1,189	612	612
30,451	30,550	1,197	616	616
30,551	30,650	1,205	620	620
30,651	30,750	1,213	624	624
30,751	30,850	1,221	628	628
30,851	30,950	1,229	632	632
30,951	31,050	1,237	636	636
31,051	31,150	1,245	640	640
31,151	31,250	1,253	644	644
31,251	31,350	1,261	648	648
31,351	31,450	1,269	652	652
31,451	31,550	1,277	656	656
31,551	31,650	1,285	660	660
31,651	31,750	1,293	664	664
31,751	31,850	1,301	668	668
31,851	31,950	1,309	672	672
31,951	32,050	1,317	676	676
32,051	32,150	1,325	680	680
32,151	32,250	1,333	684	684
32,251	32,350	1,341	688	690
32,351	32,450	1,349	692	696
32,451	32,550	1,357	696	702
32,551	32,650	1,365	700	708
32,651	32,750	1,373	704	714
32,751	32,850	1,381	708	720
32,851	32,950	1,389	712	726
32,951	33,050	1,397	716	732
33,051	33,150	1,405	720	738
33,151	33,250	1,413	724	744
33,251	33,350	1,421	728	750
33,351	33,450	1,429	732	756

If Your Taxable Income is... At Least	But Not Over	1 Or 3 Is	2 Or 5 Is	4 Is
33,451	33,550	1,437	736	762
33,551	33,650	1,445	740	768
33,651	33,750	1,453	744	774
33,751	33,850	1,461	748	780
33,851	33,950	1,469	752	786
33,951	34,050	1,477	756	792
34,051	34,150	1,485	760	798
34,151	34,250	1,493	764	804
34,251	34,350	1,501	768	810
34,351	34,450	1,509	772	816
34,451	34,550	1,517	776	822
34,551	34,650	1,526	780	828
34,651	34,750	1,535	784	834
34,751	34,850	1,545	788	840
34,851	34,950	1,554	792	846
34,951	35,050	1,563	796	852
35,051	35,150	1,572	800	858
35,151	35,250	1,582	804	864
35,251	35,350	1,591	808	870
35,351	35,450	1,600	812	876
35,451	35,550	1,610	816	882
35,551	35,650	1,619	820	888
35,651	35,750	1,628	824	894
35,751	35,850	1,638	828	900
35,851	35,950	1,647	832	906
35,951	36,050	1,656	836	912
36,051	36,150	1,665	840	918
36,151	36,250	1,675	844	924
36,251	36,350	1,684	848	930
36,351	36,450	1,693	852	936
36,451	36,550	1,703	856	942
36,551	36,650	1,712	860	948
36,651	36,750	1,721	864	954
36,751	36,850	1,731	868	960
36,851	36,950	1,740	872	966
36,951	37,050	1,749	876	972
37,051	37,150	1,758	880	978
37,151	37,250	1,768	884	984
37,251	37,350	1,777	888	990
37,351	37,450	1,786	892	996
37,451	37,550	1,796	896	1,002
37,551	37,650	1,805	900	1,008
37,651	37,750	1,814	904	1,014
37,751	37,850	1,824	908	1,020
37,851	37,950	1,833	912	1,026
37,951	38,050	1,842	916	1,032
38,051	38,150	1,851	920	1,038
38,151	38,250	1,861	924	1,044
38,251	38,350	1,870	928	1,050
38,351	38,450	1,879	932	1,056
38,451	38,550	1,889	936	1,062
38,551	38,650	1,898	940	1,068
38,651	38,750	1,907	944	1,074
38,751	38,850	1,917	948	1,080
38,851	38,950	1,926	952	1,086
38,951	39,050	1,935	956	1,092
39,051	39,150	1,944	960	1,098
39,151	39,250	1,954	964	1,104
39,251	39,350	1,963	968	1,110
39,351	39,450	1,972	972	1,116
39,451	39,550	1,982	978	1,122
39,551	39,650	1,991	984	1,128
39,651	39,750	2,000	990	1,134
39,751	39,850	2,010	996	1,140
39,851	39,950	2,019	1,002	1,148
39,951	40,050	2,028	1,008	1,156
40,051	40,150	2,037	1,014	1,164
40,151	40,250	2,047	1,020	1,172
40,251	40,350	2,056	1,026	1,180
40,351	40,450	2,065	1,032	1,188

Continued on next page.

1999 California Tax Table – Continued

Filing status: 1 or 3 (Single; Married filing Separate)   2 or 5 (Married filing Joint; Qualifying Widow(er))   4 (Head of Household)

If Your Taxable Income Is... At Least	But Not Over	The Tax For Filing Status 1 Or 3 Is	2 Or 5 Is	4 Is
40,451	40,550	2,075	1,038	1,196
40,551	40,650	2,084	1,044	1,204
40,651	40,750	2,093	1,050	1,212
40,751	40,850	2,103	1,056	1,220
40,851	40,950	2,112	1,062	1,228
40,951	41,050	2,121	1,068	1,236
41,051	41,150	2,130	1,074	1,244
41,151	41,250	2,140	1,080	1,252
41,251	41,350	2,149	1,086	1,260
41,351	41,450	2,158	1,092	1,268
41,451	41,550	2,168	1,098	1,276
41,551	41,650	2,177	1,104	1,284
41,651	41,750	2,186	1,110	1,292
41,751	41,850	2,196	1,116	1,300
41,851	41,950	2,205	1,122	1,308
41,951	42,050	2,214	1,128	1,316
42,051	42,150	2,223	1,134	1,324
42,151	42,250	2,233	1,140	1,332
42,251	42,350	2,242	1,146	1,340
42,351	42,450	2,251	1,152	1,348
42,451	42,550	2,261	1,158	1,356
42,551	42,650	2,270	1,164	1,364
42,651	42,750	2,279	1,170	1,372
42,751	42,850	2,289	1,176	1,380
42,851	42,950	2,298	1,182	1,388
42,951	43,050	2,307	1,188	1,396
43,051	43,150	2,316	1,194	1,404
43,151	43,250	2,326	1,200	1,412
43,251	43,350	2,335	1,206	1,420
43,351	43,450	2,344	1,212	1,428
43,451	43,550	2,354	1,218	1,436
43,551	43,650	2,363	1,224	1,444
43,651	43,750	2,372	1,230	1,452
43,751	43,850	2,382	1,236	1,460
43,851	43,950	2,391	1,242	1,468
43,951	44,050	2,400	1,248	1,476
44,051	44,150	2,409	1,254	1,484
44,151	44,250	2,419	1,260	1,492
44,251	44,350	2,428	1,266	1,500
44,351	44,450	2,437	1,272	1,508
44,451	44,550	2,447	1,278	1,516
44,551	44,650	2,456	1,284	1,524
44,651	44,750	2,465	1,290	1,532
44,751	44,850	2,475	1,296	1,540
44,851	44,950	2,484	1,302	1,548
44,951	45,050	2,493	1,308	1,556
45,051	45,150	2,502	1,314	1,564
45,151	45,250	2,512	1,320	1,572
45,251	45,350	2,521	1,326	1,580
45,351	45,450	2,530	1,332	1,588
45,451	45,550	2,540	1,338	1,596
45,551	45,650	2,549	1,344	1,604
45,651	45,750	2,558	1,350	1,612
45,751	45,850	2,568	1,356	1,620
45,851	45,950	2,577	1,362	1,628
45,951	46,050	2,586	1,368	1,636
46,051	46,150	2,595	1,374	1,644
46,151	46,250	2,605	1,380	1,652
46,251	46,350	2,614	1,386	1,660
46,351	46,450	2,623	1,392	1,668
46,451	46,550	2,633	1,398	1,676
46,551	46,650	2,642	1,404	1,684
46,651	46,750	2,651	1,410	1,692
46,751	46,850	2,661	1,416	1,700
46,851	46,950	2,670	1,422	1,708
46,951	47,050	2,679	1,428	1,716
47,051	47,150	2,688	1,434	1,725
47,151	47,250	2,698	1,440	1,734
47,251	47,350	2,707	1,446	1,744
47,351	47,450	2,716	1,452	1,753
47,451	47,550	2,726	1,458	1,762
47,551	47,650	2,735	1,464	1,771
47,651	47,750	2,744	1,470	1,781
47,751	47,850	2,754	1,476	1,790
47,851	47,950	2,763	1,482	1,799
47,951	48,050	2,772	1,488	1,809
48,051	48,150	2,781	1,494	1,818
48,151	48,250	2,791	1,500	1,827
48,251	48,350	2,800	1,506	1,837
48,351	48,450	2,809	1,512	1,846
48,451	48,550	2,819	1,518	1,855
48,551	48,650	2,828	1,524	1,864
48,651	48,750	2,837	1,530	1,874
48,751	48,850	2,847	1,536	1,883
48,851	48,950	2,856	1,542	1,892
48,951	49,050	2,865	1,548	1,902
49,051	49,150	2,874	1,554	1,911
49,151	49,250	2,884	1,560	1,920
49,251	49,350	2,893	1,566	1,930
49,351	49,450	2,902	1,572	1,939
49,451	49,550	2,912	1,578	1,948
49,551	49,650	2,921	1,584	1,957
49,651	49,750	2,930	1,590	1,967
49,751	49,850	2,940	1,596	1,976
49,851	49,950	2,949	1,602	1,985
49,951	50,050	2,958	1,608	1,995
50,051	50,150	2,967	1,614	2,004
50,151	50,250	2,977	1,620	2,013
50,251	50,350	2,986	1,626	2,023
50,351	50,450	2,995	1,632	2,032
50,451	50,550	3,005	1,638	2,041
50,551	50,650	3,014	1,644	2,050
50,651	50,750	3,023	1,650	2,060
50,751	50,850	3,033	1,656	2,069
50,851	50,950	3,042	1,662	2,078
50,951	51,050	3,051	1,668	2,088
51,051	51,150	3,060	1,674	2,097
51,151	51,250	3,070	1,680	2,106
51,251	51,350	3,079	1,686	2,116
51,351	51,450	3,088	1,692	2,125
51,451	51,550	3,098	1,698	2,134
51,551	51,650	3,107	1,704	2,143
51,651	51,750	3,116	1,710	2,153
51,751	51,850	3,126	1,716	2,162
51,851	51,950	3,135	1,722	2,171
51,951	52,050	3,144	1,728	2,181
52,051	52,150	3,153	1,734	2,190
52,151	52,250	3,163	1,740	2,199
52,251	52,350	3,172	1,746	2,209
52,351	52,450	3,181	1,752	2,218
52,451	52,550	3,191	1,758	2,227
52,551	52,650	3,200	1,764	2,236
52,651	52,750	3,209	1,770	2,246
52,751	52,850	3,219	1,776	2,255
52,851	52,950	3,228	1,782	2,264
52,951	53,050	3,237	1,788	2,274
53,051	53,150	3,246	1,794	2,283
53,151	53,250	3,256	1,800	2,292
53,251	53,350	3,265	1,806	2,302
53,351	53,450	3,274	1,812	2,311
53,451	53,550	3,284	1,818	2,320
53,551	53,650	3,293	1,824	2,329
53,651	53,750	3,302	1,830	2,339
53,751	53,850	3,312	1,836	2,348
53,851	53,950	3,321	1,842	2,357
53,951	54,050	3,330	1,848	2,367
54,051	54,150	3,339	1,854	2,376
54,151	54,250	3,349	1,860	2,385
54,251	54,350	3,358	1,866	2,395
54,351	54,450	3,367	1,872	2,404
54,451	54,550	3,377	1,878	2,413
54,551	54,650	3,386	1,884	2,422
54,651	54,750	3,395	1,890	2,432
54,751	54,850	3,405	1,898	2,441
54,851	54,950	3,414	1,906	2,450
54,951	55,050	3,423	1,914	2,460
55,051	55,150	3,432	1,922	2,469
55,151	55,250	3,442	1,930	2,478
55,251	55,350	3,451	1,938	2,488
55,351	55,450	3,460	1,946	2,497
55,451	55,550	3,470	1,954	2,506
55,551	55,650	3,479	1,962	2,515
55,651	55,750	3,488	1,970	2,525
55,751	55,850	3,498	1,978	2,534
55,851	55,950	3,507	1,986	2,543
55,951	56,050	3,516	1,994	2,553
56,051	56,150	3,525	2,002	2,562
56,151	56,250	3,535	2,010	2,571
56,251	56,350	3,544	2,018	2,581
56,351	56,450	3,553	2,026	2,590
56,451	56,550	3,563	2,034	2,599
56,551	56,650	3,572	2,042	2,608
56,651	56,750	3,581	2,050	2,618
56,751	56,850	3,591	2,058	2,627
56,851	56,950	3,600	2,066	2,636
56,951	57,050	3,609	2,074	2,646
57,051	57,150	3,618	2,082	2,655
57,151	57,250	3,628	2,090	2,664
57,251	57,350	3,637	2,098	2,674
57,351	57,450	3,646	2,106	2,683
57,451	57,550	3,656	2,114	2,692
57,551	57,650	3,665	2,122	2,701
57,651	57,750	3,674	2,130	2,711
57,751	57,850	3,684	2,138	2,720
57,851	57,950	3,693	2,146	2,729
57,951	58,050	3,702	2,154	2,739
58,051	58,150	3,711	2,162	2,748
58,151	58,250	3,721	2,170	2,757
58,251	58,350	3,730	2,178	2,767
58,351	58,450	3,739	2,186	2,778
58,451	58,550	3,749	2,194	2,785
58,551	58,650	3,758	2,202	2,794
58,651	58,750	3,767	2,210	2,804
58,751	58,850	3,777	2,218	2,813
58,851	58,950	3,786	2,226	2,822
58,951	59,050	3,795	2,234	2,832
59,051	59,150	3,804	2,242	2,841
59,151	59,250	3,814	2,250	2,850
59,251	59,350	3,823	2,258	2,860
59,351	59,450	3,832	2,266	2,869
59,451	59,550	3,842	2,274	2,878
59,551	59,650	3,851	2,282	2,887
59,651	59,750	3,860	2,290	2,897
59,751	59,850	3,870	2,298	2,906
59,851	59,950	3,879	2,308	2,915
59,951	60,050	3,888	2,314	2,925
60,051	60,150	3,897	2,322	2,934
60,151	60,250	3,907	2,330	2,943
60,251	60,350	3,916	2,338	2,953
60,351	60,450	3,925	2,346	2,962
60,451	60,550	3,935	2,354	2,971
60,551	60,650	3,944	2,362	2,980
60,651	60,750	3,953	2,370	2,990
60,751	60,850	3,963	2,378	2,999
60,851	60,950	3,972	2,386	3,008
60,951	61,050	3,981	2,394	3,018
61,051	61,150	3,990	2,402	3,027
61,151	61,250	4,000	2,410	3,036
61,251	61,350	4,009	2,418	3,046
61,351	61,450	4,018	2,426	3,055

Continued on next page.

1999 California Tax Table — Continued

Filing status: 1 or 3 (Single; Married filing Separate) 2 or 5 (Married filing Joint; Qualifying Widow(er)) 4 (Head of Household)

At Least	But Not Over	1 Or 3 Is	2 Or 5 Is	4 Is	At Least	But Not Over	1 Or 3 Is	2 Or 5 Is	4 Is	At Least	But Not Over	1 Or 3 Is	2 Or 5 Is	4 Is
61,451	61,550	4,028	2,434	3,064	68,451	68,550	4,679	2,994	3,715	75,451	75,550	5,330	3,638	4,366
61,551	61,650	4,037	2,442	3,073	68,551	68,650	4,688	3,002	3,724	75,551	75,650	5,339	3,647	4,375
61,651	61,750	4,046	2,450	3,083	68,651	68,750	4,697	3,010	3,734	75,651	75,750	5,348	3,656	4,385
61,751	61,850	4,056	2,458	3,092	68,751	68,850	4,707	3,018	3,743	75,751	75,850	5,358	3,666	4,394
61,851	61,950	4,065	2,466	3,101	68,851	68,950	4,716	3,026	3,752	75,851	75,950	5,367	3,675	4,403
61,951	62,050	4,074	2,474	3,111	68,951	69,050	4,725	3,034	3,762	75,951	76,050	5,376	3,684	4,413
62,051	62,150	4,083	2,482	3,120	69,051	69,150	4,734	3,043	3,771	76,051	76,150	5,385	3,694	4,422
62,151	62,250	4,093	2,490	3,129	69,151	69,250	4,744	3,052	3,780	76,151	76,250	5,395	3,703	4,431
62,251	62,350	4,102	2,498	3,139	69,251	69,350	4,753	3,061	3,790	76,251	76,350	5,404	3,712	4,441
62,351	62,450	4,111	2,506	3,148	69,351	69,450	4,762	3,070	3,799	76,351	76,450	5,413	3,721	4,450
62,451	62,550	4,121	2,514	3,157	69,451	69,550	4,772	3,080	3,808	76,451	76,550	5,423	3,731	4,459
62,551	62,650	4,130	2,522	3,166	69,551	69,650	4,781	3,089	3,817	76,551	76,650	5,432	3,740	4,468
62,651	62,750	4,139	2,530	3,176	69,651	69,750	4,790	3,098	3,827	76,651	76,750	5,441	3,749	4,478
62,751	62,850	4,149	2,538	3,185	69,751	69,850	4,800	3,108	3,836	76,751	76,850	5,451	3,759	4,487
62,851	62,950	4,158	2,546	3,194	69,851	69,950	4,809	3,117	3,845	76,851	76,950	5,460	3,768	4,496
62,951	63,050	4,167	2,554	3,204	69,951	70,050	4,818	3,126	3,855	76,951	77,050	5,469	3,777	4,506
63,051	63,150	4,176	2,562	3,213	70,051	70,150	4,827	3,136	3,864	77,051	77,150	5,478	3,787	4,515
63,151	63,250	4,186	2,570	3,222	70,151	70,250	4,837	3,145	3,873	77,151	77,250	5,488	3,796	4,524
63,251	63,350	4,195	2,578	3,232	70,251	70,350	4,846	3,154	3,883	77,251	77,350	5,497	3,805	4,534
63,351	63,450	4,204	2,586	3,241	70,351	70,450	4,855	3,163	3,892	77,351	77,450	5,508	3,814	4,543
63,451	63,550	4,214	2,594	3,250	70,451	70,550	4,865	3,173	3,901	77,451	77,550	5,516	3,824	4,552
63,551	63,650	4,223	2,602	3,259	70,551	70,650	4,874	3,182	3,910	77,551	77,650	5,525	3,833	4,561
63,651	63,750	4,232	2,610	3,269	70,651	70,750	4,883	3,191	3,920	77,651	77,750	5,534	3,842	4,571
63,751	63,850	4,242	2,618	3,278	70,751	70,850	4,893	3,201	3,929	77,751	77,850	5,544	3,852	4,580
63,851	63,950	4,251	2,626	3,287	70,851	70,950	4,902	3,210	3,938	77,851	77,950	5,553	3,861	4,589
63,951	64,050	4,260	2,634	3,297	70,951	71,050	4,911	3,219	3,948	77,951	78,050	5,582	3,870	4,599
64,051	64,150	4,269	2,642	3,306	71,051	71,150	4,920	3,229	3,957	78,051	78,150	5,571	3,880	4,608
64,151	64,250	4,279	2,650	3,315	71,151	71,250	4,930	3,238	3,966	78,151	78,250	5,581	3,889	4,617
64,251	64,350	4,288	2,658	3,325	71,251	71,350	4,939	3,247	3,976	78,251	78,350	5,590	3,898	4,627
64,351	64,450	4,297	2,666	3,334	71,351	71,450	4,948	3,256	3,985	78,351	78,450	5,599	3,907	4,636
64,451	64,550	4,307	2,674	3,343	71,451	71,550	4,958	3,266	3,994	78,451	78,550	5,609	3,917	4,645
64,551	64,650	4,316	2,682	3,352	71,551	71,650	4,967	3,275	4,003	78,551	78,650	5,618	3,926	4,654
64,651	64,750	4,325	2,690	3,362	71,651	71,750	4,976	3,284	4,013	78,651	78,750	5,627	3,935	4,664
64,751	64,850	4,335	2,698	3,371	71,751	71,850	4,986	3,294	4,022	78,751	78,850	5,637	3,945	4,673
64,851	64,950	4,344	2,706	3,380	71,851	71,950	4,995	3,303	4,031	78,851	78,950	5,646	3,954	4,682
64,951	65,050	4,353	2,714	3,390	71,951	72,050	5,004	3,312	4,041	78,951	79,050	5,655	3,963	4,692
65,051	65,150	4,362	2,722	3,399	72,051	72,150	5,013	3,322	4,050	79,051	79,150	5,664	3,973	4,701
65,151	65,250	4,372	2,730	3,408	72,151	72,250	5,023	3,331	4,059	79,151	79,250	5,674	3,982	4,710
65,251	65,350	4,381	2,738	3,418	72,251	72,350	5,032	3,340	4,069	79,251	79,350	5,683	3,991	4,720
65,351	65,450	4,390	2,746	3,427	72,351	72,450	5,041	3,349	4,078	79,351	79,450	5,692	4,000	4,729
65,451	65,550	4,400	2,754	3,436	72,451	72,550	5,051	3,359	4,087	79,451	79,550	5,702	4,010	4,738
65,551	65,650	4,409	2,762	3,445	72,551	72,650	5,060	3,368	4,096	79,551	79,650	5,711	4,019	4,747
65,651	65,750	4,418	2,770	3,455	72,651	72,750	5,069	3,377	4,106	79,651	79,750	5,720	4,028	4,757
65,751	65,850	4,428	2,778	3,464	72,751	72,850	5,079	3,387	4,115	79,751	79,850	5,730	4,038	4,766
65,851	65,950	4,437	2,786	3,473	72,851	72,950	5,088	3,396	4,124	79,851	79,950	5,739	4,047	4,775
65,951	66,050	4,446	2,794	3,483	72,951	73,050	5,097	3,405	4,134	79,951	80,050	5,748	4,056	4,785
66,051	66,150	4,455	2,802	3,492	73,051	73,150	5,106	3,415	4,143	80,051	80,150	5,757	4,066	4,794
66,151	66,250	4,465	2,810	3,501	73,151	73,250	5,116	3,424	4,152	80,151	80,250	5,767	4,075	4,803
66,251	66,350	4,474	2,818	3,511	73,251	73,350	5,125	3,433	4,162	80,251	80,350	5,776	4,084	4,813
66,351	66,450	4,483	2,826	3,520	73,351	73,450	5,134	3,442	4,171	80,351	80,450	5,785	4,093	4,822
66,451	66,550	4,493	2,834	3,529	73,451	73,550	5,144	3,452	4,180	80,451	80,550	5,795	4,103	4,831
66,551	66,650	4,502	2,842	3,538	73,551	73,650	5,153	3,461	4,189	80,551	80,650	5,804	4,112	4,840
66,651	66,750	4,511	2,850	3,548	73,651	73,750	5,162	3,470	4,199	80,651	80,750	5,813	4,121	4,850
66,751	66,850	4,521	2,858	3,557	73,751	73,850	5,172	3,480	4,208	80,751	80,850	5,823	4,131	4,859
66,851	66,950	4,530	2,866	3,566	73,851	73,950	5,181	3,489	4,217	80,851	80,950	5,832	4,140	4,868
66,951	67,050	4,539	2,874	3,576	73,951	74,050	5,190	3,498	4,227	80,951	81,050	5,841	4,149	4,878
67,051	67,150	4,548	2,882	3,585	74,051	74,150	5,199	3,508	4,236	81,051	81,150	5,850	4,159	4,887
67,151	67,250	4,558	2,890	3,594	74,151	74,250	5,209	3,517	4,245	81,151	81,250	5,860	4,168	4,896
67,251	67,350	4,567	2,898	3,604	74,251	74,350	5,218	3,526	4,255	81,251	81,350	5,869	4,177	4,906
67,351	67,450	4,576	2,906	3,613	74,351	74,450	5,227	3,535	4,264	81,351	81,450	5,878	4,186	4,915
67,451	67,550	4,586	2,914	3,622	74,451	74,550	5,237	3,545	4,273	81,451	81,550	5,888	4,196	4,924
67,551	67,650	4,595	2,922	3,631	74,551	74,650	5,246	3,554	4,282	81,551	81,650	5,897	4,205	4,933
67,651	67,750	4,604	2,930	3,641	74,651	74,750	5,255	3,563	4,292	81,651	81,750	5,906	4,214	4,943
67,751	67,850	4,614	2,938	3,650	74,751	74,850	5,265	3,573	4,301	81,751	81,850	5,916	4,224	4,952
67,851	67,950	4,623	2,946	3,659	74,851	74,950	5,274	3,582	4,310	81,851	81,950	5,925	4,233	4,961
67,951	68,050	4,632	2,954	3,669	74,951	75,050	5,283	3,591	4,320	81,951	82,050	5,934	4,242	4,971
68,051	68,150	4,641	2,962	3,678	75,051	75,150	5,292	3,601	4,329	82,051	82,150	5,943	4,252	4,980
68,151	68,250	4,651	2,970	3,687	75,151	75,250	5,302	3,610	4,338	82,151	82,250	5,953	4,261	4,989
68,251	68,350	4,660	2,978	3,697	75,251	75,350	5,311	3,619	4,348	82,251	82,350	5,962	4,270	4,999
68,351	68,450	4,669	2,986	3,706	75,351	75,450	5,320	3,628	4,357	82,351	82,450	5,971	4,279	5,008

Continued on next page.

1999 California Tax Table - Continued

Filing status: 1 or 3 (Single; Married filing Separate) 2 or 5 (Married filing Joint; Qualifying Widow(er)) 4 (Head of Household)

If Your Taxable Income is... At Least	But Not Over	1 Or 3 is	2 Or 5 is	4 is	If Your Taxable Income is... At Least	But Not Over	1 Or 3 is	2 Or 5 is	4 is	If Your Taxable Income is... At Least	But Not Over	1 Or 3 is	2 Or 5 is	4 is
82,451	82,550	5,981	4,289	5,017	88,451	88,550	6,539	4,847	5,575	94,451	94,550	7,097	5,405	6,133
82,551	82,650	5,990	4,298	5,026	88,551	88,650	6,548	4,856	5,584	94,551	94,650	7,106	5,414	6,142
82,651	82,750	5,999	4,307	5,036	88,651	88,750	6,557	4,865	5,594	94,651	94,750	7,115	5,423	6,152
82,751	82,850	6,009	4,317	5,045	88,751	88,850	6,567	4,875	5,603	94,751	94,850	7,125	5,433	6,161
82,851	82,950	6,018	4,326	5,054	88,851	88,950	6,576	4,884	5,612	94,851	94,950	7,134	5,442	6,170
82,951	83,050	6,027	4,335	5,064	88,951	89,050	6,585	4,893	5,622	94,951	95,050	7,143	5,451	6,180
83,051	83,150	6,036	4,345	5,073	89,051	89,150	6,594	4,903	5,631	95,051	95,150	7,152	5,461	6,189
83,151	83,250	6,046	4,354	5,082	89,151	89,250	6,604	4,912	5,640	95,151	95,250	7,162	5,470	6,198
83,251	83,350	6,055	4,363	5,092	89,251	89,350	6,613	4,921	5,650	95,251	95,350	7,171	5,479	6,208
83,351	83,450	6,064	4,372	5,101	89,351	89,450	6,622	4,930	5,659	95,351	95,450	7,180	5,488	6,217
83,451	83,550	6,074	4,382	5,110	89,451	89,550	6,632	4,940	5,668	95,451	95,550	7,190	5,498	6,226
83,551	83,650	6,083	4,391	5,119	89,551	89,650	6,641	4,949	5,677	95,551	95,650	7,199	5,507	6,235
83,651	83,750	6,092	4,400	5,129	89,651	89,750	6,650	4,958	5,687	95,651	95,750	7,208	5,516	6,245
83,751	83,850	6,102	4,410	5,138	89,751	89,850	6,660	4,968	5,696	95,751	95,850	7,218	5,526	6,254
83,851	83,950	6,111	4,419	5,147	89,851	89,950	6,669	4,977	5,705	95,851	95,950	7,227	5,535	6,263
83,951	84,050	6,120	4,428	5,157	89,951	90,050	6,678	4,986	5,715	95,951	96,050	7,236	5,544	6,273
84,051	84,150	6,129	4,438	5,166	90,051	90,150	6,687	4,996	5,724	96,051	96,150	7,245	5,554	6,282
84,151	84,250	6,139	4,447	5,175	90,151	90,250	6,697	5,005	5,733	96,151	96,250	7,255	5,563	6,291
84,251	84,350	6,148	4,456	5,185	90,251	90,350	6,706	5,014	5,743	96,251	96,350	7,264	5,572	6,301
84,351	84,450	6,157	4,465	5,194	90,351	90,450	6,715	5,023	5,752	96,351	96,450	7,273	5,581	6,310
84,451	84,550	6,167	4,475	5,203	90,451	90,550	6,725	5,033	5,761	96,451	96,550	7,283	5,591	6,319
84,551	84,650	6,176	4,484	5,212	90,551	90,650	6,734	5,042	5,770	96,551	96,650	7,292	5,600	6,328
84,651	84,750	6,185	4,493	5,222	90,651	90,750	6,743	5,051	5,780	96,651	96,750	7,301	5,609	6,338
84,751	84,850	6,195	4,503	5,231	90,751	90,850	6,753	5,061	5,789	96,751	96,850	7,311	5,619	6,347
84,851	84,950	6,204	4,512	5,240	90,851	90,950	6,762	5,070	5,798	96,851	96,950	7,320	5,628	6,356
84,951	85,050	6,213	4,521	5,250	90,951	91,050	6,771	5,079	5,808	96,951	97,050	7,329	5,637	6,366
85,051	85,150	6,222	4,531	5,259	91,051	91,150	6,780	5,089	5,817	97,051	97,150	7,338	5,647	6,375
85,151	85,250	6,232	4,540	5,268	91,151	91,250	6,790	5,098	5,826	97,151	97,250	7,348	5,656	6,384
85,251	85,350	6,241	4,549	5,278	91,251	91,350	6,799	5,107	5,836	97,251	97,350	7,357	5,665	6,394
85,351	85,450	6,250	4,558	5,287	91,351	91,450	6,808	5,116	5,845	97,351	97,450	7,366	5,674	6,403
85,451	85,550	6,260	4,568	5,296	91,451	91,550	6,818	5,126	5,854	97,451	97,550	7,376	5,684	6,412
85,551	85,650	6,269	4,577	5,305	91,551	91,650	6,827	5,135	5,863	97,551	97,650	7,385	5,693	6,421
85,651	85,750	6,278	4,586	5,315	91,651	91,750	6,836	5,144	5,873	97,651	97,750	7,394	5,702	6,431
85,751	85,850	6,288	4,596	5,324	91,751	91,850	6,846	5,154	5,882	97,751	97,850	7,404	5,712	6,440
85,851	85,950	6,297	4,605	5,333	91,851	91,950	6,855	5,163	5,891	97,851	97,950	7,413	5,721	6,449
85,951	86,050	6,306	4,614	5,343	91,951	92,050	6,864	5,172	5,901	97,951	98,050	7,422	5,730	6,459
86,051	86,150	6,315	4,624	5,352	92,051	92,150	6,873	5,182	5,910	98,051	98,150	7,431	5,740	6,468
86,151	86,250	6,325	4,633	5,361	92,151	92,250	6,883	5,191	5,919	98,151	98,250	7,441	5,749	6,477
86,251	86,350	6,334	4,642	5,371	92,251	92,350	6,892	5,200	5,929	98,251	98,350	7,450	5,758	6,487
86,351	86,450	6,343	4,651	5,380	92,351	92,450	6,901	5,209	5,938	98,351	98,450	7,459	5,767	6,496
86,451	86,550	6,353	4,661	5,389	92,451	92,550	6,911	5,219	5,947	98,451	98,550	7,469	5,777	6,505
86,551	86,650	6,362	4,670	5,398	92,551	92,650	6,920	5,228	5,956	98,551	98,650	7,478	5,786	6,514
86,651	86,750	6,371	4,679	5,408	92,651	92,750	6,929	5,237	5,966	98,651	98,750	7,487	5,795	6,524
86,751	86,850	6,381	4,689	5,417	92,751	92,850	6,939	5,247	5,975	98,751	98,850	7,497	5,805	6,533
86,851	86,950	6,390	4,698	5,426	92,851	92,950	6,948	5,256	5,984	98,851	98,950	7,506	5,814	6,542
86,951	87,050	6,399	4,707	5,436	92,951	93,050	6,957	5,265	5,994	98,951	99,050	7,515	5,823	6,552
87,051	87,150	6,408	4,717	5,445	93,051	93,150	6,966	5,275	6,003	99,051	99,150	7,524	5,833	6,561
87,151	87,250	6,418	4,726	5,454	93,151	93,250	6,976	5,284	6,012	99,151	99,250	7,534	5,842	6,570
87,251	87,350	6,427	4,735	5,464	93,251	93,350	6,985	5,293	6,022	99,251	99,350	7,543	5,851	6,580
87,351	87,450	6,436	4,744	5,473	93,351	93,450	6,994	5,302	6,031	99,351	99,450	7,552	5,860	6,589
87,451	87,550	6,446	4,754	5,482	93,451	93,550	7,004	5,312	6,040	99,451	99,550	7,562	5,870	6,598
87,551	87,650	6,455	4,763	5,491	93,551	93,650	7,013	5,321	6,049	99,551	99,650	7,571	5,879	6,607
87,651	87,750	6,464	4,772	5,501	93,651	93,750	7,022	5,330	6,059	99,651	99,750	7,580	5,888	6,617
87,751	87,850	6,474	4,782	5,510	93,751	93,850	7,032	5,340	6,068	99,751	99,850	7,590	5,898	6,626
87,851	87,950	6,483	4,791	5,519	93,851	93,950	7,041	5,349	6,077	99,851	99,950	7,599	5,907	6,635
87,951	88,050	6,492	4,800	5,529	93,951	94,050	7,050	5,358	6,087	99,951	100,000	7,606	5,914	6,642
88,051	88,150	6,501	4,810	5,538	94,051	94,150	7,059	5,368	6,096					
88,151	88,250	6,511	4,819	5,547	94,151	94,250	7,069	5,377	6,105	OVER $100,000 YOU MUST FILE				
88,251	88,350	6,520	4,828	5,557	94,251	94,350	7,078	5,386	6,115	FORM 540.				
88,351	88,450	6,529	4,837	5,566	94,351	94,450	7,087	5,395	6,124					

FRANCHISE TAX AND CORPORATION INCOME TAX RATES

BANK AND CORPORATION FRANCHISE TAX

Corporations, other than banks and financial institutions, are taxed at the rate of 8.84% (see ¶ 809).

For the rate on banks and financial institutions (see ¶ 809).

For the rate on S corporations (see ¶ 803).

The minimum franchise tax is $800 for existing corporations (see ¶ 809).

For the 1999 income year, the minimum franchise tax for certain new, small corporations that incorporate during 1999 for their first two years of business is reduced to $300 and $500, respectively (see ¶ 809). Corporations that incorporate in California after 1999 are exempt from the minimum franchise tax for their first and second taxable years.

CORPORATION INCOME TAX

The rate is the same as the franchise tax on corporations other than banks and financial institutions (see above and ¶ 809).

ALTERNATIVE MINIMUM TAX

The alternative minimum tax rate is 6.65% (see ¶ 809a).

PART II
RETURN PREPARATION GUIDE
RESIDENTS: PREPARING INDIVIDUAL FORM 540

¶ 25 How Residents Are Taxed

The computation of tax on a resident return (Form 540) begins with "federal adjusted gross income." Modifications (see ¶ 30) are made for law differences, then modified itemized deductions (see ¶ 31) or the standard deduction (see ¶ 29) are subtracted to arrive at "taxable income."

After the tax liability is determined, personal exemption and dependent exemption credits (see ¶ 28) are subtracted. Various other special credits are also allowed (see ¶ 33).

Special California rate provisions (see ¶ 32) deal with (1) the alternative minimum tax, (2) the penalty or recapture tax on premature distributions of IRAs, Keogh plans, or other qualified retirement plans, (3) the penalty tax on nonexempt withdrawals from medical savings accounts, (4) the separate tax on lump-sum distributions, and (5) the tax on minor children's unearned income ("kiddie tax").

The deadline for filing the 1999 Form 540 and paying the tax is the same as the federal deadline—April 17, 2000, for calendar-year taxpayers (see ¶ 34). California grants an automatic extension of time to file to October 16, 2000.

¶ 25

Paragraph references throughout this discussion are to explanations in the Guidebook. The CCH CALIFORNIA STATE TAX REPORTER should also be consulted for further details on any point.

● *Tax form outline*

The following chart illustrates the steps that an individual must follow in completing a 1999 California return.

CALIFORNIA RESIDENT

References to page numbers and line numbers below are to pages and lines of California Form 540 or Schedule CA(540). References to paragraph numbers are to the paragraphs of this discussion.

FILING STATUS

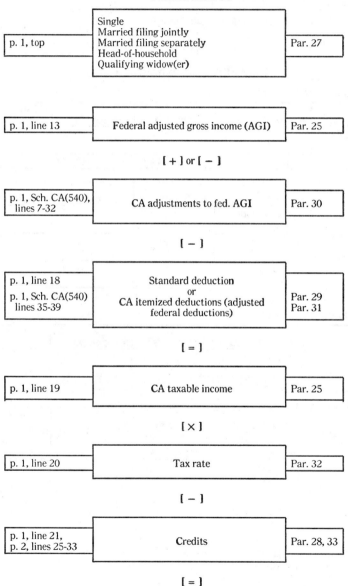

| p. 1, top | Single
Married filing jointly
Married filing separately
Head-of-household
Qualifying widow(er) | Par. 27 |

| p. 1, line 13 | Federal adjusted gross income (AGI) | Par. 25 |

[+] or [−]

| p. 1, Sch. CA(540), lines 7-32 | CA adjustments to fed. AGI | Par. 30 |

[−]

| p. 1, line 18
p. 1, Sch. CA(540) lines 35-39 | Standard deduction
or
CA itemized deductions (adjusted federal deductions) | Par. 29
Par. 31 |

[=]

| p. 1, line 19 | CA taxable income | Par. 25 |

[×]

| p. 1, line 20 | Tax rate | Par. 32 |

[−]

| p. 1, line 21, p. 2, lines 25-33 | Credits | Par. 28, 33 |

[=]

¶ 25

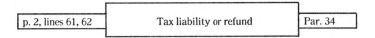

| p. 2, lines 61, 62 | Tax liability or refund | Par. 34 |

¶ 26 Return Filing Requirements

California Forms: Forms 540, 540A, 540EZ, 540 2EZ.

The following filing levels apply in 1999 (see ¶ 104):

1999 Filing Threshold Amounts

Gross income more than:

	Age on 12/31/99	No dependents	1 dependent	2 or more dependents
Single or unmarried	Under 65	10,899	18,466	24,141
	65 or older	14,499	20,174	24,714

	Age on 12/31/99	No dependents	1 dependent	2 or more dependents
Married	Under 65 (both spouses)	21,798	29,365	35,040
	65 or older (one spouse)	25,398	31,073	35,613
	65 or older (both spouses)	28,998	34,673	39,213

Adjusted gross income more than:

	Age on 12/31/99	No dependents	1 dependent	2 or more dependents
Single or unmarried	Under 65	8,719	16,286	21,961
	65 or older	12,319	17,994	22,534

	Age on 12/31/99	No dependents	1 dependent	2 or more dependents
Married	Under 65 (both spouses)	17,438	25,005	30,680
	65 or older (one spouse)	21,038	26,713	31,253
	65 or older (both spouses)	24,638	30,313	34,853

Income filing levels are determined by reference to federal gross and adjusted gross income.

For purposes of the filing thresholds, (1) single persons include taxpayers filing as heads of households and qualifying widowers and (2) married couples include taxpayers filing either jointly or separately.

¶ 26

Special filing levels apply for the filing of a separate return by a dependent (see ¶ 104).

For information regarding which taxpayers may file Forms 540A, 540EZ, and 540 2EZ, see ¶ 104.

See ¶ 103 for a discussion as to who is considered a "resident" of the state.

● *Military personnel*

Members of the Armed Forces who are residents stationed in California are subject to the same return filing requirement amounts as other taxpayers (see ¶ 103).

¶ 27 Filing Status

The filing status on the California return is generally the same as the filing status on the federal Form 1040 (see ¶ 110).

However, there are exceptions to this rule for married taxpayers who file joint federal returns:

Military: Spouses who file a joint federal return and who had different states of residence at any time during the year have the option of filing separate California returns if one spouse was an active member of the Armed Forces (Form 540). The tax should be figured both jointly and separately in order to determine the more favorable filing status.

Part-year residents and nonresidents: This exception is discussed at ¶ 63.

Factors in determining which filing status is advantageous are discussed at ¶ 110.

¶ 28 Personal and Dependent Exemptions

California provides credits against the tax for personal and dependent exemptions in lieu of deductions from income (see ¶ 109).

The 1999 tax credit amounts are as follows:

Single	$ 72
Married, separate return	72
Married, joint return	144
Head of household	72
Surviving spouse	144
Dependent	227
Visually impaired person (additional)	72
Elderly person (additional)	72

The dependent exemption credit is decreased from $253 to $227 for the 1999 taxable year and is indexed for inflation in taxable years beginning after 1999.

A physician's statement must be filed with the first return on which the visually impaired exemption credit is claimed (Instructions to Form 540).

The exemption dependent credits must be reduced for taxpayers whose federal adjusted gross income exceeds the threshold amounts specified for the taxpayer's filing status (see ¶ 109).

¶ 29 Standard Deduction

The election of a California taxpayer to itemize or to claim a standard deduction is independent of the federal election (see ¶ 303). Taxpayers may choose the more favorable tax treatment.

The California standard deduction amounts for 1999 are as follows:

Filing status	Amount
Single	$2,711
Married, joint return	5,422
Married, separate return	2,711
Head of household	5,422
Qualifying widow(er)	5,422

The above amounts are not increased (as under federal law) if the taxpayer is elderly or blind.

The standard deduction amount for dependents is limited to the greater of (a) $700 or (b) the individual's earned income plus $250.

¶ 30 Modifications to Federal Adjusted Gross Income

California Forms: Sch. CA (540), Sch. D, Sch. D-1, FTB 3801, FTB 3805V, FTB 3805Z, FTB 3806, FTB 3807, FTB 3809, FTB 3885A.

The computation on Form 540 starts with federal adjusted gross income; modification adjustments are listed to reflect federal/state law differences. The adjustments are grouped as subtractions and as additions on California Schedule CA (540). They are aggregated and then netted before entry on Form 540.

The California Schedule CA (540) has two parts. Part I reports the subtractions and additions to federal adjusted gross income. Part II reports the modified federal itemized deductions. Part II adjustments are explained at ¶ 31.

The most commonly made modifications to adjusted gross income are discussed in the following paragraphs. Other modifications are discussed in FTB Pub. 1001.

1. Interest on state obligations (see ¶ 217): Interest on bonds of states other than California or on obligations issued by municipalities of other states is added back to federal adjusted gross income.

Notes:

a. Interest from investment in an enterprise zone is deductible under California, but not federal, law (see ¶ 239).

b. Interest on Community Energy Authority bonds issued in California is deductible under California, but not federal, law (see ¶ 201).

2. Interest on federal obligations (See ¶ 217): Interest on federal obligations is exempt and, consequently, is subtracted from federal adjusted gross income. See also ¶ 217 for the pass-through of tax-exempt interest from a mutual fund.

Interest income from Federal Farm Credit banks, Federal Home Loan banks, the Student Loan Marketing Association (SLMA), the Resolution Funding Corporation, the Production Credit Association, the Commodity Credit Corporation, Certificates of Accrual on Treasury Securities (CATS), and Treasury Investment Growth Receipts (TIGRS) is also exempt interest that is subtracted from federal adjusted gross income; however, interest from Fannie Maes, Ginnie Maes, or FHLMC securities is taxable in California and, therefore, no modification is made to federal adjusted gross income for interest from these instruments.

3. **Depreciation** (see ¶ 310, ¶ 310a): California depreciation is generally the same as federal (the "modified accelerated cost recovery system" under IRC Sec. 168) for assets placed in service after 1986. California also allows the same asset expense allowance deduction as federal for IRC Sec. 179 property for assets placed in service after 1986 and before 1993 and for assets placed in service after 1998. However, for taxable years beginning after 1992 and before 1999, the maximum allowable IRC Sec. 179 deduction for California purposes was lower than that allowed under federal law; see ¶ 310a for a detailed discussion.

California adopts the federal 39-year depreciation recovery period for nonresidential real property acquired after May 12, 1993, but only for property placed in service after 1996 in taxable years beginning after 1996. Thus, for California purposes, nonresidential real property placed in service before 1997 in taxable years beginning before 1997 continues to be depreciated over a 31.5-year recovery period.

Further differences in the amount of depreciation claimed for federal and California purposes may arise due to California provisions that allow taxpayers operating in specified depressed areas to claim accelerated write-offs for certain property (see ¶ 310f).

ACRS is allowed federally for assets placed in service after 1980 and before 1987. However, for California purposes, assets placed in service before 1987 are depreciated over the period of useful life, or guidelines periods established in the appropriate federal Revenue Procedure, using sum-of-the-years digits, declining balance, straight-line, or other pre-ACRS federal method.

Note: The differences between federal and California deductions are adjusted on FTB 3885A. The net adjustment may be an addition or a subtraction.

4. **Capital gains and losses** (see ¶ 512): California law and federal law prior to the 1997 tax year treat all capital gains realized after 1986 as ordinary income. However, for tax years beginning after 1996, federal law subjects long-term capital gains to a lower tax rate.

Differences between the amount of capital gain or loss recognized for California and federal purposes can occur both in the year a gain or loss is recognized and also in loss carryover years. For the 1999 taxable year, differences can occur between the gain or loss allowed for federal and California purposes because (1) California does not permit capital loss carrybacks (see ¶ 514); (2) California, but not federal, law excludes gain on the sale or disposition of qualified assisted housing developments (see ¶ 502b); and (3)

¶ **30**

California requires certain adjustments to basis not required by federal law and makes certain federal adjustments inapplicable (see ¶ 534).

Differences between pre-1987 California and federal laws that can affect the reporting of capital gain and loss include:

(1) A difference in capital loss carryover; see ¶ 514.

(2) The pre-1987 holding periods and taxable percentages of capital gains for California were different from the federal.

(3) The California adjustment to capital gains computed for purposes of the investment interest expense deduction was different from the federal adjustment.

(4) For years prior to 1987, the federal 50% limitation on long-term capital loss deductions did not apply for California purposes.

(5) Dividends from mutual funds were treated as ordinary income for California purposes.

(6) Because of the various differences between California and federal law mentioned above, the California basis may not always be the same as the federal basis of the property. Examples of such situations are as follows:

(A) valuation of property acquired by inheritance (see ¶ 525);

(B) depreciation of business property (see ¶ 310, ¶ 310a);

(C) basis adjustment of property for moves into California (see ¶ 502a);

(D) basis adjustments for California and federal credits (see ¶ 131, ¶ 140); and

(E) basis in the stock of an S corporation (see ¶ 232).

(7) Gain or loss may be reported in different tax years for California purposes because changes to the federal law affecting the computation of gain or loss were not adopted by California until subsequent years.

Schedule D, Form 540, is used to calculate the differences, and the appropriate modification is carried to California Schedule CA (540).

See ¶ 512—¶ 520a for further details.

5. **State income tax refund:** Any California income tax refunds included in federal adjusted gross income are subtracted from federal adjusted gross income.

6. **Unemployment compensation** (see ¶ 201): Unemployment compensation included on the federal return is not taxed by California and is subtracted from federal adjusted gross income.

7. **Social security benefits** (see ¶ 201): California does not tax Social Security benefits. Any Social Security benefits included in federal adjusted gross income are subtracted.

8. **Railroad retirement benefits** (see ¶ 201, ¶ 205): Both tier 1 and tier 2 railroad retirement benefits, including ridesharing benefits and sick pay, received under the Federal Insurance Contributions and Railroad Retirement Act are subtracted from federal adjusted gross income.

¶ 30

9. **California lottery winnings** (see ¶ 201): Any California lottery winnings included in federal adjusted gross income are subtracted.

10. **IRA and Keogh distributions** (see ¶ 318): The California and federal deductible dollar limits are the same for post-1986 tax years. For pre-1987 tax years, the amounts differed; consequently, the amount taxable on a distribution will differ. Differences may also arise if the taxpayer changed residence during the time he or she made contributions to the IRA or Keogh plan.

A worksheet to compute differences in the tax treatment of distributions for federal and California purposes is included in FTB Pub. 1005, Pension and Annuity Guidelines.

11. **Net operating loss** (see ¶ 309): The California NOL is determined under the same rules as the federal NOL except that no carrybacks are allowed and the amount of loss eligible for carryover to future years is generally limited to 50% of the California net operating loss. In addition, a California NOL may be carried forward for only five years rather than the 20 years permitted under federal law (15 years for losses incurred in tax years beginning before August 6, 1997). Special rules apply for "new" and "small" businesses and for NOLs resulting from disasters or claimed by taxpayers operating in enterprise zones, the former Los Angeles Revitalization Zone (LARZ), local agency military base recovery areas (LAMBRAs), or targeted tax areas.

Calculation of the California NOL is made on FTB 3805V and the appropriate adjustment is entered on California Schedule CA (540). The order in which net operating losses are absorbed is computed on a separate worksheet (which is not filed with the return). Calculation of the NOL for enterprise zone businesses is made on FTB 3805Z. FTB 3806 is used to calculate the NOL for taxpayers who operated in the former LARZ, FTB 3807 is used to calculate the NOL for taxpayers operating in LAMBRAs, and FTB 3809 is used to calculate the NOL for taxpayers operating in targeted tax areas.

12. **Recycling revenues** (see ¶ 201): The income received by a taxpayer for recycling empty beverage containers is exempt for California purposes and is subtracted if included in federal adjusted gross income.

13. **Expenses related to tax-exempt income** (see ¶ 31): Expenses related to federally tax-exempt income that were disallowed as a deduction in computing federal adjusted gross income are subtracted for California purposes. Expenses incurred to purchase or carry obligations that are tax-exempt under California but not federal law are added to federal adjusted gross income.

Note: These modifications, to the extent not business-related, are made to federal itemized deductions.

14. **Income from exercising California qualified stock options** (see ¶ 207): Compensation received from exercising a California qualified stock option is excluded from California gross income and may be subtracted if the compensation was included in federal adjusted gross income.

¶ 30

15. Ridesharing and employee commuter deductions (see ¶ 240): An exclusion from gross income is available to an employee for amounts received from his or her employer for certain ridesharing or commuting arrangements.

16. Pensions and annuities (see ¶ 205, ¶ 206): California rules for taxing pensions and annuities are basically the same as federal; however, the taxable amount may differ because of federal/California differences in the years when contributions were made. For further information see FTB Pub. 1005.

17. Passive activity loss (see ¶ 326): California generally adopts federal rules for computing the limitation on deducting passive activity losses. However, California does not conform to the federal passive activity loss rules relating to rental real estate losses suffered by certain taxpayers who materially participate in real property trades or businesses. Differences may also exist because the amount of passive income and loss may differ. Taxpayers must segregate California adjustments that relate to passive activities from California adjustments that relate to nonpassive items (see ¶ 326). This calculation is made on FTB 3801.

18. Other gains or losses (see ¶ 519): Although California law on the computation of gain from sales of business property and certain involuntary conversions is the same as federal, the amount of gain or loss may differ because of federal/California basis differences. These amounts are reported on Schedule D-1.

19. Original issue discount (see ¶ 236): California treatment of original issue discount is the same as federal except for debt instruments issued in 1985 and 1986.

20. Alimony (see ¶ 204): Alimony received by a nonresident alien that was not included in the taxpayer's federal gross income is treated as an addition on Schedule CA (540).

21. Income from specially treated sources: See the indicated paragraphs for possible federal/California differences in the taxation of the following items: (1) noncash patronage dividends from farmers' cooperatives or mutual associations (see ¶ 231); and (2) interest income from investment in enterprise zones (see ¶ 239).

22. Income from S corporations (see ¶ 232): Shareholders of California S corporations add or subtract, as appropriate, the difference between their distributive shares of federal and California S corporation income or loss.

Shareholders of S corporations (by federal election) that have not elected California S corporation status receive notification of the amounts actually distributed or made available to them. These amounts are treated as dividends.

23. Income from partnerships and limited liability partnerships (see ¶ 612, ¶ 617): Partners add or subtract, as appropriate, the difference between their distributive shares of federal and California partnership income or loss.

24. Income from limited liability companies (see ¶ 618): Members and persons with economic interests in an LLC add or subtract, as appropriate, the difference between their shares of federal and California LLC income

¶ 30

in the same manner as partners must include their distributive shares of partnership income in their taxable income.

25. **Income from trusts and estates** (see ¶604a): Trust or estate beneficiaries add or subtract, as appropriate, the difference between their shares of federal and California trust or estate income or loss.

26. **Business expenses incurred in discriminatory clubs** (see ¶301, ¶322): California prohibits a business expense deduction for expenditures at a club that restricts membership or use on the basis of age, sex, race, religion, color, ancestry, or national origin. There is no similar federal prohibition.

27. **Wages** (see ¶201): If there is a difference in wages because of an employee's fringe benefits, also reported on the W-2, an adjustment must be made because California does not adopt the federal rules; the amount of federal wages reported on the W-2 is subtracted and the amount reported as California wages is added.

28. **Crime hotline rewards** (see ¶245): Any rewards received from a government authorized crime hotline are excluded from gross income.

29. **Water conservation rebates** (see ¶243): California excludes from gross income specified water conservation rebates received from local water agencies or suppliers.

30. **Conservation and environmental cost-share payments** (see ¶242): Certain cost-share payments received by forest landowners from the Department of Forestry and Fire Protection are subtracted from federal gross income.

¶ 31 Itemized Deductions

California Form: Sch. CA (540).

California itemized deductions are based on federal itemized deductions, with the modifications discussed below. These modifications are independent of the adjustments to federal AGI discussed at ¶30, even though both are calculated on Schedule CA (540).

Taxpayers may elect either the standard deduction or itemized deductions for California purposes, regardless of which was elected for federal purposes (see ¶29). A federal Schedule A must be completed if the taxpayer did not itemize federally but chooses to itemize on the California return. A copy of the federal Form 1040 and all supporting federal forms and schedules must be attached to Form 540 if the taxpayer filed federal schedules other than Schedules A and B.

The adjustments are:

(a) *Taxes* (see ¶306): State, local, and foreign income taxes (including state disability insurance—SDI) claimed on federal Schedule A are not allowable deductions for California purposes and are subtracted from federal itemized deductions.

(b) *California Lottery losses* (see ¶322): California Lottery losses are not deductible for California purposes. The amount of such losses, as shown on federal Schedule A, must be subtracted from federal itemized deductions.

¶ 31

(c) *Federal obligation expense* (see ¶ 305): Because California does not tax interest from federal obligations, any expenses relating to such interest that have been deducted for federal purposes on Schedule A should be subtracted from federal itemized deductions.

(d) *State obligation expense* (see ¶ 305): Because California taxes interest from state or local obligations of states other than California, which is exempt for federal purposes, any expenses related to this interest that were not entered on federal Schedule A may be added to federal itemized deductions.

(e) *Employee business expense deduction for depreciation* (see ¶ 310): If the employee business expense deduction claimed federally included depreciation of assets placed in service prior to 1987, the depreciation component is recomputed for California purposes because business property was depreciated under a different method for California and federal purposes prior to 1987. Also, if the maximum IRC Sec. 179 deduction was taken for property placed in service in tax years beginning after 1992 and before 1999, the federal and California amounts will differ (see ¶ 310a).

(f) *Adoption-related expenses* (see ¶ 128): California allows a credit for specified adoption-related expenses. If the taxpayer claims the California adoption costs credit for the same amounts deducted on the federal Schedule A, these amounts must be subtracted on California Schedule CA (540).

(g) *Investment interest expense* (see ¶ 305): This item is generally treated the same for California as for federal purposes. However, taxpayers filing federal Form 4952 must file the corresponding California FTB 3526. Differences, if any, are reported on Schedule CA (540). Differences may occur because of the capital gain component in computing pre-1987 investment interest expense; the pre-1987 holding period and taxable percentages of capital gains were different under California law.

(h) *Federal mortgage interest credit:* California does not have a credit comparable to the federal mortgage interest credit. If federal miscellaneous itemized deductions on Schedule A were reduced by the amount of this credit, California itemized deductions may be increased by the same amount on Schedule CA (540).

(i) *Limitation for high-income taxpayers* (see ¶ 303): The itemized deductions of taxpayers with adjusted gross incomes over a threshold amount must be reduced by the lesser of (1) 6% (3% under federal law) of the excess of adjusted gross income over the threshold amount or (2) 80% of the amount of the itemized deductions otherwise allowable for the tax year. A worksheet is provided in the Schedule CA (540) Instructions for calculation of the adjustment.

(j) *Federal estate and generation-skipping transfer taxes:* California does not allow deductions for federal tax paid on income with respect to a decedent or for tax paid on generation-skipping transfers. Accordingly, amounts deducted on federal Schedule A for these items must be subtracted on California Schedule CA (540).

(k) *Legislators' travel expenses* (see ¶ 301): California does not follow the federal rule allowing legislators to deduct expenses for every legislative day. California allows legislators to deduct only those expenses incurred on days that the legislators are actually away from their districts overnight. Amounts deducted for federal purposes on Schedule A that do not qualify for California purposes must be subtracted from federal itemized deductions.

(*1*) *Contributions of qualified appreciated stock* (see ¶ 312): California law, unlike federal law, does not allow a taxpayer to deduct the full fair market value of qualified appreciated stock contributed to a private foundation. Because California still requires a reduction of the fair market value to reflect the long-term capital gain that would be realized upon the stock's sale for purposes of claiming the deduction, California taxpayers must subtract the value difference from federal itemized deductions.

¶ 32 Tax Rates

California Forms: Sch. P (540), Sch. G-1, FTB 3800, FTB 3803, FTB 3805P.

The tax rates are progressive, ranging from 1% to 9.3% of taxable income (see ¶ 112). The tax tables are reproduced on pages 33 through 37. The tax rate schedules are reproduced on pages 31 and 32, but are used only to determine tax if taxable income is over $100,000.

● *Alternative minimum tax*

The California alternative minimum tax is imposed·at the rate of 7%. It is generally calculated in the same manner as for federal purposes, but there are differences (see ¶ 112a).

The California AMT is computed on Schedule P (540).

California incorporates the IRC Sec. 53 credit for "prior year minimum tax" (see ¶ 33).

● *Tax on premature distributions of IRAs, Keogh plans, annuities, and life insurance contracts*

Both California and federal law impose a penalty tax on premature distributions from IRAs, Keogh plans, other self-employed plans, annuity plans, and "modified endowment contracts," to the extent the distribution is included in income (see ¶ 206). The amount of the premature distribution includible in income for California purposes may differ from that allowed federally because of differences in deductibility of contributions in pre-1987 tax years (see ¶ 318).

The California penalty is 2.5%.

Form FTB 3805P is used to make the computation.

● *Tax on nonexempt withdrawals from medical savings accounts*

Distributions from a medical savings account for nonmedical purposes are subject to a 10% penalty tax (15% under federal law). For further information see ¶ 246. Form FTB 3805P is used to make the computation.

● *Separate tax on lump-sum distributions*

Taxpayers with lump-sum distributions of retirement income compute and pay a separate tax on these distributions if they elected to pay the separate federal tax (see ¶ 206). The California tax, which is computed on Schedule G-1, is determined under the same rules as the federal tax. The tax is transferred from Schedule G-1 to Form 540 and is added to the regular tax.

● *Tax on minor child's unearned income ("kiddie tax")*

California incorporates the federal "kiddie tax" provisions applicable when a child who is not yet 14 by the close of the tax year and who has a parent living at such time has unearned income in excess of $1,400 (see ¶ 113). The tax is computed on FTB 3800, which parallels federal Form 8615.

Under certain circumstances, a parent may elect to include the unearned income of a child on the parent's return. If the parent elects to exercise this option, FTB 3803 must accompany the parent's return.

¶ 33 Credits Against the Tax

> *California Forms:* Form 540A, Form 540EZ, Sch. P (540), Sch. S, FTB 3501, FTB 3507, FTB 3510, FTB 3521, FTB 3523, FTB 3535, FTB 3540, FTB 3546, FTB 3547, FTB 3548, FTB 3553, FTB 3805Z, FTB 3807, FTB 3808, FTB 3809.

The order of using the various tax credits is specified in the instructions to the California 540 return, with each credit identified by a code number. If there are more than three credits claimed, the taxpayer must attach the appropriate credit form and summarize each credit on California Schedule P (540).

Following is a brief description of the allowable credits.

1. Child care expense credits (see ¶ 123): Tax credits are allowed for employers who construct child care facilities, establish child care programs, contribute to child care information and referral services, or contribute to qualified child care plans. These credits are claimed on Form 3501. Unused credit may be carried over until exhausted.

2. Renter's credit (see ¶ 122): For taxable years beginning after 1997, a nonrefundable credit is available to qualified renters. For the 1999 taxable year, the amount of the credit is (1) $120 for married couples filing joint returns, heads of households, and surviving spouses, provided adjusted gross income is $51,300 or less, and (2) $60 for other individuals, provided adjusted gross income is $25,650 or less. Unused credits may not be carried over.

3. Joint custody head-of-household, dependent parent credits (see ¶ 125a): For the 1999 taxable year, these credits, which cover both dependent children and dependent parents, equal the lesser of 30% of the California tax liability or $288. A worksheet is provided in the 540 Instructions for computation purposes. Qualifications that must be met in order to claim the credits are discussed at ¶ 125a. Unused credit may not be carried over.

4. Research and development credit (see ¶ 139): California generally allows the federal credit for increasing research activities with the following changes:

    (a) research must be conducted within California to qualify;

    (b) the applicable California credit percentage is 12% of the excess of qualified research expenses for the tax year over the "base amount";

(c) California modifies the formula used by those taxpayers that elect to compute the amount of the credit using an alternative method;

(d) California does not allow a credit against personal income tax for basic research payments;

(e) the California credit applies to expenses paid or incurred in taxable years beginning after 1986 and is available indefinitely thereafter, whereas the federal credit does not apply to amounts paid or incurred after June 30, 1995, and before July 1, 1996, or after June 30, 1999;

(f) California limits the "gross receipts" that may be taken into account for purposes of calculating the base amount;

(g) the California credit may be carried over; and

(h) for taxable years beginning after 1997, California law disallows the credit for expenses incurred to purchase property for which a sales and use tax exemption for teleproduction or other postproduction property is claimed.

A married couple filing separately has the option of one taking the full credit or of dividing it equally between them.

FTB 3523 is used to compute the credit. Unused credit from nonpassive activities may be carried over until exhausted.

5. **Credit for income taxes paid to other states** (see ¶ 116): A credit is allowed for income taxes paid to certain states and possessions, but no credit is allowed for income taxes paid to any city, the federal government, or a foreign country. A list of the states and possessions for which the credit is allowed appears at ¶ 116.

The credit for income taxes paid to other states is available only for net income taxes (excluding any kind of alternative minimum tax or other tax on preference items) paid to another state on income with its source in the other state that is also taxed by California. The latter requirement rules out the credit for tax paid on income from intangible property because such income is deemed under California law to be attributable to California as the state of residence. The amount of the credit is limited to that proportion of the total California tax payable as the double-taxed income bears to the total income taxed by California.

Schedule S, showing computation of the credit, must be attached to the California return along with a copy of the other state's tax return.

There is no carryover of this credit.

6. **Excess state disability insurance credit** (see ¶ 120): Excess employee contributions for California disability insurance are treated as a refundable income tax credit. For 1999, the credit amount is the amount contributed in excess of $158.84. Excess contributions may occur when a taxpayer works for more than one employer during the tax year. The amount of the credit is calculated on a worksheet included in the Instructions to Form 540.

Note: If more than the maximum was withheld by a single employer, or at a higher rate, the excess amount must be claimed as a refund from the employer rather than as a tax credit.

¶ 33

7. **Personal exemption credits** (see ¶ 109): Credits are allowed for personal and dependency exemptions (see ¶ 28).

8. **Disabled access expenditures credit** (see ¶ 129): California allows eligible small businesses a credit for 50% of up to $250 of the disabled access expenditures paid or incurred by those businesses to comply with the federal Americans with Disabilities Act. Except for the amount, the credit is similar to the federal credit allowed under IRC Sec. 44. The credit is computed on FTB 3548. Unused credit may be carried over until exhausted.

9. **Farmworker housing credit** (see ¶ 126): California allows a nonrefundable credit for the lesser of (1) up to 50% of qualified amounts paid or incurred for the construction or rehabilitation of farmworker housing in California or (2) the amount certified by the Tax Credit Allocation Committee. Unused credit may be carried over until exhausted.

10. **Low-income housing credit** (see ¶ 127): California allows a low-income housing credit for owners of residential rental projects that provide low-income housing located in California. The credit is similar to the federal credit computed under IRC Sec. 42. The California Tax Credit Allocation Committee certifies to the taxpayer on Form 3521A the amount of the credit for each year in the credit period.

The credit is computed on FTB 3521. A copy of Form 3521A must be provided to the FTB upon request. Unused credit may be carried over until exhausted.

11. **Enterprise zone credit for wages earned** (see ¶ 135): The California credit is 5% of qualified wages received from an enterprise zone business. For each dollar of income in excess of qualified wages, the credit is reduced by 9¢. The credit is non-refundable. There is no carryover of unused credits. Designated zones are listed at ¶ 102b.

FTB 3553 is used to calculate the amount of the credit.

12. **Enterprise zone hiring and sales tax credits** (see ¶ 133 and ¶ 134): The amount of the California hiring credit is 50% of qualified wages paid to a qualified employee in his or her first year of employment, 40% in the second year, 30% in the third year, 20% in the fourth year, and 10% in the fifth year. The credit is limited to tax attributable to income from the enterprise zone. An employer's deduction for salaries and wages must be offset by the amount of the credit. California enterprise zones are listed at ¶ 102b as well as in FTB 3805Z. Unused amounts may be carried over.

The amount of sales or use tax paid on the purchase of machinery or parts used in an enterprise zone may also be claimed as a credit against tax. Unused credit may be carried over to future years.

The enterprise zone credits are computed on FTB 3805Z. A separate FTB 3805Z must be attached to the taxpayer's return for each enterprise zone in which the business area invests.

13. **Local agency military base recovery area (LAMBRA) hiring and sales tax credits** (see ¶ 133, ¶ 136): Hiring and sales tax credits substantially similar to enterprise zone credits are available to qualified LAMBRA businesses.

¶ 33

The credits are computed on FTB 3807. The amount claimed by a taxpayer for both of the LAMBRA credits combined may not exceed the amount of tax attributable to LAMBRA income. Unused credit may be carried over to succeeding taxable years and applied to tax on income from the area.

14. Targeted tax area hiring and sales and use tax credits (see ¶ 133, ¶ 137): Tax credits are provided for employers who hire certain disadvantaged individuals within a targeted tax area. A tax credit is also available for businesses that purchase machinery or equipment to be used within the area. The credits are similar to those available to enterprise zone businesses and are computed on FTB 3809.

15. Manufacturing enhancement area hiring credit (see ¶ 138): A hiring credit substantially similar to the credit available to enterprise zone businesses may be claimed by qualified manufacturing enhancement area businesses. The credit is computed on FTB 3808.

16. Credit for prior year minimum tax (see ¶ 141): California incorporates the IRC Sec. 53 credit for alternative minimum tax paid in a prior year by a taxpayer who is not liable for the AMT in the current year; the credit is based on preference items that defer tax liability rather than permanently reduce the tax. The amount allowable as a credit in any tax year is limited to the regular California personal income tax for the year, less (a) the refundable credits that have no carryover provisions and (b) the credit for taxes paid to other states. Unused credit may be carried over. The credit is computed on FTB 3510.

17. Enhanced oil recovery credit (see ¶ 142): California allows certain independent oil producers an enhanced oil recovery credit equal to ⅓ of the federal credit allowed under IRC Sec. 43, provided the costs for which the credit is claimed are attributable to projects located within California. FTB 3546 is used to compute the credit. Unused credit may be carried forward for up to 15 years.

18. Senior head-of-household credit (see ¶ 125): A credit is available to qualified seniors. A worksheet to compute the credit is included in the Instructions to Form 540.

19. Prison inmate labor credit (see ¶ 143): A credit is available to employers for 10% of the wages paid to certain prison inmates. FTB 3507 is used to calculate the credit. There is no carryover of this credit.

20. Manufacturer's investment credit (see ¶ 140): California allows a credit against net tax in an amount equal to 6% of the amount paid or incurred after 1993 for qualified property placed in service in this state that, with the exception of certain industries, is also depreciable IRC Sec. 1245 property.

The credit is computed on FTB 3535. Unused credit may be carried forward for up to eight years (10 years for certain small businesses).

21. Adoption costs credit (see ¶ 128): A credit is available for up to 50% of the costs directly related to the adoption of a U.S. citizen or legal resident minor child who was in the custody of a state or county public agency. A

¶ 33

worksheet is provided in the Form 540 Instructions to compute the credit. Unused credit may be carried over until exhausted.

22. **Salmon and steelhead trout habitat credit** (see ¶ 124): California allows a credit against net tax for up to 10% of the costs associated with qualified salmon and steelhead trout habitat restoration and improvement projects. However, the Department of Fish and Game is authorized to reduce the amount of the credit that may be claimed. Unused credit may be carried over until exhausted.

23. **Credit for costs of transporting donated agricultural products** (see ¶ 130): California allows a credit against net tax for 50% of the costs paid or incurred in connection with the transportation of agricultural products donated to nonprofit charitable organizations. FTB 3547 is used to compute the credit. Unused credit may be carried over until exhausted.

24. **Rice straw credit** (see ¶ 144): For taxable years beginning after 1996 and before 2008, California allows a credit equal to $15 for each ton of California-grown rice straw purchased during the taxable year. Unused credit may be carried forward for up to 10 years.

25. **Credit for community development investments** (see ¶ 145): For taxable years beginning after 1996 and before 2002, California allows a credit equal to 20% of each qualified deposit that is made into a community development financial institution and certified by the California Organized Investment Network.

● *Carryover credits*

Other credits for which carryovers may still exist (and the years for which they were available) include the following:

1. water conservation credit (1980—1982);

2. solar pump (agricultural) credit (1981—1983);

3. solar energy installation credit (1985—1988);

4. energy conservation credit (1981—1986);

5. ridesharing credits (1981—1986 and 1989—1995);

6. commercial solar energy credit (1987—1988);

7. political contributions credit (1987—1991);

8. residential rental and farm sales credit (1987—1991);

9. agricultural products credit (1989—1991);

10. orphan drug research credit (1987—1992);

11. qualified parent's infant care credit (1991—1993);

12. commercial solar electric system credit (1990—1993);

13. recycling equipment credit (1989—1995);

14. low-emission vehicle credit (1991—1995); and

15. Los Angeles Revitalization Zone hiring and sales and use tax credits (1992—1997).

All of the above credit carryovers may be claimed on FTB 3540. See prior editions of the GUIDEBOOK for details about these credits.

¶ 33

¶ 34 When and Where to File and Pay Tax

The due date for filing California Form 540 and paying the tax is the same as the federal due date—April 17, 2000, for calendar-year taxpayers (see ¶ 105, ¶ 107). Returns made by fiscal year taxpayers are due on or before the 15th day of the fourth month after the close of the fiscal year. Returns made by mail are considered timely if properly addressed and postmarked on or before the due date.

Returns are filed with the Franchise Tax Board (FTB). However, the address to which they are sent differs depending on (1) whether an amount is due or a refund is expected and (2) the type of form used.

Refund requests made on Forms 540, 540A, 540EZ, 540NR, 540X, and 541 are sent to P.O. Box 942840, Sacramento, CA 94240-0000. Refund requests made on scannable Forms 540 and 540A are sent to P.O. Box 942840, Sacramento, CA 94240-0009.

Both regular and scannable returns for which an amount is due are sent to P.O. Box 942867, Sacramento, CA 94267-0001. For all other forms, the appropriate address is noted on the return.

Checks or money orders should be made payable to the "Franchise Tax Board" with the taxpayer's social security number written on the check or money order.

● *E-file*

The FTB also accepts electronic filing of returns through the e-file program. Detailed information concerning this program is available at the FTB's website at http://www.ftb.ca.gov/elecserv.

● *Military personnel*

The due date for returns by members of the armed forces is the same as for other taxpayers, except that it may be postponed in certain cases (i.e., duty outside the U.S., service in a combat zone). See ¶ 106.

¶ 35 Extensions

California Forms: FTB 3519, FTB 3537, FTB 3538, FTB 3563.

The Franchise Tax Board (FTB) will grant "paperless" personal income tax extensions to individuals, partnerships, and fiduciaries for returns required to be filed by April 17, 2000. Thus, such persons will be granted an automatic six-month extension to October 16, 2000. The automatic extension does not extend the time for paying the tax. Tax payments must be accompanied by the appropriate form: FTB 3519 (Payment Voucher for Automatic Extension for Individuals); FTB 3537 (Payment Voucher for Automatic Extension for Limited Liability Companies); FTB 3538 (Payment Voucher for Automatic Extension for Limited Partnerships, LLPs, and REMICS); or FTB 3563 (Payment Voucher for Automatic Extension for Fiduciaries). Taxpayers should send FTB 3519 or FTB 3563 to the FTB at P.O. Box 942867, Sacramento, CA 94267-0051. FTB 3537 and FTB 3538 are sent to the FTB at P.O. Box 942857, Sacramento, CA 94257-0651.

Payment extensions may be granted for a reasonable period by the FTB (see ¶ 107). There is no prescribed form. Extensions of up to 90 days are also available to disaster victims (see ¶ 107).

Taxpayers abroad: Taxpayers who are outside the United States on the return due date are automatically granted an additional two-month extension of time to file (see ¶ 106). Consequently, the extended due date for such taxpayers is December 15th. However, interest accrues on any unpaid tax from the original due date of the return. Any additional extensions must be applied for in writing with a letter of explanation.

¶ 36 Estimated Tax

For the 2000 taxable year, estimated tax payments are generally due if (1) the 1999 or 2000 California tax (less withholding and allowable credits) exceeds $200 ($100 for married persons filing separately), (2) less than 80% of the 1999 tax was withheld, (3) less than 80% of the 2000 tax will be withheld, or (4) less than 80% of the 2000 California adjusted gross income consists of items subject to withholding (see ¶ 107a).

The California alternative minimum tax (see ¶ 32) is not included in determining any required estimated tax payments.

Estimated tax is paid in quarterly installments on the same dates as federal payments: April 15, June 15, September 15, and January 15. The January 15 installment need not be made if the taxpayer files a tax return and pays the balance of tax due by February 1. When a due date falls on a Saturday, Sunday, or other legal holiday, payments are due on the next business day.

Married couples may file separate or joint estimated tax payment vouchers, but no joint Form 540-ES can be made if the spouses have different tax years or are legally separated.

Form 540-ES is used for paying estimated tax.

¶ 37 State Tax Assistance

The Franchise Tax Board (FTB) offers various taxpayer assistance programs ranging from providing trained volunteers to assist taxpayers at no cost in completing their tax returns to in-state toll-free telephone assistance. The toll-free numbers are included in the Instructions to Form 540.

In addition, the FTB has several district offices located in principal cities throughout the state. These offices and their addresses are printed in the 540 Instruction booklet.

¶ 38 Forms

Forms may be ordered directly from the state at the following address:

Franchise Tax Board

Tax Forms Request Unit

P.O. Box 307

Rancho Cordova, CA 95741-0307

California income tax forms and publications may also be downloaded from the Internet or obtained through automated telephones. The Internet address and telephone numbers are listed in the Form 540 Instruction booklet.

¶ 39 Interest

The California rate of interest on underpayments and overpayments of tax is based on the federal underpayment rate (see ¶ 709). The interest rate is redetermined semiannually and is as follows:

January 1, 1996—June 30, 1996	9%
July 1, 1996—December 31, 1996	9%
January 1, 1997—June 30, 1997	9%
July 1, 1997—December 31, 1997	9%
January 1, 1998—June 30, 1998	9%
July 1, 1998—December 31, 1998	9%
January 1, 1999—June 30, 1999	8%
July 1, 1999—December 31, 1999	7%
January 1, 2000—June 30, 2000	8%

¶ 40 Penalties

A penalty of 5% per month, up to a maximum of 25%, is imposed for failure without reasonable cause to file a return. If the failure to file is fraudulent, the penalty is 15% per month, up to a maximum of 75%.

The penalty for failure to pay income tax when it is due is 5% of the unpaid amount plus 1/2% per month. If the penalties for failure to file and failure to pay are both applicable, the penalty imposed is the higher of (1) the penalty for failure to pay or (2) the total of the penalty for failure to file and the penalty for failure to furnish information.

A minimum penalty of the lesser of $100 or 100% of the tax liability is imposed if the return is not filed within 60 days of the due date.

Other penalties are discussed at ¶ 710.

NONRESIDENTS AND PART-YEAR RESIDENTS: PREPARING RETURN FORM 540NR

¶ 60 How Nonresidents Are Taxed

Nonresidents compute California tax as if they were California residents, then determine the portion of the computed tax that equals the proportion of California-source adjusted gross income (AGI) to total AGI.

The computation of taxable income on a nonresident return (Form 540NR) begins with federal AGI. Modifications (see ¶ 67) are made for law differences, then modified itemized deductions (see ¶ 68) or the standard deduction (see ¶ 65) are subtracted to arrive at "taxable income."

After tax liability is determined, personal exemption and dependent exemption credits (see ¶ 64) are subtracted. The resulting amount is prorated to determine California tax liability. California-source income, as set out on Schedule CA (540NR), is divided by total adjusted gross income from all sources to arrive at the proration percentage.

Further reduction to California tax is available by way of various other special credits (see ¶ 70).

Special California rate provisions (see ¶ 69) deal with (1) the alternative minimum tax, (2) the penalty and recapture tax on premature distributions of IRAs, Keogh plans, or other qualified retirement plans, (3) the penalty tax on nonexempt withdrawals from medical savings accounts, (4) the separate tax on lump-sum distributions, and (5) the tax on minor children's unearned income ("kiddie tax").

¶ 60

Paragraph references throughout are to explanations in the GUIDEBOOK. The CCH CALIFORNIA STATE TAX REPORTER should also be consulted for further details on any point.

¶ 61 How Part-Year Residents Are Taxed

A part-year resident is taxed on income received while residing in California and, except for retirement income received for services performed while residing in California (see ¶ 405), on income derived from sources in California during any period of nonresidency.

Computation of income for part-year residents, as for nonresidents, begins with federal adjusted gross income. Part-year residents use the same form (Form 540NR) as nonresidents and execute the same computational steps, as follows: California adjustments to federal AGI are made (see ¶ 67), followed by subtraction of modified itemized deductions (see ¶ 68) or the standard deduction (see ¶ 65). After tax liability is determined, personal exemption and dependent exemption credits are subtracted (see ¶ 64) and the result is prorated to determine California tax. California adjusted gross income (i.e., from California sources, as specified in Schedule CA (540NR)) is divided by total adjusted gross income from all sources to arrive at the proration percentage.

Various other "special" credits reduce the California tax base. These special credits include prorated credits, credits that are taken in full, and carryover credits (see ¶ 70).

Special California rate provisions (see ¶ 69) deal with (1) the alternative minimum tax, (2) the penalty or recapture tax on premature distributions of IRAs, Keogh plans, or other qualified retirement plans, (3) the penalty tax on nonexempt withdrawals from medical savings accounts, (4) the separate tax on lump-sum distributions, and (5) the tax on minor children's unearned income ("kiddie tax").

Paragraph references throughout are to explanations in the GUIDEBOOK. The CCH CALIFORNIA STATE TAX REPORTER should also be consulted for further details on any tax point.

¶ 62 Return Filing Requirements

California Form: Form 540NR.

Nonresidents: Nonresident taxpayers must file California returns if they have income from California sources and at least the following federal gross or adjusted gross income amounts, which are the same as for residents (see ¶ 104):

1999 Filing Threshold Amounts

Gross income more than:

	Age on 12/31/99	No dependents	1 dependent	2 or more dependents
Single or unmarried	Under 65	10,899	18,466	24,141
	65 or older	14,499	20,174	24,714

	Age on 12/31/99	No dependents	1 dependent	2 or more dependents
Married	Under 65 (both spouses)	21,798	29,365	35,040
	65 or older (one spouse)	25,398	31,073	35,613
	65 or older (both spouses)	28,998	34,673	39,213

Adjusted gross income more than:

	Age on 12/31/99	No dependents	1 dependent	2 or more dependents
Single or unmarried	Under 65	8,719	16,286	21,961
	65 or older	12,319	17,994	22,534

	Age on 12/31/99	No dependents	1 dependent	2 or more dependents
Married	Under 65 (both spouses)	17,438	25,005	30,680
	65 or older (one spouse)	21,038	26,713	31,253
	65 or older (both spouses)	24,638	30,313	34,853

Regardless of the above threshold amounts, a return must be filed for any tax liability of $1 or more. This may occur, for example, if California adjustments to federal income (e.g., non-California municipal bond interest) cause California taxable income to be higher than federal.

For purposes of the filing thresholds, (1) single persons include taxpayers filing as heads of households and qualifying widowers and (2) married couples include taxpayers filing either jointly or separately.

A "nonresident" is an individual who is not a resident. Case law dealing with the question of residency is found at ¶ 103.

Part-year residents: Part-year residents are subject to the same income-filing-level requirements as nonresidents.

A "part-year resident" is informally defined as an individual who moves into or out of California during the taxable year.

¶ 62

● *Military personnel*

Nonresidents stationed in California under military orders are not considered residents. Consequently, their military pay is not subject to California taxation (see ¶ 103). However, servicepersons are taxed on all other income derived from California sources.

A California resident stationed outside California under permanent military orders is considered a nonresident.

The spouses of military personnel who come to California are California residents if they are here for other than "temporary or transitory purposes."

● *Attachment of federal return*

A copy of the taxpayer's federal return and all supporting documents must be attached to the Form 540NR.

¶ 63 Filing Status

Unmarried taxpayers: Single taxpayers are required to use their federal filing status.

Married taxpayers: If a husband and wife file a joint federal income tax return, one of the spouses was a California resident for the entire year, and the other spouse was a nonresident for all or any portion of the taxable year, a joint nonresident return (Form 540NR) must be filed. There are two exceptions to this rule. A couple filing a joint federal income tax return may file either separate returns or a single joint return in California if (1) either spouse was an active member of the military during the taxable year or (2) either spouse was a nonresident of California for the entire taxable year and had no income from a California source during the taxable year. If one of these exceptions applies, the tax should be figured both jointly and separately to determine the more favorable status.

¶ 64 Personal and Dependent Exemptions

California provides tax credits for personal and dependent exemptions in lieu of deductions from income as provided under federal law (see ¶ 109).

The 1999 credit amounts are:

Single	$ 72
Married, separate return	72
Married, joint return	144
Head of household	72
Surviving spouse	144
Dependent	227
Visually impaired person (additional)	72
Elderly (additional)	72

The dependent exemption credit is decreased from $253 to $227 for the 1999 taxable year and is indexed for inflation in taxable years beginning after 1999.

¶ 63

A doctor's statement verifying a visual impairment must be attached to the first 540NR return on which the exemption credit is claimed (Instructions to Form 540).

The exemption credits must be reduced for taxpayers whose federal adjusted gross income exceeds the threshold amounts specified for the taxpayer's filing status (see ¶ 109).

¶ 65 Standard Deduction

The election of a nonresident or part-year resident to itemize or to claim a standard deduction is independent of the federal election (see ¶ 303). Taxpayers may choose the more favorable tax treatment.

The California standard deduction amounts for 1999 are:

Filing status	Amount
Single	$2,711
Married, joint return	5,422
Married, separate return	2,711
Head of household	5,422
Surviving spouse	5,422

The above amounts are not increased (as under federal law) if the taxpayer is elderly or blind.

Individuals who can be claimed on another's tax return are limited to the greater of (1) $700 or (2) the amount of earned income plus $250.

¶ 66 Income Attributable to California

California Form: Sch. CA (540NR).

Nonresidents: Nonresidents are generally taxed on California-source adjusted gross income (see ¶ 230).

Part-year residents: Generally, part-year residents must include in adjusted gross income for California purposes income from all sources attributable to any part of the tax year during which they resided in California, and income from California sources for that portion of the year during which they resided elsewhere (see ¶ 230).

● *"Accrual rule" applicable to part-year residents*

Although under California law items of income and deduction are recognized at the same time as they are federally, a special "accrual" rule applies to part-year residents in determining whether items *that are not from California sources* are attributable to the period of residency and thus taxable by California (see ¶ 405). Such items are attributed to the period of time in which they *accrue,* even if the part-year resident operates on the cash basis.

Example: A New York resident moves to and becomes a resident of California in March. The taxpayer, who operates on the cash basis, receives a bonus in April for services performed for his former New York employer prior to his move to California. Although for federal purposes the taxpayer "recognizes" this bonus in April while he was a California resident, the bonus is not taxed by California, because the bonus accrued while the taxpayer was a nonresident.

● *Attribution rules*

The rules of attribution for various types of income are discussed in the following paragraphs (see also ¶ 230). The details are reported on Schedule CA (540NR).

● *Income from trade or business*

Business income of a nonresident is attributed in full to California if the nonresident's trade or business is carried on entirely in California (see ¶ 230). On the other hand, if the nonresident's trade or business is conducted entirely outside of California, none of the income is attributed to California.

Where a trade or business is partly within California and partly in other states, the manner in which the income is attributed depends on the relationship of the segments of the taxpayer's business. If the California business activity is separate and distinct from that carried on elsewhere (e.g., a California hotel but an out-of-state manufacturing activity), only the income from the California portion is reported to California. On the other hand, if the in-state and out-of-state portions are integral parts of a single trade or business (i.e., "unitary"), business income is apportioned by a formula as discussed below.

The term "business income" means all income that arises from the conduct of the business operations of a taxpayer. Typically it includes those items reported on federal Schedules C or C-EZ. "Nonbusiness income" is all other income. Nonbusiness income is allocated, rather than apportioned, by rules described in the following paragraphs.

Formula: The apportionment formula prescribed is the same as the one generally used for the California corporation franchise tax: the average ratio of California property, payroll, and sales (double-weighted) to total property, payroll, and sales. For a discussion of formula apportionment and rules regarding its application, see Chapter 13 of the GUIDEBOOK.

● *Compensation for personal services*

Nonresidents: Nonresidents are taxed on compensation for personal services performed in California (see ¶ 230). The attribution rules for a number of specific occupations are as follows:

Salespersons: Nonresident salespersons determine the portion of commission income attributable to California by the ratio of sales volume in California to total sales volume.

Performers/athletes: Nonresident performers or athletes include gross amounts received for performances or athletic events in California.

Professionals: Fees received by nonresident professionals (e.g., doctors, lawyers, accountants) for services performed in California are taxable.

Employees: Nonresident employees, excluding sales personnel, include total compensation for any period during which they are continuously employed in California.

Transportation workers: Nonresident transportation employees may prorate compensation on whatever basis is used by their employers to measure services. For example, proration may be based on the number of days worked or the number of miles traveled in California compared to days or miles everywhere.

Part-year residents: All compensation received by part-year residents during the period of residency is taxable and attributed in full to California. Such income received during nonresidency is attributed under the rules applicable to nonresidents.

Military personnel: Federal law prohibits the taxation of military pay of nonresident servicemen while they are stationed in California, even though such income would be considered taxable to a nonresident under the regular rules (see ¶ 224). Also exempt from tax is pay of a nonresident military person that is attributed to a resident spouse by the community property laws.

● *Interest, dividend, rent, and royalty income*

Nonresidents: A nonresident's income from interest or dividends that is not related to a trade or business is not taxed by California unless the nonresident buys the stock or obligations in California or places orders with brokers in California so regularly as to constitute doing business, in which case the income is California-source adjusted gross income and must be reported in full (see ¶ 230). Special rules apply for purposes of determining whether a nonresident's interest and dividends from qualifying investment securities are California-source income (see ¶ 230).

Royalty income from intangibles such as patents or franchises is taxable only if the intangible has a business situs in California. A business situs in California is established when (1) the property is employed as capital or (2) control of the property is localized in connection with a business in California so that its use becomes an asset of the business.

Rental income received by a nonresident from real estate or from tangible personal property located in California is California-source adjusted gross income regardless of whether it is related to a trade or business.

Part-year residents: All income, of whatever kind, received by part-year residents during the period of residency is taxable and allocable to California. Such income received during nonresidency is attributed under the rules applicable to nonresidents.

● *Pensions and annuities*

Nonresidents: Nonresidents' retirement income received after 1995 is not subject to California income tax even if the income is received for services performed in California (see ¶ 230 and ¶ 405).

Part-year residents: Part-year residents who move into California are taxed on pension income from non-California sources only to the extent the income accrues after the taxpayer becomes a California resident. Part-year residents who move out of California are subject to California income tax only on their retirement income received during the period of their California residency (see ¶ 405).

● *Gains or losses from disposition of property*

Nonresidents: Gain or loss from sale of real or tangible personal property in California is California-source income whether or not related to business activities (see ¶ 230).

Gain or loss from stock and bond sales made by a nonresident is not attributable to California unless the nonresident buys such property in California or places orders in California so regularly so as to constitute doing business in California, in which case the profits from such transactions would be considered California-source income. Special rules apply for purposes of determining whether gain or loss from the sale of qualifying investment securities by a nonresident is California-source income (see ¶ 230).

Part-year residents: Gains and losses derived from any source during the period of residency are California-source income to part-year residents. Such income received during nonresidency is attributed under the rules applicable to nonresidents.

● *Income from trusts and estates*

Nonresidents: The information needed to complete the beneficiary's 540NR return, including the portion attributable to California and the character of each item, is shown on Schedule K-1 (Form 541).

A nonresident beneficiary is taxed on the portion of the beneficiary's distributive share of the trust's or estate's modified federal taxable income from sources in California (see ¶ 604a). Income or loss has the same character when passed through to a beneficiary as it had to the trust or estate. Dividends and interest from estate or trust stocks and bonds is not income from sources within the state and is not taxable to a nonresident unless the property is used by the estate or trust so as to acquire a business situs in California. The source of a nonresident's income from other trust or estate property that has not acquired a business situs in the state is determined by the fiduciaries under the general rules for allocation and apportionment (see Chapter 13).

Part-year residents: The information needed to complete the beneficiary's 540NR return, including the portion attributable to California and the character of each item, is shown on Schedule K-1 (Form 541).

A part-year resident beneficiary is taxed on the beneficiary's entire share of the modified federal income of an estate or trust if he or she is a resident on the last day of the entity's tax year (see ¶ 604a). Beneficiaries are taxed in the same manner as nonresidents if the last day of the entity's tax year falls during the period of nonresidency. Income or loss has the same character when passed through to the beneficiaries as it had to the trust or estate.

Part-year residents qualify for a credit for tax paid to other states on their income from trusts or estates that is also taxed by California (see ¶ 116).

● *Income from partnerships and limited liability partnerships*

Nonresidents: The information needed to complete the partner's 540NR return is shown on Schedule K-1 (Form 565). Amounts allocated outside California are shown as differences between California income and income reported on the federal return.

¶ 66

Nonresident partners are taxed on the part of their distributive shares of partnership income or loss derived from California sources (see ¶ 613).

Nonresident partners qualify for a credit for tax paid to certain states of residence on partnership income that is also taxed by California (see ¶ 117).

Part-year residents: Part-year resident partners are taxed on their entire distributive shares of partnership income if they are California residents on the last day of the partnership's tax year (see ¶ 613); otherwise, they are taxed in the same manner as nonresident partners.

Part-year resident partners qualify for a credit for tax paid to other states on partnership income taxed by California (see ¶ 116).

● *Income from S corporations*

Nonresidents: Nonresidents apply the S corporation apportionment percentage to their distributive shares of S corporation income to determine their portion taxable to California. The percentage is reported on Schedule K-1 (Form 100S), which is sent to the shareholders by the S corporation.

Shareholders of federal S corporations that have elected California C corporation status will not receive Schedule K-1 (Form 100S). They will receive, instead, notification of the amounts actually distributed or made available to them. These amounts are treated as taxable dividends (see ¶ 232).

Nonresidents qualify for a credit for taxes paid to certain states of residence on their S corporation income taxed by California (see ¶ 117).

Part-year residents: Part-year resident shareholders are taxed on their entire distributive shares of S corporation income, as modified for California purposes, if they are California residents on the last day of the S corporation's tax year (see ¶ 232); otherwise, they are taxed in the same manner as nonresident shareholders.

Part-year resident shareholders qualify for a credit for taxes paid to other states on S corporation income taxed by California (see ¶ 116).

● *Alimony income*

Alimony received by a part-year resident during the period of residence is attributed to the state.

Alimony paid by a California resident to a nonresident is not taxable to the recipient (see ¶ 204, ¶ 313). Alimony paid either by a nonresident or part-year resident during a period of nonresidency is not deductible by the payor.

¶ 67 Modifications to Federal Adjusted Gross Income

California Forms: Sch. CA (540NR), Sch. D, Sch. D-1, FTB 3801, FTB 3805V, FTB 3805Z, FTB 3806, FTB 3807, FTB 3808, FTB 3809, FTB 3885A.

Nonresidents and part-year residents make the following three kinds of California modification adjustments on Schedule CA (540NR):

(1) addition and subtraction modifications to federal adjusted gross income to arrive at total adjusted gross income from all sources using California law;

(2) adjustments to determine the portion of total adjusted gross income that is subject to California tax (either because it is California-source income or because it is attributable to the taxpayer's period of residency); and

(3) adjustments to federal itemized deductions, should the taxpayer itemize for California purposes (see ¶ 68 for such adjustments).

The adjustments under (2) above are computed in accordance with the rules for attributing income to California (see ¶ 66).

The most common adjustments under (1) above are discussed in the following paragraphs. Other adjustments are discussed in FTB Pub. 1001.

1. Interest on state obligations (see ¶ 217): Interest earned on bonds issued by states other than California or on obligations issued by municipalities of other states is taxed by California and is added back to federal adjusted gross income. State bond interest (other than from California obligations) that passes through from S corporations, trusts, partnerships, limited liability companies, and limited and mutual funds is also treated as an addition.

2. Interest on federal obligations (see ¶ 217): Interest on federal obligations is tax-exempt and, consequently, is subtracted from federal adjusted gross income. See also ¶ 217 for the pass-through of tax-exempt interest from a mutual fund.

Interest income from Federal Farm Credit banks, Federal Home Loan banks, the Student Loan Marketing Association (SLMA), the Resolution Funding Corporation, the Production Credit Association, the Commodity Credit Corporation, Certificates of Accrual on Treasury Securities (CATS), and Treasury Investment Growth Receipts (TIGRS) is also exempt and is subtracted from federal adjusted gross income; however, interest from Fannie Maes, Ginnie Maes, or FHLMC securities is taxable by California and, therefore, no modification is made to federal adjusted gross income for interest from these instruments.

3. Depreciation (see ¶ 310): Because nonresidents and part-year residents, in computing their California tax liability on Form 540NR, first compute a taxable income figure in the same manner as full-year residents, they must make the same California depreciation modifications required of resident taxpayers, even for assets not located in California (see ¶ 310).

California depreciation is generally the same as federal (the "modified accelerated cost recovery system" under IRC Sec. 168) for assets placed in service after 1986. Under federal law, but not California law, ACRS is allowed for assets placed in service after 1980 and before 1987. California allows the same asset expense allowance deduction as federal for IRC Sec. 179 property for assets placed in service after 1986 and before 1993 and for assets placed in service after 1998 (see ¶ 310a). However, for taxable years beginning after 1992 and before 1999, the maximum allowable IRC Sec. 179 deduction was lower for California than for federal purposes; see ¶ 310a for details.

California adopts the federal 39-year depreciation recovery period for nonresidential real property acquired after May 12, 1993, but only for property placed in service after 1996 in taxable years beginning after 1996. Thus, for California purposes, nonresidential real property placed in service before

1997 in taxable years beginning before 1997 continues to be depreciated over a 31.5-year recovery period.

Further differences in the amount of depreciation claimed for federal and California purposes may arise due to California provisions that allow taxpayers operating in specified depressed areas to claim accelerated write-offs for certain property (see ¶ 310f).

Note: The differences between federal and California deductions are adjusted on FTB 3885A. The net adjustment may be an addition or a subtraction.

4. Capital gains and losses (see ¶ 512): California law and federal law treat all capital gains as ordinary income after 1986. However, for tax years beginning after 1996, federal law subjects long-term capital gains to a lower tax rate.

Differences between the amount of capital gain or loss recognized for California and federal purposes can occur both in the year a gain or loss is recognized and in carryover years.

Differences may occur for 1999 between the gain or loss recognized for federal and California purposes because (1) California does not permit capital loss carrybacks (see ¶ 514); (2) California, but not federal, law excludes gain on the sale or disposition of qualified assisted housing developments (see ¶ 502b); and (3) California requires certain adjustments to basis not required by federal law and makes certain federal adjustments inapplicable (see ¶ 534).

Differences between pre-1987 California and federal laws that can affect the reporting of capital gain and loss include:

(1) A capital loss carryover may be different for California purposes than for federal purposes.

(2) The pre-1987 holding periods and taxable percentages of capital gains for California were different than federal.

(3) The California adjustment to capital gains computed for purposes of the investment interest expense deduction was different from the federal adjustment.

(4) For years prior to 1987, the federal 50% limitation on long-term capital loss deductions did not apply for California.

(5) Dividends from mutual funds were treated as ordinary income for California.

(6) Gain or loss may be reported in different tax years for California purposes because changes to the federal law affecting the computation of gain or loss were not generally adopted by California until subsequent years.

California Schedule D is used to calculate the differences, and the appropriate modification is carried to California Schedule CA (540NR).

(7) The California and federal basis of certain assets may be different at the time of disposition because of prior and current differences between California and federal law (see ¶ 521 and following). Examples of such situations are:

(A) valuation of property acquired by inheritance (see ¶ 525);

(B) depreciation of business property (see ¶ 310, ¶ 310a);

(C) basis adjustments for California and federal credits (see ¶ 133);

(D) basis of the stock of an S corporation (see ¶ 232); and

(E) basis adjustment of property for moves into California (see ¶ 502a).

Calculation of capital gain and loss adjustments is made on California FTB 3885A.

5. State income tax refunds: Any California income tax refunds included in federal adjusted gross income are subtracted from federal adjusted gross income.

6. Unemployment compensation (see ¶ 201): The amount of unemployment compensation included on the federal return is subtracted from federal adjusted gross income.

7. Social Security benefits (see ¶ 201): The amount of Social Security benefits included in federal adjusted gross income is subtracted from federal adjusted gross income because California does not tax social security benefits.

8. Railroad retirement benefits, ridesharing benefits, and sick pay (see ¶ 205): Tier 1 and tier 2 railroad retirement benefits, including ridesharing benefits and sick pay, received under the Federal Insurance Contributions and Railroad Retirement Act are subtracted from federal adjusted gross income.

9. California lottery winnings (see ¶ 201): Any California lottery winnings included in federal adjusted gross income are subtracted.

10. IRA and Keogh distributions (see ¶ 318): The California and federal deductible dollar amounts are the same for post-1986 tax years. However, for pre-1987 tax years, the amounts differed; consequently, the amount taxable on a distribution will differ. Differences may also arise if the taxpayer changed residence during the time he or she made contributions to the IRA or Keogh plan.

A worksheet to compute differences in the tax treatment of distributions for federal and California purposes is included in FTB Pub. 1005, Pension and Annuity Guidelines.

11. Net operating loss (see ¶ 309): California's treatment of NOLs is like federal treatment except that no carrybacks are allowed and the amount of loss eligible for carryover to future years is generally limited to 50% of the net operating loss. In addition, a California NOL may be carried forward for only five years rather than the 20 years permitted under federal law (15 years for losses incurred in tax years beginning before August 6, 1997). Special rules apply to "new" and "small" businesses and to NOLs resulting from disasters or claimed by taxpayers operating in enterprise zones, the former Los Angeles Revitalization Zone (LARZ), local agency military base recovery areas (LAMBRAs), or targeted tax areas.

Calculation of the California NOL is on FTB 3805V and the appropriate adjustment entered on California Schedule CA (540NR). The NOL for enterprise zone businesses is calculated on FTB 3805Z, for former LARZ businesses is calculated on FTB 3806, for LAMBRA businesses is calculated on FTB 3807, and for targeted tax area businesses is calculated on FTB 3809.

12. Recycling revenues (see ¶ 201): The income received by a taxpayer for recycling empty beverage containers is exempt for California purposes and is subtracted if included in federal adjusted gross income.

13. Expenses related to tax-exempt income (see ¶ 305): Expenses related to federally tax-exempt income that were disallowed as a deduction in computing federal adjusted gross income are subtracted for California. Expenses incurred to purchase or carry obligations that are tax-exempt under California but not federal law are added to federal adjusted gross income.

Note: These modifications, to the extent not business-related, are made to federal itemized deductions (see ¶ 68).

14. Income from exercising California qualified stock option (see ¶ 207): Compensation received from exercising a California qualified stock option is excluded from California gross income and may be subtracted if the compensation was included in federal adjusted gross income.

15. Ridesharing and employee commuter deductions (see ¶ 240): An exclusion from gross income is available to an employee for amounts received from his or her employer for qualifying ridesharing or commuter arrangements.

16. Pensions and annuities (see ¶ 206): California rules for taxing pensions and annuities are the same as federal; however, the taxable amount may differ because of federal/California differences in the years when contributions were made. For further information see FTB Pub. 1005.

17. Passive activity loss (see ¶ 326): California generally adopts federal rules for computing the limitation on deducting passive activity losses. However, California does not conform to the the passive activity loss rules relating to rental real estate losses suffered by certain taxpayers who materially participate in a real property trade or business. Differences may also exist because the amount of passive income and loss may differ. Taxpayers must segregate California adjustments that relate to passive-activity items from California adjustments that relate to nonpassive items (see ¶ 326). This calculation is made on FTB 3801.

18. Other gains or losses (see ¶ 519): Although California law on the computation of gain from sales of business property and certain involuntary conversions is the same as federal, the amount of gain or loss may differ because of federal/California basis differences. These amounts are reported on Schedule D-1.

19. Original issue discount (see ¶ 236): California treatment of original issue discount is the same as federal except for debt instruments issued in 1985 and 1986.

20. Alimony (see ¶ 204): Alimony received by a nonresident alien that was not included in the taxpayer's federal gross income is treated as an addition on Schedule CA (540).

21. Income from specially treated sources: See the indicated paragraphs for possible federal/California differences in the taxation of the following items: (1) noncash patronage dividends from farmers' cooperatives or mutual associations (see ¶ 231); and (2) interest income from investment in enterprise zones (see ¶ 239).

22. Income from S corporations (see ¶ 66, ¶ 232): Nonresident shareholders of California S corporations add or subtract, as appropriate, the difference between their distributive shares of federal and California S corporation income or loss.

Shareholders of S corporations (by federal election) that have not elected California S corporation status receive notification of the amounts actually distributed or made available to them. These amounts are treated as dividends.

23. Income from partnerships and limited liability partnerships (see ¶ 66, ¶ 612, ¶ 617): Partners add or subtract, as appropriate, the difference between their distributive shares of federal and California partnership income or loss.

24. Income from limited liability companies (see ¶ 618): Members and persons with economic interests in an LLC add or subtract, as appropriate, the difference between their shares of federal and California LLC income in the same manner as partners must include their distributive shares of partnership income in their taxable income.

25. Income from trusts and estates (see ¶ 66, ¶ 604a): Trust or estate beneficiaries add or subtract, as appropriate, the difference between their shares of federal and California trust or estate income or loss.

26. Business expenses incurred in discriminatory clubs (see ¶ 301, ¶ 322): California prohibits a business expense deduction for expenditures at a club which restricts membership or use on the basis of age, sex, race, religion, color, ancestry or national origin. There is no similar federal prohibition.

27. Wages (see ¶ 201): If there is a difference in wages because of an employee's fringe benefits, also reported on the W-2, an adjustment must be made because California does not adopt the federal rules; the amount of federal wages reported on the W-2 is subtracted and the amount reported as California wages is added.

28. Crime hotline rewards (see ¶ 245): Any rewards received from a government authorized crime hotline are excluded from gross income.

29. Water conservation rebates (see ¶ 243): California excludes from gross income specified water conservation rebates received from local water agencies or suppliers.

30. Conservation and environmental cost-share payments (see ¶ 242): Certain cost-share payments received by forest landowners from the Department of Forestry and Fire Protection are subtracted from federal gross income.

¶ 68 Itemized Deductions

California Forms: Sch. CA (540NR), FTB 3526, FTB 3885A.

California itemized deductions are based on federal itemized deductions shown on federal Schedule A, with the modifications discussed below. These modifications are independent of the adjustments to federal adjusted gross income discussed at ¶ 67.

Taxpayers may elect either the standard deduction or itemized deductions for California purposes, regardless of which was elected for federal purposes (see ¶ 65). However, if itemized deductions are elected for California purposes, federal Schedule A must be attached to the California Form 540NR. The adjustments to federal itemized deductions are computed in Part III of California Schedule CA (540NR) ("California Adjustments—Nonresidents or Part-Year Residents").

(a) *Taxes* (see ¶ 306): State, local, and foreign income taxes (including state disability insurance—"SDI"), federal estate tax, and generation-skipping transfer taxes claimed on federal Schedule A are not allowable deductions for California purposes and are subtracted from federal itemized deductions.

(b) *California Lottery losses* (see ¶ 322): California Lottery losses are not deductible for California purposes. The amount of such losses, as shown on federal Schedule A, must be subtracted from federal itemized deductions.

(c) *Federal obligation expense* (see ¶ 305): Because California does not tax interest from federal obligations, any expenses relating to such interest that have been deducted for federal purposes on Schedule A are subtracted from federal itemized deductions for California purposes.

(d) *State obligation expense* (see ¶ 305): Because, unlike federal law, California taxes interest from state or local obligations of states other than California any expenses related to this interest that were not entered on federal Schedule A should be added to federal itemized deductions for California purposes.

(e) *Employee business expense deduction for depreciation* (see ¶ 310): If the employee business expense deduction claimed federally included depreciation of assets placed in service prior to 1987, the depreciation component is recomputed for California purposes because of California/federal differences in depreciation methods prior to 1987. For assets placed in service after 1992 and before 1999, the maximum allowable IRC Sec. 179 deduction differs under federal and California law (see ¶ 310a). Use FTB 3885A for computing the differences.

(f) *Adoption-related expenses* (see ¶ 128): California allows a credit for specified adoption-related expenses. If the taxpayer claims the California adoption costs credit for amounts deducted on the federal Schedule A, these amounts must be subtracted on California Schedule CA (540NR).

(g) *Investment expense* (see ¶ 305): This item is generally treated the same as under federal law. Taxpayers filing federal form 4952 must file the corresponding California FTB 3526. Differences, if any, are reported on Schedule CA (540NR). Differences may occur because of the capital gain component in computing pre-1987 investment interest expense; the pre-1987

¶ 68

holding period and taxable percentages of capital gains were different under California law (see ¶ 513).

(h) *Limitation for high-income taxpayers* (see ¶ 303): The itemized deductions of taxpayers with adjusted gross incomes over a threshold amount must be reduced by the lesser of (1) 6% (3% under federal law) of the excess of adjusted gross income over the threshold amount or (2) 80% of the amount of the itemized deductions otherwise allowable for the tax year. A worksheet is provided in the Schedule CA (540NR) Instructions to calculate the adjustment.

(i) *Federal mortgage interest credit:* California does not have a credit comparable to the federal mortgage interest credit. If federal miscellaneous itemized deductions on Schedule A were reduced by the amount of this credit, California itemized deductions may be increased by the same amount on Schedule CA (540NR).

(j) *Federal estate and generation-skipping transfer taxes:* California does not allow deductions for federal tax paid on income in respect of a decedent or for tax paid on generation-skipping transfers. Accordingly, amounts included on federal Schedule A for these items must be subtracted on California Schedule CA (540NR).

(k) *Legislators' travel expenses* (see ¶ 301): California does not follow the federal rule allowing legislators to deduct expenses for every legislative day. California allows legislators to deduct only those expenses incurred on days that they are actually away from their districts overnight. Amounts deducted for federal purposes on Schedule A that do not qualify for California purposes must be subtracted from federal itemized deductions.

(*l*) *Contributions of qualified appreciated stock* (see ¶ 312): California law, unlike federal law, does not allow a taxpayer to deduct the full fair market value of qualified appreciated stock contributed to a private foundation. Because California still requires a reduction of the fair market value to reflect the long-term capital gain that would be realized upon the stock's sale for purposes of claiming the deduction, California taxpayers must subtract the value difference from federal itemized deductions.

¶ 69 Tax Rates

California Forms: Sch. G-1, Sch. P (540NR), FTB 3800, FTB 3803, FTB 3805P.

Nonresidents and part-year residents pay tax at rates applied to their total income (California income plus other income) of the taxpayer. The rates are progressive, ranging from 1% to 9.3% of taxable income. Total tax is then prorated, for nonresidents and part-year residents, on the basis of the ratio of California source adjusted gross income to total income.

The tax tables are reproduced on page 33. The tax rate schedules are reproduced on page 31, but can be used only to determine the tax if California taxable income is over $100,000.

● *Alternative minimum tax*

Nonresidents and part-year residents are subject to the alternative minimum tax in the same manner as residents, except that the tax is prorated by the ratio of alternative minimum California-source adjusted gross income to total alternative minimum adjusted gross income (see ¶ 112a).

The California alternative minimum tax is imposed at the rate of 7%. It is generally computed the same as for federal purposes, but there are differences (see ¶ 112a). The alternative minimum tax is computed on Schedule P (540NR).

California incorporates the IRC Sec. 53 "credit for prior year minimum tax" (see ¶ 70).

● *Tax on premature distributions of retirement plans and life insurance plans*

Nonresidents and part-year residents are liable in the same manner as residents for the penalty or recapture tax on premature distributions from IRAs, Keogh plans, annuities, and "modified endowment contracts," to the extent the distribution is included in California-source income (see ¶ 206 and ¶ 405). The amount included for California purposes may differ from that required to be included federally because of differences in the deductibility of contributions in years prior to 1987.

The California penalty is 2.5%.

Form FTB 3805P is used to make the tax computation.

● *Tax on nonexempt withdrawals from medical savings accounts*

Distributions from a medical savings account for nonmedical purposes are subject to a 10% penalty tax (15% under federal law). For further information see ¶ 246. Form FTB 3805P is used to make the computation.

● *Separate tax on lump-sum distributions*

Nonresidents and part-year residents with lump-sum distributions of retirement income attributable to California sources compute and pay a separate tax on these distributions if they elected to pay the separate federal tax (see ¶ 206 and ¶ 405). The California tax, which is computed on Schedule G-1, is determined under the same rules as the federal tax. The tax is transferred from Schedule G-1 to Form 540NR and is added to the prorated tax on total taxable income.

● *Tax on minor child's unearned income ("kiddie tax")*

California incorporates the federal "kiddie tax" provisions applicable when a child who is not yet 14 by the close of the tax year and who has a parent living at such time has unearned income in excess of $1,400 (see ¶ 113). The tax is computed on FTB 3800, which parallels federal Form 8615. For nonresidents and part-year residents, the amounts needed to complete FTB 3800 come from the corresponding federal Form 8615 and from both the parent's and the child's Form 540NR (including California adjusted gross income amounts from Schedule CA (540NR). The tax is subject to proration.

Under certain circumstances, a parent may elect to include the unearned income of a child on the parent's return. If the parent elects to exercise this option, FTB 3803 must accompany the parent's return.

¶ 70 Credits Against Tax

California Forms: Form 540NR, Sch. P (540NR), Sch. S, FTB 3501, FTB 3507, FTB 3510, FTB 3521, FTB 3523, FTB 3535, FTB 3540, FTB 3546, FTB 3547, FTB 3548, FTB 3553, FTB 3805Z, FTB 3807, FTB 3808, FTB 3809.

Credits available to nonresidents and part-year residents are generally divided into two categories: (1) those that are prorated by the percentage of California-source adjusted gross income, and (2) those that are taken in full because they are based upon a California transaction.

Prorated credits are (1) the exemption credits, (2) the carryover credit for child and dependent care expenses, (3) the joint custody head of household credit, (4) the dependent parent credit, (5) the senior head of household credit, and (6) the carryover credit for political contributions.

If there are more than three credits claimed, the taxpayer must attach the appropriate credit form and summarize them on California Schedule P (540NR).

Major credits are treated individually in the following paragraphs, and those credits that affect only a few taxpayers are treated together at the end of ¶ 70.

1. Exemption credits (see ¶ 109): Nonresidents and part-year residents are entitled to the same credits for personal or dependent exemptions as are residents. The amounts of these credits are at ¶ 64.

2. Child care expense credits (see ¶ 123): Tax credits are available to employers for a percentage of the costs of establishing child care programs or facilities, contributing to child care information and referral services, or contributing to qualified child care plans. These credits are computed on FTB 3501. Unused credit may be carried over until exhausted.

3. Renter's credit (see ¶ 122): Nonresidents cannot claim this credit.

Part-year residents who qualify for the credit are allowed a 1/12 credit for each full month of California residence during the year.

4. Joint custody head-of-household, dependent parent credits (see ¶ 125a): For the 1999 tax year, these credits, which cover both dependent children and dependent parents, equal the lesser of 30% of the California liability or $288. Qualifications that must be met in order to claim the credit are discussed at ¶ 125a. A worksheet is provided in the Instructions to Form 540NR to compute the credit. There is no carryover of this credit.

5. Research and development credit (see ¶ 139): Nonresidents and part-year residents may generally take the same research and development credit as that provided by federal law, except:

(a) research must be conducted in California to qualify;

(b) the applicable California credit percentage is 12% of the excess of qualified research expenses for the tax year over the "base amount;"

(c) California modifies the formula used by those taxpayers that elect to compute the amount of the credit using an alternative method;

(d) California does not allow a credit against personal income tax for basic research payments;

(e) the California credit applies to expenses paid or incurred in taxable years beginning after 1986 and is available indefinitely thereafter, whereas the federal credit does not apply to amounts paid or incurred after June 30, 1995, and before July 1, 1996, or after June 30, 1999;

(f) California limits the "gross receipts" that may be taken into account for purposes of calculating the base amount;

(g) the California credit may be carried over; and

(h) California disallows the credit for expenses incurred to purchase property for which a sales and use exemption for teleproduction or other postproduction property is claimed.

A married couple filing separately has the option of taking the full credit or of dividing it equally between them.

FTB 3523 is used to compute the credit.

6. Credit for prior-year minimum tax (see ¶ 141): California incorporates the IRC Sec. 53 credit for alternative minimum tax paid in a prior year by a taxpayer who is not liable for the AMT in the current year; the credit is based on preference items that defer tax liability rather than permanently reduce the tax. The amount allowable as a credit in any tax year is limited to the regular California personal income tax for the year less the refundable credits that have no carryover provisions and the credit for taxes paid to other states. The credit is computed on FTB 3510.

7. Credit for income taxes paid other states (nonresidents) (see ¶ 117): The credit for income taxes paid other states is available for net income taxes paid to another state or possession on income also taxed by California when the state or possession of residence is one of the following: Arizona, Guam, Indiana, Oregon, and Virginia. Net tax does not include any tax comparable to the California AMT or preference tax (see ¶ 69) or any tax not based on net income.

There are two limitations: (1) the credit is limited to the same proportion of the total tax paid to the state of residence as the income taxed in both states bears to the total income taxed by the state of residence, and (2) it is similarly limited to the same proportion of the total California tax as the income taxed in both states bears to the total income taxed by California.

Schedule S is used to compute the credit.

8. Credit for income taxes paid other states (part-year residents) (see ¶ 116): For the period of time that part-year residents are residents of California, they are entitled to credit for net income taxes paid to other states. A listing of the states and possessions for which credit is allowed appears at ¶ 116. The amount of the credit is limited to the same proportion of the total California tax as the income taxed in both states bears to the total income taxed by California. See ¶ 116 for a discussion of the credit and an example of the credit calculation.

For the period of time that the part-year resident is a nonresident of California, he/she is entitled to the credit available to nonresidents as discussed above. Because the states for which credit is allowed are mutually exclusive as to treatment of residents or nonresidents, a two-step computation is required only when California-source adjusted gross income is received while a nonresident.

Schedule S is used to compute the credit. There is no carryover of this credit.

9. Excess state disability insurance credit (see ¶ 120): Excess employee contributions for California disability insurance are treated as a refundable credit against the income tax. For 1999, the credit amount is the excess of the amount contributed over $158.84. Excess contributions may occur when a taxpayer works for more than one employer during the tax year. The amount of the credit can be calculated on a worksheet included in the Instructions to Form 540NR.

Note: If more than the maximum was withheld by a single employer, or at a higher rate, the excess amount must be claimed as a refund from the employer rather than as a tax credit.

● *Other credits*

Farmworker housing credit (see ¶ 126): California allows a nonrefundable credit for the lesser of (1) up to 50% of qualified amounts paid or incurred for the construction or rehabilitation of farmworker housing in California, or (2) the amount certified by the California Tax Credit Allocation Committee. Unused credit may be carried over until exhausted.

Low-income housing credit (see ¶ 127): California allows a credit to owners of residential rental projects that provide low-income housing located in California. The credit is similar to the federal credit computed under IRC Sec. 42. The California Tax Credit Allocation Committee certifies to the taxpayer on FTB 3521A the amount of the credit for each year in the credit period.

The credit is computed on FTB 3521. A copy of FTB 3521A must be provided to the FTB upon request. Unused credit may be carried over until exhausted.

Enterprise zone hiring and sales tax credits (see ¶ 133 and ¶ 134): Tax credits are provided for employers who pay wages to qualified individuals in an enterprise zone (attach FTB 3805Z) and for business operators who purchase machinery or parts in an enterprise zone (attach FTB 3805Z). Unused credit may be carried over to succeeding tax years.

Enterprise zone credit for wages earned (see ¶ 135): A credit is available for qualified wages paid to specified enterprise zone employees (computation of the credit is on FTB 3553). There is no carryover of unused credit.

Local agency area military base recovery area (LAMBRA) hiring and sales tax credits (see ¶ 133, ¶ 136): A hiring credit and a sales tax credit substantially similar to those available to enterprise zone businesses may be claimed by qualified LAMBRA businesses.

The credits are computed on FTB 3807. The amount that may be claimed by a taxpayer for both LAMBRA credits is limited to the amount of tax attributable to LAMBRA income. Unused credit may be carried over and applied to tax on income from the area to succeeding tax years.

¶ 70

Targeted tax area hiring and sales and use tax credits (see ¶ 133, ¶ 137): Tax credits are provided for employers who hire certain disadvantaged individuals within the targeted tax area. A tax credit is also available for businesses that purchase machinery or equipment to be used within the area. The credits are computed on FTB 3809. Unused credit may be carried over and applied to tax on income from the area in succeeding tax years.

Manufacturing enhancement area hiring credit (see ¶ 138): A hiring tax credit substantially similar to the credit available to enterprise zone businesses may be claimed by qualified manufacturing enhancement area businesses. The credit is computed on FTB 3808. Unused credit may be carried over and applied to tax on income from the area in succeeding tax years.

Senior head-of-household credit (see ¶ 125): A credit is available to qualified seniors. A worksheet to compute the credit is included in the Instructions to Form 540NR.

Prison inmate labor credit (see ¶ 143): A credit is available to employers for 10% of the wages paid to certain prison inmates (FTB 3507). There is no carryover of this credit.

Manufacturer's investment credit (see ¶ 140): California allows a credit against net tax in an amount equal to 6% of the amount paid or incurred after 1993 for qualified property placed in service in this state that, except with respect to certain industries, is also depreciable IRC Sec. 1245 property.

The credit is computed on FTB 3535. Unused credit may be carried forward for up to eight years (10 years for certain small businesses).

Adoption costs credit (see ¶ 128): A credit is available for costs directly related to the adoption of a U.S. citizen or legal resident minor child who was in the custody of a state or county public agency. A worksheet is provided in the Form 540NR Instructions to compute the credit. Unused credit may be carried over until exhausted.

Salmon and steelhead trout habitat credit (see ¶ 124): California allows a credit against net tax for 10% of the qualified costs associated with certified salmon and steelhead trout habitat restoration and improvement projects. However, the amount of the credit that may be claimed is subject to reduction by the Department of Fish and Game. Unused credit may be carried over until exhausted.

Disabled access expenditures credit (see ¶ 129): California allows eligible small businesses a credit for 50% of up to $250 of the disabled access expenditures paid or incurred by those businesses to comply with the federal Americans with Disabilities Act. Except for the amount of the credit, the credit is similar to the federal credit allowed under IRC Sec. 44. The credit is computed on FTB 3548. Unused credit may be carried over until exhausted.

Enhanced oil recovery credit (see ¶ 142): California allows certain independent oil producers an enhanced oil recovery credit equal to 1/3 of the federal credit allowed under IRC Sec. 43, provided the costs for which the credit is claimed are attributable to projects located within California. FTB

¶ 70

3546 is used to compute the credit. Unused credit may be carried forward for up to 15 years.

Credit for costs of transporting donated agricultural products (see ¶ 130): California allows a credit against net tax for 50% of the costs paid or incurred in connection with the transportation of agricultural products donated to nonprofit charitable organizations. FTB 3547 is used to compute the credit. Unused credit may be carried over until exhausted.

Rice straw credit (see ¶ 144): For taxable years beginning after 1996 and before 2008, California allows a credit equal to $15 for each ton of California-grown rice straw purchased during the taxable year. Unused credit may be carried forward for up to ten years.

Credit for community development investments (see ¶ 145): For taxable years beginning after 1996 and before 2002, California allows a credit equal to 20% of each qualified deposit that is made into a community development financial institution and certified by the California Organized Investment Network.

● *Carryover credits*

Nonresidents and part-year residents may apply carryovers of certain credits that are no longer available. The credits for which such carryovers may still exist (and the years for which the credits were available) are as follows:

1. water conservation credit (1980—1982);

2. solar pump (agricultural) credit (1981—1983);

3. solar energy installation credit (1985—1988);

4. energy conservation credit (1981—1986);

5. ridesharing credits (1981—1986 and 1989—1995);

6. political contributions credit (1987—1991);

7. commercial solar energy credit (1987—1988);

8. residential rental and farm sales credit (1987—1991);

9. credit for donation of agricultural products (1989—1991);

10. orphan drug research credit (1987—1992);

11. qualified parent's infant care credit (1991—1993);

12. commercial solar electric system credit (1990—1993);

13. recycling equipment credit (1989—1995);

14. low emission vehicle credit (1991—1995); and

15. Los Angeles Revitalization Zone hiring and sales and use tax credits (1992—1997).

All of the above credit carryovers may be claimed on FTB 3540. See prior editions of the GUIDEBOOK for details about these credits.

¶ 71 When and Where to File and Pay Tax

The due date for filing Form 540NR and payment of the tax is April 17, 2000, for calendar-year taxpayers (see ¶ 105, ¶ 107). Returns made by fiscal-year taxpayers are due on or before the 15th day of the fourth month after the

¶ 71

close of the fiscal year. Returns made by mail are considered timely if properly addressed and postmarked on or before the due date.

Returns are filed with the Franchise Tax Board (FTB). However, the address to which they are sent differs depending upon whether an amount is due or a refund is expected. Refund requests are sent to P.O. Box 942840, Sacramento, CA 94240-0000. Returns for which an amount is due are sent to P.O. Box 942867, Sacramento, CA 94267-0001.

Checks or money orders are payable to the "Franchise Tax Board" with the social security number written on the check or money order.

● *E-file*

The FTB also accepts electronic filing of returns through the e-file program. Detailed information concerning this program is available at the FTB's website at http://www.ftb.ca.gov/elecserv.

● *Military personnel*

The due date for returns by members of the Armed Forces is the same as for civilians except that it may be postponed in certain cases, such as duty outside the U.S. or service in a combat zone (see ¶ 106).

¶ 72 Extensions

California Forms: FTB 3519, FTB 3537, FTB 3538, FTB 3563.

The Franchise Tax Board (FTB) will grant "paperless" personal income tax extensions to individuals, partnerships, limited liability companies, and fiduciaries for returns required to be filed by April 17, 2000. Thus, such persons will be granted an automatic six-month extension to October 16, 2000. The automatic extension does not extend the time for paying the tax. Tax payments must be accompanied by the appropriate form: FTB 3519 (Payment Voucher for Automatic Extension for Individuals); FTB 3537 (Payment Voucher for Automatic Extension for Limited Liability Companies); FTB 3538 (Payment Voucher for Automatic Extension for Limited Partnerships, LLPs and REMICS); or FTB 3563 (Payment Voucher for Automatic Extension for Fiduciaries). Taxpayers should send FTB 3519 or FTB 3563 to the FTB at P.O. Box 942867, Sacramento, CA 94267-0051. FTB 3537 and FTB 3538 are sent to the FTB at P.O. Box 942857, Sacramento, CA 94257-0651.

Payment extensions may be granted for a reasonable period by the Franchise Tax Board. There is no prescribed form; presumably a letter of explanation may be used for this purpose. Extensions of up to 90 days are also available to disaster victims (see ¶ 107).

Taxpayers abroad: An additional automatic two-month extension of time to file a return is granted to a taxpayer traveling or residing abroad on the due date (see ¶ 106). Consequently, the extended due date for such taxpayers is December 15th. However, interest accrues on any unpaid tax from the original due date of the return. Any additional extensions must be applied for in writing with a letter of explanation.

¶ 73 Estimated Tax

Nonresidents or part-year residents are required to pay estimated taxes in the same manner as residents (see ¶ 36 and ¶ 107a).

The California alternative minimum tax (see ¶ 112a) is not included in determining any required estimated tax payments.

The estimated tax is paid in quarterly installments on the same dates as federal payments: April 15, June 15, September 15, and January 15. The January 15 installment need not be made if the taxpayer files the tax return and pays the balance of tax before February 1. When the due date falls on a Saturday, Sunday, or other legal holiday, payment may be made on the next business day.

Married couples may file separate or joint estimated tax payment vouchers, but no joint payments can be made if the spouses have different tax years, or if the spouses are legally separated.

Form 540-ES is used for paying estimated tax. This form consists of a four-part payment voucher, with the due date on each voucher.

¶ 74 State Tax Assistance

The Franchise Tax Board (FTB) offers various taxpayer assistance programs ranging from providing trained volunteers to assist taxpayers at no cost in completing their tax returns to toll-free telephone assistance. The toll-free telephone numbers are included in the instruction booklet for Form 540NR.

In addition, the FTB has several district offices located in principal cities throughout the state. These offices and their addresses are printed in the 540NR Instruction booklet.

¶ 75 Forms

Forms may be ordered directly from the state at the following address:

Franchise Tax Board

Tax Forms Request Unit

P.O. Box 307

Rancho Cordova, CA 95741-0307

California income tax forms and publications may also be downloaded from the Internet. The Internet address and telephone numbers are listed in the Form 540NR Instruction booklet.

¶ 76 Interest

The California rate of interest on underpayments and overpayments of tax is based on the federal underpayment rate (see ¶ 709). The interest rate is redetermined semi-annually and is as follows:

January 1, 1996—June 30, 1996	9%
July 1, 1996—December 31, 1996	9%
January 1, 1997—June 30, 1997	9%
July 1, 1997—December 31, 1997	9%
January 1, 1998—June 30, 1998	9%
July 1, 1998—December 31, 1998	9%
January 1, 1999—June 30, 1999	8%
July 1, 1999—December 31, 1999	7%
January 1, 2000—June 30, 2000	8%

¶ 77 Penalties

A penalty of 5% per month, up to a maximum of 25%, is imposed for failure without reasonable cause to file a return. If the failure to file is fraudulent, the penalty is 15% per month, up to a maximum of 75%.

The penalty for failure to pay the income tax when it is due is 5% of the unpaid amount plus 1/2% per month. If the penalties for failure to file and failure to pay are both applicable, the penalty imposed is the higher of (1) the penalty for failure to pay or (2) the total of the penalty for failure to file and the penalty for failure to furnish information.

A minimum penalty of the lesser of $100 or 100% of the tax liability is imposed if the return is not filed within 60 days of the due date.

Other penalties are discussed at ¶ 710.

PART III

PERSONAL INCOME TAX

FEDERAL-CALIFORNIA CROSS-REFERENCE TABLE AND INDEX

Showing Sections of California Personal Income Tax Law (Revenue and Taxation Code) Comparable to Sections of Federal Law (1986 Internal Revenue Code)

Federal	California	Subject	Paragraph
IRC Sec. 1, 3	Secs. 17041, 17048	Tax Rates and Tables	¶ 112
IRC Sec. 2(a)	Secs. 17046, 17142.5	"Surviving Spouse" Defined	¶ 104a
IRC Secs. 2(b), 2(c)	Sec. 17042	"Head of Household" Defined	¶ 110
IRC Sec. 15	Sec. 17034	Effect of Changes	¶ 406
IRC Sec. 21	. . .	Credit—Child Care	. . .
IRC Sec. 23	Sec. 17052.25	Adoption Costs Credit	¶ 128
IRC Secs. 25-30A	Sec. 17039	Credits—Various	. . .
IRC Sec. 31	Sec. 19002	Credit—Tax Withheld	¶ 712a
IRC Secs. 32-34	. . .	Credits—Various	. . .
IRC Sec. 38	Sec. 17053.57	Community Development Investment Credit	¶ 145
IRC Secs. 39-40	. . .	Credits—Various	. . .
IRC Sec. 41	Sec. 17052.12	Research Expenditures Credit	¶ 139
IRC Sec. 42	Secs. 17057.5, 17058	Low-income Housing Credit	¶ 127
IRC Sec. 43	Sec. 17052.8	Enhanced Oil Recovery Credit	¶ 142
IRC Sec. 44	Sec. 17053.42	Disabled Access Credit	¶ 129
IRC Sec. 45C	. . .	Clinical Testing Credit	. . .
IRC Sec. 51-52	Sec. 17053.7	Work Opportunity Credit	. . .
IRC Sec. 53	Sec. 17063	Minimum Tax Credit	¶ 141
IRC Secs. 55-59	Secs. 17062, 17062.5, 18037.5	Alternative Minimum Tax	¶ 112a, ¶ 319
IRC Sec. 61	Secs. 17071, 17087.6, 17090, 17131, 17133, 17133.5, 17135, 17136, 17138, 17140.5, 17147.7, 17149, 17153.5, 17303, 17555	"Gross Income" defined	¶ 201
IRC Sec. 62	Sec. 17072	"Adjusted Gross Income" defined	¶ 202, ¶ 317
IRC Sec. 63	Secs. 17073, 17073.5, 17301	Standard Deduction	¶ 108, ¶ 203, ¶ 303, ¶ 321
IRC Sec. 64	Sec. 17074	"Ordinary Income" defined	. . .
IRC Sec. 65	Sec. 17075	"Ordinary Loss" defined	. . .
IRC Sec. 66	Sec. 18534	Income Where Spouses Living Apart	¶ 104a, ¶ 238
IRC Sec. 67	Sec. 17076	2% Floor on Itemized Deductions	¶ 303, ¶ 317
IRC Sec. 68	Sec. 17077	6% Floor on Itemized Deductions	¶ 303, ¶ 317

Federal	California	Subject	Paragraph
IRC Sec. 71	Sec. 17081	Spousal and Child Support Payments	Various
IRC Sec. 72	Secs. 17081, 17085, 17085.7, 17087	Annuities	¶ 205, ¶ 206
IRC Sec. 73	Sec. 17081	Services of Child	¶ 208
IRC Sec. 74	Sec. 17081	Prizes and Awards	¶ 209
IRC Sec. 75	Sec. 17081	Dealers in Tax-Exempt Securities	¶ 210
IRC Sec. 77	Sec. 17081	Commodity Credit Corp. Loans	¶ 211
IRC Sec. 79	Sec. 17081	Group Term Life Insurance	¶ 212
IRC Sec. 80	Sec. 17081	Restoration of Value of Certain Securities	. . .
IRC Sec. 82	Sec. 17081	Moving Expense Reimbursement	¶ 237
IRC Sec. 83	Sec. 17081	Property Transferred to Employee	¶ 207
IRC Sec. 84	Sec. 17081	Transfers to Political Organizations	¶ 201, ¶ 523
IRC Sec. 85	Secs. 17081, 17083	Unemployment Compensation	¶ 201
IRC Sec. 86	Secs. 17081, 17087	Social Security Benefits, etc.	¶ 201
IRC Sec. 88	Sec. 17081	Nuclear Plant Expenses	¶ 201
IRC Sec. 90	Sec. 17081	Illegal Irrigation Subsidies	¶ 201
IRC Sec. 101	Secs. 17131, 17132.6	Death Benefits	¶ 213, ¶ 215
IRC Sec. 102	Sec. 17131	Gifts and Inheritances	¶ 216
IRC Sec. 103	Secs. 17131, 17133, 17143	Interest on Government Bonds	¶ 217
IRC Sec. 104	Sec. 17131	Compensation—Injury or Sickness	¶ 218
IRC Sec. 105	Secs. 17131, 17087	Accident and Health Plans— Amounts Received	¶ 219
IRC Sec. 106	Sec. 17131	Accident and Health Plans— Employer Contributions	¶ 219
IRC Sec. 107	Sec. 17131	Rental Value of Parsonages	¶ 220
IRC Sec. 108	Secs. 17131, 17134, 17144	Income from Discharge of Indebtedness	¶ 221
IRC Sec. 109	Sec. 17131	Improvements by Lessee	¶ 222
IRC Sec. 110	Sec. 17131	Short-term Lease Construction Allowances	¶ 222a
IRC Sec. 111	Secs. 17131, 17142	Recovery of Bad Debts and Prior Taxes	¶ 223
IRC Sec. 112	Secs. 17131, 17142.5	Combat Pay of Members of Armed Forces	¶ 224
IRC Sec. 115	Sec. 17131	Income of States and Municipalities	. . .
IRC Sec. 117	Sec. 17131	Scholarship and Fellowship Grants	¶ 226
IRC Sec. 119	Sec. 17131	Employer– Furnished Meals and Lodging	¶ 227
IRC Sec. 120	Sec. 17131	Employer Contributions to Legal Services Plan	¶ 201, ¶ 243
IRC Sec. 121	Secs. 17131, 17152	One-Time Exclusion of Gain From Sale of Residence	¶ 228
IRC Sec. 122	Sec. 17131	Reduced Uniformed Services Retirement Pay	¶ 205, ¶ 224
IRC Sec. 123	Sec. 17131	Living Expenses Paid by Insurance	¶ 237

Federal	California	Subject	Paragraph
IRC Sec. 125	Sec. 17131	Employer Contributions to "Cafeteria" Plans	¶ 201
IRC Sec. 126	Secs. 17131, 17135.5	Government Payments for Environmental Conservation	¶ 201, ¶ 242
IRC Sec. 127	Secs. 17131, 17151	Educational Assistance Programs	¶ 201, ¶ 241
IRC Sec. 129	Sec. 17131	Dependent Care Assistance Programs	¶ 201
IRC Sec. 130	Sec. 17131	Personal Injury Assignments	¶ 201
IRC Sec. 131	Sec. 17131	Foster Care Payments	¶ 201
IRC Sec. 132	Secs. 17131, 17154	Fringe Benefits	¶ 201, ¶ 240
IRC Sec. 134	Sec. 17131	Military Benefits	¶ 201, ¶ 224, ¶ 237
IRC Sec. 135	Sec. 17151	Bond Income Used for Higher Education	. . .
IRC Sec. 136	Sec. 17131	Energy Conservation Subsidies	¶ 201, ¶ 244
IRC Sec. 137	Sec. 17131	Adoption Assistance Programs	¶ 248
IRC Sec. 138	Sec. 17131	Miscellaneous Non-IRC Federal Exemptions	. . .
IRC Secs. 141-50	Sec. 17143	Private Activity Bonds	¶ 217
IRC Sec. 151	Secs. 17054, 17054.1	Deductions for Personal and Dependent Exemptions	¶ 109
IRC Sec. 152	Sec. 17056	Dependents	¶ 111
IRC Sec. 161	Secs. 17201, 17274, 17275, 17278, 17299.8, 17299.9	Allowance of Deductions	¶ 300
IRC Sec. 162	Secs. 17201, 17202, 17269, 17270, 17273, 17273.1, 17286	Trade or Business Expense	Various
IRC Sec. 163	Secs. 17201, 17224, 17230, 17235, 18037.5	Interest	¶ 236, ¶ 305
IRC Sec. 164	Secs. 17201, 17220, 17222	Taxes—Deductions	¶ 306
IRC Sec. 165	Secs. 17201, 17207 17207.4	Losses—Deductions	¶ 307, ¶ 407
IRC Sec. 166	Sec. 17201	Bad Debts—Deductions	¶ 308
IRC Sec. 167	Secs. 17201, 17250.5	Depreciation	¶ 310, ¶ 537
IRC Sec. 168	Secs. 17201, 17250	Accelerated Cost Recovery System	¶ 310, ¶ 310f
IRC Sec. 169	Secs. 17201, 17250	Amortization of Pollution Control Facilities	¶ 310d
IRC Sec. 170	Secs. 17201, 17251.5, 17275.5	Charitable Contributions	¶ 312
IRC Sec. 171	Sec. 17201	Amortization of Bond Premium	¶ 314
IRC Sec. 172	Secs. 17201, 17276-76.6, 17310	Net Operating Loss Carryover	¶ 309
IRC Sec. 173	Sec. 17201	Circulation Expenditures	¶ 303, ¶ 328
IRC Sec. 174	Sec. 17201	Research and Experimental Expenditures	¶ 319
IRC Sec. 175	Sec. 17201	Soil and Water Conservation Expenditures	¶ 302, ¶ 327
IRC Sec. 178	Sec. 17201	Depreciation or Amortization of Cost of Acquiring a Lease	¶ 310c
IRC Sec. 179	Secs. 17201, 17255, 17268	Election to Expense Depreciable Assets	¶ 310a

Federal	California	Subject	Paragraph
IRC Sec. 179A	Secs. 17201, 17256	Clean-Fuel Vehicles and Refueling Property	¶ 330
IRC Sec. 180	Sec. 17201	Farm Fertilizer Expenses	¶ 302, ¶ 327
IRC Sec. 183	Sec. 17201	Hobby Losses	¶ 322, ¶ 324
IRC Sec. 186	Sec. 17201	Recovery of Antitrust Damages	¶ 307
IRC Sec. 190	Sec. 17201	Facilities for Handicapped	¶ 301
IRC Sec. 192	Sec. 17201	Contributions to Black Lung Benefit Trust	. . .
IRC Sec. 193	Secs. 17201, 17260	Tertiary Injectants	¶ 311a
IRC Sec. 194	Secs. 17201, 17278.5	Amortization of Reforestation Expenses	¶ 310e
IRC Sec. 194A	Sec. 17201	Contributions to Employer Liability Trusts	¶ 318
IRC Sec. 195	Sec. 17201	Start-Up Expenditures	¶ 320
IRC Sec. 196	Sec. 17024.5	Unused Business Credits—Deduction	. . .
IRC Sec. 197	Sec. 17279	Amortization of Goodwill	¶ 310, ¶ 319b
IRC Sec. 198	Sec. 17279.4	Expensing of Environmental Remediation Costs	¶ 310g
IRC Sec. 211	Sec. 17201	Additional Allowance of Deductions	. . .
IRC Sec. 212	Sec. 17201	Expenses for Production of Income	¶ 304
IRC Sec. 213	Sec. 17201	Medical Expenses	¶ 315
IRC Sec. 215	Secs. 17201, 17302	Spousal Support	¶ 313
IRC Sec. 216	Secs. 17201, 18037.5	Taxes and Interest Paid to Cooperative Housing Corporation	¶ 316
IRC Sec. 217	Sec. 17201	Moving Expenses	¶ 316a
IRC Sec. 219	Secs. 17201, 17507.6	Retirement Savings	¶ 318
IRC Sec. 220	Secs. 17201, 17215	Medical Savings Accounts	¶ 246, ¶ 315a
IRC Sec. 221	Secs. 17201, 17204	Interest on Education Loans	¶ 305
IRC Sec. 261	Sec. 17201	Disallowance of Deductions	¶ 300, ¶ 322
IRC Sec. 262	Sec. 17201	Personal Living and Family Expenses	¶ 322
IRC Sec. 263	Secs. 17201, 17260	Capital Expenditures	¶ 311a, ¶ 322
IRC Sec. 263A	Sec. 17201	Inventory Capitalization Rules	¶ 322, ¶ 407, ¶ 409, ¶ 416
IRC Sec. 264	Secs. 17201, 17279.5	Amounts Paid in Connection with Insurance Contracts	¶ 305, ¶ 322
IRC Sec. 265	Sec. 17280	Tax Exempt Income—Interest and Expenses	¶ 305, ¶ 322
IRC Sec. 266	Sec. 17201	Carrying Charges	¶ 322
IRC Sec. 267	Sec. 17201	Transactions Between Related Individuals	¶ 322
IRC Sec. 268	Sec. 17201	Sale of Land with Unharvested Crop	¶ 322
IRC Sec. 269	Sec. 17201	Acquisition Made to Avoid Income Tax	. . .
IRC Sec. 269A	Secs. 17201, 17287	Personal Service Corporations	¶ 412
IRC Sec. 269B	Sec. 17201	Stapled Stock	¶ 412
IRC Sec. 271	Sec. 17201	Debts Owed by Political Parties	¶ 308
IRC Sec. 272	Sec. 17201	Disposal of Coal or Domestic Iron Ore	. . .

Federal	California	Subject	Paragraph
IRC Sec. 273	Sec. 17201	Holders of Terminable Interest	¶ 322
IRC Sec. 274	Secs. 17201, 17271	Entertainment, Travel and Gift Expenses	¶ 302, ¶ 317, ¶ 322
IRC Sec. 275	Sec. 17222	Withheld Taxes	¶ 306
IRC Sec. 276	Sec. 17201	Indirect Political Contributions	¶ 322
IRC Sec. 277	Sec. 17201	Expenses by Membership Organizations	. . .
IRC Sec. 280A	Secs. 17201, 18037.5	Disallowance of Business Expenses of Home, Vacation Rentals	¶ 301, ¶ 322
IRC Sec. 280B	Sec. 17201	Demolition of Historic Structures	¶ 322
IRC Sec. 280C	Secs. 17201, 17270	Federal Credits	¶ 322
IRC Sec. 280E	Secs. 17201, 17281, 17282	Illegal Drug Sales	¶ 322
IRC Sec. 280F	Sec. 17201	Luxury Cars, etc.	¶ 310
IRC Sec. 280G	Sec. 17201	"Golden Parachute" Payments	¶ 322
IRC Sec. 280H	Sec. 17201	Salaries of Shareholder/Owners of Personal Service Corp.	. . .
IRC Sec. 301	Sec. 17321	Corporate Distributions of Property	¶ 225
IRC Sec. 302	Secs. 17321-22	Distributions in Redemption of Stock	¶ 225
IRC Sec. 303	Sec. 17321	Distributions in Redemption of Stock to Pay Death Taxes	¶ 225
IRC Sec. 304	Sec. 17321	Redemption Through Use of Related Corporations	¶ 225
IRC Sec. 305	Sec. 17321	Distributions of Stock and Rights	¶ 225
IRC Sec. 306	Sec. 17321	Dispositions of "306" Stock	¶ 225
IRC Sec. 307	Sec. 17321	Basis of Stock and Rights of Distribution	¶ 533
IRC Sec. 312	Sec. 17321	Effect on Earnings and Profits	¶ 225
IRC Sec. 316	Sec. 17321	"Dividend" Defined	¶ 225
IRC Sec. 317	Sec. 17321	"Property," "Redemption" Defined	¶ 225
IRC Sec. 318	Sec. 17321	Constructive Ownership of Stock	¶ 225
IRC Sec. 331	Sec. 17321	Gain or Loss in Corporate Liquidations	¶ 225, ¶ 511a
IRC Sec. 334	Sec. 17321	Basis of Property Received in Liquidation	¶ ¶ 225, ¶ 511a, ¶ 526a
IRC Sec. 341	Sec. 17321	Collapsible Corporations	¶ 225, ¶ 511a
IRC Sec. 346	Sec. 17321	"Partial Liquidation" Defined	¶ 225, ¶ 511a
IRC Sec. 351	Sec. 17321	Corporate Organizations— Transfer to Controlled Corporation	¶ 506
IRC Sec. 354	Sec. 17321	Exchange of Stock in Reorganization	¶ 507
IRC Sec. 355	Sec. 17321	Reorganizations— Distributions by Controlled Corporation	¶ 508
IRC Sec. 356	Sec. 17321	Receipt of Additional Consideration	¶ 509

Federal	California	Subject	Paragraph
IRC Sec. 357	Sec. 17321	Assumption of Liability	¶ 509
IRC Sec. 358	Sec. 17321	Basis to Distributees	¶ 526, ¶ 526b
IRC Sec. 367	Sec. 17321	Transfers to Foreign Corporations	¶ 510
IRC Sec. 368	Sec. 17321	Corporate Reorganizations— Definitions	¶ 507
IRC Sec. 382	Sec. 17321	Discharge of Indebtedness	¶ 221
IRC Sec. 385	Sec. 17321	Treatment of Corporate Interests as Stock or Indebtedness	. . .
IRC Sec. 401	Sec. 17501	Pension, Profit-Sharing, Stock Bonus Plans	¶ 206, ¶ 606
IRC Sec. 402	Secs. 17501, 17504	Taxability of Beneficiary of Employees' Trust	¶ 206, ¶ 318, ¶ 606
IRC Sec. 403	Secs. 17501, 17506	Taxability of Employee Annuities	¶ 206, ¶ 606
IRC Sec. 404	Secs. 17203, 17501	Deduction for Employer's Contributions to Employee Pension, Profit-Sharing, and Stock Bonus Plans	¶ 318
IRC Sec. 404A	Sec. 17501	Foreign Deferred Compensation Plans	¶ 318
IRC Sec. 406	Sec. 17501	Employees of Foreign Subsidiaries	¶ 318, ¶ 606
IRC Sec. 407	Sec. 17501	Employees of Domestic Subsidiaries	¶ 318, ¶ 606
IRC Sec. 408	Secs. 17507, 17508	Individual Retirement Accounts	¶ 206, ¶ 318
IRC Sec. 408A	Sec. 17507.6	Roth IRAs	¶ 206, ¶ 318
IRC Sec. 409	Sec. 17501	Employee Stock Ownership Plans	¶ 318
IRC Sec. 410	Sec. 17501	Minimum Participation Standards	¶ 318
IRC Sec. 411	Sec. 17501	Minimum Vesting Standards	¶ 318
IRC Sec. 412	Sec. 17501	Minimum Funding Standards	¶ 318
IRC Sec. 413	Secs. 17501, 17509	Collectively Bargained Plans	¶ 318
IRC Sec. 414	Sec. 17501	Definitions and Special Rules—Plans	¶ 318
IRC Sec. 415	Sec. 17501	Limitations on Benefits and Contributions	¶ 318
IRC Sec. 416	Sec. 17501	Top-Heavy Plans	¶ 318
IRC Sec. 417	Sec. 17501	Minimum Survivor Annuity Requirements	¶ 318
IRC Secs. 418-18E	Sec. 17501	Pension Plan Reorganizations	¶ 318
IRC Sec. 419	Sec. 17501	Welfare Benefit Plans	¶ 318
IRC Sec. 419A	Sec. 17501	Qualified Asset Account; Limitation on Additions to Account	¶ 318
IRC Sec. 420	Sec. 17501	Transfers of Excess Pension Assets to Retiree Health Accounts	. . .
IRC Sec. 421	Secs. 17501, 17502	Employee Stock Options— Employer Deductions	¶ 207
IRC Sec. 422	Sec. 17501	Incentive Stock Options	¶ 207
IRC Sec. 423	Sec. 17501	Employee Stock Purchase Plan	¶ 207
IRC Sec. 424	Sec. 17501	Stock Options—Definitions and Special Rules	¶ 207

Federal	California	Subject	Paragraph
IRC Sec. 441	Secs. 17551, 17554, 17656	Accounting Periods— Generally	¶ 400, ¶ 401
IRC Sec. 442	Secs. 17551, 17556	Accounting—Change of Period	¶ 402
IRC Sec. 443	Secs. 17551-52	Accounting—Short Period Returns	¶ 403, ¶ 404
IRC Sec. 444	Sec. 17551	Election to Keep Same Tax Year—Partnerships	¶ 401, ¶ 612
IRC Sec. 446	Sec. 17551	Methods of Accounting— General Rule	¶ 407
IRC Sec. 447	Sec. 17551	Accounting—Corporations Engaged in Farming	¶ 407
IRC Sec. 448	Sec. 17551	Restriction on Use of Cash Method	¶ 407
IRC Sec. 451	Sec. 17551	Taxable Year of Inclusion	¶ 407
IRC Sec. 453	Secs. 17551, 17560	Installment Method	¶ 411
IRC Sec. 453A	Secs. 17551, 17560	Installment Method—Dealers in Personal Property	¶ 411
IRC Sec. 453B	Sec. 17551	Gain or Loss Disposition of Installment Obligations	¶ 411
IRC Sec. 454	Secs. 17551, 17553	Obligations Issued at Discount	¶ 408
IRC Sec. 455	Sec. 17551	Prepaid Subscription Income	¶ 407
IRC Sec. 456	Sec. 17551	Prepaid Dues Income	¶ 407
IRC Sec. 457	Sec. 17551	State Deferred Compensation Plans	¶ 318
IRC Sec. 458	Sec. 17551	Returned Magazines	¶ 407
IRC Sec. 460	Secs. 17551, 17564	Long-Term Contracts	¶ 407
IRC Sec. 461	Sec. 17551	Taxable Year of Deduction	¶ 407
IRC Sec. 464	Secs. 17551, 18037.5	Deduction Limitation— Farming Syndicates	¶ 407
IRC Sec. 465	Sec. 17551	At Risk Limitation	¶ 325
IRC Sec. 467	Sec. 17551	Deferred Rental Payments	¶ 407
IRC Sec. 468	Sec. 17551	Waste Disposal Costs	¶ 407
IRC Sec. 468A	Sec. 17551	Nuclear Plant Expenses	¶ 407
IRC Sec. 468B	Sec. 17551	Settlement Funds	¶ 407
IRC Sec. 469	Secs. 17551, 17561	Passive Loss Limits	¶ 326
IRC Sec. 471	Sec. 17551	Inventories	¶ 409
IRC Sec. 472	Sec. 17551	LIFO Inventories	¶ 410
IRC Sec. 473	Sec. 17551	Liquidation of LIFO Inventories	¶ 410
IRC Sec. 474	Sec. 17551	Dollar-Value LIFO Method	¶ 410
IRC Sec. 475	Secs. 17551, 17570	Mark to market accounting	¶ 409, ¶ 517a
IRC Sec. 481	Sec. 17551	Adjustments	¶ 407
IRC Sec. 482	Sec. 17551	Allocation of Income Among Taxpayers	¶ 412
IRC Sec. 483	Sec. 17551	Imputed Interest	¶ 414
IRC Sec. 501	Secs. 17631, 17632	Exempt Organizations and Trusts	¶ 312, ¶ 605, ¶ 606
IRC Sec. 503	Secs. 17635-40	Requirements for Exemption	¶ 606
IRC Secs. 511-14	Secs. 17651, 18037.5	Unrelated Business Income	¶ 606
IRC Sec. 529	17140.3	Qualified State Tuition Programs	¶ 249
IRC Secs. 541-58	Sec. 17024.5	Personal Holding Companies	. . .
IRC Sec. 584	Sec. 17671	Common Trust Funds	¶ 611
IRC Sec. 611	Sec. 17681	Depletion—Deduction	¶ 311
IRC Sec. 612	Sec. 17681	Basis for Cost Depletion	¶ 311, ¶ 537
IRC Sec. 613	Sec. 17681	Percentage Depletion	¶ 311

Federal	California	Subject	Paragraph
IRC Sec. 613A	Sec. 17681	Limitations on Depletion—Oil, Gas and Geothermal Wells	¶ 311, ¶ 537
IRC Sec. 614	Sec. 17681	"Property" Defined	¶ 311
IRC Sec. 616	Sec. 17681	Mine Development Expenses	¶ 311a
IRC Sec. 617	Sec. 17681	Mine Exploration Expenses	¶ 311a
IRC Sec. 631	Sec. 17681	Gain or Loss in Case of Timber, Coal or Iron	¶ 520
IRC Sec. 636	Sec. 17681	Mineral Production Payments	¶ 311
IRC Sec. 638	Sec. 17681	Continental Shelf Areas	¶ 311
IRC Sec. 641	Secs. 17731, 17731.5, 17734, 17742-45.1	Estates and Trusts—Imposition of Tax	¶ 601, ¶ 604, ¶ 605
IRC Sec. 642	Secs. 17731-33, 17736	Special Rules for Credits and Deductions	¶ 604, ¶ 604a, ¶ 605
IRC Sec. 643	Secs. 17731, 17750	Estates and Trusts—Definitions	¶ 601, ¶ 604
IRC Sec. 644	Sec. 17731	Sale of Appreciated Property by Trust	¶ 604
IRC Sec. 645	Sec. 17731	Taxable Year of Trusts	¶ 401, ¶ 601, ¶ 604
IRC Sec. 646	Sec. 17731, 17751	Certain Revocable Trusts Treated as Part of Estate	¶ 604
IRC Sec. 651	Sec. 17731	Simple Trusts	¶ 604
IRC Sec. 652	Sec. 17731	Beneficiaries of Simple Trusts	¶ 604a
IRC Sec. 661	Secs. 17731, 17735	Complex Trusts—Deductions	¶ 604
IRC Sec. 662	Sec. 17731	Beneficiaries of Complex Trusts	¶ 604a
IRC Sec. 663	Sec. 17731, 17752	Special Rules Applicable to § 661 and § 662	¶ 604a
IRC Sec. 664	Sec. 17731	Charitable Remainder Trusts	¶ 604a, ¶ 605
IRC Sec. 665	Secs. 17731, 17779	Excess Distributions by Trusts—Definitions	¶ 601, ¶ 604a
IRC Sec. 666	Secs. 17731, 17779	Accumulation Distribution Allocation	¶ 604a
IRC Sec. 667	Secs. 17731, 17779	Amounts Distributed in Preceding Years	¶ 604a
IRC Sec. 668	Secs. 17731, 17779	Interest on Accumulation from Foreign Trusts	¶ 604a
IRC Sec. 671	Sec. 17731	Grantor Trusts—Trust Income	¶ 607
IRC Sec. 672	Sec. 17731	Grantor Trusts—Definitions	¶ 607
IRC Sec. 673	Sec. 17731	Reversionary Interests	¶ 607
IRC Sec. 674	Sec. 17731	Power to Control Beneficial Enjoyment	¶ 607
IRC Sec. 675	Sec. 17731	Administrative Powers	¶ 607
IRC Sec. 676	Sec. 17731	Power to Revoke	¶ 607
IRC Sec. 677	Sec. 17731	Income for Benefit of Grantor	¶ 607
IRC Sec. 678	Sec. 17731	Person Other Than Grantor Treated as Owner	¶ 607
IRC Sec. 679	Secs. 17024.5, 17731	Foreign Trusts with U.S. Beneficiaries	¶ 607
IRC Sec. 681	Sec. 17731	Limitation on Charitable Deduction—Unrelated Business Income	¶ 605
IRC Sec. 682	Secs. 17731, 17737	Income in Case of Divorce	¶ 608
IRC Sec. 683	Sec. 17731	Use of Trust as Exchange Fund	¶ 507

Federal	California	Subject	Paragraph
IRC Sec. 684	Sec. 17731	Gain on Transfers to Foreign Trusts and Estates	¶ 510a
IRC Sec. 685	Sec. 17731, 17760.5	Funeral Trusts	¶ 607
IRC Sec. 691	Sec. 17731	Income in Respect of Decedents	¶ 413
IRC Sec. 692	Secs. 17731, 17142.5	Income Taxes of Armed Forces Members on Death	¶ 224
IRC Sec. 701	Secs. 17851, 17851.5	Partners, Not Partnership, Subject to Tax	¶ 612
IRC Sec. 702	Sec. 17851	Income and Credits of Partner	¶ 614
IRC Sec. 703	Secs. 17851, 17853	Partnership Computations	¶ 614
IRC Sec. 704	Secs. 17851, 17858	Partner's Distributive Share	¶ 612a, ¶ 614
IRC Sec. 705	Sec. 17851	Determination of Basis of Partner's Interest	¶ 530, ¶ 612b
IRC Sec. 706	Sec. 17851	Taxable Years of Partner and Partnership	¶ 615
IRC Sec. 707	Secs. 17851, 17854	Transactions Between Partner and Partnership	¶ 612a, ¶ 614
IRC Sec. 708	Sec. 17851	Continuation of Partnership	¶ 615
IRC Sec. 709	Sec. 17851	Organization and Syndication Fees	¶ 614
IRC Sec. 721	Sec. 17851	Recognition of Gain or Loss Contribution	¶ 612a
IRC Sec. 722	Sec. 17851	Basis of Contributing Partner's Interest	¶ 530, ¶ 612a
IRC Sec. 723	Sec. 17851	Basis of Property Contributed to Partnership	¶ 530, ¶ 612a
IRC Sec. 724	Sec. 17851	Disposition of Contributed Property	¶ 612a
IRC Sec. 731	Sec. 17851	Recognition of Gain or Loss on Distribution	¶ 612a
IRC Sec. 732	Sec. 17851	Basis of Distributed Property	¶ 530
IRC Sec. 733	Sec. 17851	Basis of Distributee Partner's Interest	¶ 530
IRC Sec. 734	Sec. 17851	Optional Adjustment to Basis of Undistributed Property	¶ 530
IRC Sec. 735	Sec. 17851	Character of Gain or Loss on Disposition of Distributed Property	¶ 612a
IRC Sec. 736	Sec. 17851	Payments to Retiring Partner or Deceased Partner's Successor	¶ 612a, ¶ 612b
IRC Sec. 737	Sec. 17851	Precontribution Gain From Partnership Distributions	¶ 612b
IRC Sec. 741	Sec. 17851	Gain or Loss on Sale or Exchange	¶ 612b
IRC Sec. 742	Sec. 17851	Basis of Transferee Partner's Interest	¶ 530
IRC Sec. 743	Sec. 17851	Optional Adjustment to Basis of Property	¶ 530
IRC Sec. 751	Secs. 17851, 17855-57	Unrealized Receivables and Inventory Items	¶ 612b
IRC Sec. 752	Sec. 17851	Treatment of Certain Liabilities	¶ 612b
IRC Sec. 753	Sec. 17851	Partner Receiving Income in Respect of Decedent	¶ 612b
IRC Sec. 754	Sec. 17851	Electing Optional Adjustment to Basis of Partnership Property	¶ 530, ¶ 612b

Federal	California	Subject	Paragraph
IRC Sec. 755	Sec. 17851	Rules for Allocation of Basis	¶ 530, ¶ 612b
IRC Sec. 761	Sec. 17851	Terms Defined	¶ 612
IRC Secs. 771-77	Secs. 17851, 17865	Special Rules for Electing Large Partnerships	¶ 617a
IRC Sec. 851	Secs. 17088, 17088.5	Regulated Investment Company	¶ 225
IRC Sec. 852	Secs. 17088, 17145	Dividends to Shareholders of Certain Mutual Funds	¶ 217
IRC Sec. 853	Sec. 17024.5	Foreign Tax Credit for Shareholders	¶ 225
IRC Secs. 854-55	Sec. 17088	Dividends of Regulated Investment Company	¶ 217, ¶ 225, ¶ 534
IRC Secs. 856-60	Secs. 17088, 17088.6	Real Estate Investment Trusts	¶ 225, ¶ 607a
IRC Secs. 860A-860G	Sec. 17088	Real Estate Mortgage Investment Conduits	¶ 611a
IRC Secs. 860H-860L	Sec. 17088	Financial Asset Securatization Trusts	¶ 607b
IRC Secs. 861-65	Secs. 17091, 17951-54	Sources of Income	¶ 201, ¶ 230
IRC Secs. 871-79	. . .	Nonresident Aliens	¶ 238
IRC Sec. 893	Sec. 17146	Employees of Foreign Country	¶ 229
IRC Secs. 901-08	. . .	Income from Sources Outside U.S.	¶ 115, Various
IRC Sec. 911	Sec. 17024.5	Foreign Income Exclusion	¶ 230, ¶ 234
IRC Secs. 912-43	. . .	Income from Sources Within U.S. Possessions	¶ 230
IRC Secs. 951-64	. . .	Controlled Foreign Corporations—Shareholders	¶ 225
IRC Sec. 988	Sec. 17078	Foreign Currency Transactions	¶ 510a
IRC Secs. 991-99	Sec. 17024.5	Domestic International Sales Corp. (DISC)	. . .
IRC Sec. 1001	Secs. 18031, 18041.5	Determination of Gain or Loss	¶ 501
IRC Sec. 1011	Sec. 18031	Adjusted Basis for Determining Gain or Loss	¶ 534
IRC Sec. 1012	Sec. 18031	Basis of Property	¶ 521
IRC Sec. 1013	Sec. 18031	Basis of Property Included in Inventory	¶ 522
IRC Sec. 1014	Sec. 18031	Basis of Property Acquired from Decedent	¶ 525
IRC Sec. 1015	Sec. 18031	Basis of Property Acquired by Gift and Transfers in Trust	¶ 523, ¶ 524
IRC Sec. 1016	Secs. 18031, 18036	Adjustments to Basis	¶ 534, ¶ 535
IRC Sec. 1017	Secs. 18031, 18044	Discharge of Indebtedness	¶ 221, ¶ 534
IRC Sec. 1019	Sec. 18031	Property on Which Lessee Has Made Improvements	¶ 536
IRC Sec. 1021	Sec. 18031	Sale of Annuity Contract	¶ 534
IRC Sec. 1031	Secs. 18031, 18043	Exchange of Property Held for Productive Use or Investment	¶ 504
IRC Sec. 1033	Secs. 18031, 18037-37.5	Involuntary Conversions	¶ 502, ¶ 527
IRC Sec. 1035	Sec. 18031	Exchange of Insurance Policies	¶ 504a
IRC Sec. 1036	Sec. 18031	Exchange of Stock	¶ 505
IRC Sec. 1037	Sec. 18031	Exchanges of U.S. Obligations	¶ 505a

Federal	California	Subject	Paragraph
IRC Sec. 1038	Secs. 18031, 18037.5	Reacquisition of Real Property	¶ 505b
IRC Sec. 1040	Secs. 18031, 18038	Transfer of Certain Real Property	¶ 604
IRC Sec. 1041	Sec. 18031	Inter-Spousal Transfers	¶ 501a
IRC Sec. 1042	Secs. 18031, 18042	Securities Sales to ESOPs	¶ 501, ¶ 506b
IRC Sec. 1043	Sec. 18031	Sale of Property to Comply with Conflict of Interest Requirements	. . .
IRC Sec. 1044	Secs. 18031, 18044	Rollover of Publicly Traded Securities	¶ 501
IRC Sec. 1045	Secs. 18038.4, 18038.5	Rollover of Gain from Small Business Stock	¶ 513
IRC Sec. 1052	Secs. 18031, 18039	Basis Provisions from Prior Codes	¶ 529
IRC Sec. 1053	Sec. 18031	Basis of Property Acquired Before March 1913	¶ 531
IRC Sec. 1054	Sec. 18031	Basis of Stock Issued by FNMA	¶ 527a
IRC Sec. 1055	Sec. 18031	Redeemable Ground Rents	¶ 527b
IRC Sec. 1056	Sec. 18031	Basis Limitations for Player Contracts	¶ 538
IRC Sec. 1058	Sec. 18031	Transfer of Securities Under Loan Agreement	. . .
IRC Sec. 1059A	Sec. 18031	Basis or Inventor Costs on Imports	¶ 521
IRC Sec. 1060	Sec. 18031	Allocation of Transferred Business Assets	¶ 539
IRC Sec. 1081	Sec. 18031	Exchanges in Obedience to Orders of S.E.C.	¶ 503
IRC Sec. 1082	Sec. 18031	Basis for Determining Gain or Loss	¶ 532
IRC Sec. 1083	Sec. 18031	Definitions	. . .
IRC Sec. 1091	Sec. 18031	Wash Sales of Stock or Securities	¶ 514a, ¶ 528
IRC Sec. 1092	Sec. 18031	Straddle Losses	¶ 517
IRC Sec. 1202	Secs. 18152, 18152.5	Small Business Stock	¶ 513
IRC Secs. 1211-12	Secs. 18151, 18155	Limitation on Capital Losses	¶ 512, ¶ 514
IRC Sec. 1221	Sec. 18151	"Capital Asset" Defined	¶ 512a
IRC Sec. 1222	Sec. 18151	Other Terms Relating to Capital Gains and Losses	¶ 513
IRC Sec. 1223	Secs. 18151, 18037.5, 18151, 18155.5	Holding Period of Property	¶ 515
IRC Sec. 1231	Sec. 18151	Sale of Business Property and Involuntary Conversions	¶ 519
IRC Sec. 1233	Sec. 18151	Gains and Losses from Short Sales	¶ 516
IRC Sec. 1234	Sec. 18151	Options to Buy and Sell	¶ 517
IRC Sec. 1234A	Sec. 18151	Gain or Loss from Certain Terminations	¶ 512
IRC Sec. 1235	Sec. 18151	Sale or Exchange of Patents	¶ 516a
IRC Sec. 1236	Sec. 18151	Dealers in Securities	¶ 517a
IRC Sec. 1237	Sec. 18151	Real Property Subdivided for Sale	¶ 518a
IRC Sec. 1239	Sec. 18151	Gain on Depreciable Property Transferred Between Related Taxpayers	¶ 519, ¶ 519b

Federal	California	Subject	Paragraph
IRC Sec. 1241	Sec. 18151	Cancellation of Lease or Distributor's Agreement	¶ 520a
IRC Sec. 1242	Sec. 18151	Losses on Small Business Investment Company Stock	¶ 307
IRC Sec. 1243	Sec. 18151	Stock Received Pursuant to Conversion Privilege	¶ 307
IRC Sec. 1244	Sec. 18151	Losses on Small Business Stock	¶ 307
IRC Sec. 1245	Secs. 18151, 18165	Recapture of Depreciation on Personal Property	¶ 519b
IRC Secs. 1246	Sec. 17024.5	Gain on Foreign Investment Company Stock	¶ 519a
IRC Secs. 1247-48	Secs. 17024.5, 18151	Special Rules on Foreign Investment Company Stock	¶ 519a
IRC Sec. 1249	Secs. 17024.5, 18151	Patents Sold to Foreign Corporation	¶ 516a
IRC Sec. 1250	Secs. 18037.5, 18151, 18171, 18171.5	Recapture of Depreciation on Real Property	¶ 519b
IRC Sec. 1252	Sec. 18151	Recapture of Soil and Water Conservation Expenditures	¶ 519b
IRC Sec. 1253	Sec. 18151	Transfers of Franchises, Trademarks and Trade Names	¶ 319a, ¶ 516b
IRC Sec. 1254	Sec. 18151	Recapture of Intangible Drilling Costs	¶ 519b
IRC Sec. 1255	Sec. 18151	Certain Cost-Sharing Payments	¶ 519b
IRC Sec. 1256	Sec. 18151	Regulated Futures Contracts	¶ 517
IRC Sec. 1257	Sec. 18151	Wetlands or Erodible Croplands	¶ 512
IRC Sec. 1258	Sec. 18151	Recharacterization of Gain from Certain Financial Transactions	. . .
IRC Sec. 1259	Sec. 18151	Constructive Sales Treatment for Appreciated Financial Positions	¶ 517b
IRC Secs. 1271-88	Secs. 18037.5, 18151, 18177, 18178	Income from Discount Bonds, etc.	¶ 217, ¶ 236, ¶ 518
IRC Secs. 1311-14	Secs. 19057-67	Mitigation of Effect of Limitations	¶ 708, ¶ 715
IRC Sec. 1341	. . .	Repayment of Amounts Received Under Claim of Right	¶ 415
IRC Secs. 1361-79	Secs. 17087.5, 18006	Subchapter S Corporations	¶ 232
IRC Secs. 1381-83	. . .	Tax Treatment of Cooperatives	¶ 231
IRC Sec. 1385	Sec. 17086	Amounts Includible in Patron's Gross Income	¶ 231
IRC Sec. 1396	Sec. 17053.74	Empowerment Zone Employment Credit	¶ 134
IRC Sec. 1445	Secs. 18662, 18668	Withholding—Disposition of Real Estate	¶ 712
IRC Sec. 1446	Sec. 18666	Withholding—Amounts Paid to Foreign Partners	¶ 712
IRC Secs. 1491-94	. . .	Transfers of Property to Avoid Tax	. . .
IRC Secs. 3401-05	Secs. 18551, 18661-63, 18667, 18668	Withholding	¶ 712a
IRC Sec. 3406	. . .	Backup Withholding	¶ 711
IRC Secs. 3501-05	Sec. 18677	Collection of Withholding Tax	¶ 712a

Federal	California	Subject	Paragraph
IRC Secs. 4940-48	. . .	Private Foundations	¶ 605
IRC Secs. 4971-75	. . .	Pension Plans, etc.	¶ 206, ¶ 606
IRC Sec. 4980A	. . .	Excess Distributions from Qualified Plans	¶ 206
IRC Sec. 4980B	. . .	Excise Tax on Failure to Meet Health Care Continuous Coverage	. . .
IRC Sec. 5061	Sec. 19011	Electronic Funds Transfer	¶ 107
IRC Sec. 6011	Secs. 18552, 19524	General Return Requirements	¶ 616, ¶ 712a
IRC Sec. 6012	Secs. 18501, 18503-10, 18601	Returns Required	¶ 104
IRC Sec. 6013	Secs. 18521-33, 19006	Joint Returns	¶ 104, ¶ 104a, ¶ 707, ¶ 710
IRC Sec. 6014	. .	Tax Not Computed by Taxpayer	¶ 104
IRC Sec. 6031	Secs. 18535, 18633-33.5	Return of Partnership Income	¶ 616
IRC Sec. 6034	Sec. 18635	Information from Charitable Trust	¶ 605
IRC Sec. 6034A	Sec. 18505	Information to Beneficiaries	¶ 104
IRC Sec. 6036	Sec. 19089	Notice of Executor's Qualification	. . .
IRC Sec. 6039	Sec. 18636	Returns for Stock Transfers	¶ 711
IRC Sec. 6039C	Sec. 18645	Returns by Foreign Persons	¶ 711
IRC Sec. 6039D	. . .	Fringe Benefit Plans Return	¶ 711
IRC Sec. 6041	Secs. 18637, 18661	Reporting Requirements	¶ 711
IRC Sec. 6041A	Sec. 18638	Reporting Certain Payments	¶ 711
IRC Sec. 6042	Secs. 18637, 18639	Returns for Dividends	¶ 711
IRC Sec. 6043	. . .	Returns for Dividends on Liquidation	¶ 711
IRC Sec. 6044	Sec. 18640	Returns by Cooperatives	¶ 711
IRC Sec. 6045	Secs. 18641-43	Reporting by Brokers	¶ 711
IRC Sec. 6046A	. . .	Foreign Partnership Return	¶ 711
IRC Sec. 6047	Sec. 19518	Information Returns	¶ 606, ¶ 711
IRC Sec. 6048	Sec. 18505	Consistency Rule	¶ 601
IRC Sec. 6049	Secs. 18637, 18639	Returns for Interest	¶ 711
IRC Sec. 6050A	Sec. 18644	Fishing Boat Operators— Reporting Requirements	¶ 711
IRC Sec. 6050B	. . .	Reporting Unemployment Compensation	. . .
IRC Sec. 6050E	. . .	Reporting Tax Refunds	¶ 711
IRC Sec. 6050H-S	Sec. 18645	Information Returns	¶ 711
IRC Sec. 6052	Sec. 18647	Returns for Group-Term Life Insurance	¶ 711
IRC Sec. 6053	U.I. Code	Reporting Tips	¶ 711, ¶ 712a
IRC Sec. 6060	. . .	Tax Preparer Information Returns	¶ 701
IRC Sec. 6065	Secs. 18606, 18621	Verification of Returns	¶ 105
IRC Sec. 6072	Secs. 18566, 18601	Time for Filing Returns	¶ 105
IRC Sec. 6081	Secs. 18567, 18604	Extension of Time	¶ 105, ¶ 106
IRC Sec. 6091	Sec. 18621	Form of Return	¶ 105
IRC Sec. 6102	Sec. 18623	Fractional Dollar Calculations	¶ 104
IRC Secs. 6103-10	Secs. 19542-64	Secrecy and Disclosure of Returns	¶ 701, ¶ 702, ¶ 717
IRC Secs. 6111-12	Secs. 18547, 18648, 19182	Tax Shelters	¶ 710
IRC Sec. 6115	Sec. 18648.5	Disclosure Related to Quid Pro Quo Contributions	. . .
IRC Sec. 6151	Secs. 19001-06	Payment of Tax	¶ 107

Federal	California	Subject	Paragraph
IRC Sec. 6161	. . .	Extensions of Time for Payment	¶ 107
IRC Sec. 6201	Secs. 19054, 21024	Assessment Authority	¶ 208, ¶ 702
IRC Sec. 6211	Sec. 19043	"Deficiency" Defined	¶ 702, ¶ 703
IRC Sec. 6212	Secs. 19031-36, 19049, 19050	Notice of Deficiency	¶ 702
IRC Sec. 6213	Secs. 19041-48, 19051, 19332-34	Restrictions Applicable to Deficiencies	¶ 702-05
IRC Sec. 6225	Sec. 19063	SOL for Partnership Related Deficiencies	¶ 708
IRC Sec. 6233	. . .	Partnership Audits	. . .
IRC Sec. 6302	Sec. 19011	Electronic Funds Transfer	¶ 107
IRC Sec. 6311	Sec. 19222	Payment by Check or Money Order	¶ 107
IRC Sec. 6313	. . .	Fractional Dollar Calculations	¶ 107
IRC Sec. 6315	Sec. 19007	Payments of Estimated Taxes	¶ 107a
IRC Sec. 6321	Sec. 19221	Lien on Tax	¶ 609
IRC Sec. 6322	Sec. 19221	Period of Lien	. . .
IRC Sec. 6323	Secs. 19253, 21016	Priority of Lien	. . .
IRC Sec. 6325	Secs. 19206-09, 19226	Release of Lien	. . .
IRC Sec. 6331	Secs. 19231, 19236, 19262, 21019	Levy to Collect Tax	. . .
IRC Sec. 6343	Sec. 21016	Release of Levy	¶ 701a
IRC Sec. 6401	Secs. 19107, 19349, 19354	Excess of Tax Withheld	¶ 713
IRC Sec. 6402	Secs. 19301, 19323, 19362, 19363	Credits and Refunds	¶ 713, ¶ 714
IRC Sec. 6403	. . .	Overpayment of Installment	¶ 107
IRC Sec. 6404	Secs. 19104, 19109, 19116, 19431	Abatements	¶ 709
IRC Secs. 6501-04	Secs. 19057, 19058, 19065-67, 19087, 19371	Limitations on Assessment	¶ 610, ¶ 708
IRC Sec. 6511	Secs. 19306-14	Limitation on Refunds	¶ 715
IRC Sec. 6513	Sec. 19002	Time Return Filed and Tax Paid	¶ 105
IRC Sec. 6531	Sec. 19704	Statute of Limitations— Criminal Actions	. . .
IRC Sec. 6532	Secs. 19381-85, 19388-89	Suits for Refund	¶ 716, ¶ 722
IRC Sec. 6601	Secs. 19101-15	Interest on Tax Due	¶ 107, ¶ 709
IRC Sec. 6602	Sec. 19411	Interest on Erroneous Refund	¶ 722
IRC Sec. 6611	Secs. 19325, 19340-51	Interest on Overpayments	¶ 718
IRC Sec. 6621	Sec. 19521	Interest Rate	¶ 709
IRC Sec. 6622	Sec. 19521	Compounding of Interest	¶ 709
IRC Sec. 6631	Sec. 19117	Notice of Interest Charges	¶ 709
IRC Sec. 6651	Secs. 19131-32.5	Penalty—Failure to Make Return	¶ 710
IRC Sec. 6652	Sec. 19133.5	Penalty—Certain Information Returns	¶ 710
IRC Sec. 6653	. . .	Penalty—Failure to Pay Stamp Tax	¶ 710
IRC Sec. 6654	Secs. 19136-36.6	Underpayment of Estimated Tax	¶ 107a
IRC Sec. 6657	Secs. 19005, 19134	Bad Checks	¶ 710
IRC Sec. 6658	Sec. 19161	Timely Payment During Bankruptcy	¶ 710
IRC Secs. 6662-63	Sec. 19164	Penalty for Substantial Understatement	¶ 710

Federal	California	Subject	Paragraph
IRC Sec. 6672	Sec. 19708	Penalty—Failure to Collect and Pay Tax	¶ 710
IRC Sec. 6673	Sec. 19714	Penalty for Delay	¶ 710
IRC Sec. 6674	UI Code	Penalty—Fraudulent Statement	¶ 710
IRC Sec. 6682	Sec. 19176	Penalty—False Withholding Information	¶ 710
IRC Sec. 6690	. . .	Penalty—Fraudulent Statement to Pension Plan Participant	. . .
IRC Sec. 6693	Sec. 19184	Penalty—Failure to Properly Report IRA	¶ 710
IRC Sec. 6694	Sec. 19166	Understatement by Preparer	¶ 701, ¶ 710
IRC Secs. 6695-96	Secs. 19166-69, 19712	Penalties—Tax Preparers	¶ 701, ¶ 710
IRC Sec. 6698	Sec. 19172	Penalty—Partnership Returns	¶ 616
IRC Sec. 6700	Secs. 19174, 19177	Penalty for Promoting Abusive Tax Shelters	¶ 710
IRC Sec. 6701	Sec. 19178	Penalty for Aiding and Abetting Understatement	¶ 710
IRC Sec. 6702	Sec. 19179	Penalty for Frivolous Returns	¶ 710
IRC Sec. 6703	Sec. 19180	Rules for Penalties	¶ 710
IRC Sec. 6704	. . .	Penalty—Failure to Keep Records	. . .
IRC Sec. 6705	. . .	Penalty—Broker's Failure to Notify Payors	. . .
IRC Sec. 6706	Secs. 18649, 19181	OID Information	¶ 236, ¶ 710
IRC Sec. 6707	Sec. 19182	Penalty—Tax Shelters	¶ 710
IRC Sec. 6708	Sec. 19173	Tax Shelters	. . .
IRC Sec. 6714	Sec. 19182.5	Penalty; Failure to Disclose Quid Pro Quo Information	. . .
IRC Secs. 6721-24	Sec. 19183	Penalty—Failure to File Information Returns	¶ 710
IRC Sec. 6751	Sec. 19187	Procedures for Penalties	¶ 710
IRC Sec. 6851	Sec. 19081	Jeopardy Assessments	¶ 705
IRC Sec. 6861	Secs. 19086, 19092	Jeopardy Assessments	¶ 705
IRC Sec. 6863	Secs. 19083-85	Jeopardy Assessments—Stay of Collection	¶ 705
IRC Sec. 6867	Sec. 19093	Unexplained Cash	¶ 705
IRC Sec. 6871	Secs. 19088-90	Assessment in Receivership	¶ 706
IRC Sec. 6872	Sec. 19089	Suspension of Period of Assessment	¶ 706
IRC Sec. 6873	Sec. 19091	Unpaid Claims	¶ 706
IRC Sec. 6901	Secs. 19071-74	Liability of Transferees and Fiduciaries	¶ 610, ¶ 707
IRC Sec. 6903	Sec. 19512	Notice of Fiduciary Relationship	¶ 610, ¶ 707
IRC Sec. 6905	Sec. 19516	Discharge of Liability for Decedent's Taxes	¶ 610
IRC Sec. 7121	Sec. 19441	Closing Agreements	¶ 720
IRC Sec. 7122	Sec. 19702	Compromises	¶ 720
IRC Sec. 7201	Secs. 19701, 19708	Evasion of Tax	¶ 710
IRC Sec. 7202	Secs. 19708-09	Failure to Remit Withheld Tax	¶ 710
IRC Sec. 7203	Secs. 19701, 19706	Violation—Failure to File Return	¶ 710
IRC Sec. 7206	Secs. 19701, 19705	False Statements—Fraud	¶ 710
IRC Secs. 7213-16	Secs. 19542, 19542.3, 19552, 19713	Unauthorized Disclosure of Information	¶ 717
IRC Sec. 7403	Sec. 19371	Suit for Tax	. . .
IRC Sec. 7405	Sec. 19411	Recovery of Erroneous Refunds	¶ 722

Federal	California	Subject	Paragraph
IRC Sec. 7408	Sec. 19715	Injunctive Relief	¶ 710
IRC Sec. 7421	Sec. 19381	Suits to Restrain Collection Prohibited	¶ 716
IRC Sec. 7422	Secs. 19381-83, 19387-89	Actions for Refunds	¶ 716
IRC Sec. 7429	Sec. 19084	Jeopardy Assessment Review	¶ 705
IRC Sec. 7430	Secs. 19717, 21013	Recovery of Litigation Costs	¶ 701
IRC Sec. 7502	Sec. 21027	Mailing	¶ 105
IRC Sec. 7503	Gov. Code	Due Date—Holiday	¶ 105
IRC Sec. 7508	Secs. 17142.5, 18570, 18571	Extension—Members of Armed Forces	¶ 106
IRC Sec. 7508A	Sec. 18572	Extensions for Disaster Victims	¶ 105, ¶ 107
IRC Sec. 7512	Sec. 19009	Separate Accounting for Certain Collected Taxes, etc.	¶ 712a
IRC Sec. 7518	Sec. 17088.3	Capital Construction Funds for Vessels	¶ 233
IRC Sec. 7602	Sec. 19504.7	Notice of Contact of Third Parties	¶ 701
IRC Sec. 7612	Sec. 19504.5	Software Trade Secrets	¶ 717
IRC Sec. 7701	Various	Definitions	. . .
IRC Sec. 7702B	Sec. 17020.6	Qualified Long-term Care Insurance	¶ 219
IRC Sec. 7703	Sec. 17021.5	Marital Status	¶ 110
IRC Sec. 7704	Sec. 17008.5	Publicly Traded Partnerships	¶ 612
IRC Sec. 7811	Secs. 21001-26	Taxpayers' Bill of Rights	¶ 701, ¶ 701a, ¶ 701b

CALIFORNIA-FEDERAL CROSS-REFERENCE TABLE AND INDEX

Showing Sections of Federal Law (1986 Internal Revenue Code) Comparable to Sections of California Personal Income Tax Law (Revenue and Taxation Code)

California	Federal	Subject	Paragraph
Sec. 17002	IRC Sec. 7806	Definitions	. . .
Sec. 17003	IRC Sec. 7701(a)(11)	"Franchise Tax Board" defined	. . .
Sec. 17004	IRC Secs. 7701(a)(1), (14)	"Taxpayer" defined	. . .
Sec. 17005	. . .	"Individual" defined	. . .
Sec. 17006	IRC Sec. 7701(a)(6)	"Fiduciary" defined	. . .
Sec. 17007	IRC Sec. 7701(a)(1)	"Person" defined	. . .
Sec. 17008	IRC Sec. 7701(a)(2)	"Partnership" defined	¶ 612
Sec. 17008.5	IRC Sec. 7704	Publicly traded partnerships	¶ 612
Sec. 17009	IRC Sec. 7701(a)(3)	"Corporation" defined	¶ 605
Sec. 17010	IRC Sec. 7701(a)(23)	"Taxable year" defined	. . .
Sec. 17011	IRC Sec. 7701(a)(24)	"Fiscal year" defined	. . .
Sec. 17012	IRC Sec. 7701(a)(25)	"Paid or incurred" defined	. . .
Sec. 17014	. . .	"Resident" defined	¶ 103
Sec. 17015	. . .	"Nonresident" defined	¶ 103
Sec. 17016	. . .	Presumption of residence	¶ 103
Sec. 17017	IRC Sec. 7701(a)(9)	"United States" defined	. . .
Sec. 17018	IRC Sec. 7701(a)(10)	"State" defined	. . .
Sec. 17019	. . .	"Foreign country" defined	. . .
Sec. 17020	IRC Sec. 7701(a)(26)	"Trade or business" defined	. . .
Sec. 17020.1	IRC Sec. 7701(a)(42)	Substituted basis property	. . .
Sec. 17020.2	IRC Sec. 7701(a)(43)	Transferred basis property	. . .
Sec. 17020.3	IRC Sec. 7701(a)(44)	Exchanged basis property	. . .
Sec. 17020.4	IRC Sec. 7701(a)(45)	Nonrecognition transaction	. . .
Sec. 17020.5	IRC Sec. 7701(g)	Determination of gain or loss	. . .
Sec. 17020.6	IRC Sec. 7702-02B	"Life insurance contract" defined	. . .
Sec. 17020.7	IRC Sec. 7701(a)(46)	Collective bargaining agreement	. . .
Sec. 17020.8	IRC Sec. 7701(e)	Contracts for services	. . .
Sec. 17020.9	IRC Sec. 7701(a)(19)	Domestic building & loan association	. . .
Sec. 17020.11	IRC Sec. 7701(h)	Motor vehicle operating leases	. . .
Sec. 17020.12	IRC Sec. 7701(a)(20)	"Employee" defined	¶ 212
Sec. 17020.13	IRC Sec. 7701(k)	Treatment of amounts paid to charity	. . .
Sec. 17021	IRC Sec. 7701(a)(17)	"Husband" and "Wife" defined	. . .
Sec. 17021.5	IRC Sec. 7703	Marital status	¶ 110
Sec. 17022	IRC Sec. 7701(a)(15)	"Armed Forces" defined	. . .
Sec. 17023	IRC Sec. 7801	"Franchise Tax Board" defined	. . .
Sec. 17024	IRC Sec. 7701(a)(29)	"Personal Income Tax Law of 1954" defined	. . .
Sec. 17024.5	IRC Secs. 196, 541-47, 551-58, 679, 853, 911, 991-99, 1246, 1551-3322, 7806	Federal conformity program	Various
Sec. 17026	IRC Sec. 7851	Application of act	. . .
Sec. 17028	IRC Sec. 7807	Construction of code	. .

California	Federal	Subject	Paragraph
Sec. 17029	IRC Sec. 7807	Rights and liabilities under prior code	. . .
Sec. 17029.5	. . .	Basis adjustments and carryovers	. . .
Sec. 17030	IRC Sec. 7807	Reference to corresponding law	. . .
Sec. 17031	IRC Sec. 7807	Reference to prior period	. . .
Sec. 17033	IRC Sec. 7852	Severability of law	. . .
Sec. 17034	IRC Sec. 15	Effect of law changes	¶ 406
Sec. 17035	IRC Sec. 7701(a)(16)	"Withholding agent" defined	. . .
Sec. 17036	. . .	Service of notice	. . .
Sec. 17038	. . .	"Consumer price index" defined	. . .
Sec. 17039	IRC Sec. 26	"Net tax" defined	¶ 112a, ¶ 114, ¶ 121
Sec. 17041	IRC Sec. 1(g)	Rate of tax	¶ 113, ¶ 112, ¶ 309
Sec. 17041.5	. . .	Local income tax	¶ 101
Sec. 17042	IRC Secs. 2(b), (c)	"Head of household" defined	¶ 110
Sec. 17045	. . .	Joint return tax rate	¶ 104a
Sec. 17046	IRC Sec. 2(a)	"Surviving spouse" defined	¶ 104a
Sec. 17048	IRC Sec. 3	Tax table	¶ 112
Sec. 17052	. . .	California stock options	¶ 140
Sec. 17052.8	IRC Sec. 43	Enhanced oil recovery credit	¶ 142
Sec. 17052.10	. . .	Rice straw credit	¶ 144
Sec. 17052.12	IRC Sec. 41	Research & development credit	¶ 139
Sec. 17052.17	. . .	Child care facility credit	¶ 123
Sec. 17052.18	. . .	Credit for contributions to child care plan	¶ 123
Sec. 17052.25	IRC Sec. 23	Adoption costs credit	¶ 128
Sec. 17053.5	. . .	Renter's credit	¶ 122
Sec. 17053.6	. . .	Prison inmate labor credit	¶ 143
Sec. 17053.7	IRC Sec. 51	Jobs tax credit	¶ 143
Sec. 17053.12	. . .	Credit for transportation of donated agricultural products	¶ 130
Sec. 17053.14	. . .	Farmworker Housing Credit	¶ 126
Sec. 17053.33	. . .	Sales tax credit	¶ 133
Sec. 17053.34	. . .	Targeted tax area employers'credit	¶ 138
Sec. 17053.36	. . .	Credit for joint strike fighter employers	¶ 132
Sec. 17053.37	. . .	Credit for cost of joint strike fighter property	¶ 131
Sec. 17053.42	IRC Sec. 44	Disabled access credit	¶ 129
Sec. 17053.45	. . .	LAMBRA credit, sales tax equivalent	¶ 133
Sec. 17053.46	. . .	LAMBRA credit, employers	¶ 136
Sec. 17053.47	. . .	Manufacturing enhancement area employers' credit	¶ 138
Sec. 17053.49	. . .	Manufacturing and research property credit	¶ 140
Sec. 17053.57	IRC Sec. 38	Community development investment credit	¶ 145
Sec. 17053.66	. . .	Salmon and steelhead trout habitat credit	¶ 124
Sec. 17053.70	. . .	Enterprise zone sales taxcredit	¶ 133
Sec. 17053.74	IRC Sec. 1396	Enterprise zone employer'scredit	¶ 134
Sec. 17053.75	. . .	Enterprise zone employee's credit	¶ 135

California	Federal	Subject	Paragraph
Sec. 17054	IRC Sec. 151(c)	Credits for personal and dependent exemptions	¶ 109
Sec. 17054.1	IRC Sec. 151(d)	Credit reduction for high-income taxpayers	¶ 109
Sec. 17054.5	. . .	Joint custody head of household, dependent parent credits	¶ 109a
Sec. 17054.7	. . .	Senior head of household credit	¶ 125
Sec. 17055	. . .	Credits for nonresidents, part-year residents	¶ 114
Sec. 17056	IRC Sec. 152(a)	"Dependent" defined	¶ 109, ¶ 111
Sec. 17057.5	IRC Sec. 42	Low-income housing credit	¶ 127
Sec. 17058	IRC Sec. 42	Low-income housing credit	¶ 127
Sec. 17061	. . .	Credit for excess SDI contributions	¶ 120
Sec. 17062	IRC Secs. 55-59	Alternative minimum tax	¶ 112a
Sec. 17062.5	IRC Sec. 55(b)	Federal noncorporate AMT tax rate inapplicable	¶ 112a
Sec. 17063	IRC Sec. 53	Minimum tax credit	¶ 134
Sec. 17071	IRC Sec. 61	"Gross income" defined	¶ 201
Sec. 17072	IRC Sec. 62	"Adjusted gross income" defined	¶ 202, ¶ 317
Sec. 17073	IRC Sec. 63	"Taxable income" defined	¶ 108, ¶ 203
Sec. 17073.5	IRC Sec. 63	Standard deduction	¶ 203, ¶ 321
Sec. 17074	IRC Sec. 64	"Ordinary income" defined	. . .
Sec. 17075	IRC Sec. 65	"Ordinary loss" defined	. . .
Sec. 17076	IRC Sec. 67	2% floor on miscellaneous itemized deductions	¶ 303, ¶ 317, ¶ 604
Sec. 17077	IRC Sec. 68	6% limit on itemized deductions	¶ 303, ¶ 317
Sec. 17078	IRC Sec. 988	Foreign currency transactions	¶ 510a
Sec. 17081	IRC Secs. 71-90	Items in gross income	Various
Sec. 17081	IRC Sec. 72	Annuities, endowments, and life insurance proceeds	¶ 205
Sec. 17081	IRC Sec. 83	Property transfers in connection with services	¶ 207
Sec. 17083	IRC Sec. 85	Unemployment compensation	¶ 201
Sec. 17085	IRC Sec. 72	Lump-sum distributions	¶ 205, ¶ 206, ¶ 214
Sec. 17085.7	IRC Sec. 72	Levies on retirement plans and IRAs	¶ 206
Sec. 17086	IRC Sec. 1385	Patronage allocations	¶ 231
Sec. 17087	IRC Secs. 72(r), 86, 105(i)	Social security benefits, etc.	¶ 201
Sec. 17087.5	IRC Secs. 1361-79	S corporation shareholders	¶ 232
Sec. 17087.6	IRC Sec. 61	Limited liability companies	¶ 618
Sec. 17088	IRC Secs. 851-60L	RICs, REITs, REMICs, and FASITs	¶ 217, ¶ 225, ¶ 534, ¶ 607a, ¶ 607b, ¶ 611a
Sec. 17088.3	IRC Sec. 7518	Capital construction funds for vessels	¶ 233
Sec. 17090	IRC Sec. 61	Subsidized employee parking	¶ 240
Sec. 17091	IRC Sec. 865(b)	Sales of unprocessed timber	¶ 201
Sec. 17131	IRC Secs. 101-38	Exclusions—gross income	Various
Sec. 17132.6	IRC Sec. 101	Death benefits of public safety officer	¶ 213
Sec. 17133	IRC Sec. 61	Constitutional prohibition	¶ 201, ¶ 217, ¶ 314
Sec. 17133.5	IRC Sec. 61	Gain or loss from exempt bonds	¶ 201, ¶ 506a
Sec. 17134	IRC Sec. 108	Discharge of student loans	¶ 221

California	Federal	Subject	Paragraph
Sec. 17135	IRC Secs. 61, 132, 274	Automobile expenses of federal or state taxing authority agents	¶ 201
Sec. 17135.5	IRC Sec. 126	Cost-share payments received by forest landowners	¶ 201, ¶ 242
Sec. 17136	IRC Sec. 61	Forest Service payments	¶ 201
Sec. 17138	IRC Sec. 61	Water conservation rebates	¶ 243
Sec. 17140	IRC Sec. 529	Golden State Scholarshare Trust	¶ 249
Sec. 17140.3	IRC Sec. 529	Qualified state tuition program	¶ 249
Sec. 17140.5	IRC Sec. 61	Military compensation	¶ 224
Sec. 17141	. . .	Community Energy Authority	¶ 201
Sec. 17142	IRC Sec. 111	Credits, credit carryovers	¶ 223
Sec. 17142.5	IRC Secs. 112, 692, 7508	Military combat pay	¶ 106, ¶ 224
Sec. 17143	IRC Secs. 103, 141-50	Exempt interest	¶ 217
Sec. 17144	IRC Sec. 108	Exclusion for income from discharge of indebtedness	¶ 221
Sec. 17145	IRC Sec. 852	Exempt distributions from RICs¶ 217	
Sec. 17146	IRC Sec. 893	Employees of foreign countries	¶ 229
Sec. 17147.7	IRC Sec. 61	Crime hotline rewards	¶ 201, ¶ 245
Sec. 17149	IRC Secs. 61, 132	Subsidized commuter expense	¶ 240
Sec. 17151	IRC Sec. 127	Educational assistance	¶ 201, ¶ 241
Sec. 17152	IRC Sec. 121	One-time exclusion of sale	¶ 228
Sec. 17153.5	IRC Sec. 61	Recycling income	¶ 201
Sec. 17154	IRC Sec. 132	Taxable education or training benefits	. . .
Sec. 17155	U.S.-Federal Republic of Germany Income Tax Convention	Holocaust victim compensation	¶ 247
Sec. 17156.5	. . .	Japanese internment reparations	¶ 247
Sec. 17201	IRC Secs. 161-222, 261-280H	Allowance of deductions	Various
Sec. 17201	IRC Sec. 215	Alimony payments	¶ 313
Sec. 17201	IRC Sec. 280G	"Golden parachute" payments	¶ 322
Sec. 17201	IRC Sec. 179	Asset expense election	¶ 310a
Sec. 17202	IRC Sec. 162	Employee parking cash-out programs	¶ 329
Sec. 17203	IRC Secs. 162, 219, 404	"Compensation" or "earned income"	¶ 301, ¶ 318
Sec. 17204	IRC Sec. 221	Interest on student loans	¶ 305
Secs. 17207, 17207.4	IRC Sec. 165	Disaster losses	¶ 307, ¶ 407
Sec. 17215	IRC Sec. 220	Medical savings accounts	¶ 246, ¶ 315a
Sec. 17220	IRC Sec. 164	Deduction for taxes	¶ 306
Sec. 17222	IRC Sec. 275	Withheld taxes	¶ 306
Sec. 17224	IRC Sec. 163(e)	Income from OIDs	¶ 236, ¶ 305
Sec. 17230	IRC Sec. 163	Buy-down mortgage fees	¶ 305
Sec. 17235	IRC Sec. 163	Interest deduction—depressed areas	¶ 239
Sec. 17250	IRC Sec. 168, 169	ACRS depreciation	¶ 310, ¶ 310d
Sec. 17250.5	IRC Secs. 167(g), 168	Depreciation under income forecast method	¶ 310
Sec. 17251.5	IRC Sec. 170(e)	Contributions of qualified appreciated stock	¶ 312
Sec. 17255	IRC Sec. 179	Expense election dollar limitation	¶ 310a
Sec. 17256	IRC Sec. 179A	Clean fuel vehicles deduction	¶ 330
Sec. 17260(a)	IRC Sec. 193	Tertiary injectant expenses	¶ 311a

California	Federal	Subject	Paragraph
Sec. 17260(b)	IRC Sec. 263	Capital expenditures	¶ 201, ¶ 322
Sec. 17267.2	. . .	Election to expense enterprise zone property	¶ 310f
Sec. 17267.6	. . .	Election to expense targeted tax area property	¶ 310f
Sec. 17268	IRC Sec. 179	Accelerated write-off	¶ 310f
Sec. 17269	IRC Sec. 162	No deductions for expenditures at discriminatory clubs	¶ 301, ¶ 322
Sec. 17270(a)	IRC Sec. 162	Trade and business expenses	¶ 301, ¶ 322
Sec. 17270(b)	IRC Sec. 280C(c)	Targeted employment credit(s)	¶ 322
Sec. 17270(c)	IRC Sec. 280C(a)	Legislators' expenses	¶ 301
Sec. 17270.5	IRC Sec. 162	Lobbying and political expenditures	¶ 301, ¶ 322
Sec. 17271	IRC Sec. 274	80% limitation on meals and entertainment expenses	¶ 302
Sec. 17273	IRC Sec. 162(l)	Trade or business expense	¶ 301
Sec. 17273.1	IRC Sec. 162(*l*)	Self-employed health insurance	¶ 301
Sec. 17274	IRC Sec. 161	Expenses of substandard housing	¶ 322
Sec. 17275	IRC Sec. 161	Abandonment and recoupment fees	¶ 322
Sec. 17275.5	IRC Sec. 170(f)(8), (9)	Charitable contributions	¶ 312
Secs. 17276-76.6	IRC Sec. 172	Net operating loss	¶ 309
Sec. 17278	IRC Secs. 161, 1031	Interindemnity payments	¶ 301
Sec. 17278.5	IRC Sec. 194	Amortization of forestation expenditures	. . .
Sec. 17279	IRC Sec. 197	Amortization of goodwill	¶ 319b
Sec. 17279.4	IRC Sec. 198	Expensing of environmental remediation costs	¶ 310g
Sec. 17279.5	IRC Sec. 264	Interest expense deduction for company-owned life insurance	¶ 305
Sec. 17280	IRC Sec. 265	Expenses of tax-exempt income	¶ 305, ¶ 322
Secs. 17281-82	IRC Sec. 280E	Expenses of illegal activities	¶ 322
Sec. 17286	IRC Sec. 162	Illegal payments to foreign officials, etc.	¶ 322
Sec. 17287	IRC Sec. 269A	Personal service corporation formed to avoid/evade income tax	. . .
Secs. 17299.8-99.9	IRC Sec. 161	Deductions disallowed	¶ 322, ¶ 710
Secs. 17301-02	IRC Secs. 63, 215	Deductions of nonresidents	¶ 323
Sec. 17303	IRC Sec. 61	Income of part-year residents	¶ 230
Sec. 17310	IRC Sec. 172	Loss carryover-part-year residents	¶ 323
Sec. 17321	IRC Secs. 301-85	Corporate distributions, etc.	Various
Sec. 17322	IRC Sec. 302	Limitation periods	¶ 225
Sec. 17501	IRC Secs. 401-24	Deferred compensation	Various
Sec. 17502	IRC Sec. 421	California qualified stock options	¶ 207
Sec. 17504	IRC Sec. 402(a)	Lump-sum distributions	¶ 206, ¶ 318, ¶ 606
		Beneficiaries of exempt trusts	¶ 206, ¶ 318, ¶ 606
Sec. 17506	IRC Sec. 403(a)	Employee annuities	¶ 206, ¶ 318
Sec. 17507	IRC Sec. 408	Individual retirement accounts	¶ 318
Sec. 17507.6	IRC Secs. 219, 408A	Roth IRAs	. . .
Sec. 17508	IRC Sec. 408(o)	Nondeductible contributions to IRAs	¶ 318
Sec. 17509	IRC Sec. 413	Liability for funding tax	¶ 318
Sec. 17510	IRC Sec. 7701(j)	Federal thrift savings funds	¶ 606

California	Federal	Subject	Paragraph
Sec. 17551	IRC Secs. 280H, 441-83	Accounting periods and methods	Various
Sec. 17552	IRC Sec. 443	Short-period returns	¶ 403
Sec. 17553	IRC Sec. 454	Obligations issued at discount	¶ 408
Sec. 17554	IRC Sec. 441	Change of residence	¶ 405
Sec. 17555	IRC Sec. 61	Allocation of income—spouses	¶ 412
Sec. 17556	IRC Sec. 442	Change accounting period— estates	¶ 402
Sec. 17560	IRC Secs. 453, 453A	Allocable installment indebtedness	¶ 411
Sec. 17561	IRC Sec. 469	Passive activity losses and credits	¶ 326
Sec. 17564	IRC Sec. 460	Long-term contracts	¶ 407
Sec. 17565	IRC Sec. 441	Taxable year	¶ 401
Sec. 17570	IRC Sec. 475	Mark-to-market accounting	¶ 400, ¶ 409
Sec. 17631	IRC Sec. 501(a)	Exemption for employee trusts	¶ 606
Sec. 17632	IRC Sec. 501(b)	Exempt organizations— unrelated income	¶ 606
Sec. 17635	IRC Sec. 503(a)	Prohibited transactions	¶ 606
Sec. 17636	IRC Sec. 503(a)	Application to Sec. 17501	¶ 606
Sec. 17637	IRC Sec. 503(b)	"Prohibited transactions" defined	¶ 606
Sec. 17638	IRC Sec. 503(c)	Claim for exemption	¶ 606
Sec. 17639	IRC Sec. 503(e)	Security for loan	¶ 606
Sec. 17640	IRC Sec. 503(f)	Trust loan to employer	¶ 606
Sec. 17651	IRC Secs. 511, 512	Unrelated business income	¶ 606
Sec. 17671	IRC Sec. 584	Common trust funds	¶ 611
Sec. 17677	IRC Secs. 584, 6032	Return for common trust	¶ 611
Sec. 17681	IRC Secs. 611-38	Taxation of natural resources	¶ 311, ¶ 311a, ¶ 520
		Basis for cost depletion	¶ 537
Sec. 17731	IRC Secs. 641-92	Taxation of estates and trusts	Various
Sec. 17731.5	IRC Sec. 641	Determining rates and special credits	. . .
Sec. 17732	IRC Sec. 642	No deduction personal exemptions	. . .
Sec. 17733	IRC Sec. 642	Exemption credits	¶ 109
Sec. 17734	IRC Sec. 641	Nonresident beneficiaries	¶ 604a
Sec. 17735	IRC Sec. 661	Distributions to nonresidents	¶ 604
Sec. 17736	IRC Sec. 642	Modification I.R.C. Sec. 642	¶ 604
Sec. 17737	IRC Sec. 682	Alimony trusts	¶ 608
Secs. 17742-45.1	IRC Sec. 641	Effect of residence upon taxability	¶ 103, ¶ 602, ¶ 603
Sec. 17750	IRC Sec. 643	Estates and trusts—election	¶ 604
Sec. 17751	IRC Sec. 646	Certain revocable trusts treated as part of estate	¶ 604
Sec. 17752	IRC Sec. 663	Special rules applicable to IRC Secs. 661 and 662	¶ 604a
Sec. 17760.5	IRC Sec. 685	Funeral trusts	¶ 607
Sec. 17779	IRC Secs. 665-68	Accumulation distributions	¶ 604a
Sec. 17851	IRC Secs. 701-61	Partners and partnerships	Various
Sec. 17851.5	. . .	Taxation of partnerships	. . .
Sec. 17853	IRC Sec. 703	Deductions not allowed	¶ 614
Sec. 17854	IRC Sec. 707	Guaranteed payments	¶ 614
Secs. 17855-57	IRC Sec. 751	Transfer of partnership interest	¶ 612b
Sec. 17858	IRC Sec. 704	Depreciation election by partnership	¶ 614
Sec. 17865	IRC Secs. 771—777	Electing large partnerships	¶ 617a
Secs. 17948-48.2	. . .	LLP minimum tax	¶ 617
Sec. 17951	. . .	Income of nonresidents	¶ 230, ¶ 613

California	Federal	Subject	Paragraph
Sec. 17952	. . .	Income of nonresidents from intangibles	¶ 230
Sec. 17952.5	. . .	California source retirement income	. . .
Sec. 17953	. . .	Income to nonresident beneficiaries	¶ 230
Sec. 17954	. . .	Allocation of income of nonresidents	¶ 230
Sec. 17955	. . .	Nonresident income from qualifying investment securities	¶ 230
Sec. 18001	. . .	Taxes paid by resident to other state—credit	¶ 115, ¶ 116
Sec. 18002	. . .	Taxes paid by nonresident to other state—credit	¶ 115, ¶ 117
Sec. 18003	. . .	Residence of estate or trust	¶ 115, ¶ 118
Sec. 18004	. . .	Estate or trust—credit for taxes paid another state	¶ 115, ¶ 118
Sec. 18005	. . .	Resident beneficiary credit	¶ 115, ¶ 118
Sec. 18006	. . .	Resident and nonresident S corporation shareholders and partners—credit for taxes paid another state by entity	¶ 115, ¶ 116, ¶ 117, ¶ 119, ¶ 232
Sec. 18007	. . .	Report of other state tax credit	¶ 115
Sec. 18008	. . .	Tax due on other state credit	¶ 115
Sec. 18009	. . .	Interest on credit	¶ 115
Sec. 18011	. . .	Discrimination resulting from taxes paid to other state	¶ 115
Sec. 18031	IRC Sec. 1041	Inter-spousal transfers	¶ 501a
Sec. 18031	IRC Sec. 1001-92	Determination of gain or loss	¶ 501
Sec. 18031	IRC Sec. 1014	Basis of property acquired from decedent	Various
Sec. 18031	IRC Sec. 1015	Basis of property acquired by transfer in trust	¶ 525
Sec. 18031	IRC Sec. 1060	Allocation of transferred business assets	¶ 539
Sec. 18036	IRC Sec. 1016	Adjustments to basis	¶ 310f, ¶ 534
Sec. 18036.5	IRC Sec. 1016	Basis adjustment for sale of small business stock	¶ 534
Sec. 18037	IRC Sec. 1033	Certain involuntary conversions	¶ 502, ¶ 527
Secs. 18037.5	Various	Sales and exchanges under prior law	¶ 502a
Sec. 18038	IRC Sec. 1040	Transfer of certain real property	¶ 604
Sec. 18038.4	IRC Sec. 1045	Rollover of gain from small business stock	¶ 513
Sec. 18038.5	IRC Sec. 1045	Rollover of gain from small business stock	¶ 513
Sec. 18039	IRC Sec. 1052	Basis established by prior law	¶ 529
Sec. 18041.5	IRC Sec. 1001	Gain from sale of assisted housing	¶ 502b
Sec. 18042	IRC Sec. 1042	Sales to ESOP's	¶ 501, ¶ 506b
Sec. 18043	IRC Sec. 1031	Like-kind exchanges	¶ 504
Sec. 18044	IRC Sec. 1017	Rollover of gain	¶ 221
Sec. 18044	IRC Sec. 1044	Rollover of publicly traded securities gain	¶ 501
Sec. 18151	IRC Secs. 1201-98	Capital gains and losses	Various
Sec. 18152	IRC Sec. 1202	Small business stock	¶ 513
Sec. 18152.5	IRC Sec. 1202	Small business stock	¶ 512, ¶ 513
Sec. 18155	IRC Sec. 1212	Carryovers and carrybacks	¶ 512, ¶ 514

California	Federal	Subject	Paragraph
Sec. 18155.5	IRC Sec. 1223	Holding period for small business stock	¶ 515
Sec. 18165	IRC Sec. 1245	Recapture of depreciation on personal property	¶ 519b
Sec. 18171	IRC Sec. 1250	Depreciation adjustments	¶ 512, ¶ 519b
Sec. 18171.5	IRC Sec. 1250	IRC Sec. 1250(a) modified	. . .
Sec. 18177	IRC Sec. 1275	Tax-exempt obligations	. . .
Sec. 18178	IRC Sec. 1272	Original issue discount	¶ 236, ¶ 237, ¶ 512
Sec. 18180	IRC Sec. 7872	Loans with below-market interest rates	¶ 414
Secs. 18401-03	. . .	General application of administrative provisions	. . .
Sec. 18405	. . .	Relief upon noncompliance with new provisions	. . .
Secs. 18412-17	IRC Sec. 7807	Continuity of provisions with prior law	. . .
Sec. 18501	IRC Sec. 6012(a)	Returns required	¶ 104
Sec. 18503	IRC Sec. 6012(b)	Agent for making return	¶ 104
Sec. 18504	IRC Sec. 6012	Income from estate or trust	¶ 104
Sec. 18505	IRC Sec. 6012(b)	Returns filed by fiduciary	¶ 104
Sec. 18506	IRC Sec. 6012(b)	Exempt trust—unrelated business income	¶ 104, ¶ 606
Sec. 18507	IRC Sec. 6012	Nonresident—filing return	¶ 104
Sec. 18508	IRC Sec. 6012	Returns filed by joint fiduciaries	¶ 104
Sec. 18509	IRC Sec. 6012	Fiduciary as individual	¶ 104
Sec. 18510	IRC Sec. 6012(c)	Sale of residence by individual over 65	¶ 104
Sec. 18521	IRC Sec. 6013	Filing of returns	¶ 104, ¶ 104a, ¶ 110
Sec. 18522	IRC Sec. 6013(b)	Joint return after filing separate return	¶ 104a
Sec. 18523	IRC Sec. 6013(b)(1)	Elections made in separate returns	¶ 104, ¶ 104a
Sec. 18524	IRC Sec. 6013(b)(1)	Death of spouse	¶ 104, ¶ 104a
Sec. 18526	IRC Sec. 6013(b)(2)	Time limitation	¶ 104, ¶ 104a
Sec. 18527	IRC Sec. 6013(b)(3)	Credit or refund periods	¶ 104, ¶ 104a
Sec. 18528	IRC Sec. 6013(b)(3)	When return deemed filed	¶ 104, ¶ 104a
Sec. 18529	IRC Sec. 6013(b)(4)	Assessment period extended	¶ 104, ¶ 104a
Sec. 18530	IRC Sec. 6013(b)(5)	Additions to tax, penalties	¶ 104, ¶ 104a, ¶ 710
Sec. 18531	IRC Sec. 6013(b)(5)	Returns, criminal penalty	¶ 104
Sec. 18532	IRC Sec. 6013(d)	Marital status determined	¶ 104, ¶ 110
Sec. 18533	IRC Sec. 6013(e)	Liability of spouse	¶ 104, ¶ 104a
Sec. 18534	IRC Sec. 66	Liability for community income	¶ 104, ¶ 104a
Sec. 18535	IRC Sec. 6031	Returns by partnerships and LLCs	¶ 613, ¶ 616, ¶ 618
Sec. 18542	. . .	Reporting of charitable contributions	. . .
Sec. 18547	IRC Sec. 6111	Tax-shelter reporting	¶ 711
Sec. 18551	IRC Sec. 3402(a)	Filing withholding return	¶ 712a
Sec. 18552	IRC Sec. 6011(b)	Information re taxpayer	¶ 712a
Sec. 18566	IRC Sec. 6072	Time for filing returns	¶ 105
Sec. 18567	IRC Sec. 6081(a)	Extension of time	¶ 105, ¶ 106, ¶ 107
Sec. 18570	IRC Sec. 7508	Members of armed forces	¶ 106

California	Federal	Subject	Paragraph
Sec. 18571	IRC Sec. 7508	Extension—service in combat zone	¶ 106
Sec. 18572	IRC Sec. 7508A	Extensions for disaster victims	¶ 105, ¶ 108
Sec. 18601	IRC Secs. 6012(a), 6037, 6072	Filing of returns; due dates	. . .
Sec. 18604	IRC Sec. 6081	Extension of time for filing returns	. . .
Sec. 18606	IRC Secs. 6012(a), 6065	Filing of returns by receiver, trustee, or assignee of bankrupt taxpayer	. . .
Sec. 18621	IRC Secs. 6065, 6091	Form of return	¶ 105
Sec. 18621.5	. . .	Electronic filing	¶ 105
Sec. 18622	. . .	Amendment of return after federal changes	¶ 104
Sec. 18623	IRC Sec. 6102(a)	Fractional dollar calculations	¶ 104
Sec. 18624	IRC Sec. 6109	Identifying numbers	¶ 701
Sec. 18625	IRC Sec. 6107	Copy to taxpayer	¶ 701
Sec. 18626	. . .	Return defined	. . .
Sec. 18631	. . .	Nontaxable interest obligations	¶ 711
Sec. 18632	. . .	Administration of withholding	¶ 711
Sec. 18633	IRC Sec. 6031	Returns by partnerships	¶ 616
Sec. 18633.5	IRC Sec. 6031	Returns by LLCs	¶ 618
Sec. 18635	IRC Secs. 6013(a), 6034	Information from charitable trust	¶ 605
Sec. 18636	IRC Sec. 6039	Returns for stock transfers	¶ 711
Sec. 18637	IRC Sec. 6041(a)	Return required	¶ 711
Sec. 18638	IRC Sec. 6041A	Reporting payments for services	¶ 711
Sec. 18639	IRC Secs. 6041-43, 6049	Returns for interest, dividends, collections	¶ 711
Sec. 18640	IRC Sec. 6044	Returns by cooperatives	¶ 711
Sec. 18641	IRC Sec. 6045	Reporting by brokers	¶ 711
Sec. 18642	IRC Sec. 6045	Reporting—property owners	¶ 711
Sec. 18643	IRC Sec. 6045	IRS reporting form for brokers	¶ 711
Sec. 18644	IRC Sec. 6050A	Fishing boat operators— reporting requirements	¶ 711
Sec. 18645	IRC Secs. 6039A, 6050H-50S	Filing copies of federal reports	¶ 711
Sec. 18646	IRC Sec. 6050M	State agency head—reporting requirements	¶ 711
Sec. 18647	IRC Sec. 6052	Returns for group-term life insurance	¶ 711
Sec. 18648	IRC Sec. 6112	Tax-shelter reporting	¶ 711
Sec. 18648.5	IRC Sec. 6115	Disclosure related to quid pro quo contributions	. . .
Sec. 18649	IRC Sec. 1275	Original issue discount reporting	¶ 711
Sec. 18661	IRC Secs. 3402, 6041(c)	Recipient of income	¶ 711
Sec. 18662	IRC Secs. 1445, 3402	Withholding of tax— nonresidents	¶ 712, ¶ 712a
Sec. 18663	IRC Sec. 3402(a)	Withholding	¶ 712a
Sec. 18665	. . .	Change in withholding due to legislative enactments	¶ 712a
Sec. 18666	IRC Sec. 1446	Withholding exemption certificates	¶ 712
Sec. 18667	IRC Sec. 3402	Withholding—foreign partners	¶ 712, ¶ 712a

California	Federal	Subject	Paragraph
Sec. 18668	IRC Sec. 3403	Employer's liability for tax	¶ 712
Sec. 18669	. . .	Sale, transfer, or disposition of business	¶ 712
Sec. 18670	. . .	Withholding notice— delinquency	¶ 712
Sec. 18671	. . .	Withholding—state agencies	¶ 712
Sec. 18672	. . .	Liability for failure to withhold	¶ 712
Sec. 18673	. . .	Employee relief from liability	¶ 712a
Sec. 18674	. . .	Person required to withhold— compliance	¶ 712
Sec. 18675	IRC Sec. 6414	Remedies on taxes withheld	¶ 712
Sec. 18676	. . .	Withholding notice to state agencies	¶ 712
Sec. 18677	IRC Sec. 3505	Lender, surety or other person liable	¶ 712
Secs. 18781-18865	. . .	Designated contributions	¶ 312a
Sec. 19001	IRC Sec. 6151	Date tax due	¶ 107
Sec. 19002	IRC Secs. 31(a), 6513	Credit for tax withheld	¶ 712, ¶ 712a
Sec. 19004	IRC Secs. 6151, 6655	Payment prior to due date	¶ 107
Sec. 19005	IRC Sec. 6151	Remittance to FTB	¶ 107, ¶ 710
Sec. 19006	IRC Sec. 6151	Joint return liability	¶ 104a, ¶ 707
Sec. 19007	IRC Sec. 6315	Payments of estimated taxes	¶ 107a
Sec. 19008	IRC Sec. 6159	Installment payment of tax	¶ 107
Sec. 19009	IRC Sec. 7512	Failure to pay collected taxes	¶ 712a
Sec. 19010	IRC Sec. 6655	Assessing delinquent estimated taxes	¶ 107a
Sec. 19011	IRC Sec. 6302	Electronic funds transfer	¶ 107
Sec. 19023	IRC Sec. 6655(g)	Determining estimated tax for nonfinancial corporations	. . .
Sec. 19024	IRC Sec. 6655(g)	Determining estimated tax forfinancial corporations	. . .
Sec. 19025	IRC Sec. 6655(c), (d)	Determining of when estimated tax due	. . .
Sec. 19026	IRC Sec. 6655	Calculation of remaining payments after estimated tax revised	. . .
Sec. 19027	IRC Sec. 6655	Application to income years less than 12 months	. . .
Sec. 19031	IRC Sec. 6212	Deficiency assessments—FTB authority	¶ 702
Sec. 19032	IRC Sec. 6212	Examination of return	¶ 702
Sec. 19033	IRC Sec. 6212(a)	Notice of deficiency	¶ 702
Sec. 19034	. . .	Details of notice	¶ 702
Sec. 19035	IRC Sec. 6212	Joint return notice	¶ 702
Sec. 19036	IRC Sec. 6212	Addition to tax as deficiency	¶ 702
Sec. 19041	IRC Sec. 6213	Protest to assessment	¶ 702
Sec. 19041.5	. . .	Treatment of deposits	¶ 715, ¶ 716
Sec. 19042	IRC Sec. 6213	If no protest	¶ 702, ¶ 704
Sec. 19043	IRC Sec. 6211	"Deficiency and rebate" defined	¶ 702
Sec. 19044	IRC Sec. 6213	Reconsideration of assessment	¶ 702
Sec. 19045	. . .	Appeal from FTB's action	¶ 703
Sec. 19046	IRC Sec. 6213	Mailing of appeal	¶ 703
Sec. 19047	IRC Sec. 6213	Notice of SBE's determination	¶ 703
Sec. 19048	IRC Sec. 6213	Petition for rehearing	¶ 703
Sec. 19049	IRC Sec. 6212	Notice and demand for payment	¶ 704
Sec. 19050	IRC Sec. 6212	Evidence of assessment	¶ 702

California	Federal	Subject	Paragraph
Sec. 19051	IRC Sec. 6213	Mathematical error in return	¶ 702
Sec. 19054	IRC Sec. 6201	Overstatement of credit	¶ 722
Sec. 19057	IRC Sec. 6501	Limitation period on assessment	¶ 708
Sec. 19058	IRC Sec. 6501(e)	Limitation period extended	¶ 708
Sec. 19059	. . .	Limitation period after amended return	¶ 708
Sec. 19060	. . .	Limitation period following federal adjustment	¶ 708
Sec. 19061	IRC Secs. 1032, 1033(a)(2)(A)-(D)	Limitation period— involuntary conversion	¶ 708
Sec. 19062	IRC Sec. 1034	Limitation period—sale of residence	¶ 708
Sec. 19063	IRC Secs. 6225, 6501(a)	Items of federally registered partnership	¶ 708
Sec. 19064	IRC Sec. 7609	Motion to quash subpoena	¶ 708
Sec. 19065	IRC Sec. 6501(c)	Agreement to extend period	¶ 708
Sec. 19066	IRC Sec. 6501(b)	Time return deemed filed	¶ 708, ¶ 715
Sec. 19066.5	IRC Sec. 6501	SOL for foreign corporation deficiencies	¶ 1408
Sec. 19067	IRC Sec. 6501(c)	Extension by agreement	¶ 708
Sec. 19071	IRC Sec. 6901	Assessments against persons secondarily liable	¶ 610, ¶ 707
Sec. 19072	IRC Sec. 6901	Collection from person secondarily liable	¶ 610, ¶ 707
Sec. 19073	IRC Sec. 6901	Assessment and collection from transferees and fiduciaries	¶ 610, ¶ 707
Sec. 19074	IRC Sec. 6901	Limitations period for assessment of transferee or fiduciary	¶ 610, ¶ 707
Sec. 19081	IRC Sec. 6861	Jeopardy assessment	¶ 705
Sec. 19082	IRC Sec. 6862	Taxable period terminated	¶ 705
Sec. 19083	IRC Secs. 6861, 6863	Collection of jeopardy assessment; bond	¶ 705
Sec. 19084	IRC Secs. 6213, 6863	Hearing	¶ 705
Sec. 19085	IRC Sec. 6863	Appeal	¶ 705
Sec. 19086	IRC Sec. 6861	Evidence of jeopardy	¶ 705
Sec. 19087	IRC Sec. 6501(c)	Fraudulent or no return	¶ 708
Sec. 19088	IRC Sec. 6871	Assessments in bankruptcy or receivership	¶ 706
Sec. 19089	IRC Secs. 6036, 6872	Notice; suspension of period	¶ 706
Sec. 19090	IRC Sec. 6871	Deficiency claims	¶ 706
Sec. 19091	IRC Sec. 6873	Unpaid claim	¶ 706
Sec. 19092	IRC Sec. 6861	Regulations	. . .
Sec. 19093	IRC Sec. 6867	Unexplained cash	¶ 705
Sec. 19101	IRC Sec. 6601(a)	Interest on tax due	¶ 709
Sec. 19102	IRC Sec. 6601(b)	Interest on extensions	¶ 107
Sec. 19103	IRC Sec. 6601(b)	Last date for payment	¶ 709
Sec. 19104	IRC Sec. 6404	Interest on deficiency	¶ 709
Sec. 19105	IRC Sec. 6601	No interest period	¶ 709
Sec. 19106	IRC Sec. 6601(e)	Interest on penalty	¶ 709
Sec. 19107	. . .	Overpayment applied to spouse's deficiency	¶ 709
Sec. 19108	. . .	Overpayment applied to another year's deficiency	¶ 709
Sec. 19109	IRC Sec. 6404(h)	Abatement of interest	¶ 709

California	Federal	Subject	Paragraph
Sec. 19110	. . .	Overpayment—estate or trust	¶ 709
Sec. 19111	IRC Sec. 6601(e)	Notice and demand—10 day waiver	¶ 709
Sec. 19112	. . .	Interest waived	¶ 709
Sec. 19113	IRC Sec. 6601(f)	Satisfaction by credit	¶ 709
Sec. 19114	IRC Sec. 6601(g)	When interest may be collected	¶ 709
Sec. 19115	IRC Sec. 6601(h)	Inapplicability to estimated tax	¶ 709
Sec. 19116	IRC Sec. 6404(g)	Suspension of interest and penalties	¶ 709, ¶ 710
Sec. 19117	IRC Sec. 6631	Notice of interest charges	¶ 709
Sec. 19131	IRC Sec. 6651	Penalty—failure to make return	¶ 710
Sec. 19132	IRC Sec. 6651	Penalty for tax not paid	¶ 710
Sec. 19132.5	IRC Sec. 6651	Waiver of penalties for victims of Northridge earthquake	. . .
Sec. 19133		Penalty—failure to furnish information	¶ 702, ¶ 710
Sec. 19133.5	IRC Sec. 6652	Penalty—failure to report small business stock gain	¶ 710
Sec. 19134	IRC Sec. 6657	Bad check penalty	¶ 710
Sec. 19136	IRC Sec. 6654	Penalty—payments estimated tax	¶ 107a
Sec. 19136.2	IRC Sec. 6654	Application of federal safe-harbor provision	¶ 107a
Sec. 19136.3	IRC Sec. 6654	Waiver of estimated tax underpayment penalty	¶ 107a, ¶ 710
Sec. 19136.4	IRC Sec. 6654	No additions to tax for underpayments	¶ 107a
Sec. 19136.5	IRC Sec. 6654	Penalty waiver	¶ 107a
Sec. 19136.6	IRC Sec. 6654	Penalty waiver	¶ 107a
Sec. 19161	IRC Sec. 6658	Timely payment during bankruptcy	¶ 710a
Sec. 19164	IRC Secs. 6662-65	Accuracy-related penalty	¶ 710
Sec. 19166	IRC Sec. 6694	Penalty—preparer understatement	¶ 710
Sec. 19167	IRC Sec. 6695	Penalties—tax preparers	¶ 710
Sec. 19168	IRC Sec. 6696	Penalties—tax preparers	¶ 710
Sec. 19169	IRC Sec. 6695(f)	Penalty—negotiating client's refund check	¶ 710
Sec. 19172	IRC Sec. 6698	Penalty—partnership returns	¶ 616, ¶ 618
Sec. 19173	IRC Sec. 6708	Penalty—tax shelters	¶ 710
Sec. 19174	IRC Sec. 6700	Penalty—tax shelters	¶ 710
Sec. 19175	. . .	Penalty—information returns	¶ 710, ¶ 711
Sec. 19176	IRC Sec. 6682	Penalty—false withholding information	¶ 710
Sec. 19177	IRC Sec. 6700	Penalty—abusive tax shelters	¶ 710
Sec. 19178	IRC Sec. 6701	Penalty—aiding and abetting tax understatement	¶ 710
Sec. 19179	IRC Sec. 6702	Penalty—frivolous return	¶ 710
Sec. 19180	IRC Sec. 6703	Penalty—burden of proof	. . .
Sec. 19181	IRC Sec. 6706	Penalty—original issue discount reporting	¶ 710
Sec. 19182	IRC Secs. 6111, 6707	Penalty—tax shelters	¶ 710
Sec. 19182.5	IRC Sec. 6174	Penalty—failure to disclose quid pro quo information	. . .
Sec. 19183	IRC Secs. 6652, 6721-24	Penalty—certain information returns	¶ 710
Sec. 19184	IRC Sec. 6693	Penalty—failure to properly report IRA	¶ 710

California	Federal	Subject	Paragraph
Sec. 19187	IRC Sec. 6751	Procedures for penalties	¶ 710
Secs. 19191-94	. . .	Voluntary disclosure agreements	¶ 721
Sec. 19201	. . .	Judgment for tax	. . .
Sec. 19202	. . .	Entry of judgment	. . .
Sec. 19203	. . .	Abstract as lien	. . .
Sec. 19204	. . .	Extension of lien	. . .
Sec. 19205	. . .	Execution of judgment	. . .
Sec. 19206	IRC Sec. 6325	Release of lien	. . .
Sec. 19207	IRC Sec. 6325	Release of unenforceable lien	. . .
Sec. 19208	IRC Sec. 6325	Certificate of release	. . .
Sec. 19209	IRC Sec. 6325	Cost for certificate	. . .
Sec. 19221	IRC Sec. 6321	Lien on tax	¶ 609
Sec. 19222	IRC Sec. 6311	Lien for dishonored checks	. . .
Sec. 19223	. . .	Lien against trust	¶ 609
Sec. 19224	. . .	Service of notice of fiduciary	¶ 609
Sec. 19225	. . .	Administrative review	¶ 701a
Sec. 19226	IRC Sec. 6325	Release of third-party liens	. . .
Sec. 19231	IRC Sec. 6331	Warrant to collect tax	. . .
Sec. 19232	. . .	Warrant as writ of execution	. . .
Sec. 19233	. . .	Fees for warrant	. . .
Secs. 19234-35	. . .	Fees as obligation of taxpayer	. . .
Sec. 19236	IRC Sec. 6331	Seizure of property	. . .
Sec. 19251	. . .	Remedies are cumulative	. . .
Sec. 19252	. . .	FTB as representative	. . .
Sec. 19253	IRC Sec. 6323	Priority of lien	. . .
Sec. 19254	. . .	Collection and filing enforcement fees	¶ 710
Sec. 19256	IRC Sec. 7504	Fractional dollar amount	. . .
Sec. 19262	IRC Secs. 6331, 6335	Seizure and sale of personal property	. . .
Sec. 19263	IRC Secs. 6338, 6342	Bill of sale; disposition of excess	. . .
Sec. 19264	. . .	Earnings withholding tax order	. . .
Sec. 19301	IRC Sec. 6402	Credit for overpayment	¶ 713
Sec. 19302	. . .	Credit and refund approval	¶ 713
Sec. 19306	IRC Sec. 6511(a)	Time limit for refund	¶ 715
Sec. 19307	. . .	Return as claim for refund	¶ 713, ¶ 715
Sec. 19308	IRC Sec. 6511(c)	Effect of assessment extension	¶ 715
Sec. 19309	IRC Sec. 6511(c)	Claims filed before assessment extension	¶ 715
Sec. 19311	IRC Sec. 6511	Time limit following federal adjusted return	¶ 715
Sec. 19312	IRC Sec. 6511(d)	Time limit where bad debts or worthless securities	¶ 715
Sec. 19313	IRC Sec. 6511(g)	Federally registered partnerships	¶ 715
Sec. 19314	. . .	Overpayment used as offset	¶ 715
Sec. 19321	. . .	Final action	¶ 713
Sec. 19322	. . .	Claim for refund	¶ 713
Sec. 19323	IRC Sec. 6402	Disallowance of claim	¶ 713
Sec. 19324	. . .	Appeal from FTB's action	¶ 714
Sec. 19325	. . .	Refunds resulting from federal law	¶ 714, ¶ 718
Sec. 19331	. . .	Failure to mail notice	¶ 714
Sec. 19332	IRC Sec. 6213	Mailing of appeals	¶ 714
Sec. 19333	IRC Sec. 6213	SBE determination	¶ 714
Sec. 19334	IRC Sec. 6213	Petition for rehearing	¶ 714

California	Federal	Subject	Paragraph
Sec. 19335	. . .	Payment of tax protested	¶ 714
Sec. 19340	IRC Sec. 6611(b)	Interest on overpayments	¶ 718
Sec. 19341	IRC Sec. 6611(e)	Refunds made within certain time	¶ 718
Sec. 19342	. . .	Notice of disallowance	¶ 718
Sec. 19343	. . .	Finality of notice	¶ 718
Sec. 19344	. . .	Appeal to SBE	¶ 718
Sec. 19345	. . .	Hearing	¶ 718
Sec. 19346	. . .	Finality of determination	¶ 718
Sec. 19347	. . .	Suit to recover interest	¶ 718
Sec. 19348	. . .	Failure of FTB to give notice	¶ 718
Sec. 19349	IRC Sec. 6401	Payments not entitled to interest	¶ 718
Sec. 19350	. . .	No interest on barred claim	¶ 718
Sec. 19351	IRC Sec. 6611(b)	Payment deemed made on due date	¶ 718
Sec. 19354	IRC Sec. 6401(b)	Excess of tax withheld	. . .
Sec. 19355	. . .	Refunding excess	. . .
Sec. 19361	IRC Sec. 6414	Employer's overpayment	. . .
Sec. 19362	IRC Sec. 6402	Credits against estimated tax	. . .
Sec. 19363	IRC Sec. 6402	Interest on overpayments of estimated tax	¶ 718
Sec. 19371	IRC Secs. 6502, 7403	Suit for tax	¶ 708
Sec. 19372	. . .	Prosecution of suit	. . .
Sec. 19373	. . .	Writ of attachment	. . .
Sec. 19374	. . .	Evidence of delinquency	. . .
Sec. 19375	. . .	Suit in any court	. . .
Sec. 19376	. . .	Collection of tax	. . .
Sec. 19377	IRC Sec. 6301	Agreements with collection agencies	. . .
Sec. 19378	IRC Sec. 6301	Collection and transfer of funds	. . .
Sec. 19381	IRC Sec. 7421	Injunction actions prohibited	¶ 716
Sec. 19382	IRC Sec. 7422	Action to recover void tax	¶ 716
Sec. 19383	IRC Sec. 7422	Credit for overpayment	¶ 716
Sec. 19384	IRC Sec. 6532	Time for filing	¶ 716
Sec. 19385	IRC Sec. 6532	No FTB notice of action	¶ 716
Sec. 19387	IRC Sec. 7422	Service of summons and complaint	¶ 716
Sec. 19388	IRC Secs. 6532, 7422(f)	Location of trial	¶ 716
Sec. 19389	IRC Sec. 6532	Defense of action	¶ 716
Sec. 19390	. . .	Failure to sue within time limit	¶ 716
Sec. 19391	IRC Sec. 6612	Interest on judgment	¶ 716
Sec. 19392	. . .	Judgment against FTB	¶ 716
Sec. 19411	IRC Secs. 6602, 7405	Recovery of erroneous refunds	¶ 722
Sec. 19412	. . .	Court of trial	¶ 722
Sec. 19413	. . .	Prosecution of suit	¶ 722
Sec.19431	IRC Sec. 6404	Illegal levy	. . .
Sec. 19441	IRC Secs. 7121-23	Closing agreements	¶ 719
Sec. 19442	. . .	Settlement of tax disputes	¶ 719
Sec. 19443	. . .	Offers in compromise	¶ 720
Sec. 19501	IRC Sec. 7621(a)	FTB—administering the law	¶ 701
Sec. 19502	IRC Sec. 7621(b)	FTB—establishment of districts	¶ 701
Sec. 19503	IRC Sec. 7805	FTB regulations	¶ 701
Sec. 19504	IRC Sec. 7602	FTB's powers	¶ 701

California	Federal	Subject	Paragraph
Sec. 19504.5	IRC Sec. 7612	Software trade secrets	¶ 717
Sec. 19504.7	IRC Sec. 7602	Notice of contact of third parties	¶ 701
Sec. 19505	IRC Sec. 7803	FTB—appointment and removal	¶ 701
Sec. 19506	. . .	FTB deputies	¶ 701
Sec. 19507	. . .	FTB—temporary appointments	¶ 701
Sec. 19508	. . .	FTB—salaries	¶ 701
Sec. 19509	. . .	FTB—bond	¶ 701
Sec. 19511	IRC Sec. 7622	FTB—oath	¶ 701
Sec. 19512	IRC Sec. 6903	Fiduciary assuming taxpayer's duties	¶ 610
Sec. 19513	. . .	Tax clearance on estate	¶ 610
Sec. 19514	. . .	FTB action on certificate	¶ 610
Sec. 19515	. . .	No release from liability	¶ 610
Sec. 19516	IRC Sec. 6905	Fiduciary personally liable	¶ 610
Sec. 19517	. . .	FTB assessment of tax	¶ 610
Sec. 19518	IRC Sec. 6047	Information returns—self-employed retirement trusts	¶ 606
Sec. 19519	. . .	Disability insurance—refund or credit	. . .
Sec. 19521	IRC Secs. 6621-22	Current interest rate for deficiencies and refunds	¶ 709
Sec. 19522	. . .	Federal tax changes	¶ 102a
Sec. 19523	. . .	Disqualification of appraiser	¶ 710
Sec. 19524	IRC Sec. 6011	Regulations for returns on magnetic media	¶ 616
Sec. 19525	IRC Sec. 7623	Rewards for informers	¶ 701
Sec. 19526	. . .	Taxpayer cross-reference file	. . .
Sec. 19528	. . .	Information on state licensees	. . .
Sec. 19530	. . .	Preserving tax returns	¶ 717
Sec. 19531	. . .	Fees for publications	. . .
Sec. 19532	. . .	Priority for application of collected amounts	. . .
Sec. 19533	. . .	Priority of payments	. . .
Sec. 19542	IRC Secs. 6103, 7213	Secrecy of returns	¶ 717
Sec. 19542.1-42.3	IRC Sec. 7213	Illegal disclosures	. . .
Sec. 19543	IRC Sec. 6103(b)	"Business affairs" defined	. . .
Sec. 19544	IRC Sec. 6103(b)	Nondisclosure of audit methods	¶ 717
Sec. 19545	IRC Sec. 6103(h)	Disclosure—judicial order	¶ 717
Sec. 19546-46.5	IRC Sec. 6103(f)	Disclosure to legislative committee	¶ 717
Sec. 19547	IRC Sec. 6103(h)	Disclosure to Attorney General	¶ 717
Sec. 19548	. . .	Disclosure to Calif. Parent Locator Service	¶ 717
Sec. 19549	IRC Sec. 6103(b)	"Return" defined	¶ 717
Sec. 19551	IRC Sec. 6103(d)	Disclosure to proper authorities	¶ 717
Sec. 19552	IRC Secs. 6103, 7213	Unwarranted disclosure	¶ 717
Sec. 19553	IRC Sec. 6103	Disclosure to Director of Social Services	¶ 717
Sec. 19554	IRC Sec. 6103	Locating owners of unclaimed property	¶ 717
Sec. 19555	IRC Sec. 6103	Unearned income information	¶ 717
Sec. 19557	IRC Sec. 6103	Student loan applicants	¶ 717
Sec. 19558	. . .	Disclosure to Public Employees' Retirement System	¶ 717

California	Federal	Subject	Paragraph
Sec. 19561	. . .	Fee for copies of returns	¶ 717
Sec. 19562	IRC Sec. 6103	Charge for reasonable cost	¶ 717
Sec. 19563	IRC Sec. 6108	Publication of statistics	¶ 717
Sec. 19564	IRC Sec. 6108	High income taxpayer report	¶ 717
Sec. 19565	IRC Sec. 6104	Disclosure of information	¶ 717
Sec. 19581	. . .	Use of federal forms	Specimen return
Sec. 19582	. . .	Simplification of tax forms	. . .
Sec. 19583	. . .	Forging spouse's signature	¶ 710
Sec. 19701	IRC Secs. 7203, 7206	Violation—failure to file return	¶ 710
Sec. 19701.5	. . .	Forging spouse's signature	¶ 710
Sec. 19702	. . .	Prosecutor's compromise	¶ 710
Sec. 19703	. . .	Evidence of failure to file	¶ 710
Sec. 19704	IRC Sec. 6531	Statute of limitations— violations	¶ 710
Sec. 19705	IRC Sec. 7206	False statements—fraud	¶ 710
Sec. 19706	IRC Sec. 7203	Failure to file return	¶ 710
Sec. 19707	. . .	Venue	¶ 710
Sec. 19708	IRC Sec. 7202	Failure to remit withheld tax	¶ 710
Sec. 19709	IRC Sec. 7202	Failure to withhold tax as misdemeanor	¶ 710
Sec. 19710	. . .	Writ of mandate	
Sec. 19711	IRC Sec. 7205	Penalties—employees	¶ 710
Sec. 19712	IRC Sec. 6695	Misdemeanor conviction for endorsing client's refund check	¶ 710
Sec. 19713	IRC Sec. 7215	Failure to set up withholding account	¶ 710
Sec. 19714	IRC Sec. 6673	Delay tactics	¶ 710
Sec. 19715	IRC Sec. 7408	Penalties—injunctive relief	¶ 710
Sec. 19717	IRC Sec. 7430	Recovery of litigation costs	¶ 701
Sec. 19718	. . .	Wage statements for immigrants	. . .
Sec. 19720-21	. . .	Penalty for fraudulently obtaining refunds	¶ 710
Secs. 21001-14	IRC Secs. 6404(f), 7430, 7521, 7811	Taxpayers' bill of rights	¶ 701a, ¶ 701b
Sec. 21015	. . .	Relief from penalties	¶ 710
Sec. 21015.5	. . .	Tax lien and levy protections	¶ 701a
Secs. 21016-27	IRC Secs. 6103(e)(8), 6201(d)(4), 6331, 7433, 7435, 7502, 7524, 7811	Taxpayer's bill of rights	¶ 701a, ¶ 701b

CHAPTER 1

PERSONAL INCOME TAX

IMPOSITION OF TAX, RATES, EXEMPTIONS, RETURNS

¶ 101 Overview of Personal Income Tax

The California personal income tax was first enacted in 1935 and has been amended on numerous occasions since then. It constitutes Part 10 of Division 2 of the Revenue and Taxation Code. Administrative provisions applicable to both personal and corporate income taxpayers are encompassed by Part 10.2 of Division 2 of the Revenue and Taxation Code.

The law is administered by the Franchise Tax Board, composed of the State Controller, the Director of the Department of Finance, and the Chair of the State Board of Equalization.

California's personal income tax is generally patterned after the federal income tax. Moreover, interpretations of federal income tax law by the Internal Revenue Service and the courts have typically been followed in the administration of analogous provisions of California law. However, there remain significant differences between federal and California income tax laws. See ¶ 102a for an explanation of the federal conformity program established in 1983.

Personal income tax is imposed on the entire taxable income of California residents and on the income of nonresidents derived from sources within

California. It applies to individuals, estates, and trusts. Tax is computed on a graduated scale, at rates ranging from 1% to 9.3% (see ¶ 112). Under certain circumstances, tax is reduced by a credit for tax paid to another state or by various other credits (see ¶ 114 et seq.).

● *No local income tax*

California law specifically prohibits the imposition of an income tax by any city, county, or other local jurisdiction, and also prohibits local jurisdictions from imposing a tax on the earnings of nonresident employees unless the same tax is imposed on resident employees.

In *County of Alameda, County of Contra Costa, County of Santa Clara v. City and County of San Francisco* (1971) (CCH CALIFORNIA TAX REPORTS ¶ 15-014.81), the California Court of Appeal held that a San Francisco nonresident commuter tax was unconstitutional. However, in *Beresford David Weekes, et al. v. City of Oakland, et al.* (1978) (CCH CALIFORNIA TAX REPORTS ¶ 15-014.15), the California Supreme Court upheld the validity of a 1% tax imposed on employee compensation by the City of Oakland. The Court held that the tax was a license tax rather than an income tax.

¶ 102 Scope of Chapter

This chapter discusses the questions of who is subject to the tax and who qualifies as a "resident," requirements for filing returns and payment of tax, the base upon which tax is imposed, and the rates of tax.

¶ 102a Federal Conformity Program

Law: Secs. 17024.5, 19522 (CCH CALIFORNIA TAX REPORTS ¶ 15-019).

Prior to 1983, California personal income tax law was wholly self-contained. However, California statutes duplicated many provisions of federal law. This situation was remedied in 1983 when California law was completely restructured to incorporate much of the federal law by reference and to concentrate primarily on the *differences* between California and federal law.

California has incorporated most of the 1986 Tax Reform Act, the 1987 Revenue Act, the 1988 Technical and Miscellaneous Revenue Act (TAMRA), the Revenue Reconciliation Act of 1989, the Revenue Reconciliation Act of 1990, and the Tax Extension Act of 1991. California has also incorporated some of the provisions of the Energy Policy Act of 1992 and the Unemployment Compensation Amendments of 1992. California conformed in 1993 and 1994 to several of the amendments made to the Internal Revenue Code (IRC) by the Revenue Reconciliation Act of 1993. In 1995, California conformed to some of the amendments made by the federal Self-Employed Health Insurance Act of 1995. California adopted additional amendments to the IRC in 1996 that were made by the Revenue Reconciliation Act of 1993, the Small Business Job Protection Act of 1996, the Health Insurance Portability and Accountability Act of 1996, and the public laws governing state income taxation of pension income and tax benefits for service personnel in Bosnia and Herzegovina, Croatia, or Macedonia. In 1997, California conformed to most of the remaining amendments made by the Revenue Reconciliation Act of 1993, the Small Business Job Protection Act of 1996, the Health Insurance Portability and Accountability Act of 1996, and the Uruguay Round Agreements Act of 1994 (also known as the General Agreement on Tariffs), as well as to several amendments made by the Taxpayer Bill Rights of 1996 and the Taxpayer Relief Act of 1997. California adopted the majority of the remaining amendments made by the Taxpayer Relief Act of 1997 in 1998, as well as amendments made by the Balanced Budget Act of 1997. Any federal provisions that have not been incorporated—with the corresponding impact on the filing of the California personal income tax return—are discussed at appropriate paragraphs in the GUIDEBOOK.

For taxable years beginning after 1997, California incorporates much of the Internal Revenue Code as in effect on January 1, 1998, and for taxable years beginning after 1998, California also incorporates many of the amendments made by the IRS Restructuring and Reform Act of 1998. Because of the extent of the state conformity to federal law, the state income tax return has been designed to reflect a modification format. The computation of income begins with federal adjusted gross income, to which state modifications are then made. Accordingly, the GUIDEBOOK includes a guide to aid in the preparation of California individual income tax returns (see ¶ 25 *et seq.*).

● *Federal regulations apply to California*

When federal law has been incorporated into California law, as explained above, federal regulations issued under the law in both temporary and final form are applicable for California purposes unless they conflict with California law or California regulations.

● *Federal elections apply to California*

In most cases, federal conformity relieves a taxpayer from making a separate election for California purposes when an election is required. California law provides that a proper federal election is deemed to be a proper election for California purposes unless otherwise provided in California law or regulations. A copy of the federal election must be furnished to the Franchise Tax Board (FTB) upon request.

A taxpayer may make an election for federal purposes and not for California purposes, or vice versa, when the law permits a choice. In such cases, the taxpayer must file a proper election or timely statement with the FTB setting forth relevant information and clearly expressing an intent to elect differently for California purposes. This rule does not apply where a California regulation has requirements that are substantially different from the federal requirements.

● *Federal approval applies to California*

Federal conformity also simplifies the requirement of obtaining approval from taxing authorities when such approval is required. The law provides that whenever a taxpayer is required to file an application or seek consent, proper action taken for federal purposes is deemed to be effective for California purposes, unless otherwise provided by California law or regulations. A copy of any such application must be furnished to the FTB upon request.

¶ 102a

A taxpayer may take certain actions for federal purposes and not for California purposes, or vice versa, when the law permits a choice and approval or consent is required. The rules discussed above, relating to elections, apply with equal force to these situations.

¶ 102b Special Programs for Economic Incentives

California Forms: FTB 3805Z, FTB 3806, FTB 3807, FTB 3808, FTB 3809.

The Employment and Economic Incentive Act and the Enterprise Zone Act were enacted by the California legislature in 1984 to provide economic incentives for investment, employment, and development in designated enterprise zones and programs areas. Effective January 1, 1997, these two Acts were repealed and reenacted under a new Enterprise Zone Act. The new Enterprise Zone Act consolidated the previously existing enterprise zones and program areas to create "new" enterprise zones that continue to provide incentives similar to those previously available to enterprise zone and program area taxpayers. In addition, carryover of unused credits or deductions attributable to business activities under previously designated enterprise zones and program areas is specifically permitted. These programs are administered by the California Trade and Commerce Agency. Effective for taxable years beginning after 1997, enterprise zones are subject to audit at least every five years. If an enterprise zone fails to successfully comply with a corrective plan after receiving a failing grade, the zone will be dedesignated. However, businesses located in a zone that loses its designation may continue to receive tax incentives for the remaining life of the zone.

The Trade and Commerce Agency has designated the following enterprise zones: Agua Mansa, Altadena/Pasadena, Antelope Valley, Bakersfield, Calexico, Coachella Valley, Delano, Eureka, Fresno, Kings County, Lindsay, Long Beach, Los Angeles (Central City), Los Angeles (Eastside), Los Angeles (Northeast Valley), Los Angeles (Mid-Alameda Corridor), Los Angeles (Harbor Area), Madera, Merced/Atwater, Oakland, Oroville, Pittsburg, Porterville, Richmond, Sacramento (Floren Perkins), Sacramento (Northgate/Norwood), Sacramento (Army Depot), San Diego-SanYsidro/Otay Mesa, San Diego-Southeast/Barrio Logan, San Francisco, San Jose, Santa Ana, Shafter, Shasta Metro, Shasta Valley, Stockton, Watsonville, West Sacramento, and Yuba/Sutter.

The special tax incentives available to businesses operating within enterprise zones may be claimed only for costs paid or incurred after the zone is designated and before the designation expires (Instructions to Form 3805Z). The effective date of the original designation for former enterprise zones and program areas remains the original designation date for the "new" enterprise zones.

The various enterprise zone deductions and credits are reported on FTB 3805Z.

In addition to the economic incentives available in enterprise zones, special tax incentives were provided for taxable years beginning after 1991 and before 1998 to encourage investment, employment, and rebuilding in areas constituting the Los Angeles Revitalization Zone (LARZ). Credit carryovers are reported on FTB 3540 and FTB 3806 and deductions applicable to the LARZ are reported on FTB 3806.

As a means of stimulating business and industrial growth to offset revenue losses occasioned by military base closures, a number of income tax incentives are available to businesses conducted within designated local agency military base recovery areas (LAMBRAs), provided those businesses increase their number of employees by one or more during the first two taxable years after commencing business within the LAMBRA. Deductions and credits applicable to LAMBRAs are reported on FTB 3807.

The California Trade and Commerce Agency has designated the following LAMBRAs: George Air Force Base in Victorville, Castle Air Force Base in Atwater, Mare Island Naval Shipyard in Vallejo, Norton Air Force Base in San Bernadino, and Mather Field/McClellan Air Force Base in Sacramento. Conditional designation has also been granted to Alameda Naval Air Station and Tustin Marine Corps Air Station.

To encourage private investment and employment within a targeted tax area, special tax incentives are provided for taxable years beginning after 1997 to eligible businesses. The Trade and Commerce Agency has designated Tulare County as the targeted tax area. Deductions and credits applicable to the targeted tax area are reported on FTB 3809.

Finally, for taxable years beginning after 1997, businesses conducted within manufacturing enhancement areas are eligible for an employer's credit for certain wages paid to disadvantaged individuals. The cities of Brawley and Calexico in Imperial County are designated as manufacturing enhancement areas. The credit is reported on FTB 3808.

● *Enterprise Zone Act*

This program provides special tax incentives and other benefits for businesses established in designated depressed areas. The tax incentives are as follows:

1. Income tax credits for sales or use tax paid on purchases of certain machinery and equipment—see ¶ 133.

2. Income tax credits to employers for certain wages paid to disadvantaged individuals—see ¶ 134.

3. Income tax credits to employees who are disadvantaged individuals—see ¶ 135.

4. Tax-exemption of income from investments in enterprise zones—see ¶ 239.

5. Accelerated write-off of certain machinery and equipment costs—see ¶ 310f.

6. Carryover of 100% of net operating losses for up to 15 years—see ¶ 309.

¶ 102b

● *Los Angeles Revitalization Zone*

The following special tax incentives for investment, employment, and rebuilding apply to the Los Angeles Revitalization Zone (LARZ):

1. For taxable years beginning prior to 1998, income tax credits for sales or use tax paid on purchases of certain building materials, equipment, and machinery—see ¶ 114.

2. For taxable years beginning prior to 1998, income tax credits for wages paid to certain individuals—see ¶ 114.

3. Tax exemption of income from LARZ investments earned prior to December 1, 1998—see ¶ 239.

4. Accelerated write-off of certain property purchased prior to December 1, 1998, for LARZ use—see ¶ 310f.

5. Carryover for up to 15 years of 100% of net operating losses incurred prior to the 1998 taxable year—¶ 309.

● *Local Agency Military Base Recovery Area Act*

Income tax incentives provided for businesses conducted within a designated local agency military base recovery area include the following:

1. Income tax credits for sales and use tax paid or incurred for certain equipment, components, and depreciable property—see ¶ 133.

2. Income tax credits for wages paid to disadvantaged individuals or displaced employees—see ¶ 136.

3. Accelerated write-off of the cost of certain depreciable business assets—see ¶ 310f.

4. Carryover of 100% of net operating losses for up to 15 years—see ¶ 309.

● *Targeted tax area*

Income tax incentives provided for businesses conducted within a targeted tax area include the following:

1. Income tax credits for sales and use tax paid or incurred for certain equipment, machinery, and parts—see ¶ 133.

2. Income tax credits for wages paid to disadvantaged individuals—see ¶ 137.

3. Accelerated write-off of the cost of certain depreciable business assets—see ¶ 310f.

4. Carryover of 100% of net operating losses for up to 15 years—see ¶ 309.

● *Manufacturing enhancement areas*

Businesses conducted within a manufacturing enhancement area are eligible for income tax credits for wages paid to disadvantaged individuals or displaced employees—see ¶ 138.

¶ 102b

¶ 103 Who Is a Resident

Law: Secs. 17014-16, 17745 (CCH CALIFORNIA TAX REPORTS ¶ 15-101, 16-357).

Comparable Federal: None.

California law defines "resident" to include:

1. Every individual who is in the state for other than a temporary or transitory purpose. (As explained below, it does not matter whether such an individual's domicile, or permanent home, is in California or elsewhere.)

2. Every individual who is domiciled in the state but who is outside the state for a temporary or transitory purpose.

All individuals who are not "residents," as defined above, are "nonresidents."

● *Temporary or transitory purpose*

A regulation (Reg. 17014) containing several examples of "temporary or transitory purpose" indicates: "the underlying theory . . . is that the state with which a person has the closest connection during the taxable year is the state of his residence."

California law specifically provides that an individual whose permanent home is in California, but who is absent from the state for an uninterrupted period of at least 546 days under an employment-related contract, will generally be considered to be outside the state for other than a temporary or transitory purpose and, therefore, will not be treated as a resident subject to California tax. A return to California for not more than 45 days during a taxable year will not affect the nonresident status of such an individual. However, if the individual has intangible income exceeding $200,000 in any taxable year during which the employment-related contract is in effect, or if the principal purpose of the individual's absence from the state is to avoid California personal income tax, the individual will not be considered a nonresident. The same rules will apply to a spouse who accompanies such an individual.

An individual who is in California no more than six months during the year and who maintains a permanent home at the place of his or her domicile outside the state is deemed to be in California for temporary or transitory purposes, provided that the individual does not engage in any activity other than that of a seasonal visitor, tourist, or guest. (Note that this is not a statutory presumption, as is the nine-month presumption discussed below.)

● *Effect of domicile*

"Residency" is not the same as "domicile," which is an individual's permanent home, the place to which the individual, whenever absent, intends to return. One may be domiciled outside California, and still be considered a California resident by remaining in the state for other than temporary or transitory purposes. Conversely, California domiciliaries may be considered nonresidents if they remain outside the state for purposes that are neither temporary nor transitory. It is not necessary to demonstrate residency in any particular foreign state or country to avoid being considered a California resident—see the *Vohs* case, discussed below.

Certain United States officials who are domiciled in California are classified as "residents" for income tax purposes. This applies to elected officials, congressional staff members, and presidential appointees subject to Senate confirmation, other than military and foreign service career appointees.

● *Nine-month presumption*

California law provides that "every individual who spends in the aggregate more than nine months of the taxable year within this state shall be presumed to be a resident." The nine-month presumption is not conclusive and may be overcome by satisfactory evidence.

Conversely, presence within the state for less than nine months does not necessarily mean that the individual is not a resident. This point was made in *Appeal of Raymond T. and Ann B. Stefani* (1984) (CCH CALIFORNIA TAX REPORTS ¶ 15-101.752), involving a California professor who taught at a school in Switzerland while on sabbatical leave from his California position. Additionally, a regulation (Reg. 17016) provides that "a person may be a resident even though not in the state during any portion of the year."

● *Nine-month presumption overcome*

The presumption based on nine-months' residence, described above, was overcome by the taxpayer in *Appeal of Edgar Montillion Woolley* (1951) (CCH CALIFORNIA TAX REPORTS ¶ 15-101.73). The taxpayer, a well known actor, maintained his permanent home in New York State. He was in California continuously for a period of a little over a year in 1944 and 1945, including over nine months in 1945. During that, time he made two motion pictures and appeared in radio broadcasts. While in California, he lived in a hotel on a weekly basis. His departure was delayed because of illness and a studio strike. The State Board of Equalization (SBE) held that he was in California only for a temporary or transitory purpose and, therefore, was not a resident.

Another case in which the nine-month presumption was overcome is *Appeal of Joseph and Rebecca Peskin* (1962) (CCH CALIFORNIA TAX REPORTS ¶ 15-101.734). Over a period of several years the taxpayer spent from six to ten months in California each year. He engaged in extensive business activities and owned property in California. He overcame the presumption of residence by showing that he was more closely connected with Illinois than with California.

● *Nine-month presumption upheld*

The presumption based on nine-months' residence was upheld in *Appeal of Ralph V. and Marvelle J. Currier* (1969) (CCH CALIFORNIA TAX REPORTS ¶ 15-101.262). The taxpayer was employed in a job that required him to move frequently in the course of his employment, but he lived with his family in California for 2½ years. The SBE decided that the taxpayer was domiciled in Arizona but that, because his stay in California was for an indefinite period, he was a California resident.

¶ 103

● *Less than nine months in California*

In *Appeal of Morgan C. and Ann M. Jones* (1972) (CCH CALIFORNIA TAX REPORTS ¶ 15-101.736), the taxpayers argued unsuccessfully that a presumption of nonresidency arises from living in California for a period of less than nine months. However, although the taxpayers were registered to vote in Texas, had Texas drivers' licenses, and Texas automobile registration plates, the SBE held that the taxpayers were California residents in 1961, when they lived in the state for eight months, and in 1962, when they lived in the state for only five months.

● *Military personnel—In general*

Military personnel are subject to special treatment with respect to residency. Under Legal Ruling No. 300 (CCH CALIFORNIA TAX REPORTS ¶ 15-105.30), issued by the Franchise Tax Board (FTB) in 1965, California military personnel are treated as nonresidents when they leave the state under permanent military orders to serve at out-of-state posts of duty. If the serviceperson retains a California domicile and has a spouse who remains a California resident, the resident spouse is taxable on one-half of their community income. Out-of-state military personnel serving at posts of duty in California are treated as nonresidents unless California domicile is adopted. If California domicile is adopted, California will tax the entire income received during the period of residence. Declarations filed with military service branches showing California as the state of legal residence will be treated as presumptive evidence of California residence. The 1965 ruling resulted from a 1963 decision of the SBE: *Appeal of Harold L. and Miriam J. Naylor* (CCH CALIFORNIA TAX REPORTS ¶ 15-105.301). See also ¶ 224.

FTB Pub. 1032 (Tax Information For Military Personnel) also provides information on determining resident status for military personnel.

● *Effect of temporary military assignment*

In *Appeal of Cecil L. and Bonai G. Sanders* (1971) (CCH CALIFORNIA TAX REPORTS ¶ 15-105.302), the SBE declined to follow the *Naylor* case, discussed above, where a serviceman spent most of the year outside California under military orders designating a "permanent change of station." Instead, the SBE held that the taxpayer's out-of-state duty was clearly "temporary rather than permanent or indefinite."

● *Civil employees of military*

The special rules for military personnel do not apply to civilian employees of the military. See *Appeal of Ronald L. and Joyce E. Surette* (1983) (CCH CALIFORNIA TAX REPORTS ¶ 15-101.3312), where a civilian employee of the U.S. Army and his wife spent three years in West Germany on an Army assignment. They continued to own a California home and maintained California driver's licenses and voter registrations in California. The SBE held that they were California residents throughout the three-year period.

In *Appeal of Dennis W. and Emiko Leggett* (1984) (CCH CALIFORNIA TAX REPORTS ¶ 15-101.20), the taxpayer, a civilian employee of the U.S. Navy, spent at least ten months a year aboard ships. His wife lived in California and reported one-half of his income as her share of community income. The SBE held that he was a California resident and that his entire income was taxable.

● *Business assignments outside California—In general*

Several decisions of the SBE have involved taxpayers whose domicile admittedly was California, but who claimed nonresident status when they were out of the state on business assignments or projects for varying periods. The cases turn largely on the extent to which the taxpayers sever their ties to California and establish connections elsewhere, and the extent to which out-of-state activities appear to require long or indefinite periods of time to accomplish.

● *Business assignment cases favorable to taxpayer*

In *Appeal of Richard H. and Doris J. May* (1987) (CCH California Tax Reports ¶ 15-101.99), the taxpayer was employed by a Washington wholesaler to service sales areas in Washington and Oregon. The taxpayer and his wife had all of their business interests in Washington, maintained most bank accounts in Washington and Oregon, were registered Washington voters, had Washington drivers' licenses, and had all their legal, accounting, and medical needs met by Washington and Oregon professionals. In holding that the taxpayer and his wife were Washington residents, the SBE held that the fact that they erroneously claimed residency for purposes of the California home-owners property tax exemption on their California condominium and for the federal exclusion of gain from the sale of a personal residence were factors to consider but were not conclusive with respect to residence.

In *Appeal of Berry Gordy, Jr.* (1986) (CCH California Tax Reports ¶ 15-101.42), where the taxpayer filed a 1969 California part-year resident return, the SBE held that the state with which a person has the closest connections is the state of residence, and that the taxpayer had the closest connections with Michigan, where he owned several houses, had the majority of his business interests, registered and licensed his cars, and voted, and where his attorney, accountant, physician, dentist, and insurance agent were all located.

In *Appeal of Jeffrey L. and Donna S. Egeberg* (1985) (CCH California Tax Reports ¶ 15-101.3381), the taxpayer was an engineer employed by a nuclear engineering firm in California. He spent 17 months in Europe on an assignment that was expected to last at least 3 years. The family and household goods were moved to Europe, memberships in California were terminated, and other ties with California were severed. Despite retention of some important California relationships, the SBE held that the taxpayer and his wife were not California residents during their absence from the state.

In *Appeal of Robert C. and Grace L. Weaver* (1985) (CCH California Tax Reports ¶ 15-101.88), the taxpayer was an engineer employed by an aircraft manufacturer in California. He spent two years on Kwajalein Island on a "long-term foreign assignment" that was described as "more than one year and indefinite in nature." The taxpayer and his wife took an active part in social activities on Kwajalein, their minor daughter attended school there, and they established other connections there. However, they retained owner-ship of a home, stored an automobile and other possessions, and maintained some financial connections in California. The SBE held that their absence from California was for other than a temporary or transitory purpose, and concluded that they were not California residents during their absence from the state.

In *Appeal of Tommy H. and Leila J. Thomas* (1983) (CCH CALIFORNIA TAX REPORTS ¶ 15-101.338), the taxpayer made a commitment in 1977 to move to Iran for two or three years. He kept his home in California, maintained some other connections with the state, and left two daughters in school in California, but severed other connections. Due to the political unrest in Iran, the taxpayer's commitment was canceled and he returned to California after about a year overseas. The SBE held that he was not a California resident during his absence from the state.

In *Appeal of James E. Duncan* (1982) (CCH CALIFORNIA TAX REPORTS ¶ 15-101.507), the taxpayer moved to Texas to accept an executive position with the intention of remaining indefinitely. Although he left the Texas position and returned to California after only seven months, the SBE held that he acquired a new domicile in Texas during his employment there and that, therefore, he was not a California resident during the relevant period.

In *Appeal of David A. and Frances W. Stevenson* (1977) (CCH CALIFORNIA TAX REPORTS ¶ 15-101.506), the taxpayer was an untenured professor at a California university. He spent a period of 14 months in Europe working for most of that time under a research grant from the Fulbright Commission. The SBE accepted the taxpayer's contention that he intended to remain in Europe for at least two years and, consequently, held that he was not a California resident while he was absent from the state.

In *Appeal of Christopher T. and Hoda A. Rand* (1976) (CCH CALIFORNIA TAX REPORTS ¶ 15-101.482), the taxpayer was a specialist in Near Eastern affairs and was fluent in Arabic and Persian. He had traveled widely in the Near East and elsewhere, and was married to an Egyptian national. He lived in California for several years, beginning in 1966, and was assumed to be domiciled in California. He moved to Libya in July 1970 to take a job there, but moved back to California four months later because he lost the job. The SBE held that the taxpayer was a nonresident for the four-months that he was in Libya because he "intended and expected to remain in in the Near East either permanently or indefinitely."

In *Appeal of Richards L. and Kathleen K. Hardman* (1975) (CCH CALIFORNIA TAX REPORTS ¶ 15-101.481), a professional writer was held to be a nonresident in 1969 when he spent most of the year in England, even though his absence from the state in 1969 and 1970 lasted only 13 months. The taxpayer and his wife severed most of their connections with California before their departure, and it appeared that they originally expected to stay in England for several years.

● *Business assignment cases unfavorable to taxpayer*

In *Appeal of David A. Abbott* (1986) (CCH CALIFORNIA TAX REPORTS ¶ 15-101.3143), the taxpayer was held by the SBE to be a California resident during his seven-month employment in Maryland because his absence was for a temporary or transitory purpose. His wife and two children remained in their California home while he lived in a hotel for his entire stay outside the state. He owned other property in California and also retained his driver's license, automobile registration, and bank accounts in California.

In *Appeal of Frank J. Milos* (1984) (CCH CALIFORNIA TAX REPORTS ¶ 15-101.317), the taxpayer spent four years working as an engineer on Johnson Island. His wife and children remained in California and he retained other connections with California. He contended that he was no longer domiciled in California because he could not find employment in the state. The SBE held that he retained his California domicile and was a California resident during the entire period. For another case involving employment on Johnson Island, with somewhat similar facts and the same result, see *Appeal of John A. Purkins* (1984) (CCH CALIFORNIA TAX REPORTS ¶ 15-101.331).

In *Appeal of Albert L. and Anna D. Tambini* (1984) (CCH CALIFORNIA TAX REPORTS ¶ 15-101.339), the taxpayer spent about a year on an assignment of "indefinite" duration in Spain, with an agreement that his employer would transfer him back to California upon completion of the assignment. The SBE held that he was a California resident during the period involved.

In *Appeal of Harold L. and Wanda G. Benedict* (1982) (CCH CALIFORNIA TAX REPORTS ¶ 15-101.339), the taxpayer was an airline flight engineer. He was transferred by his employer to an Australian base station, where he remained for about ten months and then returned to California. Although he retained close connections with California, he contended that he was no longer a California resident because he did not intend to return to California. The SBE held that he was a California resident throughout the period involved.

In *Appeal of Nelson and Doris DeAmicis* (1982) (CCH CALIFORNIA TAX REPORTS ¶ 15-101.89), the taxpayer worked on Ascension Island for a year in 1976 and 1977. He argued that he had established residence there after he and his wife had agreed to a trial separation. However, he did not sever his principal personal and family California connections and he did not establish connections with Ascension Island. The SBE held that he was a California resident during the period involved.

In *Appeal of Pierre E.G. and Nicole Salinger* (1980) (CCH CALIFORNIA TAX REPORTS ¶ 15-101.333), the taxpayer spent about a year on a business assignment in Europe, but maintained many close connections with California. The SBE cited some of the cases discussed above, and held that the taxpayer remained a California resident during the period involved. Also, to the same effect, see *Appeal of David C. and Livia P. Wensley* (1981) (CCH CALIFORNIA TAX REPORTS ¶ 15-101.864); in this case the taxpayer spent 18 months on a business assignment in Germany, in a situation generally similar to the *Salinger* case. See also *Appeal of Robert J. Addington, Jr.* (1982) (CCH CALIFORNIA TAX REPORTS ¶ 15-101.867), involving a one-year stay in England on an assignment that was expected to last for two or three years. Also, see *Appeal of Russell R. Stephens, Jr.* (1985) (CCH CALIFORNIA TAX REPORTS ¶ 15-101.3351), where the taxpayer spent 18 months on a work assignment in Saudi Arabia.

In *Appeal of Robert J. and Kyung Y. Olsen* (1980) (CCH CALIFORNIA TAX REPORTS ¶ 15-101.382), the taxpayer had a work assignment in Iran from December 1974 to December 1976. His wife and five children stayed in their

¶ 103

California home while he was away. Although he spent 90% of the year 1976 in Iran, the SBE held that he was outside the state for temporary or transitory purposes and was a California resident throughout the period.

In *Appeal of Alexander B. and Margaret E. Salton* (1977) (CCH CALIFORNIA TAX REPORTS ¶ 15-101.336), the taxpayer spent about two years on a job assignment in Japan. The SBE cited the *Broadhurst* case, discussed below, at some length, and held that the taxpayer was a California resident throughout the period involved.

In *Appeal of William and Mary Louise Oberholtzer* (1976) (CCH CALIFORNIA TAX REPORTS ¶ 15-101.38), the taxpayer was a California engineer who worked in France for approximately eighteen months under a contract with his employer for that period. He kept a home and a car in California, and left a daughter there to finish her schooling. Although he was treated as a resident of France under French law, the SBE held that he was a California resident during the years in question.

In *Appeal of David J. and Amanda Broadhurst* (1976) (CCH CALIFORNIA TAX REPORTS ¶ 15-101.335), the taxpayer worked for the United Nations in Argentina from April 1971 to December 1972. His family stayed in the house they owned in California. The SBE cited some of the cases discussed above and held that he remained a California resident in 1971. To the same effect, see *Appeal of Wilbert L. and Doris Penfold* (1986) (CCH CALIFORNIA TAX REPORTS ¶ 15-101.318); in this case the taxpayer worked at numerous locations outside California for 30 years, usually remaining at each site for approximately one year.

In *Appeal of Malcolm A. Coffman* (1976) (CCH CALIFORNIA TAX REPORTS ¶ 15-101.381), the taxpayer spent five months in Australia in 1970 on a short-term assignment with the idea of possibly returning later for a long-term assignment. He arranged for a long-term assignment shortly after his return to California, and went to Australia again early in 1971. The SBE held that he was a California resident throughout 1970.

In *Appeal of Anthony V. and Beverly Zupanovich* (1976) (CCH CALIFORNIA TAX REPORTS ¶ 15-101.334), the taxpayer worked from December 1967 to February 1971 as a tugboat seaman in the Vietnam war zone. The SBE held that he was a California resident in 1968 and 1969, noting that, "although appellant's absence turned out to be rather lengthy, his family life, his social life, and much of his financial life remained centered in California throughout the years in question." The SBE's opinion discusses the significance of "connections," and indicates that the connections maintained by a taxpayer "are important both as a measure of the benefits and protection that the taxpayer has received from the laws and government of California, and also as an objective indication of whether the taxpayer entered or left this state for temporary or transitory purposes."

In *Appeal of John B. and Beverly A. Simpson* (1975) (CCH CALIFORNIA TAX REPORTS ¶ 15-101.332), an engineer was held to be a resident in 1971 although he spent the period from October 1970 to May 1972 on an assignment in Australia. In this case, the taxpayer's family stayed in California, and his assignment was originally scheduled for only one year.

● *Mixed residence of spouses—Community income*

When one spouse is domiciled in California, works outside the state, and establishes nonresident status, while the other spouse remains a California resident, the resident spouse may be taxable on one-half of the nonresident spouse's income because it is deemed to be community income. See cases to this effect cited at ¶ 238. (However, as explained at ¶ 238, in case of a permanent separation of the spouses, their earnings are separate income; in this event the resident spouse would not be required to report any of the nonresident spouse's earnings.)

● *Seamen held to be California residents*

In *Appeal of Charles F. Varn* (1977) (CCH CALIFORNIA TAX REPORTS ¶ 15-101.708), the taxpayer was a merchant seaman on a ship that never called at California ports. On June 8, 1971, he married a California resident who continued to live in California and who filed a separate California income tax return for 1971. The SBE held that the taxpayer acquired a California domicile when he married, and that he was a California resident for the remainder of the year.

In *Appeal of Olav Valderhaug* (1954) (CCH CALIFORNIA TAX REPORTS ¶ 15-101.26), the SBE held that a seaman who was in a California port three months of the year was a resident because California was the state with which he had the closest connection during the year. The seaman's wife and children lived in California for the full year. See also cases involving similar situations of merchant seamen decided by the SBE in later years, particularly *Appeal of Fernandez* (1971) (CCH CALIFORNIA TAX REPORTS ¶ 15-101.70), *Appeal of Haring* (1975) (CCH CALIFORNIA TAX REPORTS ¶ 15-101.703), *Appeal of Miller* (1975) (CCH CALIFORNIA TAX REPORTS ¶ 15-101.704), *Appeal of Laude* (1976) (CCH CALIFORNIA TAX REPORTS ¶ 15-101.707), and *Appeal of Estill William Fairchild* (1983) CCH CALIFORNIA TAX REPORTS ¶ 15-101.7092); the SBE held in each case that the taxpayer was domiciled in California and was outside the state for only a temporary or transitory purpose.

● *Seamen not California residents*

In *Appeal of John Jacobs* (1985) (CCH CALIFORNIA TAX REPORTS ¶ 15-101.653), the taxpayer was an unmarried sea captain who was assigned by his employer to operations in the Persian Gulf. Although he had a California driver's license and some other connections with California, he had no home or business interests in the state. The SBE held that he was not a California resident, because his connections with California were insignificant, even though he had closer connections with California than elsewhere.

Another case holding that a merchant seaman was *not* a California resident was *Appeal of Thomas J. Tuppein* (1976) (CCH CALIFORNIA TAX REPORTS ¶ 15-101.652). The taxpayer worked exclusively for California shipping companies, and was assumed to be domiciled in California. Although he was in California frequently for a few days between voyages, he spent a total of less than one month a year in the state. On the other hand, he spent longer periods in foreign countries and in Hawaii, and he maintained bank accounts and owned real estate in such locations. The SBE concluded that his closest connections were not with California and that he did not receive "sufficient

¶ 103

benefits from the laws and government of California to warrant his classification as a resident."

In *Appeal of Richard W. Vohs* (1973) (CCH CALIFORNIA TAX REPORTS ¶ 15-101.651), the SBE held that a merchant seaman was *not* a California resident despite the fact that his closest connections were with California. The taxpayer had been born and raised in California, was domiciled in the state, voted in the state, had a California driver's license, and had other connections in the state. The SBE held that the taxpayer was outside California for other than a temporary or transitory purpose, and commented that "a taxpayer need not establish that he became a resident of any particular state or country in order to sustain his position that he was not a resident of California."

● *Resident though domiciled elsewhere*

In *Appeal of German A. Posada* (1987) (CCH CALIFORNIA TAX REPORTS ¶ 15-101.453), the taxpayer was apparently a Colombian domiciliary, but was found to be a California resident for jeopardy assessment purposes. The taxpayer spent considerable time in California during the years at issue, obtaining a California driver's license, registering a car and boat there, and, after living for a time with friends in the state, prepaying six months rent on a California apartment. The SBE conceded that the taxpayer had "few contacts" with California, and that many of the usual indicia of residency, such as voter registration and bank accounts, were lacking, but concluded that this was evidence of the taxpayer's "nomadic nature" rather than of nonresidency in California.

In *Appeal of George D. Yaron* (1976) (CCH CALIFORNIA TAX REPORTS ¶ 15-101.154), the taxpayer had substantial business interests and other connections in both California and Vietnam. Although he was considered a resident of Vietnam under the laws of that country and was assumed not to be domiciled in California, the SBE held that he was a California resident.

In *Appeal of Mary G. Steiner* (1954) (CCH CALIFORNIA TAX REPORTS ¶ 15-101.26), the SBE held that an individual who resided in California for a substantial portion of the year was a California resident although it appeared that her domicile was in Florida. The individual involved owned property in Utah, had bank accounts in Utah and Florida, voted in Florida, paid property taxes there under a "resident" classification, and contributed to a church there. She rented a furnished apartment in California on a month-to-month basis and spent about half her time in the state.

A somewhat similar situation was involved in *Appeal of Lucille F. Betts* (1954) (CCH CALIFORNIA TAX REPORTS ¶ 15-101.26). The individual in this case was a widow who claimed residence in New Jersey, where she owned property, maintained bank accounts, voted, etc. She lived in a hotel in California and, because of transportation difficulties, did not return to New Jersey for a period of years during World War II. The SBE held that she was a California resident, relying on the nine-month presumption discussed above.

● *Substantial connections with California*

In *Appeal of Beldon R. and Mildred Katleman* (1980) (CCH CALIFORNIA TAX REPORTS ¶ 15-101.401), the taxpayer owned and managed a Las Vegas hotel and casino for several years until it burned down in 1960. From 1960 to 1970 he was engaged in efforts to reconstruct or develop the property. In 1962 he purchased a large home in California. Thereafter he spent a considerable amount of time and developed substantial connections in California. Although he maintained important connections in Nevada throughout the years involved, the SBE held that he was a California resident in 1962 and subsequent years.

In *Appeal of Jerald L. and Joan Katleman* (1976) (CCH CALIFORNIA TAX REPORTS ¶ 15-101.153), the taxpayer had important ties with Illinois, including voting and filing state income tax returns there. The SBE held that he was a California resident, on the basis of a closer connection with California and also upon the fact the he "enjoyed substantial benefits and protection from the laws and government of California."

In *George and Elia Whittell v. Franchise Tax Board* (1964) (CCH CALIFORNIA TAX REPORTS ¶ 15-101.261), decided by the California Court of Appeal, it was held that the taxpayers were California residents, even though they had a large home in Nevada, voted there, filed federal tax returns there, and had many other connections with that state. The taxpayers spent most of their time in California and had important family and business connections in the state.

In *Appeal of Ada E. Wrigley* (1955) (CCH CALIFORNIA TAX REPORTS ¶ 15-101.26), the SBE held that the taxpayer was a resident of California despite these factors: important business interests in Chicago; maintenance of a home and club membership there; exercise of her voting privilege there; principal banking activity there; and maintenance of three other large homes outside of California. The SBE indicated: "Long continued preference for (spending her time in) California, when coupled with her extensive and long continued financial interests within the state, the burial of her husband in California, the retention of two large homes within the state and the exchange of her large apartment in Chicago for smaller quarters there, convinces us that . . . California had become her principal place of abode."

● *Nonresidency found despite substantial California connections*

In *Corbett v. Franchise Tax Board* (1985) (CCH CALIFORNIA TAX REPORTS ¶ 15-101.607), the taxpayers maintained important business, social, and other connections with Illinois, including voter registration and drivers' licenses there. Nonetheless, the SBE held that they were California residents because in the years involved they spent 6 1/2 to 8 1/2 months of each year in California, owned a substantial California home, and had important social and family connections with the state. However, a court of appeal reversed the SBE's decision, and held that the taxpayers were not California residents.

In *Fred C. Klemp v. Franchise Tax Board* (1975) (CCH CALIFORNIA TAX REPORTS ¶ 15-101.557), the California Court of Appeal overruled the SBE and held that the taxpayers were not California residents, despite the fact that they owned a home in California and spent more time in California than they spent in the state of their domicile, Illinois. The court mentioned several factors that showed a closer connection with Illinois than with California. These included: voter registration, automobile registration, drivers' licenses,

¶ 103

business offices and accounting, investment counselor, doctor, dentist, church affiliation, safe deposit box, all in Illinois.

● *Importance of supporting evidence*

In *Appeal of C.I. Schermer* (1961) (CCH CALIFORNIA TAX REPORTS ¶ 15-101.604), the SBE sustained the findings of the FTB that the taxpayer became a resident in 1952, on the basis of bank accounts opened, credit applications filed, and the renting of an apartment. Taxpayer offered oral argument in opposition, but failed to supply affidavits of business associates or relatives concerning the amount of time spent in California. Since the taxpayer was an attorney, the SBE noted that it was reasonable to assume he would have maintained detailed records of his time as a basis for charging clients, and he failed to introduce these records in support of his position.

● *Indefinite intentions regarding California stay*

Appeal of George W. and Gertrude S. Davis (1964) (CCH CALIFORNIA TAX REPORTS ¶ 15-101.505) involved the intent of the taxpayers as a factor in determining residence. When the taxpayers initially came to California, they were uncertain whether, or when, they would depart. Accordingly, they were considered to have come for an indefinite period and were held to be residents for purposes of the California income tax.

● *"Nonresident alien" was California resident*

In *Appeal of Riad Ghali* (1971) (CCH CALIFORNIA TAX REPORTS ¶ 15-101.263), an Egyptian citizen was held to be a California resident despite the fact that he was classified as a nonresident alien for federal tax purposes. During the period in question, the taxpayer had no lawfully permanent status in the United States but was allowed to remain in this country because he was in disfavor with the Egyptian government and was afraid to return to that country. Nevertheless, he was held to be a California resident on the basis of his continued residence in the state over a period of years and, accordingly, was taxed on gain from sale of oil and gas leases in Mexico.

● *Professors on out-of-state assignments*

In *Appeal of Thomas K. and Gail G. Boehme* (1985) (CCH CALIFORNIA TAX REPORTS ¶ 15-101.753), the SBE held that a California university professor and his wife remained California residents throughout a 22-month assignment to a university study center in Egypt. The taxpayers rented out their California home on a month-to-month rather than a long-term basis, continued to claim the California homeowner's property tax exemption for it, left their family car in California, kept various California bank and charge accounts, and maintained a number of other contacts with California during their stay in Egypt. To the same effect, see *Appeal of Mortimer and Catherine Chambers* (1987) (CCH CALIFORNIA TAX REPORTS ¶ 15-101.753), involving a university professor who taught in Germany for two years.

Appeal of William F. and June A. Massy (1972) (CCH CALIFORNIA TAX REPORTS ¶ 15-101.751) involved the residence status of a Stanford University professor who spent a year in Pennsylvania as a visiting professor. The taxpayer moved to Pennsylvania with the understanding that a permanent

¶ 103

position would become available there. The SBE held that the taxpayer was not a California resident during the period in question.

● *Airline pilots transferred to California*

Appeal of Warren L. and Marlys A. Christianson (1972) (CCH CALIFORNIA TAX REPORTS ¶ 15-101.10) involved the residence status of an airline pilot (and family) in 1967 and 1968. He was transferred in 1966 from Texas to California to fly on military charter flights from California to Southeast Asia. Although he bought a home in California, he maintained business interests in Texas and other ties to that state. He argued that his presence in California was temporary because it was related to the uncertain duration of the Vietnam conflict. The SBE held that the taxpayer was a resident of California, although still domiciled in Texas. The SBE's opinion discusses the distinction between "residence" and "domicile," and comments that, "oftentimes in our mobile society they are not the same." See also the 1972 and 1973 decisions of the SBE in *Appeal of Donald E. and Betty J. MacInnes* (CCH CALIFORNIA TAX REPORTS ¶ 15-101.101) and *Appeal of Henry C. Berger* (CCH CALIFORNIA TAX REPORTS ¶ 15-101.102), involving other pilots transferred to California during the same time period; these taxpayers were also held to be California residents, although they were registered voters in other states and had other ties to those states.

● *Federal civil service employees*

In *Appeal of Paul Peringer* (1980) (CCH CALIFORNIA TAX REPORTS ¶ 15-101.265), the taxpayer was a federal civil service employee who had been transferred several times during his government career. Although he had been stationed in California for several years before and during the taxable years, he argued that his job location was not "permanent" and also challenged California's constitutional power to tax a federal employee domiciled in another state. The SBE's holding that he was a California resident, and this was affirmed by the California Court of Appeal. To the same effect, see *Appeal of George M. and Georgia M. Webster* (1977) (CCH CALIFORNIA TAX REPORTS ¶ 15-101.264), involving a taxpayer who had been a federal employee in California for 16 years.

● *Professional sports*

In *Appeal of Jimmy J. Childs* (1983) (CCH CALIFORNIA TAX REPORTS ¶ 15-101.131), the taxpayer was a professional football player with the St. Louis Cardinals. During the year in question (1979), he spent eight months in Missouri and four months in California, where he stayed with his parents during the off-season. He filed a nonresident Missouri return, in which he stated that his home address was in California. The SBE held that he was a resident of California.

Appeal of Richard and Carolyn Selma (1977) (CCH CALIFORNIA TAX REPORTS ¶ 15-101.132) involved a native Californian, admittedly domiciled in California, who played baseball for the Philadelphia Phillies. During the off-season he worked in California as a part-time bartender. He filed nonresident Pennsylvania tax returns in which he stated that he was a California resident and had numerous connections with California. The SBE held that he was a

¶ 103

California resident. To the same effect, see *Appeal of Robert D. and Susan Owchinko* (1985) (CCH CALIFORNIA TAX REPORTS ¶ 15-101.133); in this case the taxpayer played for the Cleveland Indians in the year involved and also played winter baseball in Puerto Rico. See also *Appeal of Joe and Gloria Morgan* (1985) (CCH CALIFORNIA TAX REPORTS ¶ 15-101.133), in which the taxpayer played for the Houston Astros and kept a house or apartment in Houston.

● *Effect of homeowner's property tax exemption*

In *Appeal of Robert and Nancy D. Hanley* (1981) (CCH CALIFORNIA TAX REPORTS ¶ 15-101.863), the taxpayer-husband spent about eight months in Florida and only 137 days in California during the year involved. He owned a home in Florida and managed a business there. However, his wife remained in California, where the couple also had business and other interests and where they claimed a California home as their permanent residence for purposes of the homeowner's property tax exemption. The SBE held that they were California residents.

● *Factors affecting residency*

As the illustrative cases summarized above indicate, there is no easy rule of thumb for determining when an individual is a California resident. All of the surrounding circumstances must be considered in making a residency determination. An FTB publication entitled "Guidelines for Determining Resident Status--1998" (FTB Pub. 1031) provides the following list of some factors that should be considered, with a cautionary note that the list is only a partial one:

(1) the amount of time you spend in California versus amount of time you spend outside California;

(2) the location(s) of your spouse and children;

(3) the location of your principal residence;

(4) where you were issued your driver's license;

(5) where your vehicles are registered;

(6) where you maintain your professional licenses;

(7) where you are registered to vote;

(8) the locations of banks where you maintain accounts;

(9) the locations of your doctors, dentists, accountants, and attorneys;

(10) the locations of the church or temple, professional associations, and social and country clubs of which you are a member;

(11) the locations of your real property and investments;

(12) the permanence of your work assignments in California; and

(13) the location of your social ties.

● *Court action to determine residence status*

A person who is alleged to be a California resident can obtain a determination of the fact of his or her residence by the Superior Court by first protesting a notice of proposed deficiency issued by the FTB (see ¶ 702). If the action of the FTB is unfavorable, he or she must then appeal to the SBE (see ¶ 703). If the SBE also rules unfavorably, an action must then be brought in the Superior Court to determine the issue of residency. All of this can be done without first paying the underlying tax.

● *Special rule for trust beneficiaries*

A resident beneficiary of a trust is presumed to continue to be a resident when he or she receives an accumulation distribution from the trust within 12 months after leaving the state and returns to the state within 12 months after receiving the distribution (see ¶ 604a).

● *California-federal comparison*

Although in some respects the California rules relating to residence are similar to federal provisions regarding resident aliens, the two laws deal with quite different situations. Therefore, no attempt is made here to compare them.

¶ 104 Returns—Who Required to File—Forms

> *Law:* Secs. 18501-34, 18622-23, (CCH CALIFORNIA TAX REPORTS ¶ 15-121, 89-101, 89-107, 89-157, 89-161).
>
> *Comparable Federal:* Secs. 6012-14, 6102 (CCH STANDARD FEDERAL TAX REPORTS ¶ 36,442, 36,460, 36,480, 37,860).
>
> *California Forms:* Form 540, Form 540A, Form 540EZ, Form 540 2EZ, Form 540NR, Form 541, Form 565, Form 568, FTB 3595.

● *Who must file*

For the 1999 tax year, California law requires that an income tax return be filed for every individual who has income in excess of the following amounts:

1999 Filing Threshold Amounts

Gross income more than:

	Age on 12/31/99	No dependents	1 dependent	2 or more dependents
Single or unmarried	Under 65	10,899	18,466	24,141
	65 or older	14,499	20,174	24,714

	Age on 12/31/99	No dependents	1 dependent	2 or more dependents
Married	Under 65 (both spouses)	21,798	29,365	35,040
	65 or older (one spouse)	25,398	31,073	35,613
	65 or older (both spouses)	28,998	34,673	39,213

Adjusted gross income more than:

	Age on 12/31/99	No dependents	1 dependent	2 or more dependents
Single or unmarried	Under 65	8,719	16,286	21,961
	65 or older	12,319	17,994	22,534

	Age on 12/31/99	No dependents	1 dependent	2 or more dependents
Married	Under 65 (both spouses)	17,438	25,005	30,680
	65 or older (one spouse)	21,038	26,713	31,253
	65 or older (both spouses)	24,638	30,313	34,853

For filing threshold purposes, (1) single persons include taxpayers filing as heads of households and qualifying widowers and (2) married couples include couples filing either jointly or separately.

A fiduciary (except for fiduciaries acting on behalf of certain grantor trusts—see ¶ 607) must file a California return if (1) in the case of a fiduciary acting on behalf of an individual, the individual is single and has adjusted gross income over $6,000, the individual is married and has adjusted gross income over $12,000, or the gross income of the individual exceeds $8,000 or (2) in the case of a fiduciary acting on behalf of an estate or trust, the estate or trust owes alternative minimum tax, the estate has adjusted gross income over $1,000, the trust has adjusted gross income over $100, or the gross income of the estate or trust exceeds $8,000.

For purposes of determining their personal income tax filing requirements, individuals and fiduciaries must include in their gross income any income from the sale of a primary residence, even if such income qualifies for

¶ 104

the gross income exclusion available for sales of primary residences (discussed at ¶ 502a).

A fiduciary must also file a California return for *every* decedent for the year of death, and for all prior years in which the decedent should have filed returns but failed to do so.

Anyone who is a nonresident for all or any part of the year is required to file a return, regardless of the amount of income, if any tax is due.

An individual for whom a federal dependent exemption may be claimed must file a separate state income tax return if the individual's gross income from all sources exceeds the amount of the basic standard deduction allowed to the individual under federal law.

Married couples may elect to file separate returns or a joint return. For a discussion of joint returns, see ¶ 104a.

Although partnerships are not taxed as such, they are required to file returns in some cases (see ¶ 616). A charitable trust is subject to special reporting requirements (see ¶ 605). See ¶ 606 regarding returns of employees' trusts.

Every common trust fund for which a trust company, bank, or corporation acts must file a return, regardless of the amount of gross or net income. The fiduciary return form is used for this purpose.

● *Return forms*

The principal return forms are as follows:

	540, 540A,
Resident individuals...	540EZ, 540 2EZ
Nonresident and part-year residents	540NR
Amended individual return	540X
Estates and trusts...	541
Partnerships	565
Limited liability companies (LLCs) classified as partnerships and single member LLCs that are disregarded and treated as a sole proprietorship	568

A copy of the federal return and schedules must accompany the 540NR. It must also accompany the 540 if the taxpayer attached any federal schedules other than Schedule A or B to the federal return.

● *Use of Form 540A*

California Form 540A is similar to federal Form 1040A. A taxpayer may use Form 540A only if, for the taxable year to be reflected in the return:

  1. the taxpayer was a full-year resident;

  2. the taxpayer's only income was from wages, salaries, tips, interest, dividends, tier 1 and tier 2 railroad retirement benefits, unemployment compensation, social security benefits, taxable scholarships and fellowship grants, or fully or partially taxable pensions, annuities, or IRA distributions;

¶ 104

3. the taxpayer is making adjustments to only one or more of the following sources of income: California state income tax refund, unemployment compensation, social security and tier 1 and tier 2 railroad retirement benefits, California nontaxable interest and dividends, IRA distributions (other than Roth IRA distributions), and pensions and annuities;

4. the taxpayer's itemized deductions are the same for state and federal purposes (except for state, local, and foreign taxes);

5. the taxpayer does *not* claim any tax credits other than exemption credits and the nonrefundable renter's credit;

6. the taxpayer has federal adjusted gross income of $100,000 or less;

7. only the following payments are made: withholding shown on Form(s) W-2, W-2G, and 1099-R, estimated tax payments, payments made with an extension voucher, and excess SDI and VDPI payments; and

8. state wages do not differ from federal wages.

● *Use of Form 540EZ*

California Form 540EZ is similar to federal Form 1040EZ. Single or joint filers who are under age 65, are not blind, and have no dependents may use Form 540EZ if, for the taxable year to be reflected in the return:

1. the taxpayer was a full-year resident;

2. the taxpayer's only income was from wages, salaries, tips, taxable interest of $400 or less, taxable scholarships or fellowship grants, or unemployment compensation;

3. the taxpayer has no adjustments to income other than the subtraction of unemployment benefits received (see ¶ 201);

4. the taxpayer does not claim any itemized deductions;

5. the taxpayer does not claim any tax credits other than the personal exemption credit and the nonrefundable renter's credit;

6. the taxpayer does *not* pay any tax other than withholding shown on Form W-2 that is computed using the tax table;

7. the taxpayer has federal adjusted gross income of $50,000 or less; and

8. the taxpayer does not claim excess SDI.

● *Use of Form 540 2EZ*

Beginning with the 1999 taxable year, Form 540 2EZ is available and is intended for use by taxpayers who prepare their own returns by hand. The form is similar to Form 540EZ. However, it contains special tax tables that have the standard deduction and personal and dependent exemption credits built in so that the taxpayer has to perform fewer mathematical calculations.

Single or joint filers who are under age 65, are not blind, can not be claimed as a dependent by another taxpayer, and are qualified to claim less than four dependents may use Form 540 2EZ if, for the taxable year to be reflected in the return, the taxpayer:

    1. was a full-year resident;

    2. had income only from wages and interest of less than $400;

    3. did not receive unemployment compensation;

    4. does not claim any itemized deductions or make any adjustments to income;

    5. had gross income of $50,000 or less if using the single or head of household filing status or $100,000 or less if using the married filing joint or qualifying widower filing status; and

    6. did not apply a 1998 overpayment to the tax due in 1999.

● *Form for nonresidents—Full or part year*

A person who was a nonresident for any part of the year must file a return on Form 540NR, regardless of status at the end of the year. Any change in residence status should be fully explained on the return or in an attached statement.

● *Reproduction of forms*

Most Franchise Tax Board (FTB) forms may be reproduced, along with their supplemental schedules, and the reproductions filed in lieu of the corresponding official forms. Details of specifications and conditions for reproducing forms, and for computer-prepared forms, may be obtained from the Franchise Tax Board, Tax Forms Request Unit, P.O. Box 307, Rancho Cordova, California 95741-0307.

● *Whole-dollar reporting*

California law is the same as federal law with respect to whole-dollar reporting (sometimes referred to as "cents-less" reporting). If any amount required to be shown on a return, statement, or other document is other than a whole dollar, the fractional part of a dollar may be rounded to the nearest dollar; that is, amounts under 50¢ are dropped and amounts from 50¢ to 99¢ are increased to the next dollar.

● *Use of address label*

If possible, taxpayers should peel off and use the pre-addressed (piggyback) address labels that come with their return forms. This assists in expediting return processing. The return form should be filled in completely, including, in particular, all applicable lines on pages 1 and 2. This also assists in return processing and will expedite any refund that may be due.

● *"Special handling required" notice*

Taxpayers or practitioners may attach FTB 3595 (Special Handling Required) to the front of the California personal income tax return on top of the W-2 form if (1) FTB 5805F (Underpayment of Estimated Tax by Farmers or Fishermen) or FTB 5805 (Underpayment of Estimated Tax by Individuals and Fiduciaries) is attached, (2) the taxpayer or the taxpayer's spouse is

¶ 104

deceased, (3) the taxpayer was the victim of a disaster, (4) the taxpayer was out of the country on the original due date of the return, (5) the taxpayer is filing an amended return (Form 540X) in response to a notice of proposed assessment, or (6) the taxpayer was out of the country as a result of military service in a combat zone.

● *Reporting federal changes*

A California taxpayer filing an amended federal return is required to file an amended California return within six months after filing the federal return if the change increases the amount of California tax due. Also, if any change or correction is made in gross income or deductions by federal authorities, or if gross income or deductions are changed by renegotiation of government contracts or subcontracts, such changes must be reported to the FTB within six months after the final determination of the federal change or correction or renegotiation if any such change increases the amount of California tax due. Effective for federal determinations that become final after 1999, the "date of a final federal determination" is defined as the date that each adjustment or resolution resulting from an IRS examination is assessed pursuant to IRC Sec. 6203. The federal determination is presumed to be correct unless the taxpayer overcomes the burden of establishing that the determination is erroneous. This principle has been approved in many appeals decided by the State Board of Equalization (SBE) over the years.

● *Effect of failure to report federal changes*

Failure to comply with the requirements for reporting federal changes may result in extending the statute of limitations on deficiency assessments (see ¶ 708).

● *Effect of presumed correctness of federal report*

In *Norman P. Calhoun et al. v. Franchise Tax Board* (1978) (CCH CALIFORNIA TAX REPORTS ¶ 15-401.11), the FTB assessed California tax on the basis of a federal audit report that showed an understatement of gross income. The federal tax was approved in a U.S. District Court case. Subsequently, the California Supreme Court applied the legal theory of "collateral estoppel" to justify the imposition of the California tax, based on the similarity of California and federal definitions of "gross income."

In *Appeal of M. Hunter and Martha J. Brown* (1974) (CCH CALIFORNIA TAX REPORTS ¶ 89-538.11), the SBE held that the FTB—not the taxpayer—must bear the burden of proof where a fraud penalty is proposed based on a federal audit report. The SBE upheld the assessment of California tax because of the presumed correctness of the federal determination, but held that the same presumption does not apply to a fraud penalty. However, the SBE has held in several cases that the presumption of federal correctness does apply to the 5% negligence penalty (see ¶ 710); that is, the burden of proof with respect to the negligence penalty is on the taxpayer. See *Appeal of Casper W. and Svea Smith* (1976) (CCH CALIFORNIA TAX REPORTS ¶ 15-101.862).

¶ 104a Joint Returns

Law: Secs. 17045-46, 18521-22, 18533-34, 19006 (CCH CALIFORNIA TAX REPORTS ¶ 15-124, 15-133, 15-151, 89-107).

Comparable Federal: Secs. 2, 66, 6013 (CCH STANDARD FEDERAL TAX REPORTS ¶ 3210, 5018).

Individuals must generally use the same filing status for California purposes as they use federally (see ¶ 110).

● *Joint and several liability of spouses*

Subject to certain conditions and limitations, the joint and several liability for tax on the aggregate income in a joint return may be revised in a court proceeding for dissolution of the marriage. The court order becomes effective when the Franchise Tax Board (FTB) is served with or acknowledges receipt of the order. If the gross income exceeds $50,000 or the tax liability that a spouse is relieved of exceeds $2,500, a "tax revision clearance certificate" must be obtained from the FTB.

Also, applicable to any liability due after October 10, 1999, an individual who has filed a joint return may elect separate liability if the individual is no longer married to, is legally separated from, or for at least 12 months has been living apart from the person with whom the joint return was filed. This election must be made within two years after the FTB has begun collection activities with respect to the individual. However, the running of the period of limitations does not begin until the date of the first collection activity after October 10, 1999. An individual making this election has the burden of proving his or her portion of any deficiency. An election may be partially or completely invalidated if (1) at the time of signing the return, the individual had actual knowledge of any item giving rise to a deficiency or portion thereof or (2) any assets were transferred between joint filers as part of a fraudulent scheme or to avoid tax.

Furthermore, if relief is not specifically available under the separate liability provisions, equitable relief may still be provided if, taking into account all the facts and circumstances, it would be inequitable to hold the individual liable.

For separate liability purposes, an item giving rise to a deficiency must generally be allocated in the manner it would have been allocated if the taxpayers had filed separate returns. However, an item otherwise allocable to one individual may be allocated to the other individual to the extent the item gave rise to a tax benefit to the other individual. Also, the FTB may provide for a different manner of allocation in the case of fraud on the part of one or both of the individuals.

The FTB must give notice to a joint filer of the other joint filer's election of separate liability, and the FTB must not make its determination with respect to the election earlier than 30 days after such notification. If an individual is denied a separate liability election, the individual may appeal that determination to the SBE.

Federal law contains comparable provisions for electing separate liability.

CCH Example: Separate Liability Election

Joe and Jennifer Jackson, who are separated, file a joint return for 1999 reporting $60,000 of wage income earned by Joe, $60,000 of wage income earned by Jennifer, and $7,000 of investment income on the couple's jointly owned assets. The FTB assesses a $400 tax deficiency for $5,000 of unreported investment income from assets held in Joe's name. Jennifer knew about a bank account in Joe's name that generated $1,000 of interest income, but she had no actual knowledge of Joe's other separate investments. If Jennifer properly elects separate liability, she will not be liable for $320 of the tax deficiency, which is the amount attributable to the $4,000 of unreported income of which she had no actual knowledge ($400 × [$4,000 ÷ $5,000]). However, she will be liable for $80 of the tax deficiency, which is the amount attributable to the $1,000 of unreported interest income from the bank account ($400 × [$1,000 ÷ $5,000]).

Both California and federal laws also contain provisions that relieve an innocent spouse from liability for additional tax and penalties in certain cases of wrongdoing in joint-return situations (see ¶ 710 for further discussion of these provisions). However, the "actual knowledge" standard for separate liability is narrower than the "knew or should have known" standard for innocent spouse relief. This may make separate liability available under circumstances in which innocent spouse relief is not.

● *Effect of mixed residence status*

A nonresident joint California return is required if one spouse was a resident for the entire taxable year and the other spouse was a nonresident for all or any portion of the taxable year. However, this rule does not apply to active military personnel and their spouses.

● *Returns by surviving spouse*

A joint return must be filed by a surviving spouse whose husband or wife dies during the taxable year if this status is elected federally.

● *Change from separate to joint return*

Spouses who have filed separate California and federal returns may refile on a joint California return, provided they meet certain limitations as to the time for refiling and if they refile federally. This change may be made even if all previous separate liabilities of the individuals have not been paid.

Under both California and federal laws, a change from a joint return to separate returns is permitted only if separate returns are filed on or before the due date.

For statute of limitations and delinquency penalty purposes, both California and federal laws provide special rules for determining the date on which a joint return is deemed to be filed in situations where one or both of the spouses previously filed a separate return. If only one spouse previously filed a separate return, the result depends on the amount of income of the spouse who did not file a separate return. In this situation, the amount of income specified by California law is different from that specified by federal. The statutes should be consulted in case of any question about these rules.

¶ 105 Returns—Time and Place for Filing

Law: Secs. 6707, 11003, Government Code; Secs. 18621-21.5, 18566-67, 18572 Revenue and Taxation Code (CCH CALIFORNIA TAX REPORTS ¶ 89-104, 89-151, 89-159).

Comparable Federal: Secs. 6072, 6081, 6091, 7508A (CCH STANDARD FEDERAL TAX REPORTS ¶ 37,720, 37,780, 37,800).

California Forms: Form 540, Form 540A, Form 540EZ, FTB 3519, FTB 3537, FTB 3538, FTB 3563, FTB 3582, FTB 8453, FTB 8633.

● *Due dates*

As is the case with the federal return, calendar-year income tax returns are due on April 15 following the close of the calendar year. Fiscal-year returns must be filed by the 15th day of the fourth month following the close of the fiscal year. California returns of taxpayers residing or traveling abroad are due two months later than the regular due date; that is, calendar-year returns of such taxpayers are due on June 15 (see ¶ 106).

● *Final returns*

The final California return of a decedent is due on April 15 following the close of the calendar year in which death occurred or, in the case of a fiscal-year taxpayer, within 3½ months after the close of the 12-month period beginning on the first day of the fiscal year. This is the same as the federal rule.

As under federal law, the final California return of an estate or trust is due within 3½ months after the close of the month in which the estate or trust is terminated.

● *Extensions of time*

The Franchise Tax Board (FTB) may grant an extension or extensions of time for filing any return, declaration, statement, or other document for a period up to six months from the regular due date, or for a longer period in the case of a taxpayer who is abroad (see ¶ 106). See ¶ 107 regarding extensions of time for payment of tax.

The FTB will grant "paperless" personal income tax extensions to individuals, partnerships, and fiduciaries for the 1999 tax year. Thus, such persons will be granted an automatic six-month extension to October 16, 2000. The automatic extension does not extend the time for paying tax. Tax payments must accompany FTB 3519 (Payment Voucher for Automatic Extension for Individuals), FTB 3537 (Payment Voucher for Automatic Extension for Limited Liability Companies), FTB 3538 (Payment Voucher for Automatic Extension for Limited Partnerships, LLPs and REMICS), or FTB 3563 (Payment Voucher for Automatic Extension for Fiduciaries). See ¶ 710 for a discussion of the penalty for failure to pay an adequate amount of tax by the regular due date.

In addition, the FTB may postpone certain tax-related deadlines, including the deadline for filing a return, for a period of up to 90 days for individual taxpayers affected by a presidentially-declared disaster. The deadlines that may be postponed are the same as those that may be postponed by reason of a taxpayer's service in a combat zone (see ¶ 106). See ¶ 709 for a discussion concerning the abatement of interest available to taxpayers granted such an extension.

An extension of time for filing the California return extends the statute of limitations on assessments to a date four years after the extended due date, even though the return may actually be filed earlier (see ¶ 708).

See ¶ 107 for interest charged during extension periods.

● *Filing by mail*

Returns and requests for extensions of time filed by mail are deemed to be filed on the date they are placed in the United States mail, provided they are properly addressed and the postage is prepaid. The date of the postmark is ordinarily deemed to be the date of mailing, although it may be possible to prove that the return was actually mailed on an earlier date. It is obviously desirable to mail early enough to be sure the postmark is timely. When the due date falls on a Saturday, Sunday, or other legal holiday, returns are due on the next business day. Federal law provides that the postmark date on a properly mailed return will be deemed to be the delivery date. (Note that a postage meter date is not a "postmark.")

CCH **CCH Tip: Returns Sent by Private Delivery Services**

If private delivery services are used to mail a return, the return should be sent in time to be *received* by the due date.

Returns should be mailed to the FTB in Sacramento, or filed with any regional or district office of the FTB. The regular Sacramento address for filing personal income tax returns and the special address for returns that show a refund due, are indicated on the return form.

● *E-file*

The FTB also accepts electronic filing of returns through the e-file program. Detailed information concerning this program is available at the FTB's website at http://www.ftb.ca.gov/elecserv.

● *Filing using electronic technology*

Personal income tax returns and other documents that are filed using electronic technology must be in a form prescribed by the FTB and are not complete unless an electronic filing declaration (FTB 8453) is signed by the taxpayer. The declaration must be retained by the document preparer or the taxpayer and must be furnished to the FTB upon request. Tax preparers may apply to participate in the electronic filing program by submitting an application (FTB 8633) to the FTB. Tax payments must be accompanied by FTB 3582 (Payment Voucher for Electronically Transmitted Returns).

● *FTB offices*

The FTB has branch offices in principal cities throughout California and also in Chicago and New York. Automated telephones (listed in telephone directories as "Forms Requests") in California offices record the requester's name, address, and the tax forms ordered.

¶ 106 Extensions of Time for Persons Outside the United States

Law: Secs. 17142.5, 18567-71 (CCH CALIFORNIA TAX REPORTS ¶ 89-104).

Comparable Federal: Secs. 6081, 7508 (CCH STANDARD FEDERAL TAX REPORTS ¶ 43,586).

California Form: FTB 3519.

● *Taxpayers abroad*

Taxpayers who are "abroad" can ordinarily obtain an unlimited extension of time for filing California returns, to cover the entire period of their absence from the country. A taxpayer who is outside the United States on the return due date is automatically granted a two-month extension of time; thus, the April 15 date for a calendar-year return is extended to June 15. This extension, combined with the automatic six-month paperless extension, extends the due date to December 15th. However, interest accrues on any unpaid tax from the original due date of April 15 and late payment penalties may be imposed on any tax still unpaid as of June 15.

To obtain further extensions of time, the taxpayer must continue to file timely requests periodically during his or her sojourn abroad. California has not defined "abroad" by regulation. Under comparable federal regulations, "abroad" is defined as outside the United States and Puerto Rico, and taxpayers who are abroad are granted an automatic extension of time to June 15 for calendar-year federal returns.

● *Armed Forces and merchant marine*

California grants automatic extensions of time to members of the United States Armed Forces and merchant marines who serve outside the boundaries of the 50 states of the United States and the District of Columbia. The extension also applies to the spouses of such individuals. The extension runs to a date 180 days after a serviceperson or merchant marine returns to the United States, and applies to filing returns, paying taxes, filing protests, filing claims for refund, and filing appeals to the State Board of Equalization. There is no comparable federal provision.

Members of the Armed Forces who serve in combat zones or hazardous duty areas (Bosnia, Herzegovina, Croatia, and Macedonia) or who are hospitalized as a result of injuries received while serving in combat zones or hazardous duty areas may postpone the deadline for filing income tax returns and paying taxes (other than income taxes withheld at the source or employment taxes) by (1) the amount of time they served in a combat zone or hazardous duty area,

(2) the period of time they were hospitalized as a result of injuries sustained in the zone or area, or (3) the period of time they were missing in action from the zone or area, plus (4) 180 days following the end of their service, hospitalization, or missing status. In addition, an individual performing services as part of Operation Joint Endeavor outside of the U.S. while deployed away from the individual's permanent duty station, whether or not serving in one of the previously listed areas, is considered to be performing services in a qualified hazardous duty area for purposes of the suspended filing, payment, and appeal time requirements.

The combat zone/hazardous duty area extension also applies to deadlines for tax assessments, tax collections, levies, the granting of a credit or refund of taxes, filing a claim for a refund or credit, and the filing of a suit for a refund or a credit.

¶ 107 Payment of Tax

Law: Secs. 18567, 18572, 19001-08, 19011, 19102 (CCH CALIFORNIA TAX REPORTS ¶ 89-104, 89-231, 89-430).

Comparable Federal: Secs. 5061, 6151, 6153, 7508A (CCH STANDARD FEDERAL TAX REPORTS ¶ 38,080, 38,100, 38,105).

California Form: FTB 3567BK.

The entire balance of tax due must be paid with the income tax return. Where tax has been withheld or a prepayment has been made during the year, the withholding or prepayment is deducted to arrive at the balance due with the return. See ¶ 107a regarding payment of estimated tax; see ¶ 712 and ¶ 712a regarding withholding.

● *Extension of time*

The Franchise Tax Board (FTB) may grant a reasonable extension of time for payment of tax whenever, in its judgment, good cause exists. Where an extension of time is granted, interest is charged from the regular due date to the date of payment. The interest rate is the rate charged on deficiencies, as explained at ¶ 709.

In addition, the FTB may postpone certain tax-related deadlines, including the deadline for payment of tax, for a period of up to 90 days for individual taxpayers affected by a presidentially-declared disaster. The deadlines that may be postponed are the same as those that may be postponed by reason of a taxpayer's service in a combat zone (see ¶ 106). See ¶ 709 for a discussion concerning the abatement of interest available to taxpayers granted such an extension.

● *Installment payments*

The FTB may allow taxpayers experiencing financial hardships to pay their tax in installment payments. Applicable interest (see ¶ 709) and penalties over the life of the installment period apply. Effective October 10, 1999, the FTB must enter into an agreement to accept payment of an individual's liability in installments if, as of the date the individual offers to enter into the agreement, all of the following apply: (1) the aggregate amount of the liability, excluding interest or penalties, does not exceed $10,000; (2) the individual and, if the individual has filed a joint return, the individual's spouse has not during the preceding five years failed to file a return, failed to pay any tax required to be shown on the return, or entered into an installment agreement for payment of tax; (3) the FTB determines that the individual is financially unable to pay the liability in full when due; (4) the agreement requires full payment of the liability within three years; and (5) the individual agrees to comply with the tax law for the period the agreement is in effect. If an independent administrative review is requested within 30 days of the date of rejection of an offer of an installment agreement or termination of an agreement, the administrative review will stay the collection of tax.

Also, operative for proposed installment agreements submitted after December 31, 2000, a levy may not be issued on the property or rights to property of any person with respect to any unpaid tax during any period for which an installment offer is pending, an installment agreement is in place, or a review of an installment agreement rejection or termination is pending. However, the levy restrictions do not apply to (1) any unpaid tax if the taxpayer waives the restrictions or if the FTB determines that the collection of tax is jeopardized; (2) any levy that was first issued before the date that the proceeding commenced; and (3) at the discretion of the FTB, any unpaid tax for which the taxpayer makes an offer of an installment agreement subsequent to a rejection of an offer of an installment agreement with respect to that unpaid tax.

The period of limitations for the FTB to bring an action to recover unpaid tax is suspended for the period during which the FTB is prohibited under the above provisions from making a levy.

To request an installment payment arrangement a taxpayer should file FTB 3567BK, Installment Agreement Request. A taxpayer requesting an installment payment plan need not submit a financial statement if the taxpayer (1) has filed all required returns, (2) owes no more than $10,000, and (3) agrees to pay the income tax liability by electronic funds transfer within three years.

Generally, any failure by the taxpayer to comply fully with the agreed-upon payment plan, other than for reasonable cause, ends the agreement, provided (1) the FTB notifies the taxpayer of the termination at least 30 days before the termination date and (2) such notice includes an explanation of the reason for the intended termination of the agreement. However, notice is not required if (1) the FTB determines that collection of the tax is in jeopardy or (2) there is mutual consent to terminate, alter, or modify the agreement. Taxpayers may seek administrative review by the Taxpayers' Advocate of any such termination. However, the administrative review will not stay the collection of tax.

● *Deferment for servicepersons*

The federal Soldiers and Sailors Civil Relief Act provides for the deferment of collection of state income taxes from servicepersons if their ability to pay is materially impaired by reason of their entering military service. Also, see ¶ 106 regarding automatic extension of time granted to certain individuals.

¶ 107

● *Payment by mail*

A payment is deemed to be made on the date it is mailed, provided it is properly addressed and the postage is prepaid. The federal rule is similar. See ¶ 105 for comment regarding the effect of a postmark date.

● *Payment by check*

Payment of personal income tax in the form of a check must be made payable in United States funds.

To expedite processing, payments for separate purposes (e.g., balance due on return and estimate payment) should not be combined in one check. The taxpayer's social security number should be shown on each check. Also, returns and payments of estimated tax should be mailed in separate envelopes.

● *Payment by credit card*

Beginning with the 1999 taxable year, taxpayers can use Discover/NOVUS, MasterCard, or American Express cards to pay their personal income taxes, including any amounts past due.

● *Payment by electronic funds transfer*

Upon taxpayer request, the FTB will allow payments to be made by electronic funds transfer. Once permission is granted, a 10% penalty is imposed if payments are not made in this manner (see ¶ 710). See also ¶ 807, regarding mandated requirements for use of electronic funds transfers by corporations in certain situations.

¶ 107a Payment of Estimated Tax

Law: Secs. 19007, 19010, 19136-36.6 (CCH CALIFORNIA TAX REPORTS ¶ 16-351, 89-245, 89-410, 89-413).

Comparable Federal: Secs. 6315, 6654 (CCH STANDARD FEDERAL TAX REPORTS ¶ 40,450).

California Forms: Form 540-ES, FTB 5805, FTB 5805F.

California law, including the special treatment for farmers and fishermen, is the same as federal law except for the following:

1. certain California exceptions to penalties for underpayments of estimated tax, as outlined below, are different than those under federal law;

2. California modifies the percentage of tax required to be paid under the annualized installment income method;

3. California does not include alternative minimum taxable income or adjusted self-employment taxable income for purposes of calculating estimated tax when a taxpayer uses the annualized income installment method; and

4. for taxable years beginning after 1999, federal law concerning the payment of estimated tax by certain high-income individuals differs from California law (see below).

¶ 107a

● *California exceptions*

California imposes no penalty for underpayment—and therefore requires no estimated-tax payments—in the situations described below.

1. Either the actual tax (after deduction of credits) for the preceding year or the estimated tax for the current year is under $200 for a single person or a married couple filing jointly, or $100 for a married person filing separately. Prior to the 1999 taxable year, these amounts were $100 and $50, respectively. Federal law does not impose a penalty for underpayment of estimated tax if the actual tax is less than $1,000 after withholding.

2. Four estimated tax payments were made equal to at least 80% (90% for federal purposes) of the tax shown on the return (if no return is filed, 80% of the tax) or payments equal to 100% of the tax shown on the return for the prior year (the safe harbor). Unless a taxpayer uses the annualized installment method (discussed below), each required installment must be 25% of the required annual payment. (For limitations on the use of the preceding year's tax, see below.)

3. Eighty percent of the actual tax for the preceding year was covered by withholding, or 80% of the estimated tax for the current year is covered by withholding.

4. Eighty percent of the adjusted gross income for the current year consists of items subject to withholding. (This does not apply if the employee files a false or fraudulent withholding exemption certificate.)

5. The prior year's return covered a full 12 months and there was no tax liability on that return.

⒞⒞ℋ CCH Examples: Estimated Tax Payment Exceptions

For 2000, single taxpayer A's estimated tax before withholding is $400. His withholding is $310. A does not have to pay estimated tax, because his estimated net tax (after deduction of withholding) is less than $200.

Taxpayer B's estimated tax before deducting withholding is $2,000. Her withholding is $1,600. B does not have to pay estimated tax, because withholding amounts to 80% of the estimated tax.

Taxpayer C's tax for the preceding year was $1,000 and his withholding for that year was $800. C does not have to pay estimated tax for the current year, regardless of the amount of his estimated income, because the preceding year's withholding was 80% of the tax.

Taxpayer D's estimated adjusted gross income for the current year is $20,000, consisting of wages of $16,000 and dividends of $4,000. D is not required to pay estimated tax, because her wages subject to withholding amount to 80% of her adjusted gross income.

¶ 107a

● *Annualized income installment method*

Under both California and federal law, taxpayers who do not receive their taxable income evenly throughout the year may elect to annualize their income for purposes of matching their estimated tax payments to the period when income is actually earned. However, California excludes "alternative minimum taxable income" and "adjusted self-employment income" for purposes of the annualized estimated income tax computations. In addition, California's installment payments are lower than the required federal amounts: 20% for the first installment (22.5% for federal purposes), 40% for the second installment (45% for federal purposes), 60% for the third installment (67.5% for federal purposes), and 80% for the fourth installment (90% for federal purposes). A worksheet is provided in FTB 5805 to assist taxpayers in determining the amount required to be paid under the annualized installment method.

● *Limitations on use of preceding year's tax for high-income taxpayers*

For taxable years beginning after 1998, under both California law and federal law prior to its amendment by the Tax and Trade Relief Extension Act of 1998 (TTREA), taxpayers whose adjusted gross income for the current year exceeds $150,000 ($75,000 if married filing separately) are required to pay 105% of the prior year's tax as estimated tax instead of the 100% payment required for other taxpayers. The percentage is increased to 112% if the preceding tax year begins in 2001, and is decreased to 110% if the preceding tax year begins in 2002 or thereafter. California has not yet incorporated an amendment made by the TTREA to the safe harbor rule for federal purposes that requires payment of 106% of the preceding year's tax if the preceding tax year begins in 1999 or 2000.

● *Dates of payment*

For calendar year taxpayers, estimated tax is payable in quarterly installments, on April 15, June 15, September 15, and January 15. If a due date for payment falls on a Saturday, Sunday, or legal holiday, it is extended to the next day that is not a Saturday, Sunday, or legal holiday. If the individual's tax situation changes during the year, payments for the remaining installments may be revised accordingly.

For fiscal year taxpayers, estimated tax payments are due by the 15th day of the fourth, sixth, and ninth months of the fiscal year and the first month of the following fiscal year.

● *Early return and full payment in place of fourth installment*

If a final return for the year is filed and the full amount of tax is paid by taxpayers generally before February 1, or by farmers or fishermen before March 2, it has the same effect as a payment of estimated tax on January 15.

● *Penalty for underpayment*

A penalty is imposed for underpayment of estimated tax, computed as a percentage of the underpayment, for the period of the underpayment. However, no penalty will be imposed for any underpayment of 1998 estimated tax

¶ 107a

if the underpayment was created or increased (1) as the result of a rollover distribution from an IRA to a Roth IRA (see ¶ 206) or (2) by any amendment made by 1998 conformity legislation (Ch. 7 (S.B. 519) and Ch. 322 (A.B. 2797), Laws 1998).

The penalty rate is the same as the interest rate on deficiencies and refunds, which is established semi-annually as explained at ¶ 709. However, the penalty rate is not compounded.

The amount of underpayment subject to penalty is based on 80% of tax for taxpayers generally and 66⅔% for farmers and fishermen (for definition of "underpayment," see ¶ 806a).

The underpayment penalty may be waived for newly retired or disabled individuals and in cases of unusual circumstances.

Also, no underpayment penalty will apply if the underpayment is attributable solely to changes made to the laws of other states concerning the allowance of credits for taxes paid to another state.

● *Reporting underpayment penalties*

Where the figures on a return indicate that there has been (or may have been) an underpayment of estimated tax, the taxpayer should attach FTB 5805 or FTB 5805F (for farmers and fishermen) to show computation of the penalty or to explain why no penalty is due. (Federal Forms 2210 and 2210F should not be used with California returns.)

● *Penalty for failure to pay*

Civil and criminal penalties are imposed for willful failure to make timely payments of estimated tax.

● *New residents, nonresidents, estates and trusts*

New residents and nonresidents are subject to the requirements for paying estimated tax as set forth above. The Instructions to FTB 5805 indicate that if the taxpayer had no California tax liability for the previous year, no estimated tax is due in the first taxable year of residence. Estates and trusts are subject to California estimated tax requirements, as they are under federal law.

¶ 108 Tax Base

Law: Sec. 17073 (CCH California Tax Reports ¶ 15-420).

Comparable Federal: Sec. 63 (CCH Standard Federal Tax Reports ¶ 6020).

The income tax rates (except for the alternative minimum tax discussed at ¶ 112a) are applied to the amount of taxable income, which is defined at ¶ 203.

¶ 109 Exemption Credits

> *Law:* Secs. 17054, 17054.1, 17056, 17733 (CCH CALIFORNIA TAX REPORTS ¶ 15-207, 15-210, 16-363).
>
> *Comparable Federal:* Sec. 151 (CCH STANDARD FEDERAL TAX REPORTS ¶ 8000).
>
> *California Forms:* Form 540, Form 540A, Form 540EZ.

Tax credits are allowed for personal exemptions. The credits are deducted from tax computed on taxable income without benefit of such exemptions. The credit applies to the separate tax on lump-sum distributions.

Following are the credits for the years shown:

	1995	1996	1997	1998	1999
Single person	$66	$67	$68	$70	$72
Married, separate return	66	67	68	70	72
Married, joint return	132	134	136	140	144
Head of household	66	67	68	70	72
Surviving spouse	132	134	136	140	144
Dependent	66	67	68	253	227
Blind person—additional	66	67	68	70	72
Estate	10	10	10	10	10
Trust	1	1	1	1	1
Elderly—additional	66	67	68	70	72

● *Heads of households*

As noted above, for heads of households, the exemption credit is $72 for 1999. Also, California allows an exemption credit for the dependent who qualifies the taxpayer as head of household ($227 in 1999 and adjusted for inflation thereafter).

California, unlike federal, law will allow a dependent credit even if a taxpayer fails to provide an identification number for the dependent on the taxpayer's personal income tax return.

● *Reduction of credits for high-income taxpayers*

The exemption credits are reduced if a taxpayer's federal adjusted gross income exceeds a threshold amount. For 1999, with respect to single taxpayers, each credit is reduced by $6 for each $2,500 or fraction thereof by which the taxpayer's federal adjusted gross income exceeds $119,813. For a married taxpayer or a surviving spouse filing a joint return, each credit is reduced by $12 for each $2,500 or fraction thereof by which the taxpayer's federal adjusted gross income exceeds $239,628. For married taxpayers filing separately, each credit is reduced by $6 for each $1,250 of federal adjusted gross income over $119,813. For heads of households, each credit is reduced by $6 for each $2,500 of federal adjusted gross income over $179,720.

A worksheet is provided in the Form 540 Instructions to assist taxpayers in determining the amount of the exemption credit reduction.

● *Inflation adjustment*

The annual inflation adjustment for the exemption credits is based on the change in the price level from June of the previous year to June of the current year, measured by the California Consumer Price Index as modified for rental equivalent ownership.

● *Nonresidents and part-year residents*

Nonresidents and part-year residents are allowed reduced credits for personal exemptions, on the basis of the ratio of California adjusted gross income to total adjusted gross income. The phase-out of exemption credits for high-income taxpayers (discussed above) must be applied before proration of the credits. See ¶ 121.

● *California-federal differences*

California has not incorporated the following federal provisions adopted by the Tax Reform Act of 1986: (1) the repeal of the additional exemption for blind individuals (California retains an additional $72 exemption credit) and (2) the repeal of the additional exemption for the elderly (California law adopts a $72 exemption credit for the elderly).

For 1999, the federal personal exemption is phased out for individuals with adjusted gross incomes over $126,600, for heads of household with adjusted gross incomes over $158,300, for married persons filing jointly and surviving spouses with adjusted gross incomes over $189,950, and for married persons filing separately with adjusted gross incomes over $94,975. Although California conforms to this procedure in principle, the reduction computation and the threshold amounts differ from federal law (see above).

¶ 110 Filing Status

> *Law:* Secs. 17021.5, 17042, 18521, 18532 (CCH CALIFORNIA TAX REPORTS ¶ 15-121—15-133, 15-207, 89-107).
>
> *Comparable Federal:* Secs. 2, 7703 (CCH STANDARD FEDERAL TAX REPORTS ¶ 3210, 43,970).

For California purposes, an individual must use the filing status used on his or her federal return for the same taxable year or, if no federal return was filed, the status that the individual would have used on a federal return.

Married taxpayers are also required to use their federal filing status, except that married taxpayers who file a joint federal return may file either joint or separate California returns if (1) either spouse was an active member of the military or (2) one spouse was a nonresident for the entire year and had no California-source income. A joint nonresident income tax return is required of a husband and wife who file a joint federal return if one of the spouses was a California resident for the entire taxable year and the other was a nonresident for all or any part of the tax year and had California-source income.

The determination of whether an individual is married, a "surviving spouse," a "head of household," or blind is made as of the close of the taxable year. A joint return may be filed if one spouse dies during the taxable year.

The Franchise Tax Board may revise a taxpayer's filing status if it is based on an incorrect federal filing status.

● *Head of household*

The federal law defining "head of household" is incorporated into California law by reference. Outlined below are the basic California and federal requirements.

1. The taxpayer must be "unmarried;" this means a single person or a married person who qualifies under the special rules discussed below.

2. The taxpayer must maintain as his or her home a household that is the principal place of abode, for more than half the year, of an individual who is within specified classes of dependents. In *Appeal of William Tierny* (1997) (CCH CALIFORNIA TAX REPORTS ¶ 15-130.195), the State Board of Equalization (SBE) allowed a taxpayer who was not legally married at the end of the taxable year to include one-half of the time that he occupied the same household with his ex-wife and children to determine whether his household was his children's principal place of abode for more than one-half of the taxable year. The SBE reasoned that taxpayers who share their income with their children to the extent that they provide more than half of the children's support during the calendar year and pay for more than half of the expenses necessary to maintain a household are entitled to some relief. In *Appeal of Barbara Godek* (1999) (CCH CALIFORNIA TAX REPORTS ¶ 15-130.20), the SBE extended the *Tierney* reasoning to a taxpayer who was legally married at the end of the taxable year before her divorce, but was "treated as not married" for the taxable year under the controlling statute.

3. The taxpayer must furnish over half of the cost of maintaining the household.

CCH **CCH Example: Married Individual as Head of Household**

Barbara and her daughter Monica lived in the same house with Barbara's husband from January 1, 1999, through March 9, 1999 (68 days). During the period from March 10, 1999, through December 31, 1999, Barbara and Monica lived together for an additional 163 days without Barbara's husband. Barbara and her husband were still married at the end of 1999, but they qualified to be "treated as not married" for the year. Barbara may count 34 days (1/2 of the 68 days) plus 163 days in calculating the number of days that her household was the principal place of abode for Monica in 1999. Because the total of 197 days is more than 1/2 of the year, Barbara qualifies for head of household filing status for the year.

In *Appeal of Patrick R. Lobo* (1999) (CCH CALIFORNIA TAX REPORTS ¶ 15-130.22), the SBE held that a taxpayer's unrelated 37-year old dependent was not a foster child and, thus, was not a qualifying individual for head of household filing purposes, because the foster relationship did not begin until after the dependent became an adult. The SBE noted that although there is no statutory definition of a "foster child" in the California tax laws, the term is intended to refer to an individual who was under the age of 18 at the time the foster child relationship began.

¶ 110

A checklist is included in the Instructions for Form 540 to assist taxpayers in determining whether they qualify for the head of household filing status.

A federal amendment made by the Small Business Job Protection Act of 1996 makes a taxpayer ineligible to claim head of household status if the taxpayer fails to provide the correct taxpayer identification number for his or her dependent. California has not yet adopted this amendment.

● *Unrelated individuals living together*

As indicated above, both California and federal laws require a specified relationship to qualify for "head of household" classification. This means that unrelated individuals living together do not qualify, even though one may furnish the chief support and be entitled to an exemption credit for a dependent. See *Appeal of Stephen M. Padwa* (1977) (CCH CALIFORNIA TAX REPORTS ¶ 15-130.11), cited in several later cases.

● *Married individuals treated as "unmarried"*

Certain married individuals may be treated as "unmarried" for purposes of determining their filing status. This applies where the individual lives apart from his or her spouse for the last six months of the year and maintains a home for a dependent child, under certain limited conditions. An individual who qualifies gains an immediate federal tax advantage, because the federal tax rates for a single person are lower than those for a married person filing separately. It should be observed, however, that there is no comparable California tax advantage, because the California tax rates for these two categories are the same. The principal California advantage of the "unmarried" classification is that it puts the individual in a position where he or she may, under the rules discussed above, get the benefit of the lower rates that go with "head-of-household" classification. ("Head-of-household" classification is, of course, also advantageous on the federal return.)

● *Effect of interlocutory decree*

For both federal and California tax purposes, a husband and wife are, by law, deemed *not* to be legally separated during the period between issuance of an interlocutory decree of divorce and issuance of the final decree. They are therefore considered to be married until issuance of the final decree.

¶ 111 Definition of Dependents

     Law: Sec. 17056 (CCH CALIFORNIA TAX REPORTS ¶ 15-210).

     Comparable Federal: Sec. 152 (CCH STANDARD FEDERAL TAX REPORTS ¶ 8007).

California law is the same as federal law. The term "dependent" means any of the following persons over half of whose support, for the calendar year in which the taxable year of the taxpayer begins, was received from the taxpayer (or is treated as received from the taxpayer under the multiple support rules described below):

     (a) a son or daughter of the taxpayer, or a descendant of either;

     (b) a stepson or stepdaughter of the taxpayer;

     (c) a brother, sister, stepbrother, or stepsister of the taxpayer;

(d) the father or mother of the taxpayer, or an ancestor of either;

(e) a stepfather or stepmother of the taxpayer;

(f) a son or daughter of a brother or sister of the taxpayer;

(g) a brother or sister of the father or mother of the taxpayer;

(h) a son-in-law, daughter-in-law, father-in-law, mother-in-law, brother-in-law, or sister-in-law of the taxpayer; or

(i) an individual (other than taxpayer's spouse) whose principal place of abode is the taxpayer's home and who is a member of the taxpayer's household.

● *Multiple-support agreements*

A taxpayer may satisfy the requirement of supporting a dependent even though he or she did not furnish over half the support, in certain "multiple support" situations. Under these rules, a taxpayer may claim a dependent for whom the taxpayer contributed less than one-half (but more than 10%) of the support, provided the taxpayer is a member of a group that contributed over one-half the support, and provided the other members of the group can meet the limitations imposed in these special provisions.

● *Support paid from community income*

Where all of the income is community income neither spouse contributes *over* half of their dependents' support, so technically neither is entitled to the credit for dependents on a separate return. However, as a practical matter, the credit is allowed under such circumstances to either spouse.

● *Divorced or separated parents*

The law provides detailed rules for determining which spouse is considered to have furnished over half the support of a child where the parents are divorced or separated. California law is the same as federal, with the minor exception noted at ¶ 125a.

In Legal Ruling No. 93-3 (1993) (CCH CALIFORNIA TAX REPORTS ¶ 15-210.38), the Franchise Tax Board indicated that a divorced, custodial parent who waives the federal dependent exemption deduction is precluded from claiming the corresponding state dependency credit.

● *Effect of classification as "dependent"*

The rules discussed above merely provide the *definition* of a "dependent." A taxpayer may or may not be allowed a *credit* for a person who qualifies as a "dependent," depending on the amount of the dependent's income and other conditions. Under a federal regulation that California follows, a claimed dependent must have less than the federal exemption amount in gross income for the calendar year in which the taxable year of the taxpayer begins, except when the dependent is the taxpayer's child and is under 19 years old or is a full-time student for at least five months during the calendar year in which the taxpayer's taxable year begins and is under 24 years old.

Regardless of whether or not a taxpayer is entitled to a credit, classification as a "dependent" may affect the deduction for medical expenses (see ¶ 315).

¶ 112 Tax Rates

> *Law:* Secs. 17041, 17048, 23081, 23091, 23097 (CCH CALIFORNIA TAX REPORTS ¶ 10-007, 10-041, 10-117, 15-151, 15-152).

> *Comparable Federal:* Sec. 1 (CCH STANDARD FEDERAL TAX REPORTS ¶ 3160).

California personal income tax is imposed on taxable income, as shown in the schedules and tables in Part I of this book. For the definition of "taxable income," see ¶ 203. The current progressive rates are 1% to 9.3%.

A minimum tax of $800 is imposed on limited partnerships, limited liability partnerships (LLPs), and limited liability companies (LLCs) that are treated as partnerships or that are disregarded and treated as sole proprietorships (see ¶ 618), unless a limited partnership, LLP, or LLC did no business in California during the income year and its income year was 15 days or less.

Also, a special tax is imposed on the active conduct of any trade or business by certain grandfathered publicly traded partnerships that elect to continue to be treated as partnerships rather than corporations (see ¶ 612).

● *Inflation adjustment*

Indexing of the rate brackets is based on the amount of inflation, or deflation, as measured by the change in the California Consumer Price Index from June of the prior year to June of the current year. The rate brackets for high-income taxpayers (discussed above) are indexed annually for inflation.

● *Use of tax tables*

The tax rate *schedules* are shown in Part I. Also shown are the tax *tables* used to determine the amount of tax on the return. The tables, rather than the rate schedules, *must* be used for all California returns except when the taxpayer's taxable income is over $100,000.

Married couples filing joint returns receive "split-income" benefits that are built into the tax tables (Part I).

The rates for estates and trusts are the same as for single individuals.

● *Tax rates for nonresidents*

Nonresidents and part-year residents are taxed as though they were residents, but with the tax computed according to the ratio of California adjusted gross income to adjusted gross income from all sources (a special proration formula applies to the alternative minimum tax; see ¶ 112a). California adjusted gross income includes the following: for any period during which the taxpayer was a resident of the state, all items of adjusted gross income regardless of source; and for any period during which the taxpayer was not a resident of the state, only those income items attributable to California sources.

¶ 112

¶ 112a Alternative Minimum Tax

Law: Secs. 17039, 17062, 17062.5 (CCH California Tax Reports ¶ 15-155).

Comparable Federal: Secs. 55-59 (CCH Standard Federal Tax Reports ¶ 5101—5450).

California Forms: Sch. P (540), Sch. P (540NR), Sch. P (541).

The alternative minimum tax, which is in addition to regular tax, is imposed under both California and federal law in an amount equal to the excess (if any) of the tentative minimum tax for the taxable year over regular tax for the taxable year.

● *"Regular tax" defined*

For California alternative minimum tax purposes, "regular tax" is the personal income tax before reduction for any credits against tax.

● *Federal-California differences*

The California tentative minimum tax rate is 7%. For federal purposes, for tax years ending before May 7, 1997, the tentative minimum tax rate is (1) 26% of the first $175,000 of a taxpayer's alternative minimum taxable income (AMTI) in excess of the exemption amount and (2) 28% of any additional AMTI in excess of the exemption amount. For tax years ending after May 6, 1997, the federal, but not California, minimum tax rate is lowered to reflect the reduction in the federal capital gains rate.

For nonresidents or part-year residents, the California tentative minimum tax is computed as if the taxpayer were a full-year resident, then multiplied by the ratio of California adjusted gross income to total adjusted gross income from all sources. California adjusted gross income includes (1) for any period during which the taxpayer was a California resident, all items of adjusted gross income, regardless of source and (2) for any period during which the taxpayer was not a resident of California, only those items of adjusted gross income derived from sources within the state. There is no equivalent computation for federal purposes.

California, like federal law, includes as an item of tax preference (TPI) an amount equal to one-half of the amount of gain realized from the disposition of certain small business stock excluded from gross income. For tax years ending after May 6, 1997, federal, but not California, law reduces the amount of tax preference from 50% to 42% of gain on the sale of small business stock excluded from gross income.

California modifies federal law disallowing the standard deduction and the deduction for personal exemptions for alternative minimum tax computation purposes to disallow only the standard deduction. California also modifies federal law to exclude from AMTI the income, adjustments, or items of tax preference attributable to a trade or business of a taxpayer who (1) owns or has an ownership interest in a trade or business and (2) has aggregate gross receipts, less returns and allowances, of less than $1,000,000 during the taxable year from all trades or businesses owned by the taxpayer or in which the taxpayer has an ownership interest. For purposes of computing the taxpayer's gross receipts, only the taxpayer's proportionate interest in a trade or business in which the taxpayer has an ownership interest is included.

"Aggregate gross receipts, less returns and allowances" is the sum of (1) the gross receipts of the trades or businesses that the taxpayer owns, and (2) the proportionate interest of the gross receipts of the trades or businesses in which the taxpayer has an ownership interest and the pass-through entities in which the taxpayer holds an interest. The term includes gross income from the production of both business income and nonbusiness income.

California specifically does not incorporate federal provisions (1) designating tax-exempt interest on specified private activity bonds as a TPI and (2) allowing an alternative minimum tax foreign tax credit. However, California allows the following credits to reduce a taxpayer's regular tax below the tentative minimum tax, before the allowance of the minimum tax credit: (1) the former solar energy credits; (2) the renter's credit; (3) the research credit; (4) the manufacturer's investment credit; (5) the former orphan drug research credit; (6) the low-income housing credit; (7) the credit for excess unemployment compensation contributions; (8) the credits for taxes paid to other states; (9) the credit for withheld tax; (10) the personal, dependent, blind, and senior exemption credits; (11) the credits for sales and use tax paid or incurred in connection with the purchase of qualified property used in an enterprise zone, a former program area, the former Los Angeles Revitalization Zone, or the targeted tax area; and (12) the enterprise zone, former program area, former Los Angeles Revitalization Zone, and targeted tax area hiring credits.

Also, California, but not federal, law includes as an item of tax preference the amount by which the charitable deduction for charitable gifts or contributions made by individuals or the charitable deduction for amounts paid or permanently set aside for charitable purposes for trusts and estates would be reduced if all capital gain property were taken into account at its adjusted basis.

Although California does conform to changes made to federal law by the Small Business Job Protection Act of 1996, different effective dates apply. The federal amendment requiring that the amount of the alternative minimum tax net operating loss (NOL) that may be utilized in any taxable year be appropriately adjusted to take into account the amount of the special energy deduction claimed for the year is effective for California purposes for taxable years beginning after 1996 and for federal purposes for tax years beginning after 1990. The rules for determining the AMTI of taxpayers with residual interests in real estate mortgage investment conduits apply for California purposes to taxable years beginning after 1996 and for federal purposes to tax years beginning after 1986 unless the taxpayer elects to apply the provision to tax years beginning after August 20, 1997.

Finally, California (but not federal) law increases the exemption amounts and the exemption phaseout amounts for taxable years beginning after 1998, and indexes these amounts for inflation beginning with the 2000 taxable year (see discussion below).

● *Computation of AMTI*

For both federal and California purposes, AMTI is regular taxable income after certain adjustments, increased by the amount of TPIs. However, as discussed above, for purposes of calculating AMTI, qualified taxpayers ex-

¶ 112a

clude income, adjustments, or items of tax preference from their trade or business.

The following are the applicable adjustments and TPIs:

Adjustments: The following adjustments must be made to the deductions claimed or the methods used in calculating regular taxable income:

(1) *excess depreciation:* for personal property placed in service after 1986 and before 1999, taxpayers who used the MACRS depreciation system in calculating their regular tax liability must recompute their regular tax liability using the 150% declining-balance method; however, a taxpayer must switch from the declining-balance method to the straight-line method in the first tax year in which the straight-line method yields a higher deduction than the declining-balance method; the AMT depreciation adjustment is eliminated for all MACRS property other than property depreciated using the 200% declining balance method for regular tax purposes, effective for property placed in service after 1998;

(2) *capitalizable expenses:* certain expenses that would ordinarily be treated as TPIs if deducted in the current year will not be treated as TPIs if the taxpayer elects to amortize them over a specified amortization period for regular tax purposes;

(3) *long-term contracts:* the percentage-of-completion method must be substituted for the completed-contract method to determine alternative minimum taxable income; for certain small construction contracts, simplified procedures for allocation of costs must be used;

(4) *alternative minimum tax NOL deduction:* NOL deductions must be recomputed on the same basis as AMTI (that is, reduced by TPIs and other adjustments); an alternative NOL may not offset more than 90% of the AMTI for a tax year without regard to the NOL deduction;

CCH Tip: Computation of AMTI NOL Deduction

The Franchise Tax Board's legal division has taken the position that AMTI NOL is computed without reference to the exclusion available to taxpayers involved in a trade or business with gross receipts of $1 million or less (Question and Answer No. 2, 1997 CPA/FTB Liaison Meeting, October 16, 1997).

---

(5) *certified pollution control facilities:* the five-year depreciation method must be replaced by the alternative depreciation system specified by federal law (straight-line method, without regard to salvage value); however, a facility placed in service after 1998 is depreciated using the IRC Sec. 168 straight-line method;

(6) *alternative tax itemized deductions:* in determining AMTI, no deduction is allowed for miscellaneous itemized deductions (including certain interest and medical expenses that are less than 10% of adjusted gross income (AGI)); state, local, and foreign real property taxes and state and local personal property taxes are not deductible for alternative minimum tax purposes; the overall limitation on itemized deductions of 6% of AGI (3% of

AGI for federal purposes) does not apply for alternative minimum tax purposes;

(7) *adjusted gain or loss:* gain or loss from the sale or exchange of business property during the tax year or from a casualty to business or income-producing property must be recomputed for AMT purposes by using the AMT adjusted tax basis rather than the regular tax adjusted basis of the property;

(8) *passive farm tax shelter losses:* taxpayers who are not material participants in a farming business may not deduct passive farming losses from AMTI; however, a loss determined upon the disposition of the taxpayer's entire interest in a tax shelter farming activity is not considered a loss from a tax shelter farm activity and is deductible in computing AMTI;

(9) *passive nonfarm business activity losses:* the rules limiting deductibility of other passive activity losses for regular tax purposes are subject to the following adjustments: (a) the amount of passive loss denied is reduced by the amount of insolvency; (b) passive activity losses must be computed on the same basis as AMTI (that is, reduced by TPIs and other adjustments, including the adjustment for passive farm losses); and (c) qualified housing interests are not included in computing passive business activity losses;

(10) *incentive stock options:* a taxpayer must include in AMTI the excess (if any) of (a) the fair market value of an incentive stock option at the time the taxpayer's rights in the option are freely transferable or are no longer subject to a substantial risk of forfeiture over (b) the price paid for the option; the adjustment is limited for California purposes to California incentive stock options and California qualified stock options;

(11) *tax recoveries:* refunds of taxes that are included in computing AGI for regular tax purposes (e.g., state and local personal property taxes and state, local, and foreign real property taxes) are not included in gross income for purposes of determining AMTI; and

(12) *depreciation of grapevines:* California (but not federal) law provides that if grapevines are replanted as a result of phylloxera infestation or Pierce's disease and are being depreciated over five years instead of 20 years for regular tax purposes, they must be depreciated over 10 years for AMT purposes.

Items of tax preference: The following TPIs must be added back in computing AMTI:

(1) *appreciation on charitable property contributions:* under California (but not federal) law, the excess of the charitable deduction claimed for capital gains property over its adjusted basis must be added back;

(2) *excess depreciation on property placed in service prior to 1987:* for nonrecovery real property, leased personal property, pollution control facilities, leased recovery property, 19-year real property, and low-income housing, the excess of accelerated depreciation deductions over normal depreciation is a TPI;

(3) *excess deductions from oil or mineral operations:* the excess of the depletion deduction claimed by a taxpayer (other than an independent oil and gas producer) for an interest in a mineral deposit over its adjusted basis at the

¶ 112a

end of the tax year must be added back, as must the amount by which an integrated oil company's excess intangible drilling costs exceed 65% of net income from oil, gas, and geothermal properties; and

(4) *excluded gain on sale of small business stock:* one-half of the amount of gain excluded from gross income on the sale or disposition of qualified small business stock (as calculated for California personal income tax purposes) is a TPI.

● *Exemption amount*

The California and federal alternative minimum tax is imposed on alternative minimum taxable income minus the exemption amount. For both California and federal purposes, the exemption amounts are reduced by 25¢ for each $1 that alternative minimum taxable income exceeds the beginning phase-out level, until the exemption is completely phased out.

For the 1999 taxable year, the exemption amounts for California purposes are as follows:

	Exemption amount	Phaseout begins at	Phaseout ends at
Married filing jointly and surviving spouse	$58,749	$220,308	$455,304
Single and head of household....	$44,062	$165,231	$341,479
Married filing separately and estates and trusts..........	$29,374	$110,153	$227,649

For married individuals filing separately, AMTI is adjusted so that the maximum amount of the exemption phase-out is the same for married taxpayers filing jointly. California, but not federal, law requires the Franchise Tax Board to index for inflation both the exemption amounts and the phase-out of exemption amounts.

For federal purposes, the exemption amounts are as follows:

	Exemption amount	Phaseout begins at	Phaseout ends at
Married filing jointly and qualifying spouse..........	$45,000	$150,000	$330,000
Single and head of household....	$33,750	$112,500	$247,500
Married filing separately and estates and trusts..........	$22,500	$75,000	$165,000

In the case of a child under 14 years old, the maximum exemption amount is the lesser of (1) the exemption available to an individual taxpayer (for the 1999 tax year, $44,062 for California purposes and $33,750 for federal purposes) or (2) the sum of the child's earned income plus $5,100.

¶ 113 Children Under 14 with Unearned Income (Kiddie Tax)

Law: Sec. 17041(g) (CCH CALIFORNIA TAX REPORTS ¶ 15-151).

Comparable Federal: Sec 1(g) (CCH STANDARD FEDERAL TAX REPORTS ¶ 3160—3180).

California Forms: FTB 3800, FTB 3803.

California conforms to federal law for purposes of calculating the amount of income tax for children under 14 years of age who have "investment income" in excess of a certain amount ($1,400 for 1999). The "kiddie" tax is computed on Form 3800 (Tax Computation for Children with Investment Income), which parallels federal Form 8615. California also conforms to the federal provision permitting a parent to report the interest and dividends of a child (more than $700 but less than $7,000 for 1999) on the parent's return.

The tax is designed to prevent parents from shifting investment income to a child in a lower bracket, and equals the greater of:

(1) the income tax on the child's taxable income figured at the child's rates without benefit of a personal exemption; or

(2) the total of:

(a) the "parental tax" (defined below); plus

(b) the income tax figured at the child's rates on the amount of the child's taxable income that remains after subtracting out the child's "net investment income" (defined below).

● *"Investment income," "net investment income," "parental tax" defined*

"Investment income" is all income other than wages, salaries, professional fees, and other amounts received as pay for work actually done.

"Net investment income" is investment income reduced by the greater of:

(1) $1,400 (for 1999); or

(2) $700 (for 1999) plus the child's itemized deductions that are directly connected with the production of his or her investment income.

"Parental tax" is the difference in tax on the parent's income figured with and without the child's net investment income.

● *Election to claim child's unearned income on parent's return*

A parent may elect to include on the parent's return the unearned income of a child whose income in 1999 is more than $700 but less than $7,000 and consists solely of interest, dividends, or Alaska Permanent Fund dividends. The child is treated as having no gross income and does not have to file a tax return if the child's parent makes the election. However, the election is not available if estimated tax payments were made in the child's name and taxpayer identification number for the tax year or if the child is subject to backup withholding.

To report the unearned income of a child on the parent's 1999 return, FTB 3803 (comparable to federal Form 8814) must accompany the parent's return. In addition to the child's gross income in excess of $1,400 being taxed at the parent's highest marginal rate, additional tax liability must be reported equal to the lesser of $105 or 1% of the child's income exceeding $700 ($105 or 15% of the child's income exceeding $700, for federal purposes). Special rules apply to unmarried taxpayers and married taxpayers filing separate returns, see Instructions to FTB 3803.

¶ 113

CHAPTER 1A

PERSONAL INCOME TAX
CREDITS

¶ 114 Credits—In General

Law: Secs. 17024.5(b)(10), 17039, 17055 (CCH CALIFORNIA TAX REPORTS, ¶ 15-020, 15-109, 15-114, 15-201, 15-202).

Comparable Federal: None.

California Forms: Form 540, Form 540NR, Sch. P (540), Sch. P (540NR), Sch. P (541), FTB 3540, FTB 3801-CR.

In addition to the credits for personal and dependency exemptions (see ¶ 109), California law provides a variety of credits that may be used to reduce taxable income. However, as discussed at ¶ 112a, certain credits may not be used to reduce the taxpayer's regular tax, plus the tax imposed on lump-sum distributions from employees' trusts, below the taxpayer's tentative minimum tax. If the taxpayer claims more than three credits, the appropriate form for each credit must be filed and the credits must be summarized on Schedule P (Alternative Minimum Tax and Credit Limitations). If three or less credits are claimed, they may be entered directly on Form 540. Also, some credits may be limited because they arise from passive activities (see ¶ 326). The taxpayer must file FTB 3801-CR (Passive Activity Credit Limitations) if the taxpayer claims any of the following credits and the credits arise from passive activities: low-income housing credit (see ¶ 127), research and development credit (see ¶ 139), or orphan drug research credit carryover (see below).

Although federal tax credits are not applicable under California law, certain California credits are similar to their federal counterparts. California also has many credits for which there are no comparable federal credits, and there are some federal credits that have no California counterparts.

● *Carryover credits*

Expired credits for which carryovers may be claimed (and the years for which the credits were available) include the following:

    1. water conservation credit (1980—1982);

    2. solar pump credit (1981—1983);

    3. solar energy credit (1985—1988);

    4. energy conservation credit (1981—1986);

    5. ridesharing credits (1981—1986 and 1989—1995);

    6. political contributions credit (1987—1991);

    7. commercial solar energy credit (1987—1988);

    8. residential rental and farm sales credit (1987—1991);

    9. food donation credit (1989—1991);

    10. orphan drug research credit (1987—1992);

    11. qualified parent's infant care credit (1991—1993);

    12. commercial solar electric system credit (1990—1993);

    13. recycling equipment credit (1989—1995);

    14. low-emission vehicle credit (1991—1995); and

    15. Los Angeles Revitalization Zone hiring and sales and use tax credits (1992—1997).

All of the above credit carryovers may be claimed on FTB 3540. See prior editions of the GUIDEBOOK TO CALIFORNIA TAXES for details about these credits.

● *Credit sharing*

Unless a personal income tax credit provision specifies some other sharing arrangement, two or more taxpayers (other than a husband and wife) may share a tax credit in proportion to their respective shares of the creditable costs. Partners may divide a credit in accordance with a written partnership agreement. In the case of a husband and wife filing separately, either may claim the whole of the credit or they may divide it equally between them.

● *Limitation on credit claimed by taxpayers with interest in a disregarded entity*

If a taxpayer owns an interest in a disregarded business entity, credits claimed for amounts paid or incurred by the business are limited to the difference between the taxpayer's regular tax figured with the income of the disregarded entity and the taxpayer's regular tax figured without the disregarded entity's income. If the disregarded entity reports a loss, the taxpayer may not claim the credit for the year of the loss, but can carry over the credit amount received from the disregarded entity.

● *Reduced credits for nonresidents and part-year residents*

Nonresidents and part-year residents are allowed reduced tax credits, with some exceptions. Generally, credits are allowed according to the ratio of California-source adjusted gross income to adjusted gross income from all sources. Thus, if California income is 50% of the total, allowable credits are 50% of total credits. However, this rule is subject to the following exceptions:

1. the renter's credit (¶ 122) is allowed in proportion to the period of residence;

2. credits for taxes paid to other states (¶ 116 and ¶ 117) are allowed in full; and

3. credits which are conditional upon a transaction occurring wholly within California are allowed in full.

¶ 115 Credit for Taxes Paid Other States—General

Law: Secs. 18001-11 (CCH CALIFORNIA TAX REPORTS ¶ 15-350—15-368, 89-211).

Comparable Federal: Secs. 901-5 (CCH STANDARD FEDERAL TAX REPORTS ¶ 4301, 28,480—28,542).

California Form: Sch. S.

In an effort to relieve double taxation, the California law allows in some cases a credit against the California tax for income tax paid to another state or to a territory or possession of the United States. (Note: Reference to territories or possessions is frequently omitted in the following discussion for the sake of simplicity; "other state" should be understood to include also territories or possessions.) Detailed rules for such credits in different situations are set forth below in ¶ 116—¶ 119, inclusive. General rules applicable to credits in all situations are included in this paragraph.

No credit is allowed for income taxes paid to cities or to foreign countries. However, some foreign taxes on gross receipts may be taken as a *deduction*—see ¶ 306.

● *Tax based on net income*

The credit is allowed only for taxes of another state based on *net income* (excluding any tax comparable to the alternative minimum tax). It therefore does not apply to a tax imposed on *gross income*. In *Appeal of Jesson* (1957) (CCH CALIFORNIA TAX REPORTS ¶ 15-350.11), the State Board of Equalization held that the Alaska gross production tax on gold mining royalties was not based on net income and therefore is not eligible for credit against the California tax.

● *Credit to estates and trusts and partnerships*

Credit is allowed to estates or trusts as well as to individuals. Credit may be allowed to an individual for taxes that were paid to another state by an estate or trust of which the individual is a beneficiary or by a partnership of which the individual is a partner. See ¶ 118—¶ 119 for details.

● *Timing of credit*

A taxpayer may not take credit for tax paid another state until the tax is actually paid. If the other-state tax has already been paid, the credit may be claimed at the time of filing the California return; if not, it may be claimed later by means of a refund claim. The claim for credit must be supported by filing Schedule S together with a copy of the return filed with the other state.

The credit may be applied only against the California tax for the year in which the income is taxed by both states; it may not be applied against the California tax of the later year in which the other-state tax is paid. In other words, the credit may be taken only on the return for the year in which the taxes accrued, irrespective of whether the taxpayer's returns are filed on the cash basis or the accrual basis.

● *Effect of joint or separate returns*

In the case of a husband and wife who file separate returns in California and a joint return in the other state, each is allowed a credit based upon the portion of the other-state tax allocable to his or her own income; the total tax paid to the other state is prorated to each on the basis of the income that is included in the joint return and also taxed in the California separate returns. Where a joint return is filed in California, the entire amount of taxes paid by either or both to the other state may be claimed as a credit, regardless of whether a joint return or separate returns are filed in the other state.

● *Refunds must be reported*

If after paying tax to another state the taxpayer obtains a refund or credit of any part of such tax, such refund or credit must be reported immediately to the Franchise Tax Board. The reduction in the credit against the California tax must be computed and the resulting increase in the net California tax paid, with interest.

¶ 115

In *Appeal of Daniel W. Fessler* (1981) (CCH CALIFORNIA TAX REPORTS ¶ 15-350.85), the taxpayer claimed credit based upon $726 withheld from his wages by the State of New York. The taxpayer's New York return showed a tax of only $130; he had claimed, but not yet received, a New York refund of $596. The State Board of Equalization held that the credit should be based upon the correct New York tax of $130, since the larger amount withheld was only an estimate of the anticipated tax liability.

● *California-federal differences*

There are many differences between the California credits for taxes paid to other states and the foreign tax credit in the federal law. The federal credit is allowed for income taxes generally; the California credit is allowed only for taxes based on *net income* (excluding any tax comparable to the alternative minimum tax). Federal credit is allowed only where the taxpayer elects to take the credit instead of using the foreign tax as a deduction; California requires no election, since it allows no deduction for income taxes under any circumstances. Federal law allows a cash-basis taxpayer an election as to the year in which the credit may be claimed; California permits the credit only in the year the taxes accrued.

¶ 116 Credit for Taxes Paid Other States—Residents

Law: Secs. 18001, 18006 (CCH CALIFORNIA TAX REPORTS ¶ 15-350, 15-367, 15-368).

Comparable Federal: Secs. 901-5 (CCH STANDARD FEDERAL TAX REPORTS ¶ 4301, 4306, 4310, 4313, 4319).

California Forms: Sch. R, Sch. S.

Credit is allowed California residents for *net income* taxes paid to another state (not including any tax comparable to California's alternative minimum tax) on income subject to the California income tax, subject to the conditions discussed below.

Credit is allowed only if the other state does *not* allow California residents a credit for California taxes. The purpose is to prevent the allowance of credits by both states at the same time. Under this rule credit is allowable only for taxes paid to the following states and possessions:

Alabama	Michigan
American Samoa	Minnesota
Arkansas	Mississippi
Colorado	Missouri
Connecticut	Montana
Delaware	Nebraska
District of Columbia (unincorporated business tax and income tax, the latter for dual residents only—see below)	New Hampshire (business profits tax)
	New Jersey
	New Mexico
Georgia	New York
Hawaii	North Carolina
Idaho	North Dakota
Illinois	Ohio
Iowa	Oklahoma
Kansas	Pennsylvania
Kentucky	Puerto Rico
Louisiana	Rhode Island
Maine	South Carolina
Maryland	Utah
Massachusetts	Vermont

¶ 116

Virginia (dual residents only—see below)   Wisconsin
Virgin Islands
West Virginia

Credit is allowed for District of Columbia and Virginia taxes paid by certain U.S. officials who are treated as dual residents (see ¶ 103).

California residents who are included in nonresident composite partnership or S corporation returns filed with any of the above-listed states or with Arizona, Indiana, Oregon, or Virginia may also claim a credit for their share of income taxes paid to those states. In *Appeal of Gregory K. Soukup and Mary Jo Carr* (1994) (CCH CALIFORNIA TAX REPORTS ¶ 15-350.53), the State Board of Equalization (SBE) held that taxpayers who filed a composite Indiana return were entitled to credit on their California return for income taxes paid to Indiana because their election to file a composite return made them ineligible to claim the credit in Indiana.

Partners, S corporation shareholders, and limited liability company members are allowed a credit for their pro rata share of tax paid to other states (see ¶ 119).

● *Must be nonresident of other state*

Credit is ordinarily allowed only for taxes (not including any tax comparable to California's alternative minimum tax) paid on net income that is taxable by the other state *irrespective* of residence or domicile of the recipient. See below for exceptions. In other words, the income taxed by the other state must be derived from sources within that state, under the California interpretation of what constitutes income from sources within that state. The credit is intended to apply in a situation in which the California resident is taxed by the other state as a *nonresident* of that state, and not to a situation where the taxpayer is taxed as a resident by both states. The effect of this rule is to deny or limit the credit in cases where the taxpayer is treated as a resident of the other state as well as of California, and to deny credit in almost all cases for tax paid on income from intangible property. Such income (dividends, interest, etc.) is deemed under California law to be attributable to California as the state of residence and therefore not derived from sources in another state, on the theory that intangible property generally has its situs at the domicile of the owner. See below for discussion of cases to this effect. This rule would not apply in the rare case where an intangible asset has acquired a "business situs" outside of California; see ¶ 230 for explanation of "business situs."

The general requirement that the taxes paid to the other state be imposed without regard to the taxpayer's residence or domicile does not apply to certain United States governmental officials, who are considered to be California residents as explained at ¶ 103. The purpose of this exception presumably is to insure that such officials will not be denied credit if they are treated as residents by the other state as well as by California.

● *"Alternative minimum taxes" do not qualify*

The credit does not apply to any preference, alternative, or minimum tax paid to other states that is comparable to California's alternative minimum tax (see ¶ 112a). However, the credit may be applied against the taxpayer's alternative minimum tax, if the taxpayer is liable for that tax (see ¶ 112a).

¶ 116

● *Limitation on amount*

The amount of the credit is limited to the same proportion of the total California tax as the income taxed by both states bears to the total income taxed by California. The purpose of this rule is to ensure that the credit allowed will not be any greater than the California tax actually paid on the income that has been subjected to double taxation. In *Appeal of John and Olivia A. Poole* (1963) (CCH CALIFORNIA TAX REPORTS ¶ 15-350.60), the SBE held that the word "income" for purposes of this limitation means the equivalent of "adjusted gross income" as defined in the California law.

If the taxpayer has income from a trade or business activity conducted both within and outside of California, the taxpayer must use Schedule R for purposes of calculating the income apportionable to California for which the credit may be claimed.

● *Procedure to determine credit*

If you are a California resident (or part-year resident), here are the steps to take to determine the credit:

1. Find out from the list above whether the other state qualifies for California credit.

2. Determine what items of income are taxed to you as a *nonresident* by the other state and also taxed by California. We shall call this the "double-taxed income." (As explained above, U.S. officials are not subject to the *nonresident* limitation—they should include at this point all income that is taxed by both states.)

3. Determine the net amount of the "double-taxed income" that is actually subject to tax by California after deducting any expenses which apply specifically to that income (such as depreciation, etc.). This computation should be made by applying the California rules for determination of adjusted gross income to the "double-taxed income."

4. Apply the limitation described under the heading "*Limitation on amount*," above.

5. The credit is the lower of two amounts: (a) the amount computed under step 4, or (b) the actual tax paid to the other state.

(CCH)   **CCH Example: Computation of Credit**

		California	State "X"
(a)	Total gross income	$25,000	$10,000
(b)	Gross income taxed in both states.......................	10,000	10,000
(c)	Deductions directly attributable to income on line (b)	1,000	1,000
(d)	Other deductions, not directly attributable to any income	4,500	3,000
(e)	Taxable income	19,500	6,000
(f)	Tax paid (illustrative amounts)	1,205	285

Step 1—Assume that State "X" qualifies for California credit and that you are being taxed by "X" as a nonresident.
Step 2—"Double-taxed income" $10,000
Step 3—Net amount of "double-taxed income" taxed by both states 9,000
Step 4—Limitation:
   9,000/24,000 × $1,205= 452
Step 5—Credit—actual tax paid to "X" 285

● *Decisions of courts and State Board of Equalization*

In *Appeal of Willis M. and Ruth A. Allen* (1986) (CCH CALIFORNIA TAX REPORTS ¶ 15-350.80), the taxpayer paid income and minimum taxes to both California and Minnesota, and included both taxes in the formula for determining the credit. The SBE held that the minimum tax on tax-preference items was not included in calculating the tax credit for taxes paid to another state.

In *Appeals of Michael A. DeBenedetti and Frances, Jr., and Joy Purcell* (1982) (CCH CALIFORNIA TAX REPORTS ¶ 15-305.301), the taxpayers were California stockholders of a corporation that was taxed by Oregon as a "tax-option" (S) corporation. The taxpayers argued that the stock had acquired a "business situs" in Oregon, because it was pledged there to secure indebtedness of another corporation. The SBE held that the source of the dividend income was in California, and denied credit for the Oregon tax.

In *Appeal of Stanley K. and Beatrice L. Wong* (1978) (CCH CALIFORNIA TAX REPORTS ¶ 15-350.301), the taxpayers were California residents who claimed credit for income tax paid to the state of Hawaii. The income taxed by Hawaii consisted of (1) interest on a note resulting from the sale of a Hawaii condominium and (2) dividends on stock of a family corporation located in Hawaii. The taxpayers argued that the note and the stock certificates were physically located in Hawaii and had acquired a "business situs" there. The SBE held that the source of the income was in California and denied the credit. To the same effect, see *Appeal of Marvin and Alice Bainbridge* (1981) (CCH CALIFORNIA TAX REPORTS ¶ 15-350.81), involving interest received on a contract for sale of Hawaii land.

The case of *Theo Christman v. Franchise Tax Board* (1976) (CCH CALIFORNIA TAX REPORTS ¶ 15-350.32) involved a taxpayer who was a California stockholder in a "tax-option" (S) corporation that operated in Georgia. His share of the corporation's income was taxed directly to him under Georgia's "tax-option" rules. He paid Georgia tax on the income and claimed credit against his California tax. The California Court of Appeal denied the credit on the grounds that the source of the income was California, despite the fact that

¶ 116

the corporation was treated—in effect—as a partnership for purposes of federal and Georgia taxes. To the same effect, see *Appeal of Estate of Donald Durham* (1974) (CCH CALIFORNIA TAX REPORTS ¶ 15-350.32), and *Appeal of Maude Peterson* (1978) (CCH CALIFORNIA TAX REPORTS ¶ 15-350.15).

In *Appeal of Leland M. and June N. Wiscombe* (1975) (CCH CALIFORNIA TAX REPORTS ¶ 15-350.77), a California resident received salary from an Alabama corporation for services rendered in California. The salary was taxed by Alabama, and the taxpayer claimed California tax credit for the tax paid to Alabama. The SBE denied the credit on the ground that the income was from a California source and was not properly taxed by Alabama to a nonresident, even though Alabama insisted on taxing it.

In *Appeal of Hugh Livie, et al.* (1964) (CCH CALIFORNIA TAX REPORTS ¶ 15-350.301), a California resident paid Puerto Rico income tax on the gain realized upon liquidation of a Puerto Rico corporation. The SBE held that the Puerto Rico tax was not allowable as a credit against California tax, since the income was derived from a California source. See also *Appeal of Allan H. and Doris Rolfe* (1978) (CCH CALIFORNIA TAX REPORTS ¶ 15-350.30), applying the same principle to disallow credit for Iowa tax.

¶ 117 Credit for Taxes Paid Other States—Nonresidents

Law: Secs. 18002, 18006 (CCH CALIFORNIA TAX REPORTS ¶ 15-358, 15-367, 15-368).

Comparable Federal: Secs. 901-5 (CCH STANDARD FEDERAL TAX REPORTS ¶ 4301, 4306, 4310, 4313, 4319).

California Forms: Sch. R, Sch. S.

● *Conditions for credit*

Credit is allowed nonresidents for *net income* taxes (excluding minimum or preference taxes comparable to California's alternative minimum tax) paid to the taxpayer's state of residence on income which is also taxed by California, subject to the following conditions:

(a) Credit is allowed only where the state of residence either (1) does not tax income of California residents at all, or (2) allows California residents a credit for California taxes. In other words, California does not allow credit to a resident of another state unless the other state will do as well for residents of California. This is commonly referred to as the reciprocity requirement. The states that qualify under this rule are listed below.

(b) Credit is allowed only where the other state does *not* allow its residents a credit in the same situation. Where the other state would allow a credit *even though* California also allowed one, this rule prevents the allowance of the credit by California. The purpose is to keep a taxpayer from getting credits from both states at the same time.

Because of above rules (a) and (b), credit is currently allowable to nonresidents only for taxes paid to the following states and territories:

Arizona

Guam

Indiana

Oregon

Virginia

However, in *Appeal of Daniel Q. and Janice R. Callister* (1999) (CCH CALIFORNIA TAX REPORTS ¶ 15-358.25), the State Board of Equalization held that nonresidents were entitled to a credit for a portion of the local income tax surcharges they paid to another state because the other state required its counties to impose that portion of the surcharge. The portion of the local surcharges that the state required counties to impose was recognized as a state, rather than local, tax.

● *Limitations on amount*

The maximum credit amount is limited to the lesser of the following two amounts: (1) the same proportion of the total tax paid to the state of residence as the income taxed in both states bears to the total income taxed by the state of residence; or (2) the same proportion of the total California tax as the income taxed in both states bears to the total income taxed by California. The total California tax for this purpose is the tax after deducting credit for personal exemptions.

In computing limitations (1) and (2), follow the principles set forth in the example in ¶ 116. As with resident individuals, if the taxpayer has income from a trade or business activity conducted both within and outside of California, the taxpayer must use Schedule R for purposes of calculating the income apportionable to California for which the credit may be claimed.

● *Nonresident S corporation shareholders, partners, and LLC members*

. Nonresident S corporation shareholders, nonresident partners, and nonresident limited liability company members are entitled to this credit for the pro rata share of taxes paid to another state (see ¶ 119). The taxes are treated as if paid by the individuals, and thus the conditions discussed above apply in determining this credit. Nonresident beneficiaries are not entitled to this credit (FTB Information Letter No. 89-427, CCH CALIFORNIA TAX REPORTS ¶ 17-434.25).

¶ 118 Credit for Taxes Paid Other States—Estates and Trusts

Law: Secs. 18003-05 (CCH CALIFORNIA TAX REPORTS ¶ 15-363).

Comparable Federal: Secs. 901-5 (CCH STANDARD FEDERAL TAX REPORTS ¶ 4301, 4306, 4310, 4313, 4319).

California Form: Sch. S.

Two types of credits are allowed in connection with estates and trusts: (1) credit may be allowed to the estate or trust itself where its income is taxed by two states; and (2) credit may be allowed to a resident beneficiary for taxes paid by the estate or trust to another state.

● *Credit to estate or trust*

Credit is allowed to an estate or trust where it is treated as a "resident" of California and also of another state. For this purpose, it is considered to be a

¶ 118

"resident" of any state that taxes its income irrespective of whether the income is derived from sources within that state. There are no reciprocal provisions for granting this credit as there are for resident and nonresident individuals as outlined above in ¶ 116 and ¶ 117, so the credit is allowable against net income taxes imposed by any state. The credit is subject to the following limitations:

(a) the amount of the credit may not exceed the same proportion of the total tax paid to the other state as the income taxed in both states bears to the total income taxed in the other state; and

(b) the amount of the credit is limited to the same proportion of the total California tax as the income taxed in both states bears to the total income taxed by California.

In *Appeal of Estate of Marilyn Monroe, Deceased* (1975) (CCH CALIFOR-NIA TAX REPORTS ¶ 15-363.15), the estate was taxed on substantial income by both New York State and California. The State Board of Equalization denied the estate's claim for credit for the New York tax, on the ground that the estate was not a "resident" of both states, since Marilyn Monroe was not a California resident at the time of her death and "only estates of resident decedents are residents of California" for tax-credit purposes.

● *Credit to beneficiary*

Credit is also allowed to the *beneficiary* of an estate or trust where a beneficiary who is a California resident pays California tax on income that has been taxed to the estate or trust in another state. The credit is subject to the following limitations:

(a) the amount of the credit may not exceed the same proportion of the total tax paid to the other state by the estate or trust as the income taxed to the *beneficiary* in California and also to the *estate* or *trust* in the other state bears to the total income taxed by the other state; and

(b) the amount of the credit is limited to the same proportion of the total California tax paid by the beneficiary as the income taxed to the *beneficiary* in California and also to the *estate* or *trust* in the other state bears to the beneficiary's total income taxed by California.

The purpose of these rules is to limit the credit to the amount of other-state tax and also to the amount of California tax actually paid on the net income that has been subjected to tax by both states. Computation of the limitations is similar in principle to that shown above in the example at ¶ 116, although it may become somewhat more complicated where credit to a beneficiary is involved.

● *Credit on distribution of accumulated income*

In Legal Ruling No. 375 (1974) (CCH CALIFORNIA TAX REPORTS ¶ 15-363.47), the Franchise Tax Board discussed the tax credit for accumulated distributions made by a Minnesota trust to California beneficiaries. The ruling held that the beneficiaries were entitled to credit against their California tax for taxes paid to Minnesota by the trust. The credit was the amount that would have been allowed if the trust income had been distributed ratably in the year of distribution and the five preceding years, to conform to the method of taxing the distribution to the beneficiaries.

¶ 119 Credit for Taxes Paid Other States—Partners, S Corporation Shareholders, and LLC Members

Law: Sec. 18006 (CCH CALIFORNIA TAX REPORTS ¶ 15-367—15-368).

Comparable Federal: Secs. 901-5 (CCH STANDARD FEDERAL TAX REPORTS ¶ 28,460—28,542).

California Form: Sch. S.

Resident partners, S corporation shareholders, and limited liability company (LLC) members are allowed a credit for their pro rata share of taxes paid another state by the partnership, S corporation, or LLC itself on income that is also taxed by California; the taxes are treated as if paid by the partners, shareholders, or members. A resident S corporation shareholder may claim the credit only if (1) the other state imposing the taxes does not recognize S corporations or (2) the other state taxes S corporations and the California S corporation has elected to be an S corporation in the other state. The credit is computed using the same formula outlined at ¶ 116 above under the heading "Procedure to determine credit."

A nonresident partner, S corporation shareholder, or LLC member is allowed a credit for his or her pro rata share of taxes paid by the partnership, S corporation, or LLC to the nonresident's state of residence on income also taxed by California. The taxes are treated as if paid by the nonresident partner, shareholder, or member. For conditions governing determination of the credit, see ¶ 117 above.

¶ 120 Excess SDI Credit

Law: Sec. 17061, Revenue and Taxation Code; Sec. 1185 Unemployment Insurance Code (CCH CALIFORNIA TAX REPORTS ¶ 15-234).

Comparable Federal: None.

California Forms: Form 540, Form 540A.

An income-tax credit is allowed for any excess employee contributions for disability insurance under the Unemployment Insurance Code. As explained at ¶ 1806, an employee who works for more than one employer during the year is entitled to recover any amounts withheld from wages in excess of the tax on the maximum wage limit (amount over $158.84 withheld in 1999), plus interest. An employee who files an income tax return recovers any such excess by claiming credit on the return. If the claim is disallowed, the employee may file a protest within 30 days with the Employment Development Department. Amounts withheld by a single employer that exceed the tax on the maximum wage limit must be recovered from the employer.

¶ 121 Tax Credits—Priorities

Law: Sec. 17039 (CCH CALIFORNIA TAX REPORTS ¶ 15-204).

Comparable Federal: None.

The law provides rules for the order in which various tax credits are to be applied. These rules are necessary because of the variety of provisions for carryovers, refundability, etc., in the various credits. The law provides that credits shall be allowed against "net tax" (the regular tax plus the tax on lump-sum distributions less exemption credits, but in no event less than the tax on lump-sum distributions) in the following order:

1. credits, except the credits in categories 4 and 5 below, with no carryover or refundable provisions;

2. credits with carryovers that are not refundable;

3. credits with both carryover and refundable provisions;

4. the minimum tax credit;

5. credits for taxes paid to other states; and

6. credits with refundable provisions but no carryover (withholding, excess SDI).

¶ 122 Renter's Credit

Law: Sec. 17053.5 (CCH CALIFORNIA TAX REPORTS ¶ 15-222).

Comparable Federal: None.

California Forms: Form 540, Form 540A.

A nonrefundable credit is allowed to anyone who is a "qualified renter," as explained below. The credit is not related in any way to the amount of rent paid. For the 1999 taxable year, the amount of the credit is $120 for married couples filing joint returns, heads of households, and surviving spouses, provided adjusted gross income is $51,300 or less, and $60 for other individuals, provided adjusted gross income is $25,650 or less. The adjusted gross income limits are adjusted annually for inflation.

● *"Qualified renter" defined*

To be a "qualified renter" for purposes of claiming this credit, an individual must be a California "resident," as explained at ¶ 103, and have rented a principal residence in California for at least one-half of the year.

An individual is *not* a "qualified renter"—and, therefore, gets no credit—if any of the following conditions described below exist.

1. Someone living with the individual claims the individual as a dependent (see ¶ 111) for income tax purposes. (The Franchise Tax Board takes the position that this applies where the individual is claimed as a "dependent" for either California or federal income-tax purposes.)

2. Either husband or wife has been granted the homeowner's property-tax exemption (see ¶ 1704) during the taxable year. This does not apply to a spouse who is not granted the homeowner's exemption, if both maintain separate residences for the entire year.

3. The property rented is exempt from property taxes (see ¶ 1704), unless the taxpayer, landlord, or owner pays possessory interest taxes or makes payments that are substantially equivalent to property taxes.

¶ 122

● *Special rules for married couples*

If a husband and wife file separate returns, the credit for a married couple may be taken by either or divided equally between them, except as follows:

1. if either spouse is not a California resident for part of the year, the credit is divided equally and prorated as described below for the period of nonresidency; or

2. if both spouses are California residents and maintain separate residences for the entire year, the credit must be divided equally between them; there is no option for one to take the full credit.

● *Heads of household—Welfare recipients*

In *Appeals of Juanita A. Diaz and Constance B. Watts* (1989) (CCH CALIFORNIA TAX REPORTS ¶ 15-222.55), the taxpayers were entitled to claim the head-of-household renter's credit rather than the individual renter's credit, even though more than half the expenses of maintaining their households were paid by Aid to Families with Dependent Children (AFDC).

● *Part-year residents*

A person who is a resident for only part of the year (provided he or she qualifies, as explained above) is allowed 1/12 credit for each full month of California residence during the year.

● *How to claim credit*

The credit should be claimed on the income tax return, with the appropriate supporting schedule.

¶ 123 Employers' Credits for Child Care Programs

Law: Secs.17052.17, 17052.18 (CCH CALIFORNIA TAX REPORTS ¶ 15-380).

Comparable Federal: None.

California Form: FTB 3501.

Childcare program start-up credit: For tax years beginning before 2003, an employer may take a credit for 30% of start-up costs incurred in establishing a child care program or constructing a facility to be used by the children of the taxpayer's employees. This 30% credit is also available for an employer's contributions to California child care information and referral services, such as those that identify local child care services, offer information describing these resources to employees, and make referrals of employees to child care services when there are vacancies.

Additionally, a taxpayer who owns a commercial building and is not required by local law to provide child care services may claim the 30% credit for (1) start-up costs incurred in establishing a child care program to be used primarily by employees of tenants leasing space in the building, or (2) contributions to child care information and referral services that will benefit those same employees.

Any taxpayer wishing to claim a credit for child care program start-up costs must disclose to the Franchise Tax Board the number of children the program will legally accommodate.

The credit may not reduce the taxpayer's net tax by more than $50,000 in any one tax year. Amounts in excess of $50,000 may not be claimed and may not be carried over. However, if the available credit for the current year combined with a credit carryover from a prior year exceeds $50,000, the excess amount may be carried over until exhausted.

The employer may not take a deduction for the portion of expenses equal to the credit amount. The cost basis of the facility is reduced by the amount of credit. A taxpayer can elect to take depreciation in lieu of claiming the credit. In any event, the taxpayer may take depreciation on the cost of the facility in excess of the credit.

If the child care center is disposed of or ceases operation within 60 months after completion, a proportionate share of the credit will be recaptured in the taxable year of the disposition or nonuse.

Childcare plan credit: For tax years beginning before 2003, employers may take a credit for contributions made to a qualified childcare plan on behalf of a qualified dependent of a qualified employee. The amount of the credit is 30% of the cost of plan contributions paid directly to the child care program or provider, up to a maximum credit of $360 per year for each qualified dependent. A qualified dependent must be under the age of 12 years. A "qualified employee" is an employee of the taxpayer who is performing services for the taxpayer in California. The credit may not be claimed for payments made to a person who qualifies as a dependent of the employee or the employee's spouse or who is the employee's child or stepchild under 19 years of age at the close of the taxable year. A qualified plan includes a plan that provides services at the work site, at child care centers, at home, or at a dependent care center (which is a specialized facility for short-term illnesses of an employee's dependents), as long as the facilities meet any applicable state licensing requirements.

If child care is for less than 42 weeks, the employer may claim a prorated portion of the credit, computed by the ratio of number of weeks of care to 42. The employer may not take a deduction for the portion of expenses equal to the credit amount. Unused credit may be carried forward until exhausted.

If an employer claims a credit for contributions to a qualified care plan used at a facility owned by the employer, the basis of the facility must be reduced by a corresponding amount in the taxable year the credit is allowed.

¶ 124 Salmon and Steelhead Trout Habitat Credit

Law: Sec. 17053.66 (CCH CALIFORNIA TAX REPORTS ¶ 15-386).

Comparable Federal: None.

California Forms: Form 540, Sch. P (540).

For taxable years beginning after 1996 and before 2000, a credit is allowed for the lesser of (1) 10% of qualified costs associated with salmon and steelhead trout habitat restoration and improvement projects, up to a maximum of $50,000 per taxpayer, or (2) the amount certified by the Department of Fish and Game. For the 1995 and 1996 taxable years the amount of credit that could be claimed was not limited to the amount certified by the Department of Fish and Game. The credit must be claimed on the return for the taxable year during which the costs were incurred. However, credit amounts that exceed net tax may be carried over to succeeding taxable years until the credit is exhausted.

The Salmon and Steelhead Trout Habitat Restoration and Improvement Project credit may be claimed upon certification by the Department of Fish and Game that a project (1) meets the objectives of the Salmon, Steelhead Trout, and Anadromous Fisheries Program Act and contributes to the increased natural production of salmon and steelhead trout and (2) is not otherwise required under California law.

In computing the credit, the costs associated with a qualifying project must be reduced by the amount of any grant or cost-share payment for the project made by a public entity.

¶ 125 Senior Head of Household Credit

Law: Sec. 17054.7 (CCH CALIFORNIA TAX REPORTS ¶ 15-218).

Comparable Federal: None.

California Form: Form 540.

California allows a "senior head of household" to claim a credit equal to 2% of taxable income, up to a maximum of $883 (for 1999). To qualify, a taxpayer must (1) be at least 65 years old as of the end of the taxable year and (2) have qualified as the head of household (see ¶ 110) for either of the two taxable years preceding the current taxable year by maintaining a household for a qualifying individual who died during either of those preceding taxable years. Additionally, the credit is limited to taxpayers whose adjusted gross income does not exceed a statutory maximum that is adjusted annually for inflation. The maximum adjusted gross income for 1999 is $46,863.

¶ 125a Credits for Joint Custody Head of Household, Dependent Parent

Law: Sec. 17054.5 (CALIFORNIA TAX REPORTS ¶ 15-208, 15-209).

Comparable Federal: None.

California Form: Form 540.

For the 1999 tax year, the California joint custody head of household credits equal the lesser of 30% of the net tax or $288. The credits cover both dependent children and dependent parents. The credits are subject to the same annual inflation adjustment as the exemption credits (see ¶ 109). However, neither may be claimed if the taxpayer used either the head of household or qualifying widow(er) filing status (Instructions to Form 540).

● *Dependent child*

To claim the credit as "joint custody head of household" for purposes of a dependent child the taxpayer must: (1) be unmarried at the end of the year; (2) maintain a home that is the principal place of abode of the taxpayer's dependent or descendant for no less than 146 days but no more than 219 days of the year, under a decree of dissolution or separate maintenance, or under a written custody agreement prior to the issuance of such a decree where proceedings have been initiated; and (3) furnish over half the cost of household expenses.

● *Dependent parent*

A "qualified taxpayer," for purposes of claiming the dependent parent credit, is one who: (1) is married but living apart from the spouse for the last half of the tax year; (2) files separately; (3) furnishes over half of the cost of maintaining the household that is the principal residence of the dependent parent; and (4) does not qualify to file as a head of household or as a surviving spouse. The dependent parent does not have to live in the taxpayer's home for purposes of claiming the dependent care credit.

¶ 126 Farmworker Housing Credit

> *Law:* Sec. 17053.14 (CCH CALIFORNIA TAX REPORTS ¶ 15-331).
>
> *Comparable Federal:* None.
>
> *California Forms:* Form 540, Sch. P (540)

A credit is allowed for the lesser of (1) up to 50% of qualified amounts paid or incurred for the construction or rehabilitation of farmworker housing, or (2) the amount certified by the California Tax Credit Allocation Committee (the "Committee"). For taxable years beginning after 1998, the credit is determined by reference to "eligible costs" instead of "qualified amounts." The credit may not be claimed until the first taxable year in which construction or rehabilitation of the housing is completed and the housing is actually occupied by eligible farmworkers. No other credit or deduction may be claimed for the qualified amounts used to compute the credit. However, unused credit may be carried over until exhausted. The credit is subject to recapture if the Committee determines that certification was obtained as a result of fraud or misrepresentation or if the taxpayer does not comply with program requirements.

"Qualified farmworker housing" means housing located within California that satisfies the requirements of the Farmworker Housing Assistance Program, as outlined in the Health and Safety Code. For purposes of the credit, "qualified amounts" are those costs paid or incurred after 1996 to construct or rehabilitate qualified farmworker housing to meet the requirements of the Employee Housing Act and any general improvement costs directly related thereto. For taxable years beginning after 1998, "eligible costs" are the total costs for finance, construction, excavation, installation, and permits paid or incurred to construct or rehabilitate qualified farmworker housing. Both "qualified amounts" and "eligible costs" include, but are not limited to, costs for improvements to ensure compliance with laws governing access for persons with disabilities and costs related to reducing utility expenses. However, "eligible costs" do not include land and costs financed by grants and below-market financing. Only those amounts certified by the Committee prior to being paid or incurred may be claimed for purposes of the credit.

To qualify for the credit, a taxpayer must (1) submit an application for credit certification to the Committee prior to paying or incurring any costs; (2)

ensure that the construction or rehabilitation of the property is done in conformity with the Farmworker Housing Assistance Program; (3) own or operate, or ensure the ownership or operation of, the farmworker housing in compliance with the provisions governing the availability of the credit, including making the housing available to farmworkers for 30 years; and (4) enter into a written agreement with the Committee guaranteeing that the program requirements have been satisfied.

¶ 127 Low-Income Housing Credit

Law: Sec. 17058 (CCH California Tax Reports ¶ 15-330).

Comparable Federal: Sec. 42 (CCH Standard Federal Tax Reports ¶ 4380).

California Form: FTB 3521.

California provides a credit computed under federal law (as modified) for investors in qualified low-income housing projects in California. The credit is applied against the net tax, and may reduce tax liability to below the "tentative minimum tax."

The California credit is claimed over a four-year period, rather than over a 10-year period as under federal law. Generally, for buildings that receive credit allocations after 1989, the percentage of costs for which credit may be claimed in the first three years is the highest percentage allowed federally in the month the building is placed in service. For the fourth year, the percentage is the difference between 30% and the sum of the credit percentage for the first three years. However, with respect to credits allocated after 1989 for (1) new buildings that are federally subsidized, and (2) existing buildings that are at risk of conversion to market rental rates, the percentage of creditable costs in the first three years is the same as the federal percentage applicable to subsidized new buildings, while for the fourth year the percentage is the difference between 13% and the sum of the credit percentages for the first three years. The California provisions require a "compliance period" of 30 consecutive tax years, rather than the 15-year federal period. However, unlike federal law, California has no recapture provision (see IRC Sec. 42(i)(1)). If the credit exceeds the taxpayer's net tax for the taxable year, the excess may be carried forward to succeeding years.

When the basis of a building that has been granted a low-income housing tax credit is increased and exceeds the basis at the end of the first year of the four-year credit period, the taxpayer is eligible for a credit on the excess basis. This additional credit is also taken over a four-year period beginning with the taxable year in which the increase in qualified basis occurs.

California does not incorporate a federal provision that allows low-income housing investors, for the first tax year ending after October 24, 1990, to elect to claim 150% of the low-income housing credit otherwise allowable and to accept a corresponding pro rata reduction in the low-income housing credit taken in subsequent tax years. California also does not incorporate the federal provision allowing a taxpayer to reduce the credit for the portion of the first year that the housing remains unoccupied and claim such an amount in the year following the allowable credit period.

The credit is computed on FTB 3521, which must be attached to the return. A Certificate of Final Award of California Low-Income Housing Tax

Credits (FTB 3521A) issued by the California Tax Credit Allocation Committee must be provided to the FTB upon request.

¶ 128 Adoption Costs Credit

Law: Sec. 17052.25 (CCH CALIFORNIA TAX REPORTS ¶ 15-384).

Comparable Federal: Sec. 23.

California Form: Form 540.

California provides a credit for an amount equal to 50% of the specified costs paid or incurred by a taxpayer for the adoption of any U.S. citizen or legal resident minor child who was in the custody of a state or county public agency. The credit may not exceed $2,500 per child and may be claimed only for specified costs directly related to the adoption.

The adoption cost credit may be claimed only for the taxable year in which the decree or order of adoption is entered; however, the costs that are included may have been incurred in previous taxable years. The credit may be carried over until the total credit of $2,500 is exhausted. Any personal income tax deduction for any amount paid or incurred by the taxpayer upon which the credit is based must be reduced by the amount of the adoption cost credit.

The California credit is similar to the federal tax, with the following exceptions:

(1) the amount of the California credit is lower (50% of qualifying costs v. the 100% allowed under the federal credit);

(2) the dollar cap on the California credit is lower ($2,500 per child v. the federal limit of $5,000 per child or $6,000 per special needs child);

(3) unlike the federal credit, California's credit is not phased out on the basis of the taxpayer's adjusted gross income;

(4) the expenses that may be claimed for purposes of the federal credit include any reasonable and necessary adoption fees, court costs, attorney fees, and other expenses that are directly related to the adoption proceedings; whereas California specifies that expenses include adoption fees charged by the Department of Social Services or a licensed adoption agency, travel expenses related to adoption, and unreimbursed medical fees related to adoption;

(5) California's requirements concerning the adoptive child's citizenship, residency, and custodial status do not apply for purposes of claiming the federal credit; and

(6) California's credit may be carried over until exhausted, whereas there is a five-year carryover limit on the federal credit.

¶ 129 Disabled Access Expenditures Credit

Law: Sec. 17053.42 (CCH CALIFORNIA TAX REPORTS ¶ 15-338).

Comparable Federal: Sec. 44.

. *California Form:* FTB 3548.

California allows eligible small businesses a credit in an amount equal to 50% of up to $250 of the eligible access expenditures paid or incurred by those businesses to comply with the federal Americans with Disabilities Act. Thus, a

California credit of up to $125 is allowed. Except for the credit amount, the California credit is the same as the credit allowed under federal law.

An "eligible small business" is a business that elects to claim the credit and either (1) had gross receipts (less returns and allowances) of $1,000,000 or less for the preceding taxable year or (2) had no more than 30 full-time employees during the preceding taxable year.

"Eligible access expenditures" include all reasonable amounts paid or incurred to (1) remove architectural, communication, physical, or transportation barriers that prevent a business from being accessible to, or usable by, disabled individuals, (2) provide qualified interpreters or other effective methods of making aurally delivered materials available to hearing impaired individuals, (3) provide qualified readers, taped texts, or other effective methods of making visually delivered materials available to visually impaired individuals, (4) acquire or modify equipment or devices for disabled individuals, or (5) provide other similar services, modifications, materials, or equipment. However, amounts paid or incurred in connection with any new facility first placed in service after November 5, 1990, are not eligible access expenditures.

If the credit allowable exceeds "net tax" for the year, the excess may be carried over to succeeding years until exhausted.

Any deduction allowed for the same expenditures for which the credit is claimed must be reduced by the amount of the credit. In addition, amounts for which the credit is claimed may not be used to increase the basis of the property.

¶ 130 Credit for Costs of Transporting Donated Agricultural Products

Law: Sec. 17053.12 (CCH CALIFORNIA TAX REPORTS ¶ 15-341).

Comparable Federal: None.

California Form: FTB 3547.

California allows taxpayers engaged in the business of processing, distributing, or selling agricultural products to claim a credit equal to 50% of the costs paid or incurred in connection with the transportation of agricultural products donated to nonprofit charitable organizations.

Upon the delivery of donated agricultural products by a taxpayer, the nonprofit charitable organization must provide a certificate to the taxpayer stating (1) that the products were donated in accordance with requirements specified in the Food and Agriculture Code, (2) the type and quantity of products donated, (3) the distance transported, (4) the name of the transporter, (5) the name and address of the taxpayer donor, and (6) the name and address of the donee. The certification must be provided to the Franchise Tax Board upon request.

If the credit is claimed, any deduction allowed for the same costs must be reduced by the amount of the credit allowed. Unused credit may be carried over until exhausted.

¶ 131 Credit for Cost of Joint Strike Fighter Property

Law: Sec. 17053.37 (CCH CALIFORNIA TAX REPORTS ¶ 15-390).

Comparable Federal: None.

For taxable years beginning after 2000 and before 2006, a taxpayer under an initial contract or subcontract to manufacture property for ultimate use in a Joint Strike Fighter may claim a nonrefundable credit for 10% of the qualified cost of qualified property placed in service in California. A "Joint Strike Fighter" is the next generation air combat strike aircraft being developed and produced under a multiservice, multinational project being conducted by the U.S. government.

For purposes of the credit, "qualified property" is either of the following: (1) tangible personal property that is "IRC Sec. 1245 property" used by the taxpayer primarily in the manufacturing, processing, or fabricating of a product for ultimate use in a Joint Strike Fighter; or (2) the value of any capitalized labor costs that are direct costs allocable to the construction or modification of property described in (1) above. "Qualified property" does not include any furniture, inventory, or equipment used to store finished products, or tangible personal property used for administration, general management, or marketing.

A "qualified cost" is any cost that satisfies all of the following conditions: (1) is paid or incurred by the taxpayer for the construction, reconstruction, or acquisition of qualified property after the year 2000 and before 2006; (2) is an amount upon which the taxpayer has paid sales or use tax; and (3) is properly chargeable to the taxpayer's capital account.

No credit for the cost of Joint Strike Fighter property is allowed if the manufacturer's investment credit (see ¶ 140) is claimed for the same property. Also, no credit for Joint Strike Fighter property is allowed unless it is reflected within the bid upon which the Joint Strike Fighter contract or subcontract is based. Furthermore, no credit is allowed if the qualified property is removed from California, disposed of to an unrelated party, or used for a nonqualifying purpose in the same taxable year in which the taxpayer first places the property in service in California. If qualified property is removed from California, disposed of to an unrelated party, or used for a nonqualifying purpose within one year from the date the taxpayer first places the property in service in California, the amount of the credit allowed for that property is subject to recapture.

Excess credit may be carried forward to the taxpayer's eight succeeding taxable years, if necessary, until the credit is exhausted.

¶ 132 Credit for Joint Strike Fighter Employers

Law: Sec. 17053.36 (CCH CALIFORNIA TAX REPORTS ¶ 15-390).

Comparable Federal: None.

For taxable years beginning after 2000 and before 2006, a taxpayer under an initial contract or subcontract to manufacture property for ultimate use in a Joint Strike Fighter may claim a nonrefundable credit for a percentage of qualified wages paid or incurred with respect to qualified employees. A "qualified employee" is an individual who performs services for the taxpayer in California, at least 90% of which are directly related to the taxpayer's Joint Strike Fighter contract or subcontract. See ¶ 131 for the definition of a "Joint Strike Fighter."

The credit is equal to 50% of qualified wages paid during the taxable year 2001, 40% for 2002, 30% for 2003, 20% for 2004, and 10% for 2005. However, the credit may not exceed $10,000 per year per employee (or a proportional amount for any employee who is a qualified employee for only part of the taxable year). "Qualified wages" are wages paid or incurred by the taxpayer, with respect to qualified employees, that are direct costs allocable to property manufactured by the taxpayer in California for ultimate use in a Joint Strike Fighter.

No credit is allowed unless it is reflected within the bid upon which the Joint Strike Fighter contract or subcontract is based.

Excess credit may be carried forward to the taxpayer's eight succeeding taxable years, if necessary, until the credit is exhausted.

¶ 133 Tax-Incentive Credit—Sales Tax Equivalent

> *Law:* Secs. 17053.33, 17053.45, 17053.70 (CCH CALIFORNIA TAX REPORTS ¶ 15-988, 15-979e, 15-997, 15-999c, 15-999j).
>
> *Comparable Federal:* None.
>
> *California Forms:* FTB 3805Z, FTB 3807, FTB 3809.

● *Enterprise zones*

An income-tax credit is allowed for the amount of sales or use tax paid on the purchase of machinery or parts used for specific purposes in "enterprise zones." Detailed rules are provided in the law. Designated enterprise zones are listed at ¶ 102b.

The credit applies to purchases up to a value of $1,000,000 of machinery and parts used for (1) fabricating, processing, assembling, and manufacturing, (2) production of renewable energy resources, or (3) pollution control mechanisms. Effective for taxable years beginning after 1997, the credit may also be claimed for purchases of (1) data processing and communications equipment and (2) motion picture manufacturing equipment central to production and postproduction work.

The total amount of both the enterprise zone sales and use tax credit and the enterprise zone hiring credit (see ¶ 134), including any carryover from prior years, is limited to the amount of income tax attributable to income from the enterprise zone. If the taxpayer also operates a business elsewhere, a special apportionment formula is used to determine the amount of income attributable to the zone. The amount of the taxpayer's business income attributable to California is first determined by applying the apportionment formula discussed at ¶ 1305-1308. For purposes of apportioning income to the enterprise zone, however, the sales factor is eliminated from the standard apportionment formula and the business income used in the apportionment formula is limited to California-based income rather than worldwide income.

If the credit allowable exceeds the "net tax" for the year, the excess may be carried over and applied against the tax on income from the enterprise zone in succeeding years. Any sales tax claimed as a credit on "qualified property" may not also increase the basis of such property.

The sales and use tax credit may be used to reduce an enterprise zone taxpayer's regular tax below the tentative minimum tax (see ¶ 112a).

A taxpayer may claim the credit for use tax paid on qualified property only if qualified property of a comparable quality and price is not timely available for purchase in California.

● *Local agency military base recovery areas*

A credit is also allowed for sales or use tax paid or incurred by a local agency military base recovery area (LAMBRA) business for certain property purchased for exclusive use in a recovery area. The credit is substantially similar to the sales tax equivalent credit allowed for property purchased by enterprise zone or program area businesses except that, for purposes of LAMBRA businesses, the credit applies to (1) high technology equipment; (2) aircraft maintenance equipment; (3) aircraft components; or (4) property that is depreciable under IRC Sec. 1245(a)(3).

If a taxpayer is allowed a LAMBRA credit for qualified property, the taxpayer is limited to only one credit under the Personal Income Tax Law with respect to that property. If the qualified property is disposed of, or is no longer used by, the taxpayer within the LAMBRA at any time before the close of the second taxable year after the property is placed in service or if the taxpayer has not increased the number of employees by one or more during the first two taxable years after commencing business within a LAMBRA, the credit that was allowed will be recaptured in the year of noncompliance.

The amount claimed by a taxpayer for both of the LAMBRA credits (the sales tax credit and the hiring credit) combined may not exceed the amount of tax attributable to income from the area. The special apportionment formula used for purposes of calculating the enterprise zone and targeted tax area sales and use tax credits is also used to calculate the LAMBRA credit.

● *Targeted tax area*

For taxable years beginning after 1997 and before the date a targeted tax area designation becomes inoperative, a similar credit is allowed for sales or use tax paid on the purchase of machinery and parts used for (1) fabricating, processing, assembling, and manufacturing; (2) producing renewable energy resources; (3) air or water pollution control mechanisms; (4) data processing and communications; and (5) motion picture production, to be used exclusively within the targeted tax area (discussed at ¶ 102b).

The amount that may be claimed for all of a taxpayer's targeted tax area credits combined is limited to the amount of tax that would be imposed on the taxpayer's business income attributable to the area as if that attributable income represented all of the taxpayer's income that was subject to personal income tax. If the taxpayer also operates outside that area, a special apportionment formula is used to determine the amount of income attributable to the targeted tax area. The amount of business income attributable to California is first determined by applying the apportionment formula discussed at ¶ 1305-1308. For purposes of determining the amount attributable to the

¶ 133

targeted tax area, however, the sales factor is eliminated from the standard apportionment formula and the business income used in the formula is limited to California-based income rather than worldwide income.

If a taxpayer is allowed a targeted tax area credit for qualified property, the taxpayer is limited to only one credit under the Personal Income Tax Law with respect to that property.

If the credit allowable exceeds the amount that may be claimed for the year, the excess may be carried over and added to the credit in succeeding years until the credit is exhausted.

A taxpayer who claims the credit may not also increase the basis of the qualifying property by the amount of sales tax paid or incurred.

¶ 134 Tax-Incentive Credit—Enterprise Zone Employers

Law: Sec. 17053.74 (CCH CALIFORNIA TAX REPORTS ¶ 15-983).

Comparable Federal: Sec. 1396 (CCH STANDARD FEDERAL TAX REPORTS ¶ 33,793, 33,794).

California Form: FTB 3805Z.

A tax credit is allowed to employers for a portion of "qualified wages" paid to certain "qualified employees" who are hired to work in an enterprise zone. General business deductions that are otherwise allowable for wages paid to such individuals must be reduced by the amount of any credit claimed. Detailed rules are provided in the law. Designated enterprise zones are listed at ¶ 102b.

"Qualified wages" are generally the amounts, not in excess of 150% of the minimum wage, paid to qualified disadvantaged employees. However, with respect to up to 1,350 otherwise qualified disadvantaged individuals employed in the Long Beach enterprise zone in certain aircraft manufacturing activities, "qualified wages" is expanded to include that portion of hourly wages that does not exceed 202% of the minimum wage.

An individual is a "qualified employee" if (1) 90% of the individual's services in an enterprise zone for the taxpayer during the taxable year are directly related to the conduct of the taxpayer's enterprise zone trade or business; (2) the individual performs at least 50% of his or her services for the taxpayer during the taxable year in an enterprise zone; (3) the individual was hired after designation of the area as an enterprise zone; and (4) immediately preceding the qualified employee's employment with the taxpayer, he or she was a qualified disadvantaged individual, a resident of a targeted employment area, or an employee who qualified the employer for the enterprise zone or program area hiring credits in effect prior to 1997.

A "qualified disadvantaged individual" is any of the following individuals who, immediately preceding employment with the taxpayer, was: (a) an individual who was eligible for services under the federal Job Training Partnership Act (JTPA) or its successor, who was receiving, or was eligible to receive, subsidized employment, training, or services funded by the JTPA or its successor; (b) an individual who was eligible to be a voluntary or mandatory registrant under the Greater Avenues for Independence (GAIN) Act or its successor; (c) an economically disadvantaged individual 14 years of age or older; (d) a dislocated worker; (e) a disabled individual who was eligible for, enrolled in, or had completed a state rehabilitation plan or was a service-connected disabled veteran, veteran of the Vietnam era, or veteran who was recently separated from military service; (f) an ex-offender, including an individual placed on probation without a finding of guilt; (g) a person who was eligible for, or a recipient of, benefits from certain specified public assistance programs; (h) a member of a federally recognized Indian tribe, band, or other group of Native American descent; (i) a resident of a targeted employment area; (j) an employee who qualified the employer for a hiring credit under a former enterprise zone or program area; or (k) a member of a targeted group under IRC Sec. 51(d).

The amount of the credit is 50% of "qualified wages" in the first year of employment, 40% in the second year, 30% in the third year, 20% in the fourth year, and 10% in the fifth year. For purposes of computing the credit, seasonal workers are treated as continuously employed.

The total amount of the enterprise zone hiring credit and the enterprise zone sales and use tax credit (see ¶ 133), including any carryover from prior years, is limited to the tax attributable to income from the enterprise zone. If the taxpayer also operates outside the zone area, a special apportionment formula is used to determine the amount of income attributable to the zone area. The amount of business income attributable to California is first determined by applying the standard apportionment formula discussed at ¶ 1305-1308. For purposes of determining the amount of income attributable to the enterprise zone, however, the sales factor is eliminated from the standard apportionment formula and the income used in the apportionment formula is limited to California-based income rather than worldwide income.

The credit is reduced by any credit allowed under the federal work opportunity credit. If an involved employee is terminated within a prescribed period (generally, roughly one year), any credit that was allowed is recaptured (included in income) in the year of termination. The law provides several exceptions to the operation of this recapture rule.

If the credit allowable exceeds the "net tax" for the year, the excess may be carried forward and added to the credit in succeeding years.

The hiring credit may be used to reduce an enterprise zone taxpayer's regular tax below the tentative minimum tax (see ¶ 112a).

¶ 135 Tax-Incentive Credit—Enterprise Zone Employees

Law: Sec. 17053.75 (CCH CALIFORNIA TAX REPORTS ¶ 15-984).

Comparable Federal: None.

California Form: FTB 3553.

A limited tax credit is allowed to "qualified employees" for wages received from an enterprise zone business. The amount of the credit is 5% of "qualified wages," defined as wages subject to federal unemployment insurance, up to a maximum of $525 per employee. For each dollar of income received by the taxpayer in excess of "qualified wages," the credit is reduced by nine cents. The credit is not refundable and cannot be carried forward. The amount of the credit is further limited to the amount of tax that would be imposed on income from employment in the enterprise zone, computed as though that income represented the taxpayer's entire taxable net income.

An individual is a "qualified employee" if (1) the individual is not an employee of the federal government, the State of California, or any political subdivision of the State, (2) 90% of the individual's services in an enterprise zone for the taxpayer during the taxable year are directly related to the conduct of the taxpayer's enterprise zone trade or business, and (3) the individual performs at least 50% of his or her services for the taxpayer during the taxable year in an enterprise zone.

Designated enterprise zones are listed at ¶ 102b.

¶ 136 Tax-Incentive Credit—Local Agency Military Base Recovery Area Employers

Law: Sec. 17053.46 (CCH California Tax Reports ¶ 15-999k).

Comparable Federal: None.

California Form: FTB 3807.

Local agency military base recovery area (LAMBRA) employers are allowed a credit for qualified wages paid to specified disadvantaged individuals or displaced employees. LAMBRAs are discussed at ¶ 102b. Only those employers with a net increase of one or more employees during the first two taxable years after commencing business within a LAMBRA are eligible to claim the credit. The credit that may be claimed during the first year of business operations within a LAMBRA is 50% of "qualified wages," which is defined as that portion of hourly wages that does not exceed 150% of the minimum wage established by the California Industrial Welfare Commission. For the second, third, fourth, and fifth years of operation, the credit is reduced to 40%, 30%, 20%, and 10%, respectively. For purposes of computing the credit, seasonal workers are considered continuously employed. The total amount of wages paid or incurred by a LAMBRA employer for which the credit may be claimed is limited to $2 million.

● *"Disadvantaged individual," "displaced employee" defined*

To qualify as a "displaced employee," a person must be a military base employee who was displaced as a result of a base closure. To qualify as a "disadvantaged individual" a person must be (1) determined eligible for services under the federal Job Training Partnership Act, (2) a voluntary or mandatory registrant under California's Greater Avenues for Independence Act, or (3) certified by the state Employment Development Department as eligible for the federal Targeted Jobs Tax Credit Program. Beginning with the 1999 taxable year, (3) above is replaced with the following criteria: (1) an economically disadvantaged individual age 16 years or older; (2) a dislocated worker; (3) an individual who is enrolled in or has completed a state rehabilitation plan or is a service-connected disabled veteran, veteran of the Vietnam era, or veteran who is recently separated from military service; (4) an ex-offender; (5) a recipient of specified federal, state, or local public assistance programs; or (6) a member of a federally recognized Indian tribe, band, or other group of Native American descent. A "displaced employee" or "disadvantaged individual" must also be a person hired after the area in which the person's services are performed was designated a LAMBRA, at least 90% of whose services for the employer during the taxable year were directly related to the conduct of the employer's LAMBRA business, and at least 50% of whose services for the employer during the taxable year were performed within the LAMBRA.

● *Limitations on credit, carryover of unused amounts*

If a taxpayer is allowed a LAMBRA credit for qualified wages, the taxpayer is limited to only one credit under the Personal Income Tax Law with respect to those amounts paid. The employer's wage payment credit must be reduced by the federal work opportunity credit and by the former state jobs tax credit.

The amount of credit claimed for both the LAMBRA sales tax credit (discussed at ¶ 133) and the LAMBRA credit for qualified wages may not exceed the tax that would be imposed on the income attributed to the taxpayer's business activities within a LAMBRA. If the taxpayer's business also operates outside of the LAMBRA, a special apportionment formula is used to determine the amount of income attributable to the LAMBRA. The amount of business income attributable to California is first determined by applying the standard apportionment formula discussed at ¶ 1305-1308. For purposes of determining the amount of income attributable to the LAMBRA, however, the sales factor is eliminated from the standard apportionment formula and the income used in the apportionment formula is limited to California-based income rather than worldwide income.

Unused credit may be carried over and applied to tax on income from the area in succeeding tax years until the credit is exhausted.

If an employee is terminated within a prescribed period (generally, roughly one year), any credit that was allowed is recaptured (included in income) in the year of termination. In addition, any credit claimed is recaptured in the second taxable year if the employer fails to increase its number of jobs by one or more after commencing business within the LAMBRA. The law provides several exceptions to the recapture rules.

¶ 137 Tax-Incentive Credit—Targeted Tax Area Employers

Law: Sec. 17053.34 (CCH CALIFORNIA TAX REPORTS ¶ 15-979c).

Comparable Federal: None.

California Form: FTB 3809.

For taxable years beginning after 1997, targeted tax area employers are allowed a credit for qualified wages paid qualified employees. Targeted tax areas are discussed at ¶ 102b. Only those employers involved in the following business activities described in the Standard Industrial Classification Manual (SIC Manual) are eligible to claim the targeted tax area credit: manufacturing; transportation; communications; electric, gas, and sanitary services; and wholesale trade. The credit that may be claimed for the first year of employment is 50% of "qualified wages," which is defined as that portion of hourly wages that does not exceed 150% of the minimum wage established by the California Industrial Welfare Commission. For the second, third, fourth, and fifth years of operation, the credit is reduced to 40%, 30%, 20%, and 10%, respectively. For purposes of computing the credit, seasonal workers are considered continuously employed.

● *Qualified employee*

An individual is a "qualified employee" if (1) he or she was hired after designation of the area as a targeted tax area; (2) 90% of the individual's services for the employer during the taxable year are directly related to the conduct of the employer's trade or business located in the targeted tax area; (3) the individual performs at least 50% of his or her services for the taxpayer during the taxable year in a targeted tax area; and (4) the individual is, or immediately preceding employment with the taxpayer was, any of the following:

(a) eligible for services under the federal Job Training Partnership Act (JTPA) or its successor, who was receiving, or was eligible to receive, subsidized employment, training, or services funded by the JTPA or its successor;

(b) eligible to be a voluntary or mandatory registrant under the Greater Avenues for Independence (GAIN) Act or its successor;

(c) an economically disadvantaged individual 14 years of age or older;

(d) a qualifying dislocated worker;

(e) a disabled individual eligible for, enrolled in, or having completed a state rehabilitation plan, or a service-connected disabled veteran, a veteran of the Vietnam era, or a veteran recently separated from military service;

(f) an ex-offender, including an individual placed on probation without a finding of guilt;

(g) a person who was eligible for, or a recipient of, benefits from certain specified public assistance programs;

(h) a member of a federally recognized Indian tribe, band, or other group of Native American descent;

(i) a resident of a targeted tax area; or

(j) a member of a targeted tax group for purposes of the federal Work Opportunity Credit, or its successor.

● *Limitations and carryovers*

The total amount of the targeted tax area hiring credit and the targeted tax area sales and use tax credit (see ¶ 133), including any carryover from prior years, is limited to the tax attributable to income from the area. If the taxpayer also operates outside the targeted tax area, a special apportionment formula is used to determine the amount of income attributable to the area. The amount of business income attributable to California is first determined by applying the standard apportionment formula discussed at ¶ 1305-1308. For purposes of determining the amount of income attributable to the targeted tax area, however, the sales factor is eliminated from the standard apportionment formula and the income used in the apportionment formula is limited to California-based income rather than worldwide income.

If an employee is terminated within a prescribed period (generally, roughly one year), any credit that was allowed with respect to that employee is recaptured (included in income) in the year of termination. The law provides several exceptions to the operation of this recapture rule.

If the amount of the credit exceeds the employer's tax for the taxable year, the excess may be carried over to succeeding taxable years until exhausted.

¶ 138 Tax-Incentive Credit—Manufacturing Enhancement Area Employers

Law: Sec. 17053.47 (CCH CALIFORNIA TAX REPORTS ¶ 15-978c).

Comparable Federal: None.

California Form: FTB 3808.

For taxable years beginning after 1997, manufacturing enhancement area employers are allowed a credit for qualified wages paid to specified disadvantaged individuals or displaced employees. Manufacturing enhancement areas are discussed at ¶ 102b. Only those employers involved in certain business activities as described in Codes 2011 to 3999 of the Standard Industrial Classification Manual (SIC Manual) are eligible to claim the manufacturing enhancement area credits. The credit that may be claimed for the first year of employment is 50% of "qualified wages," which is defined as that portion of hourly wages that does not exceed 150% of the minimum wage established by the California Industrial Welfare Commission. For the second, third, fourth, and fifth years of employment, the credit is reduced to 40%, 30%, 20%, and 10%, respectively. For purposes of computing the credit, seasonal workers are considered continuously employed. The total amount of wages that may be taken into account for purposes of claiming the credit may not exceed $2 million per taxable year.

● *"Qualified taxpayer" and "qualified disadvantaged individual" defined*

A "qualified taxpayer" is a taxpayer engaged in a manufacturing trade or business within the area that, once the area has been designated as a manufacturing enhancement area, hires at least 50% of the business' employees from the county in which the area is located, 30% of whom are qualified disadvantaged individuals.

An individual is a "qualified disadvantaged individual" if (1) he or she was hired after designation of the area as a manufacturing enhancement area; (2) 90% of the individual's services for the employer during the taxable year are directly related to the conduct of the employer's trade or business located in the manufacturing enhancement area; (3) the individual performs at least 50%of his or her services for the taxpayer during the taxable year in a manufacturing enhancement area; and (4) immediately preceding employment with the taxpayer, the individual was any of the following:

(a) determined eligible for services under the federal Job Training Partnership Act (JTPA) or any successor program;

(b) a voluntary or mandatory registrant under the Greater Avenues for Independence (GAIN) Act or any successor program; or

(c) certified eligible by the Employment Development Department under the Targeted Jobs Tax Credit Program or any successor program, whether or not the program is in effect.

● *Limitations and carryovers*

The total amount of the credit, including any carryover from prior years, is limited to the tax attributable to income from the manufacturing enhancement area. If the taxpayer also operates outside the area, a special apportionment formula is used to determine the amount of income attributable to the area. The amount of business income attributable to California is first determined by applying the apportionment formula discussed at ¶ 1305-1308. For purposes of determining the amount of income attributable to the manufacturing enhancement area, however, the sales factor is eliminated from the standard apportionment formula and the income used in the apportionment formula is limited to California-based income rather than worldwide income.

The credit is reduced by the amount of any federal work opportunity credit allowed for the same wages. If an employee is terminated within a prescribed period (generally, roughly one year), any credit that was allowed with respect to that employee is recaptured (included in income) in the year of termination. The law provides several exceptions to the operation of this recapture rule.

If the amount of the credit exceeds the employer's tax for the taxable year, the excess may be carried over to succeeding taxable years until exhausted.

¶ 139 Research and Development Credit

Law: Sec. 17052.12 (CCH CALIFORNIA TAX REPORTS ¶ 15-312).

Comparable Federal: Sec. 41 (CCH STANDARD FEDERAL TAX REPORTS ¶ 4350).

California Form: FTB 3523.

California provides a credit for increased research expenditures that is similar to that provided by federal law with the exceptions noted below.

(1) The applicable California percentage is 12% (11% for taxable years beginning before 1999) of the excess of qualified research expenses for the tax

year over a specified percentage of the taxpayer's average annual gross receipts for the four preceding taxable years (the "base amount"). The federal percentage is 20% of the excess of qualified expenses over the base amount. Also, under both California and federal law, taxpayers may elect to use an alternative method of computing the credit that uses reduced credit rates and fixed-base percentages. However, as under the standard computation method, California substitutes lower credit amounts for the federal amounts under the alternative method. California uses 1.32%, 1.76%, and 2.20% for the three tiers used to compute the amount of the credit under the alternative method. The federal percentages are 1.65%, 2.20%, and 2.75%.

(2) California does not allow a credit against personal income tax for basic research payments. Under federal law, a credit equal to 20% of basic research payments is allowed.

(3) Research must be conducted in California to qualify for the California credit. Federal law provides that research must be conducted in the United States.

(4) The California credit may be carried over. The federal credit is part of the general business credit subject to the limitations imposed by IRC Sec. 38.

(5) The California credit applies to expenses paid or incurred in taxable years beginning after 1986 and is available indefinitely thereafter, whereas the federal credit does not apply to amounts paid or incurred after June 30, 1995, and before July 1, 1996, or after June 30, 1999.

(6) For purposes of determining the base amount under California law, only the gross receipts from the sale of property that is held primarily for sale to customers in the ordinary course of the taxpayer's trade or business and delivered or shipped to a purchaser within California, regardless of F.O.B point or other conditions of sale, may be taken into account.

(7) California law, but not federal law, disallows the credit for expenses incurred to purchase property for which a sales and use tax exemption for teleproduction or other postproduction property is claimed (see ¶ 1504).

● *Special rules for start-up companies*

California conforms to federal law providing special rules to determine the fixed-base percentage used in determining the amount of the credit that may be claimed by start-up companies.

● *Interaction with research deduction*

For both California and federal purposes, taxpayers do not have the option of electing to forego the research and development credit. Accordingly, taxpayers may not avoid the reduction in the research expense deduction that is required whenever the research expense credit is claimed; see ¶ 319, ¶ 322.

¶ 140 Manufacturer's Investment Credit

Law: Sec. 17053.49 (CCH CALIFORNIA TAX REPORTS ¶ 15-315).

Comparable Federal: None.

California Form: FTB 3535.

California allows qualified taxpayers to claim a credit against net tax in an amount equal to 6% of the qualified cost incurred after 1993 for construction, reconstruction, acquisition, or lease of qualified property that is placed in service in California.

A "qualified cost" is generally an amount upon which the taxpayer has paid sales or use tax and that is properly chargeable to the taxpayer's capital account. In the case of leased property, the credit is computed on the basis of the original cost to the lessor. Qualified costs also include the value of any capitalized labor costs that are directly allocable to the construction or modification of qualified property even though sales and use tax is not paid for such services. In Legal Ruling 98-1 (1998) (CCH CALIFORNIA TAX REPORTS ¶ 15-315.25), the Franchise Tax Board announced that capitalized costs of labor paid or incurred by a qualified taxpayer for engineering and design services are qualified costs for purposes of the manufacturer's investment credit only if under the taxpayer's normal method of accounting they would be properly treated as direct costs of labor capitalized to an item of qualified property, pursuant to IRC Sec. 263A.

"Qualified property" generally means tangible personal property that is depreciable IRC Sec. 1245 property or computer software used primarily in specified manufacturing, research, pollution control, or recycling activities or in maintaining, repairing, measuring, or testing property used in such activities. For those taxpayers involved in specified manufacturing, biotech, or biopharmaceutical activities, or for property placed in service after 1995, space vehicle, satellite, or communication activities, "qualified property" also includes special purpose buildings and foundations that are constructed or modified for use primarily in a manufacturing, processing, refining, or fabricating process or as a research or storage facility used in connection with such a process. Taxpayers involved in activities related to semiconductor equipment manufacturing may also claim the credit for costs related to such special purpose buildings and foundations for property placed in service after 1996. In addition, for taxable years beginning after 1997, taxpayers engaged in computer programming services, prepackaged software design, and computer integrated systems design may claim the credit for purchases of computers and computer peripheral equipment used primarily to develop or manufacture prepackaged software or specified custom software.

In addition to those specifically discussed above, "qualified taxpayers" are persons engaged in certain categories of business described in the federal Standard Industrial Classification Manual, 1987 edition.

Unused credit may be carried forward for eight years. However, in the case of a "small business" (with gross receipts or net assets of less than $50 million or a total credit of less than $1 million for the tax year), the carryover period is 10 years. For taxable years beginning after 1996, the 10-year carryover period is also available to taxpayers engaged in certain biopharmaceutical or biotechnology activities if the taxpayers have not received U.S. Food and Drug Administration approval for any product.

⚌ CCH Example: Credit Carryforward for Small Business

Assume that as of the last day of the 1999 taxable year, a qualified taxpayer is a "small business" for purposes of the manufacturer's investment credit. During the 1999 taxable year, the taxpayer purchased qualified property for $500, entitling the taxpayer to a $30 credit. However, the taxpayer's entire $30 credit exceeds the taxpayer's net tax for 1999, requiring the taxpayer to carry forward the entire credit to succeeding taxable years. The taxpayer is entitled to carry forward the credit to each of its 10 succeeding taxable years, if necessary, until the credit is exhausted, regardless of whether the taxpayer is a small business in any of its succeeding taxable years.

If the property is removed from the state, disposed of to an unrelated party, or used for a purpose not qualifying for the credit within one year of the date the property is first placed in service in California, the credit will be recaptured by adding the credit amount to the net tax of the taxpayer. Also, no credit is allowed for any property for which the former Los Angeles Revitalization Zone sales and use tax credit was claimed or for which a sales and use tax exemption or refund claim was allowed (see ¶ 1504).

The cost basis of the property is not reduced by the amount of the credit.

¶ 141 Credit for Prior Year Minimum Tax

Law: Sec. 17063 (CCH CALIFORNIA TAX REPORTS ¶ 15-155).

Comparable Federal: Sec. 53 (CCH STANDARD FEDERAL TAX REPORTS ¶ 5002).

California Form: FTB 3510.

California allows a credit in the form of a carryover to taxpayers who have incurred California alternative minimum tax in prior years but not in the current tax year.

The credit is computed in the same manner as the federal credit under IRC Sec. 53 ("credit for prior year minimum tax") with the substitution of certain California figures in place of the federal. Both the federal and California credits are based on the amount of alternative minimum tax paid on "deferral preferences" (items that defer tax liability) as distinct from "exclusion items" (items that permanently reduce tax liability).

The credit is computed on FTB 3510, and for a taxpayer claiming this credit for the first time, most of the figures needed for the computation come from Schedule P (540) of the prior year's California personal income tax return. The credit may not exceed the excess of (1) the regular tax reduced by all credits except refundable credits without carryover provisions, the portion of any credit that reduces the tax below the tentative minimum tax, and the portion of any credit that reduces the alternative minimum tax, over (2) the tentative minimum tax for the taxable year (see ¶ 112a). Unused credit may be carried forward indefinitely.

● *Nonresidents and part-year residents*

Nonresidents and part-year residents prorate the credit according to the ratio of (a) California-source alternative adjusted gross income to (b) total alternative minimum adjusted gross income. This ratio is computed on FTB 3510.

Unused credits may be carried forward indefinitely.

¶ 142 Enhanced Oil Recovery Credit

Law: Sec. 17052.8 (CCH CALIFORNIA TAX REPORTS ¶ 15-335).

Comparable Federal: Sec. 43 (CCH STANDARD FEDERAL TAX REPORTS, ¶ 4,387).

California Form: FTB 3546.

California allows certain independent oil producers a credit equal to 1/3 of the enhanced oil recovery credit allowed under federal law. Thus, a California credit is allowed in an amount equal to up to 5% of the taxpayer's qualified costs attributable to qualified enhanced oil recovery projects. However, California modifies the federal definition of "qualified enhanced oil recovery project" to include only projects located within California.

The credit is not available to certain retailers, refiners, and related persons who are not eligible for the percentage depletion specifically allowed to independent producers and royalty owners.

If a taxpayer elects under federal law not to have the credit apply, the election is binding and irrevocable for California purposes. Also, if the taxpayer's costs qualify for another credit, the taxpayer must make an election between credits.

No deduction is allowed for costs for which the credit is allowed. Also, the basis of any property for which a credit is allowed must be reduced by the amount of the credit attributable to the property.

Any amount of the credit exceeding "net tax" for the taxable year may be carried forward for up to 15 years.

¶ 143 Prison Inmate Labor Credit

Law: Sec. 17053.6 (CCH CALIFORNIA TAX REPORTS ¶ 15-382).

Comparable Federal: None.

California Form: FTB 3507.

California allows a credit equal to 10% of the wages paid to prison inmates employed under a prisoner employment joint venture agreement with the Director of Corrections. The credit is in addition to any other deduction to which the employer is entitled. There is no carryover allowed for unused credits.

¶ 144 Rice Straw Credit

Law: Sec. 17052.10 (CCH California Tax Reports ¶ 15-344).

Comparable Federal: None.

California Forms: Form 540, Sch. P (540).

For taxable years beginning after 1996 and before 2008, California allows a credit equal to $15 for each ton of California-grown rice straw purchased during the taxable year.

To qualify for the credit, a taxpayer must (1) request certification from the Department of Food and Agriculture, providing all documents necessary to verify that the purchase qualifies for the credit, (2) retain a copy of the certification, and (3) provide a copy of the certification to the Franchise Tax Board upon request.

The credit will be allowed only if the purchaser is an "end user" of the rice straw. An "end user" is anyone who uses rice straw for processing, the generation of energy, manufacturing, export, the prevention of erosion, or any other purpose other than open burning that consumes the rice straw.

No deduction will be allowed for the purchase of rice straw for which a credit is claimed. Unused credit may be carried forward for up to ten years.

¶ 145 Community Development Investment Credit

Law: Sec. 17053.57 (CCH California Tax Reports ¶ 15-388).

Comparable Federal: Sec. 38.

California Forms: Form 540, Sch. P (540).

For taxable years beginning after 1996 and before 2002, a nonrefundable credit is available in an amount equal to 20% of each qualified deposit made into a community development financial institution. However, the amount that may be claimed by a taxpayer is limited to the amount certified by the California Organized Investment Network (COIN).

A "community development financial institution" (CDFI) is a private financial institution located in California that (1) is certified by COIN, (2) has community development as its primary mission, and (3) makes loans in California urban, rural, or reservation-based communities.

A "qualified deposit" is a deposit that does not earn interest, or an equity investment, of $50,000 or more. The deposit/investment must be made for at least 60 months. If the qualified deposit is withdrawn before the end of the 60-month period and not redeposited or reinvested in another CDFI within 60 days, the entire amount of any credit previously claimed is subject to recapture. If a taxpayer reduces the amount on deposit before the end of the 60-month period, but does not reduce the amount below $50,000, an amount equal to 20% of the total reduction will be recaptured.

Unused credit may be carried forward for the next four taxable years.

CHAPTER 2

PERSONAL INCOME TAX
GROSS INCOME

¶ 201 Gross Income—In General

> *Law:* Secs. 17071, 17081, 17083, 17087, 17091, 17131-36, 17141, 17147.7, 17151, 17153.5, 17154 (CCH California Tax Reports ¶ 15-401, 15-465, 15-468, 15-469, 15-470b, 15-484, 15-511, 15-517, 15-533, 15-539, 15-546, 15-598, 15-626, 15-630, 15-638).
>
> *Comparable Federal:* Secs. 61, 62, 84-86, 88, 90, 120, 125-27, 129-132, 136, 865(b) (CCH Standard Federal Tax Reports ¶ 5502, 6400, 6410, 6420, 6470, 7240, 7320, 7330, 7350, 7380, 7420, 12,691, 27,040).
>
> *California Forms:* Sch. CA (540), Sch. D, Sch. D-1, Sch. CA (540NR), FTB 3805Z, FTB 3806.

California conforms, as a general rule, to most of the federal provisions concerning gross income as of the current IRC tie-in date (see ¶ 102a). The following paragraphs will detail the California-federal differences as to what is included in gross income for the 1999 taxable year.

"Gross income" is broadly defined to include income derived from any source whatever, except as otherwise specifically provided by statute. The California law incorporates the federal definition by reference. This means that the same items are included under both laws, unless a specific exception is spelled out. However, even if an item is included in both California and federal gross income, the amounts to be included may differ because of prior law or other differences. The following list highlights differences in California and federal gross income that should be reported on Sch. CA (540) or Sch. CA (540NR) (other relevant forms are indicated):

1. California does not include in income the following benefits, which are taxed to some extent under federal law: social security, unemployment, and railroad retirement benefits, which include pensions, ridesharing benefits, and sick pay.

2. Income from certain annuities and pension and profit-sharing plans—see ¶ 205 and ¶ 206.

3. Taxable and nontaxable interest—see ¶ 217.

4. Nonresident's military compensation attributable to resident spouse—see ¶ 224.

5. Dividends and other corporate distributions—see ¶ 225.

6. Patronage allocations from cooperatives—see ¶ 231.

7. Sales and exchanges (Sch. D, Sch. D-1, Sch. D (541))—see ¶ 228 and Chapter 5.

8. Income of nonresidents (Form 540NR, Sch. CA (540NR))—see ¶ 230.

9. Except for the treatment of certain sales of unprocessed timber, California does not follow the special federal provisions for Domestic International Sales Corporations (DISCs), personal holding companies, foreign investment companies, foreign trusts, etc.

10. California qualified stock options—see ¶ 207.

11. Income from investments in depressed areas (FTB 3805Z and FTB 3806)—see ¶ 239.

12. Compensation received by an employee for participating in a ridesharing arrangement, including free or subsidized parking, monthly transit passes; for commuting in a carpool, a vanpool, a private commuter bus or buspool, a ferry, or a subscription taxipool; or for bicycling to or from work, traveling to or from a telecommuting facility, or using any other alternative transportation method—see ¶ 240.

13. Income from original issue discount (OID) on debt instruments issued in 1985 or 1986—see ¶ 236.

14. California provides an exclusion for income derived from an obligation of a Community Energy Authority under certain provisions of the California Government Code.

15. Winnings from the California lottery are exempt from California tax. Such winnings are subject to federal tax as wagering gains, except to the extent that they may be offset by wagering losses—see ¶ 307.

However, income taxes are imposed on the income that retailers realize on the sale of lottery tickets. This also includes extra cash bonuses that the Lottery Commission pays to lottery game retailers, according to percentages of lottery prizes, because they are compensation for the sale of lottery tickets (Letter, Franchise Tax Board, CCH CALIFORNIA TAX REPORTS ¶ 15-441.40).

16. Any amount received by the consumer for recycling empty beverage containers is exempt from the California tax.

17. Certain water conservation rebates are treated as refunds or price adjustments rather than as income—see ¶ 243.

18. Rewards received from a government authorized crime hotline—see ¶ 245.

19. Certain compensation received by Holocaust and internment victims—see ¶ 247.

¶ 202 Definition of "Adjusted Gross Income"

> *Law:* Sec. 17072 (CCH CALIFORNIA TAX REPORTS ¶ 15-417).
>
> *Comparable Federal:* Secs. 62, 162 (CCH STANDARD FEDERAL TAX REPORTS ¶ 6002, 8001).

The California definition of "adjusted gross income" incorporates the federal definition as of a fixed date (see ¶ 102a), except as otherwise provided. The exceptions are noted in the following paragraphs.

¶ 203 Taxable Income

> *Law:* Secs. 17073, 17073.5 (CCH CALIFORNIA TAX REPORTS ¶ 15-420, 15-704).
>
> *Comparable Federal:* Sec. 63 (CCH STANDARD FEDERAL TAX REPORTS ¶ 6020).

The federal law defining "taxable income" is incorporated in the California law by reference. With the exceptions listed below, California law is the same as federal as of the current IRC tie-in date (see ¶ 102a).

1. California allows no deduction for personal exemptions.

2. California standard deduction amounts are different from the federal (see ¶ 321).

3. California has not adopted the federal additional standard deductions for aged and blind individuals (see ¶ 321). However, California provides additional personal exemption credits for such taxpayers (see ¶ 109).

Taking into account these differences, California "taxable income" may be defined briefly as adjusted gross income reduced either by the standard deduction or by itemized deductions.

¶ 204 Alimony

> *Law:* Sec. 17081 (CCH CALIFORNIA TAX REPORTS ¶ 15-431).
>
> *Comparable Federal:* Sec. 71 (CCH STANDARD FEDERAL TAX REPORTS ¶ 6090).
>
> *California Form:* Sch. CA (540).

California law is the same as federal law as of the current IRC tie-in date (see ¶ 102a), except with respect to alimony received by a nonresident alien. Generally, alimony and separate maintenance payments received pursuant to a divorce, dissolution, or legal separation are taxable to the spouse who receives the payments. Any amount received for support of minor children is not taxable.

Alimony paid by a California resident to a nonresident is not taxable to the recipient (see ¶ 313). Alimony paid either by a nonresident or by a part-year resident during a period of nonresidence is not deductible by the payor (but see ¶ 313, ¶ 323).

In *Appeal of Sara J. Palevsky* (1979) (CCH CALIFORNIA TAX REPORTS ¶ 15-431.175), the State Board of Equalization held that certain payments received under a property settlement agreement were fully taxable, despite the fact that the payor spouse had agreed to claim an income tax deduction for only two-thirds of the payments.

¶ 205 Annuities

> *Law:* Secs. 17081, 17085, 17131 (CCH CALIFORNIA TAX REPORTS ¶ 15-435, 15-471, 15-480).
>
> *Comparable Federal:* Secs. 72, 122 (CCH STANDARD FEDERAL TAX REPORTS ¶ 6100, 7280).

California law is substantially the same as federal. The law provides, in general, that amounts paid under an annuity contract must be included in gross income. However, amounts representing a return of capital may be excluded. The excludable portion is determined by dividing the cost of the annuity by the expected return and multiplying the result by the annuity payment received. The three-year basis recovery provision repealed under federal law for individuals with annuity starting dates after July 1, 1986 (former IRC Sec. 72(d)), was repealed for California purposes for individuals who have an annuity starting date after December 31, 1986 (or for individuals who elect out of using the three-year rule who have an annuity starting date after July 1, 1986, and before 1987). Detailed rules are provided for various special situations.

The Small Business Job Protection Act of 1996 added a simplified alternative method for determining the portion of an annuity payment from a qualified employer retirement plan that represents a nontaxable return of basis. Under the simplified method, the portion of each annuity payment that represents a nontaxable return of basis is generally equal to the employee's total investment in the contract as of the annuity starting date divided by the number of anticipated payments. The anticipated payments are determined by reference to a statutory table that lists various ages and the corresponding anticipated number of payments. The simplified method of taxing annuity distributions may be used for federal purposes in cases where the annuity starting date is after November 18, 1996, and for California tax purposes in taxable years beginning after 1996.

See ¶ 215 for a discussion of the rules applicable when an annuity is transferred for consideration.

● *Self-employed retirement plans, IRAs*

For discussion of treatment of annuities or other payments received under a self-employed retirement plan or an individual retirement account, see ¶ 206.

● *Annuites received under Railroad Retirement Act*

Annuity or pension payments received under the federal Railroad Retirement Act are exempt from California tax.

● *Inherited annuity*

See ¶ 405 for discussion of the *Kelsey* case, where annuity income earned by a decedent outside California was taxed to a survivor under the rules for income from annuities, although the income was classified as "income in respect of a decedent" and could not have been taxed to the decedent if he had become a California resident.

● *Annuities held by non-natural persons*

Annuities held by partnerships, trusts, and other non-natural persons are not entitled to the same preferential treatment as are annuities held by individuals. Instead, tax is imposed on the excess of (1) the sum of the net surrender value of the contract at the end of the tax year plus any amounts distributed under the contract to date, over (2) the investment in the contract (the aggregate amount of premiums paid under the contract minus policy-holder dividends or the aggregate amounts received under the contract that have not been included in income). This special rule applies for both California and federal purposes with respect to amounts invested in annuity contracts after February 28, 1986.

¶ 206 Income from Pension and Profit-Sharing Plans

> *Law:* Secs. 17085, 17501, 17504, 17506, 17507, 17507.6, 23712 (CCH CALIFORNIA TAX REPORTS ¶ 16-105, 16-109, 16-114, 16-118, 16-119, 16-119A, 16-127).
>
> *Comparable Federal:* Secs. 72, 401, 402-03, 408, 408A, 530 (CCH STANDARD FEDERAL TAX REPORTS ¶ 6100, 17,733, 18,207, 18,902).
>
> *California Forms:* Sch. G-1, FTB 3805P, FTB Pub. 1005.

The general plan of taxing income from pension and profit-sharing plans is the same under California and federal laws. There are, however, significant differences in the taxation of distributions depending on when the contributions giving rise to the distributions were made (see the summaries below). California conformed for post-1986 tax years to the extensive changes in the federal law applicable to tax years beginning after 1986 and to technical changes made by the Tax Reform Act of 1986. In 1989, California conformed to the several changes made by the federal Technical and Miscellaneous Revenue Act of 1988 in the distribution rules, the basis recovery rules, the nondiscrimination rules, and the provisions affecting rollovers. In 1990, California incorporated several amendments made by the Revenue Reconciliation Act of 1989, including changes in the rules relating to elective deferrals and to transfers of interests in individual retirement accounts (IRAs), government plans, and church plans as a result of domestic relations orders. For taxable years beginning after 1992, California incorporated changes made in the federal law by the Unemployment Compensation Amendments of 1992 that liberalize the rules governing rollovers.

For taxable years beginning after 1996, California conformed to an amendment made by the Health Insurance Portability and Accountability Act of 1996 concerning premature distributions from individual retirement plans when the distributions are used to pay medical expenses. For taxable years beginning after 1996, California conformed to amendments made by the Small Business Job Protection Act of 1996 that (1) authorize Savings Incentive Match Plans for Employees (SIMPLEs), (2) repeal certain aggregation rules for pension plans benefitting owner-employees, (3) allow foreign situs trusts to be treated as qualified pension plans, (4) modify the minimum participation standards for pension plans, and (5) make other changes concerning pension simplification. California also incorporated changes made by the Taxpayer Relief Act of 1997 concerning IRAs, including provisions authorizing "Roth IRAs" and Education IRAs (see ¶ 318 as well as discussion below). California also incorporates other Taxpayer Relief Act amendments effective for taxable years beginning after 1997, including those concerning pension plans of irrigation companies that are government entities; employee stock ownership plans provided by S corporations; deduction limitations for SIMPLEs; qualification requirements for pension, profit-sharing, and stock bonus plans; an increase in the full funding percentage and amortization period for defined benefit pension plans; and limits on elective contributions to IRC Sec. 401(k) plans for self-employed persons. Finally, effective for taxable years beginning after 1997, California adopts amendments made by the IRS Restructuring and Reform Act of 1998 that include clarifications regarding Roth IRAs (see discussion below and at ¶ 318).

Generally, both California and federal laws tax benefits received under qualified pension or profit-sharing plans to the employee only when actually distributed to the employee. Such distributions are usually taxed as though they were an annuity, under the rules set forth in ¶ 205, the consideration for which is the amount (if any) contributed by the employee under the plan. Certain nonforfeitable rights to receive annuities are taxed in the year in which the employer pays for the annuity contract. Certain lump-sum distributions are subject to special treatment; as explained below. See also ¶ 318.

Qualifed retirement income received after 1995 by a former California resident is not taxable by California. See ¶ 405 for a more detailed discussion.

● *Special rules for some organizations*

Special rules are provided for the taxation of employee annuities where the employer is a tax-exempt charitable-type organization or school, where the plan is not subject to the rules discussed above. Such annuities are only partially taxable, under a formula providing for an "exclusion allowance." The California rules are the same as the federal.

● *Nonqualified plans*

Both California and federal laws provide special rules for taxing the beneficiary of a *nonqualified* employee pension or profit-sharing plan or annuity, in cases where the employee's rights are forfeitable at the time the employer's contribution is made. The general effect is to tax the employee in the year the employee's rights are no longer subject to a substantial risk of forfeiture.

● *Lump-sum distributions*

If an employee's benefits are paid in one taxable year of the employee because of death or termination of employment, the taxable amount is subject to special treatment as a "lump-sum distribution." The taxable amount is the total distribution less (1) employee contributions and (2) any unrealized appreciation on employer securities included in the distribution.

Both California and federal law have eliminated capital gain treatment for lump-sum distributions made after 1986 that are at least partly attributable to pre-1974 participation in a qualified pension plan. However, a taxpayer who reached age 50 before 1986 may elect to apply an exception that allows capital gain treatment.

For tax years beginning before 2000, both California and federal law allow five-year averaging for a single lump-sum distribution received by an individual who has attained the age of 59½. An amendment made by the Small Business Job Protection Act of 1996, which is incorporated by California, repeals the five-year averaging method for tax years beginning after 1999. Prior law rules applicable to individuals who attained age 50 before 1986 remain in effect.

● *Self-employed plans*

For purposes of both federal law and California law, the rules for self-employed plans are generally the same as for employee plans, as set forth above. However, there will be differences in the *amounts* taxable in California and federal returns because of differences in the deductibility of contributions in prior years. As explained at ¶ 318, for pre-1987 tax years, California allowed smaller deductions than federal. Also, the interest element in the redemption of certain federal retirement bonds issued before 1984 was recoverable tax-free for California purposes.

The difference between allowable California and federal contributions is recoverable free of California tax. See below for summary of amounts recoverable tax-free.

As to the *timing* of the tax-free recovery, where distributions are received over a period of years, it has been the Franchise Tax Board's (FTB) policy to treat the amounts involved as part of the "investment in the contract" that is recoverable tax-free under the annuity rules.

For a discussion of the taxability of distributions from self-employed plans when the taxpayer's status changed from resident to nonresident, or vice-versa, see ¶ 405.

● *Individual retirement accounts*

The California treatment of distributions from IRAs is the same as the federal, except that California permits tax-free recovery of the following:

1. Contributions that were not allowed as California deductions.

2. Interest earned in 1975 or 1976 on a 1975 contribution, as explained below.

As to the *timing* of the tax-free recovery of amounts contributed prior to 1987, the amount of contributions not allowed as California deductions is considered to be the cost basis of the IRA account and no income is reportable for California purposes until the basis is recovered. Each year, the amount reportable federally is reduced for California purposes by California basis until such basis is recovered.

As for the recovery of post-1986 contributions, or at the election of the taxpayer, contributions made after July 1, 1986, the federal annuity rule is adopted in California and the portion of each distribution recognized federally is recognized for California purposes. Under this rule, the amount invested is recovered ratably, depending on the period of expected return.

Tax-free basis of IRA account of taxpayers who have changed residency: As to a taxpayer who was a nonresident when making contributions to an IRA but is a resident when receiving distributions, the tax-free basis of the account consists of the total of (1) contributions not allowed as a deduction for California and (2) the earnings on the IRA while a nonresident of California, minus federal nondeductible contributions (federal basis) (FTB Pub. 1005).

● *1975 contribution to IRA*

For California tax purposes, any 1975 contribution to an IRA is treated, in effect, as a separate grantor trust. Any interest earned on a 1975 contribution in 1975 or 1976 was subject to California tax as earned, and of course will not be subject to California tax when it is distributed at a later time. However, as a result of 1977 legislation, any income earned after 1976 on a 1975 contribution is not taxable until it is distributed. So far as contributions to the account for years subsequent to 1975 are concerned, the account automatically qualifies under California law even though it was established before the California law providing for IRAs was enacted.

● *Roth IRAs*

As explained in further detail at ¶ 318, both California and federal law recognize a "Roth IRA'" for tax years beginning after 1997. For both California and federal purposes, earnings from a Roth IRA are tax-free and qualified distributions are not included in gross income or subject to a penalty on early withdrawals.

Under both California and federal law, if an individual converts or rolls over a distribution from a regular IRA to a Roth IRA in 1998 and the individual's adjusted gross income does not exceed $100,000, the amount taxable as a distribution from the regular IRA is spread ratably over a four-year period, unless the individual elects to recognize all such income in the year of conversion.

In Legal Ruling 98-3 (CCH CALIFORNIA TAX REPORTS ¶ 16-118.20), the FTB discusses what portion of a distribution from a regular IRA that is rolled over to a Roth IRA during 1998 is subject to California personal income tax if an individual changes from resident to nonresident, or vice versa, during the four taxable years over which the income is spread. In general, the individual must include in gross income the ratable portion of the distribution for the periods during which the individual is a California resident.

CCH **CCH Example: Distribution After Change in Residency**

Karen, a California resident, rolls over a distribution from a regular IRA to a Roth IRA in 1998. The amount of the distribution that must be included in gross income is spread ratably over four years. During the second year of the four-year period, Karen becomes a California nonresident. Karen must include in California adjusted gross income only the portion of the distribution reportable under the four-year rule before she became a nonresident. For the taxable year of the distribution, the includible amount would simply be one-fourth of the taxable distribution. However, for the year of the change in residency, the includible amount would be one-fourth of the taxable distribution multiplied by a fraction, the numerator of

> which is the number of days in the year in which Karen was a California resident and the denominator of which is the total number of days in the taxable year.

● *Education IRAs*

As explained in further detail at ¶ 318, taxpayers with modified adjusted gross income below certain levels may contribute up to $500 per child per year to an education IRA, effective for both California and federal purposes for tax years beginning after 1997. Earnings on contributions will be distributed tax-free provided that they are used to pay the child's post-secondary education expenses.

● *Income attributable to nondeductible contributions to traditional IRAs*

As explained at ¶ 318, California law provides that any income attributable to the nondeductible portion of contributions to traditional IRAs is not taxable to the beneficiary until the income is distributed.

● *Simplified employee pension (SEP) plans*

As explained at ¶ 318, California law conforms generally to federal law permitting employer contributions to an employee's individual retirement plan through a "simplified employee pension" (SEP) plan. The employer's contributions to the employee's SEP-IRA are excluded from the employee's gross income. The employee's contributions to the SEP-IRA are separate and apart from the employer's contributions and may be deducted from the employee's gross income in the same manner, and to the same extent, as any IRA contribution (see ¶ 318). SEP distributions are subject to tax on the basis of the same rules that apply to distributions from an IRA (see above).

● *Savings incentive match plans for employees (SIMPLE plans)*

Certain small employers may establish SIMPLE plans structured as IRAs or as qualified cash or deferred arrangements. Employees are not taxed on account assets until distributions are made, and employers generally may deduct contributions to such plans. SIMPLE plans are not subject to nondiscrimination rules or some of the other complex requirements applicable to qualified plans.

● *Summary of amounts recoverable free of California tax*

SELF-EMPLOYED PLANS

1963-1970: All 1963-1970 contributions recoverable tax-free (no California deduction).

1971-1973: No 1971-1973 contributions recoverable tax-free (California deduction same as federal).

1974-1986: Excess of 1974-1986 federal deduction over California deduction recoverable tax-free.

1987 and subsequent years: No contributions recoverable tax-free (California deduction same as federal).

¶ 206

All years: Interest element in redemption of "retirement bonds" issued before 1984 recoverable tax-free.

DEDUCTIBLE INDIVIDUAL RETIREMENT ACCOUNTS

1975: All 1975 contributions recoverable tax-free (no California deduction).

1975 and 1976: Income from 1975 contributions recoverable tax-free (income was taxed currently).

1976-1981: No 1976-1981 contributions recoverable tax-free (California deduction same as federal).

1982-1986: Excess of 1982-1986 federal deduction over California deduction recoverable tax-free.

1987 and subsequent years: No contributions recoverable tax-free (California deduction same as federal).

All years: Interest element in redemption of "retirement bonds" issued before 1984 recoverable tax-free.

SIMPLIFIED EMPLOYEE PENSION PLANS

1979-1986: Excess of 1979-1986 federal deduction over California deduction recoverable tax-free.

1987 and subsequent years: No contributions recoverable tax-free (California deduction same as federal).

Note: This summary assumes that the taxpayer was a California resident during the contribution year, as well as during the year of distribution. In case there has been a change of residence, see ¶ 405.

● *Premature distributions*

Both California and federal laws impose a penalty tax on premature distributions (before age 59½) from self-employed plans, annuity plans, IRAs, and "modified endowment contracts," to the extent the distribution is includible in income. The California penalty is 2½% of the distribution, while the federal penalty is generally 10% of the distribution. The penalty is inapplicable to premature distributions from IRAs if the distributions are used to pay (1) medical expenses in excess of 7.5% of a taxpayer's adjusted gross income; (2) health insurance premiums if a taxpayer is unemployed and either received 12 consecutive weeks of unemployment compensation or, if self-employed, would have received such benefits but for the fact that he or she was self-employed; (3) qualified first-time homebuyer expenses; or (4) qualified higher education expenses. Also, the penalty does not apply to any post-1999 distribution from a qualified retirement plan or IRA if the distribution is made on account of an FTB notice to withhold from the plan or IRA (an IRS levy on the plan or IRA for federal purposes).

"Qualified higher education expenses" include tuition, fees, books, and school supplies for the taxpayer, the taxpayer's spouse, or a child or grandchild of the taxpayer or the taxpayer's spouse. "Qualified first-time homebuyer distributions" are withdrawals of up to $10,000 during the taxpayer's lifetime that are used to buy or build a home that is the principal residence of the taxpayer, his or her spouse, or a child, grandchild, or ancestor of the taxpayer or the taxpayer's spouse.

> (CCH)   **CCH Tip: Requirement to File FTB 3805P**
>
> A taxpayer that is liable for the penalty tax on premature distributions is required to file form FTB 3805P whether or not he or she meets the threshold individual income tax filing requirements. The return filing deadline is the same for filing the individual income tax return (see ¶ 105).

● *Excess contributions, accumulations, or distributions*

California does not have taxes similar to those imposed under IRC Sec. 4973 (tax on excess contributions to individual retirement arrangements) or IRC Sec. 4974 (tax on excess accumulation in qualified retirement plans).

● *Rollovers*

Both California and federal laws permit tax-free "rollovers" from one tax-qualified retirement plan to another, under certain conditions. However, a lump sum distribution from a pension plan that is rolled over into an IRA while the recipient is a nonresident of California may not be accorded the same tax-free treatment. In *Appeal of Roy and Phyllis Watts* (1997) (CCH CALIFORNIA TAX REPORTS ¶ 16-118.40, the State Board of Equalization held that such a rollover did not have to be added to the recipient's California basis in the IRA when the recipient became a California resident. Although California allows a taxpayer to treat as nontaxable basis for California purposes the amount of annual contributions to an IRA (and the earnings thereon) made while the taxpayer was a resident of another state, this adjustment is permitted to avoid double taxation should the state of prior residence seek to tax distributions from the IRA. There was, however, no such risk in *Watts*. The taxpayer deferred tax on the lump sum distribution by rolling it over into his IRA. By subsequently moving to California, he then escaped taxation by his state of former residence, which did not tax IRA distributions received by nonresidents. Consequently, the requested adjustment was not necessary to avoid double taxation.

● *Cross references*

See ¶ 205 regarding taxability of payments received under the Railroad Retirement Act. See ¶ 405 regarding taxability of distributions from self-employed plans after change of residence.

¶ 207 Employee Stock Options and Purchase Plans

Law: Sec. 17081 (CCH CALIFORNIA TAX REPORTS ¶ 15-462, 16-123).

Comparable Federal: Secs. 83, 421-24 (CCH STANDARD FEDERAL TAX REPORTS ¶ 6380, 19,602—20,100).

Except as noted below, California law is substantially the same as federal. However, the federal provision allowing an income tax deduction when the value of an option is included in both a decedent's gross income and federal gross estate does not apply for California purposes.

¶ 207

● *California qualified stock options*

The favorable tax treatment afforded by federal law to incentive and employee stock options applies for California purposes to California qualified stock options. Accordingly, a taxpayer who exercises a qualifying stock option may postpone paying tax until disposing of the option or the underlying stock. A "California qualified stock option" is a stock option (1) designated by the corporation issuing the stock option as a California qualified stock option at the time the option is granted, (2) issued by a corporation to its employees after 1996 and before 2002, and (3) exercised by a taxpayer either while employed by the issuing corporation or within three months after leaving the employ of the issuing corporation. A taxpayer who becomes permanently and totally disabled may exercise the option within one year of leaving the employ of the issuing corporation. The favorable tax treatment of California qualified stock options is available only to a taxpayer whose earned income from the corporation granting the option does not exceed $40,000 for the taxable year in which the option is exercised, and only to the extent that the number of shares transferable by the taxpayer's exercise of qualified options does not exceed a total of 1,000 shares and those shares have a combined fair market value of less than $100,000.

¶ 208 Services of Child

> *Law:* Sec. 17081 (CCH CALIFORNIA TAX REPORTS ¶ 15-438).

> *Comparable Federal:* Secs. 73, 6201 (CCH STANDARD FEDERAL TAX REPORTS ¶ 6150, 38,502).

California law is the same as federal.

Income from services of a child is includible in the gross income of the child, and not in the income of the parent. All expenditures, by parent or child, attributable to such income are treated as paid or incurred by the child.

Under certain circumstances, an assessment on the child's income is treated as an assessment against the parent as well as the child.

¶ 209 Prizes and Awards

> *Law:* Sec. 17081 (CCH CALIFORNIA TAX REPORTS ¶ 15-441).

> *Comparable Federal:* Sec. 74 (CCH STANDARD FEDERAL TAX REPORTS ¶ 620).

California law is the same as federal.

Prizes and awards are specifically designated as being includible in taxable income, with two exceptions. The exceptions relate to (1) the value of certain employee achievement awards, and (2) amounts received in recognition of achievement of charitable, scientific, artistic, etc., nature. To be eligible for the charitable award exemption the recipient must be selected without any action on his or her part and must not be required to render substantial future services. Also, the award must be transferred by the payor to a charity designated by the recipient. The federal law is incorporated in California's by reference.

¶ 210 Dealers in Tax-Exempt Securities

Law: Sec. 17081 (CCH CALIFORNIA TAX REPORTS ¶ 15-444).

Comparable Federal: Sec. 75 (CCH STANDARD FEDERAL TAX REPORTS ¶ 6250).

California follows the federal rules.

Dealers in tax-free municipal bonds may be required to make an adjustment to gross income with respect to such securities sold during the year. The cost, or other basis, of certain municipal bonds sold by a dealer must be reduced by an amount equivalent to the amortization of bond premiums that would otherwise be allowable as a deduction if the interest on the bonds were fully taxable. Exceptions are provided for certain cases where the bonds are sold within 30 days after acquisition, or where the bonds mature, or are callable, more than 5 years after acquisition. Special rules are provided where dealers use different inventory methods.

The federal law is incorporated in California's by reference. However, in view of the fact that certain municipal bond interest is taxable for California but not federal purposes, and interest on U.S. bonds is taxable for federal but not California purposes, there will be cases where the rules apply under one law but not under the other.

¶ 211 Commodity Credit Loans

Law: Sec. 17081 (CCH CALIFORNIA TAX REPORTS ¶ 15-449).

Comparable Federal: Sec. 77 (CCH STANDARD FEDERAL TAX REPORTS ¶ 6300).

California follows the federal law.

The taxpayer may elect to treat as income amounts received as loans from the Commodity Credit Corporation.

¶ 212 Employees' Group Term Life Insurance

Law: Secs. 17020.12, 17081 (CCH CALIFORNIA TAX REPORTS ¶ 15-452).

Comparable Federal: Secs. 79, 7701(a)(20) (CCH STANDARD FEDERAL TAX REPORTS ¶ 6360, 43,880).

California follows the federal law.

An employee must include in income an amount equivalent to his or her employer's cost of group term life insurance to the extent the cost exceeds (1) the cost of $50,000 of coverage plus (2) any contribution by the employee to purchase the insurance. Exceptions are provided where the employer, or a charitable organization, is the beneficiary. An exemption is also provided for insurance under a qualified pension or profit-sharing plan (see ¶ 206).

The federal law is incorporated in California's by reference, including federal rules concerning the determination of cost under a discriminatory plan.

¶ 213 Certain Death Benefits

Law: Secs. 17131, 17132.6 (CCH CALIFORNIA TAX REPORTS ¶ 15-471).

Comparable Federal: Sec. 101 (CCH STANDARD FEDERAL TAX REPORTS ¶ 6502).

● *Life insurance*

In general, life insurance proceeds are nontaxable except for the interest element. (However, see ¶ 215 for an exception to the general rule.) If proceeds are held by an insurer under an agreement to pay interest, the interest received is fully taxable. If the proceeds are paid in installments that include an interest element, the interest element is taxable. The California law is the same as federal.

● *Survivors of state employees, etc.*

Both California and federal law exclude from gross income certain survivor benefits paid as an annuity to the spouse, former spouse, or child of a public safety officer killed in the line of duty.

¶ 214 Life Insurance—Other Than Death Benefits

Law: Secs. 17081, 17085 (CCH CALIFORNIA TAX REPORTS ¶ 15-435).

Comparable Federal: Sec. 72 (CCH STANDARD FEDERAL TAX REPORTS ¶ 6102).

California law conforms to the federal provisions regarding the taxability of amounts received on life insurance contracts other than death benefits, interest, or annuities. Under these provisions, the proceeds from life insurance or endowment contracts are includible in income subject to an exclusion factor determined by reference to the investment in, and expected return from, such contracts. If an insured elects within 60 days after maturity of a policy to take the proceeds as an annuity rather than a lump sum, the lump sum proceeds will not be deemed to be constructively received. California also incorporates the federal penalty on premature distributions from "modified endowment contracts," but substitutes a different penalty rate (see ¶ 206).

¶ 215 Life Insurance or Annuity Transferred for Consideration

Law: Secs. 17081, 17131 (CCH CALIFORNIA TAX REPORTS ¶ 15-435, 15-471).

Comparable Federal: Secs. 72(g), 101(a), 101(g) (CCH STANDARD FEDERAL TAX REPORTS ¶ 6102, 6502).

California follows federal law.

Where the recipient of the proceeds has acquired a life insurance contract for a valuable consideration, the general rule is that the proceeds are exempt only to the extent of the consideration given and the premiums subsequently paid. An exception to the general rule exempts life insurance proceeds from taxation in cases where the transferee is the insured, a partner of the insured, or a corporation in which the insured is an officer or shareholder. Also exempted are transfers where basis for the contract is determined by reference to basis in the hands of the transferor.

As to annuities transferred for a valuable consideration, the general rule is that the cost of the annuity (determined for purposes of computing the tax-free recovery of cost) is computed by reference to the actual value of the consideration paid on transfer, plus premiums and other sums subsequently paid. An exception is provided for certain tax-free exchanges.

● *Accelerated death benefits*

California conforms to the federal law allowing an exclusion from gross income when accelerated death benefits are received under a life insurance contract on the life of a terminally or chronically ill individual or when amounts are received from the sale or assignment to a viatical settlement provider of any portion of the death benefits under a life insurance contract on the life of a terminally or chronically ill individual. In the case of a chronically ill individual, (1) the exclusion applies only if amounts are received under a rider or other provision of a contract that is treated as a qualified long-term care insurance contract, and (2) the excludable amount is capped at $190 per day (for 1999).

¶ 216 Gifts, Inheritances, Tips, etc.

> *Law:* Sec. 17131 (CCH CALIFORNIA TAX REPORTS ¶ 15-474).

> *Comparable Federal:* Sec. 102 (CCH STANDARD FEDERAL TAX REPORTS ¶ 6550).

California law incorporates the federal law by reference. The value of property received as a gift, bequest, devise, or inheritance is nontaxable but the income from such property is taxable.

Tips received by a waiter are taxable income and are not exempt as gifts. See *Hugo Rihn v. Franchise Tax Board* (1955) (CCH CALIFORNIA TAX REPORTS ¶ 15-401.14), decided by the California Court of Appeal.

The State Board of Equalization (SBE) held in *Appeal of Ida A. Rogers* (1956) (CCH CALIFORNIA TAX REPORTS ¶ 15-474.47) that voluntary payments by a corporation to the widow of one of its employees constituted gifts and were not taxable income. A similar result was reached by the SBE in *Appeal of Irma Livingston* (1956) (CCH CALIFORNIA TAX REPORTS ¶ 15-474.47), as to voluntary payments to surviving children of a deceased employee.

¶ 217 Tax-Free Interest

> *Law:* Secs. 17088, 17133, 17143, 17145 (CCH CALIFORNIA TAX REPORTS ¶ 15-477, 15-558, 15-601).

> *Comparable Federal:* Secs. 103, 141-150, 852, 1286 (CCH STANDARD FEDERAL TAX REPORTS ¶ 6600, 7707—7930, 26,260, 32,980).

> *California Forms:* Sch. CA (540), Sch. CA (540NR).

California's treatment of interest on certain governmental obligations differs from federal rules, as explained below.

See ¶ 305 for treatment of interest expense related to tax-free interest.

● *Interest exempt*

Interest on the following obligations is exempt from California tax:

(a) Bonds and other obligations of the United States, territories of the United States, and Puerto Rico. (Interest on Philippine Islands obligations issued on or after March 24, 1934, is not exempt. Interest on District of Columbia obligations issued after December 24, 1973, is not exempt).

(b) Bonds (not including other obligations) of the State of California or of political subdivisions thereof, issued after November 4, 1902.

If there is a separation of the ownership between the tax-exempt bond and the right to receive interest, the payments or accruals on the stripped bond and stripped coupon are treated in the manner provided under the federal law, which requires allocation of basis to prevent artificial losses.

Interest on bonds issued by a territorial government (e.g., Alaska or Hawaii) continues to be exempt after the territory becomes a State.

The exemption set forth in (a) above does not extend to interest received on refunds of United States taxes. This point is not covered in the regulations or any published ruling, but it has been the Franchise Tax Board's administrative policy to deny the exemption. The Attorney General has ruled (NS 4570, 10-28-42) that interest on postal savings accounts is taxable. Interest on bonds of other States is not exempt.

See ¶ 506a for the treatment of gain or loss from the sale of such bonds.

Interest on Housing Authority bonds (issued by housing projects created under the Housing Authorities Law) is exempt if the bonds are issued by a project located in California, but is taxable if the bonds are issued by a project located outside the state. Such interest would presumably be exempt from federal tax.

● *California-federal differences*

The above exemptions are quite different from those under federal law, which exempt interest on obligations of *any* state or political subdivision thereof and which extend only limited exemptions to certain United States obligations.

Interest on "arbitrage bonds" or private activity bonds issued by state or local governments is subject to federal tax; California has not adopted these provisions so the interest on any such bonds issued in California would be exempt from California tax. (The federal rule would have no effect on California tax so far as interest on bonds of other states is concerned, since California already taxes interest on such bonds.)

● *Status of federal agency obligations*

Whether interest from federal agency obligations is taxable for California purposes is generally governed by federal law (*Letter*, FTB, June 3, 1992, CCH CALIFORNIA TAX REPORTS ¶ 15-601.28).

In a 1984 letter (CCH CALIFORNIA TAX REPORTS ¶ 15-601.131), the Franchise Tax Board (FTB) held that interest on securities guaranteed by the

Government National Mortgage Association (GNMA) is not exempt, because such securities are only a remote and contingent liability of the United States. The ruling notes that Federal National Mortgage Association (FNMA) and Federal Home Loan Mortgage Corporation (FHLMC) securities have always been considered subject to California tax. To the same effect, see *Appeal of John LaMontaine* (1986) (CCH CALIFORNIA TAX REPORTS ¶ 15-601.132 and *Appeal of Marie Delahunte* (1986) (CCH CALIFORNIA TAX REPORTS ¶ 15-601.132).

Additional sources of nontaxable interest include obligations of the Student Loan Marketing Association (SLMA), Federal Home Loan banks, the Resolution Funding Corporation, the Production Credit Association, Federal Farm Credit banks, and the Commodity Credit Corporation (*Letter*, FTB, August 30, 1984, CCH CALIFORNIA TAX REPORTS ¶ 15-601.25; *Letter*, FTB, June 3, 1992, CCH CALIFORNIA TAX REPORTS ¶ 15-601.28). Interest from CATS (Certificates of Accrual on Treasury Securities) and TIGRS (Treasury Investment Growth Receipts) is also exempt because those obligations have been found to be government securities under federal law.

● *Interest on notes*

In *Appeal of M.G. and Faye W. Odenheimer* (1964) (CCH CALIFORNIA TAX REPORTS ¶ 15-477.11), the State Board of Equalization held that interest on a promissory note of a California municipality, issued for purchase of land to be used as a parking lot, qualified for exemption from the California personal income tax.

● *Mutual funds*

California generally adopts the federal treatment of regulated investment companies (RICs) and their shareholders. However, California has its own rules governing exempt-interest dividends and does not adopt the federal treatment of undistributed capital gains.

As to the pass-through of tax-exempt income, California provides that the flow-through treatment is allowed if, as of the close of each quarter, at least 50% of the value of a management company's assets consists of obligations that pay interest that is exempt from taxation by California. State and federal tax-exempt obligations may be combined for purposes of meeting the 50% test.

Also, California conforms to a federal provision that limits the amount of a distribution allowable as an exempt-interest dividend. With respect to the company's taxable year, if the aggregate amount designated by the company as an exempt-interest dividend is greater than the excess of (1) the amount of interest it received that was exempt from California taxation or excludable from gross income under federal law, over (2) the amounts that would be disallowed as deductions for expenses related to exempt income under California or federal law, the portion of the distribution designated as an exempt-interest dividend that will be allowed as an exempt-interest dividend is only that proportion of the designated amount that the excess bears to the designated amount.

It should be noted that the flow-through treatment applies to interest from federal obligations that would be exempt if held directly by an individ-

¶ 217

ual. Therefore, interest received from certain agency bonds (e.g., GNMA, FNMA, etc.) is not exempt interest from federal obligations.

Amounts designated as "exempt-interest dividends" are treated by recipients as nontaxable income.

See ¶ 206 regarding exemption of interest element upon redemption of individual retirement bonds.

¶ 218 Compensation for Injury or Sickness

Law: Sec. 17131 (CCH California Tax Reports ¶ 15-480).

Comparable Federal: Sec. 104 (CCH Standard Federal Tax Reports ¶ 6662).

California adopts by reference the federal law as of the current IRC tie-in date (see ¶ 102a).

Amounts received as accident or health insurance benefits, damages, workers compensation etc., on account of personal injuries or sickness, are tax-exempt. The exemption does not apply to amounts received as reimbursement for medical expenses that were allowed as deductions in prior years. Nor does it apply to (1) punitive damages, whether or not related to a claim for damages from personal injury or sickness, or (2) damages for emotional distress, except to the extent of any amounts received for medical care attributable to the emotional distress or attributable to a physical injury or sickness. Also, this exemption generally does not cover employer contributions to accident and health plans for *employees;* see ¶ 219 for discussion of special rules covering such plans. These rules are the same as the federal rules. However, the amount includible in income on account of reimbursed medical expenses may be different because of a difference in the extent to which the expenses were deductible in an earlier year.

¶ 219 Amounts Received Under Accident and Health Plans

Law: Sec. 17131 (CCH California Tax Reports ¶ 15-484, 15-487).

Comparable Federal: Secs. 105-06, 7702B (CCH Standard Federal Tax Reports ¶ 6700—6800).

California generally conforms to federal law. However, California does not incorporate the federal provision requiring that sick pay benefits received under the Railroad Unemployment Insurance Act be included in gross income.

Certain amounts paid under an employer-financed accident or health plan to reimburse an employee for expenses incurred by the employee for medical care of the employee or the employee's spouse or dependents are excludible from gross income, unless received in reimbursement for medical expenses previously deducted. These rules also cover payments made for loss of use of a member or function of the body, or for disfigurement. Such plans are subject to detailed rules designed to prevent discrimination.

Employer-provided coverage under an accident or health plan (including amounts contributed to an employee's medical savings account) are also excluded from an employee's gross income. However, employer-provided coverage for long-term care service provided through a flexible spending or similar arrangement must be included in an employee's gross income.

In *Appeal of Frank A. Aiello* (1987) (CCH CALIFORNIA TAX REPORTS ¶ 15-487.35), lump-sum payments made by a former employer to "buy out" its obligations to provide retired employees with group health benefits was taxable income and not an excludable health benefit.

¶ 220 Rental Value of Parsonages

> *Law:* Sec. 17131 (CCH CALIFORNIA TAX REPORTS ¶ 15-490).
>
> *Comparable Federal:* Sec. 107 (CCH STANDARD FEDERAL TAX REPORTS ¶ 6850).

The California exemption for the rental value of a minister's dwelling is the same as under the federal law.

In *Appeal of Nickolas Kurtaneck* (1987) (CCH CALIFORNIA TAX REPORTS ¶ 15-490.25), the State Board of Equalization (SBE) reviewed applicable federal regulations and rulings and denied the housing exclusion to an ordained minister who taught biblical studies at an independent, nonaffiliated university. The SBE held that the institution was not operated as an integral agency of a church.

¶ 221 Discharge of Indebtedness

> *Law:* Secs. 17131, 17134, 17144, 17330 (CCH CALIFORNIA TAX REPORTS ¶ 15-491, 15-492).
>
> *Comparable Federal:* Secs. 108, 382 (CCH STANDARD FEDERAL TAX REPORTS ¶ 7002).
>
> *California Forms:* Sch. CA (540), Sch. CA (540NR).

California generally incorporates federal law that provides that, if a debt of a taxpayer is canceled or forgiven, the taxpayer must include the canceled amount in gross income. Exceptions to the general rule are provided in bankruptcy situations, where the debtor/taxpayer is insolvent, or where the canceled debt is qualified real property business indebtedness or qualified farm indebtedness. Additionally, California conforms to federal legislation that (1) repealed the stock-for-debt exception to the rules on cancellation-of-indebtedness income for insolvent and bankrupt taxpayers and (2) enacted an exclusion from gross income for certain income realized from the discharge of qualified real property business indebtedness.

Under the discharge of indebtedness rules, the income-tax consequences of debt discharge may be deferred—but not permanently avoided—by reducing tax "attributes" such as capital losses or capital loss carryovers and the basis of depreciable property. Certain debt reductions are treated as purchase-price adjustments.

● *Cancellation of student loans*

Both California and federal law allow an exclusion from gross income for income from the discharge of qualified student loans. To qualify for the exclusion, the loan must (1) be made by the federal, state, or local government or a public benefit hospital corporation that is treated as a public entity and (2) contain a provision stating that all or part of the indebtedness will be discharged if the recipient works for a specified period of time in a specified profession for any of a broad class of employers. A discharged student loan

¶ 220

made by an educational organization also qualifies for the exclusion if (1) the student works in an occupation or area with unmet needs and (2) the work is performed for, or under the direction of, a tax-exempt charitable organization. A qualified student loan also includes any student loan made by an educational organization or tax-exempt charitable organization to refinance a loan pursuant to a program that imposes the above-mentioned public service requirements.

The discharge of a loan made pursuant to the California State University's Forgivable Loan Program is excludable from California gross income if the discharge is made in connection with the recipient's performance of services for the California State University.

● *California-federal differences*

Although, as stated above, federal law concerning discharge of indebtedness income has generally been incorporated by California, federal and California results may be quite different because of federal credit carryovers that do not apply to California. For example, federal law requiring the reduction of tax attributes refers to foreign tax credit carryovers, which are not applicable for California tax purposes. In addition, for purposes of both the reduction of tax attributes and the exclusion of income from the discharge of qualified farm indebtedness, California's treatment of other credit carryovers is slightly modified. Under federal law, a taxpayer who does not elect to reduce the basis of depreciable assets or inventory realty by the amount of a discharged obligation must instead reduce certain listed tax attributes, including general business credit carryover reductions of 33⅓¢ for each dollar excluded. California modifies this provision to (1) refer instead to carryovers of credits allowed under California law and (2) require reduction of only 11.1¢ for each dollar excluded. For both federal and California purposes, a taxpayer may elect to apply the amount discharged to reduce the basis of his or her depreciable property in lieu of applying the excluded amount against tax attributes.

Under both California and federal law, income from the discharge of certain farm indebtedness may be excluded even if the farmer is not insolvent or bankrupt, but the amount that may be excluded is limited to the sum of (1) the aggregate adjusted bases of the taxpayer's trade, business, and income-producing property in the year following the discharge year and (2) the taxpayer's "adjusted" tax attributes. For federal purposes, the taxpayer adjusts the general business credit carryover attribute by tripling it. For California purposes, the taxpayer multiplies the credit carryover figure by nine rather than by three.

¶ 222 Lessee Improvements

Law: Sec. 17131 (CCH California Tax Reports ¶ 15-493).

Comparable Federal: Sec. 109 (CCH Standard Federal Tax Reports ¶ 7020).

An exemption is granted to lessors on income derived upon termination of a lease in the form of improvements made by a lessee. The federal law is incorporated into California's by reference.

¶ 222a Lessee Construction Allowances

Law: Sec. 17131 (CCH CALIFORNIA TAX REPORTS ¶ 15-494).

Comparable Federal: Sec. 110 (CCH STANDARD FEDERAL TAX REPORTS ¶ 7030).

Under both California and federal law, certain tenants may exclude from gross income construction allowances received from lessors and used for additions or improvements to retail space. The exclusion applies only with respect to nonresidential real property that is (1) held under a lease of 15 years or less and (2) used in the tenant's retail trade or business.

¶ 223 Recoveries of Bad Debts, Prior Taxes, etc.

Law: Secs. 17131, 17142 (CCH CALIFORNIA TAX REPORTS ¶ 15-496).

Comparable Federal: Sec. 111 (CCH STANDARD FEDERAL TAX REPORTS ¶ 7060).

The federal law is incorporated in California's by reference.

Amounts may be excluded from gross income to the extent they represent recovery of prior-year deductions that did not reduce income tax. The portion of the federal provision dealing with credit and credit carryovers is modified to refer to California credits. Detailed rules are provided.

● *California-federal difference*

The California rule is the same as the federal, but the effect of the rule may be different under the two laws because the deduction in the earlier year of the item recovered may have resulted in a tax benefit under one law but not under the other. This could result from a difference in treatment of the item in question in the year of deductibility, or it could be the result of differences in taxable income having no relation to the item in question.

● *Cases decided by State Board of Equalization*

In *Appeal of Percival M. and Katharine Scales* (1963) (CCH CALIFORNIA TAX REPORTS ¶ 15-496.11), the State Board of Equalization (SBE) held that taxes and carrying charges on real property deducted in one period, without a corresponding reduction in tax liability, could not be excluded from income when recovered in a subsequent year upon sale of the property. The SBE said the "tax benefit" rule was not intended to have such broad application. To the same effect, see *Appeal of H.V. Management Corporation* (1981) (CCH CALIFORNIA TAX Reports ¶ 10-470.11), a case that involved gain on sale of a partnership interest. Also to the same effect, see *Appeal of Argo Petroleum Corporation* (1982) (CCH CALIFORNIA TAX REPORTS ¶ 10-470.11), which involved sale of an oil and gas lease.

¶ 224 Military Compensation

Law: Secs. 17131, 17140.5, 17142.5 (CCH CALIFORNIA TAX REPORTS ¶ 15-499, 15-555).

Comparable Federal: Secs. 112, 122, 134, 692 (CCH STANDARD FEDERAL TAX REPORTS ¶ 7080, 7100, 25,320).

Except for the exclusion described in (c) below, the California exemptions for military pay are the same as the federal. This applies also to forgiveness of taxes of service members who die as a result of serving in a "combat zone" or "qualified hazardous duty area" (as defined in ¶ 106). The federal law is incorporated in California's by reference.

The following military compensation is exempt from California tax:

(a) educational benefits received under federal or state law;

(b) compensation of enlisted personnel and commissioned officers for active service in a "combat zone" or "qualified hazardous duty area" while hospitalized as a result of such service; and

(c) military compensation of a person not domiciled or taxable in California, but attributable to a resident spouse because of community property laws.

Expenses attributable to service pay that is exempt from tax are not deductible (see ¶ 322).

● *Effect of residence status on taxability*

Under the federal Soldiers' and Sailors' Civil Relief Act, a nonresident serviceperson may not be taxed by California on service pay received for services in California, even though he or she may be stationed in the state during the entire year, and despite the fact that such income would be considered taxable to a nonresident under the regular rules. However, all other income of a nonresident serviceperson from California sources is subject to California tax. Under Legal Ruling No. 300, issued by the Franchise Tax Board in 1965, a person who enters military service from California will be treated as a nonresident when he or she leaves the state under permanent military orders to serve at another post of duty (see ¶ 103).

● *Lump-sum readjustment payments*

A lump-sum readjustment payment received under a claim of right may be treated differently for California tax purposes than for federal, because of a special provision in the federal law (see ¶ 415).

¶ 225 Dividends and Other Corporate Distributions

> *Law:* Secs. 17024.5(b), 17088, 17088.5, 17088.6, 17321, 17322 (CCH CALIFORNIA TAX REPORTS ¶ 15-558, 16-001—16-089).
>
> *Comparable Federal:* Secs. 301-46, 851-60, 951-52, 995 (CCH STANDARD FEDERAL TAX REPORTS ¶ 7160, 15,202—16,351, 26,601—26,780, 29,020, 29,040, 29,520).
>
> *California Forms:* Sch. CA (540), Sch. CA (540NR).

Although California and federal law regarding dividends and other corporate distributions are generally the same, California has not completely conformed to current federal law. In addition, prior differences in California and federal law may still affect the cost basis of property. Both current California-federal differences and prior-year differences are discussed below.

¶ 225

The principal provisions of the federal law to which California conforms may be summarized very briefly as follows:

(a) Any distribution out of earnings and profits of the current year or out of earnings and profits accumulated after February 28, 1913, is a "dividend" (IRC Sec. 316).

(b) Certain liquidating distributions are treated as payments in exchange for stock (IRC Sec. 302-03).

(c) A redemption of stock that is "essentially equivalent to the distribution of a taxable dividend" is to be treated as such. This may apply to acquisition of a corporation's stock by an affiliated corporation (IRC Sec. 304). Detailed rules are provided for some situations. Certain types of redemptions are not to be treated as taxable dividends. These include "disproportionate distributions," termination of a shareholder's interest, and redemption of stock to pay death taxes.

(d) Certain stock dividends may be nontaxable (IRC Sec. 305).

(e) Detailed rules are provided for the computation of "earnings and profits" so that a determination can be made regarding the taxability of a corporate distribution in the hands of shareholders (IRC Sec. 312).

(f) Special treatment is provided for distributions by "collapsible corporations" (IRC Sec. 341)—see ¶ 511a.

● *Distributions from mutual funds*

California adopts the federal tax treatment of regulated investment companies (RICs) and their shareholders (IRC Sec. 852), with certain modifications. See ¶ 217 for a discussion of the pass-through of RIC income that is exempt from California personal income tax.

● *Constructive dividends*

Following federal cases involving the same issue, the State Board of Equalization held in *Appeal of Howard N. and Thelma Gilmore* (CCH CALIFORNIA TAX REPORTS ¶ 16-004.231) that unsupported travel and entertainment expenses disallowed to a closely-held corporation were taxable as constructive dividends to the individual shareholders. Later cases have been decided to the same effect.

● *Current California-federal differences*

Current differences between California and federal law are summarized briefly as follows:

(1) Federal law provides for "consent dividends" (applicable to "personal holding companies," etc.). There is no comparable California provision.

(2) Federal limitations periods for waivers of stock attribution are modified for California purposes.

(3) California has not adopted a special federal rule governing generation-skipping transfers.

¶ 225

(4) The federal provision relating to distributions by foreign corporations, foreign investment companies, and foreign personal holding companies is not applicable for California purposes.

(5) Under both California and federal law, a corporate distribution may be a nontaxable return of capital if there are no "earnings and profits" out of which the distribution is made. However, the amount of "earnings and profits" of a corporation may be different for California tax purposes than it is for federal tax purposes. Such a difference may result in a particular distribution being nontaxable under one law but a taxable dividend under the other.

(6) California does not incorporate the special federal provisions for Domestic International Sales Corporations (DISC). Accordingly, a DISC is taxed under California law in the same manner as other corporations, and the special federal treatment of its dividends has no effect for California tax purposes. The DISC system was largely replaced in 1985 by a new system of Foreign Sales Corporations (FSCs). California has nothing comparable to the special federal provisions for certain distributions by FSCs.

● *Prior-year differences*

In addition to the differences listed above, there were prior-year differences that may continue to affect computations of basis. These prior-year differences concern:

(1) federal rules for distributions by World War I "personal service corporations;"

(2) rules for corporate liquidations in 1954, 1955, and 1956;

(3) special California provisions for 1935 or 1936 distributions by a "personal holding company;"

(4) effective dates (all before 1972) of provisions regarding redemption of stock through an affiliate, and "collapsible corporations;"

(5) various amendments in 1954 and 1955, regarding distribution of stock dividends and rights, etc.;

(6) various amendments, in 1981 and before, relating to special rules for redemption of stock to pay death taxes;

(7) 1958 federal amendments to special rules for 12-month liquidations;

(8) 1964-1978 difference in rules for "sidewise attribution" in stock ownership rules;

(9) 1954-1961 difference in special rules regarding distributions of property with a government-secured loan; and

(10) 1969-1971 differences in rules for taxation of stock dividends.

¶ 226 Scholarship and Fellowship Grants

Law: Sec. 17131 (CCH CALIFORNIA TAX REPORTS ¶ 15-511).

Comparable Federal: Sec. 117 (CCH STANDARD FEDERAL TAX REPORTS ¶ 7170).

California conforms to federal law.

Certain scholarship and fellowship grants and tuition grants are excluded from taxable income. In the case of graduate teaching or research assistants of exempt educational institutions, the amount of *any* tuition reduction for education at the employing institution may be excluded.

¶ 227 Meals and Lodging Furnished by Employer

Law: Sec. 17131 (CCH California Tax Reports ¶ 15-514).

Comparable Federal: Sec. 119 (CCH Standard Federal Tax Reports ¶ 7220).

California conforms to the federal law as of the current tie-in date (see ¶ 102a).

The value of meals and lodging furnished by an employer for the convenience of the employer is excluded from gross income, provided (1) the meals are furnished on the business premises of the employer and (2) the employee is required to accept the lodging on the employer's premises as a condition of employment.

A federal amendment made by the IRS Restructuring and Reform Act of 1998 that California has not yet incorporated, eases the requirements for the exclusion. Pursuant to the federal amendment, all meals furnished to employees on the employer's premises are treated as furnished for the convenience of the employer as long as more than one-half of the meals provided to employees on the employer's premises are actually furnished for the convenience of the employer. The federal amendment is effective for all tax years beginning before, on, or after July 22, 1998.

 CCH Caution: Federal Exclusion of Value of Meals

Individuals should check with their employers if they think they are being allowed to exclude the value of employer-provided meals for federal purposes solely because the meals were provided to more than 50% of the employees on the employer's premises. The value of meals excluded on this basis must be added back to the employee's federal adjusted gross income for California purposes.

¶ 228 Gain on Sale or Exchange of Personal Residence

Law: Secs. 17131, 17152 (CCH California Tax Reports ¶ 15-521).

Comparable Federal: Sec. 121 (CCH Standard Federal Tax Reports ¶ 7260).

Effective for sales and exchanges occurring after May 6, 1997, both California and federal law allow an individual taxpayer to exclude from his or her gross income up to $250,000 ($500,000 for married taxpayers filing jointly) of gain realized on the sale or exchange of his or her residence if the taxpayer owned and occupied the residence as a principal residence for an aggregate period of at least two of the five years prior to the sale or exchange. The exclusion amount is based on federal filing status, and not on California filing status. The exclusion applies only to one sale or exchange every two years, except that any pre-May 7, 1997, sale or exchange for which an exclusion was allowed under prior law (see discussion below) is not taken into account for this purpose. The California rules are generally the same as the federal, except that under California law, but not federal, a portion of the two-year ownership and use requirement is waived for individuals who served in the Peace Corps (the period waived is the length of the time of service, up to a maximum of 18 months).

Under California law incorporating federal law prior to its amendment by the IRS Restructuring and Reform Act of 1998, if a taxpayer does not meet the two-year ownership and use requirement due to a change in place of employment, health, or unforeseen circumstances, a prorated amount of the realized gain is excludable. A technical correction made by the IRS Restructuring and Reform Act to federal law provides that the amount of the exclusion, not the realized gain, is prorated. California has not as yet incorporated the federal amendment.

● *Prior law*

For sales and exchanges occurring prior to May 7, 1997, California and federal laws provided a $125,000 once-in-a-lifetime elective exclusion for gain on sale or exchange of a principal residence by taxpayers who were at least 55 years old ($62,500 for a married person filing separately). The exclusion amount was based on federal filing status, and not on California filing status. As with the currently effective exclusion, the California rules were generally the same as the federal. However, like the post-May 6, 1997, exclusion, California afforded special treatment to individuals who served in the Peace Corps.

If the once-in-a-lifetime exclusion was elected, it had to be applied against the full amount of the gain.

See ¶ 502 concerning a provision that allows nonrecognition of gain in situations involving involuntary conversion and ¶ 502a for a discussion of the former provision allowing nonrecognition of gain on the pre-May 7, 1997, sale and replacement of a personal residence.

¶ 229 Employees of Foreign Country

Law: Sec. 17146 (CCH CALIFORNIA TAX REPORTS ¶ 15-563).

Comparable Federal: Sec. 893 (CCH STANDARD FEDERAL TAX REPORTS ¶ 28,320).

Exemption is granted for compensation for services of an employee of a foreign country, provided certain conditions are met. California law incorporates the federal law by reference.

¶ 230 Gross Income of Nonresidents

Law: Secs. 17303, 17951-55 (CCH CALIFORNIA TAX REPORTS ¶ 15-109, 15-114, 15-605, 15-609).

Comparable Federal: Secs. 861-65, 911-12, 931-33 (CCH STANDARD FEDERAL TAX REPORTS ¶ 26,960, 26,991, 27,000, 27,020, 27,029, 28,020, 28,024, 28,820, 28,860, 28,900).

California Forms: Form 540NR, Sch. CA (540NR), Sch. R.

Gross income of nonresidents includes only gross income from sources within California. A nonresident member of a partnership or similar organization must include his or her distributive share of income from California sources. A nonresident beneficiary of an estate or trust must include distributable income of the estate or trust from California sources.

Nonresidents are taxed as though they were residents but with the tax computed according to the ratio of California-adjusted gross income to total income. See ¶ 112 for details.

A part-year resident is taxed on income regardless of source during the period of California residence.

● *Pension income*

A former California resident's qualified retirement income received after 1995 is not subject to California income tax, even if accrued while the nonresident resided in California. The current exclusion from gross income encompasses income or distributions received from most tax-exempt trusts, simplified employee pensions, annuity plans and contracts, individual retirement plans, government plans, and deferred compensation plans of state and local governments and tax-exempt organizations, and it also encompasses specified distributions from nonqualified plans.

● *Income from tangible property*

Any income from ownership, control, management, sale or transfer of real or tangible personal property in California is income from California sources. In *Appeal of L.N. Hagood* (1960) (CCH CALIFORNIA TAX REPORTS ¶ 15-605.77), the State Board of Equalization (SBE) held that since U.S. oil and gas leases of lands in California are real property, the income arising out of the granting of purchase options relative thereto is taxable income from California sources to a nonresident.

● *Income from intangible property*

In general, income of nonresidents from intangible property has its source at the state of residence of the owner and is therefore not taxable by California (but see next paragraph). Alimony income is considered to be derived from an intangible asset and is not taxable to a nonresident.

Income from intangible personal property, including gain on its sale or exchange, is attributable to California if the property has a business situs in the state. Such property is deemed to have a business situs in the state if it is employed as capital in California or its use and value become an asset of a business, trade or profession in the state. Even if the property does not have a business situs in California, if a nonresident deals in the property in California with sufficient regularity as to constitute doing business in the state, the income from such activity is taxable in California.

In *Appeal of Robert M. and Ann T. Bass et al.,* (1989) (CCH CALIFORNIA TAX REPORTS ¶ 15-605.673), the SBE held that a nonresident's distributive share of income from a limited partnership that was headquartered in California and that was engaged in the acquisition, holding, monitoring, and disposition of stocks and other securities was not subject to California income tax, because the limited partnership was not doing business in California.

¶ 230

Income from qualifying investment securities is not taxable by California if an individual's only contact with the state with respect to the securities is through a broker, dealer, or investment adviser located in California. Special rules apply in the case of income from qualifying investment securities distributed to a nonresident by an investment partnership, a qualifying estate or trust, or a regulated investment company. Income from qualifying investment securities is taxable by California if (1) the income is from investment activity that is interrelated with a California trade or business in which the nonresident owns an interest and the primary activities of the trade or business are separate and distinct from the acts of acquiring, managing, or disposing of qualified investment securities and (2) the income is from qualifying investment securities that are acquired with the working capital of a California trade or business in which the nonresident owns an interest.

● *Payment for contract termination*

In *Appeal of Edward and Carol McAneeley* (1980) (CCH CALIFORNIA TAX REPORTS ¶ 15-605.411), the taxpayer, a professional hockey player, was a Canadian resident employed by a California team. He received a $17,500 payment for termination of his California contract. The SBE held that the termination payment was not taxable by California, because the payment was for the sale of an intangible property right that had its situs in Canada.

● *Income from business*

Income of a business, trade, or profession carried on within the state is taxable. If such income is derived from both within and without the state, and if the part conducted outside the state is distinct and separate, only the gross income from the California operations need be reported. If, however, there is any business relationship between the parts within and without the state (flow of goods, etc.) so that the net income from sources outside the state cannot be accurately determined, the gross income from the entire business must be reported. In such cases, a portion of the net income is attributed to California, ordinarily—but not always—by use of the apportionment formula described at ¶ 1305. Taxpayers complete Sch. R for purposes of determining the amount of business income apportionable to California. See Chapter 13 for discussion of methods of apportionment, what constitutes business income subject to apportionment, etc.

In *Appeal of Chester A. and Mary E. Johnson* (1981) (CCH CALIFORNIA TAX REPORTS ¶ 15-605.95), the taxpayers were Australian residents whose pet-food business operated in both California and Iowa. The taxpayers computed their income attributable to California by using a federal formula provided by Internal Revenue Code Section 911. The SBE upheld the Franchise Tax Board (FTB) in requiring the use of the three-factor formula required under prior law.

● *Compensation for services*

Compensation for personal services performed in California is considered attributable to California. This includes fees of nonresidents for professional services. Employees engaged in transportation activities are taxed on the portion of their total compensation properly allocable to California; the regulations provide specific rules for this determination. Service pay of nonresident service personnel in California is not subject to California tax—see ¶ 224. In addition, when a nonresident receives pension income that is based on services rendered in California, the income is not taxable by California—see ¶ 405.

In *Wilson et al. v. Franchise Tax Board* (1993) (CCH CALIFORNIA TAX REPORTS ¶ 15-605.415), a nonresident professional football player's income was properly apportioned to California on the basis of the ratio of the athlete's duty days spent in California to the athlete's total duty days. "Duty days" included all days from the beginning of the official preseason training through the last game, including postseason games, in which the team competed during the taxable year.

In *Paul L. and Joanne W. Newman v. Franchise Tax Board* (1989) (CCH CALIFORNIA TAX REPORTS ¶ 15-605.162), a nonresident actor's income from a motion picture was properly apportioned according to a formula that divided his working days in California by his total working days on the picture, with "working days" including all the days on which, by contract, he was exclusively committed to his employer and on call at the employer's discretion, and not merely those days on which he actually performed.

In *Appeal of Joseph Barry Carroll* (1987) (CCH CALIFORNIA TAX REPORTS ¶ 15-605.414), compensation paid to a nonresident professional basketball player employed by the Golden State Warriors was apportioned to California on the basis of a "working day" or "duty day" formula that included days spent in training camp, practice sessions, and team travel. The taxpayer argued that he was paid for games only, and not practice or travel days, but produced no evidence to that effect. Accordingly, the SBE computed his California-source income on the basis of the ratio of training camp, practice, travel, and game days spent in California to total training camp, practice, travel, and game days.

In *Appeal of Edwin O. and Wanda L. Stevens* (1986) (CCH CALIFORNIA TAX REPORTS ¶ 15-605.27), the SBE held that benefits, sick leave, and vacation pay earned while working and residing in California are California source income and taxable in the state, even though the right to such benefits accrued during employment and residence in another state.

In *Appeal of Karl Bernhardt* (1984) (CCH CALIFORNIA TAX REPORTS ¶ 15-605.23), the taxpayer was a member of the Canadian Armed Forces who worked temporarily for Sperry Univac in California as a part of his service training. His salary was paid into a Canadian bank in Canadian funds. The SBE held that the salary was subject to California tax.

In *Appeal of George and Sheila Foster* (1984) (CCH CALIFORNIA TAX REPORTS ¶ 15-605.413), the taxpayer was an Ohio resident, where he played professional baseball for Cincinnati. He contended that $400,000 of his $985,000 salary for 1979 represented a "signing bonus" for signing a renegotiated contract, and that the "bonus" was not subject to apportionment by California according to the usual "working-days" formula. The SBE held that the $400,000 was a "playing bonus," subject to apportionment, and was not a "signing bonus" attributable to the state of residence.

In *Appeal of Dennis F. and Nancy Partee* (1976) (CCH CALIFORNIA TAX REPORTS ¶ 15-605.41), the taxpayer was a nonresident professional football

¶ 230

player with the San Diego Chargers. Here also, the SBE upheld the FTB's determination of the portion of the taxpayer's total salary allocable to California on the basis of the number of "working days" spent in the State. The taxpayer argued for use of the "games-played" formula used in other sports—see the *Krake* case, discussed below.

In *Appeals of Philip and Diane Krake, et al.* (1976) (CCH CALIFORNIA TAX REPORTS ¶ 15-605.412), the twelve taxpayers were nonresident members of the Los Angeles Kings professional hockey team. The SBE upheld the FTB's application of the "games-played" formula to total salaries, to determine the portion allocable to California. The taxpayers argued that a portion of their salary should be allocated to off-season activities before applying the "games-played" formula. However, the SBE agreed with the FTB's contention that the "games-played" method, as applied to regular season games, is a practical and reasonable method that produces approximately the same result as the "working-days" method for baseball, basketball, and hockey players.

● *Burden of proof*

Appeal of Robert L. Webber (1976) (CCH CALIFORNIA TAX REPORTS ¶ 15-605.15), involved an actor who was a New York resident. Part of his earnings for his personal services came from a wholly-owned corporation. The question at issue was the amount of his income for services performed in California. The SBE held that the taxpayer had submitted sufficient evidence to shift the burden of proof to the FTB, concluding that the latter had not borne that burden and holding in favor of the taxpayer. For another case involving similar issues, see *Appeal of Janice Rule* (1976) (CCH CALIFORNIA TAX REPORTS ¶ 15-605.16). See also *Appeal of Oscar D. and Agatha E. Seltzer* (1980) (CCH CALIFORNIA TAX REPORTS ¶ 15-605.332); in this case a corporate executive who was an Oregon resident was subjected to California tax on one-third of his income, because he did not overcome the presumption of correctness of the FTB's determination.

● *Royalty income*

In Legal Ruling No. 345 (1970) (CCH CALIFORNIA TAX REPORTS ¶ 15-605.49), it was held that royalty income received by an author on the sale of books is compensation for personal services and is taxable at the place the services are performed. Where a nonresident author's writing was done in California, his royalties received from a New York publisher were subject to California tax.

● *Covenant not to compete*

In *Appeal of Al Dean and Clara Washburn* (1982) (CCH CALIFORNIA TAX REPORTS ¶ 15-605.451), the taxpayer was a Utah resident who received income from a covenant not to compete that had been executed when he was a California resident. The SBE cited federal cases and held that the source of the income was the place (California) where the agreement was executed. See also *Appeal of Ray R. and Nellie A. Reeves* (1979) (CCH CALIFORNIA TAX REPORTS ¶ 15-605.31), which held to the same effect as to payments received for a covenant not to compete and for patent rights and trade formulas.

¶ 230

● *Change of residence status*

See ¶405 regarding determination of income subject to California tax when status changes from resident to nonresident or vice versa.

● *California-federal differences*

Although the federal law includes some rules comparable to the California law, the differences are so numerous that no attempt is made here to describe them. Any such comparison would be applicable only to nonresident aliens, since United States citizens and resident aliens are taxable for federal purposes on all their income from whatever source, with certain specific exemptions. California law has nothing comparable to the special federal provisions for earned income and deductions of Americans living and working abroad.

¶231 Patronage Allocations from Cooperatives

> *Law:* Sec. 17086 (CCH CALIFORNIA TAX REPORTS ¶ 15-582).
>
> *Comparable Federal:* Secs. 1381—1383, 1385 (CCH STANDARD FEDERAL TAX REPORTS ¶ 33,700—33,740, 33,760).
>
> *California Form:* Sch. CA (540).

Although California eliminated several differences with federal law in 1987, it retained the difference in the treatment of agricultural cooperative patronage dividends.

The California law provides optional methods of taxing non-cash patronage allocations from farmers' cooperatives and mutual associations. An election must be made to include such allocations in income either in the year the dollar amount of allocations is made known, or in the year the allocation is redeemed or realized. For a detailed discussion of the rules for such elections, see *Appeal of J.H. Johnson and Sons, Inc.* (1979) (CCH CALIFORNIA TAX REPORTS ¶ 15-582.13).

Generally, the federal rules require that allocations be included in income in the year they are received. The federal rules provide that cooperatives will not be allowed a deduction for patronage dividends and per-unit retain certificates unless the patrons include such amounts in taxable income, whether they are actually received or merely allocated.

¶232 S Corporation Shareholders

> *Law:* Secs. 17087.5, 18006, 23800-10 (CCH CALIFORNIA TAX REPORTS ¶ 15-368, 15-578).
>
> *Comparable Federal:* Secs. 1361-79 (CCH STANDARD FEDERAL TAX REPORTS ¶ 33,421—33,680).
>
> *California Form:* FTB 3830.

The California taxation of shareholders of federal S corporations that have elected S corporation status for California purposes is the same as federal.

Under long-standing federal law, as adopted by California, the shareholders of qualified S corporations report the current corporate income as though they had earned it individually, thus avoiding a tax at the corporate level for federal purposes and most of the corporate tax for California purposes (California imposes a reduced corporate tax rate on S corporation income prior to its pass-through to shareholders—see ¶ 803). Shareholders are entitled to a credit for their pro rata share of taxes paid to another state by the S corporation on income also taxed by California (see ¶ 116 and ¶ 117).

In *Appeal of Blaine B. and Bobbi J. Quick* (1999) (CCH CALIFORNIA TAX REPORTS ¶ 15-491.34), the State Board of Equalization (SBE) held that the exclusion of income from the cancellation of an insolvent S corporation's debt at the corporate level did not increase the shareholders' basis in the S corporation's stock, because the exclusion of income from the cancellation of debt was available only at the entity level and did not pass through to the shareholders.

In *Appeal of Merwyn P. Merrick, Sr. and Margaret F. Merrick* (1975) (CCH CALIFORNIA TAX REPORTS ¶ 15-578.46), the stockholders of a "tax-option" (S) corporation received distributions representing the proceeds of sale of the corporation's plant. The SBE held that the distributions were taxable as ordinary dividends.

See discussion at ¶ 715 of the *Winkenbach* case, involving the application of the doctrine of "equitable recoupment" where income was erroneously taxed to a corporation and later taxed to the individual stockholders.

● *Nonresident shareholders*

Nonresident shareholders are taxed on the portion of their distributive shares of an S corporation's income or loss, as modified for California purposes, that is derived from sources within the state.

To ensure that all nonresident shareholders pay their taxes, the law requires each S corporation to submit to the Franchise Tax Board FTB 3830 listing the names of all shareholders and statements from all nonresident shareholders that they consent to California's jurisdiction to tax their California S corporation income on the pro rata basis of their ownership interest. Nonresident shareholders may elect to file a single group return in the same manner as nonresident partners (see ¶ 613 for a discussion).

● *Part-year resident shareholders*

A part-year resident shareholder is taxed on his or her entire distributive share of S corporation income or loss, as modified for California purposes, if the shareholder is a California resident on the last day of the S corporation's income year (Instructions for Schedule CA (540NR)). A part-year resident shareholder who is a nonresident on the last day of the S corporation's income year is taxed in the same manner as a nonresident shareholder.

¶ 233 Merchant Marine Act Exemptions

Law: Sec. 17088.3 (CCH CALIFORNIA TAX REPORTS ¶ 15-591).

Comparable Federal: Sec. 7518 (CCH STANDARD FEDERAL TAX REPORTS ¶ 43,645).

California Form: Sch. CA (540).

Under Sec. 607 of the federal Merchant Marine Act, commercial fishermen and carriers can deposit part of their income in a special reserve fund to acquire or construct vessels, and can reduce their federal taxable income accordingly. Federal law provides detailed rules for treatment of deposits, withdrawals from the fund, etc. California conforms to the federal law for taxable years beginning after 1996.

¶ 234 Cost-of-Living and Peace Corps Allowances

Law: None (CCH CALIFORNIA TAX REPORTS ¶ 15-568).

Comparable Federal: Sec. 912 (CCH STANDARD FEDERAL TAX REPORTS ¶ 28,660).

California Form: Sch. CA (540).

California has no provisions comparable to a federal law specifically excluding from income certain cost-of-living allowances of civilian officers and employees of the U.S. Government residing outside the U.S., and certain allowances of Peace Corps volunteers. In *Appeal of Sammie W. and Harriet C. Gillentine* (1975) (CCH CALIFORNIA TAX REPORTS ¶ 15-565.11), the taxpayer (presumably a California resident) received a cost-of-living allowance as a U.S. Government employee stationed in Hawaii; the State Board of Equalization held that the allowance was subject to California income tax.

¶ 235 Relocation Payments

Law: Sec. 7269, Government Code (CCH CALIFORNIA TAX REPORTS ¶ 15-585).

Comparable Federal: Public Law 91-646.

Both California and federal laws provide that a person who is displaced from real property by a public entity may receive tax-exempt governmental assistance in the form of relocation payments.

California law also allows taxpayers to exclude from gross income tenant relocation assistance payments if such payments are required by state law or local ordinance.

¶ 236 Income from Original Issue Discount

Law: Secs. 17024.5, 17224, 18151, 18178 (CCH CALIFORNIA TAX REPORTS ¶ 15-575, 15-744, 16-691, 16-695).

Comparable Federal: Secs. 163(e), 1271-88, 6706 (CCH STANDARD FEDERAL TAX REPORTS ¶ 9102, 32,740—33,000, 40,875).

California Forms: Sch. CA (540), Sch. CA (540NR).

The reporting of income from original issue discount by the holder of debt instruments is the same under California law as federal as of the current IRC tie-in date (see ¶ 102a), except for a difference in the treatment of OID for 1985 and 1986 (see below).

"Original issue discount" is the excess of the stated redemption price of a debt instrument at maturity over its issue price.

The holder of a debt instrument issued at discount after July 1, 1982, must generally include in gross income the sum of the daily portions of the OID for each day during the taxable year on which the holder held the debt instrument. The holder of a debt instrument issued at discount after May 27, 1969, and before July 2, 1982, is required to include in income a ratable monthly portion of the "original issue discount" multiplied by the number of complete months and fractions thereof that the holder held the debt instrument during the taxable year. The income must be reported currently even though the taxpayer may use the cash basis of accounting. Special rules prescribe the determination of the daily portion of OID where the principal is subject to acceleration and where a subsequent holder pays an acquisition premium. These special rules extend to pooled debt instruments, effective for California purposes in taxable years beginning after 1997 and for federal purposes in tax years beginning after August 5, 1997.

The difference between the amount of OID included on the federal return and the amount included on the California return for tax years that began in 1985 or 1986 for debt instruments that were issued after 1984 must be reported as income for California purposes by the holder in the tax year in which the debt instrument matures or is otherwise disposed. The issuer of the debt instrument reports California/federal OID differences in the same year that the holder reports the income from such differences.

California conforms to the federal law used to determine how much original issue discount a purchaser of tax-exempt stripped bonds or coupons must attribute to those bonds or coupons. California also conforms to the federal provision that splits the yield on certain high-yield OID obligations into a deductible interest element and a nondeductible element representing return on equity.

The Franchise Tax Board has taken the position that OID on "stripped" U.S. Treasury obligations is interest on U.S. obligations and is exempt from California taxation. Such obligations include securities such as TIGRs and CATs, which are issued by investment firms (see ¶ 217).

¶ 237 Expense Reimbursements

Law: Secs. 17081, 17131 (CCH CALIFORNIA TAX REPORTS ¶ 15-458, 15-524).

Comparable Federal: Secs. 82, 123, 132 (CCH STANDARD FEDERAL TAX REPORTS ¶ 6374, 7300, 7420).

Specific rules are provided for certain types of expense reimbursement. California law incorporates the federal law by reference.

● *Moving expenses*

California adopts federal law allowing a taxpayer to exclude from gross income as a qualified fringe benefit any amount received by the taxpayer from an employer for moving expenses that would have been deductible by the taxpayer if they had not been reimbursed.

Moving expense deductions are discussed at ¶ 316a.

● *Loss on sale of home*

Generally, reimbursement for a loss on sale of a personal residence would be includible in income because the loss would be a personal one and nondeductible. However, where the loss is incurred in another state in connection with a move to California, the taxpayer might take the position that the reimbursement is compensation for services outside California during the period before he became a California resident and therefore is not taxable in California (see ¶ 405). On the other hand, the Franchise Tax Board (FTB) has taken the position that such a reimbursement is, in effect, a bonus for future services in California and is taxable.

    CCH **CCH Tip: Reimbursement of Loss May Be Excludable**

Under the FTB's reasoning, it would appear that reimbursement for a loss on the sale of a personal residence in connection with a move from California to another state would not be includible in California income.

Appeal of William H. Harmount and Estate of Dorothy E. Harmount (1977) (CCH CALIFORNIA TAX REPORTS ¶ 15-458.30) involved a taxpayer who moved in 1970 from Illinois to California. As an inducement to accept employment in California, the new employer reimbursed the taxpayer for certain expenses, including $5,031 for expenses in connection with the sale of an Illinois home. The State Board of Equalization held that the reimbursement represented compensation for services to be performed in California, subject to California tax. To the same effect, see *Appeal of Peter M. and Anita B. Berk* (1984) (CCH CALIFORNIA TAX REPORTS ¶ 15-609.332). See also the *Frame* case, discussed at ¶ 405, holding in effect that the source of the reimbursement income is irrelevant if the income "accrues" after the taxpayer becomes a California resident.

● *Living expenses*

Reimbursement from an insurance company for excess living expenses paid as a result of destruction (or threatened destruction) of the taxpayer's home by fire or other casualty is excluded from gross income under both California and federal law.

¶ 238 Community Income

    Law: Sec. 771, Family Code (CCH CALIFORNIA TAX REPORTS ¶ 15-428).

    Comparable Federal: Secs. 66, 879 (CCH STANDARD FEDERAL TAX REPORTS ¶ 6050, 28,160).

In general, in the absence of an agreement to the contrary, earnings of spouses who are domiciled in California and are not permanently separated are community property. On separate returns, any community income or deductions must be split equally between the spouses. The credit for a dependent supported by community funds may be taken by either spouse.

Where the spouses are separated with no intention of resuming the marital relationship, the earnings of each spouse during the period of separation are his or her separate property. This is the effect of a provision of the Family Code.

The California provision described above is generally comparable, in effect, to a federal provision (IRC Sec. 66) enacted in 1981. However, the federal provision was substantially revised, retroactively, in 1984. The federal law now provides relief for the "innocent spouse" in certain community-property situations, and empowers the Internal Revenue Service to treat community income as separate under certain conditions.

Where one spouse is a nonresident alien, community property laws are inapplicable to some extent for federal income tax purposes; California has not conformed.

Several decisions of the State Board of Equalization (SBE) have held a California-resident wife taxable on one-half of her nonresident husband's earnings, on the ground that the husband was domiciled in California and his earnings were therefore community property. See *Appeal of Annette Bailey* (1976) (CCH CALIFORNIA TAX REPORTS ¶ 15-101.252), where the husband was a resident of Canada; *Appeal of Nancy B. Meadows* (1980) (CCH CALIFORNIA TAX REPORTS ¶ 15-605.14), where the husband was a resident of Alabama; and *Appeal of Robert M. and Mildred Scott* (1981) (CCH CALIFORNIA TAX REPORTS ¶ 15-101.316), where the husband was out of the state on military assignments. Also, see *Appeal of George F. and Magdalena Herrman* (1962) (CCH CALIFORNIA TAX REPORTS ¶ 15-101.25), where the husband was a resident and domiciliary of the State of Washington: the SBE held the wife taxable on one-half of the husband's income because she was entitled to it under Washington law. To the same effect, see *Appeal of Roy L. and Patricia A. Misskelley* (1984) (CCH CALIFORNIA TAX REPORTS ¶ 15-101.255); in this case the husband was a resident and domiciliary of Nevada.

In *Appeal of Richard and Eva Taylor* (1989) (CCH CALIFORNIA TAX REPORTS ¶ 15-101.257), a wife was liable for tax on her community share of her husband's foreign earnings, and he was liable for tax on his community share of her California earnings because even though the husband established and maintained foreign residence, both spouses remained California domiciliaries.

¶ 239 Income from Investments in Depressed Areas

Law: Secs. 17233, 17235 (CCH CALIFORNIA TAX REPORTS ¶ 15-985, 15-999d).

Comparable Federal: None.

California Forms: FTB 3805Z, FTB 3806.

California allows a deduction for net interest received from loans made to a trade or business located in an enterprise zone (see ¶ 102b). It does not apply to anyone who has an ownership interest in the debtor. A similar exclusion was available for interest received prior to December 1, 1998, on loans made after June 30, 1992, to businesses located in the Los Angeles Revitalization Zone (LARZ).

The deduction for interest received from loans made to an enterprise zone business is reported on FTB 3805Z.

¶ 240 Ridesharing and Employee Commuter Deductions

Law: Secs. 17090, 17149 (CCH CALIFORNIA TAX REPORTS ¶ 15-640).

Comparable Federal: Sec. 132 (CCH STANDARD FEDERAL TAX REPORTS ¶ 7420).

California Forms: Sch. CA (540), Sch. CA (540NR).

Compensation or the fair market value of nonwage benefits furnished by an employer to an employee for participation in any employer-sponsored ridesharing program in California is excluded from the employee's California gross income. This includes compensation or benefits received for the following items:

(1) commuting in a vanpool, subscription taxipool, carpool, buspool, private commuter bus, or ferry;

(2) transit passes for use by employees or their dependents, other than transit passes for use by dependents who are elementary or secondary school students;

(3) free or subsidized parking for employees who participate in ridesharing arrangements;

(4) bicycling to or from work;

(5) travel to or from a telecommuting facility; or

(6) use of any other alternative transportation method that reduces the use of a motor vehicle by a single occupant for travel to or from that individual's place of employment.

Unlike the California gross income exclusion for the value of parking provided to ridesharing participants, the federal exclusion is subject to a cap.

Cash allowances received by an employee pursuant to a parking cash-out program (see ¶ 329), unless used for ridesharing purposes, must be included in the employee's gross income.

¶ 241 Employee Educational Assistance Plans

Law: Sec. 17151 (CCH CALIFORNIA TAX REPORTS ¶ 15-539).

Comparable Federal: Sec. 127 (CCH STANDARD FEDERAL TAX REPORTS ¶ 7350).

California Forms: Sch. CA (540), Sch. CA (540 NR).

With the exception of the expiration date, California law is substantially the same as federal law concerning the exclusion of up to $5,250 of employer-provided educational assistance benefits from an employee's gross income. The exclusion applies for federal purposes only to expenses paid for courses beginning before June 30, 2000, whereas California has no expiration date. However, under both federal and California law the exclusion is inapplicable to payments made for graduate level courses that begin after June 30, 1996.

¶ 242 Payments for Conservation and Environmental Protection

Law: Secs. 17131, 17135.5 (CCH California Tax Reports ¶ 15-536).

Comparable Federal: Sec. 126 (CCH Standard Federal Tax Reports ¶ 7330).

California incorporates the federal exclusion for cost-sharing payments received under certain conservation and environmental protection programs.

● *Payments received by forest landowners*

In addition, California provides a specific exclusion from gross income for cost-share payments received by forest landowners from the Department of Forestry and Fire Protection pursuant to the California Forest Improvement Act of 1978 or from the United States Department of Agriculture, Forest Service, under the Forest Stewardship Program and the Stewardship Incentives Program, pursuant to the federal Cooperative Forestry Assistance Act. The amount of any excluded payment must not be considered for a determination of the basis of property acquired or improved or in computation of any deduction to which the taxpayer may otherwise be entitled.

¶ 243 Water Conservation Rebates

Law: Sec. 17138 (CCH California Tax Reports ¶ 15-642).

Comparable Federal: None.

California Forms: Sch. CA (540), Sch. CA (540NR).

A California law treats certain water conservation rebates received by taxpayers from local water agencies or suppliers as refunds or price adjustments rather than as income for personal income tax purposes. To qualify, a rebate must be for the taxpayer's expenses in purchasing or installing water conservation water closets or urinals that meet specified performance standards and use no more than (1) 1.6 gallons per flush in the case of a water closet or (2) 1 gallon per flush in the case of a urinal.

¶ 244 Energy Conservation Subsidies

Law: Sec. 17131 (CCH California Tax Reports ¶ 15-548b).

Comparable Federal: Sec. 136 (CCH Standard Federal Tax Reports ¶ 7560).

California incorporates the federal gross income exclusion for subsidies received from a public utility for the purchase or installation of an energy conservation measure designed to reduce the consumption of electricity or natural gas or to improve the management of energy demand with respect to a dwelling unit.

¶ 245 Crime Hotline Rewards

Law: Sec. 17147.7 (CCH California Tax Reports ¶ 15-644).

Comparable Federal: None.

California Forms: Sch. CA (540), Sch. CA (540NR).

Rewards received from a crime hotline are excludable from gross income if the hotline is established by a government agency or a California nonprofit charitable organization and is authorized by a government entity. Employees of a government agency or nonprofit charitable organization that contributes reward funds to the crime hotline are ineligible to claim this exclusion.

¶ 246 Medical Savings Accounts

Law: Secs. 17201, 17215 (CCH CALIFORNIA TAX REPORTS ¶ 15-891).

Comparable Federal: Secs. 138, 220 (CCH STANDARD FEDERAL TAX REPORTS ¶ 7630, ¶ 12,670).

With the exception of the amount of penalties imposed on unauthorized withdrawals, California law is the same as federal law. Employer's contributions to a medical savings account (MSA) and any interest or dividends earned on an MSA are excluded from a taxpayer's gross income.

Withdrawals made from an MSA are also exempt if used to pay unreimbursed qualified medical expenses of the taxpayer, spouse, and dependents (which are essentially the same as those expenses that qualify for an itemized deduction). Distributions from an MSA for nonmedical purposes are treated as taxable income and are subject to a 10% penalty (15% under federal law), unless the distribution is made after the taxpayer reaches age 65, becomes disabled, or dies. The penalty is reported on FTB 3805P.

● *Medicare Plus Choice MSAs*

Under both California and federal law, certain seniors are permitted to establish Medicare Plus Choice MSAs, effective for tax years beginning after 1998. The tax treatment of Medicare Plus Choice MSAs is similar to that of regular MSAs, with the following exceptions: (1) tax-free distributions from the Medicare Plus Choice MSA may be used only for the qualified medical expenses of the account holder; (2) the Secretary of Health and Human Services, rather than the account holder's employer, makes tax-free contributions to the Medicare Plus Choice MSA; and (3) a Medicare Plus Choice MSA may only be used in conjunction with a high deductible Medicare Plus Choice MSA health plan (MSA health plan).

An MSA health plan is a new type of health plan that requires a certain deductible to be satisfied before a senior citizen's medical expenses are reimbursed. The amount of the annual deductible under an MSA health plan may not exceed $6,000 in 1999. This amount will be indexed for inflation in subsequent years. Contributions to a Medicare Plus Choice MSA are subject to an annual limitation, which is 75% of the individual's deductible for the required MSA health plan.

A penalty of 50% is imposed to the extent that nonqualifying distributions exceed the amount by which the value of the MSA plan as of December 31 of the preceding tax year exceeds 60% of the MSA plan's deductible amount. For purposes of this penalty, all payments and distributions not used to pay the qualified medical expenses of the account holder during any tax year are treated as one distribution.

¶ 247 Holocaust and Internment Victim Compensation

Law: Secs. 17155, 17156.5 (CCH CALIFORNIA TAX REPORTS ¶ 15-598).

Comparable Federal: United States-Federal Republic of Germany Income Tax Convention.

Under California's Holocaust Victim Compensation Relief Act, as under federal law, payments or property received as compensation pursuant to the German Act Regulating Unresolved Property Claims are excludable from an individual's gross income. The basis of any property received pursuant to the German Act is the fair market value of the property at the time of receipt by the individual.

Applicable to taxable years beginning after 1998, California law, but not federal law, allows Holocaust victims, or their heirs or beneficiaries, to exclude from gross income settlements received for claims against any entity or individual for any recovered asset. For purposes of the expanded exclusion, "Holocaust victim" means any person who was persecuted by Nazi Germany or any Axis regime during any period from 1933 to 1945. In addition, "recovered asset" means any asset of any kind, including any bank deposits, insurance proceeds, or artwork owned by a Holocaust victim during any period from 1920 to 1945, inclusive, and any interest earned on the asset, that was withheld from that victim or the victim's heirs or beneficiaries from and after 1945 and that was not recovered, returned, or otherwise compensated to the victim or his or her heirs or beneficiaries until after 1994.

California law, but not federal law, also excludes from gross income reparation payments made by the Canadian government for the purpose of redressing the injustice done to persons of Japanese ancestry who were interned in Canada during World War II, effective for taxable years beginning after 1998.

¶ 248 Adoption Assistance Programs

Law: Sec. 17131 (CCH CALIFORNIA TAX REPORTS ¶ 15-548c).

Comparable Federal: Sec. 137 (CCH STANDARD FEDERAL TAX REPORTS ¶ 7600).

Under both California and federal law, an employee may exclude from his or her gross income amounts paid or expenses incurred for the employee's adoption expenses as part of an employer's written, nondiscriminatory, adoption assistance program. The maximum amount that may be excluded is $5,000 of qualified expenses per child ($6,000 for a child with special needs). The exclusion is available for taxable years beginning after 1996 and before 2002.

¶ 249 Qualified State Tuition Program

Law: Secs. 17140, 17140.3 (CCH CALIFORNIA TAX REPORTS ¶ 15-551).

Comparable Federal: Sec. 529 (CCH STANDARD FEDERAL TAX REPORTS ¶ 22,601).

California Forms: Sch. CA (540), Sch. CA (540NR).

Under both California and federal law, distributions or earnings from a qualified state tuition program are generally excludable from a beneficiary's and contributor's gross income to the extent that such distributions are used to pay for the beneficiary's higher education expenses, including expenses for room and board, at a qualifying educational institution. California's qualified state tuition program is entitled the "Golden State Scholarshare Trust" program.

CCH Tip: Contributors May Remove Funds from Account

If the beneficiary of a Scholarshare account does not ever attend a qualified educational institution, or if there are still funds in the account after the beneficiary graduates from a qualified educational institution, the funds can be transferred to a Scholarshare account for the benefit of another family member. Alternatively, the contributor to the account may cancel the account and take back the available funds, but must pay taxes on any earnings, as well as a penalty.

CHAPTER 3

PERSONAL INCOME TAX
DEDUCTIONS

¶ 300 Deductions—Generally

Law: Sec. 17201 (CCH California Tax Reports, ¶ 15-701).

Comparable Federal: Secs. 161-219, 261-280H (CCH Standard Federal Tax Reports ¶ 8402—12,662; 13,502—14,801).

California Forms: Sch. CA (540), Sch. CA (540NR), FTB 3526, FTB 3805V, FTB 3885A, FTB 3885F, FTB 3885L, FTB 3885P.

In general, California conforms to federal law regarding deductions that may be taken to reduce taxable income, but there are some differences that are discussed in the following paragraphs. As under federal law, some deductions may be used to reduce gross income and others may be used to reduce adjusted gross income. Any differences between the amounts of the California deductions and the federal deductions must be reported on Sch. CA (540) or Sch. CA (540NR) (see ¶ 30, ¶ 31).

In addition, some deductions may be limited because they arise from passive activities (see ¶ 326).

¶ 301 Trade or Business Expenses

Law: Secs. 17201, 17203, 17269, 17270, 17270.5, 17273, 17273.1, 17278 (CCH California Tax Reports ¶ 15-711, 15-714, 15-715, 15-727, 15-734, 15-741, 15-862, 15-880, 15-943).

Comparable Federal: Secs. 162, 190, 280A (CCH Standard Federal Tax Reports ¶ 8520, 8580, 12,260, 12,290).

California Forms: Sch. CA (540), Sch. CA (540NR).

All ordinary and necessary expenses of a trade or business are deductible. The California law is the same as the federal, except as follows:

(a) California prohibits deduction of certain types of expenses (illegal activities, etc.), as explained at ¶ 322.

(b) California has not adopted special federal rules for travel expenses of state legislators.

(c) Where a federal tax credit is allowed for wages to provide new jobs, the wages are disallowed as a federal deduction; however, such wages are still allowed as a California deduction. (However, wages subject to the various hiring credits available to employers operating in economic incentive areas, described at ¶ 102b, are not allowed as a California deduction.)

(d) California denies a business expense deduction for expenditures made at, or payments made to, a club that engages in discriminatory practices.

(e) California has not adopted the federal provision denying a deduction for certain lobbying and political expenditures.

● *"Ordinary" and "necessary" expenses*

It should not be assumed that an item of expense that is allowed under federal law will always be allowed by California, because the interpretations of different taxing authorities concerning what are "ordinary" and "necessary" business expenses are not always uniform. Also, expenses that would normally be deductible under federal law are not allowed by California when they are attributable to income that is not taxed by California—see ¶ 322.

● *Principal place of business*

Both California and federal law expand the definition of a taxpayer's "principal place of business" for purposes of claiming a home office expense deduction, effective for taxable years beginning after 1998. Under the expanded definition, a home office qualifies as a taxpayer's "principal place of business" if (1) the office is used by the taxpayer to conduct business-related administrative or management activities, and (2) there is no other fixed business location where such activities take place. However, the expanded definition does not eliminate the requirement, for both federal and California purposes, that the office be used by the taxpayer exclusively on a regular basis as a place of business. Also, if the taxpayer is an employee, the taxpayer's use of the home office must be for the convenience of the taxpayer's employer.

 CCH Tip: Commuting from Home Office Deduction

Although the expenses of commuting from an individual's residence to a local place of business are generally classified as nondeductible commuting expenses, such expenses may be deductible as ordinary and necessary business expenses for taxable years beginning after 1998 if the individual uses his or her home as a principal place of business. For example, an anesthesiologist whose residence is her principal place of business may be able to deduct the expenses of traveling between her home and the hospitals at which she performs her primary duties.

● *Self-employed health insurance costs*

For both California and federal purposes, self-employed taxpayers are allowed to deduct a percentage of the amounts they have paid for medical insurance for themselves and their families, not to exceed the taxpayer's earned income from the taxpayer's trade or business. California law provides that amounts used as "earned income" for purposes of computing a taxpayer's federal deduction (rather than the earned income computed using California amounts) must be used for purposes of computing the taxpayer's state deduction. This deduction may be taken even if the taxpayer does not itemize deductions.

For California and federal purposes, the deduction is 60% for tax years beginning during 1999 through 2001; 70% for tax years beginning during

2002; and 100% for tax years beginning after 2002. California's deduction was limited to 40% for the 1997 and 1998 taxable years, whereas federal law allowed a 40% deduction during the 1997 tax year and a 45% deduction for the 1998 tax year.

● *Automobile expenses*

The Internal Revenue Service has followed a policy of allowing fixed per diem allowances and automobile mileage rates in lieu of itemized details for certain deductible expenses. For transportation expenses paid or incurred during the period of January 1, 1999, through March 31, 1999, the federal standard mileage rate for business-related automobile expense deductions is 32.5¢ per mile. Thereafter, the rate is reduced to 31¢ per mile. It is the policy, generally, of the Franchise Tax Board (FTB) to conform to the federal practice in these areas, so taxpayers may assume conformance with the federal rates in the absence of an announcement or ruling by the FTB. California also conforms to federal law allowing a U.S. postal service rural mail carrier to deduct the amount of qualified reimbursements received for expenses incurred for the use of the mail carrier's vehicle for the collection and delivering of mail on the carrier's route.

 CCH Observation: Lowering of Standard Mileage Rate

For the first time ever, the standard mileage rate for business use of an automobile is lower than the rate for the preceding year. The IRS initially prescribed an effective date of January 1, 1999, for the new 31¢ rate, but subsequently announced that it would postpone the effective date of the new rate until April 1, 1999, in order to give employers and employees additional time to implement the new rate.

● *Physicians' deduction for interindemnity payments*

California conforms to federal law allowing physicians to deduct certain interindemnity payments made to provide protection from malpractice liability.

● *Architectural adaptations to accommodate the handicapped*

Both California and federal law allow a deduction of certain expenditures for the removal of architectural and transportation barriers to the handicapped and the elderly. California and federal law allowing a credit for disabled access expenditures is discussed at ¶ 129. Amounts for which a credit is claimed may not be deducted.

¶ 302 Meals, Entertainment, and Travel Expenses

Law: Secs. 17201, 17271 (CCH CALIFORNIA TAX REPORTS ¶ 15-711, 15-929).

Comparable Federal: Secs. 162, 170, 274 (CCH STANDARD FEDERAL TAX REPORTS ¶ 8450, 14,402).

● *Meal and beverage expenses*

With certain exceptions, taxpayers may deduct only 50% of business-related meal and beverage expenses, including the cost of meals incurred during business travel away from home. The 50% limit is also applicable to unreimbursed expenses incurred by employees on behalf of their employer (see ¶ 317).

Also, the deduction is generally not allowed unless taxpayers establish that (1) the meal and beverage expenses were directly related to the active conduct of their trade or business; or (2) in the case of expenses directly preceding or directly following a bona fide business discussion, that the expenses were associated with the active conduct of their trade or business.

An exception is provided allowing deductions by taxpayers for the cost of their own meals while away on business. Food and beverage expenses deemed lavish or extravagant under the circumstances are not deductible.

The deductible percentage of meals provided to employees subject to Department of Transportation hours-of-service rules is increased for both California and federal purposes for tax years beginning after 1997, reaching an 80% deduction by the year 2008. In addition, meals provided at an eating facility for employees are fully deductible by the employer, instead of possibly being subject to the 50% limitation, effective for tax years beginning after 1997. For this purpose, the employee is treated as having paid an amount for the meal equal to the direct operating costs of the facility that are attributable to the meal.

● *Entertainment expenses*

Taxpayers may deduct only 50% of the cost of business entertainment expenses. They must establish that (1) the expenses were directly related to the active conduct of their trade or business; or (2) in the case of entertainment expenses directly preceding or directly following a bona fide business discussion, that the expenses were associated with the active conduct of their trade or business.

Generally, taxpayers may not deduct more than 50% of the face value of entertainment tickets. However, the full amount paid for tickets to sporting events may be deducted if: (1) the event benefits a charity; (2) the proceeds go to the charity; and (3) the event uses volunteers to perform substantially all the event's work.

Under federal law that is not incorporated into California law, no deduction is allowed for club dues paid or incurred for membership in any business, pleasure, social, athletic, luncheon, sporting, airline, or hotel club.

¶ 302

● *Travel expenses*

Taxpayers may not deduct the cost of travel that in itself constitutes a form of education. For example, a language teacher may not deduct the cost of visiting a foreign country merely for the purpose of maintaining familiarity with the country's language and culture.

In addition, a taxpayer's employment away from home for more than one year will be treated as indefinite, rather than temporary; thus, no deduction for travel expenses will be allowed in connection with such employment. However, both California and federal law allow a deduction to federal employees traveling on temporary duty status in connection with the investigation of a federal crime, even if they are away from home for more than one year. A technical correction made by the IRS Restructuring and Reform Act of 1998 also makes the federal exception to the one-year rule applicable to federal employees traveling on temporary duty status in connection with the *prosecution* of a federal crime. The change is effective for federal purposes for amounts paid or incurred with respect to tax years ending after August 5, 1997, but has not yet been incorporated for California purposes.

Charitable travel expenses may be deducted only if there is no significant element of personal pleasure, recreation, or vacation in such travel.

Also, taxpayers may not deduct the expenses of attending a convention, seminar, or similar meeting in connection with their investment activities. The convention, meeting, or seminar must now relate to the taxpayer's trade or business. The convention, seminar, or meeting must offer significant business related activities, e.g., participation in meetings, workshops, or lectures.

A deduction for travel expenses of a spouse, dependent, or any other individual accompanying a person on a business trip is disallowed unless (1) the accompanying individual is an employee of the person paying or reimbursing the travel expenses, (2) the accompanying individual's travel is also for a bona fide business purpose, and (3) the expenses would otherwise be deductible by the accompanying individual.

¶ 303 Itemized Deductions

> *Law:* Secs. 17076, 17077, 17201, 17207, 17208.4, 17220 (CCH CALIFORNIA TAX REPORTS ¶ 15-701, 15-747, 15-750, 15-801, 15-878).
>
> *Comparable Federal:* Secs. 63, 67, 68, 163, 164, 165, 170, 213, 217 (CCH STANDARD FEDRAL TAX REPORTS ¶ 6020, 6060, 9102—9802, 11,675, 12,540, 12,620).
>
> *California Forms:* Sch. CA (540), Sch. CA (540NR).

Individuals may take the standard deduction or itemize deductions for California purposes, whether or not they itemize federally. California has conformed to most of the federal itemized deduction provisions.

Following are the major differences between California and federal itemized deductions:

(1) state, local, and foreign income taxes, and state disability insurance tax (SDI) may be deducted for federal but not California purposes (see ¶ 306);

¶ **303**

(2) the contribution carryover from pre-1987 tax years could differ;

(3) there may be a California-only carryover from a disaster loss that occurred as a result of fire in 1985, storms or floods in 1986, forest fires or earthquakes in 1987, earthquakes in 1989, fire in 1990 or 1991, fire, storms and floods, earthquakes, or riots and arson in 1992, fire or storms and floods in 1993, earthquakes or fires in 1994, storms and flooding in 1995, storms or flooding in 1996, 1997, or 1998, or the freeze in the winter of 1998-99 (see ¶ 307);

(4) miscellaneous itemized deductions for expenses related to producing income taxed under federal law, but not California, are not deductible for California purposes, and vice versa (see ¶ 322);

(5) expenses (e.g., employee business expenses) that include depreciation on assets placed in service before 1987 or after 1992 could differ (see ¶ 310, ¶ 310a);

(6) the deduction for interest on certain home mortgages may differ (see ¶ 305);

(7) deductions including an element of gain or loss may differ because of differences in California and federal bases (see ¶ 521); and

(8) itemized deductions for high-income taxpayers must be reduced by 6% of adjusted gross income for California purposes instead of the federal 3% reduction (see below).

● *2% floor on miscellaneous itemized deductions*

Certain unreimbursed employee expenses, expenses of producing income, and other qualifying expenses are deducted as miscellaneous itemized deductions federally and for California purposes. For both California and federal purposes, most miscellaneous itemized deductions are subject to a 2% floor. Only the portion of the total amount of such deductions in excess of 2% of the taxpayer's federal adjusted gross income is deductible.

Following are the most common expenses subject to the 2% floor:

professional society dues;

employment-related educational expenses;

office-in-the-home expenses;

expenses of looking for a new job;

professional books, magazines, journals and periodicals;

work clothes and uniforms;

union dues and fees;

certain unreimbursed employee business expenses;

safe deposit box rental;

tax counsel and assistance;

cost of work-related small tools and supplies;

investment counsel fees;

fees paid to an IRA custodian; and

certain expenses of a partnership, grantor trust, or S corporation that are incurred for the production of income.

Following are the most common expenses not subject to the 2% floor:

certain adjustments when a taxpayer restores amounts held under a claim of right;

amortizable bond premium;

gambling losses to the extent of gambling winnings;

deductions allowable in connection with personal property used in a short sale;

impairment-related work expenses of a handicapped individual that are for deductible attendant care services at the individual's place of work, and other expenses in connection with the place of work that are necessary for the individual to be able to work;

mutual fund shareholder expenses; and

nonbusiness casualty losses.

● *Overall limitation for high-income taxpayers*

The itemized deductions of taxpayers in high-income brackets must be reduced by the lesser of (1) 6% (3% under federal law) of the excess of adjusted gross income over the threshold amount or (2) 80% of the amount of the itemized deductions otherwise allowable for the tax year. For 1999, the California threshold amounts are $119,813 for a single taxpayer or a married taxpayer filing a separate return, $179,720 for a head of household, and $239,628 for a surviving spouse or a married taxpayer filing a joint return. The threshold amounts are adjusted annually for inflation. The federal threshold amount for 1999 is $126,600 ($63,300 for married taxpayers filing separate returns).

For both California and federal purposes, the limitation does not apply to deductions for medical expenses, casualty and theft losses, wagering losses, or investment interest expenses.

¶ 304 Expenses for Production of Income

Law: Sec. 17201 (CCH California Tax Reports ¶ 15-875).

Comparable Federal: Sec. 212 (CCH Standard Federal Tax Reports ¶ 12,520).

California Forms: Sch. CA (540), Sch. CA (540NR).

California law is generally the same as federal law. Taxpayers may deduct all ordinary and necessary expenses incurred (1) for the production or collection of income, (2) for the management, conservation, or maintenance of property held for the production of income, or (3) in connection with the determination, collection, or refund of any tax.

   CCH Observation: Application of 2% Floor

Deductions for the expenses of producing income are generally subject to the 2% floor on miscellaneous itemized deductions. However, expenses attributable to property held for the production of

---

> rents or royalties are subtracted from gross income to arrive at
> adjusted gross income (i.e., as above-the-line deductions) and, thus,
> their deduction is not subject to the 2% floor.

For California purposes, however, deductible expenses must relate to income that is taxable by California; see ¶ 322. Moreover, it should be noted that, although federal and California law are formally the same, different taxing authorities may take different views concerning whether an item of expense is "ordinary" and "necessary." In practice, therefore, deductions allowed under one law may not always be allowed under the other.

In *Appeal of Glenn M. and Phylis R. Pfau* (1972) (CCH CALIFORNIA TAX REPORTS ¶ 15-875.28), the taxpayers claimed a deduction for campaign expenses in an election for municipal court judge. The State Board of Equalization (SBE) denied the deduction, following a former California regulation and federal cases decided under the comparable federal statute.

In *Appeal of Bernard B. and Dorothy Howard* (1961) (CCH CALIFORNIA TAX REPORTS ¶ 15-875.88), the SBE held that legal and accounting fees incurred while the taxpayer was a resident of California, but applicable to a federal tax controversy involving years prior to the establishment of California residence, were not deductible under item (3) above. The SBE based its decision on the fact that such expenses were connected with income not taxable in California; therefore, they were nondeductible under the rule denying deductions for expenses applicable to tax-exempt income (see ¶ 322).

¶ 305 Interest

> *Law:* Secs. 17072, 17201, 17204, 17224, 17230, 17279.5, 17280 (CCH CALIFORNIA TAX REPORTS ¶ 15-744, 15-892, 15-903).
>
> *Comparable Federal:* Secs. 163, 221, 264, 265(a)(2), 265(a)(6) (CCH STANDARD FEDERAL TAX REPORTS ¶ 9102, 12,692, 13,501, 14,050).
>
> *California Forms:* FTB 3526, Sch. CA (540), Sch. CA (540NR).

California conforms to federal law concerning the deductibility of interest expenses, except as discussed below.

● *Tax-exempt interest*

Interest expense incurred to purchase or carry tax-exempt obligations is not deductible under either California or federal law (see ¶ 217). The same rule applies to shareholders of mutual funds holding such obligations and distributing tax-exempt interest on them (see ¶ 217). However, the amount of nondeductible interest may differ due to differences between California and federal law regarding tax-exempt obligations.

● *Personal interest*

No deduction for personal interest is available.

Qualified residence interest is not subject to the same treatment as personal interest; see below.

● *Investment interest*

A deduction is allowed for investment interest up to the amount of net investment income. The deduction is calculated on FTB 3526. Net capital gain from the disposition of investment property is generally excluded from investment income. However, taxpayers may elect to include as much of their net capital gain investment income as they choose in calculating the investment interest limitation for federal purposes if they also reduce the amount of net capital gain eligible for the special federal capital gain tax. Taxpayers are allowed to make a similar election for California purposes; however, as discussed at ¶ 512, California treats capital gains as ordinary income.

Any amount not allowed as a deduction for any taxable year because of this limitation may be carried over and treated as deductible investment interest in the succeeding taxable year.

The limitation on itemized deductions for high-income taxpayers does not apply to investment interest expenses (see ¶ 303).

● *Mortgage interest*

A deduction is allowed for a limited amount of interest paid or accrued on (1) debts incurred to acquire a principal or second residence and (2) home equity debts. The aggregate amount of acquisition indebtedness must not exceed $1 million, and the aggregate amount of home equity indebtedness must not exceed $100,000. Interest attributable to debt over such limits is nondeductible personal interest.

California law provides that payments made to the California Housing Finance Agency by first-time home buyers under a "buy-down mortgage plan" are considered payments of interest for purposes of the interest deduction. Such payments are made under Section 52514 of the Health and Safety Code, to reimburse the agency for its cost of subsidizing the borrower's interest cost. Although there is no comparable provision in the federal law, it might be argued that the payments are made in lieu of interest and therefore should be treated as interest for federal as well as California purposes.

● *Interest on company-owned life insurance*

An employer is generally precluded from claiming a deduction for interest paid or incurred on money borrowed to fund an insurance policy or an endowment or annuity contract covering the life of *any* individual for whom the taxpayer has an insurable interest. However, an employer may still deduct interest paid or incurred to purchase life insurance policies, annuities, and endowment contracts for a limited number of officers and 20% owners if (1) the aggregate amount of debt with respect to the policies and contracts does not exceed $50,000 per key person and (2) the interest rate does not exceed a specified amount. See ¶ 301 for limitations on the deductibility of premiums on company-owned life insurance.

● *Student loan interest*

Under both California and federal law, an above-the-line deduction is allowed for interest due and paid on qualified education loans after 1997, up to a maximum of $1,000 for 1998 and increasing to $2,500 by the year 2001. The

¶ 305

maximum deduction for the 1999 tax year is $1,500. The deduction may be claimed only for the first 60 months of interest payments and is subject to gradual phase-outs for individuals with modified adjusted gross income (AGI) of $40,000 or more ($60,000 for joint filers), with complete phase-outs for individuals with modified AGI of $55,000 or more ($75,000 for joint filers). For purposes of this deduction, modified AGI includes income from social security benefits as well as amounts contributed to an individual retirement account. The modified AGI figures are adjusted for inflation for taxable years beginning after 2002.

 CCH Caution: Deductible Amounts Won't Be Indexed

Although the maximum deductible amounts of student loan interest increase over a four-year phase-in period, these amounts are not scheduled to be indexed for inflation thereafter.

● *Miscellaneous interest*

See ¶ 316 regarding deductibility of interest by tenant-stockholders of cooperative housing corporations. See ¶ 414 for special rules regarding imputed interest on certain installment contracts. See ¶ 416 regarding capitalization of interest during the construction period of real property.

¶ 306 Taxes

> *Law:* Secs. 17201, 17220, 17222 (CCH CALIFORNIA TAX REPORTS ¶ 15-747).
>
> *Comparable Federal:* Secs. 164, 275 (CCH STANDARD FEDERAL TAX REPORTS ¶ 9500, 14,500).
>
> *California Forms:* Form 540A, Sch. CA (540), Sch. CA (540NR).

California law is the same as federal except that California specifically prohibits the deduction of "state, local, and foreign income, war profits, and excess profits taxes," and California does not allow the deduction of California SDI tax (see below). California also prohibits the deduction for personal income tax purposes of any tax imposed under the bank and corporation tax law. However, some such taxes may be used as the basis for claiming credits—see ¶ 114—¶ 119.

Under both California and federal law, the following taxes may be deducted:

(1) state, local, and foreign real property taxes;

(2) state and local personal property taxes; and

(3) other state, local, and foreign taxes relating to a trade or business, or to property held for production of income (except income taxes—see below).

● *Taxes based on gross receipts*

A tax on gross receipts may be deductible under category (3) above, if it can avoid classification as an income tax, since it presumably is incurred "for the production or collection of income."

In *Scott Beamer v. Franchise Tax Board* (1977) (CCH CALIFORNIA TAX REPORTS ¶ 15-747.41), the California Supreme Court held that the Texas "occupation tax" on oil and gas production is not "on or according to or measured by income or profits" and therefore is deductible.

● *Self-employment tax*

A deduction for one-half of a taxpayer's federal self-employment tax liability for the taxable year is available under both California and federal law.

● *Foreign taxes*

Numerous rulings and decisions over the years have held specific foreign taxes nondeductible under the income-tax prohibition. Following is a partial listing, in alphabetical order by state or country:

ALASKA—gross production tax on oil royalties—*Appeal of Jesson* (1957) (CCH CALIFORNIA TAX REPORTS ¶ 15-350.11).

ARGENTINA—tax withheld on royalties—*Appeal of Don Baxter, Inc.* (1964) (CCH CALIFORNIA TAX REPORTS ¶ 10-561.203).

AUSTRALIA—tax withheld on dividends—*Appeal of Siff* (1975) (CCH CALIFORNIA TAX REPORTS ¶ 15-747.152).

BRAZIL—same as Argentina, above.

CANADA—tax withheld on dividends, interest, and trust distributions—*Appeal of Bochner* (1974) (CCH CALIFORNIA TAX REPORTS ¶ 15-747.13), *Appeal of Siff* (1975) (CCH CALIFORNIA TAX REPORTS ¶ 15-747.152).

HAWAII—gross income tax—*Robinson et al. v. Franchise Tax Board* (1981) (CCH CALIFORNIA TAX REPORTS ¶ 15-747.157).

ITALY—same as Argentina, above.

JAPAN—tax withheld on royalties and dividends—*Appeal of Everett* (1973) (CCH CALIFORNIA TAX REPORTS ¶ 15-747.431), *Appeal of Siff* (1975) (CCH CALIFORNIA TAX REPORTS ¶ 15-747.152).

MEXICO—tax withheld on royalties, dividends, and interest—*Appeal of Don Baxter, Inc.* (1964) (CCH CALIFORNIA TAX REPORTS ¶ 10-561.203), *Appeal of Mabee* (1966) (CCH CALIFORNIA TAX REPORTS ¶ 15-747.153), *Appeal of Blankenbeckler* (1969) (CCH CALIFORNIA TAX REPORTS ¶ 15-747.154).

NETHERLANDS—tax withheld on dividends—*Appeal of Siff* (1975) (CCH CALIFORNIA TAX REPORTS ¶ 15-747.152).

PHILIPPINES—same as Argentina, above.

SOUTH AFRICA—tax withheld on dividends—*Appeal of Haubiel* (1973) (CCH CALIFORNIA TAX REPORTS ¶ 15-747.15), *Appeal of Siff* (1975) (CCH CALIFORNIA TAX REPORTS ¶ 15-747.152).

UNITED KINGDOM—tax withheld on dividends—*Appeal of Siff* (1975) (CCH CALIFORNIA TAX REPORTS ¶ 15-747.152).

¶ 306

● *SDI tax*

California does not allow a deduction for the employees' tax under the unemployment insurance law (commonly referred to as SDI—see ¶ 1806). A 1977 Tax Court decision *(Trujillo)* allowed a federal deduction for the SDI tax on the ground that it is, in effect, a state income tax; however, as explained above, California denies any deduction for income taxes. See *Appeal of Arnold E. and Mildred H. Galef* (1979) (CCH CALIFORNIA TAX REPORTS ¶ 15-747.511).

However, California does allow a credit for excess SDI if two or more of the taxpayer's employers withheld more than the maximum amount for the year (see ¶ 120).

● *Auto license fees*

California motor vehicle license fees, except for registration fees, weight fees (trucks only), and county or district fees, are based on value and are deductible as personal property taxes. The deductible and nondeductible portions included in the total license fee are shown on the renewal notice for vehicle registration.

● *Postponed property taxes*

Where payment of property taxes is postponed, as explained at ¶ 1704a, the taxes are treated as if paid for income tax purposes and are deductible in the taxable year when the required certificate is submitted to the tax assessor.

● *Cross-references*

See ¶ 316 regarding deductibility of taxes by tenant-stockholders of cooperative housing corporations. See ¶ 416 regarding capitalization of taxes during the construction period of real property.

¶ 307 Losses

Law: Secs. 17201, 17207, 17207,4, 17208.4 (CCH CALIFORNIA TAX REPORTS ¶ 15-750, 15-753, 15-756, 15-759).

Comparable Federal: Secs. 165, 186, 1242—44 (CCH STANDARD FEDERAL TAX REPORTS ¶ 9802, 12,210, 32,453, 32,470, 32,490).

California Form: FTB 3805V.

Under both California and federal laws, an ordinary loss deduction is allowed for a loss that is not compensated for by insurance or otherwise. As to individual taxpayers, losses are limited to the following:

(a) those incurred in a trade or business;

(b) those incurred in a transaction entered into for profit; or

(c) those arising from casualty or theft, to the extent the total of such losses, after excluding the first $100 of each loss, exceeds 10% of federal adjusted gross income. Casualty, theft, and wagering losses are not subject to the limitations on high income taxpayers explained at ¶ 303.

Casualty losses are measured, generally, by the loss in value of the property; however, in any event the deduction is limited by the amount of the cost or other basis of the property. (See *Appeal of Dominic and Mary Barbaria*

(1981) (CCH CALIFORNIA TAX REPORTS ¶ 15-750.191), where a deduction was denied because the property lost had been fully depreciated.)

Federal law disallows income tax deductions for certain losses if the losses may be claimed as federal estate-tax deductions. Although California law generally provides that references to federal estate tax should be ignored, the Franchise Tax Board has announced that estate administration expenses can be deducted for California income tax purposes or California estate "pickup" tax purposes, but not both (*Tax News*, FTB, May 1988, CCH CALIFORNIA TAX REPORTS ¶ 16-363.751).

● *Theft losses*

Theft losses are deductible only in the year of discovery, unlike other losses, which are deductible in the year sustained.

● *Disaster losses*

Special California legislation allows losses due to the following causes, including related casualties, to be carried forward for up to five years if they were sustained in presidentially-designated disaster areas or in California counties or cities proclaimed to be in a state of disaster by the Governor:

(1) forest fire occurring in 1985 in California;

(2) storm or flooding occurring in 1986 in California;

(3) forest fire during 1987;

(4) earthquake or aftershock occurring in 1987 in California;

(5) earthquake or aftershock occurring in 1989 in California;

(6) fire during 1990 in California;

(7) the Oakland/Berkeley Fire of 1991;

(8) storm or flooding occurring in February 1992 in California;

(9) earthquake or aftershock occurring in April 1992 in Humboldt County;

(10) riots or arson occurring in April or May 1992 in California;

(11) earthquakes occurring in San Bernardino County in June and July 1992;

(12) the Fountain Fire in Shasta County or the fire in Calaveras County in August 1992;

(13) storm or flooding occurring in the Counties of Alpine, Contra Costa, Fresno, Humboldt, Imperial, Lassen, Los Angeles, Madera, Mendocino, Modoc, Monterey, Napa, Orange, Plumas, Riverside, San Bernardino, San Diego, Santa Barbara, Sierra, Siskiyou, Sonoma, Tehama, Trinity, and Tulare and the City of Fillmore in January 1993;

(14) fire in Los Angeles, Orange, Riverside, San Bernardino, San Diego, or Ventura County during October or November 1993;

(15) earthquake or aftershock in Los Angeles, Orange, and Ventura counties on or after January 17, 1994;

(16) fire in San Luis Obispo County in August 1994;

(17) storms or flooding during 1995;

(18) storms or flooding during December 1996 or January 1997;

(19) storms or flooding during February 1998; and

(20) the freeze during the winter of 1998-99.

All of these losses may be taken in the year prior to the casualty, pursuant to an adopted federal provision. Also, a loss resulting from a disaster declared by the Governor may be claimed in the year prior to the casualty whether the President has declared the area a disaster or not. Fifty percent of any loss remaining after the five-year carryover period may be carried forward for the next 10 years.

Both the President and the Governor declared a state of disaster in the counties of Los Angeles, Orange, and San Diego as a result of the firestorms that occurred in October 1996. However, California legislation has not been enacted that extends the special disaster loss carryover and carryback provisions to losses resulting from this disaster.

A taxpayer is allowed to carry over only disaster losses that exceed taxable income increased by the sum of (1) the personal exemption deduction and (2) the lower of (a) $3,000 ($1,500 for married taxpayers filing separately) or (b) the amount by which losses from sales or exchanges of capital assets exceed gains from such sales or exchanges.

● *Wagering losses*

Wagering losses are deductible only to the extent of wagering gains. However, see ¶ 322 regarding disallowance of deductions for expenses of illegal activities or California lottery losses.

● *Worthless securities*

Losses from worthless securities that are capital assets are considered losses from the sale or exchange of the securities on the last day of the taxable year in which the securities become worthless. As under federal law, such losses are therefore subject to the limitations on deduction of capital losses.

In *Appeal of Everett R. and Cleo F. Shaw* (1961) (CCH CALIFORNIA TAX REPORTS ¶ 15-759.292), the State Board of Equalization held that a worthless stock loss was not deductible in the year claimed, where the company that issued the stock later expressed an intent to continue operations with a possibility of future earnings.

● *Losses on "small business corporation" stock*

Current treatment of losses on "small business corporation" stock is discussed at ¶ 513.

● *Violation of public policy*

A loss deduction may be disallowed on the ground that the loss is the result of actions that are violative of public policy. See *Appeal of Anthony H. Eredia* (1981) (CCH CALIFORNIA TAX REPORTS ¶ 15-750.288), involving a loss of money advanced to a narcotics dealer.

¶ 307

● *Cross references*

See ¶ 518 for treatment of losses on redemption of United States Savings Bonds. See ¶ 324 for discussion of special rules regarding farm and hobby losses. See ¶ 325 for "at risk" limitations on deductible losses. See ¶ 326 for a discussion of passive losses.

See ¶ 512 regarding losses on "capital assets." See ¶ 514a regarding disallowance of loss on "wash sales."

¶ 308 Bad Debts

> *Law:* Sec. 17201 (CCH CALIFORNIA TAX REPORTS ¶ 15-762).
>
> *Comparable Federal:* Secs. 166, 271 (CCH STANDARD FEDERAL TAX REPORTS ¶ 10,502, 14,306).

California law is the same as federal law. "Nonbusiness" bad debts are treated as short-term capital losses (one year or less).

¶ 309 Net Operating Loss Deduction

> *Law:* Secs. 17041, 17276—17276.6 (CCH CALIFORNIA TAX REPORTS ¶ 15-814, 15-986, 15-998, 15-999f).
>
> *Comparable Federal:* Sec. 172 (CCH STANDARD FEDERAL TAX REPORTS ¶ 12,002).
>
> *California Forms:* FTB 3805V, FTB 3805Z, FTB 3806, FTB 3807, FTB 3809.

Post-1986 Tax Years

California generally conforms to the federal net operating loss (NOL) deduction for losses incurred in taxable years beginning after 1984, with the exception of the following:

(1) for an NOL sustained in a tax year beginning after 1986, but before 1991 or after 1992, California law generally allows 50% of the loss to be carried forward for up to five years (rather than the federal 100% carryover for up to 20 years; 15 years for NOLs incurred in tax years beginning before August 6, 1997);

(2) for tax years beginning in 1991 and 1992, California generally did not allow NOL deductions; however, California extends the carryover period as follows: (a) by one additional year for an NOL sustained in a tax year beginning in 1991 and (b) by two additional years for an NOL sustained in a tax year beginning before 1991;

(3) special rules apply to NOLs incurred by small businesses, new businesses, bankrupt taxpayers, and qualified enterprise zone, former Los Angeles Revitalization Zone, local agency military base recovery area, and targeted tax area businesses (see discussion below);

(4) California does not allow an NOL carryback to prior years; and

(5) an NOL sustained by a nonresident or part-year resident is limited to the sum of (a) the portion of the NOL attributable to the part of the year in which the taxpayer is a resident, plus (b) the portion of the NOL that, during the portion of the year when the taxpayer is not a resident, is attributable to California-source income and deductions.

In *Appeal of Harminder S. and Harpal Chana* (1995) (CCH CALIFORNIA TAX REPORTS ¶ 15-814.11), nonresident taxpayers who had California source NOLs that did not exceed their income from all sources were unable to carry over any of those losses to offset income in a later year. The fact that the taxpayers' California source NOLs exceeded their California source income for that year did not entitle the taxpayers to carry over an NOL. Nonresident taxpayers must first determine whether there is an overall NOL by computing the loss on the basis of *all* of the taxpayers' taxable income as though the taxpayers were full-year residents. Then, if an overall NOL is sustained, the taxpayers must determine how much of that overall NOL is attributable to California sources.

● *Carryover for new and small businesses*

A business that commences activity in this state after 1993 (a new business) or a business that has total receipts of less than $1 million for the tax year (a small business) may deduct 100% of an NOL that is equal to or less than its net loss attributable to the new or small business as follows: (1) for a new business, the carryover period is eight years if the loss is attributable to its first year of business, seven years if the loss is attributable to its second year of business, and six years if the loss is attributable to its third year of business; and (2) for a small business, the carryover period is five years, regardless of the year to which the loss is attributable. Taxpayers involved in certain biopharmaceutical or other biotechnology activities that have not received regulatory approval for any product from the U.S. Food and Drug Administration are also eligible for the extended NOL carryover available to new businesses, effective for taxable years beginning after 1996. A new or small business that incurs an NOL that exceeds its net loss may carry forward 50% of the excess to each of the five taxable years following the taxable year of the loss.

Under the analysis provided in FTB Legal Ruling 96-5 (see ¶ 15-814.20 in the CCH CALIFORNIA TAX REPORTS), an existing business will be considered a "new business" if it undertakes a new activity within California that is classified under a different *division* of the Standard Industrial Classification (SIC) Manual than its existing business activity. If a taxpayer acquires assets of an existing trade or business that is doing business in California, the trade or business thereafter conducted by the taxpayer or related persons will be considered a new business only if the fair market value of the acquired assets is 20% or less of the total assets of the trade or business. The same divisional approach is used to determine whether a business qualifies for the "small business" NOL deduction. For purposes of determining whether a business's gross receipts are under the $1,000,000 eligibility limit for a small business, each business activity will be examined separately if the activities are classified under different SIC Manual divisions.

● *Carryover for enterprise zone, LARZ, LAMBRA, and targeted tax area businesses*

Enterprise zones, local agency military base recovery areas (LAMBRAs), and the targeted tax area, are economically deprived regions in which the state and local governments provide an array of tax and other incentives for taxpayers (see ¶ 102b). The Los Angeles Revitalization Zone (LARZ) was also designated as an area in which businesses could receive a variety of tax incentives, including an NOL deduction. Because the designation was repealed December 1, 1998, qualified taxpayers may claim only NOL carryovers for losses sustained prior to the 1998 taxable year. However, a taxpayer may receive a LARZ NOL in 1998 as a pass-through NOL from a 1997 fiscal-year partnership, S corporation, or limited liability company.

The NOL deduction available to taxpayers in these designated areas is the same as California's regular NOL deduction except that 100% of the NOLs incurred by businesses operating in these regions may be carried forward to each taxable year ending before the expiration date for the zone or area or for up to 15 taxable years following the year of the loss, whichever is longer. Taxpayers that also conduct business outside of the designated zone or area must apportion loss to the area by multiplying the business's total loss by a two-factor apportionment formula, comprised of the property and payroll factors. This special apportionment formula is effective for enterprise zone taxpayers in taxable years beginning after 1997. Because the loss attributable to the area may be claimed only against income attributable to the area, further calculations are also required. The amount of business income is first determined using the standard apportionment formula described in ¶ 1305-1308. For purposes of determining the amount of business income attributable to the zone or area, however, the sales factor is eliminated from the standard apportionment formula and the income used in the apportionment formula is limited to California-based income rather than worldwide income.

In order to claim the special NOL, a taxpayer must make an irrevocable election designating whether the loss is being claimed for a business located in an enterprise zone, LARZ, LAMBRA, or targeted tax area and attach a copy of the election form to a timely tax return. An enterprise zone, LARZ, LAMBRA, or targeted tax area NOL may be used only to offset income from the zone, area, or former zone for which the NOL is claimed. In addition, if a taxpayer elects to claim an enterprise zone, LARZ, LAMBRA, or targeted tax area NOL, no other type of NOL may be carried over. A worksheet is provided in the FTB 3805Z, FTB 3806, FTB 3807, and FTB 3809 booklets to assist taxpayers in determining the most advantageous NOL.

The NOL deduction for enterprise zone businesses is claimed on FTB 3805Z. LARZ businesses claim the NOL carryover deduction on FTB 3806 and the LAMBRA NOL is claimed on FTB 3807. The NOL deduction for targeted tax area businesses is claimed on FTB 3809. The LAMBRA NOL is subject to recapture if the taxpayer does not satisfy the net increase in jobs requirement discussed at ¶ 102b.

● *Carryover for bankrupt taxpayers*

A 10-year carryover period applies to NOLs attributable to taxable years beginning after 1986 and before 1994 that are incurred by a taxpayer that was under the jurisdiction of the court in a federal Title 11 (bankruptcy) or similar case during the taxable year in which the loss was incurred.

¶ 309

● *Effect of certain deductions and exclusions on computation of NOL*

California generally follows federal law under which certain deductions and exclusions may not be taken into account in computing an NOL deduction. However, California modifies federal law to disallow the California gross income exclusion provided to personal income taxpayers for gain on the sale of certain small business stock (see ¶ 513).

¶ 310 Depreciation

> *Law:* Secs. 17201, 17250, 17250.5 (CCH California Tax Reports ¶ 15-765—15-769, 15-785, 15-954).
>
> *Comparable Federal:* Secs. 167-68, 197, 198, 280F (CCH Standard Federal Tax Reports ¶ 11,002, 11,250, 12,260, 12,280, 12,450, 15,100).
>
> *California Forms:* FTB 3885A, FTB 3885F, FTB 3885L, FTB 3885P, Sch. CA (540), Sch. CA (540NR), Sch. D.

California has adopted federal depreciation provisions (the modified accelerated cost recovery system, or MACRS) for personal income tax purposes. However, California did not fully conform to an increase in the IRC Sec. 179 deduction allowance applicable for federal purposes to property placed in service after 1992 and before 1999 (see ¶ 310a). Assets placed in service before 1987 continue to be depreciated under pre-1987 California rules (see the discussion of assets placed in service before 1987, below). Property placed in service in 1987 in a taxable year which began in 1986, is depreciated under pre-1987 California law, unless the taxpayer elects to have the post-1986 law apply.

In addition, California has not conformed to a federal amendment made by the Revenue Reconciliation Act of 1993 that allows special recovery periods that permit faster write-offs for qualified Indian reservation property that is placed in service after 1993 and before 2004.

The following summary of MACRS applies to federal and California post-1986 asset acquisitions:

The 1986 Tax Reform Act (TRA) modified the Accelerated Cost Recovery System (ACRS) for property placed in service after 1986, except for property covered by transitional rules. Four classes of property were added: (1) 7-year property; (2) 20-year property; (3) residential rental property (generally, 27.5 years); and (4) nonresidential real property (31.5 years). The Revenue Reconciliation Act of 1993 extended for federal purposes the recovery period for nonresidential real property acquired after May 12, 1993, to 39 years. California conforms to the 39-year recovery period for nonresidential real property, but only for property placed in service after 1996 in taxable years beginning after 1996.

The 3-year, 5-year, and 10-year classes were also revised by the TRA, and more accelerated depreciation was provided within these classes. Property within the 15-year and 20-year classes is depreciated under the TRA modifications by methods that maximize the depreciation deduction. However, commercial real estate and residential rental property are depreciated over longer periods than under pre-TRA provisions.

● *Depreciation methods according to class (IRC Sec. 168)*

Under the federal MACRS method as incorporated by California, there are six classes of recovery property: 3-year, 5-year, 7-year, 10-year, 15-year, and 20-year. Prescribed depreciation methods are assigned to each class, as follows:

     (1) for 3-year, 5-year, 7-year, and 10-year classes, depreciation is by the 200% declining-balance method, switching to straight line when the latter yields a larger deduction;

     (2) for 15-year and 20-year property, depreciation is by the 150% declining-balance method, switching to straight line when the latter yields a larger deduction; and

     (3) for residential rental property and nonresidential real property, straight-line depreciation is to be used.

The taxpayer may make an irrevocable election to treat all property in one of the classes under the straight-line method. Property is statutorily placed in one of the classes.

● *Alternative depreciation system (IRC Sec. 168)*

An alternative system is provided for property used predominantly outside the U.S., tax-exempt use property, tax-exempt bond-financed property, and certain other property. In addition, the alternative method must be used for computing the portion of the depreciation allowance treated as a tax preference item for purposes of the alternative minimum tax. The allowable depreciation deductions for luxury cars and listed property used 50% or less in business are also determined under the alternative system.

Under this alternative depreciation system, the cost of property is recovered over the property's Asset Depreciation Range (ADR) midpoint life by the straight-line method. In computing the depreciation preference for alternative minimum tax purposes, recovery of the cost of personal property is calculated by the 150% declining-balance method.

An irrevocable election may be made to use the alternative depreciation system for all property in any class.

● *Disease-infested vineyards*

The depreciation period under MACRS for any grapevine replaced in a California vineyard is reduced from the 10-year period normally allowed for fruit-bearing vines to a five-year period if the vine is replaced (1) in a taxable year beginning after 1991 as a direct result of phylloxera infestation or (2) in a taxable year beginning after 1996 as a direct result of Pierce's Disease infestation. If an election is made to use the alternative depreciation method (discussed above), such grapevines will have a 10-year class life rather than the 20-year class life normally specified for such vines.

● *Luxury autos (IRC Sec. 280F)*

There are limits on the allowable recovery deduction for passenger automobiles in a given tax year. For automobiles first placed in service during 1999, the limits are as follows: $3,060 for the first recovery year; $5,000 for the

¶ 310

second year; $2,950 for the third year; and $1,775 for each succeeding tax year in the recovery period.

> ### ⓒCCH Observation: Limits Apply to All Auto Depreciation
>
> The limits on depreciation deductions for automobiles used in a trade or business apply to all types of depreciation deductions for automobiles, including IRC Sec. 179 expensing deductions.

Under both California and federal law, the amount of the deduction that may be claimed for electric passenger vehicles built by an original equipment manufacturer is tripled and the cost of an installed device that equips a nonclean-burning fuel vehicle to be propelled by clean-burning fuel is exempt from the deduction limitations. An amendment made by the IRS Restructuring and Reform Act of 1998, not yet incorporated by California, clarifies for federal purposes that the higher depreciation limits for clean-fuel vehicles may be claimed for years following the regular depreciation period, as well as during the regular depreciation period.

● *Listed property (IRC Sec. 280F)*

Special depreciation rules apply to property that is classified as "listed property" that is not used more than 50% of the time for business purposes. The depreciation of such property must be determined using the alternative depreciation method discussed above. If the percentage of business use was originally more than 50% and drops below that percentage in a subsequent tax year, the excess depreciation deduction claimed in the years that it was predominantly used in a trade or business must be recaptured.

"Listed property" includes (1) a passenger automobile, (2) other property used as transportation, (3) property that is generally used for purposes of entertainment, recreation, or amusement, (4) computers or peripheral equipment (except those used exclusively at regular business establishments), and (5) cellular telephones and other similar telecommunications equipment.

Assets Placed in Service Before 1987

The California rules for depreciation of assets placed in service before 1987 are the same as the federal rules in effect before the 1981 introduction of ACRS, except for the California prohibition against use of the "ADR" ranges. However, there are differences in the special rules for depreciation (or amortization) for certain classes of property, as explained below. Also, there have been many differences in prior years that may still have an effect on current depreciation; because of this possible effect, the prior-year differences are explained in some detail.

The basic rules for depreciation in the federal law (IRC Sec. 167) were incorporated in the California law by reference. However, California did not adopt the federal ACRS provisions (IRC Sec. 168) that apply to assets placed in service after 1980 and before 1987. As to assets not covered by ACRS, there is still a difference from the federal rules, in that Franchise Tax Board (FTB) Regulation 17208 specifically prohibits the use of the 20% "ranges" that are

¶ 310

permitted under federal regulations. Thus, the California rules for pre-1987 asset additions are still essentially the same as they were before 1981.

The federal law was amended in 1984, 1985, and 1986 to provide special rules for ACRS depreciation of luxury automobiles and of property not used principally in business. The California law applicable to pre-1987 assets was amended in 1985 to conform in principle to the pre-1986 federal rules; however, the California rules are based on the depreciation allowances under the ADR system, discussed below, rather than on the ACRS system.

● *California depreciation rules for pre-1987 assets*

In general, California depreciation methods and rates for pre-1987 assets are the same as the federal methods and rates applicable to assets placed in service during the years 1971 to 1980, inclusive. California has not conformed for pre-1987 assets to the mandatory federal Accelerated Cost Recovery System (ACRS) that was adopted in 1981 for tangible assets placed in service after 1980, except for certain residential property as explained at ¶ 310h. The federal ACRS allows generally a much faster write-off of tangible depreciable property; however, the pre-1981 rules still apply to current federal depreciation on assets acquired before 1981, and also to depreciation on assets that are not covered by ACRS.

● *Depreciation based on useful life*

Under the California rules for pre-1987 assets, property must be depreciated over its estimated useful life (economic life as well as physical life). The taxpayer could determine the useful life by any means that produced a reasonable result, or could elect to use the useful life that is specified under the Federal Class Life Asset Depreciation Range System (known as ADR). The ADR system was in effect for federal purposes during the years 1971 to 1980, and is still applicable to assets acquired during that period and to assets not covered by ACRS. California adopted the ADR system in 1976, for assets placed in service after 1970, and it is still in effect for assets placed in service before 1987, although California uses only the standard ADR rates and does not permit use of the "ranges" of 20% above or below the standard rate.

● *Useful life under ADR system*

Under the ADR system, the useful life for each class of property is specified in Federal Revenue Procedure 83-35, which superseded Revenue Procedure 77-10. The classes of assets and their prescribed useful life (called the "Asset Guideline Period") are listed in previous editions of the GUIDEBOOK.

There are no ADR classes for buildings, except for farm buildings. A taxpayer that elected ADR could determine the useful life of buildings by using the old federal guideline lives under Revenue Procedure 62-21 as in effect from 1962 to 1970, or may determine the useful life in some other way that produced a reasonable result. The old guideline lives for buildings were as follows:

¶ 310

Apartment buildings, hotels, theaters .... 40 years
Factories, garages, machine shops, office buildings,
   dwellings .... 45 years
Loft buildings, banks .... 50 years
Wholesale and retail business buildings, warehouses, grain
   elevators .... 60 years

A complete table with guideline lives can be found in Revenue Procedure 83-35, 1983-1 CB 745, or see pre-1988 editions of the GUIDEBOOK TO CALIFORNIA TAXES.

In *Appeal of Morris M. and Joyce E. Cohen* (1973) (CCH CALIFORNIA TAX REPORTS ¶ 15-769.273), the State Board of Equalization (SBE) overruled the FTB and allowed the taxpayers to use a shorter life for 1968 depreciation than the guideline life shown in Rev. Proc. 62-21, discussed above. The taxpayers used a 25-year life for a new apartment building. The FTB used the 40-year life shown in Rev. Proc. 62-21, but offered no explanation or evidence to support the use of the longer life. The SBE stated that Rev. Proc. 62-21 was only a guide and could not be arbitrarily applied with no objective standard, and concluded that the FTB's action in the particular circumstances of this case was "arbitrary and capricious."

● *California depreciation methods*

In accordance with federal rules for property that is not covered by the Accelerated Cost Recovery System, California permits a variety of depreciation methods for assets placed in service before 1987 as follows:

1. Straight-line method. This is the time-honored method, applicable to both tangible and intangible property (other methods, described below, apply only to tangible property). Under this method, the cost basis of the property, less salvage value, is written off ratably over the property's estimated useful life.

2. 200% declining-balance method. This method may be used only for new personal property with a useful life of three years or more, and for certain new residential rental property on which at least 80% of the gross rentals come from dwelling units.

3. Sum-of-the-years-digits method. This method may be used wherever the 200% declining-balance method may be used.

4. 150% declining-balance method. This method may be applied to used personal property and to new real estate.

5. 125% declining-balance method. This method may be applied to used residential rental property having a remaining useful life of twenty years or more.

6. Other "consistent methods" (e.g., sinking-fund method), with limitations on the total amount deductible during the first two-thirds of the useful life.

In accordance with the federal rules for property not covered by ACRS, California ordinarily allowed only a part of a full year's depreciation in the first year, based on the portion of the year in which the property was in service. A taxpayer that elected the ADR system could also elect to use one of two first-year conventions: (1) the half-year convention, or (2) the modified

¶ 310

half-year convention. In the year property is sold the depreciation allowable may be reduced or eliminated, in cases where excessive depreciation was taken in prior years; this conforms to a 1962 federal ruling (Rev. Rul. 62-92, 1962-1 C.B. 29).

● *Salvage value*

In computing California depreciation for pre-1987 asset additions, salvage value must be taken into account in two ways. First, in all methods except declining-balance, salvage value must be deducted from the asset's cost basis in computing the annual write-off based on useful life. Second, regardless of method, no asset may be depreciated below a reasonable salvage value. However, as to depreciable personal property (except livestock) with a useful life of three years or more, the salvage value taken into account may be reduced by up to 10% of the basis of the property.

Generally, salvage value is the amount estimated to be recoverable by the taxpayer at the end of the asset's useful economic life.

● *Change of depreciation method*

California follows the federal rules for changing depreciation methods for pre-1987 asset additions, as set forth in Revenue Ruling 74-11. Application for permission to change should be made within the same time as the application to the Internal Revenue Service, and a copy of the federal form should be submitted to the FTB. California follows the federal rules in permitting changes from certain accelerated methods to the straight-line method without consent.

● *Prior-year differences*

There have been many differences over the years between California and federal rules for depreciation. Since these differences may still affect current depreciation computations or the adjusted basis of property, they are summarized briefly in the following comments.

Since 1977, the California regulations have authorized taxpayers to develop and utilize a formula for converting federal depreciation into state depreciation (see Reg. 17208). Any such formula is subject to FTB approval. It appears, however, that use of such a formula would not be practicable where federal depreciation is determined under ACRS.

Prior to the introduction of the ADR system in 1971, the federal rules provided guidelines for depreciation rates, published in 1962 in Revenue Procedure 62-21. Assets placed in service after 1970 and before 1987 are governed by the ADR system.

The original federal provisions for accelerated depreciation methods were enacted in 1954, but California did not conform until 1959. During the period 1954-1958 the FTB maintained the position that in failing to adopt conforming legislation in those years the California legislature had issued a mandate that the accelerated depreciation methods were not allowable for California purposes. The FTB was sustained in this position by the SBE in *Appeal of Garrett Freightlines, Inc.* in 1957, and in *Appeal of William S. and Camilla A. Andrews* (CCH CALIFORNIA TAX REPORTS ¶ 15-769.25) in 1959.

¶ **310**

Where this situation created a difference between California and federal depreciation in the years 1954-1958, the FTB permitted taxpayers to eliminate this difference over a period of years on a somewhat arbitrary basis, in order to avoid the necessity of continuing detailed separate computations of depreciation for California tax purposes.

Use of the 200% declining balance and sum-of-the-years-digits methods was suspended under federal law for the period October 10, 1966, to March 9, 1967. California did not follow this federal suspension.

The California law was amended in 1977 to conform to a 1976 federal amendment permitting a change from accelerated methods to the straight-line method on real estate. The California amendment permitted the change in the first taxable year ending after 1976; the federal amendment applied to the first year ending after 1975. (The corporation tax law was not amended in 1977 to conform to this personal income tax amendment.)

Special Depreciation and Amortization Rules

● *Nonresidents and part-year residents*

Because nonresidents and part-year residents, in figuring their California tax liability on Form 540NR, first compute a taxable income figure in the same manner as full-year residents, they must make the same California depreciation modifications required of resident taxpayers, even for assets not located in California (*Letter*, FTB, July 10, 1989, CCH CALIFORNIA TAX REPORTS ¶ 15-605.29).

● *Motion picture films, books, copyrights, etc.*

Special rules have been applied over the years to the depreciation or amortization of production costs of motion picture films. The major film studios maintaining their own distribution systems amortize such costs over estimated useful lives as have been established by their own experience, or by industry averages. Independent producers, on the other hand, are permitted to use an estimated receipts method to develop a formula for cost amortization. This formula uses estimated total receipts as the denominator and periodic receipts as the numerator in arriving at the proportion of production cost to be amortized in each period. The use of this formula by independent producers was upheld by the SBE in *Appeal of Filmcraft Trading Corporation* (1957) (CCH CALIFORNIA TAX REPORTS ¶ 11-229.60). The rule was further clarified in *Appeal of King Bros. Productions, Inc.* (1961) (CCH CALIFORNIA TAX REPORTS ¶ 12-585.70). Similar treatment is accorded production costs of television films. The federal rules are substantially the same. In 1986, technical changes to the federal law applicable to property placed into service after March 28, 1985, were made by the Tax Reform Act of 1986; these were adopted by California applicable to post-1986 assets.

Taxpayers may elect to compute depreciation using the income forecast method for property such as film, video tape, sound recordings, copyrights, books, patents, and other property of a similar character approved by federal regulation. If such an election is made, the depreciation claimed must take into account the amount of income expected to be earned in connection with the property before the close of the 10th tax year following the tax year that

¶ 310

the property was placed in service, which means that 11 tax years are taken into account. Depreciation is determined using the income forecast method by multiplying the property's cost (less estimated salvage value) by a fraction, the numerator of which is the income generated by the property during the year and the denominator of which is the total estimated income to be derived from the property during its useful life. Use of the income forecast method applies for federal purposes to property placed in service after September 13, 1995, and for California purposes to taxable years beginning after 1996. However, the income forecast method may not be used to compute depreciation for intangible property amortizable under IRC Sec. 197 or for consumer durables subject to rent-to-own contracts.

● *"Safe harbor" transactions*

The federal Economic Recovery Act of 1981 permits the transfer of depreciation benefits and investment tax credits between taxpayers under certain conditions. This is accomplished by so-called "safe harbor" rules that treat as a lease what would otherwise be treated as a sale. Since California has not conformed to these federal provisions, California follows prior federal rulings and may treat as a sale a transaction that is treated as a lease under the federal rules. See Legal Ruling 419 (1981) (CCH CALIFORNIA TAX REPORTS ¶ 15-769.20) for discussion of the effect of this difference on the taxpayers involved.

¶ 310a Asset Expense Election (IRC "Sec. 179" Election)

Law: Secs. 17201, 17255 (CCH CALIFORNIA TAX REPORTS ¶ 15-834).

Comparable Federal: Sec. 179 (CCH Standard Federal Tax Reports ¶ 12,120).

California Forms: FTB 3885A, Sch. D.

California has adopted the federal asset expense election for assets placed in service after 1986. However, California did not conform to the amendment made by the Revenue Reconciliation Act of 1993 that increased the expense allowance for federal purposes from $10,000 to $17,500 for tax years beginning after 1992 and before 1997. For taxable years beginning after 1996, California conformed to an amendment made by the Small Business Job Protection Act of 1996 that phased in further increases in the expense allowance for federal purposes, but the increases were phased in using a modified schedule for California purposes during the 1997 and 1998 tax years. For federal purposes, the expense allowance was increased to $18,000, $18,500, $19,000, $20,000, $24,000, and $25,000 for property placed in service in tax years beginning in 1997, 1998, 1999, 2000, 2001 or 2002, and 2003 or thereafter, respectively. For California purposes, the expense allowance was increased to $13,000 for property placed in service in 1997 and to $16,000 for property placed in service in 1998, and thereafter is increased to the same amounts as under federal law. Because depreciable basis must be reduced by any IRC Sec. 179 deduction, the depreciable basis of property placed in service after 1992 may differ for federal and state purposes.

For both federal and California purposes, the deduction is reduced, but not below zero, by the excess of the total investment in qualified property over $200,000 in the tax year. The excess of the deduction over otherwise allowable depreciation is recaptured if the property ceases to be used predominately in

¶ 310a

the trade or business before the end of its recovery period. The deduction cannot exceed the taxable income derived from the trade or business during the tax year.

California conforms to a federal provision that denies IRC Sec. 179 expensing for air conditioning and heating units and certain property used (1) outside the United States, (2) in connection with furnishing lodging, (3) by tax-exempt organizations, or (4) by governments and foreign persons. The provision is effective for federal purposes for property placed in service after 1990 and for California purposes for taxable years beginning after 1996.

¶ 310b Additional First-Year Depreciation (Pre-1987)

Law: Former Sec. 17260 (CCH CALIFORNIA TAX REPORTS ¶ 15-834).

Comparable Federal: Former Sec. 179 (CCH STANDARD FEDERAL TAX REPORTS ¶ 12,120).

Under pre-1987 California law, a special first-year depreciation allowance was allowed on tangible personal property having a useful life of six years or more. This deduction was in addition to the regular depreciation on the balance of the cost. It was limited to 20% of the cost of such property, and could be claimed only with respect to $10,000 ($20,000 on a joint return) of property additions each year. It did not apply to trusts. In the case of a partnership, the dollar limitation applied to the partnership and to each partner.

For the post-1986 asset expense election that replaced the first-year allowance, see ¶ 310a.

¶ 310c Amortization of Cost of Acquiring a Lease

Law: Sec. 17201 (CCH CALIFORNIA TAX REPORTS ¶ 15-831).

Comparable Federal: Sec. 178 (CCH STANDARD FEDERAL TAX REPORTS ¶ 12,100).

California law incorporates the federal law by reference.

For purposes of amortizing the cost of acquiring a lease, the term of the lease includes all renewal options (and any other period for which the parties to the lease reasonably expect the lease to be renewed) if less than 75% of such cost is attributable to the unexpired term of the lease on the date of its acquisition. In determining the unexpired term of the lease, the taxpayer may not take into consideration any period for which the lease may subsequently be renewed, extended, or continued pursuant to an option exercisable by the lessee.

¶ 310d Amortization of Pollution Control Facilities

Law: Sec. 17250 (CCH CALIFORNIA TAX REPORTS ¶ 15-797).

Comparable Federal: Sec. 169 (CCH STANDARD FEDERAL TAX REPORTS ¶ 11,502).

California Form: FTB 3580.

California incorporates federal law allowing an accelerated (60-month) write-off of pollution control facilities, with the following modifications:

    1. the California deduction is available only for facilities located in California; and

2. the "state certifying authority" in cases involving air pollution is the State Air Resources Board and in cases involving water pollution is the State Water Resources Control Board.

FTB 3580 may be used to file an election with the Franchise Tax Board for an accelerated write-off.

¶ 310e Amortization of Reforestation Expenditures

Law: Secs. 17201, 17278.5 (CCH CALIFORNIA TAX REPORTS ¶ 15-868).

Comparable Federal: Sec. 194 (CCH STANDARD FEDERAL REPORTS ¶ 12,330).

California law is the same as federal, except that California limits the deduction to expenses associated with qualified timber located in California.

The taxpayer may elect to write off certain "reforestation expenditures" over a period of 84 months. This applies to direct costs of forestation or reforestation, including seeds, labor, equipment, etc. The amortization period begins on the first day of the second half of the taxable year of the expenditures. The limit of amortizable expenditures for a taxable year is $10,000 ($5,000 in case of a separate return of a married individual).

¶ 310f Accelerated Write-Offs for Economic Incentive Areas

Law: Secs. 17266, 17267.6, 17268, 18036 (CCH CALIFORNIA TAX REPORTS ¶ 15-987, 15-979d, 15-999e, 15-999*l*).

Comparable Federal: None.

California Forms: FTB 3805Z, FTB 3807, FTB 3809, Sch. D.

Under the tax incentive programs enacted by California, explained at ¶ 102b, accelerated write-offs are allowed for certain property as explained below.

● *Property used in enterprise zones, LAMBRAs, and the targeted tax area*

Taxpayers can expense 40% of the cost of IRC Sec. 1245 property that is purchased for use exclusively in a business conducted in an enterprise zone, a targeted tax area, or, effective for taxable years beginning after 1998, a local agency military base recovery area (LAMBRA). The cost that may be taken into account is limited to $100,000 for the taxable year that an area is designated as a qualifying zone or area, $100,000 for the first taxable year thereafter, $75,000 for the second and third taxable years after the year of designation, and $50,000 for each taxable year after that. For taxable years beginning before 1997, the deduction for program areas was basically the same (see ¶ 102b for a discussion of program areas).

A different computation was utilized for LAMBRA businesses for taxable years beginning before 1999. The deduction allowed for the cost of qualified property for taxable years beginning before 1999 was simply the cost of qualified property (with no percentage cap) up to the following amounts:

¶ 310e

Year of designation as enterprise zone	$ 5,000
1st year thereafter	$ 5,000
2nd year thereafter	$ 7,500
3rd year thereafter	$ 7,500
Each year thereafter	$10,000

If this treatment is elected, the asset expense election described at ¶ 310a is not allowed. The election is not available to estates or trusts or for property acquired from certain related persons.

The expense deduction is recaptured (included in income) if the property ceases to be used in the zone or area at any time before the close of the second taxable year after the property was placed in service. The deduction claimed by LAMBRA businesses may also be recaptured if the taxpayer does not satisfy the net increase in jobs requirement (see ¶ 102b).

A taxpayer's basis in the property must be adjusted to reflect the expense deduction.

The enterprise zone deduction is claimed on FTB 3805Z, the LAMBRA deduction is claimed on FTB 3807, and the targeted tax area deduction is claimed on FTB 3809; see ¶ 102b.

● *Property used in the Los Angeles Revitalization Zone (Prior law)*

Taxpayers could elect to expense the cost of any IRC Sec. 1245 property purchased prior to December 1, 1998, for exclusive use in a trade or business conducted within the zone.

Property acquired from certain related persons did not qualify for this treatment. Furthermore, the election was not available to estates and trusts.

Like the expense deduction available to taxpayers in other areas or zones, the deduction is subject to recapture (included in income) if the property ceases to be used in the zone at any time before the second taxable year after the property was placed in service and the taxpayer's basis in the property must be adjusted to reflect the expense deduction.

¶ 310g Expensing of Environmental Remediation Costs

Law: Secs. 17201, 17279.4 (CCH CALIFORNIA TAX REPORTS ¶ 15-874a).

Comparable Federal: Sec. 198 (CCH STANDARD FEDERAL TAX REPORTS ¶ 12,465).

Effective for taxable years beginning after 1997 and before 2001, taxpayers may elect to currently deduct costs paid or incurred in connection with the abatement or control of hazardous substances at a qualified contaminated site. The election is available for federal purposes for qualifying costs paid or incurred after August 5, 1997. A federal election, or lack thereof, is binding for California purposes.

To claim the deduction, (1) the property must be held by the taxpayer for use in a trade or business, for the production of income, or as stock in trade or inventory; and (2) the taxpayer must receive certification from a state environmental agency that the site is in a targeted area at or on which there has been a release, threat of release, or disposal of a hazardous substance.

¶ 310f

¶ 310h ACRS Depreciation for Residential Rental Property (Pre-1987)

Law: Former Sec. 17250.5 (CCH California Tax Reports ¶ 15-788).

Comparable Federal: Sec. 168 (CCH Standard Federal Tax Reports ¶ 11,250).

The California law was amended in 1984 to allow ACRS depreciation, in accordance with federal law, on certain new residential rental property as defined below. The provision was repealed applicable to assets placed in service after 1986. For depreciation of post-1986 assets, see ¶ 310.

The property must have been located in California, and construction must have commenced after June 30, 1985. It must comply with the definition of "rental property" in IRC Sec. 167(j)(2)(B), which means that at least 80% of the gross rentals must come from dwelling units (such property also qualified for 200% declining-balance depreciation under California's regular depreciation rules, as explained at ¶ 310).

This provision applied to certain low-income housing, as defined in IRC Sec. 168(c)(2)(F). In this case, depreciation was determined in accordance with Sec. 168(b)(4), as amended in 1984. This provides for a 15-year recovery period, with an accelerated write-off in the early years.

¶ 311 Depletion and Natural Resources

Law: Sec. 17681 (CCH California Tax Reports ¶ 16-325).

Comparable Federal: Secs. 611-14, 636, 638 (CCH Standard Federal Tax Reports ¶ 24,520, 24,540, 24,560, 24,600, 24,680, 24,720).

California law is the same as federal for tax years beginning after 1992.

● *Percentage depletion*

Both California and federal law allow percentage depletion on specified types of depletable assets. This allowance is computed as a percentage of gross income from the property, with a limitation based on 50% of the taxable income from the property before the depletion allowance (100% in the case of oil and gas properties). Under both California and federal law, the 100% taxable income limit is suspended for tax years beginning after 1997 and before 2000 for oil and gas production from marginal properties. Federal law (IRC Sec. 614), adopted in California for post-1986 tax years, provides detailed definitions of the term "property" and provides for aggregation of separate interests into one "property" under certain conditions. For pre-1987 tax years, California law did not include these provisions but did follow the general pattern of the federal law.

● *Oil and gas wells and geothermal deposits*

California fully conforms to the federal law on percentage depletion for oil and gas wells and geothermal deposits. Under the incorporated federal law, the following depletion rates apply: (1) 22% for domestic regulated natural gas and natural gas sold under a fixed contract; (2) 10% for qualified natural gas from geopressurized brine; (3) 15% for domestic crude oil and natural gas from wells of certain independent producers and royalty owners, limited to 65% of the taxpayer's taxable income before the depletion allowance; and (4) 15% for geothermal deposits located in the United States.

For taxable years beginning before 1993, instead of conforming to federal law, California provided a 22% depletion rate for oil, gas, and geothermal wells, up to a maximum of 50% of the taxpayer's taxable income from the property before the depletion allowance. California also imposed a limit on depletion, applicable when the accumulated depletion allowed or allowable exceeded the taxpayer's adjusted interest in the property.

● *Depletable assets other than oil, gas, and geothermal*

California also adopts federal percentage depletion provisions for depletable assets other than oil, gas, and geothermal deposits.

In pre-1987 tax years California law provided its own depletion percentages. See the 1986 and prior editions of this GUIDEBOOK.

● *Continental shelf areas*

California law conforms to IRC Sec. 638, concerning continental shelf areas. Therefore, natural resources include those located in seabeds and the subsoil of submarine areas adjacent to the territorial waters of the United States over which the United States has exclusive rights, in accordance with international law, in regard to the exploration and exploitation of natural resources.

¶ 311a Development and Exploration Expenses of Mines, etc.

Law: Secs. 17260, 17681 (CCH CALIFORNIA TAX REPORTS ¶ 16-329, 16-333).

Comparable Federal: Secs. 193, 263(c), 616-17 (CCH STANDARD FEDERAL TAX REPORTS ¶ 5350, 12,310, 13,700, 24,640, 24,660).

Development and exploration expenditures in connection with a mine or other mineral deposit (other than an oil, gas, or geothermal wells) may be deducted currently or may be deferred (as to development expenses only), at the taxpayer's election, subject to the following general rules:

(a) Exploration expenses are those paid or incurred prior to the development period. Deductions for such expenses are subject to "recapture" when the mine reaches the productive stage.

(b) Development expenses are those paid or incurred after the existence of ores or minerals in commercially marketable quantities has been established. There is no dollar limitation on such deductions.

(c) Alternatively, development expenses may be capitalized and amortized on a ratable basis over a ten-year period depending on the units of ores or minerals produced and sold. However, the election to capitalize and amortize applies only to the excess of development expenditures paid or incurred during the taxable year over the net receipts during the year from the sale of ores or minerals produced. California has adopted federal rules for post-1986 expenditures.

Both California and federal laws permit the taxpayer to elect to expense intangible drilling and development costs of oil, gas, and geothermal wells.

Pre-1987 Tax Years

For pre-1987 tax years, the California law regarding mine development and exploration expenses was substantially the same as the federal, although the federal law was not incorporated in California's by reference. (However, federal law regarding expensing of intangible costs of oil, gas, and geothermal wells was incorporated in California's by reference.)

California did not conform to the following federal provisions for pre-1987 expenditures:

1. the deduction of "tertiary injectant expenses"; and

2. elective ten-year amortization of certain expenditures that would be treated as federal "tax preferences" if they were expensed.

¶ 312 Contributions

Law: Secs. 17201, 17251.5, 17275.5 (CCH California Tax Reports ¶ 15-801).

Comparable Federal: Secs. 170, 501(k) (CCH Standard Federal Tax Reports ¶ 11,675).

California Forms: Sch. CA (540), Sch. CA (540NR)

The California contribution deduction is generally the same as federal as of the current IRC tie-in date (see ¶ 102a), with the exception of (1) the amount that may be deducted for qualified appreciated stock donated to a private foundation (see below) and (2) the federal denial of a deduction for contributions to organizations that conduct lobbying activities for which a deduction is disallowed (see ¶ 301).

● *Educational institutions*

Federal law (IRC Sec. 501(k)) provides that for purposes of determining whether a contribution to a child care organization is deductible, an organization is considered operated for "educational purposes" if (1) it provides care of children away from their home; (2) substantially all the care is for purposes of enabling individuals to be gainfully employed; and (3) the services are available to the general public.

California conforms to the federal provision permitting a deduction for 80% of the contribution to universities and colleges, even though the taxpayer receives the right to purchase athletic tickets to school events.

● *Qualified appreciated stock*

Federal, but not California, law allows a taxpayer who contributes qualified appreciated stock to a private foundation after June 30, 1996, to claim a deduction for the fair market value of the stock. The deduction is limited under California law to the stock's fair market value less the long-term capital gain that would have been realized if the stock had been sold at fair market value.

¶ 312

● *Carryovers*

California follows federal law, which allows a five-year carryover of contributions that exceed the percentage limit and specifies how the carryover is to be absorbed in succeeding tax years.

● *Automobile expense*

California conforms to federal law allowing taxpayers to claim a fixed automobile mileage rate of 14¢ per mile for use of an automobile in activities for the benefit of an organization that qualifies for deductible contributions.

● *Substantiation*

California conforms to federal provisions that allow a deduction for charitable contributions only if the contributions are verified under regulations prescribed by the Secretary of the Treasury (the Franchise Tax Board for California purposes). Both California and federal law also require charitable contributions of $250 or more to be substantiated in order to be deducted.

¶ 312a Designated Contributions

Law: Secs. 18711—18865 (CCH CALIFORNIA TAX REPORTS ¶ 89-113).

Comparable Federal: None.

California Form: Form 540.

California permits taxpayers to make certain contributions by designating the desired amounts (full dollar amounts) on their returns as additions to their tax liability. Thus, the designated amounts increase the balance payable on the return or reduce the refund, if any. The contributions, funds, and accounts listed on the 1999 returns are as follows:

1. The California Fund for Senior Citizens, which is used for the California Senior Legislature and other activities on behalf of older persons.

2. The Rare and Endangered Species Preservation Program.

3. The State Children's Trust Fund for the Prevention of Child Abuse.

4. The Alzheimer's Disease and Related Disorders Fund.

5. The California Breast Cancer Research Fund.

6. The California Public School Library Protection Fund.

7. The California Firefighters' Memorial Fund.

8. The California Drug Abuse Resistance Education (D.A.R.E.) Fund.

9. The California Mexican American Veterans' Memorial Fund.

10. The Emergency Food Assistance Program Fund.

11. The California Peace Officer Memorial Foundation Fund.

12. The Birth Defects Research Fund.

A taxpayer who is 65 years of age or older and who is entitled to claim an additional personal exemption credit may designate an amount not to exceed the amount of the credit as a contribution to the California Seniors Special Fund. The amount of the contribution need not be reduced to reflect any income-based reduction in the amount of the credit.

All the above designated contributions are permitted as charitable contributions (see ¶ 312).

¶ 313 Alimony

> *Law:* Sec. 17201 (CCH California Tax Reports ¶ 15-882).
>
> *Comparable Federal:* Sec. 215 (CCH Standard Federal Tax Reports ¶ 12,570).
>
> *California Forms:* Sch. CA (540), Sch. CA (540NR).

Alimony payments includible in income of the spouse who receives the payments (see ¶ 204) are deductible in computing adjusted gross income of the California resident spouse who makes the payments. California disallows the deduction for alimony paid by a nonresident.

(CCH **CCH Observation: New York Law Ruled Unconstitutional**

It should be noted that the U.S. Supreme Court in *Lunding, et ux. v. New York Tax Appeals Tribunal* (1998) (CCH California Tax Reports ¶ 15-882.65) struck down as unconstitutional a similar New York law that disallowed a deduction for alimony paid by a nonresident.

A California-federal difference could arise in a case in which a California court holds a foreign divorce invalid. For federal tax purposes, the deductibility of alimony paid under a state divorce decree is not affected by another state's declaration that the divorce is invalid. The rule is designed to avoid the uncertainty that could arise from conflicting state determinations regarding the validity of divorces.

● *Paid to nonresident*

Alimony paid by a California resident is deductible where paid to a former spouse who is not a California resident, although the former spouse is not taxable on the income. This has been the policy of the Franchise Tax Board for many years, following two 1951 decisions of the California Court of Appeal. These cases are *Ada Davis Francis, Executrix v. McColgan* (CCH California Tax Reports ¶ 15-882.43) and *M.B. Silberberg, Executor v. Franchise Tax Board* (CCH California Tax Reports ¶ 15-882.43).

¶ 314 Amortization of Bond Premium

> *Law:* Secs. 17133, 17201 (CCH California Tax Reports ¶ 15-811).
>
> *Comparable Federal:* Sec. 171 (CCH Standard Federal Tax Reports ¶ 11,850).

Deduction is allowed at the taxpayer's election for amortization of premium on bonds the income of which is taxable under the California law. California law incorporates the federal law by reference. However, the amortization may apply to different bonds because of the differences in taxability of government bond interest. This means that amortization may be deductible on a given bond on the California return and not on the federal, or vice versa. Both federal and California law treat amortizable bond premium deductions as interest.

As to nontaxable bonds, no deduction is allowed but amortization of premium must nevertheless be taken into account in computing the adjusted basis of the bond at time of sale or other disposition. This adjustment may be different for California purposes than for federal because the particular bond involved may be taxable for California purposes but not federal, or vice versa.

In some computations of adjusted basis involving amortization of premium on bonds, the result will be different for California purposes than for federal. This is because California did not conform to certain amendments to federal law affecting the computation of amortization until subsequent years, so that the computations of amortization may be different even though the two laws are now the same.

Amortization is not allowed on any portion of bond premium attributable to conversion features of the bond.

Special rules are provided for dealers in tax-exempt securities. See ¶ 210.

¶ 315 Medical Expenses

Law: Sec. 17201 (CCH CALIFORNIA TAX REPORTS ¶ 15-155, 15-878).

Comparable Federal: Sec. 213 (CCH STANDARD FEDERAL TAX REPORTS ¶ 12,540).

California Forms: Sch. CA (540), Sch. CA (540NR).

With the exception of the amount that may be claimed for self-employed health insurance costs (see ¶ 301), California law is the same as federal with respect to the deductibility of medical expenses, including the disallowance of a medical expense deduction for unnecessary cosmetic surgery.

A deduction is permitted for medical and dental expenses, not compensated for by insurance or otherwise, to the extent that such expenses paid for medical and dental care of the taxpayer, a spouse, and dependents exceed 7½% of federal adjusted gross income (10% for purposes of the alternative minimum tax). The definition of "dependent" is the same as for purposes of the exemption credit for dependents (see ¶ 111), and is determined without reference to the gross income of the dependent. For taxable years beginning after 1996, the definition of "medical care" is expanded for both California and federal purposes to include amounts paid for qualified long-term care services and eligible long-term care premiums paid under qualified long-term care insurance contracts. For the 1999 taxable year, "eligible long-term care premiums" are amounts not in excess of the following: $210 for persons attaining age 40 or less by the close of the taxable year; $400 for persons attaining an age over 40 but not over 50 by the close of the taxable year; $800 for persons attaining an age over 50 but not over 60 by the close of the taxable year; $2,120 for persons attaining an age over 60 but not over 70 by the close of the taxable year; and $2,660 for persons attaining an age over 70 by the close of the taxable year.

The limitation on itemized deductions for high-income taxpayers does not apply to medical expenses (see ¶ 303).

¶ 315a Medical Savings Accounts

Law: Secs. 17201, 17215 (CCH CALIFORNIA TAX REPORTS ¶ 15-891).

Comparable Federal: Sec. 220 (CCH STANDARD FEDERAL TAX REPORTS ¶ 12,670).

California law is the same as federal as of the current IRC tie-in date (see ¶ 102a), with the exception of the penalty amount imposed on withdrawals from a medical savings account (MSA) that are used for nonqualified expenses (see ¶ 246 for a discussion of the penalty).

Taxpayers that claim a federal deduction for contributions to an MSA may claim the same deduction on their California return. The deduction is not subject to the 7.5% floor for itemized medical expense deductions (discussed at ¶ 315). Under both California and federal law, a contribution made after the end of the taxable year is considered to have been made on the last day of the year, provided that the contribution is on account of such taxable year and is made no later than the due date of the return.

¶ 316 Tenant Expenses—Cooperative Apartment and Housing Corporations

Law: Sec. 17201 (CCH CALIFORNIA TAX REPORTS ¶ 15-885).

Comparable Federal: Sec. 216 (CCH STANDARD FEDERAL TAX REPORTS ¶ 12,600).

California law is the same as federal as of the current IRC tie-in date (see ¶ 102a).

Deductions are allowed to tenant-stockholders in cooperative apartment and housing corporations for amounts representing taxes and interest paid to such corporations.

¶ 316a Moving Expenses

Law: Secs. 17072, 17076, 17134.5 (CCH CALIFORNIA TAX REPORTS ¶ 15-889).

Comparable Federal: Sec. 217 (CCH STANDARD FEDERAL TAX REPORTS ¶ 12,623).

California Forms: Sch. CA (540), Sch. CA (540NR).

California adopts federal provisions that allow an above-the-line deduction for moving expenses incurred in connection with the commencement of work at a new principal place of work.

The treatment of an employer's moving expense reimbursements for purposes of calculating an employee's gross income is discussed at ¶ 237.

¶ 317 Employee Business Expenses

Law: Secs. 17072, 17076, 17077, 17201 (CCH CALIFORNIA TAX REPORTS ¶ 15-701).

Comparable Federal: Secs. 62(a), 67, 68, 162, 274 (CCH STANDARD FEDERAL TAX REPORTS ¶ 6002, 6060, 8520, 8580, 14,402).

California and federal unreimbursed employee business expenses are considered miscellaneous itemized deductions rather than adjustments to gross income. As explained at ¶ 303, only the total amount of miscellaneous itemized deductions in excess of 2% of the taxpayer's federal adjusted gross income is deductible.

¶ 316

California also incorporates the 50% limit on deductions for business meals and entertainment expenses (see ¶ 302). The 50% limit is computed before the 2% floor is applied. A deduction is allowed even if reimbursement comes from a third party rather than from the employer. Reimbursed employee business expenses that are included in the taxpayer's gross income are deducted from gross income.

¶ 318 Payments to Pension or Profit-Sharing Plans

Law: Secs. 17201, 17203, 17501, 17504-09, 17551, 23712 (CCH CALIFORNIA TAX REPORTS ¶ 16-105, 16-114, 16-118, 16-119, 16-119A, 16-227).

Comparable Federal: Secs. 194A, 219, 402, 404—419A, 457, 530 (CCH STANDARD FEDERAL TAX REPORTS ¶ 7320, 12,350, 12,650, 12,681, 18,330, 18,902—19,250, 19,265—19,290, 19,295, 21,531, 22,711).

California generally conforms to the federal rules for deduction of contributions to retirement plans by employers, employees, and the self-employed. The federal law is incorporated in California's by reference (see ¶ 102a). For taxable years beginning before 1987, California law provided for important differences, as explained below.

Under both laws, a contribution made after the end of the taxable year is considered to have been made on the last day of the year, provided the contribution is on account of such taxable year and is made no later than the due date of the return. Except for individual retirement accounts (IRAs), the due date for this purpose includes any extensions.

California, in 1989, adopted several of the 1988 TAMRA changes relating to rollovers of pension funds, applicable to taxable years beginning after 1986. The rules relating to multiple distributions do not apply to distributions received in taxable years beginning prior to 1987. In 1990 California conformed, effective for post-1989 tax years, to a variety of changes made by the federal Revenue Reconciliation Act of 1989, affecting among other things the minimum vesting rules and the ceiling on pension plan contributions for retiree medical and life insurance benefits, as well as amendments made by the federal Pension Protection Act, which strengthened the minimum funding rules. Effective for tax years beginning after 1996, California conforms to amendments made by the Small Business Job Protection Act of 1996 authorizing Savings Incentive Match Plans for Employees (SIMPLE plans) and redefining "active participant" in a pension plan for purposes of determining eligibility for an IRA. California also conforms to amendments made by the Taxpayer Relief Act of 1997, including amendments expanding the eligibility for and the role of IRAs by establishing Roth IRAs and Education IRAs (see below) for taxable years beginning after 1997. California also adopts certain amendments regarding Roth IRAs made by the IRS Restructuring and Reform Act of 1998, also effective for taxable years beginning after 1997.

● *Payments by employers*

Detailed rules are provided for deduction of employers' payments made under an employees' trust or annuity plan or other arrangement for deferring compensation. The California rules are the same as the federal, except for the differences explained below.

California has not conformed to federal provisions that impose special excise taxes on insufficient distributions, inadequate funding, prohibited transactions, etc. However, California does impose a penalty tax on premature distributions (before age 59½) from self-employed plans and individual retirement accounts although at a lower rate than under federal law (see ¶ 206).

See below regarding employer contributions to self-employed retirement plans and to individual retirement accounts.

To the extent the California and federal laws are comparable, it is the stated policy of the Franchise Tax Board (FTB) to follow all federal rules and regulations. Where the federal rules require advance approval of a plan, California will accept the federal approval and it is not necessary to file a separate application with the state.

● *Self-employed retirement plans (Keoghs)*

Both California and federal laws allow deductions for contributions to self-employed retirement plans, commonly known as "H.R. 10" or "Keogh" plans.

Under federal law, which California follows, a self-employed individual who maintains a defined contribution plan may contribute and deduct the lesser of $30,000 or 25% of earned income. The contribution and deduction limits for defined benefit plans are the lesser of $90,000 or 100% of average compensation for the three highest consecutive years of active plan participation. The $90,000 limitation for defined benefit plans is subject to annual cost-of-living adjustments. The adjusted amount for 1999 is $130,000. For taxable years beginning after 1995, California law provides that amounts used as "earned income" for purposes of computing a taxpayer's federal deduction (rather than the earned income computed using California amounts) must be used for purposes of computing the corresponding state deduction.

For pre-1987 tax years, California had allowed a deduction of 10% of earned income for contributions to these plans, with a maximum of $2,500 and no minimum. The federal law had allowed a deduction with varying limits that have been higher than California's since 1974.

● *Individual retirement accounts—Current law*

Both California and federal laws allow deductions for contributions to individual retirement accounts or for the purchase of individual retirement annuities or bonds. These arrangements are commonly known as "IRAs." The California IRA deduction in taxable years beginning after 1986 is the same as the federal.

Contributions to an IRA are deductible by an individual taxpayer up to a maximum of the lesser of $2,000 per year or 100% of the individual's compensation, subject to an adjusted gross income limitation discussed below. For taxable years beginning after 1995, California law provides that amounts used as "compensation" for purposes of computing a taxpayer's federal deduction (rather than the earned income computed using California amounts) must be used for purposes of computing the corresponding state deduction. A husband and wife may each establish and contribute to an IRA. The deduction limitations generally apply separately to each spouse.

¶ 318

For taxable years beginning after 1996, under both California and federal law, a nonworking spouse may make a deductible contribution of up to $2,000 to an IRA, so that the maximum amount deductible by a married couple is the lesser of $4,000 or the combined compensation of both spouses. Prior to 1997, the aggregate deduction for a married couple filing jointly when only one spouse worked was $2,250 if a spousal IRA was maintained. However, the maximum deductible contribution to either spouse's IRA was $2,000, even though the aggregate deduction was $2,250.

"Active participant" in a qualified retirement plan: If an individual is an active participant in an employer-sponsored retirement plan, the $2,000 deduction limitation is gradually reduced and eventually eliminated when the taxpayer has a designated amount of adjusted gross income. For married taxpayers filing a joint return for the 1999 taxable year, the deduction for contributions to an IRA for an active participant is reduced when adjusted gross income is between $51,000 and $61,000 and is completely eliminated at $61,000. For all other taxpayers (except married taxpayers filing separately), the deduction for contributions to an IRA for an active participant is reduced for the 1999 taxable year when adjusted gross income is between $31,000 and $41,000 and is completely eliminated at $41,000. For a married taxpayer filing a separate return, no deduction is allowed if adjusted gross income is $10,000 or more.

Prior to the 1998 taxable year, an individual was treated as an active participant in his or her spouse's employer-sponsored retirement plan and thus was subject to the deduction limitations for active participants on the basis of his or her spouse's active participation. Beginning with the 1998 taxable year, the maximum deductible IRA contribution for an individual who is not an active participant, but whose spouse is, is phased out at higher adjusted gross income levels, between $150,000 and $160,000.

⨎ CCH Example: Deductible IRAs for Married Individuals

Fred is covered by a 401(k) plan sponsored by his employer. His wife, Wilma, is not employed. For 1999, they file a joint return reporting adjusted gross income (AGI) of $130,000. Wilma may make a deductible contribution to an IRA for 1999 because she is not an active participant in an employer-sponsored plan and the couple's combined AGI is below $150,000. However, Fred may not make a deductible contribution to an IRA for 1999 because the couple's combined AGI exceeds the applicable phase-out range of $51,000 to $61,000 for active participants who are married and file jointly.

Generally, for both California and federal purposes, an "active participant" is an individual who actively participates in (1) a qualified pension, profit-sharing, or stock bonus plan, (2) a qualified annuity plan, (3) a simplified employee pension (SEP), (4) a plan established for employees by the United States, a state or political subdivision of a state, or a federal or state instrumentality, or (5) effective for tax years beginning after 1996, a SIMPLE retirement account.

¶318

Earnings on nondeductible contributions are not taxed until they are withdrawn.

"Roth IRAs": Both California and federal law recognize a "Roth IRA'" for tax years beginning after 1997. Contributions to a Roth IRA are not deductible, however earnings from a Roth IRA are tax-free and qualified distributions are not included in gross income or subject to a penalty on early withdrawals. To qualify for tax-free treatment, a distribution must be (1) made when the taxpayer is at least 59½ years of age, (2) made to a beneficiary or the taxpayer's estate after his or her death, (3) attributable to the taxpayer's becoming disabled, or (4) made for the purpose of purchasing a first home (up to $10,000 in expenses). In addition, the Roth IRA must be held for at least five years prior to the withdrawal. Unlike deductible IRAs, contributions to Roth IRAs are allowed even after the owner of the Roth IRA reaches the age of 70½.

The maximum contribution to a Roth IRA is the lesser of $2,000 (reduced by deductible contributions to other IRAs), or the individual's compensation for the year. However, the maximum yearly contribution amount is phased out at certain adjusted gross income levels. Income phase-outs are at $95,000 to $110,000 of adjusted gross income for single filers, $150,000 to $160,000 of adjusted gross income for joint filers, and $0 to $10,000 of adjusted gross income for married individuals filing a separate return.

Education IRAs: Joint filers with modified adjusted gross income below $150,000 ($95,000 for single filers) may contribute up to $500 per child per year to an education IRA, effective for both California and federal purposes for tax years beginning after 1997. Earnings on contributions will be excluded from gross income and be distributed tax-free provided that they are used to pay the child's post-secondary education expenses. A federal election to waive the application of the exclusion, or the lack of such an election, is binding for California purposes.

The $500 annual contribution is phased out for joint filers with modified adjusted gross income of $150,000 to $160,000, and for single filers with modified adjusted gross income of $95,000 to $110,000. The $500 maximum annual contribution is reduced by an amount that bears the same ratio to $500 as the excess of the contributor's modified adjusted gross income for the tax year over $150,000, or $95,000, bears to $10,000 for joint filers or $15,000 for single filers.

"Qualified education expenses" include tuition, fees, books, supplies, and equipment required for the enrollment of a designated beneficiary at an eligible educational institution. The term also includes room and board to the extent of the minimum room and board allowance applicable to the student as determined by the institution in calculating costs of attendance for federal financial aid programs.

The balance remaining in an education IRA must be distributed within 30 days after a beneficiary reaches age 30 or dies under age 30.

¶ 318

CCH Tip: Transfer of Education IRA Balances

Before a beneficiary reaches age 30, the balance of an education IRA may be transferred or rolled over to another education IRA for a member of the former beneficiary's family in order to further defer or possibly avoid payment of tax on the earnings in the account.

● *Individual retirement accounts—Prior law*

The basic California IRA deduction for all pre-1987 years was the lesser of $1,500 or 15% of the individual's compensation or earned income, with an additional deduction (since 1977) for a "nonworking spouse," up to an overall limit of $1,750. These California amounts were the same as the federal deductions allowed for years before 1982.

An important difference in the pre-1987 California law was that no California IRA deduction was available to individuals covered by other plans (this was also the rule in the federal law before 1982).

Because of the pre-1987 differences in California and federal deductible contribution limits, there could be a difference in the California and federal taxable amounts of IRA distributions (see ¶ 206).

● *Simplified employee pension (SEP) plans*

Under both California and federal law, an employer may provide for a simplified employee pension (SEP) plan for his or her employees. Ordinarily, an SEP plan will take the form of an IRA established by the employer into which the employer makes contributions for the benefit of the employee's SEP-IRA account. The contributions may be deducted by the employer and are excluded from the employee's gross income. The employer may take a deduction for an amount equal to the lesser of (1) 15% of the employee's compensation (not including the employer's SEP contribution) or (2) $30,000. The employer's SEP contribution deduction limitation is separate and apart from the employee's $2,000 IRA contribution deduction limitation (see discussion of IRAs above). Thus, the employee may also contribute and deduct from gross income up to the maximum IRA amount of $2,000. However, the amount of the employee's IRA contribution may be limited by the employee's active participation in an employer-sponsored plan (in this case, the SEP).

In the case of a self-employed individual, the individual's "compensation" is his or her "earned income," as determined for purposes of computing the taxpayer's federal deduction (rather than the earned income computed using California amounts).

● *Savings Incentive Match Plans for Employees (SIMPLE Plans)*

Both California and federal law authorize Savings Incentive Match Plans for Employees (SIMPLE plans) for tax years beginning after 1996. Under a SIMPLE plan, employees may make elective contributions of up to $6,000 per year and employers must make matching contributions. Assets in the account

¶ 318

are not taxed until they are distributed to an employee, and employers may deduct contributions to employees' accounts. In addition, the SIMPLE plan is not subject to the nondiscrimination rules (including top-heavy provisions) required of qualified plans. A SIMPLE plan may be structured as an IRA or as a 401(k) plan. However, an employer's deduction for contributions to a SIMPLE 401(k) plan is limited to the greater of (1) 15% of the total compensation of plan participants for the taxable year or (2) the amount the employer is required to contribute to the plan for the year.

To establish a SIMPLE plan, an employer must have 100 or fewer employees who received at least $5,000 in compensation from the employer in the preceding year. The employer may not maintain other qualified plans (there is a federal exception concerning SIMPLE IRAs for noncollectively bargained employees).

"Contribution formulas": Employers must satisfy one of two contribution formulas. Under the matching contribution formula, employers are generally required to match employee contributions on a dollar-for-dollar basis, up to 3% of an employee's compensation for the year. However, an employer may also elect to limit its match, for all eligible employees, to a smaller percentage of compensation (not less than 1%). The election may not be made in more than two out of five years. Under an alternative formula, an employer may elect to make a contribution of 2% of compensation for each employee who has earned at least $5,000 in compensation and who is eligible to participate in the SIMPLE plan.

● *Contributions to union pension plans*

California conforms to the federal rules regarding deductibility of members' contributions to union pension plans. This means, generally, that the contributions are not deductible, since the employee ordinarily has a vested interest or the right to a return of his or her contributions. See *Appeal of Allen B. Crane* (1978) (CCH CALIFORNIA TAX REPORTS ¶ 16-109.92) and *Appeal of Allan I. and Ivy L. Berr* (1980) (CCH CALIFORNIA TAX REPORTS ¶ 16-109.921) (5% of the contributions in question was allowed as a deduction, because that portion was forfeitable upon termination of union membership).

¶ 319 Research and Experimental Expenditures

Law: Sec. 17201 (CCH CALIFORNIA TAX REPORTS ¶ 15-821).

Comparable Federal: Secs. 59(e), 174 (CCH STANDARD FEDERAL TAX REPORTS ¶ 5480, 12,040).

Research and experimental expenditures may be deducted currently, or may be amortized over a 60-month period at the election of the taxpayer. For both California and federal purposes, the option to deduct or amortize research and experimental expenditures applies only to expenditures that are "reasonable under the circumstances."

The federal law allows a tax credit for certain increases in research expenditures (IRC Sec. 41); California allows a similar credit (see ¶ 137).

¶ 319a Trademark or Trade Name Expenditures

Law: Sec. 18151 (CCH CALIFORNIA TAX REPORTS ¶ 15-827, 16-672).

Comparable Federal: Former Sec. 167(e), Sec. 1253 (CCH STANDARD FEDERAL TAX REPORTS ¶ 1991, 1993, 32,640—32,644).

California incorporates special federal rules governing the deductibility of payments made in connection with the transfer of a trademark, trade name, or franchise. Such amounts, when paid or incurred in the conduct of a trade or business during the taxable year, are currently deductible if (1) they are contingent on the productivity, use, or disposition of the trademark, trade name, or franchise; (2) they are paid as part of a series of amounts payable at least annually throughout the term of the transfer agreement; and (3) the payments are substantially equal in amount or are to be paid pursuant to a fixed formula. Transfer payments that do not meet the above requirements are generally subject to amortization over a 15-year period for post-August 10, 1993, transfers (see ¶ 310).

● *Prior law*

For transfers occurring after October 2, 1989, and before August 11, 1993, a single payment in discharge of a principal amount could be amortized over the shorter period of 10 years or the term of the agreement if the principal sum did not exceed $100,000. Prior to October 2, 1989, no depreciation or amortization deduction was allowed for trademark or trade name expenditures, including acquisition expenditures.

¶ 319b Goodwill and Other Intangibles

Law: Sec. 17279 (CCH CALIFORNIA TAX REPORTS ¶ 15-874).

Comparable Federal: Sec. 197 (CCH STANDARD FEDERAL TAX REPORTS ¶ 12,450—12,455).

California incorporates IRC Sec. 197, which provides for the amortization, over a 15-year period, of goodwill and certain other intangibles used in a trade or business or for the production of income. Amortization of intangibles is available for acquisitions made after August 10, 1993, or, on an elective basis, for all property acquired after July 25, 1991, for federal purposes and for taxable years beginning after 1993 for California purposes. For property acquired in a tax year beginning before 1994, the amount that may be amortized may not exceed the adjusted basis of that intangible as of the first day of the first tax year beginning in 1994 and that amount is amortized ratably from that day until 15 years after the month in which the intangible was acquired.

The following intangibles are subject to amortization unless specifically excluded by federal law: (1) goodwill, going concern value, and covenants not to compete entered into in connection with the acquisition of a trade or business; (2) workforce in place; (3) information base; (4) know-how; (5) any customer-based intangible; (6) any supplier-based intangible; (7) any license, permit, or other right granted by a governmental unit or agency; and (8) any franchise, trademark, or trade name.

¶ 320 Start-Up Expenditures

Law: Sec. 17201 (CCH CALIFORNIA TAX REPORTS ¶ 15-872).

Comparable Federal: Sec. 195 (CCH STANDARD FEDERAL TAX REPORTS ¶ 12,370).

"Start-up" expenditures may be treated as deferred expenses, at the election of the taxpayer, and amortized over a period of 60 months (or more). California law incorporates the federal law as of the current IRC tie-in date (see ¶ 102a).

¶ 321 Standard Deduction

Law: Sec. 17073.5 (CCH CALIFORNIA TAX REPORTS ¶ 15-704).

Comparable Federal: Sec. 63 (CCH STANDARD FEDERAL TAX REPORTS ¶ 620).

California conforms to federal law allowing taxpayers to elect a standard deduction in lieu of itemizing deductions, with the exception of the amount of the deduction.

For 1999, the California standard deduction for a head of household, surviving spouse, or a married couple filing a joint return is $5,422. For others, the deduction is $2,711.

Both federal and California law limit the standard deduction of a person who is claimed as a dependent. For 1999, the deduction is limited to the greater of (1) $700 or (2) the earned income of the dependent plus $250.

 CCH Example: Deduction for Employed Dependent

Matthew, age 16, has $300 of interest income from a savings account and $2,000 of earned income from a summer job in 1999. Assuming Matthew is eligible to be claimed as a dependent on his parents' tax return, his standard deduction is $2,250: the greater of (1) $700 or (2) the $2,000 of earned income plus $250.

Both federal and California law provide for inflation adjustments to the standard deduction as explained at ¶ 109.

As under federal law, the following may not take the standard deduction: (1) a married individual filing separately when the other spouse itemizes; (2) an individual making a short-period return because of a change in the annual accounting period; or (3) an estate, trust, common trust fund, or partnership. Federal law also denies the standard deduction to nonresident aliens, but California does not.

¶ 322 Items Not Deductible

> *Law:* Secs. 17201, 17269, 17270, 17274-75, 17280-82, 17286, 17299.8-9.9 (CCH CALIFORNIA TAX REPORTS ¶ 15-715, 15-717, 15-727, 15-898, 15-900, 15-905, 15-933, 15-943—15-955, 15-974, 15-977, 89-410).
>
> *Comparable Federal:* Secs. 162, 183, 261-68, 273, 274, 276, 280A, 280B, 280C, 280E, 280G (CCH STANDARD FEDERAL TAX REPORTS ¶ 8520, 8580, 12,170, 12,240, 13,502—14,200, 14,313, 14,850, 14,900, 14,950, 15,000, 15,050, 15,800).
>
> *California Forms:* Sch. CA (540), Sch. CA (540NR).

The federal law making certain items expressly nondeductible is incorporated in California's by reference as of the current IRC tie-in date (see ¶ 102a). There are, however, several specific differences that are explained below.

● *California-federal differences*

California provides for the following categories of nondeductible items not provided under federal law:

1. expenses of certain illegal activities in addition to those specified federally, or of other activities that directly tend to promote or are otherwise related to such activities;

2. certain expenses attributable to substandard housing, as explained below;

3. abandonment fees on open-space easements and timberland tax-recoupment fees, as explained below;

4. in connection with the denial of deductions for illegal bribes, etc., California provides for disallowance of certain payments that would be unlawful under U.S. laws;

5. deductions for remuneration of personal services that are not reported in required statements to employees (see ¶ 712a) or in required information returns (see ¶ 711) may be disallowed at the discretion of the Franchise Tax Board;

6. deductions for interest, taxes, depreciation, and amortization are denied to property owners who fail to file proper information returns as explained at ¶ 711; and

7. California denies a business expense deduction for expenditures made at, or payments paid to, a club that engages in discriminatory practices.

Federal law that generally prohibits a current deduction for capital expenditures (IRC Sec. 263(a)) does not apply to expenditures for which a deduction is allowed under California law for enterprise zone property.

● *Illegal activities*

The California law has two quite similar provisions that deny deductions for expenses of illegal activities. The first provision applies to activities defined in Chapters 9, 10, and 10.5 of Title 9, Part 1, of the Penal Code of California. Chapter 9 refers to lotteries; Chapter 10 covers gaming; Chapter 10.5 applies to touting, etc., in connection with horse racing. The purpose is to deny deduction of expenses against income from gambling. The law specifically provides that wagering losses may be deducted as an offset to wagering gains, but it has been held that this does not apply to bookmakers. See *Appeal of M.R. and J.V. Van Cleave* (1955) (CCH CALIFORNIA TAX REPORTS ¶ 15-953.58), decided by the State Board of Equalization (SBE), and *Herman E. Hetzel v. Franchise Tax Board* (1958) (CCH CALIFORNIA TAX REPORTS ¶ 15-953.58), decided by the California District Court of Appeal. These cases disallowed deductions claimed by bookmakers for wagering losses and taxed them on their entire gross winnings. The SBE reached a similar result in cases regarding payouts to pinball machine winners—see *Appeals of C.B. Hall, Sr., et al.* (CCH CALIFORNIA TAX REPORTS ¶ 15-953.16) and *Appeal of Arnerich et al.* (CCH CALIFORNIA TAX REPORTS ¶ 15-953.34).

The second provision of this type applies to a variety of activities defined in certain chapters of the Penal Code and the Health and Safety Code. These chapters cover a wide range of criminal activities, including larceny, robbery, burglary, forgery, counterfeiting, lewd conduct, prostitution, drug trafficking, etc. This provision includes a prohibition against deductions for cost of goods sold.

Under prior law it has been held that a deduction (or exclusion) is allowable for cost of goods sold in an illegal business.

In *Appeal of Felix L. Rocha* (1977) (CCH CALIFORNIA TAX REPORTS ¶ 15-953.89), the taxpayer was engaged in the illegal sale of narcotics. The SBE cited several federal court decisions as precedents and allowed a deduction for the cost of the narcotics sold; the SBE pointed out that the deduction represented, in effect, an exclusion from gross receipts for a return of capital.

● *Substandard rental housing*

California denies deductions for interest, taxes, depreciation, or amortization attributable to substandard rental housing. This applies to both occupied and unoccupied housing that violates laws or codes relating to health, safety, or building, where (1) the property is not renovated within six months after notice of violation is given or (2) good faith compliance efforts have not been commenced. It also applies to employee housing that has not been brought into compliance with the conditions stated in a written notice of violation issued under the Employee Housing Act within 30 days of the date of such notice or the date prescribed in the notice. Exceptions are provided for cases where the substandard condition results from a natural disaster or from a change in standards (unless there is danger to occupants), or where failure to renovate is due to unavailability of credit. This provision was applied to deny deductions for interest, taxes, and depreciation in *Appeal of Robert J. and Vera Cort* (1980) (CCH CALIFORNIA TAX REPORTS ¶ 15-974.18). Other cases have held to the same effect. In *Appeal of Bryan H. Hillstrom* (1983) (CCH CALIFORNIA TAX REPORTS ¶ 15-974.36), deductions were disallowed even though the notice of violation had been issued to a prior owner and the current owner was not aware of the notice or the substandard condition.

● *Fees under environmental laws*

California denies deductions for abandonment fees paid to terminate an open-space easement, and also for tax recoupment fees imposed by the Government Code under the program for timberland preserves (see also ¶ 534).

¶ 322

● *Expenses for which credits are allowable*

California incorporates the portion of IRC Sec. 280C that disallows a deduction for that portion of qualified research expenses or basic research expenses that is equal to the amount of the credit allowed for such expenses (see ¶ 137). California does not incorporate the rest of IRC Sec. 280C, which disallows a deduction for that portion of expenses for which a federal employment credit is allowed.

● *Other nondeductible items*

Differences between federal and California rules as to what is tax-exempt income may also result in differences in expenses that are nondeductible. For example, California exempts certain interest income, whereas federal does not. Expenses attributable to such income that would be deductible for federal tax purposes would not be deductible for California purposes. Also, California does not permit deduction of expenses attributable to income that was not taxed by California.

 CCH Example: Nondeductible Lottery Expenses

California lottery losses may not be deducted from lottery winnings for California purposes, because the expenses are attributable to the production of income not taxed by California.

In addition, where income is received before the taxpayer became a California resident, expenses attributable to that income are not deductible for California purposes, even though the income is of a type that California would tax to a resident. In *Harry R. Haldeman and Joanne H. Haldeman v. Franchise Tax Board* (1983) (CCH CALIFORNIA TAX REPORTS ¶ 15-711.23), the California Court of Appeal denied deduction of legal and other expenses claimed as either business expenses (see ¶ 301) or expenses of producing income (see ¶ 304). The taxpayer (Haldeman) incurred expenses of $125,000 in the years 1974-1976 as a result of his involvement in the Watergate affair when he was White House Chief of Staff before he became a California resident in June 1973. The court held that the expenses could not be deducted against income of $106,000 received during 1974-1976 for television appearances and newspaper articles, even though this income was made possible by his involvement in Watergate.

See the following paragraphs for other possible federal or California nondeductible items:

¶ 323 Deductions of Nonresidents

> *Law:* Secs. 17301-10 (CCH CALIFORNIA TAX REPORTS ¶ 15-109, 15-114, 15-814, 15-882).
>
> *Comparable Federal:* None.
>
> *California Form:* Sch. CA (540NR).

As explained at ¶ 112, the tax on nonresidents and part-year residents is a proportion of the tax that would be payable if they were full-year residents, the proportion being determined by the ratio of California adjusted gross income to total adjusted gross income. In computing California adjusted gross income for this purpose, only deductions that are attributable to California are allowable.

In computing California income, no deduction is allowed for alimony paid while the taxpayer was not residing in California. However, it should be noted that the U.S. Supreme Court struck down as unconstitutional a similar New York law in *Lunding, et ux. v. New York Tax Appeals Tribunal* (1998) (CCH CALIFORNIA TAX REPORTS ¶ 15-882.65).

A net operating loss carryover (see ¶ 309) is deductible for California purposes even if the loss was sustained while the taxpayer was not a state resident.

In computing the tax that would be payable if the taxpayer were a full-year resident, the usual rules for itemizing deductions are applicable; that is, deductions should normally be itemized if they amount to more than the standard deduction (see ¶ 321).

¶ 324 Farm and Hobby Losses

> *Law:* Sec. 17201 (CCH CALIFORNIA TAX REPORTS ¶ 15-845).
>
> *Comparable Federal:* Sec. 183 (CCH STANDARD FEDERAL TAX REPORTS ¶ 12,170).

California conforms to federal law (see ¶ 102a).

California and federal law provide special rules to restrict the tax benefit of farm and hobby losses. These rules disallow loss deductions under certain conditions and "recapture" prior deductions when property is sold.

¶ 325 "At Risk" Limitations

> *Law:* Sec. 17551 (CCH CALIFORNIA TAX REPORTS ¶ 16-243).
>
> *Comparable Federal:* Sec. 465 (CCH STANDARD FEDERAL TAX REPORTS ¶ 21,850).

California law is the same as federal (see ¶ 102a).

Detailed rules are provided to limit the deduction of certain losses to the amount of the taxpayer's economic risk. These provisions, which were designed to restrict the use of various types of tax shelters, apply to any activity engaged in as a trade or business or for the production of income. The federal law is incorporated in California's by reference.

In *Haggard and Williams* (1994) (CCH CALIFORNIA TAX REPORTS ¶ 16-243.45) the State Board of Equalization held that losses arising from a taxpayer's investment in a tax shelter that involved the purchase and lease-back of computer equipment were not deductible, because the taxpayer was protected against loss by the provisions of his purchase agreement. Although business losses generated by the leasing of depreciable property may be deducted to the extent that a taxpayer is "at risk," a taxpayer is not considered "at risk" with respect to amounts protected against loss through nonrecourse financing, guarantees, stop loss agreements, or similar arrangements.

¶ 326 Passive Activity Losses and Credits

Law: Secs. 17551, 17561 (CCH California Tax Reports ¶ 16-248c).

Comparable Federal: Sec. 469 (CCH Standard Federal Tax Reports ¶ 21,966).

California Forms: Sch. CA (540), Sch. CA (540NR), FTB 3801, FTB 3801-CR.

California incorporates, with the changes noted below, the federal law (as of the current IRC tie-in date; see ¶ 102a) that generally prohibits the use of passive losses to reduce nonpassive income.

California generally conforms to amendments made to federal law by the Small Business Job Protection Act of 1996 concerning the (1) passive activity credit that may be claimed for working interests in oil and gas property and (2) calculation of a passive activity loss when a passive activity is disposed in a taxable transaction. However, these amendments are effective for federal purposes for tax years beginning after 1986 and for California purposes for taxable years beginning after 1996.

California makes three modifications to the federal rule as incorporated:

(1) under IRC Sec. 469(d)(2), certain federal passive income credits may be carried over to later tax years if they exceed the tax attributable to the passive activity; for California purposes, credits that may be carried over are the credits for research expenses and low-income housing and the former credits for targeted jobs and orphan drug research;

(2) for purposes of California's low-income housing credit, California substitutes a $75,000 limitation in place of the federal $25,000 limitation on use of passive activity losses or credits against nonpassive rental income; and

(3) California has not conformed to federal amendments made by the Revenue Reconciliation Act of 1993 that, for tax years beginning after 1993, ease application of the passive activity loss rules to rental real estate losses suffered by certain taxpayers who materially participate in a real property trade or business.

● *Computation*

All California taxpayers who engage in passive activities must segregate California adjustments that relate to passive activities from California adjustments that relate to nonpassive activities. On FTB 3801, taxpayers must make adjustments to items of federal adjusted gross income that relate to passive activities and as to which California and federal law differ (e.g., depreciation).

On FTB 3801, the taxpayer first adjusts passive activity losses to reflect any California/federal differences (as in depreciation) and then subjects the modified figure to the passive activity loss limitation rules. The resultant figure, which is the California passive activity loss, is transferred to the form or schedule normally used to report the California adjustment amount. The adjustment is computed and then entered on the appropriate line of Schedule CA (540) or Schedule CA (540NR). If there is no California schedule or form to compute the passive activity loss adjustment (e.g., for rental real estate losses), the adjustment is computed on a special worksheet on FTB 3801 and then transferred directly to the corresponding line in either the subtraction or addition section of Schedule CA (540) or Schedule CA (540NR). To compute passive activity loss adjustment amounts for Schedule CA (540) or Schedule CA (540NR), the taxpayer should use total adjusted gross income amounts and should not start with federal income amounts.

Unallowed (i.e., excess) passive activity losses may be carried forward and subtracted from passive activity income in succeeding tax years.

Nonresidents and part-year residents: In addition to the adjustments described above, nonresidents and part-year residents must make similar adjustments to passive activity items in computing California-source adjusted gross income.

¶ 327 Expenses of Soil Conservation, etc.

> *Law:* Sec. 17201 (CCH California Tax Reports ¶ 15-824, 15-838).
>
> *Comparable Federal:* Secs. 175, 180 (CCH Standard Federal Tax Reports ¶ 12,060, 12,140, 12,160).

California law is the same as federal.

● *Soil and water conservation*

Farmers may deduct expenditures for soil and water conservation and the prevention of erosion on farmland.

● *Expenditures for fertilizer, etc.*

Farmers are permitted to elect to deduct expenditures for fertilizer and other materials designed to improve farm land, where the costs would otherwise be chargeable to capital account.

¶ 328 Circulation Expenditures of Periodicals

> *Law:* Sec. 17201 (CCH California Tax Reports ¶ 15-817).
>
> *Comparable Federal:* Sec. 173 (CCH Standard Federal Tax Reports ¶ 12,050).

Expenditures to "establish, maintain, or increase" the circulation of a periodical are deductible. This provision permits deduction of costs of increasing circulation, which would otherwise have to be capitalized, with elective three-year amortization of such expenditures. California law incorporates the federal law by reference.

¶ 329 Employee Parking Cash-Out Programs

> *Law:* Sec. 17202 (CCH California Tax Reports ¶ 15-976).
>
> *Comparable Federal:* Sec. 162 (CCH Standard Federal Tax Reports ¶ 8474).

California law allows employers a business expense deduction for expenses incurred in connection with an employee parking cash-out program. Under such a program, an employer provides a cash allowance to an employee in an amount equal to the parking subsidy that the employer would otherwise pay to provide the employee with a parking space.

¶ 330 Clean-Fuel Vehicles and Refueling Property

Law: Secs. 17024.5, 17201, 17256 (CCH CALIFORNIA TAX REPORTS ¶ 15-836).

Comparable Federal: Sec. 179A (CCH STANDARD FEDERAL TAX REPORTS ¶ 6005.1).

Federal law allowing a limited deduction from gross income for the cost of clean-fuel vehicle property and clean-fuel vehicle refueling property was incorporated by California for property placed in service after June 30, 1993, and before 1995. Under federal law, the deduction applies to property placed in service after June 30, 1993, and before 2005, but is phased out incrementally in calendar years 2002 through 2004.

Any deduction taken with respect to a clean-fuel vehicle or clean-fuel vehicle refueling property requires a reduction in the basis of the affected vehicle or property (see ¶ 534).

● *California-federal differences*

In addition to certain deductions that are prohibited under federal law, California did not allow the cost of enterprise zone, former program area, or Los Angeles Revitalization Zone property that was expensed under California law to be claimed as a deduction for clean-fuel vehicles or clean-fuel vehicle refueling property.

CHAPTER 4

PERSONAL INCOME TAX
ACCOUNTING METHODS AND BASES, INVENTORIES

¶ 400 Accounting Periods and Methods—In General

> *Law:* Secs. 17551-70 (CCH CALIFORNIA TAX REPORTS ¶ 16-201—16-273, 89-107, 89-164).

> *Comparable Federal:* Secs. 441-83 (CCH STANDARD FEDERAL TAX REPORTS ¶ 2701, 2720, 2731, 2754, 2761, 2775, 2785, 2823, 2885A, 2887, 2888, 2889, 2894, 2899, 2899I, 2899N, 2899V, 2901, 2917, 2921, 2924, 2926X, 2926Y, 2926Z, 2926ZL, 2926ZT, 2927A, 2951, 2966, 2969, 2972, 2990, 2994).

California generally incorporates federal law governing accounting periods and methods of accounting as of the current tie-in date (see ¶ 102a). However, California's requirements in connection with annualized short-period returns are somewhat different (see ¶ 403). In addition, California has a special rule with no federal counterpart authorizing the Franchise Tax Board to allocate income between separately filing spouses (see ¶ 412).

California has not yet incorporated an amendment made by the federal Tax and Trade Relief Extension Act of 1998 that disregards a cash basis taxpayer's receipt of a qualified prize option for purposes of determining the tax year for which any portion of the qualified prize is to be included in gross income. Qualified prizes are prizes or awards from contests, lotteries, jackpots, games, or similar arrangements that provide for a series of payments over a period of no less than 10 years. A qualified prize option entitles an individual to receive a single cash payment in lieu of a qualified prize, or a portion thereof, provided that the option can be exercised no later than 60 days after the contest winner becomes entitled to the qualified prize. The amendment is generally applicable for federal purposes to any qualified prize to which a person first becomes entitled after October 21, 1998, although transitional rules apply to prizes awarded earlier.

¶ 401 Accounting Periods

Law: Secs. 17551, 17565 (CCH CALIFORNIA TAX REPORTS ¶ 16-204, 16-207, 89-164).

Comparable Federal: Secs. 441, 444, 645 (CCH STANDARD FEDERAL TAX REPORTS ¶ 20,302, 20,600, 24,850).

California law is the same as federal law (see ¶ 102a). The taxpayer's tax year must be the same as federal unless a different period is initiated or approved by the Franchise Tax Board.

The taxpayer may report on a calendar year or fiscal year basis, in accordance with the taxpayer's books. If no books are kept, the taxpayer must report on the calendar year basis. A 52-53 week year may be used under certain circumstances; special rules are provided for determining the effective date of law changes in such cases. California law incorporates the federal law by referencing the Internal Revenue Code.

If a fiscal year is to be established by a new taxpayer, the year must be adopted on or before the time prescribed by law (not including extensions) for filing the return for that year.

In *Appeal of P.A. Reyff* (1958) (CCH CALIFORNIA TAX REPORTS ¶ 16-204.15), the State Board of Equalization held that the taxpayer was required to report on a calendar year basis for the particular year in question because he kept no books, even though returns were filed and accepted in later years on a fiscal year basis. The later years were not in question.

¶ 402 Change of Accounting Period

Law: Secs. 17551, 17556 (CCH CALIFORNIA TAX REPORTS ¶ 16-204).

Comparable Federal: Sec. 442 (CCH STANDARD FEDERAL TAX REPORTS ¶ 20,400).

California law is essentially the same as federal law, including the provisions on accounting-period changes by partnerships, S corporations, trusts, and personal service corporations (and the effects of the taxable income of partners, S corporation shareholders, etc.).

Federal law regarding changes of accounting period is incorporated in California law by reference.

Generally, a change of accounting period requires the approval of the taxing authorities. Application for change should be filed by the 15th day of the second month following the close of the short period. Under the conformity rules, an application for federal purposes will be considered an application for California purposes also.

See ¶ 612 for a discussion of the taxable year of a partnership.

¶ 403 Return for Short Period—Annualization of Income

Law: Sec. 17552 (CCH CALIFORNIA TAX REPORTS ¶ 16-207, 89-164).

Comparable Federal: Sec. 443 (CCH STANDARD FEDERAL TAX REPORTS ¶ 20,500).

California law is the same as federal law with minor exceptions noted below.

California law, unlike federal law, requires a short-period return when a taxpayer's year is terminated by the Franchise Tax Board because of a jeopardy assessment.

California requires a proportional reduction in the amount allowed for exemption credits when a short-period return is filed. Federal law requires a similar reduction for exemption deductions.

¶ 404 Optional Method for Short-Period Returns

Law: Sec. 17551 (CCH CALIFORNIA TAX REPORTS ¶ 16-207, 89-164).

Comparable Federal: Sec. 443 (CCH STANDARD FEDERAL TAX REPORTS ¶ 20,500).

California law is the same as federal law (see ¶ 102a).

¶ 405 Change of Status, Resident or Nonresident

Law: Sec. 17554 (CCH CALIFORNIA TAX REPORTS ¶ 15-609).

Comparable Federal: None.

When the status of the taxpayer changes from resident to nonresident, or vice versa, the determination of whether or not income is subject to California tax is made on the accrual basis, even though the taxpayer may report on the cash basis of accounting. The period in which the income is actually to be reported, however, is determined under the regular rules relating to the taxpayer's method of accounting.

The purpose of this rule, as interpreted by the State Board of Equalization (SBE) in cases discussed below, is to treat cash-basis taxpayers the same as accrual-basis taxpayers when a change of residency occurs.

CCH Example: Treatment of Cash-Basis Taxpayers

Mary, a New York resident who reports income on the cash basis, moves to California on January 1. On January 5, Mary receives a salary check for $1,000 that she earned in the preceding month. As a California resident at the time she receives and reports the income, she is subject to tax on all income regardless of its source, and in the absence of a special rule she would be taxable on the $1,000 in California. However, if her income had been reported on the accrual basis, the $1,000 would have been treated as "accrued" and reported in the preceding month before she became a California resident. The special rule permits her, as a cash-basis taxpayer, to exclude the income and produces a consistent result that is independent of the method of accounting.

● *Rules for application of accrual provision*

The purpose and application of this special provision are discussed in some detail in *Appeal of Virgil M. and Jeanne P. Money* (1983) (CCH CALIFORNIA TAX REPORTS ¶ 15-609.98). The opinion reasons that the purpose is merely to prevent differing treatment of cash and accrual basis taxpayers, and concludes that the provision is applicable only if:

1. California's sole basis for taxation is the taxpayer's residency; and

2. taxation would differ depending on whether the taxpayer used the accrual or cash method of accounting.

Applying these criteria to a situation where a California taxpayer received a military pension that started when he was a nonresident, the SBE held that the second condition was not satisfied and, therefore, the pension was taxable by California.

In the *Money* opinion, the SBE stated specifically that it had reversed its earlier reasoning regarding the intent of the law. Cases decided before 1983 should be reconsidered in the light of the rationale of the *Money* case. Some such older cases have been cited in the discussion below, because the conclusions reached in the cited cases would presumably be the same under the *Money* rationale.

● *Distributions from qualified plans for deferred compensation*

In *Appeal of Frank W. and Harriet S. Walters* (1984) (CCH CALIFORNIA TAX REPORTS ¶ 15-609.97), the SBE applied the rationale of the *Money* case, discussed above, to distributions from a qualified deferred-compensation plan. The taxpayer earned future benefits in Missouri, and moved to California after his retirement. The SBE held that his benefit payments were taxable by California, since there is no distinction between cash and accrual basis taxpayers in the treatment of distributions from qualified plans. Also, to the same effect, see *Appeal of Edward A. and Leonora F. Kodyra* (1985) (CCH CALIFORNIA TAX REPORTS ¶ 15-404.252); in this case, the pension of a retired New York policeman was taxed by California even though it was exempt from state and local taxation under New York law. Similarly, in *Daks v. Franchise Tax Board* (1999) (CCH CALIFORNIA TAX REPORTS ¶ 15-609.56) a California court of appeal held that pension benefits earned by a taxpayer as a participant in his employer's noncontributory, qualified, defined-benefit pension plan while the taxpayer was a resident of New York were taxable in California because the benefits were received by the taxpayer while he was a resident of California.

The SBE has also cited and followed the *Money* decision in a case involving a lump-sum distribution from a qualified plan. In *Appeal of Lawrence T. and Galadriel Blakeslee* (1983) (CCH CALIFORNIA TAX REPORTS ¶ 15-609.941), the taxpayer became entitled to a lump-sum distribution in 1976, before moving to California from Florida; however, she did not receive the distribution until 1978, after she became a California resident. The SBE held that the distribution was taxable by California, on the ground that California makes no distinction between cash and accrual basis taxpayers in the treatment of lump-sum distributions; this principle was affirmed in *Appeal of Ralph G. and Martha E. McQuoid* (1989) (CCH CALIFORNIA TAX REPORTS ¶ 15-609.55). It should be observed that California taxation of pensions earned

¶ 405

elsewhere does not depend on the rationale of the *Money* case. Many earlier cases held that such pensions were taxable to California residents because the right to receive the pensions was contingent upon the taxpayer's survival and therefore the income had not "accrued" when the change of residence occurred.

● *Sale of out-of-state real estate*

In the *Appeal of Estate of Albert Kahn, Deceased, and Lillian Kahn* (1986) (CCH CALIFORNIA TAX REPORTS ¶ 15-114.30), the taxpayers, having established residence in California on May 21, 1976, were not allowed to deduct rental expenses on out-of-state real estate even though the expenses were paid at the escrow for the sale of the property and even though the gain from the sale was taxable. Although binding agreements of sale had been executed prior to the establishment of California residency, escrow closed afterwards, and the gain was realized during the period of residency. The SBE applied the rationale of the *Money* case and held that the rental expenses were accrued prior to the establishment of California residency.

● *Distributions from self-employed (Keogh) or IRA plans*

Retirement income attributable to services performed outside California but received after the taxpayer becomes a resident is taxable in its entirety by California. California does not impose tax on retirement income, including income from a self-employed (Keogh) plan or an individual retirement account (IRA), received by a nonresident after 1995. Prior to 1996, California taxed retirement income of a nonresident.

See ¶ 206 for a discussion of (1) a possible recoverable tax-free California basis of a self-employed plan resulting from pre-1987 differences between California and federal law on deductibility of contributions to such a plan and (2) how to calculate the California basis of an IRA of a California resident that made nondeductible contributions to an IRA while a nonresident.

● *Income from annuities*

In *Appeal of Preston T. and Virginia R. Kelsey* (1976) (CCH CALIFORNIA TAX REPORTS ¶ 15-435.411), the taxpayer was the current beneficiary of her deceased father's retirement annuity. The annuity had been earned entirely in Pennsylvania. The SBE held that the taxpayer, as a California resident, was fully taxable under the rules for income from annuities, even though the payments were properly classifiable as "income in respect of a decedent" (see ¶ 413).

● *Liquidation of corporation*

The case of *Sweetland et al.* (1961) (CCH CALIFORNIA TAX REPORTS ¶ 15-609.92) involved a large gain realized by a shareholder upon liquidation of a corporation. The taxpayer contended that his gain was not taxable because it was the result of appreciation in value prior to the time he became a resident (and also prior to the time the California income tax law was enacted in 1935). A California court of appeal held that the entire gain was taxable in the year of liquidation, since there was no realization of income until that year. Other cases have held to the same effect.

● *Installment sales*

In cases decided before the *Money* decision, discussed above, the SBE held that installments received by nonresidents on a sale made when they were California residents were subject to California tax. See *Appeal of Sherwood R. and Marion S. Gordon* (1983) (CCH CALIFORNIA TAX REPORTS ¶ 15-605.47). Presumably these cases are not affected by the *Money* decision, since the income is from a California source and is therefore taxed regardless of residence. As to installments received by a California resident on an out-of-state sale made before becoming a California resident, the installments are not subject to California tax since the right to receive the income accrued during nonresidency. Any interest from installment sales is taxable while the taxpayer is a resident.

● *Partnership income*

In *Appeal of Jerald L. and Joan Katleman* (1976) (CCH CALIFORNIA TAX REPORTS ¶ 15-155.11), the taxpayer contended that his distributive share of certain out-of-state partnership income accrued before he became a California resident. He became a California resident late in 1968; the partnership income was for a fiscal year ended January 31, 1969. The SBE held that the income in question did not "accrue" until the end of the partnership's fiscal year, so it was all subject to California tax in the taxpayer's 1969 return.

● *Disputed or contingent income*

In *Appeal of David D. and Linda D. Cornman* (1984) (CCH CALIFORNIA TAX REPORTS ¶ 15-350.851), the taxpayer earned income in Alaska during the years 1974-1977 when he was a resident of that state. The amount of the income was subject to litigation, which was settled in 1979 after he had become a California resident. The SBE held that the income was subject to California tax.

In *Appeal of Louis E. and Echite M. Dana* (1979) (CCH CALIFORNIA TAX REPORTS ¶ 15-609.28), the taxpayer received income after he became a California resident, under a contingent-fee contract executed with other attorneys when he was a Michigan resident. The SBE held that the income was taxable by California, since uncertainty regarding the amount to be received prevented its accrual before the change of residence.

● *Expense reimbursement*

In *Appeal of James H. and Heloise A. Frame* (1979) (CCH CALIFORNIA TAX REPORTS ¶ 15-609.331), the taxpayer received approximately $50,000 from IBM as reimbursement for expenses of moving to California. The right to receive the reimbursement was clearly established before the taxpayer became a California resident; however, the SBE held that the reimbursement (partly offset by about $11,000 of deductions allowed) was taxable by California, since uncertainty as to the amount prevented accrual before the change of residence. See ¶ 237 for further discussion of treatment of reimbursed expenses when a taxpayer moves to or from California.

¶ 405

● *Stock option*

In *Appeal of Earl R. and Alleene R. Barnett* (1980) (CCH CALIFORNIA TAX REPORTS ¶ 15-609.91), the taxpayer moved to California after serving as a corporation executive in Canada for many years. Two months after he became a California resident, he exercised a stock option he had received as compensation in Canada. The SBE held that he was subject to California tax on income of over $100,000 received upon exercise of the option, since the income did not "accrue" until the option was exercised.

● *Income from trust*

Special rules apply where a resident beneficiary receives from a nonresident trustee a distribution of non-California source income that accumulated when the beneficiary was a nonresident. In such cases the taxability depends on whether the income was accrued at the time the beneficiary became a resident. If the beneficiary was a contingent or discretionary beneficiary during the period of accumulation, the income is not accrued at the time the beneficiary's status changes from nonresident to resident; it follows that the income is fully taxable in the year of distribution. Otherwise, the income is considered to be accrued at the time of change of residence and is not subject to California tax. See also ¶ 604a.

¶ 406 Tax Rate Change During Taxable Year

Law: Sec. 17034 (CCH CALIFORNIA TAX REPORTS ¶ 89-030).

Comparable Federal: Sec. 15 (CCH STANDARD FEDERAL TAX REPORTS ¶ 3285).

California law differs from federal in situations involving rate changes during the taxable year.

The general California rule is that, unless an amending act specifies otherwise, changes affecting the imposition or computation of taxes (including rates), credits, penalties, and additions to tax are applicable to taxable years beginning on or after January 1 of the year in which the amending act takes effect. All other tax-related provisions are applied beginning on the date the act takes effect.

¶ 407 Accounting Methods—General

Law: Secs. 17201, 17207, 17208.4, 17551, 17564 (CCH CALIFORNIA TAX REPORTS ¶ 15-701, 15-750, 16-232, 16-237, 16-247, 16-248b).

Comparable Federal: Secs. 165, 263A, 446-448, 451, 455-56, 458, 460, 461, 464, 467-68B, 481 (CCH STANDARD FEDERAL TAX REPORTS ¶ 6450, 9802, 13,800, 20,606, 20,621, 20,625, 20,800, 21,002, 21,510, 21,520, 21,540, 21,550, 21,802, 21,830, 21,840, 21,910, 22,270).

California Form: FTB 3834.

With minor exceptions, California law is the same as federal law.

● *Automatic consent procedure for accounting method change*

California does not follow federal law that provides for an automatic consent procedure for a change in accounting method for purposes of claiming the full deduction for any previously unclaimed depreciation or amortization allowed—see IRS Rev. Proc. 96-31; FTB Notice 96-3 (CCH CALIFORNIA TAX REPORTS ¶ 16-211.211).

● *Timing of excess disaster-loss deductions*

Both California law and federal law allow taxpayers to elect to deduct in the prior year certain excess casualty losses sustained after the end of the year in a disaster area, as determined by the President. California law provides similar treatment for specified categories of excess losses sustained in a disaster area declared by the Governor. Under California law, all of these losses may also be carried forward for five years from the year claimed. For a discussion of disaster losses, see ¶ 307.

● *Special rules for accounting methods*

See ¶ 310 for special rules regarding production costs of films, books, etc. See ¶ 416 for special rules regarding construction-period interest and taxes. See ¶ 614 for special rules regarding partnership accounting.

¶ 408 Election to Accrue Income on Noninterest-Bearing Obligations Issued at Discount

Law: Secs. 17551, 17553 (CCH CALIFORNIA TAX REPORTS ¶ 15-550).

Comparable Federal: Sec. 454 (CCH STANDARD FEDERAL TAX REPORTS ¶ 21,500).

California law is the same as federal as of the current IRC tie-in date (see ¶ 102a).

A cash basis taxpayer may elect to accrue the increment in value of noninterest-bearing bonds issued at a discount and redeemable for fixed amounts increasing at stated intervals. The election is binding for subsequent years. On certain short-term obligations issued at a discount, the discount is not considered to accrue until the obligation is disposed of.

Federal law includes a special rule for income from U.S. Savings Bonds. Since interest from such bonds is exempt from California tax (see ¶ 217), this rule is not applicable to California.

See also ¶ 236, regarding special rules for discount bonds.

¶ 409 Inventories

Law: Secs. 17201, 17551, 17570 (CCH CALIFORNIA TAX REPORTS ¶ 16-249, 16-475).

Comparable Federal: Secs. 263A, 471, 475 (CCH STANDARD FEDERAL TAX REPORTS ¶ 13,800, 22,202, 22,265).

California law is the same as federal law.

Inventories are required where the production, purchase, or sale of merchandise is an income-producing factor. Valuation must conform to the best practice in the industry and must clearly reflect income. California follows federal regulations that provide detailed rules for inventory valuation.

¶ 408

● *Uniform capitalization rules*

California adopts by reference the federal uniform rules for capitalization of costs.

The uniform capitalization rules apply to individuals, corporations, and partnerships in a trade or business who produce real or tangible personal property or acquire property for resale. Special rules apply to farmers. Under the uniform capitalization rules, taxpayers include certain expenses in inventory costs or capitalize these expenses. These expenses include the direct costs of the property and the share of any indirect costs that are allocable to that property. Indirect costs that must be included in inventory include those that benefit property produced by the taxpayer for sale to customers in a trade or business, or that are incurred in acquiring, storing, or processing property acquired for resale to others by the taxpayer. Examples include depreciation, rent, taxes, interest, storage, purchasing (buyer's wages), processing, repackaging, handling, and general and administrative costs.

The rules do not apply to any of the following: property that is used for personal purposes; timber; property that is being produced under a long-term contract; the creative expenses paid by free-lance authors, photographers, and artists; certain costs of oil and gas wells or mineral property; research and experimental expenditures; and costs (other than circulation expenditures) and those subject to 10-year amortization rules for tax preferences.

● *Inventory shrinkage*

Under both California law and federal law, a business may determine its year-end closing inventory by taking a reasonable deduction for shrinkage, even if an actual year-end inventory has not been taken to measure the amount of shrinkage.

"Shrinkage" is generally inventory loss due to undetected theft, breakage, or bookkeeping errors. In order to claim the deduction for estimated shrinkage, a business must normally take a physical count of its inventories at each business location on a regular, consistent basis. It also must make proper adjustments to its inventories and to its estimating methods to the extent its estimates are more or less than the actual shrinkage.

● *Securities and commodities dealers and traders*

For taxable years beginning after 1996, California incorporates a federal provision added by the Revenue Reconciliation Act of 1993 that requires securities dealers to use the mark-to-market method of accounting in identifying and valuing inventory. The mark-to-market accounting requirement is effective for federal purposes for tax years ending after 1993. For taxable years beginning before 1997, securities dealers were permitted, but not required, to use mark-to-market accounting for California personal income tax purposes (Legal Ruling 95-6, CCH CALIFORNIA TAX REPORTS ¶ 16-260.10).

Effective for taxable years beginning after 1997, California also incorporates an amendment to federal law that allows commodities dealers and traders of securities or commodities to elect to use mark-to-market accounting. The amendment is effective for federal purposes in tax years ending after

¶ 409

August 5, 1997. A federal election, or lack thereof, is binding for California purposes.

Under the mark-to-market rules gain or loss with respect to any security that is not inventory in a dealer's or trader's hands and that the dealer or trader holds at the close of the tax year must be recognized and taken into account. In addition, the dealer's or trader's inventory of securities must be determined by including any security that is inventory in the dealer's or trader's hands at the security's market value as of the date the inventory is determined. The amount of gain or loss that must be taken into account for a tax year under the mark-to-market rules must be determined as if the security dealer or trader sold a qualifying security for its fair market value on the last business day of the tax year. The dealer or trader may then adjust the amount of any subsequent gain or loss actually realized to reflect the gain or loss already taken into account.

A dealer or trader in securities is not required to apply the mark-to-market accounting rules to any of the following: (1) securities held for investment; (2) notes, bonds, debentures, or other evidence of indebtedness acquired or originated by the dealer or trader in the ordinary course of the trader's or dealer's trade or business and not held for sale; or (3) securities that are hedges with respect to securities that are not subject to the mark-to-market rules or that are positions, rights to income, or liabilities that are not securities in the dealer's or trader's hands. However, any security to which an exception applies must be clearly identified as such in the dealer's or trader's records as of the close of the day on which the security was acquired, originated, or entered into.

¶ 410 Inventories—Last-In, First-Out Method

> *Law:* Sec. 17551 (CCH California Tax Reports ¶ 16-253).

> *Comparable Federal:* Secs. 472-74 (CCH Standard Federal Tax Reports ¶ 22,230, 22,250, 22,260).

A taxpayer may elect to use the last-in, first-out (LIFO) method of inventory valuation. California law is the same as federal law (see ¶ 102a) including the limitation on the election of the simplified dollar-value LIFO method for small businesses.

The Franchise Tax Board will allow automobile dealers that violate the LIFO inventory conformity requirement of IRC Sec. 472(c) or 472(e)(2) to continue using the LIFO method for California purposes, provided that they qualify for relief granted under IRS Revenue Procedure 97-44 (FTB Notice 98-10 (1998) (CCH California Tax Reports ¶ 16-253.20). Taxpayers must send a copy of the memorandum submitted to the IRS, as required under Rev. Proc. 97-44, with their California tax returns for the accounting period that includes May 31, 1998. However, they will not be required to pay a settlement amount.

¶ 410

¶ 411 Installment Sales

Law: Secs. 17551, 17560 (CCH CALIFORNIA TAX REPORTS ¶ 16-217).

Comparable Federal: Secs. 453, 453A, 453B, former 453C (CCH STANDARD FEDERAL TAX REPORTS ¶ 12,401, 21,480).

California Form: FTB 3805E.

California law is the same as federal as of the current IRC tie-in date (see ¶ 102a), except that different effective dates apply for 1987, 1988, and 1989 federal amendments that were adopted by California in 1990. California's repeal of the proportionate disallowance rule applies to dispositions by California taxpayers in income years beginning after 1989. The federal repeal was effective for dispositions beginning after 1987. Under the repealed proportionate disallowance rule, certain of the seller's outstanding indebtedness at the end of the tax year was allocated between outstanding installment sales obligations and other assets. The portion of the indebtedness allocated to installment sales obligations was treated as a payment received on those obligations for installment reporting purposes.

California's repeal of the installment method for dealers in real property and adoption of special federal rules for nondealers are applicable to transactions occurring after 1989, whereas the federal provisions apply to transactions occurring after 1987.

Income reported federally on the installment basis may differ from that reported for California purposes because of federal/California differences in basis of property sold and differences in installment reporting rules applicable to the year of sale.

Income from casual sales of real or personal property other than inventory is reported on FTB 3805E if payments are received in a year after the year of sale.

● *Law applicable when installments received*

The taxation of installment sales is governed by the law in effect at the time each installment is received. To this effect, see *William S. Andrews et al. v. Franchise Tax Board* (1969) (CCH CALIFORNIA TAX REPORTS ¶ 16-217.11), involving the percent of gain to be taken into account after the law was changed in 1959. See also *Appeal of Herbert J. and Sheila Frankel* (1978 CCH CALIFORNIA TAX REPORTS ¶ 16-601.12), holding that the percent of gain to be taken into account on a 1974 installment was governed by the law as amended in 1972, although the installment sale was made in 1970.

● *Change of residence*

See ¶ 405 for discussion of treatment of installments received after an interstate move, where an installment sale was made before the change of residence.

¶ 412 Allocation of Income and Deductions—Related Organizations, etc.

Law: Secs. 17201, 17287, 17555 (CCH CALIFORNIA TAX REPORTS ¶ 15-701, 89-107).

Comparable Federal: Secs. 269A-69B, 482 (CCH STANDARD FEDERAL TAX REPORTS ¶ 14,300, 14,303, 22,280).

California law, otherwise the same as federal law, contains a unique marital provision that applies when a husband and wife file separate returns. This provision empowers the Franchise Tax Board to make any adjustments necessary to reflect the proper income of the spouses.

Under both federal and California law, the tax authorities are given broad powers to allocate income or deductions among related organizations, trades, or businesses where necessary to prevent evasion of taxes or to clearly reflect income. Specific authority is given for treatment of personal service corporations formed, or availed of, to avoid or evade income tax.

¶ 413 Income and Deductions in Respect of Decedents

Law: Secs. 17024.5, 17731 (CCH CALIFORNIA TAX REPORTS ¶ 15-552).

Comparable Federal: Sec. 691 (CCH STANDARD FEDERAL TAX REPORTS ¶ 25,300).

Income and deductions of a decedent, not reportable during his or her life, are includible in the return of the decedent's estate or heir when received or paid.

Despite the inclusion of federal law in California law by reference (see ¶ 102a), California does not allow a deduction for federal death tax attributable to the income reported. Any provision relating to federal estate tax is ignored for California purposes. Also, no deduction is allowed for the California estate tax allowed as a credit against the federal tax.

In *Appeal of Estate of Marilyn Monroe, Deceased* (1975) (CCH CALIFORNIA TAX REPORTS ¶ 15.363.15), the estate received substantial income under contracts providing for payment of a percentage of the earnings of certain films in which the actress Marilyn Monroe had appeared. She was not a California resident when she died. The State Board of Equalization held that to the extent the films were made in California, the income was from a California source and was taxable by California as "income in respect of a decedent."

See ¶ 405 for discussion of the Kelsey case, where annuity income earned by a decedent outside California was classified as "income in respect of a decedent" but was taxed to a survivor under the rules for income from annuities.

¶ 414 Imputed Interest; Loans with Below-Market Interest

Law: Secs. 17024.5, 17551, 18180 (CCH California Tax Reports ¶ 16-270, 16-698).

Comparable Federal: Secs. 483, 7872 (CCH Standard Federal Tax Reports ¶ 22,290, 44,856).

California law generally is the same as federal law. California incorporates IRC Sec. 7872, which concerns taxation of "foregone interest" on loans with below-market interest rates.

When property is sold on a deferred payment basis and no provision is made for interest, or an unreasonably low rate of interest is provided, a portion of the deferred payments is treated as interest to the buyer and to the seller.

¶ 415 Claim of Right—Effect of Repayment

Law: None (CCH California Tax Reports ¶ 15-964).

Comparable Federal: Sec. 1341 (CCH Standard Federal Tax Reports ¶ 33,380).

If an item is included in income because it appears that the taxpayer has an unrestricted right to the item, and the taxpayer is later required to repay the item, the taxpayer is permitted under federal law to reduce the income and tax for the year of repayment. There is no California statute comparable to the federal provision. However, it is clear from the case law that California applies the claim-of-right doctrine. See *Appeal of White* (1981) (CCH California Tax Reports ¶ 15-964.30). California does not, however, follow the federal law for calculating the deduction when the repaid amount exceeds $3,000.

¶ 416 Construction-Period Interest and Taxes

Law: Sec. 17201 (CCH California Tax Reports ¶ 15-858).

Comparable Federal: Former Sec. 189, Sec. 263A (CCH Standard Federal Tax Reports ¶ 12,240; 13,800).

California conforms to federal rules requiring capitalization under the uniform capitalization rules of interest and taxes incurred during the construction period of real property.

CHAPTER 5

PERSONAL INCOME TAX
SALES AND EXCHANGES, GAIN OR LOSS, BASIS

¶ 501 Gain or Loss—General Rule

Law: Secs. 18031, 18042, 18044 (CCH CALIFORNIA TAX REPORTS ¶ 16-505, 16-576a).

Comparable Federal: Secs. 1001, 1042, 1044 (CCH STANDARD FEDERAL TAX REPORTS ¶ 29,620, 31,720, 31,745).

California Forms: Sch. D, Sch. D-1.

Gain or loss on disposition of property is the difference between the adjusted basis and the amount realized. The entire gain or loss is recognized except where specifically exempted. Exceptions to the general rule are discussed in subsequent paragraphs.

Although California law is generally the same as federal law, the *effect* may be different because (1) of a difference in the basis of the property and (2) California law, unlike federal law, does not apply a lower tax rate to capital gains.

¶ 501

¶ 501a Transfers Between Spouses

Law: Sec. 18031 (CCH CALIFORNIA TAX REPORTS ¶ 16-574a).

Comparable Federal: Sec. 1041 (CCH STANDARD FEDERAL TAX REPORTS ¶ 31,700).

California law is the same as federal (see ¶ 102a). No gain or loss is recognized on a transfer of property from an individual to, or in trust for the benefit of, (1) a spouse or (2) a former spouse if the transfer is incident to a divorce. However, gain is recognized with respect to the transfer of property in trust to the extent that the liabilities assumed, plus the amount of any liabilities to which the property is subject, exceeds the total of the adjusted basis of the property transferred.

¶ 502 Involuntary Conversion

Law: Secs. 18031, 18037 (CCH CALIFORNIA TAX REPORTS ¶ 16-554).

Comparable Federal: Sec. 1033 (CCH STANDARD FEDERAL TAX REPORTS ¶ 31,540).

California Form: Sch. D-1.

California law is generally the same as federal as of the current IRC tie-in date (see ¶ 102a).

Loss (but not gain) is recognized on involuntary conversion of property due to destruction, theft, condemnation, etc. Gain is recognized, however, to the extent (1) the proceeds are not used to acquire other property similar or related in service or use or (2) the taxpayer purchases the replacement property or stock from related persons. However, a taxpayer, other than a C corporation or a partnership with majority corporate partners, may defer gain recognition if the aggregate of the amount of gain realized on the property is $100,000 or less.

The taxpayer may elect not to recognize gain even though the proceeds of the involuntary conversion are not expended *directly* on the replacement property. In this case the replacement property must be purchased within a limited period of time as specified in the law. A longer period may be allowed upon application by the taxpayer. Replacement property may consist of stock in a corporation owning qualified replacement property, provided control of the corporation is acquired. "Control" for this purpose is defined as 80% of the voting stock, plus 80% of all other classes of stock outstanding.

Special rules limit the amount of gain a taxpayer must recognize on the receipt of insurance proceeds for the taxpayer's principal residence (including a rented residence) or its contents that are involuntarily converted as a result of a presidentially declared disaster. In addition, if business or investment property is compulsorily or involuntarily converted as the result of a presidentially declared disaster, *any* tangible property of a type held for productive use in a trade or business will be treated for nonrecognition purposes as "similar or related in service or use" to the converted property.

CCH Example: Disaster-Related Involuntary Conversion

Paul's coffee cart was destroyed as a result of a presidentially-declared disaster. Before the disaster, Paul sold coffee, juices, and pastries from the cart outside a local hospital. Within two months of the cart's destruction, Paul received related insurance proceeds and immediately used all of the proceeds to purchase a computer for use in the word processing business he runs from his home. The computer will be treated as similar or related in use to the coffee cart, and Paul may elect not to recognize gain with respect to the involuntarily converted cart.

If a taxpayer who satisfies the property replacement requirement by acquiring stock in a corporation is required to reduce the basis of the acquired stock, the corporation must also reduce the adjusted basis of its assets by the amount by which the taxpayer is required to reduce the basis of the stock. The taxpayer's basis in the corporation's stock is decreased by the amount of any gain realized from the involuntary conversion that is not recognized.

¶ 502a Sale of Residence

> *Law:* Secs. 18031, 18037.5 (CCH CALIFORNIA TAX REPORTS ¶ 16-557).
>
> *Comparable Federal:* Former Sec. 1034 (CCH STANDARD FEDERAL TAX REPORTS ¶ 31,560).

California law is the same as federal law (see ¶ 102a).

Gain from the sale or exchange of the taxpayer's own residence is taxable as a capital gain because the residence is a "capital asset" (see ¶ 512a). Loss from such a sale or exchange is not deductible, either as a capital loss or as an ordinary loss (see ¶ 307). Circumstances under which taxpayers may exclude part of such gain from taxable income are discussed below.

● *Post-May 6, 1997, transactions*

Effective for transactions after May 6, 1997, taxpayers who sell or exchange property that they owned and occupied as a principal residence for at least two of the five years preceding the sale or exchange can elect a $250,000 ($500,000 for joint filers) exclusion from gross income of gain realized on the sale or exchange (see ¶ 228). This new exclusion replaces the one-time exclusion from income by taxpayers age 55 or over (discussed at ¶ 228) and the deferral of gain discussed below.

● *Pre-May 7, 1997, transactions*

Both California and federal law applicable to sales or exchanges occurring before May 7, 1997, provide for nonrecognition of gain when a principal residence is replaced by the purchase and use of another within a specified period. The cost basis of the new residence is reduced to the extent of the nonrecognized gain. However, there have been differences between state and federal law in some prior years that can result in basis differences if replacement occurred in those years and property is still held.

¶ 502a

Both state and federal law allow the nonrecognition of gain on the sale of a former residence prior to May 7, 1997, where one spouse dies before occupying the replacement home.

Prior-year differences: One prior-year difference that may affect present basis resulted from the substitution of "adjusted sales price" for "gross sales price," which applies for federal purposes to tax years after 1953 and for California purposes to taxable years after 1960.

Another such prior-year difference relates to treatment of a residence replacement as an involuntary conversion under certain circumstances. Such transactions were specifically excluded from the residence-replacement provisions under state law for the years 1955-60 and under federal law for the years 1954-57.

Replacement period: For transactions occurring before May 7, 1997, the specified replacement period begins two years before the sale of the old residence and ends two years after the sale. The replacement period is extended to four years for certain taxpayers who have a "tax home" outside the United States, and for certain service personnel serving on extended active duty.

¶ 502b Gain from Sale of Assisted Housing

Law: Sec. 18041.5 (CCH CALIFORNIA TAX REPORTS ¶ 16-573).

Comparable Federal: Former Sec. 1039 (CCH STANDARD FEDERAL TAX REPORTS ¶ 31,660).

No gain is recognized on the sale of an assisted housing development to a tenant association, organization, agency, or individual that obligates itself and its successors to make the development affordable to low-income families for (1) 30 years from the date of sale or (2) for the remaining term of existing federal government assistance, whichever is longer. The proceeds from the sale must be reinvested in residential real property, other than a personal residence, within two years of the sale. An "assisted housing development" is a multifamily rental housing development that receives federal government assistance.

● *California law prior to the 1990 tax year*

Prior to the 1990 tax year, California had a provision (Former Sec. 18035.5) concerning sales of low-income housing that was generally based on federal law (Former IRC Sec. 1039) except that:

(1) under California law, no replacement was required; gain was excluded rather than deferred as it is under federal law;

(2) there were different percentages of nonrecognition; and

(3) California law expanded the nonrecognition of gain to other qualified projects.

¶ 503 Liquidation Under S.E.C. Order

Law: Sec. 18031 (CCH CALIFORNIA TAX REPORTS ¶ 16-588).

Comparable Federal: Sec. 1081 (CCH STANDARD FEDERAL TAX REPORTS ¶ 32,020).

California law is the same as federal law (see ¶ 102a).

A shareholder is precluded from recognizing gain or loss from distributions in liquidation of a corporation pursuant to an order of the Securities and Exchange Commission under the Public Utility Holding Company Act.

¶ 504 Exchange of Property for Like Property

Law: Secs. 18031, 18043 (CCH CALIFORNIA TAX REPORTS ¶ 16-551).

Comparable Federal: Sec. 1031 (CCH STANDARD FEDERAL TAX REPORTS ¶ 31,502).

California law is the same as federal law as of the current IRC tie-in date (see ¶ 102a).

Generally, no gain or loss is recognized if property held for productive use or investment is exchanged for property of a like kind. However, under both federal and state law, an exchange of foreign real property for real property located within the U.S. may not qualify as a like-kind exchange. This disqualification from nonrecognition of gain extends to exchanges of *personal property* predominantly used outside the U.S. for personal property predominantly used in the U.S, effective for California purposes in taxable years beginning after 1997, and for federal purposes to exchanges made after June 8, 1997.

¶ 504a Exchange of Insurance Policies

Law: Sec. 18031 (CCH CALIFORNIA TAX REPORTS ¶ 16-561).

Comparable Federal: Sec. 1035 (CCH STANDARD FEDERAL TAX REPORTS ¶ 31,580).

California law is the same as federal law (see ¶ 102a).

No gain or loss is recognized on (1) the exchange of a life insurance contract for another life insurance contract or (2) certain exchanges involving endowment or annuity contracts.

¶ 505 Exchange of Stock for Stock

Law: Sec. 18031 (CCH CALIFORNIA TAX REPORTS ¶ 16-564).

Comparable Federal: Sec. 1036 (CCH STANDARD FEDERAL TAX REPORTS ¶ 31,600).

California law is the same as federal law (see ¶ 102a).

No gain or loss is recognized on an exchange of a corporation's (1) common stock for common stock of the same corporation or (2) preferred stock for other shares of its preferred stock.

¶ 505a Exchange of Certain U.S. Obligations

Law: Sec. 18031 (CCH CALIFORNIA TAX REPORTS ¶ 16-568).

Comparable Federal: Sec. 1037 (CCH STANDARD FEDERAL TAX REPORTS ¶ 31,620).

California law is the same as federal law (see ¶ 102a).

Certain designated U.S. obligations (bonds issued under chapter 31, title 31, of the United States Code) may be exchanged tax-free for other obligations issued under the same chapter.

¶ 505b Reacquisition of Property After Installment Sale

Law: Sec. 18031 (CCH CALIFORNIA TAX REPORTS ¶ 16-572).

Comparable Federal: Sec. 1038 (CCH STANDARD FEDERAL TAX REPORTS ¶ 31,640).

California law is the same as federal law (see ¶ 102a).

Certain limitations are imposed on a seller's recognized gain or loss upon repossession of certain *real* property if the property had previously been sold on the installment method.

¶ 506 Sale or Exchange of Property for Stock

Law: Sec. 17321 (CCH CALIFORNIA TAX REPORTS ¶ 16-001, 16-058).

Comparable Federal: Sec. 351 (CCH STANDARD FEDERAL TAX REPORTS ¶ 16,402).

California law is the same as federal law as of the current IRC tie-in date (see ¶ 102a). Generally, no gain or loss is recognized on a transfer of property to a corporation in exchange for its stock or securities, when the transferors are in control after the exchange.

¶ 506a Sale or Exchange of Tax-Exempt Bonds

Law: Sec. 17133.5 (CCH CALIFORNIA TAX REPORTS ¶ 16-689).

Comparable Federal: None.

The gain or loss from the sale or transfer of bonds yielding tax-exempt interest is not exempt. Federal law is the same as to state and municipal obligations.

¶ 506b Sale of Stock to ESOPs or Cooperatives

Law: Sec. 18042 (CCH CALIFORNIA TAX REPORTS ¶ 16-576).

Comparable Federal: Sec. 1042 (CCH STANDARD FEDERAL TAX REPORTS ¶ 31,722).

California generally conforms to federal law allowing taxpayers to sell qualified securities to an employee stock ownership plan (ESOP) or worker-owned cooperative and to replace such securities with other securities without recognition of the gain. However, California does not incorporate the federal provision that allows a taxpayer to defer the recognition of gain from the sale of stock of a qualified agricultural refiner or processor to an eligible farm cooperative.

¶ 506c Sale of Small Business Stock

Law: Secs. 18038.4, 18038.5 (CCH CALIFORNIA TAX REPORTS ¶ 16-576b).

Comparable Federal: Sec. 1045 (CCH STANDARD FEDERAL TAX REPORTS ¶ 31,757).

California law generally mirrors federal law allowing an individual to elect to roll over capital gain from a post-August 5, 1997, sale of qualified small business stock held for more than six months, provided that the gain from the sale is used to purchase other qualified small business stock within 60 days from the date of the original sale. However, unlike federal law, California law does not allow partnerships and S corporations to make the election. In addition, for California purposes only, a corporation's stock will not qualify for the rollover unless 80% of the corporation's payroll, measured by total dollar value, is attributable to employment located within California.

See ¶ 513 for a discussion of the capital gains exclusion applicable to sales of qualified small business stock.

¶ 507 Exchange in Connection with Reorganization

Law: Sec. 17321, (CCH CALIFORNIA TAX REPORTS ¶ 16-061, 16-083).

Comparable Federal: Secs. 354, 368 (CCH STANDARD FEDERAL TAX REPORTS ¶ 16,431, 16,750).

California law is the same as federal law as of the current IRC tie-in date (see ¶ 102a).

No gain or loss is recognized if stock or securities in a corporation that is a party to a reorganization are exchanged solely for other stock or securities in the corporation or for stock or securities in another corporation that is a party to the reorganization (a "B" type reorganization). "Reorganization" and other terms are specifically defined.

¶ 508 "Spin-Off" Reorganization

Law: Sec. 17321 (CCH CALIFORNIA TAX REPORTS ¶ 16-064).

Comparable Federal: Sec. 355 (CCH STANDARD FEDERAL TAX REPORTS ¶ 16,460).

California law is the same as federal law as of the current IRC tie-in date (see ¶ 102a).

No gain is recognized in a "spin-off" type of reorganization, provided certain tests of the business purpose of the transaction are met. This type of reorganization involves the transfer of part of a corporation's assets to a new corporation and the distribution of the new corporation's stock to the share-holders of the old corporation. Both corporations must be engaged in the active conduct of a trade or business that has been operating for at least five years, and it must be shown that the transaction was not used principally as a "device for the distribution of earnings and profits."

¶ 509 Exchanges Not Solely in Kind

Law: Sec. 17321 (CCH CALIFORNIA TAX REPORTS ¶ 16-067).

Comparable Federal: Sec. 356 (CCH STANDARD FEDERAL TAX REPORTS ¶ 16,490).

California law is the same as federal law as of the current IRC tie-in date (see ¶ 102a).

Where exchanges would be exempt except for the fact that money or other property ("boot") is received, gain is recognized up to the amount of money or other property, but no loss may be recognized. Where a distribution has the effect of a taxable dividend, it is subject to tax up to the amount of gain recognized on the transaction.

¶ 507

¶ 510 Exchanges Involving Foreign Corporations

Law: Sec. 17321 (CCH California Tax Reports ¶ 16-079).

Comparable Federal: Sec. 367 (CCH Standard Federal Tax Reports ¶ 16,640).

California law is the same as federal law as of the current IRC tie-in date (see ¶ 102a).

Certain exchanges involving foreign corporations lose their exempt status unless property is transferred to the foreign corporation for use in its active conduct of a trade or business.

¶ 510a Transfers of Property to Foreign Trusts and Estates

Law: Secs. 17024.5(b), 17731 (CCH California Tax Reports ¶ 16-398a).

Comparable Federal: Sec. 684 (CCH Standard Federal Tax Reports ¶ 29,400).

California incorporates federal law subjecting to taxation any transfer of property by a U.S. person to a foreign estate, except to the extent provided by regulations. Such a transfer is treated as a sale or exchange of the property for its fair market value. The U.S. transferor must recognize gain equal to the excess of the property's fair market value over its adjusted basis in the hands of the transferor. The gain recognition rule does not apply if the U.S. transferor (or other person) is considered to be the owner of the trust under the grantor trust rules (discussed at ¶ 607). Also, under California law only, the gain recognition rule does not apply to transfers of property to a foreign trust.

¶ 511 Foreign Currency Transactions

Law: Sec. 17078 (CCH California Tax Reports ¶ 15-573).

Comparable Federal: Sec. 988 (CCH Standard Federal Tax Reports ¶ 29,400).

California law is the same as federal law (see ¶ 102a), except that the federal provision relating to the source of income or loss does not apply for California purposes. Gains and losses resulting from foreign currency transactions are characterized as ordinary income and classified as interest income or expense.

¶ 511a Liquidation of Corporation

Law: Sec. 17321 (CCH California Tax Reports ¶ 16-052).

Comparable Federal: Secs. 331-46 (CCH Standard Federal Tax Reports ¶ 16,002, 16,351).

California law is the same as federal law as of the current IRC tie-in date (see ¶ 102a), except for provisions relating to domestic international sales corporations (DISCs) that are not recognized by California.

Gain or loss to a stockholder upon liquidation of a corporation is ordinarily a capital gain or loss because it results from the exchange of stock for assets distributed in liquidation (see also ¶ 225).

● *Relief for minority shareholders*

Relief is provided for minority shareholders in corporate liquidations if the liquidation is tax-free to a parent corporation owning 80% or more of the stock. Accordingly, minority shareholders are protected from the double impact of corporate tax on the sale of appreciated property and a personal income tax on the distribution from the corporate liquidation (see ¶ 1208).

● *Collapsible corporations*

Liquidating distributions by "collapsible corporations" may be subject to tax as ordinary income. California and federal law both deny capital gain treatment under certain circumstances where a corporation is "formed or availed of" to manufacture or construct property to avoid corporate tax on the income. These provisions may apply to a sale of stock as well as to a liquidating distribution.

¶ 512 Capital Gains and Losses—General Rules

> *Law:* Secs. 18151, 18152.5, 18155, 18171, 18178 (CCH California Tax Reports ¶ 16-600).

> *Comparable Federal:* Secs. 1201-57 (CCH Standard Federal Tax Reports ¶ 32,152—32,450).

California law is the same as federal law as of the current IRC tie-in date (see ¶ 102a), with the exceptions of the tax rate applied to capital gains and other differences discussed below.

Because California treats capital gains as ordinary income, the amount of California tax is not dependent on the holding period, and the distinction between long-term and short-term capital gains has minimal significance for California purposes. With the enactment of lower capital gains tax rates by the Taxpayer Relief Act of 1997, the length of time property is held does have major significance for federal tax purposes. Generally, for sales and exchanges after May 6, 1997, the lower long-term federal capital gains rates (10% for individuals in the 15% bracket; 20% for all other individuals) will apply if a taxpayer held the asset for more than 12 months. For sales and exchanges occurring after July 28, 1997, in tax years ending before 1998, the lower rate applied only if the property was held for more than 18 months. Under an amendment made by the IRS Restructuring and Reform Act of 1998, which California has not yet incorporated, effective for tax years ending after 1997, the lower rates once again apply to property held for more than 12 months. Even lower rates will be applied to the sale of assets held more than five years, effective for federal income tax purposes for assets sold after 2000. Prior to May 7, 1997, the maximum long-term federal capital gains tax rate was 28%.

Certain gains and losses are classified as "capital" gains and losses and are subject to special rules. Generally, capital losses are subject to restrictions, as explained at ¶ 513 and ¶ 514. Ordinarily, a gain or loss constitutes a "capital" gain or loss only if:

> (a) the asset disposed of is a "capital asset" (see below) or a noncapital asset that, under a special rule, is treated as a "capital asset" (see ¶ 519), and

> (b) the gain or loss results from a *sale or exchange,* or from something that, under a special rule, is treated as a sale or exchange (see ¶ 516-¶ 520).

¶ 512

● *Special rules*

Worthlessness of securities is arbitrarily treated as a sale or exchange (see ¶ 307). A nonbusiness bad debt is treated as a capital loss (see ¶ 308). Losses from the destruction or theft of property may also be treated as a sale or exchange under some circumstances (see ¶ 519). Gain or loss on liquidation of a corporation is ordinarily capital gain or loss (see ¶ 511a). A limited ordinary loss deduction was formerly allowed on securities of certain "small business" corporations (see ¶ 307). Losses on wash sales are not allowable (see ¶ 514a).

Losses resulting from abandonment are not subject to capital loss limitations, because they do not result from sale or exchange.

The general rules for capital gains and losses discussed above are provided under federal law incorporated by California. However, there are a number of differences between California and federal law in the numerous special rules. The differences are discussed in later paragraphs. See also ¶ 225 for special federal capital-gain treatment of dividends from mutual funds.

● *Federal-California differences*

1. California does not incorporate a federal provision that allows a 50% exclusion for gain from the sale of certain small business stock, but has adopted a substantially similar provision (see ¶ 513).

2. California does not permit capital loss carrybacks (see ¶ 514).

3. California renders inoperative for specified periods certain federal rules relating to recapture of excess depreciation (see ¶ 519b).

4. Different amounts of original issue discounts are reported for California purposes for debt instruments issued in 1985 and 1986 (see ¶ 236).

5. As noted above, California does not adopt the special federal tax rates imposed on long-term capital gains.

¶ 512a Definition of "Capital Assets"

Law: Sec. 18151 (CCH CALIFORNIA TAX REPORTS ¶ 16-614).

Comparable Federal: Sec. 1221 (CCH STANDARD FEDERAL TAX REPORTS ¶ 32,220).

California law is the same as federal law as of the current IRC tie-in date (see ¶ 102a).

The term "capital assets" includes all property *except:*

(a) inventoriable assets;

(b) property held for sale in the ordinary course of business;

(c) depreciable business property;

(d) real property used in business;

(e) certain copyrights, books, artistic works, etc.;

(f) accounts or notes receivable acquired in the ordinary course of business through sales or services; and

(g) certain government publications.

¶ 512a

See ¶519-¶520 for items that, although they are not actually capital assets, are treated under some circumstances as though they were.

¶513 Capital Gains and Losses—Amount Taken into Account

> *Law:* Secs. 18151, 18152, 18152.5, (CCH CALIFORNIA TAX REPORTS ¶16-604, 16-611).
>
> *Comparable Federal:* Secs. 1202, 1222 (CCH STANDARD FEDERAL TAX REPORTS ¶32,160, 32,172, 32,240).

Beginning in 1988, both California and federal law measure the amount of capital gains in the same manner, except as noted below. Prior to 1988, differences existed between California and federal law as follows: (1) the percentage of capital gain or loss taken into account in computing taxable income differed for California and federal purposes and (2) California (but not federal) law had special rules concerning nonproductive assets.

● *Small business stock*

California generally follows federal law allowing 50% of the gain from the sale or exchange of qualified small business stock held for more than five years to be excluded from gross income under certain conditions, provided the issuing corporation meets specified active business requirements within California. See ¶506c for a discussion of the rollover of gain allowed for sales of certain small business stock.

ⓒⒸⒽ CCH Tip: Recomputation of 1998 NOL May Be Required

The exclusion from gross income for gain on the sale of small business stock is not allowed in the computation of a California net operating loss (NOL). However, the 1998 form FTB 3805V, Net Operating Loss (NOL) Computation and Disaster Loss Limitations—Individuals, Estates, and Trusts, did not include instructions for taxpayers to add back any excluded gain from small business stock. Therefore, some taxpayers may have an overstated NOL on their 1998 form FTB 3805V. The Franchise Tax Board recommends that these taxpayers recompute their 1998 NOL using the 1999 form FTB 3805V, which accounts for the small business stock exclusion in the computation of an NOL. If there is a difference between the computed amounts, these taxpayers need to file amended 1998 returns.

Amounts excluded from gross income are treated as a tax preference item in a computation of the alternative minimum tax (see ¶112a).

Gains or losses related to small business stock sold after October 1, 1987, and before 1994 are treated in the same way as are gains or losses of any stock. Although characterized as "capital" for purposes of certain limitations, they are taxed as ordinary income or loss.

¶513

¶ 514 Deductible Capital Losses—Carryovers, Carrybacks

Law: Secs. 18151, 18155 (CCH CALIFORNIA TAX REPORTS ¶ 16-600, 16-611).

Comparable Federal: Secs. 1211-12 (CCH STANDARD FEDERAL TAX REPORTS ¶ 32,190, 32,200).

Capital losses are deductible in full both federally and for California purposes against capital gain. In addition, up to $3,000 ($1,500 for married taxpayers filing separately) of any excess of capital loss over capital gain is also deductible against ordinary income.

● *Current treatment of carryovers*

Any unused net capital loss may be carried forward, indefinitely, to offset capital gains in subsequent years and may be deducted from ordinary income up to the limitation discussed above. The California rule is the same as the federal. However, the procedure for determining the amount of capital loss that may be carried over to the succeeding year was changed for federal purposes, effective retroactively to 1987. California conformed to the federal change effective for taxable years after 1988.

Loss carryovers attributable to out-of-state transactions prior to establishment of California residence are not allowable for California tax purposes (see ¶ 405).

● *No carrybacks*

California law does not permit capital loss carrybacks by individuals under any circumstances. Federal law, on the other hand, allows individuals to claim capital loss carrybacks with respect to capital losses from "marked to market" contracts (regulated futures contracts, foreign currency contracts, nonequity options, and dealer equity options).

¶ 514a Loss from Wash Sales

Law: Sec. 18031 (CCH CALIFORNIA TAX REPORTS ¶ 16-592).

Comparable Federal: Sec. 1091 (CCH STANDARD FEDERAL TAX REPORTS ¶ 32,080).

California law is the same as federal law (see ¶ 102a). Losses on disposition of stock or securities are disallowed where substantially identical property is acquired within 30 days before or after the sale.

¶ 515 Holding Period—Special Rules

Law: Secs. 18151, 18155.5 (CCH CALIFORNIA TAX REPORTS ¶ 16-617).

Comparable Federal: Sec. 1223 (CCH STANDARD FEDERAL TAX REPORTS ¶ 32,260).

California law as to the character of gain or loss as long or short term is the same as federal law (see ¶ 102a).

Special rules are provided for determining the holding period in situations where (1) property was received in a tax-free exchange, and (2) stock was acquired through exercise of rights. Where property is acquired from a decedent and sold within one year after his or her death, the property is considered to have been held for more than one year.

Under both California and federal law, the holding period for the surviving spouse's share of community property dates from the date of original acquisition.

¶ 516 Gain or Loss on Short Sales

Law: Sec. 18151 (CCH CALIFORNIA TAX REPORTS ¶ 16-624).

Comparable Federal: Sec. 1233 (CCH STANDARD FEDERAL TAX REPORTS ¶ 32,290).

California law as to the character of gain or loss as capital or ordinary or long-term or short-term is the same as federal law as of the current IRC tie-in date (see ¶ 102a).

Gains or losses on short sales are treated as capital gains or losses to the extent the property used to close the short sale is a "capital asset." The law regarding short sales includes many special rules for determining holding period, etc., intended to close certain "loopholes" that permitted tax avoidance through conversion of short-term gains into long-term gains.

¶ 516a Sale or Exchange of Patents

Law: Sec. 18151 (CCH CALIFORNIA TAX REPORTS ¶ 16-634).

Comparable Federal: Secs. 1235, 1249 (CCH STANDARD FEDERAL TAX REPORTS ¶ 32,350, 32,580).

California law as to the character of gain or loss as (1) capital or ordinary and (2) long-term or short-term is generally the same as federal law as of the current IRC tie-in date (see ¶ 102a).

Capital gain treatment is accorded investors and certain others on gain from the sale or exchange of patent rights, or interests therein. This treatment pertains even though the transaction has certain characteristics of a license rather than a sale. The provision does not apply to transfers between certain family members, controlled corporations, etc. California law incorporates the federal law by reference, except for the federal provision that denies capital gains treatment on transactions with controlled foreign corporations.

¶ 516b Transfers of Trademarks, Trade Names, and Franchises

Law: Sec. 18151 (CCH CALIFORNIA TAX REPORTS ¶ 16-672).

Comparable Federal: Sec. 1253 (CCH STANDARD FEDERAL TAX REPORTS ¶ 32,640).

California law as to the character of gain or loss as (1) capital or ordinary and (2) long-term or short-term is the same as federal law as of the current IRC tie-in date (see ¶ 102a).

Detailed rules govern the transfer of a franchise, trademark, or trade name. Generally, the transaction is denied capital gain treatment if the transferor retains any significant power, right, or continuing interest. This provision does not apply to professional sports.

¶ 517 Gain or Loss on Options

Law: Sec. 18151 (CCH CALIFORNIA TAX REPORTS ¶ 16-627, 16-682).

Comparable Federal: Secs. 1092, 1234, 1256 (CCH STANDARD FEDERAL TAX REPORTS ¶ 32,100, 32,310, 32,700).

California law as to the character of gain or loss as capital or ordinary or long-term or short-term is the same as federal law as of the current IRC tie-in date (see ¶ 102a).

Gain or loss attributable to the sale or exchange of (or loss arising from failure to exercise) a privilege or option to buy or sell property may or may not be a capital gain or loss. The character of the gain or loss depends on the character of the optioned property in the hands of the taxpayer. The law provides special rules designed to prevent tax avoidance by means of option transactions, including the use of straddle options. Certain futures contracts must be marked to market under these rules and 40% of the gain or loss is treated as short-term while 60% is treated as long-term. The special marked-to-market rules do not apply to hedging transactions.

¶ 517a Dealers in Securities

Law: Sec. 18151 (CCH CALIFORNIA TAX REPORTS ¶ 16-637).

Comparable Federal: Sec. 1236 (CCH STANDARD FEDERAL TAX REPORTS ¶ 22,265, 32,370).

California law as to the character of gain or loss as capital or ordinary or long-term or short-term is the same as federal law as of the current IRC tie-in date (see ¶ 102a). For a discussion of the accounting methods applicable to security dealers, see ¶ 409.

Securities dealers are subject to special rules designed to prevent switching of securities in and out of the capital asset category for the purpose of realizing capital gains and ordinary losses.

¶ 517b Appreciated Financial Positions

Law: Sec. 18151 (CCH CALIFORNIA TAX REPORTS ¶ 16-687).

Comparable Federal: Sec. 1259 (CCH STANDARD FEDERAL TAX REPORTS ¶ 32,370).

California incorporates federal law, which treats specified hedging transactions as constructive sales that require the immediate recognition of gain (but not loss). The provision generally applies to "short sales against the box," futures or forward contracts, notional principal contracts, and to any other transactions as prescribed by regulations.

¶ 518 Retirement of Bonds, etc.

Law: Secs. 17024.5, 18151 (CCH CALIFORNIA TAX REPORTS ¶ 16-690—16-692).

Comparable Federal: Secs. 1271-1274 (CCH STANDARD FEDERAL TAX REPORTS ¶ 32,276, 32,277, 32,278, 4774-74D).

California law as to the character of gain or loss as capital or ordinary or long-term or short-term is the same as federal law as of the current IRC tie-in date (see ¶ 102a).

Amounts received upon retirement of bonds, etc., are ordinarily treated as amounts received in exchange therefore. The purpose of this provision is to permit such transactions to qualify for capital gain treatment. However, capital gain treatment does not apply to any obligation issued before July 2, 1982, if the issuer was neither a corporation nor a governmental unit or political subdivision. In taxable years beginning before 1998, an exemption was also available for debt obligations issued by natural persons. The exemption was repealed for federal purposes, applicable to sales, exchanges, and retirements of debt instruments issued by a natural person after June 8, 1997.

Pre-1987 Tax Years

In an effort to prevent tax avoidance, numerous special rules were provided for discount bonds, stripped bonds, etc., which resulted in some or all of the gain realized being treated as ordinary income. The federal rules regarding discount bonds and other debt instruments were extensively amended in 1984 and California conformed in 1987 for post-1986 tax years (see ¶ 236).

¶ 518a Real Estate Subdivided for Sale

Law: Sec. 18151 (CCH CALIFORNIA TAX REPORTS ¶ 16-641).

Comparable Federal: Sec. 1237 (CCH STANDARD FEDERAL TAX REPORTS ¶ 32,390).

California law as to the character of gain or loss as capital or ordinary or long-term or short-term is the same as federal law as of the current IRC tie-in date (see ¶ 102a).

In general, profits from land subdivision activities will be treated as ordinary income. However, at least a part of the gain may be treated as long-term capital gain if the taxpayer can comply fully with certain very restrictive conditions in the law. Detailed rules are provided, including a requirement that the property be held at least five years, a prohibition against substantial improvements to the property, etc.

¶ 519 Sales of Property Used in Business, etc.

Law: Sec. 18151 (CCH CALIFORNIA TAX REPORTS ¶ 16-621, 16-648).

Comparable Federal: Secs. 1231, 1239 (CCH STANDARD FEDERAL TAX REPORTS ¶ 32,272, 32,430).

California Form: Sch. D-1.

California law as to the character of gain or loss as capital or ordinary or long-term or short-term is the same as federal law as of the current IRC tie-in date (see ¶ 102a).

Capital gain treatment applies to the disposition of certain property that would not otherwise qualify for such treatment because the property is not a "capital asset" or because it is not sold or exchanged. In applying the rule, the following three classes of transactions are lumped together:

(a) sales or exchanges of "property used in the trade or business" (see below for definition of such property);

(b) involuntary conversions (including losses upon destruction, theft, or condemnation) of business property (as described in (a) above); and

(c) involuntary conversions of capital assets held for more than one year.

If, during the taxable year, the gains on all three classes of transactions exceed the losses (using 100% of each gain or loss regardless of holding period), all transactions are treated as sales or exchanges of capital assets. This means that all of the gains or losses involved are treated as capital gains or losses, applying the rules discussed in ¶ 513 in determining the amount to be taken into account in computing taxable income. If the total gains do not exceed the total losses, all gains and losses are treated as "ordinary" gains and losses. Thus, involuntary conversions of *capital assets* resulting in a loss would give rise to a fully-deductible "ordinary" loss if there were no offsetting gains.

● *"Property used in trade or business"*

Federal law is incorporated in California law by reference.

For this purpose "property used in the trade or business" includes:

(1) depreciable and real property used in a trade or business, held for more than one year;

(2) cattle and horses held for draft, breeding, dairy, or sporting purposes, provided they are held for two years or longer, and other livestock held for such purposes provided they are held for one year or longer;

(3) unharvested crops sold with land used in a trade or business and held for more than one year; and

(4) timber, coal, and iron ore, under certain circumstances—see ¶ 520.

However, depreciable and real property used in a business is *not* "property used in the trade or business" for capital gain treatment purposes if it is any of the following:

(1) inventoriable property;

(2) property held primarily for sale in the ordinary course of business;

(3) copyrights, etc., of the type included in item (e) in ¶ 512a; and

(4) certain government publications.

● *Transactions between related taxpayers*

Capital gain treatment is denied on the sale or exchange, directly or indirectly, of depreciable property between a husband and wife. This rule applies also to transactions between (1) an individual and a corporation that is 50% or more owned by such individual; (2) an executor and beneficiary of an estate, except in the case of a sale or exchange in satisfaction of a pecuniary bequest; and (3) certain related individuals.

¶519

¶519a Sale of Stock of Foreign Investment Companies, etc.

> *Law:* Sec. 17024.5 (CCH CALIFORNIA TAX REPORTS ¶ 16-658).
>
> *Comparable Federal:* Secs. 1246-48 (CCH STANDARD FEDERAL TAX REPORTS ¶ 32,520—32,560).

California has not adopted federal provisions that treat as ordinary income, rather than capital gain, the gain arising out of the sale or exchange of certain stock investments in foreign investment companies and other foreign corporations.

¶519b Recapture of Excess Depreciation, etc.

> *Law:* Secs. 18151, 18165, 18171, 18171.5 (CCH CALIFORNIA TAX REPORTS ¶ 16-656, 16-662).
>
> *Comparable Federal:* Secs. 1239, 1245, 1250-55 (CCH STANDARD FEDERAL TAX REPORTS ¶ 32,410, 32,430, 52,502, 32,600—32,680).

California law as to the character of gain or loss as capital or ordinary or long-term or short-term is the same as federal law as of the current IRC tie-in date (see ¶ 102a).

The law contains several "recapture" provisions intended to prevent possible abuse of the capital gain benefits permitted on the sale of various kinds of business property as explained at ¶ 519. The recapture provisions treat as ordinary income a portion of the gain realized upon disposition of certain property that has been subject to depreciation deductions. The amount "recaptured" depends on (1) the type of property, (2) the method of depreciation used, and (3) the period during which depreciation has been deducted. The types of property subject to this treatment are prescribed in IRC Secs. 1245 and 1250, which are incorporated into California law by reference.

The federal law was amended slightly in 1984, and California conformed in 1985. Federal law was amended by the Tax Reform Act of 1986 to provide that recapture rules also apply to percentage depletion, mining development, and mining exploration costs for binding contracts entered into before September 26, 1985, and for all dispositions after 1986. California in 1987 incorporated the federal changes applicable to post-1986 tax years. California provides for the following differences from the federal rules:

1. special federal rules for Subchapter S corporations do not apply to California for pre-1987 tax years;

2. federal provisions for recapture on pollution control facilities do not apply to California;

3. federal provisions for recapture of pre-1983 amortization of trademarks do not apply to California;

4. California provides for some exceptions to the federal rules for certain low-income housing (for pre-1987 tax years) and historic structures;

5. California substitutes different dates for various dates in the federal law, as follows:

(a) December 31, 1970, for July 24, 1969, and December 31, 1969;

(b) January 1, 1971, for January 1, 1970;

(c) December 31, 1976, for December 31, 1975; and

(d) January 1, 1977, for January 1, 1976; and

6. the federal provision treating certain deductions as deductions allowable for amortization is modified for California purposes to also apply to enterprise zone, former Los Angeles Revitalization Zone, local agency military base recovery area, and targeted tax area asset expense allowance deductions (discussed at ¶ 310f).

Even where the applicable California and federal recapture provisions are the same, the amount of recapture may of course be different because of differences in amounts deducted in prior years.

¶ 520 Gain or Loss in the Case of Timber, Coal, or Domestic Iron Ore

Law: Sec. 17681 (CCH CALIFORNIA TAX REPORTS ¶ 16-341).

Comparable Federal: Sec. 631 (CCH STANDARD FEDERAL TAX REPORTS ¶ 24,700).

California law as to the character of gain or loss as capital or ordinary or long-term or short-term is the same as federal law as of the current IRC tie-in date (see ¶ 102a).

Special rules allow a taxpayer to elect to apply capital gain treatment to the cutting of timber held for more than one year or the disposal of coal or domestic iron ore held for more than one year. This is accomplished by including gains or losses from such cutting or disposal in the class of transactions designated (a) in ¶ 519, above.

¶ 520a Cancellation of Lease or Distributor's Agreement

Law: Sec. 18151 (CCH CALIFORNIA TAX REPORTS ¶ 16-652).

Comparable Federal: Sec. 1241 (CCH STANDARD FEDERAL TAX REPORTS ¶ 32,450).

California law as to the character of gain or loss as capital or ordinary or long-term or short-term is the same as federal law as of the current IRC tie-in date (see ¶ 102a).

The law provides for capital gain treatment on: (1) amounts received by a lessee for the cancellation of a lease and (2) amounts received by a distributor for cancellation of a distributor's agreement, provided the distributor has a substantial capital investment in the distributorship.

¶ 521 Basis, General Rule

Law: Sec. 18031 (CCH CALIFORNIA TAX REPORTS ¶ 16-511).

Comparable Federal: Secs. 1012, 1059A (CCH STANDARD FEDERAL TAX REPORTS ¶ 29,680, 31,940).

Except where otherwise provided, the "basis" of property is its cost. California law is the same as federal law as of the current IRC tie-in date (see ¶ 102a).

Prior to 1961 for California purposes (and prior to 1954 for federal), certain real property taxes paid by the buyer were not deductible and were required to be capitalized. Any such taxes are includible in the basis of the property.

¶ 522 Basis, Inventoriable Property

Law: Sec. 18031 (CCH CALIFORNIA TAX REPORTS ¶ 16-514).

Comparable Federal: Sec. 1013 (CCH STANDARD FEDERAL TAX REPORTS ¶ 29,700).

The basis of inventoriable property is the last inventory value thereof. California law incorporates the federal law by reference as of the current IRC tie-in date (see ¶ 102a).

¶ 523 Basis of Property Acquired by Gift

Law: Secs. 17081, 18031 (CCH CALIFORNIA TAX REPORTS ¶ 15-465, 16-527).

Comparable Federal: Secs. 84, 1015 (CCH STANDARD FEDERAL TAX REPORTS ¶ 6400, 29,740).

California law is the same as federal law as of the current IRC tie-in date (see ¶ 102a).

The basis of property acquired by gift after 1920 is generally determined by reference to the donor's basis, except that for the purpose of determining loss, the basis is limited to the fair market value at the date the gift was made. The basis of property acquired by gift before 1921 is the fair market value at the date the gift was made.

● *Adjustment for gift tax*

The basis may be increased by federal gift tax paid, but there is a limitation on this adjustment. For gifts before 1977, the gift tax adjustment is limited to the excess of fair market value over the donor's adjusted basis. For gifts after 1976, the adjustment is limited to an amount proportionate to the appreciation in value over the donor's adjusted basis.

Prior to 1985, the California limitation on gifts after 1976 was the same as for earlier gifts.

● *Transfers between spouses*

The federal law was amended in 1984 to provide a special rule for transfers between spouses. Such transfers are treated as gifts, with carryover of basis to the transferee and with no limit on the transferee's basis for determining loss. California conformed in 1985.

● *Procedure where facts unknown*

Where the necessary facts for determination of basis are unknown to the donee, the Franchise Tax Board (FTB) is required to obtain the facts. If the FTB can not obtain sufficient facts to make the determination, the basis is the fair market value, as determined by the FTB, as of the date the property was acquired by the donor.

The provision for FTB determination of basis of gift property was applied in *Appeal of Victor and Evelyn Santino* (1975) (CCH CALIFORNIA TAX RE-

PORTS ¶ 16-527.30). The State Board of Equalization upheld the FTB's finding, based on 1926 records and market values.

¶ 524 Basis of Property Acquired by Transfer in Trust

Law: Sec. 18031 (CCH CALIFORNIA TAX REPORTS ¶ 16-527).

Comparable Federal: Sec. 1015 (CCH STANDARD FEDERAL TAX REPORTS ¶ 29,740).

California law is the same as federal law as of the current IRC tie-in date (see ¶ 102a).

The basis of property acquired by a transfer in trust (other than by gift, bequest or devise) after 1920 is the grantor's basis adjusted for gain or loss recognized to the grantor on the transfer. For such transfers before 1921, the basis is the fair market value at the date of the transfer.

The federal law was amended in 1984 to provide special basis rules for inter-spousal transfers in trust, and California conformed in 1985 (see ¶ 523).

¶ 525 Basis of Property Transmitted at Death

Law: Sec. 18031 (CCH CALIFORNIA TAX REPORTS ¶ 16-518, 16-524, 16-548).

Comparable Federal: Sec. 1014 (CCH STANDARD FEDERAL TAX REPORTS ¶ 29,720).

Federal law regarding basis of property transmitted at death is incorporated by California by reference as of the current IRC tie-in date (see ¶ 102a). However, the California law provides for important differences from the federal rules as explained below.

1. Ordinarily, the basis of property acquired by bequest, devise, or inheritance (or deemed to be so acquired) is the fair market value at date of death.

2. When federal estate tax is calculated on the basis of the value of the property at the "optional" valuation date (six months after death), that value becomes the basis. California conformed to the federal law in 1985.

3. When family farms or businesses are valued for federal estate tax purposes at less than fair market value, the reduced valuation becomes the basis. California conformed to the federal law in 1985.

4. Federal (but not California) law contains special rules for the basis of stock in certain foreign personal holding companies and Domestic International Sales Corporations (DISCs).

5. When death occurred between January 1, 1977, and November 6, 1978, and a carryover basis was elected, the basis is the carryover basis.

6. When appreciated property is received by a decedent as a gift within one year before death and the same property reverts to the donor (or spouse), a carryover basis applies.

7. The basis of individual retirement accounts and retirement bonds is zero. However, as to the portion attributable to contributions that were not deductible for state purposes, the California basis would be fair market value.

8. Special rules are provided for community property, quasi-community property, and joint tenancy property. The California and federal rules are different, as explained below.

● *Community property*

Each spouse has a 1/2 interest in California community property. With the exception of cases in which a carry-over basis was elected (as discussed in (5) above), the California basis of the *decedent spouse's* 1/2 interest in the hands of the surviving spouse (or other party) is fair market value at date of death.

● *"Quasi-community" property*

In determining the basis of property acquired from a decedent, quasi-community property is treated as community property.

"Quasi-community" property generally refers to property that was acquired while the taxpayer was domiciled outside of California and that would have been community property had the taxpayer been domiciled in California.

● *Interest of surviving spouse*

The basis of the *surviving spouse's* 1/2 interest varies according to date of death and other circumstances. Under federal law, for deaths occurring after 1947, the basis of a surviving spouse's 1/2 interest is fair market value. California basis is also fair market value for deaths occurring after 1986. Prior to 1987, the California basis of the surviving spouse's 1/2 interest was valued at cost.

● *Joint tenancy property*

The basis of joint tenancy property transmitted at death is not covered by the general rule stated at the beginning of ¶ 525, because such property is not received by "bequest, devise or inheritance." However, federal law provides that, in the case of decedents whose deaths occurred after 1953, such property is considered to have been acquired from the decedent as to the portion of the property that is includible in the estate for federal death-tax purposes. As to that portion, the basis is fair market value, under the rule stated at the beginning of ¶ 525. As to the survivor's interest, the basis is cost. This federal provision was incorporated in California law by reference so that the California basis is now the same as the federal.

Prior-Year Basis Rules

The many changes in the inheritance tax and income tax laws over the years are reflected in the following summary of the California rules for determining the basis of California community property in the hands of the survivor, covering both the decedent's and the surviving spouse's interests in the property.

(1) *if death occurred prior to April 9, 1953:* basis of decedent's 1/2 interest is fair market value at date of death and basis of surviving spouse's 1/2 interest is cost;

¶ 525

(2) *if death occurred after April 8, 1953, and before September 15, 1961:*

(a) if wife was survivor, basis of entire property is fair market value;

(b) if husband was survivor and all of wife's ½ interest went to others, basis of entire property is fair market value; and

(c) if husband was survivor and he received any part of wife's ½ interest, basis of decedent wife's ½ interest is fair market value and basis of surviving husband's ½ interest is cost;

(3) *if death occurred after September 14, 1961, and before January 1, 1987:*

(a) if decedent's entire interest went to others than the surviving spouse (prior to June 8, 1982), basis of entire property is fair market value; and

(b) if any part of decedent's interest went to surviving spouse, basis of decedent's ½ interest is fair market value and basis of surviving spouse's ½ interest is cost (excepted from this rule is the period from January 1, 1981, to June 8, 1982; see below).

(4) *if death occurred after December 31, 1986:* basis of entire property is fair market value—the same as the federal basis.

● *Death 1965-1975—Conversion of separate property*

There is a special rule for community property that was converted from separate property, applicable when death occurred between September 17, 1965, and December 31, 1975. In this case, the basis of the entire property is fair market value. Under the present law, there is no special treatment of such converted property.

● *Decisions of courts and State Board of Equalization*

In *Howard Mel v. Franchise Tax Board* (1981) (CCH CALIFORNIA TAX REPORTS ¶ 16-524.854), involving four companion cases, the bulk of the deceased husband's ½ interest in community property was left in trust upon his death in 1967, with a lifetime beneficial interest to the surviving wife. The wife claimed a stepped-up basis for her ½ interest when she sold certain items of the community property. A California Court of Appeal applied rule 3(b), above, to deny a stepped-up basis on the items in question. For a later case, citing and following the *Mel* case, see *Appeal of Georgianna Brewer* (1983) (CCH CALIFORNIA TAX REPORTS ¶ 16-524.90).

In *The Bank of California, N.A., et al. v. Franchise Tax Board* (1978) (CCH CALIFORNIA TAX REPORTS ¶ 16-524.853), the deceased husband's ½ interest in a substantial estate of community property was left to a testamentary trust. The trust provided for payments of $1,000 per month to the surviving wife for her lifetime. The surviving wife claimed a stepped-up basis for her ½ interest in certain items of the community property. The Franchise Tax Board (FTB) applied rule 3(b) above and denied the stepped-up basis. However, a California Superior Court overruled the FTB and allowed the stepped-up basis, concluding that it was the legislative intent to conform the California law to the federal. However, see discussion above of the *Howard Mel*

¶ 525

case, in which the Court of Appeal overruled the trial court and reached the opposite conclusion.

In *Appeals of Estate of William S. Hatch et al.* (1976) (CCH CALIFORNIA TAX REPORTS ¶ 16-518.20), community property (a citrus grove) was in escrow when the husband died, under an almost-completed contract of sale. The State Board of Equalization (SBE) held, following federal precedents, that decedent's 1/2 of the property constituted a right to receive "income in respect of a decedent" and that neither 1/2 of the property was entitled to a stepped-up California basis.

In *Appeal of Estate of Philip Rosenberg, Deceased* (1975) (CCH CALIFORNIA TAX REPORTS ¶ 16-524.851), the question was whether the surviving wife was entitled to a stepped-up California basis on her 1/2 interest in community property. The husband died in 1966, leaving the community property in trust for the surviving wife and children. The situation fell squarely within item (3)(b) of the discussion above. The SBE's opinion deplored the fact that the California result was different from the federal, but upheld the FTB in limiting the survivor's basis to her cost and denying a step-up to the value at date of death. See also *Appeal of Louis (L.M.) Halper Marital Trust* (1977) (CCH CALIFORNIA TAX REPORT ¶ 16-524.852), to the same effect.

● *Non-California community property*

The basis provisions of the income tax law apply to property held "under the community property laws of any state, territory or possession of the United States or any foreign country." However, the basis of non-California community property may be different from the basis of California community property as discussed above, because of differing treatment under the inheritance tax law. See the following discussion of quasi-community property.

● *"Quasi-community" property (prior law)*

"Quasi-community" property is property acquired outside California that would have been California community property if the spouse acquiring the property had been domiciled in California at the time of acquisition. Under the California inheritance tax law from 1957 to 1980, one-half of such property was includible in the estate.

● *Joint tenancy property*

Prior to 1985 California law provided a rule that was similar in principle to the federal rule, but California permitted a stepped-up basis only on the portion of the property that was subject to California inheritance tax. Since the California inheritance tax was repealed on June 8, 1982, in case of death after that date and subsequent disposition of the property before 1985, it appears that the basis of the entire property would be cost.

● *Death between January 1981 and June 1982*

Under the California inheritance tax law in effect from January 1, 1981, to June 8, 1982, property transferred to the spouse of the decedent was exempt from the tax. Thus, none of such property has a basis of fair market value, and the basis of the entire property in the hands of the surviving spouse is cost.

¶ **525**

● *Surviving joint tenant other than spouse*

When death occurred during the period January 1, 1955, to June 8, 1982, and the surviving joint tenant is other than the spouse, the basis of the decedent's interest is fair market value. However, when death occurred prior to 1955, the basis of the entire property is cost; this applies also when the surviving joint tenant was the spouse.

● *Decedent spouse's interest—Death before 1981*

When the surviving joint tenant is the spouse and death occurred prior to 1981, the basis of the decedent's interest is usually fair market value. This applies back to 1955 in cases in which the property was originally separate property of the spouses; the decedent's interest is determined by contribution to the original cost. It applies back to September 15, 1961, in cases where the property was originally "quasi-community" property (as defined in the gift tax law); the decedent is deemed to have had a ½ interest. It applies back to 1976 in cases where the property was originally California community property; the decedent's interest was ½ of the total property. When death occurred prior to 1976 and the property was originally California community property, the basis of the decedent's interest is usually cost; however, there are some exceptions, and it is suggested that the FTB be consulted in case of any question.

● *Decision of SBE*

Appeal of William F. and Dorothy M. Johnson (1976) (CCH CALIFORNIA TAX REPORTS ¶ 16-521.41) involved the basis to the survivor of joint tenancy property that had its source in community property, where death occurred in 1967. The SBE held that the basis was original cost, applying the rule set forth above.

● *California-federal differences*

The federal basis of joint tenancy property in the hands of the survivor may be different from the California basis because of differences in the death tax treatment and differences between the two laws in prior years. Where death occurred prior to 1954, the federal basis of the entire property is cost. Where death occurred after 1953, the federal basis is fair market value for the portion includible in the estate (unless a carryover basis applied under prior law) and cost for the remainder of the property. Note that the decedent's interest is always "includible in the estate" for federal estate tax purposes, even though the property may be completely relieved of tax by the marital deduction. In the case of joint tenancy property of husband and wife, where death occurs after 1981, the decedent's interest is deemed to be one-half of the property regardless of which spouse furnished the consideration.

¶ 526 Basis of Property Acquired in Tax-Free Exchange

Law: Sec. 17321 (CCH CALIFORNIA TAX REPORTS ¶ 16-073).

Comparable Federal: Sec. 358 (CCH STANDARD FEDERAL TAX REPORTS ¶ 16,550).

California law is the same as federal law as of the current IRC tie-in date (see ¶ 102a).

The basis of property acquired after February 28, 1913, in a tax-free exchange is the same as that of the property exchanged, with adjustment for "boot" received, for any amount treated as a dividend in the exchange, and for any gain or loss recognized upon the exchange.

¶526a Basis of Property Acquired in Corporate Liquidation

Law: Sec. 17321 (CCH CALIFORNIA TAX REPORTS ¶ 16-046).

Comparable Federal: Sec. 334 (CCH STANDARD FEDERAL TAX REPORTS ¶ 16,150).

California law is the same as federal law as of the current IRC tie-in date (see ¶ 102a).

Generally, the basis of property received by an individual stockholder in a corporate liquidation is the fair market value of the property at the date of liquidation.

In the case of a corporation completely liquidated within one calendar month after 1950 and before 1987, the basis of the shareholder's stock was applied to the property received and became the basis of such property. California law incorporates the federal law, including for post-1986 tax years the repeal of the one-month liquidation provisions adopted by the Tax Reform Act of 1986.

¶526b Basis of Stock After "Spin-off" Reorganization

Law: Sec. 17321 (CCH CALIFORNIA TAX REPORTS ¶ 16-073).

Comparable Federal: Sec. 358 (CCH STANDARD FEDERAL TAX REPORTS ¶ 16,550).

California law is the same as federal law as of the current IRC tie-in date (see ¶ 102a).

When stock of a new corporation is distributed to stockholders of another corporation in a "spin-off" type reorganization (see ¶ 508), the adjusted basis of the old stock is allocated between the old and new stocks.

¶527 Basis of Property Acquired upon Involuntary Conversion

Law: Secs. 18031, 18037 (CCH CALIFORNIA TAX REPORTS ¶ 16-554).

Comparable Federal: Sec. 1033 (CCH STANDARD FEDERAL TAX REPORTS ¶ 31,540).

California law is the same as federal law as of the current IRC tie-in date (see ¶ 102a).

The basis of property acquired as a result of involuntary conversion is the same as that of the property converted, with adjustment for any part of the proceeds not reinvested as required by the law and for any gain or loss recognized upon the conversion.

The rules relating to involuntary conversions of a principal residence have been changed in prior years, as explained at ¶ 502a, and the California effective dates of some changes have been different from the federal. This may result in a difference between California and federal bases for such property.

¶ 527a Basis of FNMA Stock

Law: Sec. 18031 (CCH CALIFORNIA TAX REPORTS ¶ 16-579).

Comparable Federal: Sec. 1054 (CCH STANDARD FEDERAL TAX REPORTS ¶ 31,820).

Basis is reduced for the excess of cost over fair market value (deductible as a business expense) of Federal National Mortgage Association (FNMA) stock issued to an initial holder. California law incorporates the federal law by reference as of the current IRC tie-in date (see ¶ 102a).

¶ 527b Redeemable Ground Rents

Law: Sec. 18031 (CCH CALIFORNIA TAX REPORTS ¶ 16-580).

Comparable Federal: Sec. 1055 (CCH STANDARD FEDERAL TAX REPORTS ¶ 31,840).

Redeemable ground rents are treated as being the equivalent of a mortgage. California law incorporates the federal law by reference as of the current IRC tie-in date (see ¶ 102a).

¶ 528 Basis of Securities Acquired in Wash Sale

Law: Sec. 18031 (CCH CALIFORNIA TAX REPORTS ¶ 16-592).

Comparable Federal: Sec. 1091 (CCH STANDARD FEDERAL TAX REPORTS ¶ 32,080).

The basis of stock or securities acquired in a "wash sale" is the same as that of the securities sold, increased, or decreased, as the case may be, by the difference between the cost of the new securities and the selling price of the securities which were subject to the "wash sale" rules. California law incorporates the federal law by reference as of the current IRC tie-in date (see ¶ 102a).

¶ 529 Basis Prescribed by Personal Income Tax Law of 1954

Law: Sec. 18039 (CCH CALIFORNIA TAX REPORTS ¶ 16-577).

Comparable Federal: Sec. 1052 (CCH STANDARD FEDERAL TAX REPORTS ¶ 31,780).

The basis of property acquired after February 28, 1913, in certain transactions covered by the California Personal Income Tax Law of 1954, is as prescribed in that Law.

The federal law contains a somewhat comparable provision that refers to federal Revenue Acts of 1932 and 1934. Prior to 1983 California law contained a conforming provision.

¶ 530 Basis of Partnership Property

Law: Sec. 17851 (CCH CALIFORNIA TAX REPORTS ¶ 16-401).

Comparable Federal: Secs. 701-61 (CCH STANDARD FEDERAL TAX REPORTS ¶ 25,360—25,900).

California law is the same as federal law as of the current IRC tie-in date (see ¶ 102a).

The basis of property transferred to a partnership is the transferor's basis, adjusted for any gain or loss recognized upon the transfer.

The rules for determining basis of property distributed by a partnership to a partner may be summarized very briefly as follows:

1. generally, the basis of property in the hands of the partner-distributee is the same as the basis in the hands of the partnership;

2. the basis of property distributed in liquidation of a partner's interest is the properly allocable part of the basis of the partner's partnership interest;

3. special rules to prevent tax avoidance are provided for the treatment of inventories, "unrealized receivables," and depreciable property subject to "depreciation recapture" provisions that are distributed to a partner (there are minor federal-California differences in these rules, as explained at ¶ 612b);

4. under some conditions, the partnership may adjust the basis of its assets remaining after the distribution to reflect the step-up or step-down of basis in the transfer from the partnership to the partner; and

5. the partnership may elect to adjust the basis of partnership assets to reflect the purchase price paid by a new partner for his or her interest; under some conditions the same type of adjustment may be made by a partner who receives a distribution of partnership property within two years after acquiring an interest.

¶ 531 Basis of Property Acquired Before March 1, 1913

Law: Sec. 18031 (CCH CALIFORNIA TAX REPORTS ¶ 16-578).

Comparable Federal: Sec. 1053 (CCH STANDARD FEDERAL TAX REPORTS ¶ 31,800).

For property acquired before March 1, 1913, when the fair market value at March 1, 1913, was greater than the adjusted basis otherwise determined as of that date, the basis for determining gain is such fair market value. Federal law is incorporated in California law by reference as of the current IRC tie-in date (see ¶ 102a).

¶ 532 Basis of Property Acquired Pursuant to S.E.C. Order

Law: Sec. 18031 (CCH CALIFORNIA TAX REPORTS ¶ 16-588).

Comparable Federal: Sec. 1082 (CCH STANDARD FEDERAL TAX REPORTS ¶ 32,040).

The basis of securities received in certain liquidations under order of the federal Securities and Exchange Commission is the same as that of the securities exchanged. Federal law is incorporated in California law by reference as of the current IRC tie-in date (see ¶ 102a).

¶ 532a Basis of Property Distributed Under Bank Holding Company Act (Prior Law)

Law: Sec. 18031 (CCH CALIFORNIA TAX REPORTS ¶ 16-599).

Comparable Federal: Former Sec. 1102 (CCH STANDARD FEDERAL TAX REPORTS ¶ 32,125).

California formerly incorporated a federal provision under which the basis of stock or other property distributed pursuant to federal Bank Holding Company legislation without recognition of gain was determined by allocating the adjusted basis of the stock with respect to which the distribution was made between such stock and the property so distributed. The federal provision was repealed by the Revenue Reconciliation Act of 1990. For both federal and California purposes, the repeal was generally effective November 5, 1990.

¶ 533 Basis of Rights to Acquire Stock

Law: Sec. 17321 (CCH CALIFORNIA TAX REPORTS ¶ 16-022).

Comparable Federal: Sec. 307 (CCH STANDARD FEDERAL TAX REPORTS ¶ 15,400).

California law is the same as federal law as of the current IRC tie-in date (see ¶ 102a).

When the fair market value of stock rights is less than 15% of the value of the stock on which the rights are issued, the basis of the rights is zero unless the taxpayer elects to allocate to the rights a portion of the basis of the stock.

As to the following rights, the basis of the stock is allocated between the stock and the rights according to their respective values at the time the rights are issued:

(a) all rights acquired in a taxable year beginning before 1937, *except* as to certain rights acquired before 1935 (see below); and

(b) nontaxable rights acquired in a taxable year beginning after December 31, 1936, where the value of the rights is more than 15% or the taxpayer elects to allocate as explained above.

If a stock right was acquired prior to 1935 and it constituted income under the Sixteenth Amendment to the Federal Constitution, the basis of the right is its fair market value when acquired.

Where stock rights were acquired and sold in a taxable year beginning after 1934 and prior to 1941 and the entire proceeds were reported as income, the basis of the stock is determined without any allocation to the rights.

California law incorporates the federal law by reference. California has conformed closely to the federal law for many years, although there have been minor differences in the effective dates of prior-year amendments.

¶ 534 Adjusted Basis

Law: Secs. 17088, 18031, 18036 (CCH CALIFORNIA TAX REPORTS ¶ 16-508, 16-531, 16-538).

Comparable Federal: Secs. 1011, 1016—1021 (CCH STANDARD FEDERAL TAX REPORTS ¶ 29,660, 29,760—29,840).

California law incorporates IRC Sec. 1016(a), as amended through a fixed date (see ¶ 102a), concerning adjustments to basis (see ¶ 102a). However, the following federal basis adjustments, although contained in IRC Sec. 1016(a), are inapplicable under California law:

(1) amounts related to a shareholder's stock in a controlled foreign corporation;

(2) certain federal investment tax credits;

(3) adjustments to the basis of a United States taxpayer's stock in a foreign personal holding company to reflect certain undistributed income of the company;

(4) abandonment fees paid upon the termination of an open-space easement;

(5) tax recoupment fees on timberland; and

(6) sales or use tax paid by the taxpayer in acquiring property, if the taxpayer claims the tax credit allowed for enterprise zone, former Los Angeles Revitalization Zone, local agency military base recovery area, or targeted tax area businesses on certain "qualified property" (the credit is discussed at ¶ 131).

The following basis adjustments required by IRC Sec. 1016(a) are technically incorporated by California but have no practical effect: (1) amounts specified in a shareholder's consent; (2) amortization of premium and accrual of discount on bonds and notes held by a life insurance company; (3) certain carryover basis property acquired from a decedent; (4) the adjustments to the basis of stock concerning a basis reduction for extraordinary dividends; (5) unrecognized gain resulting from an acquisition of certain qualified replacement property; and (6) the amount of the gas guzzler tax on an automobile.

California law also requires that adjustments be made for certain deducted enterprise zone, former Los Angeles Revitalization Zone, and local military base recovery area business expenses (see ¶ 310f). No comparable basis adjustments are required under federal law.

See ¶ 221 regarding basis adjustment upon discharge of indebtedness. See ¶ 536 regarding basis adjustment for lessee improvements.

¶ 535 Substituted Basis

Law: Sec. 18031 (CCH CALIFORNIA TAX REPORTS ¶ 16-534).

Comparable Federal: Sec. 1016 (CCH STANDARD FEDERAL TAX REPORTS ¶ 29,760).

"Substituted basis" is defined as the basis determined (1) by reference to the basis in the hands of a transferor or (2) by reference to other property held at any time by the taxpayer. California law incorporates federal law by reference as of the current IRC tie-in date (see ¶ 102a).

¶ 536 Lessor's Basis for Lessee's Improvements

Law: Sec. 18031 (CCH CALIFORNIA TAX REPORTS ¶ 16-541).

Comparable Federal: Sec. 1019 (CCH STANDARD FEDERAL TAX REPORTS ¶ 29,820).

Where the value of improvements by a lessee is excluded from income (see ¶ 222), there is no effect on the basis of the property to the lessor. Where the value of such improvements was included in the lessor's income, in a taxable year beginning before 1943, the basis of the lessor's property is adjusted accordingly. California law incorporates federal law by reference as of the current IRC tie-in date (see ¶ 102a).

¶ 537 Basis for Depreciation and Depletion

> *Law:* Secs. 17201, 17681 (CCH California Tax Reports ¶ 15-765, 15-778, 16-325).
>
> *Comparable Federal:* Secs. 167, 612-13 (CCH Standard Federal Tax Reports ¶ 11,002, 24,540, 24,560).

The basis for depreciation and for cost depletion is the adjusted basis for purposes of determining gain upon sale of the property, except that certain deferred development and exploration expenses includible in basis are disregarded for this purpose (see ¶ 311a). California law incorporates federal law by reference as of the current IRC tie-in date (see ¶ 102a).

For rules regarding percentage depletion, see ¶ 311.

¶ 538 Basis for Player Contracts

> *Law:* Sec. 18031 (CCH California Tax Reports ¶ 16-582).
>
> *Comparable Federal:* Sec. 1056 (CCH Standard Federal Tax Reports ¶ 31,860).

The basis of player contracts that are acquired in connection with a sports franchise is limited to the basis to the seller plus the gain recognized by the seller on the transfer. California law incorporates federal law by reference (see ¶ 102a).

¶ 539 Allocation of Transferred Business Assets

> *Law:* Sec. 18031 (CCH California Tax Reports ¶ 16-584b).
>
> *Comparable Federal:* Sec. 1060 (CCH Standard Federal Tax Reports ¶ 31,960).

California has adopted the federal residual method for allocating purchases of assets that constitute a trade or business (see ¶ 102a). Generally, under the residual method, the purchase price is allocated first to the assets to the extent of their fair market value, and then, if there is any excess, to goodwill and going concern value.

The Revenue Reconciliation Act of 1990 amended the federal law to provide that if a transferor and a transferee agree in writing as to the allocation of consideration for transferred business assets, their agreement will generally be binding for tax purposes.

CHAPTER 6

PERSONAL INCOME TAX
ESTATES AND TRUSTS, PARTNERSHIPS

¶ 601 Application of Tax to Estates and Trusts

Law: Secs. 17731, 18505 (CCH CALIFORNIA TAX REPORTS ¶ 16-351).

Comparable Federal: Secs. 641, 643, 645, 665, 6034A, 6048 (CCH STANDARD FEDERAL TAX REPORTS ¶ 24,760, 24,820, 24,850, 24,980).

California Forms: Forms 541, 541-A, 541-B, 541-ES, 541-QFT, 541-T.

The personal income tax law applies to the income of estates and to property held in trust, whether the income is accumulated or distributed. The federal law is incorporated by California as of the current IRC tie-in date (see ¶ 102a).

The tax rates for estates and trusts are the same as for resident individuals (see ¶ 112). The alternative minimum tax, discussed at ¶ 112a, applies to estates and trusts as well.

● *Estimated tax*

Generally, trusts and estates make estimated tax payments in the same manner as individuals (see ¶ 107a). However, under both California and federal law, this general rule is inapplicable to: (1) private foundations; (2) charitable trusts that are taxed on unrelated business income; (3) any estate in the first two tax years following the decedent's death; or (4) any trust in the first two tax years following the grantor's death if the trust either receives the residual of a probate estate under the grantor's will or, if the grantor died without a will, the trust is primarily responsible for the estate's taxes, debts, and administrative expenses.

Under both California and federal law, a trust or, for its final year, a decedent's estate, may elect to have any part of its estimated tax payments treated as made by a beneficiary or beneficiaries. For California purposes, the election is made on Form 541-T, which must be filed by the 65th day after the close of the estate's or trust's taxable year.

● *Consistency rule*

Under both California and federal law, beneficiaries of an estate or trust are required to (1) file their returns in a manner consistent with that reported on the trust's or estate's return or (2) file a notice of inconsistent treatment with the Franchise Tax Board (the Secretary for federal purposes) that identifies the inconsistent items. If a beneficiary fails to comply with these requirements, any adjustment necessary in order to make the treatment of the items consistent will be treated as a mathematical or clerical error subject to summary assessment procedures. If the noncompliance was the result of the beneficiary's negligence, a negligence penalty will also be imposed (see ¶ 710).

● *Returns*

Form 541 is used to report the tax information of estates and trusts unless otherwise indicated.

¶ 602 Effect of Residence upon Taxability

Law: Secs. 17742-45 (CCH CALIFORNIA TAX REPORTS ¶ 16-357).

Comparable Federal: None.

In the case of an estate, the following rules apply:

(a) if the decedent was a resident of California at the time of his or her death, all of the estate's net income is taxable, regardless of source;

(b) if the decedent was a nonresident, only income of the estate from California sources is taxable, unless income is distributed to California beneficiaries; if income is not distributed, it does not matter that either the fiduciary or beneficiary, or both, are California residents ("income in respect of a decedent" may be from a California source and therefore taxable, even though the decedent was a nonresident, where the income arose from personal services in California—see ¶ 413); and

(c) any income distributed to a beneficiary who is a California resident is taxable to the beneficiary, regardless of the source of the income.

See ¶ 604a for taxation of nonresident and part-year resident beneficiaries.

In the case of a trust, taxability depends on the residence of the fiduciaries and beneficiaries. If either the fiduciary (or all fiduciaries, if more than one) or the beneficiary (or all beneficiaries, if more than one) is a California resident, all of the income, regardless of source, is taxable. This applies only to any net income that is taxable to the trust, as distinguished from the beneficiaries. It does not apply to distributed (or distributable) income that is taxable to the beneficiaries; see ¶ 604a for treatment of such income. See also *Appeal of The First National Bank of Chicago, Trustee* (1960) (CCH CALIFORNIA TAX REPORTS ¶ 16-357.27), decided by the State Board of Equalization, in which a nonresident trustee was held taxable on the undistributed income of a trust only because its beneficiaries were California residents. In *Robert P. McCulloch v. Franchise Tax Board* (1964) (CCH CALIFORNIA TAX REPORTS ¶ 16-357.40), the California Supreme Court held that the tax on income accumulated by a nonresident trust could be collected from a resident trustee-beneficiary in the year of distribution to him. A beneficiary whose interest in a trust is *contingent* is not to be considered in determining the taxability of a trust's income.

The residence of a corporate fiduciary is determined by reference to the place where the corporation transacts the major portion of its administration of the trust.

If the taxability of the trust depends on the residence of the fiduciary and there are two or more fiduciaries, not all of whom are residents of California, the taxable income from sources outside California is apportioned to California according to the number of California fiduciaries in relation to the total number of fiduciaries. For example, suppose a trust has two fiduciaries, only one of whom is a California resident, and has net income of $10,000 from property located in New York. One-half of the income of the trust, or $5,000, is taxable for California income tax purposes. This rule has no application to income derived from sources within California (see ¶ 230); such income is fully taxable in California regardless of the residence of the fiduciary, beneficiary, or settlor.

If the taxability of the trust depends on the residence of the beneficiary and there are two or more beneficiaries, not all of whom are California residents, the taxable income from sources outside California is apportioned to California to the extent the income will eventually be distributed to beneficiaries who are California residents. To illustrate, suppose A, a resident, and B, a nonresident, are equal beneficiaries of the income of a trust established by a nonresident settlor and having a nonresident fiduciary. Its income of $10,000 is all derived from property located in New York State. All of the income is accumulated in the trust. One-half of the income, or $5,000, is taxable for California income tax purposes. As in the rule discussed in the preceding paragraph, this rule has no application to income derived from California sources.

Where there are multiple fiduciaries and also multiple beneficiaries, some of whom are California residents and some nonresidents, the practice of the Franchise Tax Board has been to apply the above rules consecutively; that is first to the fiduciaries and then to the beneficiaries, or vice versa. For example, suppose there are two fiduciaries, one of whom is a California resident, and two (equal) beneficiaries, one of whom is a California resident. One-half of the income taxable to the trust would be considered attributable to California because of the resident fiduciary. Of the remaining one-half, 50% would then be considered as California income because of the resident beneficiary, the result being that 75% of the total income is attributed to California. This practice is explained in some detail in Legal Ruling No. 238 (1959) (CCH CALIFORNIA TAX REPORTS ¶ 16-357.13).

Where a nonresident trust has a resident trustee who is also a beneficiary, taxability of the trust's income has been held to be determined only by reference to the resident's status as a trustee. See *Robert P. McCulloch v. Franchise Tax Board,* cited above.

¶ 603 Income of Estate from Community Property

Law: Reg. 17742 (CCH CALIFORNIA TAX REPORTS ¶ 16-360).

Comparable Federal: None.

Franchise Tax Board Regulation 17742 provides that the estate of a deceased spouse is taxable on the income from that part of his or her one-half of the community property that is subject to administration. Income received by the estate, but derived from the surviving spouse's share of the community property, is taxable to the surviving spouse.

Under the California Probate Code, the decedent's share of community property may pass to the surviving spouse without administration. In this case, the entire income is taxable to the surviving spouse.

¶ 604 Taxable Income of Estate or Trust

Law: Secs. 17076, 17731, 17735-36, 17551, 18038 (CCH CALIFORNIA TAX REPORTS ¶ 16-351, 16-363, 16-369, 16-379, 16-617).

Comparable Federal: Secs. 67, 641-46, 651, 661, 1040 (CCH STANDARD FEDERAL TAX REPORTS ¶ 24,760, 24,850, 24,860, 24,900, 31,680).

The taxable income of an estate or trust is computed the same as for individuals, as explained in Chapters 2-5 of this GUIDEBOOK, inclusive, with the following exceptions:

(a) unlimited deduction is allowed for income paid or set aside by an estate or complex trust under the terms of the will or trust instrument for certain charitable-type purposes (see discussion below);

(b) deduction is allowed for income required to be distributed currently to beneficiaries, the deduction not to exceed the "distributable net income;" and

(c) deduction is allowed to certain types of trusts ("complex" trusts—see ¶ 604a) for other amounts properly paid or credited or required to be distributed.

The federal law is incorporated in California's by reference as of the current IRC tie-in date (see ¶ 102a). However, California does not incorporate a federal provision that limits the taxable gain of an estate or trust where a pecuniary bequest is satisfied by the transfer of farm-type real property that has been the subject of a reduced estate-tax valuation.

In the case of an estate, California allows no deduction under items (b) and (c) above for distributions that are taxable to a nonresident beneficiary if the fiduciary fails to obtain a tax-clearance certificate as explained at ¶ 610.

● *Expenses of administration*

Expenses of administration of an estate are ordinarily deductible. However, estate administration expenses can be deducted for California income tax purposes or California estate "pickup" tax purposes, but not both (*Tax News,* FTB, May 1988, CCH CALIFORNIA TAX REPORTS ¶ 16-363.751). For federal purposes, such expenses may be deducted for federal income tax purposes or federal estate tax purposes, but not both.

● *Unlimited deduction*

The deduction described in (a) above is subject to some restrictions. Generally, the unlimited deduction is reduced or denied where the trust has "unrelated business income" or where it engages in certain "prohibited transactions." The deduction is allowed only for income actually paid out and not for income set aside by a trust. California substitutes December 31, 1970, where October 9, 1969, appears in the federal law. A trust claiming the unlimited deduction presumably would be classified as a charitable trust and treated as a corporation for California tax purposes, as explained at ¶ 605.

For both federal and California tax purposes, the above deductions are not miscellaneous itemized deductions subject to the 2% floor (see ¶ 303).

● *Electing small business trusts*

The portion of a small business trust that consists of stock in one or more S corporations is treated as a separate trust for purposes of computing the income tax attributable to the S corporation stock held by the trust and is taxed at the highest federal rate imposed on estates and trusts. Special rules also apply to the income attributable to the S corporation stock, treatment of capital losses, deductions, and credits.

● *Treatment of revocable trust as part of estate*

A qualified revocable trust may make an irrevocable election to be treated for income tax purposes as part of a decedent's estate, provided the election is made jointly by the trustee of the revocable trust and the executor of the decedent's estate by the due date for filing the estate's income tax return for its first tax year. A federal election, or lack thereof, is binding for California purposes.

¶ 604

¶ 604a Income Taxable to Beneficiaries

Law: Secs. 17731, 17734, 17779 (CCH CALIFORNIA TAX REPORTS ¶ 16-357, 16-376, 16-382).

Comparable Federal: Secs. 642, 652, 662-68 (CCH STANDARD FEDERAL TAX REPORTS ¶ 24,780, 24,880, 24,920—25,040).

California Form: FTB 5870A.

Federal law pertaining to income taxable to beneficiaries is incorporated in California law by reference as of the current IRC tie-in date (see ¶ 102a). However, California provides special rules to cover various residence situations, as explained below.

Amounts deductible under (b) and (c) of ¶ 604 are includible in the income of the beneficiaries.

Income retains the same character (capital gain, exempt income, etc.) in the hands of the beneficiary that it had in the hands of the estate or trust. In other words, the estate or trust is treated as merely a "conduit" for income that is taxable to the beneficiaries. Depreciation is apportioned between the trust or estate and the beneficiaries according to the terms of the trust instrument or on the basis of the income allocable to each.

● *Notice to estate or trust beneficiaries*

The fiduciary of an estate or trust must furnish each beneficiary (or nominee) (1) who receives a distribution from an estate or trust or (2) to whom any taxable item is allocated, a statement (in accordance with IRC Sec. 6034A) containing information necessary for the beneficiary to file his or her California income tax return.

● *Nonresident and part-year resident beneficiaries*

Nonresident beneficiaries are taxed on their distributive shares of estate or trust income only to the extent the income is derived from sources within California. Thus, four beneficiaries who were residents of Sweden were required to pay California income tax on distributions from their brother's estate because the distributions were from the sale of real estate located in California (*Appeals of Folke Jernberg et al.* (1986), CCH CALIFORNIA TAX REPORTS ¶ 16-357.83); the accumulated income from these holdings was also taxable.

A part-year resident beneficiary is taxed on his or her entire distributive share of estate or trust income if the beneficiary is a California resident on the last day of the estate's or trust's taxable year (*Information Letter No. 89-427*, FTB, July 10, 1989, CCH CALIFORNIA TAX REPORTS ¶ 16-376.30). A part-year resident beneficiary who is a nonresident on the last day of the entity's tax year is taxed in the same manner as a nonresident beneficiary.

● *Miscellaneous provisions*

In *Appeal of Proctor P. and Martha M. Jones* (1983) (CCH CALIFORNIA TAX REPORTS ¶ 16-357.79), the taxpayer, a California resident, was one of several beneficiaries of an out-of-state trust. The State Board of Equalization held that tax-exempt California municipal bond income of the trust was properly allocated exclusively to the taxpayer.

¶ 604a

Where accumulated income is distributed by a nonresident trust to a resident beneficiary, the distribution is fully taxable to the beneficiary in the year of distribution if it has not previously been taxed in California. If the beneficiary was not a resident during the period of accumulation, the income may or may not be taxable in the year of distribution (see ¶ 405). However, credit will be allowed for taxes paid to other states (see ¶ 118). The California law also provides:

(a) where taxes have not been paid on the income of a trust because a resident beneficiary's interest was merely contingent, and not vested, the income is taxable to the resident beneficiary when distributed, or distributable, to the beneficiary;

(b) even though the trust instrument provides that income accumulations are to be added to corpus, the income is nevertheless taxable as distributed, or distributable, to a resident beneficiary, if the trust failed to pay the tax when due, or no tax was paid by the trust because the interest of the resident beneficiary was merely contingent during the period of accumulation;

(c) the tax attributable to the inclusion of trust distributions in income by a resident beneficiary under (a) above is the total amount of tax that would have been paid by the beneficiary if he or she had included a ratable amount in his or her income for the shorter of the following two periods: (1) the year of distribution and the five preceding years, or (2) the period that the trust acquired or accumulated the income (the "throwback" rules discussed below do not apply in this situation); and

(d) where a resident beneficiary leaves California within 12 months prior to the date of distribution of accumulated income and returns within 12 months after the receipt of such distribution, the beneficiary is presumed to be a resident throughout the entire intervening period of distribution.

In *Robert P. McCulloch v. Franchise Tax Board* (1964) (CCH CALIFORNIA TAX REPORTS ¶ 16-357.40), the California Supreme Court held that where income was accumulated by a nonresident trust, and the tax on that income was not paid over to the state when due, it was properly includible in the resident beneficiary's income when distributed in a later year in proportion to the amount that should have been taxed to the trust in prior years.

The law divides trusts into two classes. The first type—commonly known as the "simple" trust—is one that is required to distribute all of its income currently. All other trusts and decedents' estates are included in the other category, commonly called "complex" trusts. Separate rules are provided for the determination of the amount taxable to beneficiaries of "simple" and of "complex" trusts.

Relief is provided to beneficiaries in some cases in the year of termination of an estate or trust. If the deductions of the estate or trust exceed the gross income for the last year, the excess deductions may be carried over and allowed to the beneficiaries. The same procedure applies to unused capital loss carryovers.

If the taxable year of the beneficiary is different from that of the estate or trust, the amount of distributable income that the beneficiary reports is based upon the income of the estate or trust for the taxable year of the estate or trust that ends within the beneficiary's taxable year.

¶ 605 Charitable Trusts

> *Law:* Secs. 17009, 17731, 18635 (CCH CALIFORNIA TAX REPORTS ¶ 16-354, 16-385, 89-185).

> *Comparable Federal:* Secs. 501(c)(3), 642(c), 664, 681, 4940-48, 6034 (CCH STANDARD FEDERAL TAX REPORTS ¶ 22,602, 24,780, 24,960, 25,240, 35,400—35,560, 36,640).

Under California law, a charitable trust is treated as a corporation. (This is accomplished by including trusts operated for charitable purposes within the definition of "corporation.") This means that a charitable trust should apply for tax exemption under Section 23701d of the corporation tax law and should comply with the reporting requirements discussed at ¶ 805a.

The special federal treatment of "charitable remainder annuity trusts" and "charitable remainder unitrusts" is incorporated in California law by reference.

Although California has conformed in principle to federal law by creating a special category of organizations classified as "private foundations," California has not adopted many of the complicated federal provisions relating to such organizations. California does not impose a tax on the investment income of "private foundations," nor does California impose any of the excise taxes (on self-dealing, income-accumulation, prohibited investments, lobbying, termination, etc.) that are included in the federal law. The California provisions regarding "private foundations" are almost all in the corporation tax law (see ¶ 805a).

Both California and federal laws require certain trusts, including "private foundations," to include certain provisions in their governing instruments in order to maintain their tax-exempt status, unless a state statute accomplishes the same result. The California Civil Code provides that the required provisions are deemed to be included automatically in the governing instruments of all trusts to which the requirement applies, and further provides that any provisions of trust instruments that are inconsistent or contrary are of no effect.

¶ 606 Employees' Trusts

> *Law:* Secs. 17504, 17510, 17631-40, 18506, 19518 (CCH CALIFORNIA TAX REPORTS ¶ 16-105, 16-109, 16-314, 89-110).

> *Comparable Federal:* Secs. 401-7, 501-14, 4971-75, 6047, 7701 (CCH STANDARD FEDERAL TAX REPORTS ¶ 17,773, 18,500, 22,602—22,800, 35,720—35,800, 37,080).

California law is generally the same as federal law.

A trust forming part of an employees' stock bonus, pension, or profit-sharing plan is exempt from taxation provided it meets certain requirements as summarized very briefly as follows:

(a) contributions must be made for the exclusive benefit of employees or their beneficiaries and it must be impossible for any part of the corpus or income to be diverted to any other purpose; and

(b) the plan must benefit the employees generally, under certain specific rules, and must not discriminate in favor of officers, shareholders, supervisory employees, etc.

The employee benefits under an exempt plan are taxed to the employee only when actually distributed to the employee. See ¶ 206.

California rules for employees' trusts (including self-employed plans and individual retirement accounts) conform generally to federal rules. See ¶ 206 and ¶ 318 for a detailed discussion.

An exempt employees' trust need not file a California return unless it changes its character, purpose, or method of operation, or unless it has unrelated business income. However, both California and federal laws require trustees and insurers to file information returns regarding payments made under self-employed retirement plans. Also, as to individual retirement accounts, California requires trustees and others to file copies of federal reports with the Franchise Tax Board.

¶ 607 Trusts Taxable to Grantor

Law: Secs. 17731, 17760.5 (CCH California Tax Reports ¶ 16-392).

Comparable Federal: Secs. 671-79, 685 (CCH Standard Federal Tax Reports ¶ 25,080—25,220).

California law is the same as federal law as of the current IRC tie-in date (see ¶ 102a).

Where the grantor retains an interest, as specifically defined in the Code sections cited above, in either corpus or income, the income is taxable to the grantor and not to the trust or the beneficiaries. However, under both California and federal law, qualified pre-need funeral trusts may not be treated as grantor trusts. Consequently, the tax on the annual earnings of a funeral trust is payable by the trustee, if a trustee elects this special tax treatment. A federal election to receive such treatment for a qualified pre-need funeral trust is binding for California purposes and a separate California election is not allowed.

Where income of a trust may be used to satisfy the grantor's legal obligation to support a beneficiary, the income is taxed to the grantor to the extent—and only to the extent—that the income is so used.

In *Appeal of Blake and Alice Hale* (1960) (CCH California Tax Reports ¶ 16-392.481), the State Board of Equalization held that income from a voluntary trust was taxable to the grantor when the trust instrument did not specifically provide that the trust was irrevocable, and partial or total revocations were contemplated in certain provisions.

Where the grantor in a trust of the type under discussion is not a California resident, he or she is taxed on the income of the trust only to the extent it is derived from sources within California.

There are special federal rules for taxing the income of foreign trusts to their U.S. grantors, under certain conditions. In addition, the U.S. beneficiary of a foreign trust may be treated as the grantor of the trust in certain cases in which the grantor trust rules would otherwise be frustrated.

Fiduciaries of certain grantor trusts are not required to file a return for the trust; the income, deductions, and credits of the trust are reported on the grantor's return.

¶ 607a Real Estate Investment Trusts

Law: Sec. 17088 (CCH CALIFORNIA TAX REPORTS ¶ 16-471).

Comparable Federal: Secs. 856-60 (CCH STANDARD FEDERAL TAX REPORTS ¶ 26,700, 26,720, 26,740).

California adopts by reference the federal provisions as of the current IRC tie-in date (see ¶ 102a).

A "real estate investment trust" is ordinarily treated as a business trust subject to the corporation income tax, as explained at ¶ 802a. The corporation tax law allows such organizations a deduction for income distributed, as explained at ¶ 1016.

¶ 607b Financial Asset Securitization Investment Trusts

Law: Sec. 17088 (CCH CALIFORNIA TAX REPORTS ¶ 16-474).

Comparable Federal: Secs. 860H-860L (CCH STANDARD FEDERAL TAX REPORTS ¶ 26,930, 48,810).

California incorporates federal provisions concerning financial asset securitization investment trusts (FASITs) as of the current IRC tie-in date (see ¶ 102a). A FASIT is a pass-through entity that may be used to securitize debt obligations such as credit card receivables, home equity loans, and auto loans. Securities issued by a FASIT are treated as debt for federal income tax purposes, regardless of whether instruments with similar terms issued by an entity other than a FASIT would be characterized as equity ownership interests. Consequently, a FASIT may be used to avoid imposition of a corporate level tax on investors' income and to ensure that interest paid to investors will be deductible by the loan pool's sponsor. For a detailed discussion of FASITs, see ¶ 802a.

¶ 608 Alimony Trusts

Law: Secs. 17731, 17737 (CCH CALIFORNIA TAX REPORTS ¶ 16-396).

Comparable Federal: Sec. 682 (CCH STANDARD FEDERAL TAX REPORTS ¶ 25,260).

Income of "alimony trusts" is taxable to the beneficiary and is not taxable to the trustor. This rule does not apply to any part of such income that is payable for the support of minor children.

California law incorporates federal law by reference as of the current IRC tie-in date (see ¶ 102a).

¶ 607a

¶ 609 Lien for Tax on Trust Income

Law: Secs. 19221, 19223-24 (CCH CALIFORNIA TAX REPORTS ¶ 89-320).

Comparable Federal: Sec. 6321 (CCH STANDARD FEDERAL TAX REPORTS ¶ 39,035).

California law provides that under certain conditions the amount of taxes imposed upon the grantor of a trust on the trust income (see ¶ 607) constitutes a lien on the trust property. Although federal law contains certain provisions for liens for unpaid taxes, it contains no rule similar to this one.

¶ 610 Liability of Fiduciary

Law: Secs. 19071-74, 19512-17 (CCH CALIFORNIA TAX REPORTS ¶ 89-239, 89-310).

Comparable Federal: Secs. 6501, 6901, 6903, 6905 (CCH STANDARD FEDERAL TAX REPORTS ¶ 39,910, 41,500, 41,605).

California Form: FTB 3571.

California law is the same as federal law as of the current IRC tie-in date (see ¶ 102a).

The fiduciary is personally liable for the taxes on an estate or trust under certain conditions. Federal law provides for discharge of an executor's liability under certain circumstances; there is no comparable California provision.

Where the asset value of an estate exceeds $400,000 and assets valued at more than $100,000 are distributable to one or more nonresident beneficiaries, the fiduciary of an estate must file with his or her final accounting a certificate from the Franchise Tax Board (FTB) to the effect that all California income taxes have been paid or otherwise provided for. The FTB supplies a form (FTB 3571, Request for Estate Income Tax Certificate) for applying for such a certificate. The law allows 30 days for processing such requests. There is no similar federal requirement.

A fiduciary (or other person liable for the tax) of an estate or trust may by written request filed with the FTB shorten the period of limitations on assessment, etc., to 18 months. The comparable federal provision is limited to the fiduciary of an estate.

A fiduciary should give the FTB notice in writing of the assumption of the duties, rights, etc., attaching to the fiduciary capacity. A fiduciary who wishes to be relieved of fiduciary responsibilities must give the FTB a written termination notice, accompanied by evidence of such termination. The California rule is the same as the federal rule.

In *Appeals of Dunham et al.* (1963) (CCH CALIFORNIA TAX REPORTS ¶ 16-411.30), the State Board of Equalization (SBE) held that the co-executors of an estate remained liable for additional California income tax imposed on the estate after they had been discharged from their duties by a superior court. The SBE held that failure to notify the FTB of discharge by a superior court left them responsible, in their representative capacities, for the additional tax.

¶ 611 Common Trust Funds

> *Law:* Secs. 17671, 17677 (CCH CALIFORNIA TAX REPORTS ¶ 16-309).
>
> *Comparable Federal:* Sec. 584 (CCH STANDARD FEDERAL TAX REPORTS ¶ 23,830).

California law is the same as federal law as of the current IRC tie-in date (see ¶ 102a).

Special rules are provided for common trust funds maintained by banks or trust companies. The general plan is to treat such funds as reporting entities, only the individual shares of income being taxed to the participants, as is the manner for partnerships.

¶ 611a Real Estate Mortgage Investment Conduits

> *Law:* Secs. 17088, 24874 (CCH CALIFORNIA TAX REPORTS ¶ 16-473).
>
> *Comparable Federal:* Secs. 860A-860G (CCH STANDARD FEDERAL TAX REPORTS ¶ 26,800—26,920).

California law is the same as federal law as of the current IRC tie-in date (see ¶ 102a), except that California does not impose an excise tax on prohibited transactions, but subjects real estate mortgage investment conduits (REMICs) to a minimum tax.

Trusts or partnerships that meet specified requirements may elect to be treated as a REMIC. A REMIC, which is a fixed pool of mortgages with multiple classes of interests held by investors, is not taxed on its income, but its income is taxable to the holders of its interests.

¶ 612 Partnerships—Method of Taxing

> *Law:* Secs. 17008, 17008.5, 17851, 23081, 23097, 24637 (CCH CALIFORNIA TAX REPORTS ¶ 16-209, 16-401, 16-407, 16-475).
>
> *Comparable Federal:* Secs. 444, 701-61, 7701, 7704 (CCH STANDARD FEDERAL TAX REPORTS ¶ 20,600, 25,360—25,900, 43,880, 43,980).
>
> *California Form:* Form 565.

California law is the same as federal law as of the current IRC tie-in date (see ¶ 102a), except for a minimum tax imposed by California on limited partnerships, limited liability partnerships, and limited liability companies treated as partnerships (see ¶ 112).

Partnerships are not taxable as such but are treated as reporting entities only, the distributive shares of the partners being reported and taxed in their individual returns. "Partnership" may include a syndicate, group, pool, joint venture, or other unincorporated organization. California adopts the federal provision that treats publicly traded partnerships as corporations unless (1) 90% or more of their gross income consists of qualifying passive income or (2) they are grandfathered publicly traded partnerships exempt from corporate treatment. However, for tax years beginning after 1997, a grandfathered publicly traded partnership that elects to continue its partnership status will be subject to a California tax equal to 1% of its California-source gross income attributable to the active conduct of any trade or business (a 3.5% tax on gross income attributable to the active conduct of any trade or business for federal purposes).

For a detailed discussion of limited liability partnerships, see ¶ 617. For a discussion of limited liability companies classified as partnerships, see ¶ 618.

● *Taxable year*

Generally, a partnership must use the same taxable year as the taxable year of a majority of its partners (usually a calendar year). However, certain partnerships may elect to change to a taxable year with a three-month deferral period. Federal law requires an entity making the election federally to make certain "required payments" to the IRS in exchange for deferral of the tax. California does not adopt the "required payments" requirement.

Partnership information is reported on Form 565 unless otherwise indicated.

¶ 612a Transactions Between Partner and Partnership

Law: Sec. 17851 (CCH CALIFORNIA TAX REPORTS ¶ 16-417, 16-428).

Comparable Federal: Secs. 704, 707, 721-24, 731-36 (CCH STANDARD FEDERAL TAX REPORTS ¶ 25,427, 25,480, 25,483, 25,523, 25,540, 25,600, 25,620—25,720, 25,722).

California law generally is the same as federal law (see ¶ 102a).

In keeping with the theory that a partnership is not a separate taxable entity, it has been the general rule that no gain or loss is recognized when property is transferred from a partner to a partnership or *vice versa.* Special rules applicable to specific situations have, to some extent, eroded that general rule, however. Distributions of money and distributions in liquidation of a partner's interest are subject to special rules under which gain or loss is sometimes recognized. Also, recognition treatment is accorded to distributions of appreciated property contributed by a partner when the property is distributed within seven years of its contribution (within five years for California purposes for taxable years beginning before 1998 and for federal purposes for property contributed to a partnership before June 9, 1997). See ¶ 530 for rules regarding basis of property contributed to or distributed by a partnership.

When a partner engages in a transaction with the partnership in a non-partner capacity, the partner is generally treated as an outsider. This provision does not apply, however, in the case of losses on such transactions where the partner holds more than a 50% interest in the partnership. Also, capital gain treatment is denied on certain sales or exchanges where a partner holds more than a 50% interest in a partnership or where the same group owns more than a 50% interest in two partnerships.

¶ 612b Transfer of Partnership Interest

> *Law:* Secs. 17851, 17855-57 (CCH CALIFORNIA TAX REPORTS ¶ 16-441, 16-444, 16-448).
>
> *Comparable Federal:* Secs. 736, 737, 741-55 (CCH STANDARD FEDERAL TAX REPORTS ¶ 25,740—25,880).

The sale of a partnership interest is generally considered to be the sale of a capital asset, with exceptions for cases where there are "unrealized receivables" or appreciated inventory.

The federal law is incorporated in California law by reference (see ¶ 102a). However, there are some specified California differences, as explained below.

The law provides special rules for treatment of "unrealized receivables" and appreciated inventory in the sale or liquidation of a partnership interest. The purpose is to prevent tax avoidance by converting profit on such items from ordinary income to capital gain. The federal definition of "unrealized receivables" includes the following items that are not included in the California definition: (1) stock in a Domestic International Sales Corporation (DISC); (2) stock in certain foreign corporations; and (3) certain oil, gas, and geothermal property. Also, federal law regarding appreciated inventory includes a provision relating to foreign investment companies that does not apply to California.

Under both California and federal law, if the partner receiving property in liquidation does not have enough available basis to cover the full amount of the partnership's basis in unrealized receivables and inventory, the shortfall in available basis must be accounted for. The difference between the partnership's basis in the unrealized receivables and inventory and the partner's substituted basis available for allocation is treated as a basis "decrease." The decrease is allocated first to properties with unrealized depreciation. Any remaining decrease is allocated to the properties in proportion to their respective adjusted bases.

For an example of ordinary-income treatment of "unrealized receivables" upon sale of a partnership interest, see *Appeal of Gerald H. and Dorothy A. Bense* (1979) (CCH CALIFORNIA TAX REPORTS ¶ 16-441.15).

¶ 613 Nonresident and Part-Year Resident Partners

> *Law:* Secs. 17951, 18535 (CCH CALIFORNIA TAX REPORTS ¶ 15-605, 16-467).
>
> *Comparable Federal:* None.
>
> *California Forms:* Form 540NR, Sch. CA (540NR).

● *Nonresident partners*

Nonresident partners are taxable on the portion of their distributive share of partnership income that is derived from sources within California. Such partners are taxable on any such income and may deduct their share of any loss attributable to California sources. See ¶ 230 for a discussion of taxable income of nonresidents and ¶ 117 for a credit nonresident partners may take on taxes paid other states on income also taxed by California.

An election to file a group return is available to nonresident partners of California partnerships or partnerships having California source income (this provision also applies to nonresident shareholders of S corporations). Election to file a group return relieves a nonresident partner of the responsibility of filing individually. The tax rate applicable to each partner's distributive share will be at the highest marginal rate. Only distributive deductions, those necessary to determine each partner's distributive share, are permitted (an exception is made for deferred-compensation deductions attributable to the partner's earned income from the partnership, provided this is the only earned income the partner has). Credits are restricted to those directly attributable to the partnership (e.g., as net income taxes paid to other states by the partnership) and do not include credits to which the nonresident may be otherwise entitled as an individual.

● *Part-year resident partners*

A part-year resident partner is taxed on his or her entire distributive share of partnership income if the partner is a California resident on the last day of the partnership's tax year (Instructions to Schedule CA (540NR)). A part-year resident partner who is a nonresident on the last day of the partnership's tax year is taxed in the same manner as a nonresident.

¶ 614 Computation of Partnership Income

Law: Secs. 17851-54, 17858 (CCH California Tax Reports ¶ 16-404, 16-417, 16-467).

Comparable Federal: Secs. 702, 703 (CCH Standard Federal Tax Reports ¶ 25,380, 25,400).

California law is substantially the same as federal law as of the current IRC tie-in date (see ¶ 102a), except that California deductions are not allowed to the partnership for state income taxes or political contributions.

Under both California and federal law, the taxable income of a partnership is computed in the same way as that of an individual, except that no deduction is allowed for charitable contributions or for personal items such as medical expenses. The individual partners are permitted to pick up their shares of the partnership contributions in their individual returns. Capital gains and losses of the partnership are segregated from other income so that the individual partners' shares may be picked up and combined with other capital gains and losses on their individual returns.

Guaranteed payments to partners for salary and interest are treated as though paid to an outsider, and are reported by the partners as separate items. In the case of a nonresident partner, guaranteed payments are treated as income from a California source.

A partner's share of a partnership loss may be deducted only to the extent of the adjusted basis of the partner's interest in the partnership at the end of the partnership year. However, such losses may be deducted in a subsequent year when the partner has sufficient basis to offset the loss.

Generally, elections affecting the computation of partnership income, such as depreciation, must be made on the partnership return; thus the amount of depreciation is not required to be recalculated by individual partners. However, certain elections are made by each partner separately.

See ¶ 1304 and ¶ 1305 regarding computation of California partnership income where a partnership is engaged in a unitary business with a corporate partner.

Special rules are provided for determining income of partnerships and partners, as part of the effort to restrict the use of various forms of tax shelters. These provisions include "at risk" limitations on losses (see ¶ 325), limitation on "bonus" depreciation (for pre-1987 tax years) (see ¶ 310b), limitations on deduction of syndication and organization expenses, specific rules for apportionment of income among partners, restrictions on deductions by farming syndicates, and use of the accrual method of accounting by certain farming partnerships.

¶ 615 Taxable Year in Which Income of Partner Includible

Law: Sec. 17851 (CCH CALIFORNIA TAX REPORTS ¶ 16-414).

Comparable Federal: Secs. 706, 708 (CCH STANDARD FEDERAL TAX REPORTS ¶ 25,460, 25,500).

California law is the same as federal law (see ¶ 102a).

The partner must report a distributive share of the partnership income for the taxable year (or years) of the partnership ending within or with the partner's taxable year. A partnership is limited in its choice of a taxable year (see ¶ 612). In order to adopt a taxable year other than that of its principal partners, the partnership must establish a business purpose.

¶ 616 Partnership Returns

Law: Secs. 18633, 19172, 19524 (CCH CALIFORNIA TAX REPORTS ¶ 16-464, 89-410).

Comparable Federal: Secs. 6011(e), 6031, 6698 (CCH STANDARD FEDERAL TAX REPORTS ¶ 36,581, 40,795).

California Form: Form 565.

Partnership returns are made on Form 565 and must be filed by the 15th day of the fourth month after the close of the partnership's taxable year. Returns must be filed by all partnerships (including real estate mortgage investment conduits treated as partnerships) having income from sources in California or engaging in a trade or business within California. Regardless of where the trade or business of the partnership is located, a partnership is considered to be doing business in California if any of its partners (general or limited) or other agents is conducting business in California on behalf of the partnership. Pertinent information from the return must be furnished to each partner and to each person who holds a partnership interest as a nominee for another person. The provision is the same as federal law. California also conforms to the federal reporting requirements of a partnership that has one or more exempt partners subject to the unrelated business tax. However, California does not conform to the federal requirement that all partnerships having more than 100 partners file returns on magnetic media.

California law imposes a special penalty, in addition to other penalties discussed at ¶ 710, for failure to file a timely and proper partnership return.

The penalty is $10 per month per partner, for a maximum of five months. This conforms generally to a federal penalty that is imposed at the rate of $50 per month per partner. However, the federal exception to the imposition of penalties for certain small partnerships does not apply for California purposes.

A partnership, other than a limited partnership or a limited liability partnership, carrying on no business in California and having no income from sources in California is not required to file a partnership return, even if the partnership consists of one or more California residents. However, if any partner is a California resident, a return must be filed if there is an election required to be made by the partnership, and the partners wish to obtain different California treatment with respect to the election than that chosen for federal purposes (e.g., installment method, exclusion from partnership provisions, etc.). Even if there are no partnership elections to be made and a return is not filed, a resident partner of a nonresident partnership may be required to submit information to determine whether or not there is any liability for California tax on partnership income; this may include information regarding the apportionment factors discussed in Chapter 13, as well as a copy of federal Form 1065. Limited partnerships and limited liability partnerships that have a certificate on file or are registered with the Secretary of State must file a return even if they are not doing business in California.

¶ 617 Limited Liability Partnerships

> *Law:* Secs. 16101, 16951, 16953, 16956, 16959, Corporation Code; Secs. 17948—17948.2, Revenue and Taxation Code (CCH CALIFORNIA TAX REPORTS ¶ 16-403).
>
> *Comparable Federal:* None.
>
> *California Form:* Form 565.

The formation of registered limited liability partnerships (LLPs) and the registration of foreign LLPs by legal and accounting firms is authorized in California. In addition, from January 1, 1999, through December 31, 2001, California authorizes architectural firms to operate as registered LLPs and foreign LLPs. A qualifying partnership, other than a limited partnership, may register as an LLP if all of the firm's partners are licensed, registered, or authorized to practice public accountancy or law (or, from January 1, 1999, through December 31, 2001, architecture), either in California or in another jurisdiction. A partnership that is related to an LLP and provides services related or complementary to the professional services provided by the LLP or provides services to the LLP may also register as an LLP. A partnership is considered related to an LLP if (1) at least a majority of the partners in one partnership are also partners in the other partnership; (2) at least a majority in interest in each partnership hold interest or are members in another entity and each renders services pursuant to an agreement with that other entity; or (3) one partnership controls, is controlled by, or is under common control with the other partnership.

● *LLPs subject to minimum tax*

An LLP must pay an annual nondeductible minimum tax if the LLP is doing business in California or has had its certificate of registration issued by the Secretary of State and has had a taxable year of more than 15 days. See ¶ 809 for the minimum tax rate.

● *Registration requirements*

To register as an LLP or foreign LLP, a partnership must file a registration statement with the Secretary of State and pay a fee of $70. A foreign LLP that transacts intrastate business in California without registration is subject to a penalty of $20 per day, up to a maximum of $10,000. In addition, as part of the registration requirement, all LLPs are required to provide specified amounts of security against any claims that might arise against the LLP.

¶ 617a Electing Large Partnerships

> *Law:* Sec. 17865 (CCH CALIFORNIA TAX REPORTS ¶ 16-463).
>
> *Comparable Federal:* Secs. 771--777 (CCH STANDARD FEDERAL TAX REPORTS ¶ 25,905--25,918).

California does not incorporate the federal provisions that authorize electing large partnerships, which may use simplified reporting systems and significantly reduce the number of items that must be separately reported to their partners. An "electing large partnership" is any nonservice partnership that elects to apply certain simplified reporting provisions, provided that the number of qualifying partners in the partnership was at least 100 during the preceding tax year.

An electing large partnership combines most items of partnership income, deduction, credit, and loss at the partnership level and passes through net amounts to the partners. Netting of capital gains and losses occurs at the partnership level, and passive activity items are separated from capital gains stemming from partnership portfolio income. Special rules apply to partnerships engaging in oil and gas activities.

¶ 618 Limited Liability Companies

> *Law:* Secs. 17087.6, 17941-46, 18535, 18633.5, 19172 (CCH CALIFORNIA TAX REPORTS ¶ 10-041).
>
> *Comparable Federal:* Reg. 301.7701-2 (CCH STANDARD FEDERAL TAX REPORTS ¶ 43,883).
>
> *California Forms:* Form 568, FTB 3522, FTB 3832, Sch. K-1 (568).

California authorizes the formation of limited liability companies (LLCs) and also allows foreign LLCs to qualify to do business in California. California conforms to federal "check-the-box" rules, and an LLC will be classified for California tax purposes according to the classification the LLC elects for federal purposes. The taxes and fees discussed below apply to LLCs classified as partnerships or that are disregarded and taxed as a sole proprietorship for California tax purposes. LLCs classified as corporations remain subject to the same tax return and tax payment requirements as any other corporation.

Effective January 1, 2000, California authorizes the formation of single member LLCs and allows a member of an LLC to have alter ego liability for the LLC's debts or other liabilities.

¶ 617a

● *Minimum tax*

An LLC that is classified as a partnership or that is disregarded and treated as a sole proprietorship for California tax purposes must pay an annual minimum tax if the LLC (1) is doing business in California or (2) has had its articles of organization accepted or a certificate of registration issued by the Secretary of State. The LLC is not liable for the tax if it did no business in California during the taxable year and the taxable year was 15 days or less. See ¶ 809 for the minimum tax rate. The tax is due by the 15th day of the fourth month after the beginning of the taxable year. (The taxable year of an LLC that was not previously in existence begins when the LLC is organized, registered, or begins doing business in California). If the 15th day of the fourth month of the taxable year has passed before an existing foreign LLC commences business in California or registers with the Secretary of State, the tax should be paid immediately after commencing business in California or registering with the Secretary of State.

CCH Example: When to Pay the Annual LLC Tax

DDLLC, a newly formed calendar-year taxpayer, organizes as an LLC in Delaware on June 1. DDLLC registers with the California Secretary of State on August 12, and begins doing business in California on August 13. Because DDLLC's initial tax year began on June 1, it must pay an annual LLC tax by September 15 (the 15th day of the fourth month of its short-period taxable year). Thereafter, its annual LLC tax is due on April 15th of each year.

● *Fee*

Additionally, every LLC classified as a partnership or treated as a sole proprietorship and subject to the minimum tax must pay an annual fee for the 1999 taxable year as follows: $865 if the total income of the LLC from all sources reportable to California for the taxable year is $250,000 or more, but less than $500,000; $2,595 if the total income is $500,000 or more, but less than $1 million; $5,190 if the total income is $1 million or more, but less than $5 million; and $7,785 if the total income is $5 million or more. For taxable years beginning after 1998, the Franchise Tax Board (FTB) is authorized to adjust the amount of the fees.

"Total income" means gross income plus the cost of goods sold that are paid or incurred in connection with the trade or business of the taxpayer. If, however, multiple LLCs are formed primarily to reduce the annual fees payable by members of a group of commonly controlled LLCs, the FTB may determine that the total income of a commonly controlled LLC is the aggregate total income of *all* the commonly controlled group members.

The LLC fee is due on the date the LLC return is required to be filed.

● *Returns*

LLCs classified as partnerships: An LLC classified as a partnership must file a return (Form 568) by the 15th day of the fourth month after the close of its taxable year. The LLC must attach to the return a Schedule K-1 (568) for

¶ 618

each member containing the member's name, address, and taxpayer identification number and the amount of the member's distributive share of the LLC's income, deductions, credits, etc. Also, when the LLC files its return, it must either (1) attach the agreement of each nonresident member to file a return, make timely tax payments, and be subject to personal jurisdiction in this state for purposes of the collection of income taxes (FTB 3832), or (2) pay tax on behalf of each nonconsenting nonresident member, computed by multiplying the member's distributive share of income by the highest marginal tax rate in effect. The return must be verified by a written declaration that it is made under the penalties of perjury, and it must be signed by one of the LLC members or managers. A copy of each member's Schedule K-1 (568) must be provided to that member. Unrelated business taxable income of an LLC must be separately stated to the members. Penalties are authorized for the failure to file an LLC return or provide LLC information as required by the FTB. Penalties are discussed in detail at ¶ 710.

LLCs treated as sole proprietorships: An owner of an LLC that is disregarded and treated as a sole proprietorship is required to file a California return if the LLC is doing business in California, is organized in California, or is registered with the Secretary of State. The return must contain information necessary to verify the tax liability for the minimum tax and LLC fees and must be filed by the 15th day of the fourth month after the close of the owner's income or taxable year. If the owner fails to comply with the reporting and payment requirements, the LLC will be liable for California tax at an amount equal to the highest marginal tax rate and will be subject to penalties and interest for failure to timely pay the amount due.

● *Returns of LLC members*

Persons with membership or economic interests in an LLC are required to include in their California taxable income their share of the LLC's California-source income in the same manner as partners must include their distributive share of partnership income in their taxable income (see ¶ 613, ¶ 614). As with nonresident partners of a partnership, nonresident members of an LLC may elect to file a group income tax return in lieu of filing individual returns (see ¶ 613).

● *Report to Secretary of State*

LLCs are required by Section 17060 of the Corporations Code to file with the Secretary of State a biennial report (an annual report prior to 2000) showing names of managers or members and other information. The first report must be filed within 90 days of filing original articles of organization. Thereafter, reports are due biennially by the date indicated by the Secretary of State on the form mailed to the LLC. LLCs may file a brief statement in lieu of the biennial report in cases where no changes have occured during the filing period.

CHAPTER 7

PERSONAL INCOME TAX
ADMINISTRATION, DEFICIENCIES, REFUNDS

¶ 701 Administration of Tax—General

> *Law:* Secs. 18624-25, 19501-11, 19525, 19717, 21001-26 (CCH CALIFORNIA TAX REPORTS ¶ 89-020, 89-167, 89-315, 89-510, 89-566).
>
> *Comparable Federal:* Secs. 6060, 6107, 6109, 6694-96, 7407, 7421, 7430, 7811 (CCH STANDARD FEDERAL TAX REPORTS ¶ 37,560, 37,960, 40,755—40,775, 40,833, 42,265, 42,315, 42,340).

California income tax law is administered by the Franchise Tax Board (FTB), composed of the State Controller, the Director of the Department of Finance, and the Chairman of the State Board of Equalization. The chief administrative officer is the Executive Officer of the FTB. The FTB has broad powers to prescribe necessary rules and regulations, etc.

¶ 701

If an audit of a return is concluded with no change, the FTB will notify the taxpayer to that effect; this procedure is similar to the federal one. For the procedure in case of underpayment or overpayment, see subsequent paragraphs in this chapter.

The FTB and the Internal Revenue Service (IRS) have exchanged tax-related data for many years. When an audit is conducted by either the FTB or the IRS, the results are reported to the other entity. See ¶ 104 regarding required California reporting of federal changes by taxpayers.

● *Tax-return preparers*

Tax preparers are required to (1) maintain a $5,000 bond for each individual preparing tax returns for another person; (2) provide in writing to each customer the tax preparer's name, address, telephone number, and evidence of compliance with the bonding requirements before rendering tax return preparation services; and (3) meet stringent educational requirements. Conversely, tax preparers are prohibited from (1) making deposits instead of complying with the bonding requirements; (2) making false, fraudulent, or misleading statements; (3) having taxpayers sign documents containing blank spaces to be filled in after they have been signed; (4) failing to sign taxpayers' returns; (5) failing to maintain copies of returns prepared for customers; and (6) failing to return taxpayers' records upon request.

Tax preparers must be at least age 18. Currently licensed public accountants, active members of the State Bar, employees of certain trust companies, financial institutions regulated by the state or federal government, and enrolled agents who practice before the IRS are exempt from compliance with the provisions governing tax preparers.

Federal law also provides for the regulation of "income tax preparers." California law conforms to federal requirements for furnishing copies of returns to taxpayers, retaining certain records, and providing identification numbers (social security numbers or IRS-approved alternatives) of preparers on returns and refund claims.

● *Issuance of rulings by FTB*

See ¶ 701b for a discussion.

● *FTB audit manuals*

The FTB has issued several audit manuals for the guidance of its staff. These manuals may be purchased from the Technical Analysis Section of the FTB; prices will be quoted upon request.

● *Recovery of litigation costs*

California law follows federal provisions that permit a taxpayer to recover litigation costs in a civil income tax proceeding if the taxpayer has exhausted all available administrative remedies, including the filing of an appeal before the State Board of Equalization, and the State is unable to establish that its position in the proceeding was substantially justified. Effective for costs incurred and services performed after April 7, 2000, in determining whether the position of the State was substantially justified, the court must take into

¶ 701

account whether the FTB has lost in any published California court of appeal case in another district involving substantially similar issues.

● *Taxpayers' bill of rights*

The legislature provides for the safeguarding of taxpayer privacy and property rights during the tax collection process. See ¶ 701a for a discussion.

● *Enforcement program*

Additional information returns, including returns of tax-shelter promoters, are required as explained at ¶ 711. The FTB is empowered to employ private in-state as well as out-of-state collection agencies and add their compensation to the amount of tax due. The FTB may establish a reward program for information leading to the collection of underreported taxes.

¶ 701a Taxpayers' Bill of Rights

Law: Secs. 19225, 21001-27 (CCH CALIFORNIA TAX REPORTS ¶ 89-230, 89-235, 89-510).

Comparable Federal: Sec. 7811 (CCH STANDARD FEDERAL TAX REPORTS ¶ 44,304).

Taxpayers dealing with the Franchise Tax Board (FTB) are given a wide range of protections under the "Katz-Harris Taxpayers' Bill of Rights". The provisions contained in the "Bill of Rights" are applicable to both the personal income and corporate franchise taxes. Similar "bills of rights" apply to unemployment insurance tax matters involving the Employment Development Department (see ¶ 712a) and property and sales and use tax matters involving the State Board of Equalization (SBE) (see ¶ 1506, ¶ 1708).

● *Hearing and appeal procedures*

Protest hearings before the FTB's audit or legal staff must be held at times and places that are reasonable and convenient to the taxpayer. Prior to the hearing, the taxpayer must be informed of the right to have a designated agent present. Hearings may be recorded only with prior notice to the taxpayer, who is entitled to receive a copy of any such recording. Protest hearings are discussed further at ¶ 702.

Taxpayers who appeal to the SBE and who are successful may be awarded reimbursement for reasonable fees and expenses related to the appeal that were incurred after the appeal was filed. The decision to make such an award is discretionary with the SBE, which must determine, in ruling on a reimbursement claim filed with the SBE, whether action taken by the FTB's staff was unreasonable, and in particular, whether the FTB has established that its position in the appeal was substantially justified. Effective for fees and expenses incurred after April 7, 2000, the starting point after which reasonable fees and expenses may be awarded is the date of the notice of proposed deficiency assessment rather than the date the appeal was filed. Also, effective for fees incurred after April 7, 2000, fees may be awarded in excess of the fees paid or incurred if the fees paid of incurred are less than reasonable fees.

For appeals to the SBE from an action of the FTB on a deficiency assessment protest or refund claim, the burden of proving the correctness of certain items of income reported by third parties on information returns filed with the FTB also shifts to the FTB if the taxpayer asserts a reasonable dispute with respect to the reported amounts and fully cooperates with the FTB. The items of income to which the shift applies are the same as under federal law.

Appeals to the SBE are discussed further at ¶ 703 and ¶ 714.

● *Tax levy protections*

Applicable to tax collection actions initiated after June 29, 2000, the FTB must send a notice of levy to a taxpayer at least 30 days prior to issuing a levy for unpaid tax. Also, if the FTB holds the collection of unpaid tax in abeyance for more than six months, the FTB is generally required to mail the taxpayer an additional notice prior to issuing a levy. A taxpayer may, within the 30-day period, request an independent administrative review and if a review is requested the levy action will be suspended until 15 days after there is a final determination in the review.

Except in the case of property seized as a result of a jeopardy assessment, a previously issued tax levy must be released in the following situations: (1) the expense of selling the property levied upon would exceed the taxpayer's liability; (2) the proceeds of the sale would not result in a reasonable reduction of the taxpayer's debt; (3) a determination is made by the Taxpayer Rights Advocate (a position established pursuant to the Taxpayers' Bill of Rights, with responsibility for investigating taxpayer complaints) that the levy threatens the health or welfare of the taxpayer or the taxpayer's family; (4) the levy was not issued in accordance with administrative procedures; (5) the taxpayer has entered into an installment payment agreement with the FTB to satisfy the tax liability for which the levy was made, and nothing in the agreement or any other agreement allows for the levy; (6) the release of the levy will facilitate the collection of the tax liability or will be in the best interest of the taxpayer and the State; or (7) the FTB otherwise deems the release of the levy appropriate. Certain household and other goods are exempted from levy under California's Code of Civil Procedure; the taxpayer must be notified in writing of these exemptions prior to the sale of any seized property. A taxpayer may be reimbursed for bank charges incurred as a result of an erroneous levy.

The FTB must release a levy on salary or wages as soon as practicable upon agreement with the taxpayer that the tax is not collectible. However, this requirement does not apply to any levy issued with respect to a debt that has been discharged because the tax debtor and/or the tax debtor's assets cannot be located, unless the debt is satisfied.

● *Civil actions against the FTB; litigation costs*

Taxpayers aggrieved by the reckless disregard of the FTB's published procedures on the part of an officer or employee of the FTB may bring a superior court action against the state for actual damages. In determining damages, the court must take into consideration any contributing negligence on the taxpayer's part. A taxpayer who prevails in such an action is entitled to reasonable litigation costs, but there is a penalty of up to $10,000 for filing frivolous claims.

¶ 701a

Taxpayers may also file a civil action against the State for direct economic damages and costs totaling up to $50,000 if an officer or employee of the FTB intentionally entices an attorney, certified public accountant, or tax preparer representing the taxpayer into disclosing taxpayer information in exchange for a compromise or settlement of the representative's tax liability. However, the action is not allowed if the information was conveyed by the taxpayer to the representative for the purpose of perpetuating a fraud or crime. The action must be brought within two years after the date the activities creating the liability were discoverable by the exercise of reasonable care.

● *Reliance on FTB written opinions; taxpayers' remedies*

See ¶ 701b for a complete discussion.

● *Tax liens*

A taxpayer is entitled to preliminary notice of the proposed filing or recording of a tax lien, mailed at least 30 days beforehand, and an opportunity in the interim to demonstrate by substantial evidence that the lien would be in error. Also, applicable to tax collection actions initiated after June 29, 2000, at least five business days after the date the notice of lien is filed the FTB must notify taxpayers in writing of the filing or recording of a notice of state tax lien and the taxpayer's right to an independent administrative review. A taxpayer must request a review during the 15-day period beginning on the day after the five-day period described above.

If the FTB finds that its action was in error, it must mail a release to the taxpayer and the lien recorder within seven working days. The FTB may also release a lien if it determines that the release will facilitate the collection of tax or will be in the best interest of the taxpayer and the State.

● *Unassociated payments*

If the FTB receives a payment from a taxpayer that the FTB cannot associate with the taxpayer's account, the FTB must make reasonable efforts to notify the taxpayer of this situation within 60 days after receipt of the payment.

● *Annual notice of tax delinquencies*

The FTB must mail an annual notice to each taxpayer who has a delinquent tax account, indicating the amount of the delinquency as of the date of the notice, unless a previously mailed notice has been returned to the FTB as undeliverable or the account has been discharged from accountability.

● *Other provisions*

The Taxpayers' Bill of Rights also obligates the FTB to undertake extensive taxpayer education and information programs; report annually to the legislature concerning areas of noncompliance with the tax laws; develop simplified written statements of taxpayer rights and FTB procedures; develop and implement an employee and officer evaluation program; and draw up plans to reduce the time required to resolve amended return claims for

¶ **701a**

refunds, protests, and appeals. The FTB is authorized to settle certain civil tax disputes (see ¶719). FTB officers and employees are prohibited from authorizing, requiring, or conducting an investigation or surveillance of taxpayers for reasons unrelated to tax administration.

¶701b Reliance on FTB's Advice

Law: Sec. 21012 (CCH CALIFORNIA TAX REPORTS ¶ 89-410, 89-510).

Comparable Federal: Sec. 6404(f) (CCH STANDARD FEDERAL TAX REPORTS ¶ 39,520).

Under the "Taxpayers' Bill of Rights" (see ¶701a), taxpayers may be relieved from penalties, interest, and even tax liability itself in certain cases in which there was detrimental reliance on written advice from the Franchise Tax Board (FTB).

● *Taxpayer's reliance on FTB rulings*

The following concerns the waiver of tax, penalties, and interest in situations in which the taxpayer relied on the FTB's own written advice (FTB Notice No. 89-277, CCH CALIFORNIA TAX REPORTS ¶ 89-050.25):

Waiver of tax: If a taxpayer's failure to timely file or pay is due to reasonable reliance on a Chief Counsel Ruling or an Opinion Letter, the taxpayer may be relieved—under the proper conditions (see below)—of having to pay *the tax itself,* as well as any interest, penalty, or addition to the tax.

Waiver of penalties, interest, and additions to tax only: If the taxpayer relies on FTB correspondence other than Chief Counsel Rulings or Opinion Letters, such as standard computer-generated letters issued in response to frequently asked questions, the taxpayer may be relieved—under the proper conditions (see below)—of having to pay any interest, penalty, or addition to the tax; the taxpayer will not be relieved of having to pay the tax itself.

Conditions for waiver: All of the following conditions must be met for the taxpayer to receive a waiver: (1) the taxpayer must have made a written request that the FTB indicate whether a particular activity or transaction is taxable and must have described in the request all of the facts and circumstances involved; (2) the FTB must have responded in writing, stating whether the activity was taxable or the conditions under which it would be taxable; (3) the taxpayer must have failed to remit tax in reliance on the FTB's advice; (4) the FTB's ruling must not have been revoked before the taxpayer relied on it; and (5) there must have been no change in applicable state or federal law or in the facts or circumstances of the taxpayer's case.

● *How to make a proper advance ruling request*

A written request for an advance ruling must contain the taxpayer's name, identifying number, and a statement of all facts relating to the transaction from which the tax question arises. In addition, the request must disclose if the same question arose in (1) a prior year's return, (2) an ongoing audit, protest, or appeal, or (3) litigation involving the taxpayer (FTB Notice No. 89-277, *supra*).

CCH Tip: How a Taxpayer May Seek Relief

If the FTB acts in a way that appears inconsistent with its written advice to the taxpayer, the taxpayer may seek relief following one of two courses. If the advice was not issued by the FTB's legal division, the taxpayer must file FTB 3910 (Request for Waiver of Tax, Penalty or Interest). If the advice was issued by the FTB's Chief Counsel or another member of the FTB's legal division, the taxpayer must mail a written request for relief to the Chief Counsel, enclosing (1) a copy of the original written request for an opinion and the FTB's written response, (2) documentation of the adverse action subsequently taken by the FTB, and (3) a sworn statement that describes the activity or transaction in which the taxpayer engaged and that states that the failure to remit tax was due to reliance on the FTB's opinion. The request for relief must be made separately from any protest or appeal filed by the taxpayer.

● *Oral advice*

The FTB may also respond to individual queries with nonbinding oral advice, which is purely advisory. A taxpayer who relies on such advice is not entitled to the relief provisions of the Taxpayers' Bill of Rights (FTB Notice No. 89-277, *supra*).

● *Effect of federal regulations and procedures*

The FTB will generally follow federal regulations, procedures, and rulings in situations in which the California provisions substantially conform to those of federal law. However, federal rulings and procedures are not binding on the FTB if the FTB has publicly indicated in writing that the federal ruling or procedure will not be followed (FTB Notice No. 89-277, *supra*).

¶ 702 Deficiencies—Procedure, Protests

> *Law:* Secs. 19031-36, 19041-44, 19050-51, 19133 (CCH California Tax Reports ¶ 89-101, 89-302, 89-410, 89-523).
>
> *Comparable Federal:* Secs. 6103, 6201, 6211-13 (CCH Standard Federal Tax Reports ¶ 37,880, 38,502, 38,535—55).

If the Franchise Tax Board (FTB) determines after examining an original or amended return that additional tax is payable, it may proceed in any one of the following five ways:

1. if the additional tax is due to a mathematical error, the FTB sends the taxpayer a notice and requests payment of the tax; the taxpayer has no right of protest or appeal in such cases;

2. if the FTB is of the opinion that collection of the deficiency will be jeopardized by delay, it may make a jeopardy assessment (see ¶ 705);

3. if the taxpayer fails to make a required return after notice and demand by the FTB, the FTB may estimate the income and levy the tax from any available information; in such cases the tax is immediately due

and payable, without administrative remedies prior to payment, and a special penalty of 25% of the tax is added (see ¶ 710); and

4. in other cases the FTB will mail to the taxpayer a notice of proposed deficiency assessment (sometimes referred to as an NPA), which must include an explanation of the adjustments made, a computation of the deficiency, and, applicable to notices mailed after 1999, the date determined by the FTB as the last day on which the taxpayer may file a written protest.

In *Appeal of Melvin D. Collamore* (CCH CALIFORNIA TAX REPORTS ¶ 15-350.63), involving the personal income tax, and in *Appeal of Kung Wo Company, Inc.* (CCH CALIFORNIA TAX REPORTS ¶ 89-302.69), involving the franchise tax, the State Board of Equalization held that the FTB can properly make two deficiency assessments against a taxpayer for the same taxable year.

● *Protest*

A taxpayer who does not agree with the notice of proposed deficiency assessment may file a protest. The protest must be filed within 60 days from the mailing date of the notice of proposed assessment. There is no provision for extension of time for filing a protest. Any protest filed by the last day for filing the protest, as specified by the FTB in a notice of proposed deficiency assessment mailed after 1999, will be treated as timely filed.

A protest must state the grounds on which it is based. Otherwise it is not necessary that the protest be in a particular form, although the FTB will supply a form upon request. The protest should be signed by the taxpayer; however it may be signed by the taxpayer's representative if accompanied by a power of attorney. It is not required to be under oath. There is no requirement for filing more than one copy, although it is a good idea to file an extra copy for the convenience of the FTB, along with a copy of the notice of proposed assessment. It is also suggested that the protest be filed with the FTB at Sacramento, although it may be filed if desired at one of the branch offices.

● *Oral hearing*

If an oral hearing is desired, request must be made in the protest. Unless otherwise specified in the request, the hearing usually will be arranged at the branch office of the FTB nearest to the taxpayer's address. A taxpayer who wishes to be represented by others at the hearing should so state in the written protest; arrangements will be made accordingly. The oral hearings are informal.

● *Power of attorney*

No power of attorney is required as evidence of the authority of the taxpayer's representative to discuss the case, provided the taxpayer has indicated, in the protest or otherwise, a desire to be so represented. However, a representative may not take any definite action on the taxpayer's behalf without a power of attorney definitely authorizing the representative to act. The FTB provides FTB 3520 for this purpose. There is no requirement that representatives be admitted to practice or have particular qualifications to be eligible to represent taxpayers.

¶ 702

¶ 703 Deficiencies—Appeal to State Board of Equalization

Law: Secs. 19045-48 (CCH CALIFORNIA TAX REPORTS ¶ 89-523, 89-541).

Comparable Federal: Secs. 6211-15 (CCH STANDARD FEDERAL TAX REPORTS ¶ 38,535—55).

Upon receiving notice of action by the Franchise Tax Board (FTB) on the taxpayer's protest, the taxpayer may appeal to the State Board of Equalization (SBE). The appeal must be filed by the appeal filing date specified in the FTB's notice (within 30 days of the date of the FTB's notice); in the absence of an appeal, the FTB's action becomes final at the expiration of the 30-day period as specified in the notice.

Two copies of the appeal and two copies of any supporting documents must be sent to the SBE in Sacramento, which will send a copy of each document to the FTB.

● *Requirements for appeal*

FTB Regulation 5012 covering hearing procedures before the SBE provides that the appeal must be in writing, should state the fact that an appeal is being made, and should include the following information:

(a) name of appellant (or appellants);

(b) amounts and years involved;

(c) date of notice of action by FTB;

(d) statement of facts;

(e) points and authorities in support of the taxpayer's position;

(f) statement of portion of tax the taxpayer concedes is owing; and

(g) signature of appellant (or appellants) or authorized representative.

The appeal may be supplemented at a later date, provided the original appeal is filed timely. If additional data is requested by the SBE and it is not provided by the taxpayer within the time requested (including reasonable extensions of time granted by the SBE), the appeal may be dismissed. Upon receipt of an appeal, the SBE gives the FTB an opportunity to file an answer, and gives the taxpayer an opportunity to file a reply if desired.

● *Hearing on appeal*

The SBE will set a time and place for hearing on the appeal and will so notify the taxpayer or the taxpayer's representatives. Hearings are more formal than the oral hearings before the FTB, sworn testimony being taken and other formalities observed. Taxpayers' representatives are not required to be admitted to practice before the SBE.

After the hearing, the SBE notifies the taxpayer and the FTB of its determination. Either the taxpayer or the FTB may file a petition for rehearing within 30 days of the time of the determination. If such petition is not filed, the determination becomes final at the expiration of the 30-day period; if a petition is filed, the determination becomes final 30 days after the SBE issues its opinion on the petition.

The SBE has published a booklet entitled "Appeals Procedures" and will supply a copy upon request.

● *Suit to establish residence*

See ¶ 103 for a description of a special procedure whereby a person who is alleged to be a California resident can file a suit to determine the issue of residency without first paying the tax. Otherwise, there is no provision in California law for filing suit until after the tax is paid. See ¶ 716 regarding suits for refund.

¶ 704 Final Assessment of Deficiency

Law: Secs. 19042, 19049 (CCH CALIFORNIA TAX REPORTS ¶ 89-302, 89-523).

Comparable Federal: Secs. 6213, 6402 (CCH STANDARD FEDERAL TAX REPORTS ¶ 38,545, 38,549).

A deficiency assessment becomes final, in the absence of protest, at the expiration of the 60-day period allowed for protest after mailing of the notice of proposed deficiency. If a protest is filed, the assessment becomes final at a later date as explained above in ¶ 702 and ¶ 703. When the assessment becomes final, the Franchise Tax Board mails to the taxpayer a notice and demand for payment of the tax and interest. Except as noted below, the amount is due and payable within 15 days of the date of the notice and demand.

A federal provision enacted by the IRS Restructuring and Reform Act of 1998 allows the IRS to offset past-due, legally enforceable state income tax debts that have been reduced to judgment against any federal tax refunds due to the same taxpayer after 1999.

¶ 705 Jeopardy Assessments

Law: Secs. 19081-86, 19093 (CCH CALIFORNIA TAX REPORTS ¶ 89-306, 89-535).

Comparable Federal: Sec. 6861 (CCH STANDARD FEDERAL TAX REPORTS ¶ 41,260).

If the Franchise Tax Board (FTB) finds that the collection of a tax or deficiency for any year will be jeopardized by delay, it may make an immediate assessment. As to the current period, it may declare the taxable period immediately terminated. Any such assessment is immediately due and payable, but the taxpayer may stay collection by filing within 30 days a bond in the amount of the tax and accrued interest, or other security in such amount as the FTB may require. Any jeopardy assessment is also a deficiency assessment, if such an assessment has not already been issued for that tax year and amount.

No jeopardy assessment may be made and no levy may be issued less than 30 days after notice and demand is mailed for payment or for a return and payment, unless the Chief Counsel of the FTB or the Chief Counsel's delegate personally approves, in writing, the assessment or levy.

The taxpayer may file a petition for reassessment within 30 days after the FTB furnishes the taxpayer with a written statement of the information upon which it relied in issuing the notice and demand. If the taxpayer so requests, an oral hearing will be granted, and under certain conditions the taxpayer may appeal to the State Board of Equalization (SBE). If no petition for reassessment is filed, the assessment becomes final at the end of the 30-day period.

The taxpayer or the FTB may file a civil action within 60 days in superior court to appeal the decision of the SBE. If no civil action is commenced, the SBE's determination is final.

In *Pierre Roland Dupuy* (1975) (CCH CALIFORNIA TAX REPORTS ¶ 89-556.82), the taxpayer sought an injunction against seizure and sale of his property under a jeopardy assessment. The matter reached the California Supreme Court, which discussed the constitutional questions involved and concluded that an injunction may be issued in some circumstances in the interests of "due process."

¶ 706 Bankruptcy and Receiverships

Law: Secs. 19088-91 (CCH CALIFORNIA TAX REPORTS ¶ 89-308).

Comparable Federal: Secs. 6871-73 (CCH STANDARD FEDERAL TAX REPORTS ¶ 41,410, 41,440, 41,450).

California law is generally the same as federal law.

Special provisions apply to taxpayers in bankruptcy or receivership. In such cases the tax may be assessed immediately. The running of the statute of limitations is suspended under certain circumstances. Claims for tax are adjudicated by the court before which the bankruptcy or receivership procedure is pending, despite any appeal which may be pending before the State Board of Equalization.

Anyone who is appointed trustee, receiver, assignee, or other fiduciary in a receivership or bankruptcy situation is required to give the Franchise Tax Board notice of the appointment. Failure to give timely notice may suspend the running of the period of limitations on assessments.

¶ 707 Transferee Liability

Law: Secs. 19006, 19071-74 (CCH CALIFORNIA TAX REPORTS ¶ 89-107, 89-310).

Comparable Federal: Secs. 6013, 6901-4 (CCH STANDARD FEDERAL TAX REPORTS ¶ 36,460, 41,500—41,640).

The law contains provisions permitting assessment and collection of tax from persons secondarily liable. The period of limitations is extended for assessments against transferees and fiduciaries. California law is the same as federal law.

Both California and federal laws provide for suspension of the running of the period of limitations against the transferee while the taxpayer is exercising an administrative remedy.

California law also provides that the spouse who controls the disposition of, as well as the spouse who is taxable on, community income is liable for the tax on such income. There is no comparable federal provision.

In *Appeal of Robert D. Burch* (1968) (CCH CALIFORNIA TAX REPORTS ¶ 89-541.28), the Franchise Tax Board held a husband liable for an additional assessment against his former wife, because the husband controlled the disposition of the community income involved, but contended that the husband was not entitled to appeal the wife's assessment. The State Board of Equalization permitted the appeal.

¶ 708 Statute of Limitations on Assessments

> **Law:** Secs. 18529, 19057-67, 19087, 19371 (CCH California Tax Reports ¶ 89-107, 89-302, 89-304).
>
> **Comparable Federal:** Secs. 1311-14, 6501-4, 7609 (CCH Standard Federal Tax Reports ¶ 33,300—33,360, 39,910—40,000, 43,790).

The California statute of limitations on assessments applies to the date for mailing a notice of proposed deficiency assessment, whereas the federal law applies to the date of the actual assessment of tax. The California rules governing time limits on assessment are summarized below. (The statute of limitations on tax *collection* is discussed below under "Statute of limitations on collections.")

(a) **General rule**—Taxes may be assessed up to four years after the return required to be filed by the taxpayer is filed. A return filed before the "last day prescribed by law for filing," determined without regard to any extension of time for filing, is deemed to have been filed on such last day. The federal limitation period is three years, with the same rule about returns filed before the regular due date.

(b) **Waivers**—The taxpayer may agree to an extension of the limitation period. Applicable to statute of limitations waivers requested after December 31, 2000, the Franchise Tax Board (FTB) must notify a taxpayer of his or her right to (1) refuse to extend the statute of limitations for assessments or (2) limit the extension to a particular period of time. This is the same as the federal rule. The California law has an additional provision that *automatically* extends the limitation period whenever the taxpayer has signed a waiver extending the statute of limitations for federal purposes. The automatic extension runs to six months after the expiration date of the federal waiver.

(c) **Omission of over 25% of income**—Where a taxpayer's return omits gross income in excess of 25% of the gross income stated in the return, the limitation date is six years after the return was filed. This provision is comparable to the federal rule.

(d) **False or no return**—Where no return or a false or fraudulent return was filed, there is no period of limitation on assessment or collection of tax. The California rule is the same as the federal one.

(e) **Failure to report changes or amendment of federal returns**—Where the taxpayer fails to report any change of income or deductions made by federal authorities or fails to file an amended California return when required (see ¶ 104), a notice of proposed deficiency may be mailed at any time after the change or amended return is reported to or filed with the federal government. This rule applies only to the effect of the adjustments made by the federal authorities, or to the items changed in an amended federal return.

(f) **Amended return filed or federal change reported**—When the taxpayer does file an amended return or otherwise reports a federal change within the required time (see ¶ 104), the limitation date for deficiencies "resulting from such adjustments" is two years after the filing of the amended return or report, or the date provided in (a) or (c) above, whichever is later. If an amended return is filed or a federal change is reported by the taxpayer after the prescribed time for doing so has expired, the limitation period for deficiencies is four years from the date the amended return or report is filed. Effective for federal determinations that become final after 1999, the two year limitation period applies to notifications made by the IRS, as well as by the taxpayer, within six months of the final federal determination or filing of an amended federal return.

(g) **Change from separate to joint returns**—Where taxpayers elect to change from separate to joint returns (see ¶ 104a), the otherwise applicable limitation period includes one additional year after the date of filing on the new basis.

(h) **Sale of residence**—Where the taxpayer has claimed the benefit of the special provisions regarding sale and replacement of a residence (see ¶ 502a), the limitation period is extended to four years from the date the FTB received notice from the taxpayer regarding replacement of the residence, etc. The federal rule is the same except that the period is three years.

(i) **Involuntary conversion**—If the taxpayer elects not to recognize gain on involuntary conversion where replacement property is purchased (see ¶ 502), the limitation period is extended to four years from the date the FTB receives notice from the taxpayer regarding the replacement, etc. The federal period is three years.

(j) **"Federally registered partnerships"**—The limitation date for assessments against partners is extended under certain conditions.

(k) **Installment sales between related parties**—The limitation period may be extended under certain circumstances.

(*l*) **Additional tax liability shown within 60 days of limitation date for assessment**—Where, within the 60-day period ending on the limitation date for assessment, the FTB receives from the taxpayer a signed document, other than an amended return or report required to be filed due to a federal change or correction (see ¶ 104), showing that the taxpayer owes an additional amount of tax for the taxable year, the period for assessment of that additional amount is extended to 60 days after the document is received by the FTB.

(m) **Subpoenaed person's intervention**—The statute of limitations for assessment is suspended in certain cases involving actions by taxpayers to quash subpoenas to other persons. This conforms to federal law.

● *Special rules*

In the case of members of the Armed Forces, disaster victims, and certain other taxpayers who are outside the United States for a period of time, the statute of limitations is automatically extended under certain conditions (see ¶ 106).

¶ **708**

The limitation period for an estate or trust may be shortened to 18 months (see ¶ 610).

The running of the period of limitations is suspended for any period during which the FTB is precluded from action by bankruptcy laws and for 60 days thereafter; the California rule is the same as the federal one. Also, the running of the period of limitations may be suspended where a fiduciary fails to give timely notice of his or her appointment (see ¶ 706).

California law contains nothing similar to IRC Secs. 1311-14, which mitigate the effect of the statute of limitations in certain situations where an inconsistent position is maintained.

● *Statute of limitations on collections*

California's statute of limitations on court actions to collect tax deficiencies, penalties, and interest is ten years. The period runs from the time the taxpayer's liability for tax, penalties, or interest is first determined, but does not apply in situations in which a tax lien is properly in force.

● *Decisions of State Board of Equalization*

Appeal of Orville H. and Jeanne K. Haag (1977) (CCH CALIFORNIA TAX REPORTS ¶ 89-304.154) involved the application of rule (c) above. The taxpayers failed to report $67,257 of dividends received from an S corporation. The omitted income exceeded 25% of the gross income on the return. However, the reconciliation in the return between federal and state income showed that S corporation income was reported on the federal but not on the state return. The State Board of Equalization (SBE) held that the reconciling item was sufficient to put the FTB on notice as to the possibility of additional California income; it followed that the statute of limitations was not extended and the proposed assessment was not timely.

In *Appeal of Phillip Yordan* (1958) (CCH CALIFORNIA TAX REPORTS ¶ 89-304.253), the SBE applied rule (e) above in a situation where the taxpayer did report the federal adjustments but did not do so within the specified time limit. Similarly, see *Appeal of the Pullman Company* (1972) (CCH CALIFORNIA TAX REPORTS ¶ 89-304.258), involving the comparable provision of the corporation tax law. In the *Pullman* case, state assessments for the years 1938 through 1943 were not made until 1957, based on a Tax Court settlement that became final in 1955. See also *Appeal of Vinemore Company, etc.* (1972) (CCH CALIFORNIA TAX REPORTS ¶ 11-361.15), holding that notice of a Federal Revenue Agent's Report did not constitute the required notice where the final determination was made later in a Tax Court proceeding.

¶ 709 Interest on Deficiencies

Law: Secs. 19101-17, 19521 (CCH CALIFORNIA TAX REPORTS ¶ 89-430, 89-436).

Comparable Federal: Secs. 6404, 6601, 6621, 6622 (CCH STANDARD FEDERAL TAX REPORTS ¶ 40,310, 40,340, 40,360).

California Form: FTB 3701.

Interest is charged upon deficiencies or other delinquent payments of tax (see ¶ 107 for interest charged during extension periods). Interest is compounded daily. As to certain individuals, the running of interest may be suspended for a period because of their absence from the United States—see ¶ 106.

California imposes interest on tax underpayments at the federal underpayment rate. However, while the federal rate changes on a quarterly basis, the California rate is adjusted semiannually.

Interest rates are as follows:

January 1, 1996—June 30, 1996	9%
July 1, 1996—December 31, 1996	9%
January 1, 1997—June 30, 1997	9%
July 1, 1997—December 31, 1997	9%
January 1, 1998—June 30, 1998	9%
July 1, 1998—December 31, 1998	9%
January 1, 1999—June 30, 1999	8%
July 1, 1999—December 31, 1999	7%
January 1, 2000—June 30, 2000	8%

● *Interest is mandatory*

The imposition of interest is not a penalty, but is considered to be compensation for the taxpayer's use of money. The assessment of interest is mandatory, regardless of the reason for the late payment of tax. See *Appeal of Robert M. and Mildred Scott* (1981) (CCH CALIFORNIA TAX REPORTS ¶ 89-430.25), and other cases involving this point. However, as noted below, under some circumstances interest may be waived.

● *Special rules for related taxpayers or items*

In certain cases involving related taxpayers or related items where overpayments are offset against deficiencies, no interest is charged on the portion of the deficiency extinguished by the credit for overpayment for the period subsequent to the date the overpayment was made. This rule applies in the following situations:

(a) where a deficiency owed by a husband is offset by an overpayment by his wife for the same year, or vice versa;

(b) where a deficiency owed by a taxpayer for any year is offset by an overpayment by the same taxpayer for any other year; and

(c) in the cases of estates, trusts, parents and children (including in-laws), or husbands and wives, where the correction of an error results in a deficiency for one taxpayer and an overpayment for a related taxpayer.

There are no comparable federal provisions with respect to items (a) and (c). Item (b) is somewhat similar to a federal provision whereby interest is not imposed on deficiencies satisfied by overpayment credits under certain conditions.

In *Appeal of John L. Todd* (1952) (CCH CALIFORNIA TAX REPORTS ¶ 89-430.40), the State Board of Equalization (SBE) considered the effect of this rule in a case where the tax was paid in installments. The case involved a deficiency against the husband and an overpayment of exactly the same amount by the wife. The SBE held that there was no overpayment by the wife until she paid her last installment, so interest was properly chargeable on the husband's deficiency from the due date of the return to the date of the last installment.

● *Rules for imposition of interest*

The law contains detailed rules regarding interest on deficiencies. Principal provisions of these rules are as follows:

(a) interest is assessed, collected, and paid in the same manner as the tax;

(b) interest is assessed on tax deficiencies from the due date of the tax without regard for any extension of time that may have been granted and without regard to any notice of jeopardy assessment issued prior to the last date prescribed for the payment of such deficiency;

(c) interest is normally assessed on a penalty from (1) the date of notice and demand for payment or (2) the date of the deficiency notice; however, as to certain penalties, interest is imposed from the due date of the return;

(d) if an amount is paid within 15 days following notice and demand for payment, no interest will be charged for the period after the date of the notice and demand;

(e) if tax is satisfied by an overpayment credit, interest is not imposed on such tax for any period during which interest was allowable on the overpayment;

(f) interest may be assessed and collected any time during the period within which the related tax may be collected; and

(g) no interest may be imposed for the period between 45 days after the date of final audit review and the date a notice of proposed assessment is sent to the taxpayer.

Applicable to taxable years ending after October 10, 1999, if an individual files a timely return and the Franchise Tax Board (FTB) fails to issue a notice specifically stating the taxpayer's liability and the basis for such liability within 18 months following the later of the original due date of the return or the date on which a timely return is filed, the FTB must generally suspend the imposition of interest during the period commencing on the date after the 18-month period expires until 15 days after the FTB sends the required notice. The suspension does not apply to any interest amount involving fraud or any additional amount shown on the return. Federal law is similar, except that the 18-month period is shortened to one year for federal tax years beginning after 2003. Special rules apply when a taxpayer is required to report a federal change or correction to the state. In that case, the FTB has either one or two years from the date the taxpayer or the IRS reports the federal change or correction to issue a notice before interest is suspended, depending on whether the change or correction is reported within six months or more than six months after the final federal determination.

 CCH Example: Suspension of Interest

Ken gets an automatic extension of time to file his 1999 California personal income tax return and timely files on September 1, 2000. Ken inadvertently fails to include $1,000 of interest income on the return. The FTB sends Ken the required notice on June 1, 2002, and Ken pays the tax deficiency on July 15, 2002. Ken owes

---

¶ 709

interest on the tax deficiency from April 17, 2000 (the original due date of the return), through March 1, 2002 (the last day of the 18-month period). Interest is suspended from March 2, 2002, through June 15, 2002. Interest runs again from June 16, 2002 (the 15th day after notice was provided), until July 15, 2002 (the date of payment of the tax deficiency).

● *Notice of interest charges*

Each notice issued after December 31, 2001, that states an amount of interest required to be paid must include the code section under which the interest is imposed and a description of how the interest is computed. Upon request of the taxpayer, the FTB must also provide a computation of the interest.

● *Waiver and abatement of interest*

Interest may be waived for any period for which the FTB determines that the taxpayer cannot pay because of extreme financial hardship caused by catastrophic circumstance. In addition, the FTB is authorized to abate the assessment of interest whenever

(1) a deficiency is attributable at least in part to an unreasonable error or delay of an FTB officer or employee, or

(2) a delay in payment is the result of dilatory conduct on the part of an FTB officer or employee performing a ministerial or managerial act in an official capacity, or

(3) a deficiency is based on a final federal determination of tax for the same period that interest was abated on the related federal deficiency amount, provided that the error or delay to which the deficiency is attributable occurred on or before the issuance of the final federal determination.

A request for such an abatement may be made by submitting FTB 3701 to the FTB. If a request for abatement of interest is made and the FTB mails the taxpayer a determination not to abate interest, the taxpayer may appeal the FTB's determination to the SBE within 180 days after the mailing of the notice. The FTB may also waive interest in certain cases in which the taxpayer has relied on the FTB's written advice (see ¶ 701b).

In addition, both California and federal law require the abatement of interest imposed against any individual taxpayer (excluding trusts and estates) located in a presidentially declared disaster area for any period that the FTB (IRS for federal purposes) (1) extended the taxpayer's period for filing an income tax return and paying income tax with respect to such return and (2) waived any corresponding penalties. Applicable to disasters declared after 1997 with respect to taxable years beginning after 1997, California differs from the federal law by (1) extending relief to taxpayers in Governor declared disaster areas and (2) requiring taxpayers seeking relief to have incurred a loss, in addition to being located in a disaster area.

¶ 709

● *Interest on erroneous overpayment to taxpayer*

Interest may be assessed and collected if the FTB makes an erroneous overpayment to a taxpayer. Interest accrues 30 days from the date the FTB mails notice for repayment. The FTB is required to abate interest on erroneous refunds that accrue prior to the date the demand for payment is made unless the action of the taxpayer caused the erroneous refund or the refund exceeds $50,000.

¶ 710 Penalties

> *Law:* Secs. 17299.8, 17299.9, 18633.5, 19011, 19116, 19131-36.3, 19164, 19166-67, 19169, 19172-79, 19181-87, 19701-01.5, 19705-06, 19708-09, 19711-15, 19720-21 (CCH CALIFORNIA TAX REPORTS ¶ 89-231, 89-410, 89-420).

> *Comparable Federal:* Secs. 6111-12, 6404, 6651-53, 6657-58, 6662, 6663, 6671-6674, 6693-95, 6698, 6700-06, 6707, 6721-24, 7201-07, 7408 (CCH STANDARD FEDERAL TAX REPORTS ¶ 5229P, 5230, 38,000, 38,020, 40,370-400, 40,510, 40,520, 40,540, 40,580, 40,585, 40,745-765, 40,770, 40,825-845, 40,875, 40,885, 40,905, 40,965-995, 42,005-025, 42,270).

[*Note:* See ¶ 701b for a discussion of relief provisions under the Taxpayers' Bill of Rights.]

Penalties are provided as follows:

(1) failing to report personal services remuneration—disallowance of deduction; unreported amount multiplied by the highest personal income tax rate;

(2) failing to report real estate transaction—disallowance of related deductions;

(3) failing to comply with requirement to remit payment by electronic funds transfer without reasonable cause—10% of amount paid;

(4) failing to file return without reasonable cause—5% per month, up to 25%; for individuals, after 60 days, at least the lesser of $100 or 100% of tax; if fraudulent, 15% per month, up to a 75% maximum;

(5) failing to pay amount on return by due date or within 15 days of notice and demand without reasonable cause (10 days for notices issued before 1998), or, for limited liability companies, failing to pay the income tax liability of a nonresident member when required to do so—5% of unpaid amount plus 0.5% per month of remaining tax, up to 25% of unpaid amount;

(6) failing to furnish requested information or to file return on notice and demand by Franchise Tax Board (FTB) without reasonable cause—25% of deficiency or of tax amount for which information was requested;

(7) failing to make small business stock report without reasonable cause—$50 per report; $100 if failure due to negligence or intentional disregard;

(8) dishonored check or electronic funds transfer—the lesser of $15 or amount of check; 2% of amount of check if check is for $750 or more;

(9) underpayment of estimated tax—see ¶ 107a;

(10) negligence, substantial underpayment, etc. without reasonable cause—20% of underpayment attributable to violation; 40% for gross valuation misstatements;

(11) fraud—75% of underpayment attributable to fraud;

(12) understatement by return preparer—$250 per return; $1,000 if willful or reckless;

(13) failure of tax preparer to give taxpayer copy of return, furnish identifying number, or retain copy or list—$50 for each failure up to $25,000 per return period;

(14) negotiation or endorsement of client's refund check by tax preparer—$250 per check plus criminal penalty (misdemeanor) of up to $1,000 and/or up to 1 year in jail, and costs of prosecution;

(15) failing to file partnership return—$10 multiplied by number of partners;

(16) failing to file tax shelter promoter return within 60 days of FTB request—$1,000 multiplied by number of investors;

(17) failing to maintain records to substantiate tax shelter promoter return—$1,000 multiplied by number of investors;

(18) making false statements in connection with withholding—$500;

(19) promoting abusive tax shelter—lesser of $1,000 or 100% of gross income derived or to be derived from violation; injunction to prohibit taxpayer actions;

(20) aiding or abetting understatement of tax liability—$1,000;

(21) filing frivolous return—$500;

(22) failing to meet original issue discount reporting requirements without reasonable cause—1% of aggregate issue price, up to $50,000 per issue;

(23) failing to furnish information concerning tax shelter—greater of 1% of aggregate investment or $500;

(24) failing to timely register a confidential corporate tax shelter— the greater of $10,000 or 50% of promoters fees (75% if intentional);

(25) failing to file information return or furnish payee statement— $50 per violation up to $100,000 per year for payee statements or $250,000 per year for information returns; the greater of $100 or 5% or 10% of the items to be reported, depending on the return involved, if intentional disregard of requirements;

(26) failing to provide written explanation—$10 per failure up to $5,000;

(27) failing to file information report regarding individual retirement account (IRA) or annuity—$50 per failure;

(28) overstatement of nondeductible IRA contributions without reasonable cause—$100 per overstatement;

(29) failure to timely file a return concerning Golden State Scholarshare Trust activities—$50 per failure;

¶710

(30) failing to file return or to furnish information; filing false or fraudulent return or information; aiding or abetting tax evasion; willfully failing to pay tax or estimated tax—$5,000 maximum plus criminal penalty (misdemeanor) of up to $5,000 and/or up to 1 year in jail, and costs of prosecution;

(31) instituting frivolous protest or refund proceedings—$5,000 maximum;

(32) obtaining, endorsing, or negotiating a tax refund warrant generated by the filing of a return knowing the recipient is not entitled to the refund—$5,000 maximum plus criminal penalty (misdemeanor) of up to $10,000 and/or up to 1 year in jail, and costs of investigation and prosecution; $10,000 maximum if done willfully and with intent to defraud plus criminal penalty (misdemeanor/felony) of up to $50,000 and/or up to 1 year in jail or up to 3 years in prison, and costs of investigation and prosecution;

(33) forging spouse's signature—misdemeanor; up to $5,000 and/or up to 1 year in jail;

(34) willfully making or signing a return or document containing a declaration made under penalty of perjury that the maker or signer does not believe to be materially true or correct—felony; up to $50,000 and/or up to 3 years in prison, and costs of investigation and prosecution;

(35) willfully aiding preparation or presentation of a false return or document—felony; up to $50,000 and/or up to 3 years in prison, and costs of investigation and prosecution;

(36) falsely executing or signing a bond, permit, entry, or required document—felony; up to $50,000 and/or up to 3 years in prison, and costs of investigation and prosecution;

(37) removing, depositing, or concealing taxable goods to evade tax—felony; up to $50,000 and/or up to 3 years in prison, and costs of investigation and prosecution;

(38) concealing property or destroying or falsifying records in regard to a tax settlement, closing agreement, compromise, or offer in compromise—felony; up to $50,000 and/or up to 3 years in prison, and costs of investigation and prosecution;

(39) willfully failing to file return or supply information with intent to defraud—misdemeanor/felony; up to $20,000, and/or up to 1 year in jail or 3 years in prison, and costs of investigation and prosecution;

(40) willfully making, signing, or verifying false return or statement with intent to evade tax—misdemeanor/felony; up to $20,000 and/or up to 1 year in jail or 3 years in prison;

(41) failing to collect and pay withholding—felony; up to $2,000 and/or up to 3 years in prison;

(42) failing to withhold or pay over nonresident withholding—misdemeanor; up to $1,000 and/or up to 1 year in jail, and costs of prosecution;

(43) filing false information with employer—misdemeanor; $1,000 and/or up to 1 year in jail; and

¶710

(44) failing to set up withholding account—misdemeanor; up to $5,000 and/or up to 1 year in jail.

The FTB is authorized by law to waive or not impose the penalty described in item (3) above, under certain conditions. In Legal Ruling 96-4 (CCH CALIFORNIA TAX REPORTS ¶ 89-410.45) the FTB provides examples of situations in which it will or will not use this authority.

The penalty imposed under (24) above, concerning failure to timely register a confidential corporate tax shelter will be waived if the taxpayer has complied with the federal registration requirements.

Item (31) above refers to Rev. & Tax. Code Sec. 19714 (formerly, Sec. 19414), which conforms to IRC Sec. 6673. In *Appeals of Fred R. Dauberger et al.* (1982) (CCH CALIFORNIA TAX REPORTS ¶ 89-302.316), the State Board of Equalization (SBE) commented on the flood of California "tax protester" cases and used the following language: "We take this opportunity to advise all individuals who proceed with frivolous cases that serious consideration will be given to the imposition of damages under Section 19414." (This case involved a consolidation of appeals for 32 different taxpayers.) In numerous later decisions involving similar facts, the SBE has imposed the penalty.

● *Effect of automatic extension of time*

Under the automatic-extension procedure (see ¶ 105), reasonable cause is assumed and a late-payment penalty will not be imposed if at least 90% of the tax is paid by the regular due date and the balance is paid (with the return) by the extended due date. This conforms to federal practice.

● *Procedures for imposing penalties*

Each notice issued after December 31, 2001, that imposes a penalty must include the name of the penalty, the code section under which it is imposed, and a description of the computation of the penalty. Upon request of the taxpayer, the FTB must also provide a computation of the penalty imposed.

Further, penalties imposed after December 31, 2001, generally may not be imposed unless the initial determination of the imposition of the penalty receives written approval by an authorized FTB supervisor. However, supervisory approval is not required for any penalty (1) for failure to file or failure to pay, (2) calculated through automated means, or (3) resulting from a federal change or correction required to be reported to the state.

● *Suspension of penalties*

Applicable to taxable years ending after October 10, 1999, if an individual files a timely return and the FTB fails to issue a notice specifically stating the taxpayer's liability and the basis for such liability within 18 months following the later of the original due date of the return or the date on which a timely return is filed, the FTB must generally suspend the imposition of civil penalties, additions to tax, or additional amounts during the period beginning from the date after the 18-month period expires until 15 days after the FTB sends the required notice. The suspension does not apply to any (1) penalty for failure to file or failure to pay, (2) penalty, addition to tax, or additional amount involving fraud, (3) penalty, addition to tax, or additional amount

¶710

shown on the return, or (4) criminal penalty. Federal law is similar, except that the 18-month period is shortened to one year for federal purposes for federal tax years beginning after 2003.

● *Relief for innocent spouse*

Under both California and federal laws, an innocent spouse is relieved from penalties in certain cases of wrongdoing in joint return situations. Innocent spouse relief is available if an individual establishes that (1) in signing a joint return, he or she did not know or have reason to know of any understatement on the return attributable to his or her spouse and (2) it would be inequitable to hold the individual liable.

Also, innocent spouse relief is available on a partial basis if the individual establishes that he or she did not know or have reason to know of the *extent* of an understatement on the return attributable to his or her spouse. Further, if relief is not specifically available under the innocent spouse provisions, equitable relief may still be provided if, taking into account all the facts and circumstances, it would be inequitable to hold the individual liable.

An individual seeking innocent spouse relief must elect such relief within two years after the commencement of collection activities with respect to that individual. However, the running of the period of limitations does not begin until the date of the first collection activity after October 10, 1999.

The FTB must give notice to a joint filer of the other joint filer's election of innocent spouse relief, and the FTB must not make its determination with respect to the election earlier than 30 days after such notification. If an individual is denied an innocent spouse election, the individual may appeal that determination to the SBE.

In addition to electing innocent spouse relief, a joint filer who is divorced or separated from the person with whom a joint return was filed may be eligible to elect separate liability. See ¶ 104 for a discussion of separate liability elections.

 CCH Tip: Separate Liability or Innocent Spouse Relief

The "actual knowledge" standard for separate liability is narrower than the "knew or should have known" standard for innocent spouse relief. This may make separate liability available under circumstances in which innocent spouse relief is not.

● *Bankruptcy proceedings*

Both California and federal laws provide for relief from penalties in cases where failure to pay is due to rules applicable in bankruptcy proceedings.

● *Collection and filing enforcement fees*

A collection cost recovery fee will be imposed on any taxpayer who fails to timely pay any amount of tax, penalty, addition to tax, interest, or other liability if the FTB has mailed a notice advising the taxpayer that continued failure to pay that amount may result in a collection action, including the imposition of a collection cost recovery fee. A filing enforcement cost recovery fee will be imposed on any taxpayer who fails to file a required tax return within 25 days after formal legal demand is mailed to the taxpayer by the FTB. The fees for the state's 1999-2000 fiscal year are $109 and $69, respectively. Collection and filing enforcement fees are subject to annual adjustment to reflect actual costs.

● *Decisions of State Board of Equalization*

In several cases the SBE has upheld the presumptive correctness of the FTB's imposition of penalties. For example, in *Appeal of Harold G. Jindrich* (1977) (CCH CALIFORNIA TAX REPORTS ¶ 89-523.88), the taxpayer failed to file a return and did not respond to the FTB's notice and demand for a return. The SBE upheld the imposition of two 25% penalties, under items (4) and (6) above, on the income as computed by the FTB.

In *Appeal of Terry L. Lash* (1986) (CCH CALIFORNIA TAX REPORTS New ¶ 89-410.36), the taxpayer failed to prove to the SBE that the failure to respond to notice and demand to file was due to a reasonable cause and not willful neglect. The taxpayer also failed to prove that not filing a timely return in the subsequent year was due to a reasonable cause. Reasonable cause was tested in both years by the standards of a normally intelligent and prudent businessperson.

In *Appeal of Philip C. and Anne Berolzheimer* (1986) (CCH CALIFORNIA TAX REPORTS ¶ 89-410.3611), the SBE held that an underpayment penalty was properly assessed. A New York law firm, acting as the taxpayers' agent, had filed a timely request for an extension of time for filing the taxpayers' 1981 California income tax return. Due to a programming error in the agent's computer tax software program, the capital gains for the year were incorrectly computed, resulting in an underpayment of the amount required to be paid with the extension request. The FTB assessed an underpayment penalty.

In holding that the underpayment was due to willful neglect and not reasonable cause, the SBE found inapplicable the U.S. Supreme Court rule that it is reasonable for a taxpayer to rely on the advice of an accountant or attorney on a matter of tax law. The underpayment was not due to a mistake of law; it was due to a simple mistake in computation of tax due. It is not "reasonable cause" so as to overcome a presumption of "willful neglect" to rely on an accountant or attorney for a simple computational problem as distinguished from a matter of law.

In *Appeal of Greg L. Dexter* (1986) (CCH CALIFORNIA TAX REPORTS ¶ 89-410.71), the SBE held that a return with the verification above the signature altered was not filed and signed under penalty of perjury and was an invalid return. Since the taxpayer had not filed a valid return, penalties for negligence and failure to respond were upheld and calculated on the entire tax liability.

Failure to receive a tax form does not constitute reasonable cause for failure to file—see *Appeal of Thomas P.E. and Barbara Rothchild* (1973) (CCH CALIFORNIA TAX REPORTS ¶ 89-413.57).

In *Appeal of Frank E. and Lilia Z. Hublou* (1977) (CCH CALIFORNIA TAX REPORTS ¶ 89-410.32), the taxpayers failed to respond to a notice and demand for a return. The return, as filed later, showed a tax liability of $213 which was more than offset by a $419 credit for tax withheld from salary, resulting in a refund. The SBE upheld the FTB in imposing a 25% penalty on the $213 tax liability, under item (6) above. To the same effect, see *Appeal of Sal J. Cardinalli* (1981) (CCH CALIFORNIA TAX REPORTS ¶ 89-410.25), involving penalties imposed under items (6) and (10) above. In *Appeal of Irma E. Bazan* (1982) (CCH CALIFORNIA TAX REPORTS New ¶ 89-410.2532), the SBE's opinion points out that the penalty described in item (6) above is properly measured by the FTB's estimate of the tax liability rather than the actual tax as later determined.

In *Appeal of Estate of Marilyn Monroe, Deceased* (1975) (CCH CALIFOR-NIA TAX REPORTS ¶ 89-410.26), the estate contended that there was reasonable cause for failure to file California returns, because of uncertainties as to whether the estate was subject to tax and the fact that the executor believed in good faith that no tax was due. The SBE upheld imposition of penalties ($12,810) for failure to file, commenting that "mere uninformed and unsupported belief, no matter how sincere . . . is insufficient to constitute reasonable cause. . . ."

In *Appeal of Horace H. and Mildred E. Hubbard* (1961) (CCH CALIFOR-NIA TAX REPORTS ¶ 89-410.322), the SBE upheld the penalty for failure to file, where the taxpayers had repeatedly ignored the demand of the FTB for a return based on a federal audit report.

In *Appeals of Leonard S. and Frances M. Gordon* (1960) (CCH CALIFOR-NIA TAX REPORTS ¶ 89-410.669), the SBE held that taxpayers, having previously been found guilty of filing fraudulent federal income tax returns, were also subject to the California fraud penalty provisions. (But see the *Brown* case, cited at ¶ 104, to the opposite effect.)

In *Appeal of Thomas* (1955) (CCH CALIFORNIA TAX REPORTS ¶ 89-410.26), the SBE held that a new resident of California was subject to a delinquency penalty for failure to file a return for his first year in the state. The taxpayer's income was from salary earned in California; the SBE held that he could reasonably have been expected to make inquiry regarding possible liability for California tax. However, in *Appeal of Estate of Anna Armstrong* (1964) (CCH CALIFORNIA TAX REPORTS ¶ 89-410.3617), the SBE held that the taxpayer's failure to file a timely return was due to reasonable cause when she relied on the advice of competent professional tax advisors.

Both California and federal laws provide special provisions for injunctive relief to prevent taxpayers from engaging in certain conduct (abusive tax shelters, etc.) subject to penalty.

¶ 711 Information at Source

> *Law:* Secs. 18547, 18631-32, 18636-61, 19175, 19182 (CCH CALIFORNIA TAX RE-PORTS ¶ 16-464, 89-171, 89-173, 89-175, 89-189—89-207, 89-410)
>
> *Comparable Federal:* Secs. 6039, 6039D, 6041-50R, 6052-53, 6111 (CCH STAN-DARD FEDERAL TAX REPORTS ¶ 36,800, 36,860, 36,920—37,400, 37,440—37,460).

Under California law, the Franchise Tax Board (FTB) *may* require individuals, partnerships, corporations, or other organizations engaged in trade or business in California, making payments in the course of such trade or business, to make information returns and to furnish copies to recipients of the payments. The following payments are covered:

(a) as to payees whose last known address is in California:

(1) payments of any fixed or determinable income (i.e., group term life insurance, gambling winnings, medical payments, remuneration for personal services, but excludes compensation subject to withholding as explained at ¶712a) amounting to $600 or more; "service-recipients" required to make a return under IRC Sec. 6041A must also make a return to California;

(2) payments of dividends if the payor was required to file an information return (1099) under federal law;

(3) payments of interest if the payor was required to file an information return (1099) under federal law;

(4) specified payments of interest and exempt-interest dividends aggregating $10 or more if the interest is from other states' bonds exempt from federal income tax but taxable by California (see discussion below);

(5) group life insurance benefits provided to employees, to the extent the cost of such benefits exceeds the cost of $50,000 of coverage plus the amount contributed by the employee;

(6) corporate liquidating distributions amounting to $600 or more to any stockholder;

(7) patronage dividends of cooperatives amounting to $100 or more; and

(8) original issue discount paid on a publicly offered debt instrument; and

(b) as to payees who are not residents of California, payments of compensation for services rendered in California, and payments of rents or royalties on property located in California, in the amount set forth in (a)(1) above.

● *Reporting not required*

The following payments need not be reported, regardless of amount:

(a) payments to a corporation, other than payments for attorneys' fees;

(b) partnership, estate, or trust distributions shown on their returns;

(c) rent payments to a real estate agent having a place of business in California;

(d) payments to a nonresident that are reported by the withholding agent on Forms 592 and 592-B (see ¶712);

(e) payments of income exempt from California income tax;

(f) payments by those not engaged in a trade or business;

(g) payments for merchandise, etc.;

(h) certain payments to employees of interstate carriers;

(i) certain payments by bankers acting as collection agents;

(j) payments of dividends and interest by a record owner to the actual owner;

(k) wages reported on Form W-2;

(*l*) mortgage interest statement; and

(m) acquisition or abandonment of secured property.

● *Information on cash received in trade or business*

The FTB *must* require a copy of the federal information return relating to cash received in a trade or business (Form 8300) if a federal information return was required under IRC Sec. 6050I. Under federal law, any person required to be named in the return must be furnished with written notice of the name and address of the person required to file the Form 8300 and the amount of cash required to be specified on Form 8300 as received from the person named. California has not adopted this requirement.

● *Information on tax-exempt interest and dividends*

Brokerages and mutual fund companies are required to report to the FTB payments of interest and exempt-interest dividends aggregating $10 or more in any calendar year to any person if the interest and dividends are from other states' bonds that are exempt from federal income taxation but taxable by California.

● *Procedure for reporting*

Payments are reported on federal Form 1099. All 1099-B returns must be filed on magnetic tape; other information reports may be made on magnetic tape if the volume exceeds specified limits, conforming to the federal procedure. Reports are for the calendar year and are due generally on February 28th of the following year. Extension of time for filing may be obtained by written request to the FTB. Copies of individual forms should be furnished to recipients by January 31.

● *Nontaxable distributions*

In the case of corporate distributions believed to be nontaxable, complete information should be supplied to the FTB not later than February 1, for the preceding year. The FTB will then advise the distributing corporation regarding the taxability of the distribution.

● *Stock options*

Corporations transferring stock under certain stock options are required to furnish statements (by January 31 of the following year) to the individuals involved. California incorporates the federal requirement.

● *Tips*

The California recordkeeping and reporting requirements for tips are generally the same as the federal regulations. However, under federal law, certain food or beverage establishments employing ten or more workers on a typical business day in the preceding year are required to file annual informa-

¶711

tion returns for the purpose of increasing taxpayer compliance in reporting income from tips. California has no comparable requirement.

● *Tax-shelter promoters*

Tax-shelter promoters may be required to make a detailed return describing the investment and giving full information regarding each investor involved. Also, any person required to register a California tax shelter under IRC Sec. 6111, including a confidential corporate tax shelter, is required to send a duplicate of the registration information to the FTB and to include shelter identification numbers on returns. However, a penalty will not be imposed for failure to register a confidential corporate tax shelter if the person required to register the tax shelter has complied with federal registration requirements.

● *Property owners*

Owners and transferors of real property or a mobilehome assessed by a California assessor, except for property covered by a homeowner's exemption (see ¶ 1704), may be required to file returns requested and prescribed by the FTB. The returns include the owner's social security number or other identification number prescribed by the FTB, identification of the property interest, and other information the FTB may request. Owners who fail to file within 60 days of the due date or file a misleading return will be denied deductions for interest, taxes, depreciation, or amortization paid or incurred with respect to the property.

● *Brokers*

Concerning the information return requirements imposed on brokers, California considers governmental units and agencies to be brokers if their activities otherwise qualify them as brokers. California, however, does not consider a person who manages a farm on behalf of another person to be a broker with respect to such activities.

● *Real estate transactions*

Brokers are required to make a return showing details regarding gross proceeds and other information for each customer. Closing agents who are responsible for finalizing a real estate transaction involving California property are required to forward to the FTB a copy of the required federal real estate transaction return by the date required in federal law.

Real estate transactions involving a sale or exchange of a residence for $250,000 or less are exempt from these reporting requirements if the broker receives written assurance that (1) the residence is the seller's principal residence, (2) there is no federally subsidized mortgage financing assistance with respect to the mortgage on the residence, and (3) the full amount of the gain on the sale or exchange is excludable from gross income.

● *Attorneys*

A taxpayer who makes a payment to an attorney in connection with legal services in the course of the taxpayer's trade or business must file an information return, even if the payment is made to a corporation providing legal services. The return must show the name and address of each attorney and such details regarding such payments as well as any other information that the FTB may require. Statements must also be provided to the attorneys listed on the return by January 31 of the year following the calendar year for which the information return was made.

● *Copies of federal reports required*

The FTB may require filing of copies of certain federal information reports with the FTB. This applies to (1) mortgage interest received in a trade or business; (2) direct investments in California real property by foreign persons; (3) foreclosures and abandonments; (4) exchanges of partnership interests; (5) certain dispositions of donated property; (6) payments of royalties; (7) discharges of indebtedness; (8) payments of long-term care benefits; (9) certain purchases of fish for resale; and (10) reimbursements or refunds of qualified tuition and related expenses.

The FTB *must* require a copy of the federal information report required when any person receives more than $10,000 in cash in one transaction, or in two or more related transactions, in the course of the person's trade or business.

● *Penalties*

As stated at ¶ 710, severe civil and criminal penalties may be imposed for various offenses, including failure to comply with the requirements for information returns. Also, as stated at ¶ 322, certain deductions may be disallowed in cases where required information returns are not filed.

The failure to file information returns on remuneration for personal services is also penalized under the Unemployment Insurance Code. If the failure to file is punishable under the Revenue and Taxation Code as well as the Unemployment Insurance Code, only the latter penalty will be applied.

● *Nonprofit organizations*

Under California law, the activities of a nonprofit organization constitute a "trade or business" for information reporting purposes.

● *Backup withholding*

The federal law requires 20% withholding from certain payments by employers and others that require information returns (so-called "backup withholding payments"), where the payee fails to furnish a correct identification number to the payor.

¶ 712 Withholding of Tax at Source—General

> *Law:* Secs. 18662, 18666, 18668-77 (CCH CALIFORNIA TAX REPORTS ¶ 16-726, 16-851, 16-857, 16-860, 89-335).
>
> *Comparable Federal:* Secs. 1445, 1446 (CCH STANDARD FEDERAL TAX REPORTS ¶ 33,980, 34,000).
>
> *California Forms:* Forms 587, 588, 589, 590, 590-P, 592, 592-A, 592-B, 594, 595, 597, 597-E, 597-I, 597-W, 598, 598-A, 598-B.

● *Nonresidents*

As to nonresidents, withholding is generally required on payments of compensation for personal services (including payments to independent contractors), payments for professional services, rents, patent royalties, prizes, etc., provided the income is attributable to California. (See ¶ 230 for discussion of income from sources within the state.) In addition, the Franchise Tax Board (FTB) requires withholding on payments of partnership income to domestic nonresident partners. However, under Reg. 18805-2, withholding is not required unless the income payments to a payee by the same payor exceed $1,500 during the calendar year or the payor is directed to withhold by the FTB. In addition, corporations are not required to withhold income taxes from compensation paid to nonresident directors for director services performed for the corporation within California. Withholding is also not required if the payee is a tax-exempt organization.

The tax to be withheld is computed at the rate of 7% of gross income. However, in cases such as those involving entertainers where deductible expenses are likely to be large, the FTB may upon application (through the payor's submission of a Form 588, Nonresident Withholding Waiver Request) waive the withholding requirements in whole or in part by issuing the Notice to the Withholding Agent (Form 595) or the Notice to Withhold Tax at Source (Form 594). According to the Instructions for Form 592, the FTB will generally grant a waiver if (1) the vendor/payee has a history of filing California returns; (2) the vendor/payee is currently making estimated tax payments; (3) distributions are made by publicly traded partnerships; or (4) distributions are made to brokerage firms and tiered partnerships or limited liability companies. However, waivers may not be granted for withholding on foreign partners. Waivers are effective for a maximum of two years from the date the waiver is granted.

● *Realty dispositions by foreigners, nonresidents*

California has adopted a provision similar to IRC Sec. 1445, which requires withholding of tax on dispositions of United States real property interests by foreign persons. However, the California provision differs from the federal one in that (1) the real property must be located in California, (2) the transferee must ordinarily withhold $3\frac{1}{3}\%$ of the sales price, rather than 10% as under federal law, and (3) the withholding requirement applies not only to a "foreign person" but to any transferor of California property who has a last known address outside California. However, no withholding is required if: (1) the transferor is a partnership, limited liability company, or bank; (2) the sales price does not exceed $100,000; (3) the transferee has not received written notification of the withholding requirements; or (4) the transferee relies in good faith on the transferor's written statement certifying under penalty of perjury either that the transferor is a California resident or that the property is the transferor's principal residence.

If there are multiple transferors, some of whom are nonresidents, withholding of $3\frac{1}{3}\%$ is required on the **total** sales price and allocated among the nonresident sellers.

¶712

At the request of the transferor, the FTB may reduce the rate of withholding or waive the withholding amount altogether. See the discussion below under "Procedures and returns."

Those who fail to withhold required tax in connection with a nonresident realty disposition are subject to a penalty equal to the greater of $500 or 10% of the amount that should have been withheld. A real estate escrow person who fails to give a transferee written notice of this withholding requirement is liable for the same penalty if the tax due on the transaction is not paid on time.

● *Foreign partners*

California incorporates the federal provision (IRC Sec. 1446) that requires the withholding of tax on all amounts paid by United States partnerships to foreign partners that are connected to the partnership's U.S. activities. However, the California tax is withheld at the maximum California rate, rather than at the rate specified in the federal provision, and California's withholding is limited to California-source amounts.

● *Procedures and returns*

If a payor receives a Nonresident Allocation Worksheet (Form 587) from the payee, the payor may rely on that certification to determine if withholding is required provided the form is accepted in good faith. A payor is relieved of the obligation to withhold if he or she obtains a Withholding Exemption Certificate (Form 590), Nonresident Withholding Exemption Certificate for Previously Reported Income of Partners and Members (Form 590-P), or Nonresident Withholding Exemption Certificate and Waiver Request for Real Estate Sales (Form 590-W) from the payee. Foreign (non-U.S.) partners or members may not file a Form 590-P as there is no exemption from withholding available to a foreign partner or member. Penalties (fine, or imprisonment, or both) are provided for violation of withholding requirements.

When tax is withheld as the result of a realty disposition by a nonresident, the transferee must file Copy A of Form 597 and transmit the tax within 20 days following the end of the month in which the transaction occurred. The transferor may request the FTB to reduce or eliminate withholding by filing Form 597-W, Nonresident Withholding Exemption Certificate and Waiver Request for Real Estate Sales, at the time the transferor enters into a contract of sale. The FTB will generally grant a waiver if (1) the 3⅓% withholding exceeds the estimated tax liability from the sale, (2) the transaction involves a tax-free exchange, a foreclosure, or an installment sale, or (3) the transaction involves multiple sellers, only some of whom are nonresidents (Instructions to Form 597-W). If the FTB has not responded to the request before close of escrow, the parties may request the escrow person to hold the amount of the tax in trust for 45 days pending action by the FTB.

An annual return showing the total tax withheld from nonresidents (other than foreign partners or members) must be made on Form 592 by January 31. For withholding on foreign partners or members, Form 592 must be filed by the 15th day of the fourth month after the partnership's or limited liability company's tax year ends (15th day of the sixth month if all partners or members are foreign). A separate statement of the tax withheld from each

¶712

nonresident (Form 592-B) must be attached to Form 592. Form 592-A, accompanied by payment of tax withheld, must be filed by the 20th day of the month following a month that the accumulated amount withheld exceeds $2,500. However, for withholding on foreign partners or members, Form 592-A is filed in accordance with federal rules governing the timing of withholding payments.

For realty dispositions by nonresidents, Form 597 must be used to report and transmit the amount withheld.

● *Interest on late remittances*

The interest on deficiencies (see ¶ 709) applies to delayed remittances of amounts withheld from fixed or determinable gains, profits, and income and from remittances of partnership income to foreign partners.

● *Delinquent taxes*

In addition to withholding from payments of income to nonresidents, the law provides for withholding of delinquent taxes due from both resident and nonresident taxpayers. The FTB may, by notice and demand, require such withholding and payment to the FTB by anyone, including state agencies, who is in possession or control of credits or property belonging to a delinquent taxpayer or belonging to a person who has failed to withhold as required under the law. In *Greene v. Franchise Tax Board* (1972) (CCH CALIFORNIA TAX REPORTS ¶ 89-335.42), the California Court of Appeal upheld the FTB's use of the withholding procedure to collect delinquent tax of $72. In *Franchise Tax Board v. Construction Laborers Vacation Trust for Southern California* (1983) (CCH CALIFORNIA TAX REPORTS, ¶ 89-335.47), the issue was whether the FTB was precluded by federal law (ERISA) from requiring a union vacation trust fund to withhold for unpaid personal income tax owed by union members. The U.S. Supreme Court held that federal courts did not have jurisdiction in the matter, and referred the case back to California Superior Court. In *Franchise Tax Board of California v. United States Postal Service* (1984) (CCH CALIFORNIA TAX REPORTS ¶ 89-335.40), the U.S. Supreme Court held that the Postal Service could be required to withhold delinquent California tax from its employees.

If the FTB determines that an employer withheld earnings pursuant to an earnings withholding order for taxes but failed to remit the withheld earnings to the FTB, and the employer also fails to remit the withheld earnings following notice from the FTB, the employer becomes liable for the unremitted amount, plus interest, and may be issued a deficiency assessment for such amount within seven years from the date that the amount, in the aggregate, was first withheld. When the assessment against the employer becomes final, the taxpayer's account may be credited for that amount. Collection action against the taxpayer is stayed until the earlier of the time the credit is applied or the assessment against the employer is withdrawn or revised and the taxpayer is notified thereof.

● *Date tax deemed paid*

For the purpose of filing claims for refund, any tax withheld under the California withholding provisions is deemed to have been paid on the due date (without regard to extensions of time) of the return for the taxable year with respect to which the withheld tax is allowed as a credit.

¶ 712a Withholding on Wages

> *Law:* Secs. 18551-52, 18662-66, 19002, 19009, Revenue and Taxation Code; Secs. 1151-1153, 1233—1236, 1870-1875, 13009, 13021, 13028, 13059, Unemployment Insurance Code (CCH CALIFORNIA TAX REPORTS ¶ 16-735— 16-741, 16-777, 16-783, 16-786, 16-789, 16-825, 16-851).
>
> *Comparable Federal:* Secs. 31, 3401-05, 3501-05, 6053 (CCH STANDARD FEDERAL TAX REPORTS ¶ 4060, 35,002—35,120, 35,160—35,240, 37,460).
>
> *California Form:* DE-4.

The California wage withholding system conforms closely to the federal system; for this reason, the following discussion will deal principally with the differences between the California and federal rules.

The wage withholding provisions are administered by the Employment Development Department (EDD). The withholding rules are set forth in Division 6 of the Unemployment Insurance Code (Secs. 13000 to 13101) and the regulations issued by the EDD.

● *California-federal differences*

Employers are required to withhold on all "wages", as defined below, of California residents and on "wages" of nonresidents for services performed in California. As in the federal rules, "wages" includes all remuneration for services of an employee, with specified exceptions for agricultural labor, domestic service, and other categories. Following are differences between the California and federal rules in what is subject to withholding:

    (a) California excludes wages paid to members of a crew on a vessel engaged in foreign, coastwise, intercoastal, interstate, or noncontiguous trade; federal law has no such exclusion;

    (b) federal law excludes compensation paid under certain bond purchase plans; California has no such exclusion;

    (c) federal law excludes certain foreign service; California has no such exclusion; however, such compensation would be excluded under California law if the employee is not a California "resident", as defined at ¶ 103;

    (d) California specifies that whether an individual provides equipment shall be ignored in determining whether the individual is an "employee;" and

    (e) federal withholding applies to certain payments of gambling winnings, whereas California withholding does not.

The California rules for withholding on pensions, annuities, sick pay, supplemental unemployment benefits, and other deferred income conform generally to the federal rules. Such payments are subject to withholding unless the recipient elects *not* to have tax withheld. If a recipient makes such a federal election, that election is automatically effective for California purposes also unless the recipient (and the payor) elects to have tax withheld by California. On the other hand, in the absence of a federal election, the recipient may still elect *not* to have California tax withheld. In case of certain nonperiodic qualified total distributions, the recipient may choose one of the following methods for determining the amount of California withholding: (1) the amount prescribed by Franchise Tax Board (FTB); (2) a designated dollar amount; or (3) 10% of federal withholding.

● *Withholding methods*

California provides two methods for computing the amount of tax to be withheld, as follows:

Method A—WAGE BRACKET TABLE METHOD (similar to federal "wage bracket" method); and

Method B—EXACT CALCULATION METHOD (similar to the federal "percentage" method).

California permits use of other methods in special situations, upon application. Federal rules also permit alternative methods.

With respect to supplemental wages (bonuses, overtime, commissions, sales awards, back pay including retroactive wage increases, and reimbursement of nondeductible moving expenses), an employer may either (1) add supplemental wages to regular wages and compute withholding on the whole amount or (2) apply a flat percentage rate to the supplemental wages alone, without allowance for exemptions or credits. California's supplemental withholding rate is 6%.

● *Instruction booklet*

Detailed instructions for determining the amount to be withheld, with tables and formulas, are included in a booklet entitled "Employer's Tax Guide for the Withholding, Payment, and Reporting of California Income Tax." This booklet can be obtained from offices of the FTB or the EDD.

● *Employee forms*

California provides a form (Form DE-4) for the employee's exemption certificate to determine the number of California withholding exemptions. The employee has the option of using California Form DE-4. Otherwise, the employee must use federal Form W-4 to determine the number of California exemptions. If the employer cannot determine the employee's marital status from either Form DE-4 or W-4, the employee is considered unmarried.

California conforms fully to the federal rules for exemption certificates. Thus, any certificate that complies with the federal rules is accepted also for California purposes. The requirements for complete exemption, based on absence of federal income tax liability, are the same for California as for federal; that is, a certificate that eliminates federal withholding also eliminates California withholding. An employer who makes the required special report to the Internal Revenue Service where a large number of exemptions is claimed need not make a report to the state. The FTB may require employers to submit copies of withholding exemption certificates. The law sets forth procedures to be followed if the FTB determines that the withholding exemption certificate is invalid.

¶ 712a

● *Filing of returns*

Withheld tax must be reported and paid monthly or quarterly, depending on the amounts involved, as explained below.

Statements must be furnished to employees, using federal Form W-2, by January 31 and upon termination. The Form W-2 must show the amount of disability insurance contributions (SDI) withheld (see ¶ 1806).

Generally, a report of wages must be submitted each calendar quarter showing the total tax withheld for each employee. Effective January 1, 2000, the report must also show amounts withheld from pensions, annuities, and other deferred compensation. A reconciliation return must be filed annually by January 31 (or within 10 days of termination of business).

Employers authorized under federal law to file magnetic media returns for federal withholding tax purposes must either (1) file by means of magnetic media the reports of wages that must accompany their quarterly payments of state withholding tax or (2) establish a lack of automation, severe economic hardship, current exemption from the magnetic media requirement, or other good cause for not filing reports of wages magnetically.

The due date of a withholding return, report, or statement may be extended if an employer's failure to timely file or pay tax is attributable to a state of emergency declared by the Governor.

● *Payment of tax*

An employer who is required to remit withheld federal income taxes pursuant to IRC Sec. 6302 and who has accumulated withheld state income taxes in the amount of $500 or more must remit the withheld state income taxes within the same number of banking days specified for withheld federal income taxes. The $500 threshold amount is adjusted annually for inflation. For 1999 the threshold amount is $400. An employer who is required to withhold tax, but who is not required to remit payment in accordance with IRC Sec. 6302, must remit the amount withheld during each month of each calendar quarter by the 15th day of the subsequent month if the amount withheld for any month, or cumulatively for two or more months within the quarter, is $350 or more.

Any employer whose cumulative average eighth-monthly (as described in IRC Sec. 6302) payment during any deposit period is $20,000 or more must remit the withheld state income taxes by way of electronic funds transfer within the same number of banking days specified in IRC Sec. 6302, for withheld federal income taxes. The electronic funds transfer requirement may be waived if the average withholding payment exceeding the threshold amount is not representative of the taxpayer's actual tax liability and was the result of an unprecedented occurrence. Employers not required to pay by electronic means may elect to do so with the approval of the EDD. Payment by electronic means will generally be deemed complete on the date the transfer is initiated.

Any income tax withheld that is not covered by any of the above requirements must be remitted to the state by the last day of the month following the end of the quarter. Any amounts withheld for employees'

¶ 712a

disability-insurance contributions (see ¶ 1808) are due and payable at the same time as the payments for income-tax withholding, regardless of the amounts involved.

Employers who are subject to certain requirements for accelerated payment of withheld federal taxes are required to remit withheld California taxes on the same time schedule.

The law provides detailed rules for collection of tax, liabilities and obligations of employers and employees, penalties, etc. Upon sale of a business, the purchaser may be liable for unsatisfied obligations of the seller. FTB Regulation 4320-1 specifies procedures to be followed when employers are required to withhold other-state taxes from wages paid to California residents; in these cases, where the other state's withholding requirement is greater than the California amount, no California withholding is required.

● *Compromise of withholding tax liability*

The EDD is authorized to accept partial payment in satisfaction of final, nondisputed withholding tax liabilities of certain employers if the amount offered in compromise is more than could reasonably be collected through involuntary means during the four-year period beginning on the date the offer is made.

● *Penalties*

As stated at ¶ 710, severe civil and criminal penalties are imposed on employers, employees, and others for various offenses. Also, as stated at ¶ 322, deductions for remuneration for personal services may be disallowed for failure to report the payments in required statements to employees or to independent contractors.

● *Settlement authority*

The Director of the EDD may approve the settlement of any civil tax dispute involving a reduction of tax of $7,500 or less on his or her own authority. However, the proposed settlement must be submitted to an administrative law judge for approval if (1) an appeal has been filed with the Unemployment Insurance Appeals Board, (2) the appeal has been assigned to an administrative law judge, and (3) a notice of hearing has been issued. Proposed settlements of $5,000 or more must be reviewed by the Attorney General prior to final approval, and settlements involving amounts over $7,500 must also be approved by the Unemployment Insurance Appeals Board.

● *Waiver for reliance on written advice*

The EDD is authorized to waive tax assessments, interest, additions to tax, or penalties imposed as a result of a taxpayer's failure to make a timely return or payment if the taxpayer's failure was due to the taxpayer's reasonable reliance on the written advice of a ruling by the Director or the Director's designee. If the taxpayer's action was due to reasonable reliance on written advice other than a ruling by the director or director's designee, the EDD is authorized to waive interest, additions to tax, or penalties. All of the following

¶ 712a

conditions must be met before the EDD may provide relief: (1) the taxpayer must request advice regarding the tax consequences of a particular activity or transaction and the activity or transaction must be fully described; (2) the EDD must issue a written ruling or opinion; (3) the taxpayer must have reasonably relied on that advice; and (4) the tax consequences expressed in the EDD's advice must not have been changed by a later issued opinion, statutory or case law, federal interpretation, or material facts or circumstances relating to the taxpayer. No relief will be provided if the taxpayer's request for written advice contained a misrepresentation or omission of a material fact.

Nonprofit organizations and governmental agencies are specifically excluded from the relief provisions discussed above. Relief from the assessment of unemployment insurance taxes is conditioned upon approval from the United States Secretary of Labor; however, relief from any corresponding interest and penalties may still be provided.

¶ 713 Overpayments and Refunds—Procedure

> *Law:* Secs. 19301-19302, 19321-19323 (CCH CALIFORNIA TAX REPORTS ¶ 89-237, 89-523—89-532).

> *Comparable Federal:* Secs. 6401-02 (CCH STANDARD FEDERAL TAX REPORTS ¶ 39,430—39,610).

> *California Form:* Form 540X.

Claims for refund must be in writing, signed by the taxpayer or the taxpayer's representative, and must state the specific grounds upon which they are based. They should ordinarily be filed on Form 540X, Amended Individual Income Tax Return. Claims should be filed with the Franchise Tax Board (FTB) at Sacramento, California.

Claims for refund made on behalf of a class of taxpayers must be both authorized in writing and signed by each taxpayer.

Upon examination of a refund claim, the FTB must notify the taxpayer of its action on the claim. In addition, the FTB must notify a taxpayer of the reasons for disallowing any refund claim, applicable to refund claims disallowed after April 7, 2000. It is the FTB's practice to grant the taxpayer an informal hearing, if desired, before the claim is acted upon or within 90 days after the mailing of a notice of disallowance. The law provides that the FTB may reconsider a disallowed claim at any time within the period allowed for filing a suit for refund (see ¶ 716).

A return filed within the statutory period for filing refund claims, showing a credit of more than $1 for estimated tax paid in excess of the tax due, is treated as a claim for refund. At the taxpayer's election, such overpayment may be either refunded or applied on the following year's estimated tax.

Legal Ruling No. 386 (1975) (CCH CALIFORNIA TAX REPORTS ¶ 89-526.22) discusses the question of what constitutes a valid refund claim. The ruling states that it is not necessary to use a particular form, provided the necessary information is provided. A federal revenue agent's report, filed by the taxpayer or a representative and accompanied by a refund request, will constitute a claim if sufficient explanation is provided in the report or otherwise. Under some circumstances the FTB may initiate refund action in the absence of a proper claim. See *Newman v. Franchise Tax Board* (1989) (CCH CALIFOR-

NIA TAX REPORTS ¶ 89-526.224); in this case, the California Court of Appeal held that a statement entitled "protest" qualified as a sufficient claim for refund, since it put the FTB on notice that a right was being asserted with respect to an overpayment of tax.

In FTB Notice 97-4 (CCH CALIFORNIA TAX REPORTS ¶ 89-526.781), the FTB stated its position that a refund request could be adjudicated only if the tax, together with interest and penalties, had been paid in full. Subsequently, in FTB Notice 97-8 (CCH CALIFORNIA TAX REPORTS ¶ 89-526.782), the FTB stated that it would continue to process a refund claim at the administrative level if the taxpayer paid the assessed tax, additions to tax, and penalties, but not interest. However, pending a final, controlling appellate court decision, the FTB maintained its position that payment of interest was a prerequisite to judicial review. Thereafter, in *Chen et al. v. Franchise Tax Board* (CCH CALIFORNIA TAX REPORTS ¶ 89-526.783), a California court of appeal held that payment of interest was not a prerequisite to seeking judicial review.

In case of a joint return, an overpayment may be credited against taxes due from both taxpayers and any balance is refunded to both taxpayers. In *Appeal of Elam* (1997) (CCH CALIFORNIA TAX REPORTS ¶ 89-237.25), the State Board of Equalization ordered the FTB to refund to a divorced taxpayer her portion of an overpayment from a prior year's tax return filed jointly with her ex-husband, even though the FTB had erroneously refunded the entire overpayment to the ex-husband.

¶ 714 Refund Claims—Appeal to State Board of Equalization

> *Law:* Secs. 19324-35 (CCH CALIFORNIA TAX REPORTS ¶ 89-523, 89-532, 89-541, 89-559).
>
> *Comparable Federal:* Secs. 6401-02 (CCH STANDARD FEDERAL TAX REPORTS ¶ 39,430—39,610).

If the Franchise Tax Board (FTB) disallows a claim for refund, the taxpayer may appeal to the State Board of Equalization (SBE) within 90 days from the date of mailing of the notice of disallowance. If the FTB fails to take action on a claim for six months (120 days in certain bankruptcy situations) after the claim is filed, the taxpayer may consider the claim disallowed and file an appeal to the SBE.

. Procedure on an appeal to the SBE on a refund claim is the same as on a proposed deficiency, as outlined in ¶ 703 above. Some proceedings that start out as deficiency appeals are converted into refund appeals because the taxpayer pays the tax while the proceeding is pending; in such cases the proceeding is considered after payment of the tax as an appeal from the denial of a claim for refund.

See ¶ 716 regarding suits for refund.

¶ 715 Statute of Limitations on Refund Claims

Law: Secs. 19041.5, 19066, 19306-14 (CCH California Tax Reports ¶ 89-529).

Comparable Federal: Secs. 1311-14, 6511 (CCH Standard Federal Tax Reports ¶ 33,300—33,360, 40,010).

The period of limitation for filing refund claims is outlined below.

(a) **General rule**—Generally, a refund claim must be made by the later of (1) four years after the last day prescribed for filing the return (determined without regard to any extension of time for filing), (2) one year from the date of overpayment, or (3) applicable to all claims for which the statute of limitations has not expired as of January 1, 2000, four years from the date the return was filed, if filed by the prescribed date for filing the return (including extensions). This may be compared with the federal rule of the earlier of three years from the date the return was filed or two years from the date the tax was paid. If a return is filed before the actual due date, it is treated as filed on the due date.

Effective January 1, 2000, a deposit in the nature of a cash bond made by a taxpayer to stop the running of interest after the Franchise Tax Board (FTB) has mailed a notice of proposed deficiency assessment is not a payment of tax for purposes of determining the limitations period for filing a refund claim, unless the taxpayer provides a written statement to the FTB specifying that the deposit is a payment of tax or the deficiency assessment becomes due and payable.

(b) **Waivers**—Where a waiver has been executed, *either* for California tax purposes or for federal tax purposes, extending the running of the statute of limitations on deficiency assessments, the limitation date for refunds is the same as that for mailing notices of proposed additional assessments. This is different from the federal rule, which extends the limitation period for refunds 6 months beyond the period for deficiency assessments. It should be noted, however, that where the California refund limitation date is based on a federal waiver, the date is six months after the expiration of the period for *federal* deficiency assessments, although it is not six months after the date for additional *California* assessments.

The limitation date for a California refund claim, if based upon a federal waiver, may be the same as that for a federal claim.

(c) **Special 7-year rule.**—Where the claim is based on (1) a bad debt loss, (2) a worthless security loss, or (3) erroneous inclusion of certain recoveries of no-tax-benefit deductions, the limitation period is extended to seven years from the last day prescribed for filing the return. As to bad debt and worthless security losses, this is the same as the federal; as to erroneous inclusion of certain recoveries, there is no comparable federal rule.

(d) **Changes or corrections to federal returns.**—When a change or correction to the taxpayer's federal return is made or allowed by federal authorities, as explained at ¶ 104, the limitation period is extended to a date two years after the notice or amended return is filed with the FTB, if such date is later than that set forth in (a) above.

● *Taxpayers outside United States*

In the case of members of the armed forces and certain other taxpayers who are outside the United States for a period of time, the statute of limitations is automatically extended under certain conditions (see ¶ 106).

● *Offset of refund against deficiency*

A refund that is barred under the above rules may be allowed as an offset against a deficiency, where the refund and deficiency both result from the transfer of income or deductions from one year to another. Such offset is also allowed where the refund is for the same year as the deficiency and is due to a related taxpayer. The offset must be made within seven years from the due date of the return on which the refund (overpayment) is determined. In *Appeal of Paritem and Janie Poonian* (1971) (CCH CALIFORNIA TAX REPORTS ¶ 89-237.193), the State Board of Equalization (SBE) applied the 7-year limitation strictly to deny an offset (an offset had been allowed earlier in settling the federal tax liability, presumably because the federal limitation period had not yet run).

In *Appeal of Earl and Marion Matthiessen* (1985) (CCH CALIFORNIA TAX REPORTS ¶ 89-237.195), the taxpayers claimed a barred refund as an offset to a deficiency for a later year. A refund claim had been filed within the 7-year period, but the offset was not claimed until after the deficiency had been paid. The SBE denied the claim.

In *Appeal of Wilfred and Gertrude Winkenbach et al.* (1975) (CCH CALIFORNIA TAX REPORTS ¶ 89-237.24), individuals were taxed on income that had been taxed to a corporation in an outlawed year. The situation did not permit an offset of the barred refund due the corporation against the individuals' deficiency, under the rules discussed above, because the corporation and the individuals were not "related" taxpayers as specifically defined in the law. However, the SBE allowed the offset under the doctrine of "equitable recoupment".

● *Effect of federal litigation*

In *Appeal of Valley Home Furniture* (1972) (CCH CALIFORNIA TAX REPORTS ¶ 89-529.221), the taxpayer's refund claim was based on the allowable deduction of certain salaries paid to an officer-stockholder. The Tax Court had allowed the deduction for federal tax purposes, and the officer-stockholder had paid both federal and California income tax on the salaries. Nevertheless, the refund was denied because the claim was not filed within the required period of one year after the date of overpayment. The SBE commented that the taxpayer "could easily have filed protective claims for refund pending the outcome of the federal litigation."

● *No California relief provision*

California law contains nothing similar to the federal provision enacted by the IRS Restructuring and Reform Act of 1998 that suspends the statute of limitations for the filing of refund claims during any period when an individual is financially disabled.

¶ **715**

Also, except as explained above, California law contains nothing similar to IRC Secs. 1311-14, which mitigate the effect of the statute of limitations in certain situations where an inconsistent position is maintained. In *Appeal of Skaggs Pay Less Drug Stores* (1959) (CCH CALIFORNIA TAX REPORTS ¶ 89-304.702), the taxpayer attempted to obtain a refund for an outlawed year to conform with a federal adjustment made under IRC Sec. 1311; the SBE held that no refund could be made.

A claim is deemed to be filed on the date it is mailed; the date of the postmark is ordinarily considered to be the date of mailing (Government Code Sec. 11003).

¶ 716 Suits for Refund

Law: Secs. 19041.5, 19381-92 (CCH CALIFORNIA TAX REPORTS ¶ 89-559).

Comparable Federal: Secs. 6532, 7421-22 (CCH STANDARD FEDERAL TAX REPORTS ¶ 40,220, 42,280—42,285).

Generally, suits for refund may be instituted only after the taxpayer has filed a claim for refund, and they must be based on the grounds set forth in the claim. Time limits for bringing suit are:

(a) four years from the due date of the return;

(b) one year from the date the tax was paid;

(c) 90 days after notice of action by the Franchise Tax Board (FTB) on a claim for refund; or

(d) 90 days after notice of action by the State Board of Equalization (SBE) on an appeal from the action of the FTB on a refund claim, whichever period expires the later.

Effective January 1, 2000, a deposit in the nature of a cash bond made by a taxpayer to stop the running of interest after the FTB has mailed a notice of proposed deficiency assessment is not a payment of tax for purposes of the limitations period for filing a suit for refund, unless the taxpayer provides a written statement to the FTB specifying that the deposit is a payment of tax or the deficiency assessment becomes due and payable.

If the FTB fails to take action on a refund claim within six months (120 days in certain bankruptcy situations) after the claim is filed, the taxpayer may consider the claim disallowed and proceed to bring suit.

Under the California procedure, the taxpayer may appeal to the SBE and, following an adverse decision, may then appeal to the courts by filing suit for refund. The FTB has no right to appeal against an adverse decision of the SBE.

See ¶ 103 for the special procedure whereby a person who is alleged to be a California resident can file a suit to determine the issue without first paying the tax.

The California rules regarding suits for refund are different from the federal in several respects; due to the technical nature and limited applicability of these provisions, no attempt is made here to explain the differences.

¶ 716

¶ 717 Disclosure of Information

Law: Secs. 19504.5, 19530, 19542.3, 19544-65, Revenue and Taxation Code; Sec. 17530.5, Business and Professions Code (CCH CALIFORNIA TAX REPORTS ¶ 89-224).

Comparable Federal: Secs. 6103-10, 7213-16 (CCH STANDARD FEDERAL TAX REPORTS ¶ 37,880—37,980, 42,050—42,078).

Under the California Business and Professions Code, it is a misdemeanor for anyone to disclose any information obtained in the business of preparing federal or state income tax returns or in assisting taxpayers to prepare their returns, unless the disclosure is:

(1) authorized by written consent of the taxpayer;

(2) authorized by law;

(3) necessary to the preparation of the return; or

(4) pursuant to court order.

California and federal laws provide for reciprocal exchange of information in administration of tax laws. The Franchise Tax Board (FTB) and the Internal Revenue Service have a continuing program of informing each other of findings resulting from their examinations of tax returns. To avoid duplication of effort, the two agencies may agree that a particular taxpayer's return will be examined by one or the other. Any improper disclosure or use of such information is a misdemeanor.

The California Revenue and Taxation Code provides rules and procedures regarding personal and confidential information in the files of state agencies; these rules are designed to insure privacy of such information.

Special safeguards are provided to prevent improper disclosure by the FTB of trade secrets or other confidential information with respect to any software that comes into the FTB's possession or control in connection with a tax return examination. Computer software source code and executable code are considered return information for disclosure purposes. Any person who willfully makes known to another person any computer software source code or executable code obtained in connection with a tax return examination may be punished by a fine or imprisonment or both. These provisions apply for software acquired after October 10, 1999, and, after January 8, 2000, for software acquired before October 11, 1999.

¶ 718 Interest on Overpayments

Law: Secs. 19325, 19340-51, 19363 (CCH CALIFORNIA TAX REPORTS ¶ 89-248, 89-433).

Comparable Federal: Sec. 6611 (CCH STANDARD FEDERAL TAX REPORTS ¶ 40,330).

Interest is paid upon overpayments of tax. The interest rate is the same as the rate for deficiencies, as explained at ¶ 709. The law contains specific rules regarding the period for which interest will be paid, depending on whether the tax is refunded or allowed as a credit.

With the exception discussed below, no interest will be allowed if refund or credit is made within 45 days of the date of filing a return, or within 45 days after the due date (without regard to extensions of time). In case of a late return, no interest will be allowed for any day before the date of filing.

The law contains a provision to prevent payment of interest on overpayments which are made deliberately for the purpose of obtaining interest. In any case where the Franchise Tax Board disallows interest on a refund, the taxpayer may appeal to the State Board of Equalization (SBE) and may bring suit if the action of the SBE is not favorable; detailed rules are provided for such appeals. There are no comparable federal provisions.

Where a refund is made under the special 7-year limitation period for claims based on bad debt and worthless security losses, the amount of interest paid is limited.

¶ 719 Closing Agreements

Law: Secs. 19441, 19442 (CCH CALIFORNIA TAX REPORTS ¶ 89-360).

Comparable Federal: Sec. 7121 (CCH STANDARD FEDERAL TAX REPORTS ¶ 41,880).

The Franchise Tax Board (FTB) and a taxpayer may enter into a "closing agreement" in respect to the tax for any taxable period. Such an agreement is binding and may not be reopened except upon a showing of fraud, etc. The California provision is substantially the same as the federal.

In addition, the Executive Officer and the Chief Counsel of the FTB may approve the settlement of any civil tax dispute involving a reduction of tax of $5,000 or less without the Attorney General's review or the FTB's approval. For reduction of tax settlements in excess of $5,000, the Executive Officer and the Chief Counsel are required to submit the proposed settlements to the Attorney General for review prior to presenting their recommendations to the FTB. FTB Notice No. 98-11 (1998) (CCH CALIFORNIA TAX REPORTS ¶ 89-360.702) addresses the procedures for initiating and processing a request for a settlement agreement.

If the FTB neither approves nor disapproves a recommendation for settlement within 45 days after receiving the recommendation, the recommendation is deemed approved. Disapproval requires a majority vote of the FTB, and a disapproved settlement may be resubmitted to the FTB. All settlements are final and nonappealable, except upon a showing of fraud or material misrepresentation.

In *Appeal of Wesley G. Pope* (1958) (CCH CALIFORNIA TAX REPORTS ¶ 89-360.56), the State Board of Equalization held that a check marked "payment in full" does not follow the statutory requirements of a closing agreement. Hence, the FTB was justified in making subsequent assessments after the receipt of such a payment.

¶ 720 Compromise of Tax Liability

Law: Sec. 19443 (CCH CALIFORNIA TAX REPORTS ¶ 89-360).

Federal: Sec. 7122 (CCH STANDARD FEDERAL TAX REPORTS ¶ 41,910).

California Form: FTB 4905PIT.

The executive officer and chief counsel of the Franchise Tax Board (FTB), or their delegates, jointly, may administratively compromise any final tax liability in which the reduction of tax is $7,500 or less. The FTB, itself, upon recommendation by its executive officer and chief counsel, jointly, may compromise a final tax liability in which the reduction of tax is in excess of $7,500 but less than $10,000.

For an amount to be administratively compromised, the taxpayer must establish that (1) the amount offered in payment is the most that can be expected to be paid or collected from the taxpayer's present assets or income and (2) the taxpayer has no reasonable prospects of acquiring increased income or assets that would enable the taxpayer to satisfy a greater amount of the liability than that offered. In addition, the FTB must determine that the acceptance of the offer in compromise is in the best interest of the state.

In the case of joint and several liability, the acceptance of an offer in compromise from one spouse does not relieve the other spouse from paying the liability. However, the amount of the liability must be reduced by the amount of the accepted offer.

Also, it is of course possible under California procedures, as under federal, to negotiate a "compromise" of doubtful items of income, expense, etc., in dealing with representatives of the FTB upon examination of returns or during appeal proceedings or to make a settlement of a suit after litigation has begun.

See ¶ 712a for a discussion of compromises of withholding tax liabilities.

¶ 721 Voluntary Disclosure Agreements

Laws: Secs. 19191-94 (CCH CALIFORNIA TAX REPORTS ¶ 89-360).

Comparable Federal: None.

The Franchise Tax Board (FTB) is authorized to enter into voluntary disclosure agreements with (1) qualified business entities that in good faith have previously failed to comply with California's registration and reporting requirements, and (2) qualified S corporation shareholders who in good faith have failed to comply with California's registration, reporting, and payment requirements.

Under the terms established in a voluntary disclosure agreement, the FTB may waive penalties for noncompliance with specified reporting and payment requirements for the six taxable years immediately preceding the FTB's signing of the agreement. For taxable years ending more than six years prior to the agreement, the business's income taxes, additions to tax, fees, or penalties may also be waived. However, the FTB may not waive penalties for any of the six years immediately preceding the signing of the agreement in which an S corporation shareholder was a California resident required to file a California tax return. In addition, for purposes of qualified shareholders, the FTB's waiver authority is limited to penalties or additions to tax attributable to the shareholder's California source income from the S corporation.

A "qualifying business entity" includes any out-of-state bank or non-exempt corporation (including any predecessors to the business entity) that voluntarily comes forward prior to any contact from the FTB and that has never filed a California income tax return or been the subject of an FTB inquiry regarding income tax liability. A "qualified shareholder" is a nonresident shareholder of an S corporation that has applied for a voluntary disclosure agreement and disclosed all material facts pertaining to the shareholder's liability.

¶ 722 Recovery of Erroneous Refunds

Law: Secs. 19054, 19411-13 (CCH CALIFORNIA TAX REPORTS ¶ 89-350).

Comparable Federal: Secs. 6532, 6602, 7405 (CCH STANDARD FEDERAL TAX REPORTS ¶ 40,220, 40,320, 42,255).

The Franchise Tax Board may recover erroneous refunds, with interest, subject to certain conditions. The California law is generally similar to the federal law.

In *Appeal of Albert A. Ellis, Jr.* (1972) (CCH CALIFORNIA TAX REPORTS ¶ 89-430.371), the State Board of Equalization (SBE) allowed interest on recovery of an erroneous refund, although the tax assessment in question was not a "deficiency" under the law then in effect. In *Appeal of Bruce H. and Norah E. Planck* (1977) (CCH CALIFORNIA TAX REPORTS ¶ 89-350.311), the SBE held that assessment of an erroneous refund was a "deficiency" and that interest was properly imposed under the rules for interest on deficiencies (see ¶ 709).

PART IV
Taxes on Corporate Income

FEDERAL-CALIFORNIA CROSS-REFERENCE TABLE AND INDEX

Showing Sections of California Bank and Corporation Tax Law (Revenue and Taxation Code) Comparable to Sections of Federal Law (1986 Internal Revenue Code)

Federal	California	Subject	Paragraph
IRC Sec. 11	Secs. 23151, 23501	Tax imposed	¶ 802a, ¶ 809
IRC Sec. 15	Secs. 23058, 24251	Tax rate changes during year	¶ 1105
IRC Sec. 26	Sec. 23036	"Tax" defined	¶ 809, ¶ 809a
IRC Sec. 30	. . .	Low emission motor vehicle credit	¶ 810a
IRC Sec. 38	. . .	General business credit	. . .
IRC Sec. 39	. . .	Unused credits	. . .
IRC Sec. 40	. . .	Credit for WIN programs	. . .
IRC Sec. 41	Sec. 23609	Qualified research credit	¶ 810a
IRC Sec. 42	Secs. 23610.4-10.5	Low-income housing credit	¶ 810a
IRC Sec. 43	Sec. 23604	Enhanced oil recovery credit	¶ 810a
IRC Sec. 44	Sec. 23642	Disabled access credit	¶ 810a
IRC Sec. 45C	. . .	Clinical testing credit	¶ 810a
IRC Secs. 46-50	. . .	Investment in depreciable property	. . .
IRC Secs. 51, 52	Sec. 23621	Work opportunity credit	. . .
IRC Sec. 53	Sec. 23453	Minimum tax credit	¶ 809a, ¶ 810a
IRC Secs. 55-59	Secs. 23400, 23455-59	Alternative minimum tax	¶ 809a, ¶ 1008
IRC Sec. 59A	. . .	Environmental tax	. . .
IRC Sec. 61	Secs. 24271, 24314, 24308, 24315, 24323	Gross income	¶ 901
IRC Sec. 63	Sec. 24341	Taxable income defined	¶ 808
IRC Sec. 64	Sec. 23049.1	Ordinary income defined	. . .
IRC Sec. 65	Sec. 23049.2	Ordinary loss defined	. . .
IRC Sec. 72	Secs. 24272.2, 24302	Annuities	¶ 903, ¶ 904
IRC Sec. 75	. . .	Dealers in tax-exempt securities	. . .
IRC Sec. 77	Sec. 24273	Community credit loans	¶ 911
IRC Sec. 78	. . .	Dividends from foreign corporations	. . .
IRC Sec. 80	. . .	Restoration of value of certain securities	. . .
IRC Sec. 83	Sec. 24379	Transfer of property in exchange for services	¶ 1001, ¶ 1012a
IRC Sec. 84	. . .	Property transferred to political organizations	. . .
IRC Sec. 88	Sec. 24275	Nuclear plant expenses	. . .
IRC Sec. 90	Sec. 24276	Illegal federal irrigation subsidies	. . .
IRC Sec. 101	Secs. 24301, 24302, 24305	Life insurance proceeds	¶ 902, ¶ 903, ¶ 904
IRC Sec. 102	. . .	Gifts and inheritances	. . .

Federal	California	Subject	Paragraph
IRC Sec. 103	Secs. 24272, 24301	Interest on government bonds	¶ 909
IRC Sec. 108	Secs. 24301, 24307	Income from discharge of indebtedness	¶ 907
IRC Sec. 109	Secs. 24301, 24309	Improvements by lessee	¶ 905
IRC Sec. 110	Sec. 24309.5	Lessee construction allowances	¶ 905a
IRC Sec. 111	Secs. 24301, 24310	Recovery of bad debts and prior taxes	¶ 906
IRC Sec. 118	Secs. 24324, 24325	Contributions to capital of corporation	¶ 912
IRC Sec. 126	Secs. 24301, 24308.5	Cost-sharing payments	¶ 922
IRC Sec. 136	Secs. 24301, 24326	Energy conservation subsidies	¶ 921
IRC Secs. 141-50	Sec. 24272	Private activity bonds	¶ 909
IRC Sec. 161	Secs. 24415, 24436.5, 24441, 24447, 24448	Allowance of deductions	. . .
IRC Sec. 162	Secs. 24343, 24343.2, 24343.5, 24343.7	Deductions for business expense	¶ 1001, ¶ 1017
IRC Sec. 163	Secs. 24344, 24344.5, 24344.7	Interest expense deduction	¶ 1002, ¶ 1310
IRC Sec. 164	Secs. 24345, 24346	Deduction for taxes	¶ 1003
IRC Sec. 165	Secs. 24347, 24347.5	Losses-deductions	¶ 1004, ¶ 1007
IRC Sec. 166	Sec. 24347	Deduction for bad debts	¶ 1006
IRC Sec. 167	Secs. 24349-5.4, 24368.1	Depreciation	¶ 1008, ¶ 1238
IRC Sec. 168	Sec. 24349	Accelerated cost recovery system	¶ 1008
IRC Sec. 169	Sec. 24372.3	Amortization of pollution control facilities	¶ 1008
IRC Sec. 170	Secs. 24357-59.1	Charitable contributions	¶ 1010, ¶ 1310
IRC Sec. 171	Secs. 24360-63.5	Amortizable bond premium	¶ 1011
IRC Sec. 172	Secs. 24416-16.6, 25110	Net operating loss deduction	¶ 1018
IRC Sec. 173	Sec. 24364	Circulation expenditures	¶ 1001b
IRC Sec. 174	Sec. 24365	Research expenditures	¶ 1008
IRC Sec. 175	Sec. 24369	Soil and water conservation expenditures	¶ 1001a
IRC Sec. 176	. . .	Social security payments for employees of foreign subsidiaries	. . .
IRC Sec. 178	Sec. 24373	Depreciation or amortization of lessee improvements	¶ 1008
IRS Secs. 179	Secs. 24356, 24356.8	Bonus depreciation	¶ 1008
IRS Sec. 179A	Sec. 24356.5	Clean-fuel vehicles and refueling property	¶ 1008
IRC Sec. 180	Sec. 24377	Farm fertilizer expenses	¶ 1001a
IRC Sec. 183	. . .	Hobby losses	. . .
IRC Sec. 186	Secs. 24675, 24677, 24678	Recovery of antitrust damages	¶ 1106
IRC Sec. 190	Sec. 24383	Architectural adaptations for the handicapped	¶ 1001
IRC Sec. 192	. . .	Contributions to black lung benefit trust	¶ 1010
IRC Sec. 193	. . .	Tertiary injectants	¶ 1009a
IRC Sec. 194	Sec. 24372.5	Amortization of reforestation expenses	¶ 1008
IRC Sec. 194A	. . .	Contributions to employer liability trusts	¶ 1012
IRC Sec. 195	Sec. 24414	Start-up expenses	¶ 1012b
IRC Sec. 196	Sec. 23051.5	Unused investment credits	. . .
IRC Sec. 197	Sec. 24355.5	Amortizatioin of goodwill	¶ 1008, ¶ 1214

Federal	California	Subject	Paragraph
IRC Sec. 198	Sec. 24369.4	Environmental remediation expenses	¶ 1008
IRC Sec. 216	Sec. 24382	Foreclosure of cooperative housing corporation stock	¶ 1016
IRC Sec. 220	Sec. 24343.3	Medical Savings Accounts	. . .
IRC Sec. 241	Sec. 24401	Special deductions	. . .
IRC Secs. 243-247	Secs. 24401, 24402, 24410, 24411	Dividends received by corporations	¶ 808, ¶ 908, ¶ 1014
IRC Sec. 248	Secs. 24407-09	Organizational expenditures	¶ 1008
IRC Sec. 249	Sec. 24439	Deductions of bond premium on repurchase	¶ 1002, ¶ 1214a
IRC Sec. 261	Sec. 24421	Disallowance of deductions	¶ 1017
IRC Sec. 263	Secs. 24422-23	Capital expenditures	¶ 1009a, ¶ 1017
IRC Sec. 263A	Sec. 24422.3	Inventory capitalization— inclusion	¶ 1106, ¶ 1107
IRC Sec. 264	Sec. 24424	Payments on life insurance contracts	¶ 1002, ¶ 1017
IRC Sec. 265	Sec. 24425	Deductions allocable to tax-exempt income	¶ 1002, ¶ 1017
IRC Sec. 266	Sec. 24426	Taxes and carrying charges	¶ 1017
IRC Sec. 267	Sec. 24427	Transactions between related individuals	¶ 1017
IRC Sec. 268	. . .	Sale of land with unharvested crop	¶ 1017
IRC Sec. 269	Sec. 24431	Acquisitions made to avoid tax	¶ 1110
IRC Sec. 269A	. . .	Personal service corporations formed to evade taxes	¶ 1110
IRC Sec. 269B	. . .	Stapled interests	¶ 1110
IRC Sec. 271	Sec. 24434	Debts owed by political parties	¶ 1006, ¶ 1017
IRC Sec. 272	. . .	Disposal of coal or iron ore	. . .
IRC Sec. 274	Sec. 24443	Disallowance of entertainment and gift expenses	¶ 1001, ¶ 1017
IRC Sec. 275	Sec. 24345	Certain taxes	1003¶
IRC Sec. 276	Sec. 24429	Indirect contributions to political parties	¶ 1017
IRC Sec. 277	Sec. 24437	Deduction limitation for social clubs	¶ 1017
IRC Sec. 279	Sec. 24438	Interest deduction on corporate acquisition indebtedness	¶ 1002
IRC Sec. 280B	Sec. 24442	Demolition of historic structures	¶ 1017
IRC Sec. 280C	Sec. 24440	Expenses for which credit allowed	¶ 810a, ¶ 1017
IRC Sec. 280E	Secs. 24436-36.1	Illegal sale of drugs	¶ 1017
IRC Sec. 280F	Sec. 24349.1	Depreciation-luxury cars	¶ 1008
IRC Sec. 280G	. . .	Golden parachutes	¶ 1017
IRC Sec. 280H	Sec. 24442.5	Amounts paid to employee owners	. . .
IRC Sec. 291	Sec. 24449	Preference items	¶ 809a
IRC Secs. 301-385	Secs. 24451-81	Corporate distributions and adjustments	¶ 814, ¶ 907, ¶ 908, ¶ 1206-08, ¶ 1210-11, ¶ 1213, ¶ 1213a, ¶ 1220-22, ¶ 1230, ¶ 1232

Federal	California	Subject	Paragraph
IRC Secs. 401-424	Secs. 23701p, 24601-12	Deferred compensation	¶ 908, ¶ 1012, ¶ 1012a
IRC Sec. 441	Secs. 24631, 24632, 24633.5	Accounting periods	¶ 1101
IRC Sec. 442	Sec. 24633	Change in accounting period	¶ 1102
IRC Sec. 443	Secs. 23113, 24634-36	Short-period returns	¶ 1103
IRC Sec. 444	Sec. 24637	Election to keep same tax year—S Corporations	¶ 803, ¶ 1104
IRC Sec. 446	Sec. 24651	Accounting methods	¶ 1106
IRC Sec. 447	Secs. 24652-52.5	Accounting for farm corporations	¶ 1106
IRC Sec. 448	Sec. 24654	Cash method of accounting restricted	¶ 1106
IRC Sec. 451	Sec. 24661	Taxable year of inclusion	¶ 1106
IRC Sec. 453	Secs. 24667, 24668.1	Installment method	¶ 1109
IRC Sec. 453A	Sec. 24667	Installment method	¶ 1109
IRC Sec. 453B	Sec. 24667	Installment method	¶ 1109
IRC Sec. 454	Sec. 24674	Obligation issued at discount	¶ 1111
IRC Sec. 455	Sec. 24676	Prepaid subscription income	¶ 1106
IRC Sec. 456	. . .	Prepaid dues income	¶ 1106
IRC Sec. 457	. . .	Deferred compensation plans-state governments	. . .
IRC Sec. 458	Sec. 24676.5	Returned magazines, paperbacks, records	¶ 1106
IRC Sec. 460	Secs. 24673, 24673.2	Long-term contracts	¶ 1106
IRC Sec. 461	Sec. 24681	Taxable year of deduction	¶ 1002, ¶ 1106
IRC Sec. 464	Sec. 24682	Farming expenses	¶ 1106
IRC Sec. 465	Sec. 24691	Deductions limited to amount at risk	¶ 1017, ¶ 1019
IRC Sec. 467	Sec. 24688	Deferred rental payments	¶ 1106
IRC Sec. 468	Sec. 24689	Waste disposal costs	¶ 1106
IRC Sec. 468A	Sec. 24690	Nuclear decommissioning funds	. . .
IRC Sec. 468B	Sec. 24693	Designated settlement funds	¶ 803a
IRC Sec. 469	Sec. 24692	Passive losses and credits	¶ 1002a
IRC Sec. 471	Sec. 24701	Inventories-general rule	¶ 1107
IRC Sec. 472	Sec. 24701	Inventories-LIFO	¶ 1108
IRC Sec. 473	. . .	Liquidation of LIFO inventories	¶ 1108
IRC Sec. 474	Sec. 24708	Simplified dollar value LIFO	¶ 1108
IRC Sec. 475	Sec. 24710	Mark to market accounting	¶ 1107, ¶ 1214
IRC Sec. 481	Sec. 24721	Adjustments required by changes in method	¶ 1106
IRC Sec. 482	Sec. 24725	Allocation of income among taxpayers	¶ 1106, ¶ 1110
IRC Sec. 483	Sec. 24726	Imputed interest	¶ 1106, ¶ 1112
IRC Sec. 501	Secs. 23701-01y, 23704, 23704.4, 23704.5, 23706	Exempt organizations and trusts	¶ 804, ¶ 804a
IRC Sec. 502	Sec. 23702	Feeder organizations	¶ 804a
IRC Sec. 503	Secs. 23736-36.4	Requirements for exemption	¶ 804a
IRC Sec. 504	Sec. 23704.6	Status after disqualification for lobbying	¶ 804
IRC Sec. 505	Sec. 23705	Special rules—VEBAs, etc.	¶ 804
IRC Sec. 507	Sec. 23707	Private foundation status terminated	¶ 804
IRC Sec. 508	Sec. 23708	Presumption that organization is private foundation	¶ 804
IRC Sec. 509	Sec. 23709	"Private foundation" defined	¶ 804
IRC Sec. 511	Sec. 23731	Unrelated business income	¶ 804a

Federal	California	Subject	Paragraph
IRC Sec. 512	Sec. 23732	Unrelated business taxable income	¶ 804a
IRC Sec. 513	Secs. 23710, 23734	Unrelated trade or business	¶ 804a
IRC Sec. 514	Sec. 23735	Unrelated debt-financed income	¶ 804a
IRC Sec. 515	. . .	Taxes, possessions, and foreign countries	¶ 804a
IRC Sec. 521	. . .	Farmers' cooperatives-exemption	¶ 1015
IRC Sec. 526	. . .	Shipowners' protection associations	. . .
IRC Sec. 527	Sec. 23701r	Political organizations	¶ 804
IRC Sec. 528	Sec. 23701t	Homeowners' associations	¶ 804, ¶ 914
IRC Sec. 529	Secs. 18645, 23711, 24306	Qualified state tuition program	¶ 804, ¶ 923
IRC Sec. 530	Sec. 23712	Education IRAS	. . .
IRC Secs. 531-37	. . .	Corporations improperly accumulating surplus	. . .
IRC Secs. 541-47	Sec. 23051.5	Personal holding companies	. . .
IRC Secs. 551-57	Sec. 23501.5	Foreign personal holding companies	. . .
IRC Secs. 561-65	Sec. 24402	Deduction for dividends paid	. . .
IRC Sec. 581	Sec. 23039	Definition of bank	. . .
IRC Sec. 582	Sec. 24347	Bad debts, losses, and gains	¶ 1006
IRC Sec. 585	Sec. 24348	Deduction for bad debts—banks and S and L's	¶ 1006
IRC Sec. 591	Secs. 24370, 24403	Deduction for dividends paid on deposits	¶ 1015
IRC Sec. 593	Sec. 24348	Deduction for bad debts—federal mutual savings banks	¶ 1006
IRC Sec. 594	. . .	Mutual savings banks conducting life insurance business	. . .
IRC Sec. 597	Sec. 24322	FSLIC financial assistance	¶ 912
IRC Secs. 611-12	Sec. 24831	Natural resources	¶ 1009, ¶ 1238
IRC Sec. 613	Sec. 24831	Percentage depletion	¶ 1009, ¶ 1238
IRC Sec. 613A	Sec. 24831	Oil and gas wells	¶ 1009
IRC Sec. 614	Sec. 24831	"Property" defined	¶ 1009
IRC Sec. 616	Sec. 24831	Mine development expenditures	¶ 1009, ¶ 1009a
IRC Sec. 617	Sec. 24831	Mine exploration expenditures	¶ 1009, ¶ 1009a
IRC Sec. 631	Sec. 24831	Timber, coal, iron ore	¶ 1009
IRC Sec. 636	Sec. 24831	Mineral production payments	¶ 1009
IRC Sec. 638	Sec. 24831	Continental shelf areas	¶ 1009
IRC Secs. 641-92	Sec. 24271	Estates, trusts, and beneficiaries	. . .
IRC Secs. 701-777	Secs. 23081, 23083, 23091-99.5, 24271	Partnerships	¶ 612, ¶ 1234
IRC Secs. 801-848	. . .	Insurance companies	. . .
IRC Secs. 851-855	Secs. 24870, 24872	Regulated investment companies	¶ 802a, ¶ 1015
IRC Secs. 856-860	Secs. 24870, 24872-72.7	Real estate investment trusts	¶ 802a, ¶ 1015
IRC Secs. 860A-860G	Secs. 24870, 24873, 24874	Real estate mortgage investment conduits	¶ 802a
IRC Secs. 860H-860L	Secs. 24870, 24875	Financial asset securitization trusts	¶ 802a

Federal	California	Subject	Paragraph
IRC Secs. 861-865	Sec. 25110	Income from sources within or without U.S.	¶ 817, ¶ 1308
IRC Secs. 871-879	. . .	Foreign government investment income	. . .
IRC Secs. 881-882	Sec. 24321	Income of foreign corporations	. . .
IRC Sec. 883	Sec. 24320	Operation of foreign aircraft or ships	¶ 915
IRC Secs. 884-891	. . .	Foreign corporations and nonresident aliens	. . .
IRC Sec. 892	Sec. 24327	Income of foreign governments and of international organizations	. . .
IRC Secs. 901-907	. . .	Foreign tax credit	. . .
IRC Sec. 908	. . .	Reduction of credit for international boycott participation	. . .
IRC Secs. 921-927	. . .	Foreign sales corporations	. . .
IRC Secs. 931-936	. . .	U.S. possessions	. . .
IRC Secs. 951-964	Sec. 25110	Controlled foreign corporations	¶ 817, ¶ 908
IRC Secs. 970-971	. . .	Export trade corporations	. . .
IRC Secs. 985-989	Sec. 24905	Foreign currency transactions	¶ 1202b
IRC Sec. 988	Secs. 24905, 24905.5	Hedging transactions	¶ 1214
IRC Secs. 991-999	Sec. 23051.5	DISC corporations	¶ 908
IRC Sec. 1001	Secs. 24901, 24902, 24955	Determination of gain or loss	¶ 1201
IRC Sec. 1011	Secs. 24911, 24964	Adjusted basis	¶ 1235
IRC Sec. 1012	Sec. 24912	Basis of property—cost	¶ 1215
IRC Sec. 1013	Sec. 24913	Basis of property in inventory	¶ 1216
IRC Sec. 1014	. . .	Basis of property acquired from decedent	¶ 1219
IRC Sec. 1015	Secs. 24914, 24915	Basis of property acquired by gift or transfer in trust	¶ 1217, ¶ 1218
IRC Sec. 1016	Secs. 24916, 24916.2, 24917	Adjustments to basis	¶ 1235-36
IRC Sec. 1017	Sec. 24918	Discharge of indebtedness	¶ 1235, ¶ 1239
IRC Sec. 1019	Sec. 24919	Improvements to property by lessee	¶ 1235, ¶ 1237
IRC Sec. 1021	. . .	Sale of annuities	¶ 1235
IRC Sec. 1031	Sec. 24941	Exchange of property held for productive use	¶ 1204
IRC Sec. 1032	Secs. 19061, 24942	Exchange of stock for property	¶ 1214b
IRC Sec. 1033	Secs. 19061, 24941-49.5	Involuntary conversions	¶ 1202, ¶ 1223
IRC Sec. 1035	Sec. 24950	Exchanges of insurance policies	¶ 1204a
IRC Sec. 1036	Sec. 24951	Exchange of stock	¶ 1205
IRC Sec. 1037	. . .	Exchanges of U.S. obligations	¶ 1205a
IRC Sec. 1038	Sec. 24952	Reacquisitions of real property	¶ 1205b
IRC Sec. 1042	Secs. 24954-54.1	Securities sales to ESOPs	¶ 1201
IRC Sec. 1044	Sec. 24956	Rollover of publicly traded securities	¶ 1214
IRC Sec. 1051	Sec. 24961	Basis of property acquired from affiliated corporation	¶ 1225
IRC Sec. 1052	Sec. 24962	Basis provisions from prior codes	¶ 1226
IRC Sec. 1053	Sec. 24963	Basis of property acquired before March 1, 1913	¶ 1227
IRC Sec. 1054	Sec. 24965	Basis of stock issued by FNMA	¶ 1228

Federal	California	Subject	Paragraph
IRC Sec. 1055	. . .	Redeemable ground rents	¶ 1229
IRC Sec. 1056	Sec. 24989	Basis limitation for player contracts	¶ 1240
IRC Sec. 1057	. . .	Transfers of property to foreign trust	. . .
IRC Sec. 1059	Sec. 24966	Basis after extraordinary dividend	¶ 1215
IRC Sec. 1059A	Sec. 24966.1	Basis of property imported from related persons	¶ 1215, ¶ 1216
IRC Sec. 1060	Sec. 24966.2	Allocation of asset acquisitions	¶ 1215, ¶ 1241
IRC Sec. 1081	Sec. 24981	Exchange or distribution in obedience to SEC orders	¶ 1203
IRC Sec. 1082	Sec. 24988	Basis for determining gain or loss	¶ 1233
IRC Sec. 1091	Sec. 24998	Wash sales of stock or securities	¶ 1005, ¶ 1224
IRC Sec. 1092	Sec. 24998	Straddles	. . .
IRC Secs. 1201-59	Secs. 23051.5, 24990, 24990.4-24990.7	Capital gains and losses	¶ 1008, ¶ 1201, ¶ 1209, ¶ 1214
IRC Secs. 1271-74A	Secs. 24990, 24994	Debt instruments	¶ 910, ¶ 1214a
IRC Sec. 1275	Secs. 24990, 24991	Definitions and special rules relating to debt instruments	¶ 909, ¶ 910
IRC Secs. 1276-78	Sec. 24990	Market discount on bonds	¶ 910, ¶ 1214
IRC Secs. 1281-83	Secs. 24990, 24991	Discount on short term obligations as income	¶ 1214
IRC Secs. 1286-88	Secs. 24990	Miscellaneous provisions	¶ 1214
IRC Secs. 1291-98	Secs. 24990, 24995	Passive foreign investment companies	¶ 1214
IRC Secs. 1311-14	. . .	Mitigation of effect of limitations	¶ 1408
IRC Sec. 1341	. . .	Repayment of income received under claim of right	¶ 1106
IRC Sec. 1351	. . .	Recovery of foreign expropriation losses	. . .
IRC Secs. 1361-79	Secs. 23800-11, 23813	"Subchapter S" corporations	¶ 803
IRC Sec. 1381	Secs. 24404-06	Cooperatives	¶ 1015
IRC Sec. 1382	Secs. 24404-06	Taxable income of cooperatives	¶ 1015
IRC Sec. 1383	Secs. 24404-06.5	Nonqualified notices of allocation redeemed by cooperative	¶ 1015
IRC Sec. 1385	Sec. 24273.5	Amounts includible in patron's gross income	¶ 913
IRC Sec. 1441	. . .	Withholding on nonresident aliens	¶ 1412
IRC Sec. 1445	. . .	Withholding on U.S. real estate sales	¶ 1412
IRC Sec. 1501	Secs. 23362, 23364a	Consolidated return of affiliated group	¶ 806
IRC Sec. 1502	Secs. 23363, 25106.5	Regulations	¶ 806
IRC Sec. 1503	Sec. 23364	Computation and payment of tax	¶ 806
IRC Sec. 1504	Sec. 23361	"Affiliated group" defined	¶ 806
IRC Sec. 4911	Sec. 23740	Excess expenditures to influence legislation	¶ 1017
IRC Secs. 4940-48	. . .	Taxes on private foundations	¶ 804
IRC Secs. 4971-75	. . .	Tax on failure to meet pension funding requirements	¶ 1012

Federal	California	Subject	Paragraph
IRC Sec. 6012	Various	Returns required	¶ 805, ¶ 805a
IRC Sec. 6031	Secs. 18535, 18633-33.5, 23810	Return of partnership income	. . .
IRC Sec. 6033	Sec. 23772	Annual returns by exempt organizations	¶ 805a
IRC Sec. 6037	Sec. 18601	S corporation returns	¶ 803
IRC Sec. 6038	Sec. 19141.2	Information returns on foreign corporations	¶ 1412
IRC Sec. 6038A	Sec. 19141.5	Report of 25% foreign-owned corporations	¶ 1412a
IRC Sec. 6038B	Sec. 19141.5	Report on transfers to foreign persons	¶ 1412a
IRC Sec. 6038C	Sec. 19141.5	Report of foreign corporation doing U.S. business	¶ 1412a
IRC Sec. 6039	Sec. 18636	Information returns for foreign interests	¶ 1411
IRC Sec. 6041	Secs. 18637, 25111	Information at source	¶ 1411
IRC Sec. 6041A	Sec. 18638	Reporting certain payments	¶ 1411
IRC Sec. 6042	Sec. 18639	Returns for corporate earnings and profits	¶ 1411
IRC Sec. 6043	. . .	Returns for dividends on liquidation	. . .
IRC Sec. 6044	Sec. 18640	Returns for cooperatives	. . .
IRC Sec. 6045	Secs. 18641-43	Returns for brokers	¶ 1411
IRC Sec. 6049	Sec. 18630	Returns for payment of interest	¶ 1411
IRC Sec. 6050A	Sec. 18644	Returns for fishing boat operators	¶ 1411
IRC Sec. 6050I-50S	Sec. 18645	Information returns	¶ 1410, ¶ 1411
IRC Sec. 6062	. . .	Signing of corporation returns	. . .
IRC Sec. 6065	Secs. 18606, 18621	Verification of return	¶ 805
IRC Sec. 6072	Sec. 18566	Time for filing returns	¶ 805
IRC Sec. 6081	Secs. 18567, 18604	Extension of time for filing return	¶ 805
IRC Sec. 6091	Sec. 18621	Place for filing returns or other documents	. . .
IRC Sec. 6102	Sec. 18623	Fractional dollar calculations	¶ 805
IRC Secs. 6103-04	Secs. 19543-49, 19551-55, 19562, 19565, 21023	Confidentiality of returns	. . .
IRC Sec. 6107	Sec. 18625	Duties of tax prepares	¶ 1401
IRC Sec. 6109	Sec. 18624	Identifying numbers required on documents	¶ 1401
IRC Sec. 6115	Sec. 18648.5	Disclosure related to quid pro quo information	¶ 1010
IRC Sec. 6151	Secs. 19001, 19004-06	Payment of tax	¶ 807
IRC Sec. 6155	. . .	Payment on notice and demand	¶ 1404
IRC Secs. 6161-64	. . .	Extensions of time for payment	¶ 807
IRC Sec. 6201	Sec. 21024	Burden of proof	¶ 1401a
IRC Sec. 6212	Secs. 19031-36, 19049, 19050	Notice of deficiency	¶ 1402, ¶ 1403
IRC Sec. 6213	Secs. 19041-48, 19332-34, 19051	Deficiencies—petition to tax court	¶ 1402, ¶ 1403, ¶ 1404
IRC Sec. 6225	Sec. 19063	SOL for partnership items	¶ 1408
IRC Sec. 6325	Sec. 19226	Release of liens	. . .
IRC Sec. 6331	Secs. 19231, 19236, 19262, 21019	Levy to collect tax	. . .
IRC Sec. 6335	Sec. 19262	Sale of seized property	. . .
IRC Sec. 6338	Sec. 19263	Certificate of sale	. . .

Federal	California	Subject	Paragraph
IRC Sec. 6342	Sec. 19263	Disposition of proceeds of levy or sale	. . .
IRC Secs. 6401-08	Secs. 19104, 19107, 19116, 19349, 19354, 19362-63, 19431, 21012	Abatements, credits, and refunds	¶ 1413, ¶ 1414
IRC Sec. 6425	. . .	Adjustment of overpayment of estimated income tax	¶ 806a
IRC Secs. 6501, 6503(i)	Secs. 19057-58, 19065-67, 19087, 19371	Limitations on assessments	¶ 1402, ¶ 1408
IRC Sec. 6511	Secs. 19306, 19308-14	Time limitation on filing claim for credit or refund	¶ 1415
IRC Sec. 6532	Sec. 19384	Limitation periods on suits	¶ 1416, ¶ 1421
IRC Sec. 6601	Secs. 19101-06, 19108, 19111-15	Interest on tax due	¶ 807, ¶ 1409
IRC Sec. 6602	Sec. 19411	Interest on erroneous refund	¶ 1421
IRC Sec. 6611	Secs. 19340, 19341, 19349, 19351	Interest on overpayments	¶ 806a, ¶ 1417
IRC Sec. 6621	Sec. 19521	Determination of rate of interest	¶ 1409
IRC Sec. 6651	Secs. 19131-32.5	Failure to file return or pay tax	¶ 1410
IRC Sec. 6652	Secs. 19133.5, 23772	Failure to file return	¶ 805a, ¶ 1410
IRC Sec. 6653	. . .	Failure to pay stamp tax	¶ 1410
IRC Sec. 6655	Secs. 19004, 19010, 19023-27, 19142-51	Estimated tax	¶ 806a
IRC Sec. 6657	Sec. 19134	Bad checks	¶ 1410
IRC Sec. 6658	Sec. 19161	Timely payments during pending bankruptcy	¶ 1410
IRC Sec. 6662	Sec. 19164	Accuracy-related penalty	¶ 1410
IRC Sec. 6663	Sec. 19164	Fraud penalty	¶ 1410
IRC Sec. 6664	Sec. 19164	Definitions and special rules	¶ 1410
IRC Sec. 6665	Sec. 19164	Applicable rules	¶ 1410
IRC Sec. 6673	Sec. 19714	Penalty for delay	¶ 1410
IRC Sec. 6693	Sec. 19184	Failure to file return	¶ 1410
IRC Sec. 6694	Sec. 19166	Understatement by preparer	¶ 1410
IRC Sec. 6695-96	Secs. 19167, 19168, 19712	Tax preparer penalties	¶ 1410
IRC Sec. 6700	Sec. 19177	Penalty for promoting abusive tax shelters	¶ 1410
IRC Sec. 6701	Sec. 19178	Penalty for aiding understatement of tax liability	¶ 1410
IRC Sec. 6702	Sec. 19179	Penalty for frivolous tax returns	¶ 1410
IRC Sec. 6703	Sec. 19180	Rules for penalties	¶ 1410
IRC Sec. 6706	Sec. 19181	Original issue discount reporting	¶ 1410
IRC Sec. 6707-08	Secs. 19173, 19182	Penalty for failure to provide tax shelter information	¶ 1410
IRC Sec. 6714	Sec. 19182.5	Penalty for failure to disclose quid pro quo information	. . .
IRC Secs. 6721-24	Sec. 19183	Penalty for nonfiling	¶ 1410
IRC Sec. 6751	Sec. 19187	Procedures for penalties	¶ 1410
IRC Sec. 6861	Secs. 19081, 19086, 19092	Jeopardy assessments	¶ 1405
IRC Sec. 6863	Sec. 19083	Jeopardy assessments stay of collection	¶ 1405
IRC Sec. 6867	Sec. 19093	Presumption for large amount of cash not identified	. . .

Federal	California	Subject	Paragraph
IRC Sec. 6871	Secs. 19088, 19090	Receivership—immediate assessment	¶ 1406
IRC Sec. 6872	Sec. 19089	Suspension of period on assessment	¶ 1406
IRC Sec. 6873	Sec. 19091	Unpaid claims	¶ 1406
IRC Secs. 6901-04	Secs. 19071-74	Liability of transferees and fiduciaries	¶ 1407
IRC Sec. 7121	Sec. 19441	Closing agreements	¶ 1418
IRC Sec. 7122	Sec. 19441	Compromise of tax liability	¶ 1419
IRC Sec. 7201	. . .	Attempt to evade or defeat tax	. . .
IRC Sec. 7202	Secs. 19708, 19709	Wilful failure to collect or pay over tax	¶ 1410
IRC Sec. 7203	Sec. 19706	Wilful failure to file return	¶ 1410
IRC Sec. 7206	Secs. 19701, 19705	Fraud and false statements	¶ 1410
IRC Sec. 7207	. . .	Fraudulent returns, statements, or other documents	. . .
IRC Sec. 7213	Secs. 19542, 19542.3, 19552	Unauthorized disclosure of information	. . .
IRC Sec. 7405	Sec. 19411	Recovery of erroneous refunds	¶ 1421
IRC Sec. 7421	Secs. 19081, 19381	Prohibition of suits to restrain assessment	¶ 1417
IRC Sec. 7422	Secs. 19382, 19383, 19387	Actions for refunds	¶ 1417
IRC Sec. 7430	Secs. 19717, 21013	Recovery of litigation costs	¶ 1401
IRC Sec. 7502	Sec. 21027	Mailing/delivery of returns	¶ 1401a
IRC Sec. 7518	Sec. 24272.5	Capital construction funds for vessels	¶ 916
IRC Sec. 7524	Sec. 21026	Annual notice of delinquency	¶ 1401a
IRC Sec. 7602	Secs. 19504, 19504.7	Examination of books and witnesses	¶ 1402
IRC Sec. 7609	Sec. 19064	Third-party summonses	¶ 1402, ¶ 1408
IRC Sec. 7612	Sec. 19504.5	Software trade secrets	¶ 1401
IRC Sec. 7701	Secs. 23031-38, 23041-51	Definitions	¶ 802a, ¶ 1106
IRC Secs. 7702, 7702A	Sec. 23045	Modified endowment contracts	. . .
IRC Sec. 7704	Sec. 23038.5	Publicly traded partnerships	¶ 802, ¶ 802a
IRC Sec. 7806	Secs. 23030, 23051.5, 23060	Construction of title	. . .
IRC Sec. 7811	Secs. 21001-27	Taxpayers' bill of rights	¶ 1401, ¶ 1401a
IRC Sec. 7872	Sec. 24993	Imputed interest	¶ 1112

CALIFORNIA-FEDERAL CROSS-REFERENCE TABLE AND INDEX

Showing Sections of Federal Law (1986 Internal Revenue Code) Comparable to Sections of California Bank and Corporation Tax Law (Revenue and Taxation Code)

California	Federal	Subject	Paragraph
Secs. 18401-03	. . .	General application of administrative provisions	. . .
Sec. 18405	. . .	Relief upon noncompliance with new provisions	. . .
Secs. 18412-17	IRC Sec. 7807	Continuity of provisions with prior law	. . .
Sec. 18601	IRC Secs. 6012(a), 6037, 6072	Annual income or franchise tax return	¶ 805
Sec. 18602	. . .	Paying wrong tax	¶ 805
Sec. 18604	IRC Sec. 6081	Extension of time for filing return	¶ 805
Sec. 18606	IRC Sec. 6012(b)	Returns by receivers, trustees, or assignees	¶ 805
Sec. 18621	IRC Secs. 6065, 6091	Verification of return	¶ 805
Sec. 18621.5	. . .	Electronic filing verification	¶ 805
Sec. 18622	. . .	Change in federal income tax return	¶ 805
Sec. 18623	IRC Sec. 6102	Fractional dollar calculations	¶ 805
Sec. 18624	IRC Sec. 6109	Identifying numbers	¶ 1401
Sec. 18625	IRC Sec. 6107	Copy to taxpayer	¶ 1401
Sec. 18631	. . .	Nontaxable interest obligations	¶ 1411
Sec. 18633.5	IRC Sec. 6031	Limited liability companies	¶ 802a
Sec. 18636	IRC Sec. 6039	Returns for stock transfers	¶ 1411
Sec. 18637	IRC Sec. 6041	Information returns	¶ 1411
Sec. 18638	IRC Sec. 6041A	Reporting certain payments	¶ 1411
Sec. 18639	IRC Secs. 6041-43, 6049	Returns for interest, dividends, collections	¶ 1411
Sec. 18640	IRC Sec. 6044	Returns by cooperatives	¶ 1411
Sec. 18641	IRC Sec. 6045	Reporting by brokers	¶ 1411
Sec. 18642	IRC Sec. 6045	Information returns of property owners	¶ 1411
Sec. 18643	IRC Sec. 6045	Reporting form for brokers	¶ 1411
Sec. 18644	IRC Sec. 6050A	Fishing boat operators— reporting requirements	¶ 1411
Sec. 18645	IRC Secs. 6039C, 6050H-S	Federal information returns	¶ 1411
Sec. 18647	IRC Sec. 6052	Returns for group-term life insurance	¶ 1411
Sec. 18648	IRC Sec. 6112	Tax shelter reporting	¶ 1411
Sec. 18648.5	IRC Sec. 6115	Disclosure related to quid pro quo information	. . .
Sec. 18649	IRC Sec. 1275	Information furnished to FTB	¶ 1411
Sec. 18661	IRc Sec. 3402	Recipient of income	¶ 1412
Sec. 18662	IRC Secs. 1445, 3402	Withholding of corporate tax	¶ 1412
Sec. 18665	. . .	Change in withholding due to legislative enactments	¶ 1412
Sec. 18667	IRC Sec. 3402	Withholding exemption certificates	¶ 1412
Sec. 18668	IRC Sec. 3403	Failure to withhold	¶ 1412

California	Federal	Subject	Paragraph
Sec. 18669	. . .	Sale, transfer, or disposition of business	¶ 1412
Sec. 18670	. . .	Notice to withhold	¶ 1412
Sec. 18670.5	. . .	Electronic notice to withhold	. . .
Sec. 18671	. . .	Withholding—state agencies	¶ 1412
Sec. 18672	. . .	Liability for failure to withhold	¶ 1412
Sec. 18674	. . .	Requirements for withholding agent	¶ 1412
Sec. 18675	IRC Sec. 6414	Taxpayer remedies when order to withhold	¶ 1412
Sec. 18676	. . .	Notice to withhold to state agencies	¶ 1412
Sec. 18677	IRC Sec. 3505	Lender, surety, or other person liable	¶ 1412
Sec. 19001	IRC Sec. 6151	Payment of tax	¶ 807
Sec. 19002	IRC Sec. 6513	Credit for amount withheld	¶ 805
Sec. 19004	IRC Sec. 6151	Early tax payment	¶ 807
Sec. 19005	IRC Sec. 6151	Tax payable to FTB	¶ 807
Sec. 19007	IRC Sec. 6315	Payments of estimated taxes	¶ 806a
Sec. 19009	IRC Sec. 7512	Failure to pay collected taxes	¶ 1412
Sec. 19010	IRC Sec. 6655	Assessing delinquent estimated taxes	¶ 806a
Sec. 19011	IRC Sec. 6302	Electronic funds transfer	¶ 807
Sec. 19021	. . .	Bank and financial corporation tax	¶ 806a, ¶ 807
Sec. 19022	. . .	Bank tax due date	¶ 806a, ¶ 807
Sec. 19023	IRC Sec. 6655(g)	"Estimated tax" defined	¶ 806a
Sec. 19024	IRC Sec. 6655(g)	"Estimated tax" for banks defined	¶ 806a
Sec. 19025	IRC Sec. 6655(c), (d)	Installment payments of tax	¶ 806a
Sec. 19026	IRC Sec. 6655	Revised estimate of taxes	¶ 806a
Sec. 19027	IRC Sec. 6655	Short-year estimated tax payments	¶ 806a
Sec. 19031	IRC Sec. 6212	Deficiency assessments—FTB authority	¶ 1402
Sec. 19032	IRC Sec. 6212	FTB authorized to examine return	¶ 1402
Sec. 19033	IRC Sec. 6212	Notice of additional assessment	¶ 1402
Sec. 19034	IRC Sec. 6212	Contents of notice	¶ 1402
Sec. 19036	IRC Sec. 6212	Interest, penalties, additions to tax as deficiency assessments	¶ 1402
Sec. 19041	IRC Sec. 6213	Filing protest	¶ 1402
Sec. 19041.5	. . .	Treatment of deposits	¶ 1415, ¶ 1416
Sec. 19042	IRC Sec. 6213	60-day protest period	¶ 1402, ¶ 1404
Sec. 19043	IRC Sec. 6211	Deficiency defined	¶ 1402
Sec. 19044	IRC Sec. 6213	Protest hearing	¶ 1402
Sec. 19045	. . .	Finality of action upon protest	¶ 1402
Sec. 19046	IRC Sec. 6213	Appeal to SBE	¶ 1402, ¶ 1403
Sec. 19047	IRC Sec. 6213	Determination of appeal	¶ 1402, ¶ 1403
Sec. 19048	IRC Sec. 6213	Finality of determination	¶ 1402, ¶ 1403
Sec. 19049	IRC Sec. 6212	Notice and demand	¶ 1402, ¶ 1404
Sec. 19050	IRC Sec. 6212	Certificate of mailing	¶ 1402
Sec. 19051	IRC Sec. 6213	Mathematical error	¶ 1402
Sec. 19054	IRC Sec. 6201	Overstatement of credit	¶ 1421
Sec. 19057	IRC Sec. 6501	Limitation on assessment	¶ 1402, ¶ 1408
Sec. 19058	IRC Sec. 6501(e)	Limitation period extended	¶ 1402, ¶ 1408
Sec. 19059	. . .	Assessment of deficiencies on amended returns	¶ 1408
Sec. 19060	. . .	Failure to file amended return	¶ 1408

California	Federal	Subject	Paragraph
Sec. 19061	IRC Secs. 1032, 1033(a)(2)(A)-(a)(2)(D)	Deficiency after involuntary conversion	¶ 1408
Sec. 19063	IRC Secs. 6501(a), 6225	Items of federally registered partnership	¶ 1408
Sec. 19064	IRC Sec. 7609	Motion to quash subpoena	¶ 1402, ¶ 1408
Sec. 19065	IRC Sec. 6501(c)	Federal extension for assessing deficiencies	¶ 1402, ¶ 1408
Sec. 19066	IRC Sec. 6501(b)	Time return deemed filed	¶ 1402, ¶ 1408
Sec. 19066.5	IRC Sec. 6501(c)	Suspension of SOL	¶ 1408
Sec. 19067	IRC Sec. 6501(c)	Extension by agreement	¶ 1402, ¶ 1408
Sec. 19071	IRC Sec. 6901	Collection from other than taxpayer	¶ 1407
Sec. 19072	IRC Sec. 6901	Collection from person secondarily liable	¶ 1407
Sec. 19073	IRC Sec. 6901	Assessment and collection from transferees and fiduciaries	¶ 1407
Sec. 19074	IRC Sec. 6901	Limitations period for assessment of transferee or fiduciary	¶ 1407
Sec. 19081	IRC Secs. 6851, 6861	Jeopardy assessments	¶ 1405
Sec. 19082	IRC Sec. 6862	Jeopardy assessments	¶ 1405
Sec. 19083	IRC Sec. 6863	Jeopardy assessments—stay of collection	¶ 1405
Sec. 19084	IRC Sec. 6863	Jeopardy assessments	¶ 1405
Sec. 19085	IRC Sec. 6863	Jeopardy assessments	¶ 1405
Sec. 19086	IRC Sec. 6861	Evidence of jeopardy	¶ 1405
Sec. 19087	IRC Sec. 6501(c)	Estimated assessments	¶ 1402
Sec. 19088	IRC Sec. 6871	Receivership—immediate assessment	¶ 1406
Sec. 19089	IRC Secs. 6036, 6872	Notice by receiver to FTB	¶ 1406
Sec. 19090	IRC Sec. 6871	Adjudication in receivership proceeding	¶ 1406
Sec. 19091	IRC Sec. 6873	Unpaid claims	¶ 1406
Sec. 19092	IRC Sec. 6861	Regulations	. . .
Sec. 19101	IRC Sec. 6601(a)	Interest on tax due	¶ 1409
Sec. 19102	IRC Sec. 6601(b)	Interest on extensions	¶ 1409
Sec. 19103	IRC Sec. 6601(b)	Last date for payment	¶ 1409
Sec. 19104	IRC Sec. 6404	Interest on deficiency	¶ 1409
Sec. 19106	IRC Sec. 6601(e)	Interest on penalty	¶ 1409
Sec. 19108	IRC Sec. 6601	Overpayment applied to another year's deficiency	¶ 1409
Sec. 19111	IRC Sec. 6601(e)	Notice and demand—10-day waiver	¶ 1409
Sec. 19113	IRC Sec. 6601(f)	Satisfaction by credit	¶ 1409
Sec. 19114	IRC Sec. 6601(g)	Collection and assessment of interest	¶ 1409
Sec. 19115	IRC Sec. 6601(h)	Inapplicability to estimated tax	¶ 1409
Sec. 19131	IRC Sec. 6651	Penalty for failure to file return	¶ 1410
Sec. 19132	IRC Sec. 6651	Penalty for underpayment of tax	¶ 1410
Sec. 19132.5	IRC Sec. 6651	Waiver of penalties for victims of Northridge earthquake	. . .
Sec. 19133	. . .	Penalty for failure to furnish information	¶ 1410
Sec. 19134	IRC Sec. 6657	Bad checks	¶ 1410

California	Federal	Subject	Paragraph
Sec. 19135	. . .	Penalty—unqualified and doing business	¶ 1410
Secs. 19136.4-36.6	. . .	Waiver of estimated tax underpayment penalty	¶ 806a
Sec. 19141	. . .	Failure to file annual statement	¶ 1410
Sec. 19141.2	IRC Sec. 6038	Information returns on foreign corporations	¶ 1412a
Sec. 19141.5	IRC Secs. 6038A-38C	Information returns on foreign-owned and foreign corporations, transfers to foreign persons	¶ 1410, ¶ 1412a
Sec. 19141.6	. . .	Penalty for failure to keep water's-edge records	¶ 1410
Sec. 19142	IRC Sec. 6655(a)	Underpayment of estimated tax	¶ 806a
Sec. 19144	IRC Sec. 6655(b)	Amount of underpayment	¶ 806a
Sec. 19145	IRC Sec. 6655(e)	Period of underpayment	¶ 806a
Sec. 19147	IRC Sec. 6655(d)	Exceptions to underpayment	¶ 806a
Sec. 19148	IRC Sec. 6655	Underpayment of estimated tax	¶ 806a
Sec. 19149	IRC Sec. 6655	Calculation of addition to tax	¶ 806a
Sec. 19150	IRC Sec. 6655	Underpayment for income years of less than 12 months	¶ 806a
Sec. 19151	IRC Sec. 6655	Underpayment not applicable to exempt corporation until certificate revoked	¶ 806a
Sec. 19161	IRC Sec. 6658	Timely payments during pending bankruptcy	¶ 806a, ¶ 1410
Sec. 19164	IRC Secs. 6662-65	Accuracy- and fraud-related penalties, special rules	¶ 1410
Sec. 19166	IRC Sec. 6694	Penalty—preparer understatement	¶ 1410
Sec. 19167	IRC Secs. 6695(a), (c), (d)	Penalty—tax preparers	¶ 1410
Sec. 19168	IRC Sec. 6696	Penalty—tax preparers	¶ 1410
Sec. 19169	IRC Sec. 6695(f)	Penalty—negotiating client's refund check	¶ 1410
Sec. 19173	IRC Sec. 6708	Penalty—tax shelters	¶ 1410
Sec. 19174	IRC Sec. 6700	Penalty—tax shelters	¶ 1410
Sec. 19176	IRC Sec. 6682	Penalty—withholding	¶ 1410
Sec. 19177	IRC Sec. 6700	Penalty—abusive tax shelters	¶ 1410
Sec. 19178	IRC Sec. 6701	Penalty—aiding and abetting	¶ 1410
Sec. 19179	IRC Sec. 6702	Penalty—frivolous return	¶ 1410
Sec. 19180	IRC Sec. 6703	Rules for penalties	¶ 1410
Sec. 19181	IRC Sec. 6706	Penalty for failure to report original issue discount	¶ 1410
Sec. 19182	IRC Sec. 6707	Penalty for tax shelter providers	¶ 1410
Sec. 19182.5	IRC Sec. 6714	Penalty for failure to disclose quid pro quo information	. . .
Sec. 19183	IRC Secs. 6721-24	Penalty for failure to file information return	¶ 1410
Sec. 19184	IRC Sec. 6693	Penalty for failure to properly report IRA	¶ 1410
Sec. 19187	IRC Sec. 6751	Procedures for penalties	¶ 1410
Secs. 19191-94	. . .	Voluntary disclosure agreements	¶ 1421
Sec. 19201	. . .	Request for judgment	. . .
Sec. 19202	. . .	Judgment for taxes	. . .
Sec. 19221	IRC Sec. 6321	Perfected tax lien	. . .

California	Federal	Subject	Paragraph
Sec. 19222	IRC Sec. 6311	Lien for dishonored checks	. . .
Sec. 19225	. . .	Administrative review	¶ 1401a
Sec. 19226	IRC Sec. 6325	Release of third-party liens	. . .
Sec. 19231	IRC Sec. 6331	Warrant for collection of tax	. . .
Sec. 19232	. . .	Warrant as writ of execution	. . .
Sec. 19233	. . .	Fees for warrant	. . .
Sec. 19234	. . .	Fees as obligation of taxpayer	. . .
Sec. 19235	. . .	Costs associated with sale of property	. . .
Sec. 19236	IRC Sec. 6331	Seizure of property	. . .
Sec. 19251	. . .	Remedies cumulative	. . .
Sec. 19252	. . .	FTB as representative	. . .
Sec. 19253	. . .	Priority of tax lien	. . .
Sec. 19254	. . .	Collection and filing enforcement fees	¶ 1410
Sec. 19256	IRC Sec. 7504	Fractional dollar amounts	. . .
Sec. 19262	IRC Secs. 6331, 6335	Seizure and sale of personal property	¶ 1410
Sec. 19263	IRC Secs. 6338, 6342	Bill of sale; disposition of excess	. . .
Sec. 19264	. . .	Earnings withholding tax orders	. . .
Sec. 19301	IRC Sec. 6402(a)	Overpayment—credit or refund	¶ 1413
Sec. 19302	. . .	Credit and refund approval	¶ 1415
Sec. 19306	IRC Sec. 6511(a)	Time limitation on filing claim for credit or refund	¶ 1415
Sec. 19307	. . .	Return as claim for refund	¶ 1413, ¶ 1415
Sec. 19308	IRC Sec. 6511(c)	Effect of assessment extension	¶ 1413, ¶ 1415
Sec. 19309	IRC Sec. 6511(c)	Claims file before assessment extension	¶ 1413, ¶ 1415
Sec. 19311	IRC Sec. 6511	Time limit following federal adjusted return	¶ 1413, ¶ 1415
Sec. 19312	IRC Sec. 6511(d)	Time limit where bad debts or worthless securities	¶ 1413, ¶ 1415
Sec. 19313	IRC Sec. 6511(g)	Federally registered partnerships	¶ 1413, ¶ 1415
Sec. 19314	. . .	Overpayment allowed as offset	¶ 1413, ¶ 1415
Sec. 19321	. . .	Refund claim where final action	¶ 1413
Sec. 19322	. . .	Claim for refund—grounds	¶ 1413
Sec. 19323	. . .	Notice of disallowance	¶ 1413
Sec. 19324	. . .	Finality of action upon claim	¶ 1413
Sec. 19325	. . .	Disallowance of interest on claims resulting from change in federal law	¶ 1417
Sec. 19331	. . .	Presumption of disallowance	¶ 1413
Sec. 19332	IRC Sec. 6213	Mailing of appeals	¶ 1413, ¶ 1414
Sec. 19333	IRC Sec. 6213	SBE's determination	¶ 1413, ¶ 1414
Sec. 19334	IRC Sec. 6213	Petition for rehearing	¶ 1413, ¶ 1414
Sec. 19335	. . .	Appeal as claim for refund	¶ 1413
Sec. 19340	IRC Sec. 6611(b)	Interest on overpayments	¶ 1417
Sec. 19341	IRC Sec. 6611(e)	Time period for payment without interest	¶ 1417
Sec. 19342	. . .	Notice of disallowance	¶ 1417
Sec. 19343	. . .	Finality of notice	¶ 1417
Sec. 19344	. . .	Appeal to SBE	¶ 1417
Sec. 19345	. . .	Determination of appeal	¶ 1417
Sec. 19346	. . .	Finality of determination	¶ 1417

California	Federal	Subject	Paragraph
Sec. 19347	. . .	Suit to recover interest	¶ 1417
Sec. 19348	. . .	Failure of FTB to give notice	¶ 1417
Sec. 19349	IRC Secs. 6401, 6611	Payments not entitled to refunds	¶ 1417
Sec. 19350	. . .	No interest on portion of barred claim	¶ 1417
Sec. 19351	IRC Sec. 6611(b)	Determining limitation period for interest	¶ 1417
Sec. 19355	. . .	Refunding excess	. . .
Sec. 19361	IRC Sec. 6414	Employer's overpayment	. . .
Sec. 19362	IRC Sec. 6402	Credits against estimated tax	. . .
Sec. 19363	IRC Sec. 6402	Interest on overpayments of estimated tax	¶ 806a, ¶ 1417
Sec. 19364	. . .	Overpayments of tax	¶ 806a
Sec. 19371	IRC Sec. 6502	Writ of attachment	. . .
Sec. 19372	. . .	Suit for tax	. . .
Sec. 19373	. . .	Prosecution of suit	. . .
Sec. 19374	. . .	Evidence of tax due	. . .
Sec. 19375	. . .	Bringing of action	. . .
Sec. 19376	. . .	Collection of tax	¶ 1401
Sec. 19377	IRC Sec. 6301	Agreements with collection agencies	. . .
Sec. 19378	IRC Sec. 6301	Collection and transfer of funds	. . .
Sec. 19381	IRC Sec. 7421	Injunction to prevent assessment prohibited	¶ 1416
Sec. 19382	IRC Sec. 7422	Action to recover void tax	¶ 1416
Sec. 19383	IRC Sec. 7422	Credit of overpayment	¶ 1416
Sec. 19384	IRC Sec. 6532	Time limitation on action	¶ 1416
Sec. 19385	IRC Sec. 6532	FTB's failure to mail notice	¶ 1416
Sec. 19387	IRC Sec. 7422	Service upon FTB	¶ 1416
Sec. 19388	IRC Sec. 6532	Place of action	¶ 1416
Sec. 19389	IRC Sec. 6532	Defense of action	¶ 1416
Sec. 19390	. . .	Bar of action	¶ 1416
Sec. 19391	IRC Sec. 6612	Interest on judgment rendered for overpayment	¶ 1416
Sec. 19392	. . .	Judgment against FTB	¶ 1416
Sec. 19393	. . .	Recomputation of discriminatory bank tax	. . .
Sec. 19411	IRC Secs. 6602, 7405	Action to recover refund erroneously made	¶ 1421
Sec. 19412	. . .	Location of trial	¶ 1421
Sec. 19413	. . .	Prosecution of action	¶ 1421
Sec. 19431	IRC Sec. 6404	Cancellation of illegal levy	. . .
Sec. 19432	. . .	Cancellation of tax for inactive corporations	. . .
Sec. 19441	IRC Sec. 7121-23	Closing agreements	¶ 1418
Sec. 19442	. . .	Settlement of tax disputes	¶ 1418
Sec. 19443	. . .	Offers in compromise	¶ 1419
Sec. 19501	IRC Sec. 7621(a)	FTB's powers	¶ 1401
Sec. 19502	IRC Sec. 7621(b)	FTB—establishment of districts	¶ 1401
Sec. 19503	IRC Sec. 7805	FTB—rules and regulations	¶ 1401
Sec. 19504	IRC Sec. 7602	FTB—audits	¶ 1401
Sec. 19504.5	IRC Sec. 7612	Software trade secrets	¶ 1401
Sec. 19504.7	IRC Sec. 7602	Notice of contact of third parties	¶ 1401
Sec. 19521	IRC Secs. 6621, 6622	Determination of rate of interest	¶ 1409
Sec. 19524	IRC Sec. 6011	Computerized returns	. . .
Sec. 19525	IRC Sec. 7623	Reward program	¶ 1401

California	Federal	Subject	Paragraph
Sec. 19530	. . .	Preservation of returns	¶ 1401
Sec. 19531	. . .	Fees for publications	. . .
Secs. 19532-32.1	. . .	Priority for application of collected amounts	. . .
Secs. 19542-42.3	IRC Secs. 6103, 7213	Unauthorized disclosure by FTB	. . .
Sec. 19543	IRC Sec. 6103(b)	Nondisclosure of extraneous matters	. . .
Sec. 19544	IRC Sec. 6103(b)	Nondisclosure of audit methods	. . .
Sec. 19545	IRC Sec. 6103(h)	Disclosure in tax administration proceedings	. . .
Sec. 19546-46.5	IRC Sec. 6103(f)	Disclosure to legislative committee	. . .
Sec. 19547	IRC Sec. 6103(h)	Matters represented by Attorney General	. . .
Sec. 19549	IRC Sec. 6103(b)	Definitions	. . .
Sec. 19551	IRC Sec. 6103(d)	Disclosure to proper authorities	. . .
Sec. 19552	IRC Sec. 7213	Unauthorized disclosure	. . .
Sec. 19559	. . .	Disclosure of tourist industry information	. . .
Sec. 19562	IRC Sec. 6103	Charge for reasonable cost	. . .
Sec. 19563	IRC Sec. 6108	Publication of statistics	. . .
Sec. 19565	IRC Sec. 6104	Inspection of exempt organizations' applications	. . .
Sec. 19701	IRC Sec. 7206	Failure to file—aiding and abetting	¶ 1410
Sec. 19703	. . .	Evidence of failure to file	¶ 1410
Sec. 19704	. . .	Time limit on prosecution	¶ 1410
Sec. 19705	IRC Sec. 7206	False statements and fraud	¶ 1410
Sec. 19706	IRC Sec. 7203	Wilful failure to file return	¶ 1410
Sec. 19707	. . .	Venue	¶ 1410
Sec. 19708	IRC Sec. 7202	Failure to collect or pay over tax	¶ 1410
Sec. 19709	IRC Sec. 7202	Failure to withhold tax as misdemeanor	¶ 1410
Sec. 19710	. . .	Writ of mandate	¶ 1410
Sec. 19712	IRC Sec. 6695	Endorsing client's refund check as misdemeanor	¶ 1410
Sec. 19713	IRC Sec. 7215	Failure to collect and pay withholding tax	¶ 1410
Sec. 19714	IRC Sec. 6673	Delay tactics	¶ 1410
Sec. 19715	IRC Sec. 7408	Penalties—injunctive relief	¶ 1410
Sec. 19717	IRC Sec. 7430	Recovery of litigation costs	¶ 1401
Sec. 19719	. . .	Penalty for doing business after suspension	¶ 1410
Sec. 19720-21	. . .	Fraudulently obtaining refunds	¶ 1410
Sec. 19801	. . .	Administrative agency or officer determinations	¶ 1401
Sec. 19802	. . .	Res judicata	¶ 1401
Secs. 21001-27	IRC Secs. 6103(e)(8), 6201(d)(4), 6323, 6331, 6404(f), 7430, 7433, 7435, 7502, 7521, 7524, 7811	Taxpayers' bill of rights	¶ 1401, ¶ 1401a, ¶ 1410, ¶ 1412a
Sec. 23002	IRC Sec. 7851	Application of Bank and Corporation Law	. . .
Sec. 23004	IRC Sec. 7805	Regulation authorization	. . .

California	Federal	Subject	Paragraph
Sec. 23030	IRC Sec. 7806	Definitions	. . .
Sec. 23031-35	IRC Secs. 7701(a)(10), (11), (24), (25), 7704	Definitions	. . .
Sec. 23036	IRC Sec. 26	"Tax" defined	¶ 802, ¶ 802a, ¶ 809
Sec. 23037	IRC Sec. 7701(a)(14)	"Taxpayer" defined	. . .
Sec. 23038	IRC Sec. 7701(a)(3)	"Corporation" defined	¶ 802a
Sec. 23038.5	IRC Sec. 7704	Publicly-traded partnerships	¶ 802, ¶ 802a
Sec. 23039	IRC Sec. 581	"Bank" defined	. . .
Sec. 23040	. . .	"Income from sources within State" defined	¶ 802a, ¶ 908
Sec. 23040.1	. . .	Income from qualifying investment securities	¶ 802a, ¶ 908
Sec. 23041	IRC Sec. 7701(a)(23)	"Taxable year" defined	. . .
Sec. 23042	. . .	"Income year" defined	. . .
Sec. 23043.5	IRC Sec. 7701(g)	"Fair market value—Property subject to nonrecourse debt	. . .
Sec. 23044	. . .	"International banking facility" defined	. . .
Sec. 23045	IRC Secs. 7702, 7702A-B	Modified endowment contracts	. . .
Sec. 23045.1	IRC Sec. 7701(a)(42)	"Substituted basis" defined	¶ 1106
Sec. 23045.2	IRC Sec. 7701(a)(43)	"Transferred basis" defined	¶ 1106
Sec. 23045.3	IRC Sec. 7701(a)(44)	"Exchanged basis" defined	¶ 1106
Sec. 23045.4	IRC Sec. 7701(a)(45)	"Nonrecognition transaction" defined	¶ 1106
Sec. 23045.5	IRC Sec. 7701(a)(19)	"Domestic building & loan association" defined	. . .
Sec. 23045.6	IRC Sec. 7701(a)(20)	Employee defined	. . .
Sec. 23046	IRC Sec. 7701(a)(46)	Collective bargaining agreements	. . .
Sec. 23047	IRC Sec. 7701(e)	Lease vs. service contracts	. . .
Sec. 23048	IRC Sec. 7701(i)	"Taxable mortgage pools" defined	. . .
Sec. 23049	IRC Sec. 7701(h)	Motor vehicle operating leases	¶ 1008
Sec. 23049.1	IRC Sec. 64	"Ordinary income" defined	. . .
Sec. 23049.2	IRC Sec. 65	"Ordinary loss" defined	. . .
Sec. 23050	. . .	Specific definitions	. . .
Sec. 23051	IRC Sec. 7701(a)(29)	Definition of BCTL of 1954	. . .
Sec. 23051.5	IRC Secs. 196, 541-47, 551-58, 991-99, 1246, 6048, 7806	References to federal law	¶ 801b
		Nonincorporation of federal credit provisions	¶ 1015a
		Nonincorporation of federal DISC and FSC provisions	¶ 817
		Delayed incorporation of federal OID provisions	¶ 910
Sec. 23051.7	. . .	Effect of amendments	¶ 801a, ¶ 810a
Secs. 23052-57	IRC Secs. 7807, 7852	Applications and effects	. . .
Sec. 23058	IRC Sec. 15	Tax rate changes during year	¶ 1105
Sec. 23101	. . .	"Doing business" defined	¶ 802
Sec. 23101.5	. . .	Activities not constituting doing business	¶ 802
Sec. 23102	. . .	Status of holding companies	¶ 802
Sec. 23104	. . .	Convention and trade show activities	¶ 802
Sec. 23113	IRC Sec. 443	Short year returns	. . .

California	Federal	Subject	Paragraph
Sec. 23114	. . .	Tax attaches irrespective of short period	. . .
Sec. 23151	IRC Sec. 11	Franchise and corporation income tax rate	¶ 809
Sec. 23151.1	. . .	Rate of tax of commencing or ceasing corporations	¶ 811, ¶ 812
Sec. 23151.2	. . .	Franchise tax when corporation dissolves or withdraws	¶ 813
Sec. 23153	. . .	Minimum franchise tax	¶ 809
Sec. 23154	. . .	Tax imposed in lieu of other taxes	¶ 809
Sec. 23155	. . .	Credit for erroneous taxes	. . .
Sec. 23181	. . .	Imposition of tax on banks	¶ 809, ¶ 811, ¶ 812
Sec. 23182	. . .	In lieu of other taxes	¶ 809
Sec. 23183	. . .	Annual tax on financial corporation	¶ 809, ¶ 811, ¶ 812
Sec. 23183.1	. . .	Financial corporations— determination of tax	¶ 809-12
Sec. 23183.2	. . .	Tax when financial corporation dissolves or withdraws	¶ 813
Sec. 23186	. . .	Rate of tax on banks	¶ 809, ¶ 1410
Sec. 23187	. . .	Tax receipts	¶ 809
Sec. 23188	. . .	Erroneous assessment	¶ 809
Sec. 23201	. . .	Determination of credit in year of dissolution	¶ 813
Sec. 23202	. . .	Transferees in reorganization	¶ 813
Sec. 23203	. . .	Submission of evidence for credit	¶ 813
Sec. 23204	. . .	Statute of limitations	¶ 813
Sec. 23221	. . .	Minimum tax prepayment	¶ 811
Sec. 23222	. . .	Prepayment basis for first and subsequent years	¶ 811
Sec. 23222a	. . .	Computation in case of short periods	¶ 811
Sec. 23223	. . .	Commencing business in year other than incorporation or qualification	¶ 811
Sec. 23224	. . .	Computation basis upon change from corporation income to franchise tax	¶ 811
Sec. 23224.5	. . .	Doing business after 12/31/71	¶ 811
Sec. 23225	. . .	Due date for payment in excess of minimum	¶ 811
Sec. 23226	. . .	FTB may apportion income	¶ 811
Sec. 23251	IRC Sec. 368	"Reorganization" and "control" defined	¶ 814
Sec. 23253	IRC Sec. 381	Reorganization—procedure taxable to transferee	¶ 814
Sec. 23281	. . .	Resuming business after voluntary discontinuance	¶ 813
Sec. 23282	. . .	Computation after suspension or forfeiture	¶ 813
Sec. 23301	. . .	Suspension of corporate powers for nonpayment	¶ 816
Sec. 23301.5	. . .	Suspension for failure to file	¶ 816
Sec. 23301.6	. . .	Application of suspension on foreign corporation	¶ 816

California	Federal	Subject	Paragraph
Sec. 23302	. . .	Transmittal of names by FTB to Secretary of State	¶ 816
Sec. 23303	. . .	Doing business while suspended—taxability	¶ 816
Sec. 23304.1	. . .	Contracts made during suspension	¶ 816
Sec. 23304.5	. . .	Court order rescission of contract	¶ 816
Sec. 23305	. . .	Application for certificate of revivor	¶ 816
Sec. 23305a	. . .	Endorsement of corporation's name by Secretary of State	¶ 816
Sec. 23305b	. . .	Revival without tax payment	¶ 816
Sec. 23305c	. . .	Revival sent to Secretary of State	¶ 816
Sec. 23305d	. . .	FTB's certificate as evidence of suspension	¶ 816
Sec. 23305e	. . .	Letters of good standing	¶ 816
Sec. 23305.1	. . .	Relief from contract voidability	¶ 816
Sec. 23305.2	. . .	Revival with bond or other security	¶ 816
Sec. 23305.5	. . .	Suspension of LLC corporate powers	¶ 816
Sec. 23331	. . .	Effective date of dissolution or withdrawal	¶ 813
Sec. 23332	. . .	Corporations dissolving or withdrawing before 1/1/73	¶ 812, ¶ 813
Sec. 23332.5	. . .	Tax on financial corporations	¶ 813
Sec. 23333	. . .	Maximum tax on withdrawal or dissolution	¶ 813
Sec. 23334	. . .	Issuance of tax clearance certificate by FTB	¶ 813
Sec. 23335	. . .	Request for tax clearance certificate	¶ 813
Sec. 23361	IRC Sec. 1504	"Affiliated group" defined	¶ 806
Sec. 23362	IRC Sec. 1501	Consolidated return of affiliated group	¶ 806
Sec. 23363	IRC Sec. 1502	FTB's regulations	¶ 806
Sec. 23364	IRC Sec. 1503	Parent and each subsidiary severally liable	¶ 806
Sec. 23364a	IRC Sec. 1501	Computation of tax	. . .
Secs. 23400, 23453-59	IRC Secs. 55-59	Alternative minimum tax	¶ 809a
Sec. 23453	IRC Sec. 53	Minimum tax credit	¶ 810a
Sec. 23455.5	. . .	AMT exclusion for small corporations inapplicable	¶ 810
Sec. 23501	IRC Sec. 11(b)	Rate of tax	¶ 802a, ¶ 809
Sec. 23503	. . .	Franchise tax offset	¶ 802a, ¶ 810
Sec. 23504	. . .	Change to corporation income tax liability	¶ 812
Sec. 23561	. . .	Tax payment before termination	¶ 813
Sec. 23601.5	. . .	Energy conservation credit	¶ 810a
Sec. 23604	IRC Sec. 43	Enhanced oil recovery credit	¶ 810a
Sec. 23608	. . .	Credit for transportation of donated agricultural products	¶ 810a
Sec. 23608.2	. . .	Farmworker Housing credit	¶ 810a
Sec. 23608.3	. . .	Credit for farmworker housing development loans	¶ 810a
Sec. 23609	IRC Sec. 41	Reseach expense credit	¶ 810a
Sec. 23610	. . .	Rice straw credit	¶ 810a

California	Federal	Subject	Paragraph
Secs. 23610.4-10.5	IRC Sec. 42	Credit for low-income housing	¶810a
Sec. 23612.2	. . .	Sales tax credit	¶810a
Secs. 23617, 23617.5	. . .	Child care assistance	¶810a
Secs. 23612.6-25	IRC Secs. 51-52	Additional credits against tax	¶810a
Sec. 23633	. . .	Targeted tax area's qualified property sales and use tax credit	. . .
Sec. 23634	. . .	Targeted tax area's employer's wages credit	. . .
Secs. 23636-37	. . .	Joint strike fighter credits	¶810a
Sec. 23642	IRC Sec. 44	Disabled access credit	¶810a
Sec. 23645	. . .	Sales tax credit	¶810a
Sec. 23646	. . .	Employers' wage payment credit	¶810a
Sec. 23649	. . .	Manufacturing and research property credit	¶810a
Sec. 23657	. . .	Community development investment credit	¶810a
Sec. 23666	. . .	Salmon and steelhead trout credit	¶810a
Sec. 23701	IRC Secs. 501(a), (b)	Exemption for employee trusts	¶804
Sec. 23701a	IRC Sec. 501(c)(5)	Labor, agricultural, horticultural organizations	¶804
Sec. 23701b	IRC Sec. 501(c)(8)	Fraternal orders	¶804
Sec. 23701c	IRC Sec. 501(c)(13)	Cemetery companies	¶804
Sec. 23701d	IRC Secs. 501(c)(3), (j)	Religious, charitable, educational organizations	¶804
Sec. 23701e	IRC Sec. 501(c)(6)	Business leagues, chambers of commerce	¶804
Sec. 23701f	IRC Sec. 501(c)(4)	Civic leagues or organizations	¶804
Sec. 23701g	IRC Sec. 501(c)(7)	Nonprofit recreational clubs	¶804
Sec. 23701h	IRC Sec. 501(c)(2)	Companies holding title for exempt organizations	¶804
Sec. 23701i	IRC Sec. 501(c)(9)	Employees' beneficiary associations	¶804
Sec. 23701j	IRC Sec. 501(c)(11)	Teachers' retirement associations	¶804
Sec. 23701k	IRC Sec. 501(d)	Religious organizations	¶804
Sec. 23701l	IRC Sec. 501(c)(10)	Domestic fraternal societies	¶804
Sec. 23701n	IRC Sec. 501(c)(17)	Supplemental unemployment compensation plan	¶804
Sec. 23701p	IRC Sec. 401	Self-employed individual retirement plans	¶804, ¶1012
Sec. 23701r	IRC Secs. 527, 6012(a)(6)	Political organizations	¶804
Sec. 23701s	IRC Sec. 501(c)(18)	Employee funded pension trust—pre- 6/25/59	¶804
Sec. 23701t	IRC Secs. 528, 6012(a)(7)	Homeowners' associations	¶804, ¶914
Sec. 23701u	. . .	Nonprofit public benefit corporations	¶804
Sec. 23701v	IRC Sec. 501(c)	Mobile home owners	. . .
Sec. 23701w	IRC Sec. 501(c)(19)	Veterans organizations	. . .
Sec. 23701x	IRC Sec. 501(c)(25)	Title holding companies	¶804
Sec. 23701y	IRC Sec. 501(c)(14)	Credit unions	¶804
Sec. 23701z	IRC Sec. 501(n)	Nonprofit insurance risk pools	¶804
Sec. 23702	IRC Sec. 502	Feeder organizations	¶804, ¶804a
Sec. 23703	. . .	Failure to file with attorney general	¶804, ¶805a
Sec. 23704.3	IRC Sec. 501(o)	Participation in provider-sponsored organization	¶804
Sec. 23704.4	IRC Sec. 501(e)	Child care organizations	¶804

California	Federal	Subject	Paragraph
Sec. 23704.5	IRC Sec. 501(h)	Expenditures to influence legislation	¶ 804
Sec. 23704.6	IRC Sec. 504	Status after disqualification for lobbying	¶ 804
Sec. 23705	IRC Sec. 505	Nondiscrimination requirement	¶ 804
Sec. 23706	IRC Sec. 501(c)(1)	Exemptions for state instrumentalities	. . .
Sec. 23707	IRC Sec. 507	Private foundation status terminated	¶ 804
Sec. 23708	IRC Sec. 508	Presumption that organization is private foundation	¶ 804
Sec. 23709	IRC Sec. 509	"Private foundation" defined	¶ 804
Sec. 23710	IRC Sec. 513	Bingo games	¶ 804
Sec. 23711	IRC Sec. 529	Qualified state tuition program	¶ 804, ¶ 923
Sec. 23712	IRC Sec. 530	Education IRA's	. . .
Sec. 23731	IRC Secs. 501(b), 511	Unrelated business income	¶ 802a, ¶ 804a
Sec. 23732	IRC Sec. 512	Unrelated business income	¶ 804a
Sec. 23734	IRC Sec. 513	"Unrelated trade or business" defined	¶ 804a
Sec. 23735	IRC Sec. 514	Unrelated debt-financed income	¶ 804a
Sec. 23736	IRC Sec. 503(a)	Prohibited transactions	¶ 804a
Sec. 23736.1	IRC Sec. 503(b)	"Prohibited transactions" defined	¶ 804a
Sec. 23736.2	IRC Sec. 503(a)(1)	Denial of exemption to organizations engaged in prohibited transactions	¶ 804a
Sec. 23736.3	IRC Sec. 503(a)(2)	Taxable years affected	¶ 804a
Sec. 23736.4	IRC Sec. 503(c)	Future status of organizations denied exemption	¶ 804a
Sec. 23737	. . .	Grounds for denial of exemption	¶ 804a
Sec. 23740	IRC Sec. 4911	Excess expenditures to influence legislation	¶ 804
Sec. 23741	. . .	Churches receiving rental income from other churches	¶ 804a
Sec. 23771	IRC Sec. 6012	Returns required	¶ 804a, ¶ 805a
Sec. 23772	IRC Secs. 6033, 6072(e)	Annual returns by exempt organizations	¶ 805a
Sec. 23774	. . .	Annual return of exempt corporation	¶ 805a
Sec. 23775	. . .	Exempt corporation's failure to file return	¶ 805a
Sec. 23776	. . .	Reinstatement of exempt corporation	¶ 805a
Sec. 23777	. . .	Revocation of exemption	¶ 805a
Sec. 23778	. . .	Reestablishing exemption	¶ 805a
Sec. 23800	IRC Secs. 1361-79	S corp determination	¶ 803
Sec. 23800.5	IRC Sec. 1361	Application	. . .
Sec. 23801	IRC Sec. 1362	Election	¶ 803
Sec. 23802	IRC Sec. 1363	Tax rate	¶ 803
Sec. 23802.5	IRC Sec. 1366	Determination of shareholders tax liability	. . .
Sec. 23803	IRC Sec. 1361	Credit carryover	¶ 803
Sec. 23804	IRC Sec. 1367	Cross references	¶ 803
Sec. 23804.5	IRC Sec. 1368	Certain adjustments taken into account	. . .
Sec. 23806	IRC Sec. 1371	IRC Sec. 338 election	¶ 803

California	Federal	Subject	Paragraph
Sec. 23807	IRC Sec. 1372	Partnership references	¶ 803
Sec. 23808	IRC Secs. 1373, 1379	Nonconformity to Federal	¶ 803
Sec. 23809	IRC Sec. 1374	Substituted California tax rate	¶ 803
Sec. 23810	IRC Sec. 6031	Deemed election	¶ 803
Sec. 23811	IRC Sec. 1375	Tax on passive income	¶ 803
Sec. 23813	IRC Sec. 1377	Determinations	. . .
Sec. 24251	IRC Sec. 15	Tax rate changes during year	¶ 1105
Sec. 24271	IRC Secs. 61, 641-92, 701-77	Gross income	¶ 901
Sec. 24272	IRC Secs. 103, 141-50	Interest on government bonds	¶ 909
Sec. 24272.2	IRC Sec. 72	Annuities	¶ 904
Sec. 24272.3	IRC Sec. 865(b)	Sales of unprocessed timber	¶ 817
Sec. 24272.5	IRC Sec. 7518	Capital construction funds for vessels	¶ 916
Sec. 24273	IRC Sec. 77	Commodity credit loans	¶ 911
Sec. 24273.5	IRC Sec. 1385	Noncash patronage allocations from farmers' cooperatives	¶ 913
Sec. 24275	IRC Sec. 88	Nuclear decommissioning costs	. . .
Sec. 24276	IRC Sec. 90	Illegal federal irrigation subsidies	. . .
Sec. 24301	IRC Secs. 101-36	Exclusions from gross income	. . .
Sec. 24302	IRC Secs. 72, 101(a)	Life insurance proceeds	¶ 903, ¶ 904
Sec. 24305	IRC Sec. 101(f)	Life insurance proceeds	¶ 902
Sec. 24306	IRC Sec. 529	Qualified state tuition program	¶ 923
Sec. 24307	IRC Sec. 108	Income from discharge of indebtedness	¶ 907
Sec. 24308	IRC Sec. 61	Forest Service payments	¶ 901
Sec. 24308.5	IRC Sec. 126	Cost-share payments received by forest landowners	¶ 922
Sec. 24309	IRC Sec. 109	Improvements by lessee	¶ 905
Sec. 24309.5	IRC Sec. 110	Qualified lessee construction allowances	¶ 905a
Sec. 24310	IRC Sec. 111	Recovery of bad debts and prior taxes	¶ 906
Sec. 24314	IRC Sec. 61	Gain or loss from exempt bond	¶ 1206a
Sec. 24315	IRC Sec. 61	Recycling income	¶ 918
Sec. 24320	IRC Sec. 883	Operation of foreign aircraft or ships	¶ 915
Sec. 24321	IRC Sec. 881-82	Local governmental units prohibited	¶ 915
Sec. 24322	IRC Secs. 118, 597	Contributions to capital	¶ 912
Sec. 24323	IRC Sec. 61	Rebates for water-conservation devices	¶ 920
Sec. 24324	IRC Sec. 118	Exclusion of utilities	. . .
Sec. 24325	IRC Sec. 118	Contributions to capital	¶ 912
Sec. 24326	IRC Sec. 136	Energy conservation subsidies	¶ 921
Sec. 24327	IRC Sec. 892	Foreign government investment income	. . .
Sec. 24328	. . .	Golden State Scholarshare Trust	¶ 924
Sec. 24341	IRC Sec. 63	"Net income" defined	¶ 808
Sec. 24343	IRC Sec. 162	Deductions for business expenses	¶ 1001
Sec. 24343.2	IRC Sec. 162	Expenses incurred at discriminatory clubs	. . .
Sec. 24343.3	IRC Sec. 220	Medical savings account deduction	. . .
Sec. 24343.5	IRC Sec. 162	Subsidization of employees' ridesharing	¶ 1013

California	Federal	Subject	Paragraph
Sec. 24343.7	IRC Sec. 162	Deductions for business expenses	¶ 1001, ¶ 1017
Sec. 24344	IRC Sec. 163	Interest expense deduction	¶ 1002, ¶ 1310
Sec. 24344.5	IRC Sec. 163	Deduction for discount bonds	¶ 910, ¶ 1002
Sec. 24344.7	IRC Sec. 163	Limitation on interest expense deduction	¶ 1002
Sec. 24345	IRC Secs. 164, 275	Deduction for taxes	¶ 1003
Sec. 24346	IRC Sec. 164	Apportionment of taxes on real property	¶ 1003
Sec. 24347	IRC Secs. 165, 166, 582	Losses—deductions	¶ 1004, ¶ 1006, ¶ 1007
Secs. 24347.4-47.5	IRC Sec. 165	Disaster losses	¶ 1004
Sec. 24348	IRC Secs. 166, 585, 593	Deduction for bad debts	¶ 1006
Sec. 24348.5	IRC Sec. 595	Foreclosure on property securing loans	¶ 1006
Sec. 24349	IRC Secs. 167(a), 168	Depreciation	¶ 1008
Sec. 24349.1	IRC Sec. 280F	Depreciation-luxury cars	¶ 1008
Sec. 24350	...	Limitations on use of methods and rates	¶ 1008
Sec. 24351	...	Agreement as to useful life—depreciation	¶ 1008
Sec. 24352	...	Depreciation—change in method	¶ 1008
Sec. 24352.5	...	Depreciation—salvage method	¶ 1008
Sec. 24353	IRC Sec. 167(c)	Basis for depreciation	¶ 1008, ¶ 1238
Sec. 24354	IRC Sec. 167(d)	Life tenants and beneficiaries	¶ 1008
Sec. 24354.1	...	Rules for Sec. 18212 property	¶ 1008
Sec. 24355.4	IRC Sec. 168	Depreciation of rent-to-own property	¶ 1008
Sec. 24355.5	IRC Sec. 197	Amortization of goodwill	¶ 1008
Sec. 24356	IRC Sec. 179	Bonus depreciation	¶ 1008
Sec. 24356.5	IRC Sec. 179A	Clean-fuel vehicles and refueling property	¶ 1008
Sec. 24356.6	...	Election to expense 40% of cost in targeted tax property	...
Sec. 24356.7	...	Accelerated write-off for enterprise zone property	¶ 1008
Sec. 24356.8	IRC Sec. 179	Accelerated write-off	¶ 1008
Sec. 24357	IRC Sec. 170(a), (f)(8), (9), (j)	Charitable contributions	¶ 1010, ¶ 1310
Sec. 24357.1	IRC Sec. 170(e)	Contributions of ordinary income and capital gain property	¶ 1010
Sec. 24357.2	IRC Sec. 170(f)(3)	Partial interest in property	¶ 1010
Sec. 24357.3	IRC Sec. 170(f)(4)	Valuation of remainder interest in real property	¶ 1010
Sec. 24357.4	IRC Sec. 170(f)(5)	Reduction for certain interest	¶ 1010
Sec. 24357.5	IRC Sec. 170(f)(1)	Disallowance of deduction	¶ 1010
Sec. 24357.6	IRC Sec. 170(f)(6)	Out-of-pocket expenditures	¶ 1010
Sec. 24357.7	IRC Sec. 170(h)	Qualified conservation expenditures	¶ 1010
Sec. 24357.8	IRC Sec. 170(e)	Scientific property used for research—deduction	¶ 1010
Sec. 24357.9	IRC Sec. 170	Contribution of computer technology to schools	¶ 1010
Sec. 24357.10	IRC Sec. 170(l)	Contributions in connection with athletic events	¶ 1010

California	Federal	Subject	Paragraph
Sec. 24358	IRC Sec. 170(b)	Limitations on corporate contributions	¶ 1010
Sec. 24359	IRC Sec. 170(c)	Charitable contribution defined	¶ 1010
Sec. 24359.1	IRC Sec. 170(e)	Credit or deduction for scientific equipment donated	¶ 1010
Sec. 24360	IRC Sec. 171(a)	Amortizable bond premium	¶ 1011
Sec. 24361	IRC Sec. 171(b)	Determination of bond premium	¶ 1011
Sec. 24362	IRC Sec. 171(c)	Election as to taxable bonds	¶ 1011
Sec. 24363	IRC Sec. 171(d)	Bond defined	¶ 1011
Sec. 24363.5	IRC Sec. 171(e)	Offset to interest payments	¶ 1011
Sec. 24364	IRC Sec. 173	Circulation expenditures	¶ 1001b
Sec. 24365	IRC Sec. 174	Research expenditures	¶ 1008
Sec. 24368.1	IRC Sec. 167(e)	Trademark expenditures	¶ 1008
Sec. 24369	IRC Sec. 175	Soil and water conservation expenditures	¶ 1001a
Sec. 24369.4	IRC Sec. 198	Environmental remediation expenses	¶ 1008
Sec. 24370	IRC Sec. 591	Deductions for dividends paid on deposits	¶ 1015
Sec. 24372.3	IRC Sec. 169	Amortization of pollution control facilities	¶ 1008
Sec. 24372.5	IRC Sec. 194	Amortization of reforestation expenses	¶ 1008
Sec. 24373	IRC Sec. 178	Depreciation or amortization of lessee improvements	¶ 1008
Sec. 24377	IRC Sec. 180	Farm fertilizer expenses	¶ 1001a
Sec. 24379	IRC Sec. 83	Transfer of property for services	¶ 1012a
Sec. 24382	IRC Sec. 216	Foreclosure of cooperature housing corporation stock	¶ 1016
Sec. 24383	IRC Sec. 190	Architectural adaptations for the handicapped	¶ 1001
Sec. 24384.5	IRC Sec. 163	Interest received-depressed areas	¶ 917
Sec. 24401	IRC Sec. 241	Special deductions	. . .
Sec. 24402	IRC Secs. 243-47, 561-565	Dividends received by corporations taxed by California	¶ 908, ¶ 1014
Sec. 24403	IRC Sec. 591	Deductions for credits to withdrawable shares	¶ 1015
Sec. 24404	IRC Secs. 1381-83	Agricultural cooperatives	¶ 1015
Sec. 24405	IRC Secs. 1381-83	Other cooperatives	¶ 1015
Sec. 24406	IRC Secs. 1381-83	Cooperative corporations	¶ 1015
Sec. 24406.5	IRC Sec. 1381	Gas producers' cooperatives	¶ 1015
Sec. 24407	IRC Sec. 248(a)	Organizational expenditures	¶ 1008
Sec. 24408	IRC Sec. 248(b)	"Organizational expenditures" defined	¶ 1008
Sec. 24409	IRC Sec. 248(c)	Organizational expenditures— period of election	¶ 1008
Sec. 24410	IRC Secs. 243-47	Dividends from subsidiary insurance company	¶ 908, ¶ 1014
Sec. 24411	IRC Secs. 243-47	Unitary business water's edge election	¶ 806, ¶ 1309
Sec. 24414	IRC Sec. 195	Start-up expenses	¶ 1012b
Sec. 24415	IRC Sec. 161	Interindemnity payments	¶ 1001
Secs. 24416-16.6	IRC Sec. 172	Net operating loss carryovers	¶ 803, ¶ 1018
Sec. 24421	IRC Sec. 261	Disallowance of deductions	¶ 1008, ¶ 1017
Sec. 24422	IRC Secs. 263, 263A	Capital expenditures	¶ 1008, ¶ 1017, ¶ 1107

California	Federal	Subject	Paragraph
Sec. 24422.3	IRC Sec. 263A	Capitalization of inventory-related expense	¶ 1017, ¶ 1107
Sec. 24423	IRC Sec. 263	Drilling and development costs—oil and gas	¶ 1009a, ¶ 1017
Sec. 24424	IRC Sec. 264	Payments on life insurance contracts	¶ 1002, ¶ 1017
Sec. 24425	IRC Sec. 265	Deductions allocable to tax-exempt income	¶ 1017
Sec. 24426	IRC Sec. 266	Taxes and carrying charges	¶ 1017
Sec. 24427	IRC Sec. 267	Transaction between related individuals	¶ 1017
Sec. 24429	IRC Sec. 276	Indirect contributions to political parties	. . .
Sec. 24431	IRC Sec. 269	Acquisitions made to avoid tax	¶ 1110
Sec. 24434	IRC Sec. 271	Debts owed by political parties	¶ 1006
Sec. 24436	IRC Sec. 280E	Illegal business expenses	¶ 1017
Sec. 24436.1	IRC Sec. 280E	Illegal activities	¶ 1017
Sec. 24436.5	IRC Sec. 161	Deductions on substandard housing	¶ 1017
Sec. 24437	IRC Sec. 277	Deduction limitation for social clubs	¶ 1017
Sec. 24438	IRC Sec. 279	Interest deduction on corporate acquisition indebtedness	¶ 1002
Sec. 24439	IRC Sec. 249	Deductions of bond premium on repurchase	¶ 1002, ¶ 1214a
Sec. 24440	IRC Sec. 280C(b), (c)	Federal credits	¶ 810a, ¶ 1015
Sec. 24441	IRC Sec. 161	Abandonment or tax recoupment fees	¶ 1017
Sec. 24442	IRC Sec. 280B	Demolition of historic structures	¶ 1017
Sec. 24442.5	IRC Sec. 280H	Limitation on amounts paid to employee-owners	¶ 1017
Sec. 24443	IRC Sec. 274	Disallowance of entertainment expenses	¶ 1017
Secs. 24447-48	IRC Sec. 161	Expenses disallowed	¶ 1017, ¶ 1018
Sec. 24449	IRC Sec. 291	Preference items	¶ 809a
Sec. 24451	IRC Secs. 301-85	Corporate distributions and adjustments	¶ 908, ¶ 1002, ¶ 1206-08, ¶ 1210-11, ¶ 1213-13a, ¶ 1220-22, ¶ 1230, ¶ 1232
Sec. 24452	IRC Sec. 301	Special rule for distributions received by 20% shareholder	¶ 908
Sec. 24453	IRC Sec. 302	Termination of interest	¶ 908
Sec. 24456	IRC Sec. 306	Source of gain—IRC Sec. 306(f) inapplicable	¶ 908
Sec. 24461	Sec. 337	Effective dates of 1986 TRA changes as to liquidations	¶ 1213a
Sec. 24471	IRC Sec. 381	Items of distributor or transferor corporation	¶ 908, ¶ 1213a
Sec. 24472	IRC Sec. 382	Discharge of indebtedness	¶ 907
Sec. 24481	IRC Sec. 383	Special limits on certain excess credits, etc.	¶ 908, ¶ 1213a
Sec. 24601-12	IRC Secs. 401-24	Deferred compensation	¶ 908, ¶ 1012, ¶ 1012a
Sec. 24631	IRC Sec. 441	Accounting periods	¶ 1101
Sec. 24632	IRC Sec. 441	Income year	¶ 1101

California	Federal	Subject	Paragraph
Sec. 24633	IRC Sec. 442	Change in accounting period	¶ 1102
Sec. 24633.5	IRC Sec. 441	Change of accounting period	¶ 803, ¶ 1102
Sec. 24634	IRC Sec. 443	Short-period returns	¶ 1103
Sec. 24636	IRC Sec. 443	Computation of tax in short period return	¶ 1103
Sec. 24637	IRC Sec. 444	Election to Keep Same Tax Year—S Corporations	¶ 803, ¶ 1104
Sec. 24651	IRC Sec. 446	Accounting methods	¶ 1106
Sec. 24652	IRC Sec. 447	Accounting for farm corporations	¶ 1106
Sec. 24654	IRC Sec. 448	Cash method of accounting restricted	¶ 1106
Sec. 24661	IRC Sec. 451	Taxable year of inclusion	¶ 1106
Sec. 24667	IRC Secs. 453, 453A, 453B	Installment method	¶ 1109
Sec. 24668.1	IRC Sec. 453	Installment method—property condemnations	¶ 1109
Sec. 24672	. . .	Installment income on cessation of business	¶ 1109
Sec. 24673	IRC Sec. 460	Percentage of completion accounting	¶ 803, ¶ 1106
Sec. 24673.2	IRC Sec. 460	Long term contracts	¶ 1106
Sec. 24674	IRC Sec. 454	Obligations issued at discount	¶ 1111
Sec. 24675	IRC Sec. 186	Patent infringement damages	¶ 1106
Sec. 24676	IRC Sec. 455	Prepaid subscription income	¶ 1106
Sec. 24676.5	IRC Sec. 458	Returned magazines, paperbacks, records	¶ 1106
Sec. 24677	IRC Sec. 186	Breach of contract award	¶ 1106
Sec. 24678	IRC Sec. 186	Damages received under Clayton Act	¶ 1106
Sec. 24679	. . .	Fractional part of month	¶ 1106
Sec. 24681	IRC Sec. 461	Taxable year of deduction	¶ 1003, ¶ 1106
Sec. 24682	IRC Sec. 464	Farming expenses	¶ 1106
Sec. 24685	. . .	Accrual of vacation pay	¶ 1106
Sec. 24688	IRC Sec. 467	Deferred rental payments	¶ 1106
Sec. 24689	IRC Sec. 468	Waste disposal costs	¶ 1106
Sec. 24690	IRC Sec. 468A	Nuclear decommissioning funds	¶ 1106
Sec. 24691	IRC Sec. 465	At risk	¶ 1017, ¶ 1019
Sec. 24692	IRC Sec. 469	Passive activity losses	¶ 1002a, ¶ 1106
Sec. 24693	IRC Sec. 468B	Designated settlement funds	¶ 803a
Sec. 24701	IRC Secs. 471, 472	Inventories—general rule	¶ 1107, ¶ 1108
Sec. 24708	IRC Sec. 474	Simplified dollar value LIFO	¶ 1108
Sec. 24710	IRC Sec. 475	Mark-to-market accounting	¶ 1107, ¶ 1214
Sec. 24721	IRC Sec. 481	Adjustments required by changes in method	¶ 1106
Sec. 24725	IRC Sec. 482	Allocation of income among taxpayers	¶ 1106, ¶ 1110
Sec. 24726	IRC Sec. 483	Interest on deferred payments	¶ 1106, ¶ 1112
Sec. 24831	IRC Secs. 611-38	Natural resources	¶ 1009, ¶ 1009a, ¶ 1238
Secs. 24870-75	IRC Secs. 851-60L	RICs, REITs, REMICs, and FASITs	¶ 802a, ¶ 1015
Sec. 24901	IRC Sec. 1001	Determination of gain or loss	¶ 1201
Sec. 24902	IRC Sec. 1001	Recognition of gain or loss	¶ 1201
Sec. 24905	IRC Sec. 988	Foreign currency transactions	¶ 1202b
Sec. 24905.5	IRC Sec. 988	Hedging transactions	. . .
Sec. 24911	IRC Sec. 1011	Adjusted basis	¶ 1235
Sec. 24912	IRC Sec. 1012	Basis of property—cost	¶ 1215

California	Federal	Subject	Paragraph
Sec. 24913	IRC Sec. 1013	Basis of property in inventory	¶ 1216
Sec. 24914	IRC Sec. 1015	Basis of property acquired by gift or transfer in trust	¶ 1217, ¶ 1218
Sec. 24915	IRC Sec. 1015	Adjustment for gift taxes paid	¶ 1217
Sec. 24916	IRC Sec. 1016	Adjustments to basis	¶ 1235
Sec. 24916.2	IRC Sec. 1016	Abandonment fees, open-space easement	¶ 1235
Sec. 24917	IRC Sec. 1016	Substituted basis	¶ 1236
Sec. 24918	IRC Sec. 1017	Discharge of indebtedness	¶ 1239
Sec. 24919	IRC Sec. 1019	Improvements to property by lessee	¶ 1237
Sec. 24941	IRC Sec. 1031	Exchange of property held for productive use	¶ 1204
Sec. 24942	IRC Sec. 1032	Exchange of stock for property	¶ 1214b
Sec. 24943	IRC Sec. 1033(a)	Involuntary conversions	¶ 1202
Sec. 24944	IRC Sec. 1033(a)(2), (A), (B)	Conversion into money or unrelated property	¶ 1202
Sec. 24945	IRC Sec. 1033(a)(2)(C)	Time for assessment of deficiency attributable to gain	¶ 1202
Sec. 24946	IRC Sec. 1033(a)(2)(D)	Time for assessment of other deficiencies	¶ 1202
Sec. 24947	IRC Sec. 1033(b)	Basis of property	¶ 1223
Sec. 24948	IRC Sec. 1033(c)	Property sold pursuant to reclamation laws	¶ 1202
Sec. 24949	IRC Sec. 1033(d)	Diseased livestock	¶ 1202
Sec. 24949.1	IRC Sec. 1033(e)	Livestock sold on account of drought	¶ 1202
Sec. 24949.2	IRC Sec. 1033(g)	Condemnation of real property held for productive use	¶ 1202
Sec. 24949.3	IRC Sec. 1033(f)	Environmental contamination—replacement of livestock	¶ 1202
Sec. 24949.5	IRC Sec. 1033(h)	Applicability of federal involuntary conversion rules	¶ 1202
Sec. 24950	IRC Sec. 1035	Exchanges of insurance policies	¶ 1204a
Sec. 24951	IRC Sec. 1036	Exchange of stock	¶ 1205
Sec. 24952	IRC Sec. 1038	Reacquisitions of real property	¶ 1205b
Sec. 24954	IRC Sec. 1042	Deferral of gain on roll-over sales of stock to ESOP	¶ 1201
Sec. 24954.1	IRC Sec. 1042(g)	Sales to agricultural refiners and cooperatives	¶ 1206b
Sec. 24955	IRC Sec. 1001	Rollover sales of low-income housing	¶ 1202a
Sec. 24956	IRC Sec. 1044	Rollover of publicly traded securities gain	. . .
Sec. 24961	IRC Sec. 1051	Basis of property acquired from affiliated corporation	¶ 1225
Sec. 24962	IRC Sec. 1052	Basis provisions from prior codes	¶ 1226
Sec. 24963	IRC Sec. 1053	Basis of property acquired before March 1, 1913	¶ 1227
Sec. 24964	IRC Sec. 1011	Property received from controlled corporation	¶ 1231
Sec. 24965	IRC Sec. 1054	Basis of stock issued by FNMA	¶ 1228
Sec. 24966	IRC Sec. 1059	Basis after extraordinary dividend	¶ 1215
Sec. 24966.1	IRC Sec. 1059A	Basis of property imported from related persons	¶ 1215, ¶ 1216

California	Federal	Subject	Paragraph
Sec. 24966.2	IRC Sec. 1060	Allocation of transferred business assets	¶ 1215, ¶ 1241
Sec. 24981	IRC Sec. 1081	Exchange or distribution in obedience to SEC order	¶ 1203
Sec. 24988	IRC Sec. 1082	Basis of stock received under Sec. 24981	¶ 1233
Sec. 24989	IRC Sec. 1056	Basis limitation for player contracts	¶ 1240
Secs. 24990, 24990.5	IRC Secs. 1201-97	No capital gains or losses	¶ 1008, ¶ 1214
Sec. 24990.6	IRC Sec. 1245	Character of gain or loss	. . .
Sec. 24990.7	IRC Sec. 1248	Gain on sales in foreign corporations	¶ 1209
Sec. 24991	IRC Sec. 1275	Definition of tax-exempt obligation	¶ 909, ¶ 910
Sec. 24993	IRC Sec. 7872	Imputed interest	¶ 1112
Sec. 24994	IRC Sec. 1272	Tax treatment of bonds	¶ 910, ¶ 1214a
Sec. 24995	IRC Secs. 1291-98	Passive foreign investment companies	¶ 1214
Sec. 24998	IRC Secs. 1091, 1092	Wash sales of stock or securities	¶ 1005, ¶ 1224
Sec. 25101	. . .	Apportionment	¶ 815, ¶ 1302, ¶ 1311
Sec. 25101.3	. . .	Property factor—aircraft	¶ 1306
Sec. 25101.15	. . .	In-state income of two or more taxpayers	¶ 1309
Sec. 25102	. . .	Combined return of controlled taxpayers	¶ 1110, ¶ 1309
Sec. 25103	. . .	Corporate transactions to evade tax	¶ 1110
Sec. 25104	. . .	Consolidated report	¶ 1309
Sec. 25105	. . .	Determination of control	¶ 1309
Sec. 25106	. . .	Income from intercompany dividend distribution	¶ 908
Sec. 25106.5	IRC Sec. 1502	Affiliated corporations—Combined reporting	¶ 806, ¶ 1309
Sec. 25107	. . .	Apportionment of income of international banking facility	¶ 1306, ¶ 1307, ¶ 1308
Sec. 25108	IRC Sec. 172	Net operating loss	¶ 1018
Secs. 25110-14	. . .	Unitary business water's edge election	¶ 1018, ¶ 1309a
Sec. 25120	. . .	Definitions	¶ 1302
Sec. 25121	. . .	Allocation and apportionment of income	¶ 1302
Sec. 25122	. . .	Taxability in another state	¶ 1302
Sec. 25123	. . .	Nonbusiness income	¶ 1303
Sec. 25124	. . .	Rents and royalties from real and tangible personal property	¶ 1303
Sec. 25125	. . .	Capital gains and losses from sales of real and personal property	¶ 1303
Sec. 25126	. . .	Allocation of interest and dividends	¶ 1303
Sec. 25127	. . .	Allocation of patent and copyright royalties	¶ 1303
Sec. 25128	. . .	Apportionment formula	¶ 1304, ¶ 1305
Sec. 25129	. . .	Property factor	¶ 1306
Sec. 25130	. . .	Property valuation	¶ 1306
Sec. 25131	. . .	Average value of property	¶ 1306
Sec. 25132	. . .	Payroll factor	¶ 1307

California	Federal	Subject	Paragraph
Sec. 25133	. . .	Allocation of compensation	¶ 1307
Sec. 25134	. . .	Sales factor	¶ 1308
Sec. 25135	. . .	Sales of tangible personal property	¶ 1308
Sec. 25136	. . .	Sales other than sales of tangible personal property	¶ 1308
Sec. 25137	. . .	Adjustment of formula	¶ 1304, ¶ 1305, ¶ 1305a
Sec. 25138	. . .	Purpose of act	. . .
Sec. 25139	. . .	Title	. . .
Sec. 25140	. . .	Intercompany dividends	. . .
Sec. 25141	. . .	Professional sports	¶ 1305a

CHAPTER 8

TAXES ON CORPORATE INCOME
IMPOSITION OF TAX, RATES,
EXEMPTIONS, RETURNS

¶ 801 Overview of Corporation Franchise and Income Taxes

The franchise tax was first imposed in 1929; the corporation income tax in 1937. The law is known as the Bank and Corporation Tax Law, and constitutes Part 11 of Division 2 of the Revenue and Taxation Code. Administrative provisions affecting both corporate and personal income taxpayers are in Part 10.2 of Division 2 of the Revenue and Taxation Code.

The Law is administered by the Franchise Tax Board, composed of the State Controller, the Director of the Department of Finance, and the Chair of the State Board of Equalization.

The franchise tax is imposed for the privilege of exercising the corporate franchise in California. It is imposed upon corporations organized in California and upon out-of-state ("foreign") corporations that are doing business in the state. The tax is measured by the net income (from California sources) of the preceding year, which is referred to as the "income year." Special rules are provided for beginning corporations, dissolving corporations, and corporations involved in a reorganization—see ¶ 811—¶ 814. Banks and financial corporations are taxed at a higher rate than other corporations, and in turn are relieved of certain other taxes as explained at ¶ 809.

The corporation income tax is imposed upon net income, at the basic rate of the franchise tax—see ¶ 809. It is intended to be complementary to the franchise tax, to apply to corporations that derive income from California sources but that are not subject to the franchise tax. Because the franchise tax applies in the great majority of cases (see ¶ 802), the income tax is applicable only to a relatively small number of corporations (see ¶ 802a).

The franchise and income tax rate applied to general C corporations is 8.84%. For banks and financial corporations, the tax rate is 10.84%. S corporations are taxed at a reduced rate of 1.5% (3.5% for S corporations that are financial corporations). For a discussion of the minimum tax, see ¶ 809.

The computation of income for both the franchise tax and the income tax generally follows the pattern of the federal income tax, and interpretations of the federal law by the Treasury Department and the courts are usually followed in the administration of comparable provisions of the California law. However, there are many differences between the federal and California laws. See ¶ 801b for an explanation of the federal conformity program established in 1983. There is also one important difference between the two California laws, as explained at ¶ 909: interest on obligations of the United States is not taxable for income tax purposes although it is included in the measure of the tax for franchise tax purposes.

Some corporations are exempt from both franchise and income taxes. These include insurance underwriting companies (subject to special taxes—see ¶ 1902), several categories of nonprofit organizations, and others, as explained at ¶ 804.

¶ 801a Scope of Chapter

This chapter discusses the two taxes imposed on, or measured by, corporate income: (1) the bank and corporation franchise tax; and (2) the corporation income tax. It covers the question of who is subject and who is exempt, requirements for filing returns and payment of tax, the base upon which the taxes are imposed, the rates of tax and credits against tax, and the extent to which the taxes apply in certain special situations.

¶ 801b Federal Conformity Program

Law: Sec. 23051.5 (CCH California Tax Reports ¶ 10-014).

Comparable Federal: None.

The federal conformity program adopted in 1983 for the personal income tax, as explained at ¶ 102a, has not been applied as thoroughly to corporation taxes. However, in a number of areas—including gross income, deductions, and accounting periods and methods—California corporation franchise and income tax law consists largely of incorporated federal provisions. As under the personal income tax law, references to the Internal Revenue Code (and to uncodified federal laws that relate to Internal Revenue Code provisions) are updated periodically through conforming legislation. Such references in the California law are now updated to January 1, 1998 (for income years beginning after 1997). However, California has adopted only a portion of the amendments made by the the IRS Restructuring and Reform Act of 1998.

California adopts both temporary and final federal regulations to the extent that the federal regulations do not conflict with California law or California regulations.

A proper election, application, or consent filed in accordance with the Internal Revenue Code is effective for California purposes, unless otherwise specified. To obtain different treatment for California than federal, a separate election, application, or consent must be filed with the Franchise Tax Board.

¶ 802 Corporations Subject to Franchise Tax

Law: Secs. 23038, 23038.5, 23101-04 (CCH California Tax Reports ¶ 10-030, 10-034, 12-425).

Comparable Federal: Sec. 7704 (CCH Standard Federal Tax Reports ¶ 26,700, 26,720, 26,740).

California Form: Form 100.

Every corporation doing business or incorporated in California is subject to the franchise tax, unless specifically exempted as set forth in ¶ 804. A corporation organized in California but not doing business in the state, and not expressly exempt, is subject only to a minimum tax—see ¶ 809. However, if such a corporation has income from California sources, it is subject to the income tax, as explained at ¶ 802a. If there is income from both within and without the state, a portion of the total is assigned to California as explained in Chapter 13.

● *When liability for tax attaches*

Once articles of incorporation are filed with the California Secretary of State, a corporation is subject to the franchise tax unless it is specifically exempt—see *Appeal of Mammouth Academy* (1973) (CCH California Tax Reports ¶ 10-034.21). See also *Appeal of Mission Valley East* (1974) (CCH California Tax Reports ¶ 10-117.47). In this case the Secretary of State permitted the filing of articles of incorporation, but there was a conflict of corporate name and the corporation was not permitted to pursue its business activity. The State Board of Equalization (SBE) held that the corporation was nevertheless subject to the franchise tax.

A foreign corporation not doing business in the state is not subject to the franchise tax, but is subject to the income tax if it realizes any income from sources within the state. If a foreign corporation is qualified in the state, it is required to pay the minimum franchise tax even though it does not engage in business in the state; see *Appeal of Tip Top Delights, Inc.* (1970) (CCH CALIFORNIA TAX REPORTS ¶ 10-117.28).

● *What is "doing business"*

The law defines "doing business" as "actively engaging in any transaction for the purpose of financial or pecuniary gain or profit." It also provides that certain corporations, the activities of which are limited to the receipt and disbursement of dividends and interest on securities, are not to be considered as doing business. A corporation is not "doing business" in California for franchise tax purposes if (1) it is not incorporated under the laws of California, (2) its sole activity in California is engaging in convention and trade show activities for seven or fewer calendar days during the income year, and (3) it derives no more than $10,000 of gross income reportable to California from convention and trade show activities during the income year.

In *Appeal of Amman & Schmid Finance AG et al.* (1996) (CCH CALIFORNIA TAX REPORTS ¶ 10-034.31), foreign corporations with interests in limited partnerships were not subject to the California franchise tax, because the corporations' only contact with the state was the receipt of distributive shares of the limited partnerships' California source income. Accordingly, they did not meet the active participation requirement for "doing business" in the state.

The Franchise Tax Board (FTB) has taken the position that an out-of-state limited partner in a limited partnership is not subject to the California minimum tax simply because it holds an interest in a limited partnership that is doing business in California. The FTB's position, in effect, extends the holding in *Amman & Schmid Finance AG et al.* to all limited partners, including corporate and limited partnership limited partners. In addition, the FTB has indicated that it will apply this holding to a limited liability company to the extent that the limited liability company is a limited partner in a limited partnership (*Tax News*, FTB, January 1997).

FTB Regulation 23101 provides, generally, that a foreign corporation that has stocks of goods in California and that makes deliveries in California pursuant to orders taken by employees in California is doing business in the state and is subject to the franchise tax. On the other hand, Regulation 23101 provides that a foreign corporation engaged wholly in interstate commerce is not subject to the franchise tax. (Note that these rules apply to the *franchise* tax. For the application of the corporation *income* tax, see ¶ 802a.)

In *Appeal of Hugo Neu-Proler International Sales Corporation* (1982) (CCH CALIFORNIA TAX REPORTS ¶ 12-500.528), the taxpayer was a Domestic International Sales Corporation (DISC) subject to special treatment under federal income tax law. The corporation had no employees or physical assets in California. The SBE held that the corporation was doing business in California and subject to the franchise tax, because "the exercise of appellant's corporate powers and privileges was essential to the performance of the various transactions it entered into" in California.

¶ 802

In *Appeal of Putnam Fund Distributors Inc., et al.* (1977) (CCH CALIFOR-NIA TAX REPORTS ¶ 12-425.61), the SBE held that a Massachusetts corporation engaged in promoting California sales of mutual fund shares by brokers was doing business and was subject to the franchise tax. The SBE approved the imposition of 25% failure-to-file penalties (see ¶ 1410) for a period of 10 years.

In *Appeal of Kimberly-Clark Corp.* (1962) (CCH CALIFORNIA TAX RE-PORTS ¶ 10-043.85), the SBE held that a foreign corporation qualified to do business in California was subject to the franchise tax even though it did not maintain a stock of goods within the State. It conducted extensive activities and had substantial stocks of samples, displays, and sales promotion materials in the state.

A corporation may be "doing business" even though it is in the process of liquidation. The SBE held to this effect in the case of *Appeal of Sugar Creek Pine Co.* (1955) (CCH CALIFORNIA TAX REPORTS ¶ 10-054.20). The corporation's activities involved principally perfecting title to properties that it had previously contracted to sell.

In *Appeal of American President Lines, Ltd.* (1961) (CCH CALIFORNIA TAX REPORTS ¶ 11-181.23), the SBE held that a corporation that is principally engaged in interstate and foreign commerce is nevertheless subject to the *franchise* tax on the basis of its entire income attributable to sources within the state when it engages in some *intrastate* business in California.

● *Foreign lending institutions*

The Corporations Code specifies the activities in which a foreign lending institution may engage in California without being deemed to be "doing business" in the state. The permissible activities include purchasing or making loans, making appraisals, enforcement of loans, etc., provided the activities are carried on within the limitations set forth in the law.

● *Exemption for limited activities*

The law authorizes the FTB to determine that a corporation is not subject to franchise or income tax if its only activities in California are within specified limits. A corporation may petition the FTB for such a determination. The limited activities are:

1. purchasing in California for its own or its affiliate's use outside the state if (a) the corporation has no more than 100 employees in California whose duties are limited to specified activities, or (b) the corporation has no more than 200 employees in California whose duties are limited, as specified, and the items purchased are used for the construction or modification of a physical plant or facility located outside the state; however, the combined number of employees in this state for purposes of both (a) and (b) may not exceed 200; and/or

2. presence of employees in California solely for the purpose of attending school.

¶ **802**

● *Certain organizations treated as corporations*

The tax law includes "professional corporations" within the definition of "corporation" for franchise tax purposes. Charitable trusts are treated as "corporations"—see ¶ 605.

Under both federal and California law, publicly traded partnerships are treated as "corporations" for income tax purposes unless 90% or more of their gross income consists of qualifying passive activities or they are grandfathered publicly traded partnerships exempt from corporate treatment. However, for tax years beginning after 1997, a grandfathered publicly traded partnership that elects to continue its partnership status will be subject to a California tax equal to 1% of its California-source gross income attributable to the active conduct of any trade or business (a 3.5% tax on gross income attributable to the active conduct of any trade or business for federal purposes).

Limited liability companies classified as corporations are discussed at ¶ 802a.

¶ 802a Corporations Subject to Income Tax

Law: Secs. 18633.5, 23038, 23038.5, 23501, 23503, 23731, 24870-75 (CCH CALIFOR-NIA TAX REPORTS ¶ 10-029, 10-030, 10-032, 11-751, 11-771, 11-791, 89-231).

Comparable Federal: Secs. 851-60G, 7701, 7704 (CCH STANDARD FEDERAL TAX REPORTS ¶ 26,620, 26,700—26,740, 26,780, 43,880, 43,980).

California Form: Form 100.

Generally, the corporation income tax applies to those corporations (including associations, Massachusetts or business trusts, and real estate investment trusts) that derive income from sources within California but are not subject to the franchise tax. If there is income from both within and without the state, a portion of the total is assigned to California as explained in Chapter 13.

● *Application of income tax*

The most common application of the income tax is to foreign corporations that engage in some business activity in California but that are not "doing business" in the state so as to subject them to the franchise tax. One example is a corporation that maintains a stock of goods in California from which deliveries are made to fill orders taken by independent dealers or brokers. Another example might be a corporation that has employees operating in California but has no stock of goods or other property in the state; however, the state's right to tax in such a situation may be limited under the federal legislation discussed below. Where a corporation maintains only a stock of samples in California, having no other property or agents or other activity in the state, it has generally been considered not subject to tax in California.

The income tax, rather than the franchise tax, is imposed on the unrelated business income of an exempt organization.

● *Limited activities—Application of P.L. 86-272*

The scope of the California income tax is limited by federal legislation enacted in 1959. This legislation was intended to overcome the effect of two decisions of the U. S. Supreme Court earlier in 1959: *Northwestern States Portland Cement Co. v. Minnesota* and *Williams v. Stockham Valves and Fittings, Inc.*, 358 U. S. 450, 79 S.Ct. 357. These cases ruled that individual states had broad powers to levy taxes on the income of foreign state corporations even though the business conducted within the state was exclusively in interstate commerce. The federal law (Public Law 86-272) prohibits a state from imposing a tax on income derived from interstate commerce, provided: (1) the activities within the state are limited to the solicitation of orders for sales of tangible personal property by employees or other representatives; (2) orders are sent outside the state for approval; and (3) orders are filled from stocks of goods maintained outside the state. The prohibition against tax applies also to a corporation that sells through a sales office maintained within the state by independent contractors whose activities consist solely of making sales or soliciting orders.

The Franchise Tax Board (FTB) has issued a guide to its interpretation of P.L. 86-272, discussed above. The guide discusses various types of activity that will, or will not, cause a business to lose its state-tax immunity. Activities that will subject a corporation to California taxation include property repairs, credit investigations, and collection of delinquent accounts. Certain activities that are incidental to the solicitation of sales will not cause a business to lose its state-tax immunity. However, if at any time during the income year, a company conducts activities that are not protected, all sales in this state or income earned by the company attributed to this state during any part of the income year are subject to California taxation. The guide also discusses various other problems, including use of display rooms, use of independent contractors, maintaining facilities in the state, and application of the throwback rule. It states that the protection of P.L. 86-272 does not apply to California or foreign-nation corporations or to California residents or domiciliaries. The FTB will supply a copy of the guide upon request.

In Legal Ruling No. 372 (1974) (CCH CALIFORNIA TAX REPORTS ¶ 16-851.11), the FTB held that the protection of Public Law 86-272 does not extend to salesmen soliciting orders in California; such salesmen are subject to withholding of California income tax.

As explained at ¶ 802, the FTB may determine that a corporation is subject to neither franchise nor income tax if its only activities in California are within specified limits.

Appeal of Riblet Tramway Co. (1967) (CCH CALIFORNIA TAX REPORTS ¶ 12-420.74) involved a Washington state manufacturer of ski lift facilities that were installed in California by others. The company usually inspected the facilities after they were installed; the State Board of Equalization (SBE) held that this inspection activity went beyond "solicitation" and subjected the company to California tax.

Similarly, in *Brown Group Retail, Inc. v. Franchise Tax Board* (1996) (CCH CALIFORNIA TAX REPORTS ¶ 12-420.751), an out-of-state shoe manufacturer and distributor that had no facilities or property in the state was not immune from California franchise tax under P.L. 86-272, because services performed by the taxpayer's employees went beyond the mere solicitation of orders. Although the taxpayer made no direct sales in the state, the presence in California of two of the taxpayer's employees who assisted current and potential customers with financial analysis, lease and loan negotiations, site selection, store design, marketing, etc., established a sufficient nexus with the state to subject the taxpayer to California's franchise tax.

● *Cases decided favorably to taxpayer*

In *Appeal of John H. Grace Co.* (1980) (CCH CALIFORNIA TAX REPORTS ¶ 12-425.51), the taxpayer was an Illinois corporation that leased railroad cars to industrial companies. The cars sometimes passed into or through California in interstate commerce, and the taxpayer paid the private car tax (see ¶ 2505) on the average number of cars per day in California. The SBE held that the corporation was not subject to California income tax, because it had no "activities" within the state and the railroad cars were not under its control when they were in the state.

In *Appeal of E.F. Timme & Son, Inc.* (1969) (CCH CALIFORNIA TAX REPORTS ¶ 12-420.76), the FTB contended that P.L. 86-272 was not applicable because the taxpayer did not own the goods it was selling in California. The SBE overruled the FTB and held that the taxpayer was exempt from California tax.

● *Cases unfavorable to taxpayer*

In *William Wrigley, Jr., Co. v. Wisconsin Department of Revenue* (1992) (CCH CALIFORNIA TAX REPORTS ¶ 12-420.75), the U.S. Supreme Court held that an Illinois-based corporation that had sales representatives in Wisconsin to store goods, replace goods, and restock retailers' display racks was not immune from Wisconsin franchise taxes under P.L. 86-272, because those activities went beyond mere "solicitation."

In *Appeal of Aqua Aerobic Systems, Inc.* (1985) (CCH CALIFORNIA TAX REPORTS ¶ 12-420.65), the SBE held that an Illinois manufacturer's warranty repairs exceeded "solicitation" and went beyond the protection of P.L. 86-272.

In *Appeal of Ramfjeld and Co., Inc.* (1981) (CCH CALIFORNIA TAX REPORTS ¶ 12-425.15), the taxpayer warehoused in California canned fish that it sold to U.S. military installations in California and Asia. The taxpayer was a New York corporation, with no office or employees in California. The SBE held that the corporation was subject to California income tax.

In *Appeal of CITC Industries, Inc.* (1979) (CCH CALIFORNIA TAX REPORTS ¶ 12-420.70), the taxpayer was the U.S. sales representative for a Japanese manufacturer and maintained a sales office in California. The SBE held that the taxpayer's activities went beyond the protection of P.L. 86-272. See also *Appeal of Schmid Brothers, Inc.* (1980) (CCH CALIFORNIA TAX REPORTS ¶ 12-420.79), to the same effect.

In *Appeal of Kelsey-Hayes Company* (1978) (CCH CALIFORNIA TAX REPORTS ¶ 12-585.59), the taxpayer corporation had an active California division that admittedly subjected the corporation to the franchise tax. The corporation also had limited activity in California in an entirely unrelated business. The SBE held that P. L. 86-272 was not applicable and the limited activity could be taxed on a unitary basis with related out-of-state operations, because P. L. 86-272 must be applied to the totality of the corporation's California activities.

¶ 802a

In *Appeal of Knoll Pharmaceutical Company, Inc.* (1977) (CCH CALIFOR-
NIA TAX REPORTS ¶ 12-420.72), an out-of-state manufacturer had employees
soliciting sales in California. The sales were approved and filled by a California consignee from a stock of goods maintained in the state. The SBE held that
the corporation's activities went beyond the protection of P. L. 86-272. See
also *Consolidated Accessories Corp. v. Franchise Tax Board* (1984) (CCH
CALIFORNIA TAX REPORTS ¶ 12-420.71), to the same effect.

In *Appeal of Nardis of Dallas, Inc.* (1975) (CCH CALIFORNIA TAX RE-
PORTS ¶ 12-420.78), an out-of-state corporation sold clothing through a California showroom. The SBE held that the corporation was not protected from
California tax under P. L. 86-272, because the California salesman was an
employee—not an independent contractor—and the showroom was maintained by the company, even though it was leased in the salesman's name.

In *Appeal of Snap-On Tools Corporation* (1958) (CCH CALIFORNIA TAX
REPORTS ¶ 12-425.34), the SBE held that where an out-of-state corporation
operated in California solely through independently owned distributorships, it
was not doing business in the state so as to be subject to the franchise tax.
However, because the corporation maintained consigned stocks of goods in
California from which withdrawals were made by the independent distributors, it was held subject to the income tax.

● *Noncorporate organizations subject to tax*

California adopts IRC Sec. 7704, under which publicly traded partnerships are taxed as corporations, unless 90% or more of their gross income is
qualifying passive income or they are grandfathered publicly traded partnerships exempt from corporate treatment. However, for tax years beginning
after 1997, a grandfathered publicly traded partnership that elects to continue
its partnership status will be subject to a California tax equal to 1% of its
California-source gross income attributable to the active conduct of any trade
or business (a 3.5% tax on gross income attributable to the active conduct of
any trade or business for federal purposes).

The income tax applies to certain other organizations that may be said
generally to have the characteristics of a corporation. It applies to certain
associations, to Massachusetts or business trusts, and to some non-publicly
traded limited partnerships. FTB Regulations 23038(a) and 23038(b) contain
detailed rules in this regard.

● *Regulated investment companies*

California adopts federal provisions dealing with regulated investment
companies (RICs) (commonly known as "mutual funds") as of the current IRC
tie-in date (see ¶ 801), with the exception that California allows RICs to
deduct exempt interest dividends distributed to shareholders to the extent that
the interest was included in gross income. (At the federal level, the deduction
is denied because interest from state and local bonds is excluded from federal
gross income; however, because such interest is included in gross income for
California purposes (see ¶ 909), California permits the deduction.) California
taxes a RIC the same as a taxable C corporation, except that its California
"net income" is the same as its federal "investment company taxable income"
with specified modifications.

¶ 802a

● *Real estate investment trusts*

An organization that qualifies as a "real estate investment trust" (REIT) for federal income tax purposes is treated as a business trust subject to the corporation income tax. California has conformed to the federal law regarding such organizations as of the current IRC tie-in date (see ¶ 801), adopting federal definitions and accounting methods, except that a REIT's California "net income" is the same as its federal "real estate investment company taxable income" with specified modifications. A federal election to treat certain REIT property as foreclosure property, or the lack of such an election, is binding for California purposes and a separate California election is not allowed.

For federal purposes, the IRS Restructuring and Reform Act modified the ordering rule that applies when a REIT is required to distribute earnings and profits accumulated in non-REIT years. Under the modified rule, "earliest accumulated earnings and profits" are the earliest earnings and profits accumulated in *any* tax year in which the entity did not qualify as a REIT. This facilitates the purging of non-REIT earnings and profits from existing REITs, as well as from newly electing REITs. The modification is effective for federal purposes for tax years beginning after August 5, 1997, but has not yet been incorporated for California purposes.

● *Real estate mortgage investment conduits*

California follows federal law as of the current IRC tie-in date (see ¶ 801), exempting from income or franchise taxation corporations that qualify as "real estate mortgage investment conduits" (REMICs). The income of such an entity is taxable to the holders of its interests. There are two separate interests in a REMIC, with each taxed under a different set of complex rules. California does not incorporate the federal provision that imposes a 100% tax on the net income from prohibited transactions. A REMIC is subject to the minimum tax, but not to the franchise tax, and a REMIC's income is taxable to the holders of its interests; see ¶ 802.

● *Financial asset securitization investment trusts*

California incorporates federal provisions concerning financial asset securitization investment trusts (FASITs) as of the current IRC tie-in date (see ¶ 801), with a number of modifications discussed below. A FASIT is a pass-through entity that may be used to securitize debt obligations such as credit card receivables, home equity loans, and auto loans. Securities issued by a FASIT are treated as debt for federal income tax purposes, regardless of whether instruments with similar terms issued by an entity other than a FASIT would be characterized as equity ownership interests. Consequently, a FASIT may be used to avoid imposition of a corporate level tax on investors' income and to ensure that interest paid to investors will be deductible by the loan pool's sponsor.

To qualify as a FASIT, an entity must (1) have a single ownership interest that is held by a domestic bank or C corporation, (2) not qualify as a regulated investment company, (3) issue only nonownership security instruments that meet the requirements for "regular interests," (4) have assets

¶ 802a

substantially all of which are "permitted assets," and (5) make an election to be treated as a FASIT for the year of the election and thereafter.

"Permitted assets" include for FASIT purposes cash and cash equivalents, certain permitted debt instruments, certain foreclosure property, certain instruments or contracts that represent hedges or guarantees of debt held or issued by the FASIT, contract rights to acquire permitted debt instruments or hedges, and a regular interest in another FASIT. A "regular interest" is defined for FASIT purposes as an asset-backed security issued on or after the startup date of the FASIT that (1) has fixed terms, (2) unconditionally entitles the holder to receive a specified principal amount, (3) pays interest that is either fixed, indexed to a predictable schedule based on rates that measure current variations in the cost of newly borrowed funds, or variable rates similar to those allowable for regular interests in a real estate mortgage investment conduit (REMIC), (4) is issued to the public with a premium not exceeding 25% of the stated principal amount, and (5) has a yield to maturity at issue of no more than five percentage points above the applicable federal rate for the calendar month in which the instrument is issued.

A FASIT is not generally subject to entity-level tax. Under federal law, taxes paid by the FASIT at the entity level are limited to a corporate tax on income from foreclosure and certain excise taxes on prohibited transactions such as lending. A FASIT is subject to California's minimum franchise tax (see ¶ 809), but is not subject to a California tax on prohibited transactions. All of the FASIT's assets are treated as assets and liabilities of the FASIT's owner. Any income, gain, deduction, or loss of the FASIT is accordingly directly allocable to its owner. Any securities held by the FASIT are treated as held for investment by its owner.

● *Limited liability companies*

A limited liability company (LLC) that is classified as a corporation for California tax purposes is subject to the same tax return and tax payment requirements as any other corporation. LLCs that are classified as partnerships or that are disregarded and treated as sole proprietorships are discussed at ¶ 618.

● *Credit for franchise tax*

A corporation subject to the income tax is allowed a credit for any franchise tax imposed for the same period.

¶ 803 S Corporations

Law: Secs. 23800—23813, 24416, 24633.5, 24637 (CCH CALIFORNIA TAX REPORTS ¶ 12-051, 89-133).

Comparable Federal: Secs. 1361-79 (CCH STANDARD FEDERAL TAX REPORTS ¶ 4845-4848M).

California Forms: Form 100S, FTB 3560.

Corporations electing S corporation status for federal tax purposes are deemed to have elected S corporation status for state tax purposes, unless they make an express C corporation status election using FTB 3560.

California's conformity to federal provisions recognizing S corporations as pass-through entities is partial in that (1) California imposes both a 1.5% tax and the minimum tax at the corporate level, (2) California law prohibits the election of S corporation status by savings and loan associations, banks, and financial corporations that use the reserve method of accounting for bad debts under California law, while federal law prohibits such an election by financial institutions that use the reserve method of accounting for bad debts under federal law, and (3) California imposes a minimum tax on qualified subchapter S subsidiaries.

● *Character of pass-through entity*

Under federal law, small corporations (limited by the number of shareholders) enjoy the tax advantages of partnerships while at the same time benefiting from the corporate characteristic of limited liability. Tax is not paid by the corporation, as such. Generally, items of income, loss, and credits are passed through to shareholders on a pro-rata basis. California has adopted a hybrid version of the S corporation in which both a reduced corporate tax is paid at the corporate level and income and tax attributes are passed through to shareholders.

● *Nonresident shareholders*

To ensure that all nonresident shareholders pay their taxes, the law requires each S corporation that has one or more shareholders who is a nonresident or a trust with nonresident fiduciaries to submit to the Franchise Tax Board (FTB): (1) names of all shareholders; and (2) statements from all nonresident shareholders that they consent to California's jurisdiction to tax their California S corporation income on the pro rata basis of their ownership interest. Nonresident shareholders of an S corporation may elect to file a single group return in the same manner as nonresident partners under the personal income tax law (see ¶ 613).

● *S corporation's taxable year*

California incorporates IRC Sec. 444, under which S corporations may elect a fiscal year that is the same as the corporation used in its last tax year. See ¶ 1104.

● *Reduced tax at corporate level*

S corporations that are not financial corporations compute the corporate franchise (income) tax on Form 100S, but pay this tax at the rate of 1.5% instead of the normal corporate tax rate discussed at ¶ 809. For purposes of the 1.5% tax, S corporations compute depreciation and amortization deductions using MACRS.

In *Handlery Hotels, Inc.* (1995) (CCH CALIFORNIA TAX REPORTS ¶ 12-051.15), a California court of appeal held that a corporation that made a valid election to be treated as an S corporation was not entitled to apply the lower S corporation franchise tax rate until the first income year following the corporation's valid election.

¶ 803

As under federal law, S corporations are not subject to the alternative minimum tax (¶ 810). However, they are subject to the minimum tax (see ¶ 809).

● *Financial S corporation*

The tax rate for S corporations that are also financial corporations is 3.5%.

● *Qualified subchapter S subsidiaries*

Under both California and federal law an S corporation may own a qualified subchapter S subsidiary (QSSS). However, under California (but not federal) law, a QSSS is subject to the California corporate minimum tax if it is incorporated in California, qualified to transact business in California, or doing business in California. In addition, the activities of a QSSS are imputed to the S corporation for purposes of determining whether the S corporation is "doing business" in California. An S corporation's federal election to treat a corporation as a QSSS is binding for California purposes and no separate election is allowed.

● *Separate tax on excess net passive investment income*

A separate tax is imposed on excess net passive investment income from California sources, using the full tax rate that applies to general corporations, but only when the taxpayer has excess net passive income for federal purposes. This tax is not reduced by any tax credits; however, the amount of the income subject to this tax is deductible from net income for purposes of computing the 1.5% tax.

● *NOL deductions*

An S corporation is allowed to deduct a net operating loss incurred during a year in which it elects to be treated as an S corporation. An S corporation may pass the full amount of such loss through to its shareholders in the year the loss is incurred. If a shareholder is unable to use the full amount of the loss in the year it is incurred, the shareholder may carry over 50% of the unused loss to subsequent years. The S corporation may carry forward 50% of the NOL for up to five years to offset the 1.5% tax on net income.

S corporations may also qualify for the 100% NOL carryover deduction available to (1) taxpayers engaged in the conduct of qualified businesses in enterprise zones, the former Los Angeles Revitalization Zone, local agency military base recovery areas, and the targeted tax area; and (2) "new" and "small" businesses (see ¶ 1018).

● *Combined reporting of members of a unitary business*

A corporation that elects to be treated as an S corporation is, by virtue of its election, required to be excluded from the combined report of the unitary group. However, the law contains enforcement provisions to help the FTB prevent tax avoidance or evasion.

¶ 803

● *Separate tax on built-in capital gains*

A "built-in gains" tax is imposed on gains from sales of assets, as determined under IRC Sec. 1374. The tax applies only to gains from California source income. The tax is not reduced by any credits except credits carried over from years prior to an S election. The full corporate tax rate (see ¶ 809) is applied to this income.

● *Credits available to S corporations*

Corporate credits may be claimed against the 1.5% (or 3.5% for financial S corpoations) tax, with no pass-through to shareholders. The credits are reduced to one-third of their total value because the tax rate is much lower than the regular corporate tax rate discussed at ¶ 809. Unused portions of the credit, but not the two-thirds that is denied, may be carried forward. Credit carryovers from years prior to making an S election are also subject to the one-third limitation for the first income year, but not in subsequent years. Shareholders, however, are able to take the full amount of credits to which they may be entitled as individual taxpayers.

For California purposes, credits and credit carryovers may not reduce the minimum franchise tax, built-in gains tax, excess net passive income tax, credit recaptures, the increase in tax imposed for the deferral of installment sale income, or an installment of last-in first-out (LIFO) recapture tax.

● *Passive activity losses and at-risk rules*

The federal limitations on losses and credits from passive activities (IRC Sec. 469) and the at-risk rules (IRC Sec. 465) are applied in the same manner as if the corporation were an individual. For this purpose, "adjusted gross income" of the S corporation is its "net income," as modified for California purposes, but without any charitable contributions deduction. However, the material participation rules apply as if the S corporation was a closely held corporation.

● *S corporation election; termination of status*

Generally, a federal S corporation is treated as a California S corporation, unless the corporation elects to be treated as a regular corporation for state purposes on a return filed with the FTB by the 15th day of the third month of the year in which the corporation elects federal S status. However, savings and loan associations, banks, and financial corporations that are allowed a bad debt deduction under California law are ineligible to elect S corporation status for California purposes.

Under current law, the election applies only to corporations that are incorporated or qualified to do business in California and, with one exception, only within the time frames established under federal law. An invalid election that was validated by the Secretary of the IRS under a special provision that grants the Secretary authority to validate invalid elections retroactively to tax years beginning after 1982 is recognized for California purposes only in the corporation's first income year beginning after 1996. However, a corporation may perfect an S corporation election for California purposes for any income year beginning after 1986 in those instances when the corporation merely failed to timely file a federal S corporation election if (1) the corporation and all of its shareholders reported their income for California income tax purposes on original returns consistent with S corporation status for the year the election should have been made and for each subsequent income year and (2) the corporation and its shareholders have filed with the IRS for relief and received notification from the IRS of the acceptance of an untimely filed S corporation election.

A federal S corporation that elects to continue as a regular corporation for state purposes may elect to become a California S corporation in subsequent income years unless prohibited federally. A foreign nonqualified corporation that is not doing business in California but qualifies later is deemed to have made an election as an S corporation in the income year of qualification, unless regular corporation status is chosen for that income year within the filing deadline. For purposes of the tax imposed on built-in gains and on excess passive investment income (see below), taxpayers that do elect California S corporation status are allowed to use their federal election date for purposes of applying the rules of these separate taxes.

The deadline for filing a California election to be a regular corporation is the last date allowed for filing a federal S election.

Termination of a federal S corporation election simultaneously terminates the California election; however, an S corporation may terminate its California S corporation status without terminating its federal S corporation status. In such a case, written notification must be made to the FTB.

Under federal law as adopted by California, if an S corporation terminates its election, it is ineligible to make another S corporation election for five years without the consent of the FTB (the IRS for federal purposes). However, any S corporation that terminated its election within the five-year period immediately prior to 1997 may re-elect S corporation status without the IRS's or FTB's consent.

● *Other differences from federal treatment*

The federal provisions dealing with coordination with the investment credit recapture are inapplicable as are the provisions dealing with foreign (non-US) income.

● *Taxation of shareholders*

Taxation of shareholders is discussed at ¶ 232.

¶ 803a Designated Settlement Funds

Law: Sec. 24693 (CCH California Tax Reports ¶ 11-257a).

Comparable Federal: Sec. 468B (CCH Standard Federal Tax Reports ¶ 21,950).

California follows IRC Sec. 468B, relating to the taxation of designated settlement funds, except that the tax imposed is at the regular California income tax rate. The tax is in lieu of any other income tax.

¶ 804 Exempt Corporations

> *Law:* Secs. 23701-11, 23740, 24328 (CCH CALIFORNIA TAX REPORTS ¶ 11-301, 11-313, 11-337, 11-367).
>
> *Comparable Federal:* Secs. 501, 504-05, 507-09, 527-29, 4940-48, 7428 (CCH STANDARD FEDERAL TAX REPORTS ¶ 22,602, 22,700, 22,711, 22,721, 22,740, 22,750, 22,850, 22,870, 35,400—35,560, 42320).
>
> *California Form:* FTB 3500.

The following organizations are exempt from both franchise and income tax:

(1) labor, agricultural, or horticultural organizations, with some exceptions (see comment below);

(2) fraternal organizations providing insurance benefits to their members or devoting earnings exclusively to certain charitable-type and fraternal purposes;

(3) nonprofit cemetery or crematory companies;

(4) nonprofit religious, charitable, scientific, literary, or educational organizations (including certain cooperative hospital service organizations and certain amateur athletic associations);

(5) nonprofit business leagues, chambers of commerce, etc.;

(6) nonprofit civic leagues, etc.;

(7) nonprofit social and recreational clubs;

(8) nonprofit title holding corporations;

(9) voluntary employees' beneficiary associations;

(10) teachers' retirement associations;

(11) certain religious or apostolic organizations, provided the income is reported by the individual members;

(12) certain employee-funded pension plans created before June 25, 1959;

(13) organizations providing child care to the general public;

(14) insurance underwriting companies (this is a constitutional exemption; see discussion below. Insurance companies are subject to special taxes—see ¶ 1902);

(15) nonprofit corporations engaged in port and terminal protection and development (Sec. 10703 of Corporations Code);

(16) trusts that provide for the payment of supplemental unemployment compensation benefits;

(17) trusts or plans that meet the requirements of the federal Self-Employed Individual Tax Retirement law, if not otherwise exempt as an employees' trust;

(18) political organizations (see discussion below);

(19) homeowners' associations—see ¶ 914;

(20) tenant organizations established to purchase mobile home parks for conversion into condominiums, stock cooperatives, or other resident ownership interests;

(21) veterans' organizations;

(22) nonprofit public benefit organizations;

(23) nonprofit insurance risk pools;

(24) qualified state tuition programs; and

(25) state-chartered and federally chartered credit unions.

● *California-federal comparisons*

The California exemptions are largely the same as the federal ones, although there are several differences.

The following exemptions are the same as the federal:

Item above	California law	Federal law
(1)	23701a	501(c)(5)
(2)	23701b, 23701 *l*	501(c)(8), (c)(10)
(3)	23701c	501(c)(13)
(4)	23701d, 23704	501(c)(3), 501(e), 501(j)
(7)	23701g	501(c)(7)
(8)	23701h, x	501(c)(2), (c)(25)
(9)	23701i	501(c)(9)
(10)	23701j	501(c)(11)
(11)	23701k	501(d)
(12)	23701s	501(c)(18)
(13)	23704.4	501(k)
(16)	23701n	501(c)(17)
(17)	23701p	401(a)
(21)	23701w	501(c)(19)
(24)	23711	529
(25)	23701y	501(c)(14)

Item (1) above (Sec. 23701a) is substantially the same as IRC Sec. 501(c)(5). The California exemption for agricultural cooperatives applies only if the organization is determined by the Internal Revenue Service to be exempt. (See also ¶ 1015.)

Item (5) above (Sec. 23701e) is the same as IRC Sec. 501(c)(6) except that the federal provision includes professional football leagues and California does not.

Item (6) above (Sec. 23701f) is the same as IRC Sec. 501(c)(4) except that the California law requires that the organization's assets be irrevocably dedicated to exempt purposes.

Item (23) above (Sec. 23701z) applies to any organization established pursuant to the Nonprofit Corporation Law by three or more corporations to pool self-insurance claims or losses of those corporations. Federal law provides a similar exemption to "qualified charitable risk pools" organized under state law.

Item (25) above (Sec. 23701y) applies to California state-chartered credit unions only. Federally-chartered unions are exempt from California taxation by operation of the Federal Credit Union Act.

¶ 804

The federal law contains a number of exemptions not included in the California law. On the other hand, there are no specific exemptions in the federal law comparable to California items (14), (15), (20), and (22) above.

● *Political organizations*

The California exemption for political organizations—item (18) above—with minor exceptions, is the same as the federal exemption. However, the California definition of "political organization" is slightly different from the federal. Also, California has not conformed to federal provisions that tax a nonpolitical organization on certain amounts when such organization engages in political activity.

An unincorporated political organization is automatically exempt, and is not required to file the usual application for exemption. Likewise, an *incorporated* political organization is not required to file the usual application for exemption; however, in order to avoid the minimum prepayment at the time of incorporation (see ¶ 806a and ¶ 809), such a corporation must obtain a certificate of exemption from the Franchise Tax Board (FTB). As explained at ¶ 805a, an exempt political organization is required to file an income tax return if it has taxable income in excess of $100.

● *Insurance companies*

The gross premiums tax imposed on insurance companies is "in lieu" of all other state and local taxes and licenses, including the franchise tax.

● *Dedication of assets required*

Under California law, a charitable organization is not eligible for exemption under item (4) above unless its assets are irrevocably dedicated to exempt purposes. The California law (Sec. 23701d) provides specific rules for determining whether the assets are so dedicated, and requires a provision to that effect in the articles of organization. Federal law does not include this requirement; however, the governing instrument of a charitable organization must include specific provisions regarding distribution of income, prohibited acts, etc. See further comment below on this point.

● *Use of accumulated income defeated exemption*

The State Board of Equalization (SBE) held in *Appeal of Boys Incorporated of America* (1960) (CCH CALIFORNIA TAX REPORTS ¶ 11-307.45) that the organization was not operated exclusively for exempt purposes, where it was shown that accumulated income had been used to liquidate indebtedness rather than for its avowed charitable purposes.

● *Application for exemption*

Charitable trusts are treated as corporations for California income and franchise tax purposes (see also ¶ 605). Corporations and trusts claiming an exemption must file an application (FTB 3500) with the FTB, which will advise the applicant of its decision. Applications must be accompanied by a $25 filing fee. This does not apply to insurance underwriting companies, which are exempt under the state constitution. Neither does it apply to political

¶ 804

organizations except that an *incorporated* political organization must either pay the minimum tax (see ¶ 809) or obtain a certificate of exemption.

Certain organizations are required by federal law to give notice that they are applying for tax-exempt status. In these cases, the organizations are required to file a copy of the federal notice with the FTB.

California law provides that an exempt organization shall not be disqualified on the basis that it conducts bingo games authorized by law, provided the proceeds are used exclusively for charitable purposes. Federal law provides for exemption of income from bingo games under certain conditions—see ¶ 804a.

● *Retroactivity of exemption*

The FTB may grant exempt status retroactively to years that the organization can prove it satisfied the exemption requirements. All applications for refunds must be timely filed (see ¶ 1415).

● *Private foundations*

Although California has conformed in principle to federal law by creating a special category of charitable organizations classified as "private foundations," California has not adopted many of the complicated federal provisions relating to such organizations. Also, whereas federal law imposes a tax on the investment income of such organizations and a series of excise taxes on self-dealing, income-accumulation, prohibited investments, lobbying, termination, etc., California imposes no special taxes on "private foundations" as such.

Corporations classified as "private foundations" are required to include certain provisions in their governing instruments in order to maintain their tax-exempt status, unless a state statute accomplishes the same result. The California Corporations Code imposes the restrictions of federal law on every corporation that is deemed to be a "private foundation" under federal law. The law further provides that any provisions of a corporation's governing instruments that are inconsistent or contrary are of no effect.

Organizations exempt under Sec. 23701d of the law (item (4) above) may lose their exemption by engaging in certain "prohibited transactions" or by accumulating income under certain conditions.

In *Appeal of Vinemore Company, etc.* (1972) (CCH California Tax Reports ¶ 11-361.15), the SBE revoked a hospital corporation's charitable exemption retroactively six years after the exemption was granted; the FTB had not been informed earlier of the corporation's improper activities.

● *Permissible lobbying activities*

Both California and federal laws provide for permissible levels of lobbying activities that a tax-exempt organization, which elects to apply these provisions, can engage in without losing its exempt status. However, California has not conformed to the federal provisions imposing a 25% tax on "excess expenditures."

● *No California provision for court review*

The federal law provides for court review of Internal Revenue Service rulings regarding tax-exempt status under certain conditions; there is nothing comparable in the California law.

¶804a   Taxation   of   Business   Income   of   Exempt Corporations

> *Law:* Secs. 23702, 23731-37, 23741, 23771 (CCH CALIFORNIA TAX REPORTS ¶ 11-319, 11-349, 89-231).

> *Comparable Federal:* Secs. 501-03, 511-15 (CCH STANDARD FEDERAL TAX REPORTS ¶ 22,602, 22,670, 22,680, 22,770—22,820).

California law concerning the taxation of unrelated business income of exempt organizations is substantially the same as federal law as of the current IRC tie-in date (see ¶ 801b), except that certain rentals received by one exempt church from another are exempt from California tax. Unrelated business income is subject to California income tax, rather than franchise tax. Also, California has not yet conformed to a federal amendment made by the IRS Restructuring and Reform Act of 1998 that modifies the rules for determining whether certain income derived from a subsidiary is unrelated business income of a tax-exempt organization. As modified, the rules apply to payments accrued, as well as received, by a tax-exempt organization. The modification is effective for federal purposes for tax years beginning after August 5, 1997.

California adopts by reference federal law for treatment of "unrelated debt-financed income." Under the rule, tax-exempt organizations in partnership with taxable entities treat income from debt-financed real property as unrelated business taxable income if partnership allocations are neither (1) qualified allocations, or (2) permissible disproportionate allocations. The purpose of the federal rule is to prevent the allocation of tax losses to the taxable partner.

Income from bingo games conducted by exempt organizations is exempt from California tax (Sec. 23710); however, income from games of chance is subject to the federal tax on unrelated business income.

● *Return required for business income*

Organizations otherwise exempt that are subject to tax as explained above are required to file returns reporting their income from taxable activities and to pay tax on such income, under the rules applicable to organizations that are not exempt. The due date for such returns is the same as that for information returns of exempt organizations: the 15th day of the fifth month following the period covered by the return (the 15th day of the fourth month following the close of the income year for education IRAs).

¶ 804a

¶ 805 Returns—Time and Place for Filing

Law: Secs. 18601-23 (CCH California Tax Reports ¶ 89-121—89-127, 89-142, 89-159—89-161, 89-171).

Comparable Federal: Secs. 6065, 6072, 6081, 6102 (CCH Standard Federal Tax Reports ¶ 37,720, 37,780, 37,860).

California Forms: Forms 100, 100S, FTB 3539, FTB 8633.

Corporations subject to tax are required to file an annual income or franchise tax return by the fifteenth day of the third month after the close of the income year. This is the same as the federal due date and is one month earlier than the date for filing individual income tax returns. The filing date for farmers' cooperative associations is the 15th day of the ninth month after the close of the income year.

Information returns are discussed at ¶ 1411.

● *Short-period returns*

A California short-period return is due the same day as the federal short-period return, which is the 15th day of the third calendar month following the close of the short period. If a federal short-period return is not required, the California short-period return is due within two months and 15 days after the close of the short period.

● *Extensions of time*

The Franchise Tax Board (FTB) has authority to grant extensions of time, not to exceed seven months, for filing any return, declaration, statement, or other document. An automatic extension will be granted for filing franchise or income tax returns (unless the corporation is suspended on the original due date for the return), provided the prescribed procedure is followed. The FTB will grant "paperless" extensions to corporations. Under this procedure, corporations will be granted an automatic extension to the 15th day of the 10th month following the close of the income year (fiscal-year filers) or October 15 (calendar-year filers). An extension of time for filing does not extend the time for paying the underlying tax. Interest and late payment penalties will still accrue from the date the original return was due. Tax payments must be accompanied by FTB 3539 (Payment Voucher for Automatic Extension for Corporations and Exempt Organizations). However, corporations required to pay their tax liability by electronic funds transfer (EFT) (see ¶ 807) must remit all payments by EFT to avoid penalties and, thus, do not submit FTB 3539.

Where affiliated corporations file a combined report, as explained at ¶ 1311, the FTB will accept a single FTB 3539 covering all the corporations to be included in the combined report.

● *Interest on late payments*

If the amount paid by the regular due date of the return (without regard to extensions) is less than the tax payable with the return, interest is charged from the regular due date of the return to the date of payment. Interest is charged on late payments, at the rate charged on deficiencies as explained at

¶ 1409. See ¶ 1410 regarding the penalty for failure to pay by the regular due date, in cases where an extension is granted for filing.

● *Filing by mail*

Returns and requests for extension of time filed by mail are deemed to be filed on the date they are placed in the United States mail, provided they are properly addressed and the postage is prepaid. When the due date falls on a Saturday, Sunday, or other legal holiday, returns may be filed on the following business day. The date of the postmark is ordinarily deemed to be the date of mailing. Although it may be possible to prove that the return was actually mailed on an earlier date, it is obviously desirable to mail early enough to be sure the postmark is timely. (Note that a postage meter date is not a "postmark.") If private delivery services are used, items should be sent in time to be *received* by the deadline.

Returns should be mailed to the FTB in Sacramento, or filed with any area or district office. The Sacramento mailing address is shown in the return instructions.

● *Filing using electronic technology*

Corporation franchise and income tax returns and other documents that are filed using electronic technology must be in a form prescribed by the FTB. In addition, taxpayers are required to complete and retain an electronic filing declaration, which must be furnished to the FTB upon request. Tax preparers may apply to participate in the electronic filing program by submitting an application (FTB 8633) to the FTB.

● *Form for return*

Form 100 is used to file a California corporation franchise or income tax return. Schedules on the California return provide for adjustments and other information needed for state purposes. Corporations may substitute federal schedules for California schedules as long as they attach all supporting federal schedules and reconcile any differences between federal and California figures.

Generally, a copy of federal Form 1120 or Form 1120A, Page 1, U.S. Corporation Income Tax Return, and all pertinent supporting schedules must be attached or the information from the federal return must be transferred to Schedule F, Form 100, and all pertinent schedules must be attached. If the corporation is not required to file a federal return, or has a different federal reporting requirement, the corporation must complete Schedule F, Form 100, to determine its California income. If net income is computed under California laws, generally no state adjustments are necessary.

Taxpayers should use, if possible, the return forms they receive from the FTB with their name, address, and corporate number already imprinted on the label; this is important to the FTB's handling of returns. If reproduced forms are used in lieu of the forms supplied by the FTB, the gummed label should be affixed to the reproduced form. Details of specifications and conditions for reproducing forms, and for computer-prepared forms, may be obtained from the Franchise Tax Board, Tax Forms Development and Distribution Unit, P.O. Box 1468, Sacramento, California 95812-1468.

S Corporations file Form 100S.

● *Whole dollar reporting*

The California law conforms to federal law with respect to whole dollar reporting (sometimes referred to as "cents-less" reporting). Under these rules, if any amount required to be shown on a return, statement, or other document is other than a whole dollar, the fractional part of a dollar may be rounded to the nearest dollar; that is, amounts under 50¢ are dropped and amounts from 50¢ to 99¢ increased to the next dollar.

● *Reporting federal changes*

A taxpayer filing an amended federal return is required to file an amended California return within six months if the change increases the amount of California tax due. Also, if any change or correction is made in gross income or deductions by federal authorities, or income or deductions are changed by renegotiation of government contracts or subcontracts, such changes must be reported to the FTB within six months of the date of the final determination of the federal change or correction or renegotiation if they increase the amount of California tax due. Effective for federal determinations that become final after 1999, corporate taxpayers are required to report changes or corrections to any item required to be reported on a federal tax return within six months of the federal determination of the change or correction, regardless of whether the change or correction increases the amount of tax due. The "date of the final federal determination" is defined as the date that each adjustment or resolution resulting from an IRS examination is assessed pursuant to IRC Sec. 6203. The taxpayer is required to concede the accuracy of the federal determination or state wherein it is erroneous. Failure to comply with these requirements may result in extending the running of the statute of limitations on deficiency assessments—see ¶ 1408.

● *Exempt organizations*

If an exempt-organization return (see ¶ 805a) is filed in good faith and the organization is later held to be taxable, the return filed is deemed a valid taxable return for the organization. Receivers, trustees in bankruptcy, or assignees operating the property or business of a corporation are required to file returns.

● *Report to Secretary of State*

Sections 1502 and 2117 of the Corporations Code require domestic and foreign corporations to file with the Secretary of State a biennial report (an annual report prior to 2000) showing names of officers and directors and other information. The first report must be filed within 90 days of incorporation. Thereafter, reports are due biennially by the date indicated by the Secretary of the State on the form mailed to the corporation. The tax law provides for assessment by the FTB of a penalty for failure to file this report—see ¶ 1410. Corporations may file a brief statement in lieu of the biennial report in cases where no changes have occurred during the filing period.

¶ 805

● *Effect of failure to file or pay*

A corporation that fails to file a return or to make required payments may have its corporate rights suspended—see ¶ 816.

● *Filing date for DISCs*

California has nothing comparable to the special federal provisions for Domestic International Sales Corporations (DISCs). Accordingly, the special federal filing date for such corporations has no application to California returns. See *Appeal of CerwinVega International* (1978) (CCH CALIFORNIA Tax Reports ¶ 89-410.3851, ¶ 89-416.15, ¶ 89-430.31), in which penalties were imposed on a DISC for underpayment of estimated tax and late payment of tax.

¶ 805a Returns of Exempt Organizations

> *Law:* Secs. 23703, 23771-78 (CCH CALIFORNIA TAX REPORTS ¶ 11-322, 89-124, 89-139, 89-169).
>
> *Comparable Federal:* Secs. 6012(a), 6033, 6652 (CCH STANDARD FEDERAL TAX REPORTS ¶ 36,620, 37,466).
>
> *California Forms:* Form 109, Form 199, FTB 3539.

Exempt organizations (including charitable trusts) are required to file annual information returns (Form 199).

● *Exceptions to filing requirement*

The filing of information returns is not required for the following organizations and activities:

(1) churches;

(2) exclusive religious activities of religious orders;

(3) political organizations;

(4) exempt organizations, except private foundations, with gross receipts of $25,000 or less; and

(5) exempt organizations controlled by the state or by a public body that fulfills a public function.

Some other organizations are excepted under discretionary authority of the Franchise Tax Board (FTB).

A religious organization that refuses to file because of religious convictions may be permitted to submit a notarized statement instead.

● *Requirements for returns*

Although the California requirements for information returns are generally similar to the federal requirements, there are some differences and the FTB should be consulted in case of any question. FTB 1066, Guide for Filing Exempt Organizations Group Returns, provides a simplified procedure for some organizations with branches.

¶ 805a

● *Private foundations*

California private foundations file Form 199 as do other exempt organizations. Instead of completing certain parts of the form, a private foundation may submit a completed copy of the current Form CT-2, Registry of Charitable Trusts Report (including federal Form 990) or a completed copy of federal Form 990-PF with appropriate schedules.

● *Filing with Registrar of Charitable Trusts*

In addition to the information return requirements discussed above, a charitable corporation and a trustee holding property for charitable purposes is required to register with the Registrar of Charitable Trusts, in the office of the Attorney General in Sacramento, and to file an annual report (CT-2) with the Registrar. (Some types of organizations, including churches, schools, and hospitals, are specifically exempted from this requirement.) Under the tax law, any organization that fails to file a required registration or annual report with the Registrar on or before the due date is subject to assessment of the minimum tax (see ¶ 809) and loss of its tax exemption for the period of noncompliance.

● *Filing fees*

The information returns discussed above (Form 199), with limited exceptions, must be accompanied by a $10 fee if filed on time, or by a $25 fee if filed later. (A return is considered to be filed on time if it is filed within the period allowed by an extension of time granted by the FTB.)

● *Time for filing*

The due date for information returns and statements is the 15th day of the fifth month following the end of the organization's accounting period. An exempt organization that is required to file an information return and fails to do so without reasonable cause on or before the due date is subject to a penalty for late filing, at the rate of $5 per month, with a maximum of $40. Also, a special penalty of $5 per month, with a $25 maximum, may be imposed where a private foundation fails to respond to a demand for filing.

● *Organizations penalized for failure to file*

In *Appeal of Escondido Chamber of Commerce* (1973) (CCH CALIFORNIA TAX REPORTS ¶ 89-181.90), an exempt corporation failed to file annual information returns. The corporation argued that there was reasonable cause for failure to file, stating that it was unaware of the filing requirements and did not receive the proper forms. The State Board of Equalization held that these factors did not constitute "reasonable cause."

In *Appeal of Young Women's Christian Association of Santa Monica* (1971) (CCH CALIFORNIA TAX REPORTS ¶ 11-307.22), the SBE upheld the imposition under prior law of the $100 minimum tax, plus interest, for failure to file annual information returns, despite the fact that the Internal Revenue Service did not require federal information returns for the years involved. The organization did not come within the exception for filing of returns by charitable organizations, because it did not establish compliance with the exception's requirement that the organization be "primarily supported by contributions of the general public."

● *Effect of failure to file or pay*

An exempt organization that fails to file required reports or to pay any tax due within 12 months from the close of its taxable year may have its corporate rights suspended or forfeited. Provision is made for relief from such suspension under certain conditions. Further, the FTB may revoke the organization's exemption if it fails to file any corporation franchise (income) tax return or pay any tax due.

● *Extensions of time*

The FTB may grant a reasonable extension of time for filing a return or report of an exempt organization. Exempt organizations will be granted an automatic seven-month "paperless" extension. The extended due date is the 15th day of the twelfth month following the close of the taxable year (fiscal year filers) or December 15 (calendar year filers). An extension of time for filing does not extend the time for paying tax. Tax payments must be accompanied by FTB 3539 (Payment Voucher for Automatic Extension for Corporations and Exempt Organizations).

● *Organizations with nonexempt income*

Exempt political organizations are not required to file the annual information returns or statements discussed above; however, such organizations that have more than $100 of income from sources other than contributions, dues, and political fund-raising ("exempt function income") should file a corporation income tax return. (See ¶ 804 for discussion of exemption for political organizations.)

Exempt homeowners' associations that have more than $100 of income from sources other than membership dues, fees, and assessments should file a corporation income tax return (see ¶ 914).

An exempt organization, other than a political organization, a homeowner's association, or an organization controlled by the state carrying out a state function, must file an exempt organization business income tax return (Form 109) in addition to its annual information return (Form 199) if it has gross income of $1,000 or more from an unrelated trade or business. The electronic funds transfer requirements discussed at ¶ 807 also apply to non-profit corporations with nonexempt income.

● *Filing with Secretary of State*

Sections 6210 and 8210 of the California Nonprofit Corporation Law require nonprofit corporations to file with the Secretary of State an annual report showing names of officers and other information. The tax law provides for assessment by the FTB of a penalty for failure to file this report (see ¶ 1410).

¶ 805a

¶ 806 Consolidated Returns

Law: Secs. 23361-64a (CCH CALIFORNIA TAX REPORTS ¶ 89-137).

Comparable Federal: Secs. 1501-4 (CCH STANDARD FEDERAL TAX REPORTS ¶ 34,221—34,360).

The law contains provision for filing of consolidated franchise tax returns by certain groups of railroad corporations, where the degree of affiliation through a common parent corporation is 80% or more. Unlike federal law, California law contains no general provisions allowing affiliated groups of corporations other than railroads the privilege of making consolidated returns. However, the Franchise Tax Board may require any affiliated corporations to file a consolidated return to prevent tax evasion or to clearly reflect income earned by the corporations from business in this state.

Although California permits only railroad corporations to file *consolidated returns,* California does permit or require *combined reports* by corporations owned or controlled by the same interests, under some conditions. See ¶ 1309 for further discussion of combined reporting.

¶ 806a Estimated Tax

Law: Secs. 19010, 19021-27, 19136.3 19142-61, 19363-64, 26081.5 (CCH CALIFORNIA TAX REPORTS ¶ 10-043, 89-241, 89-248, 89-416, 89-433).

Comparable Federal: Secs. 6611, 6655 (CCH STANDARD FEDERAL TAX REPORTS ¶ 40,330, 40,465).

California Forms: Form 100-ES, FTB 5806.

All corporations and exempt organizations subject to franchise or income tax, other than REMICs, are required to pay estimated tax during the income year. The estimated tax of a corporation subject to the franchise tax cannot be less than the minimum tax (see ¶ 809). If an S corporation has a qualified subchapter S subsidiary (QSSS) (discussed at ¶ 803), the S corporation's estimated tax payments must not be less than the S corporation's minimum tax plus the subsidiary's minimum tax. California law does not require corporations to file declarations, but they must file their estimated tax with payment vouchers (Form 100-ES). Banks and financial corporations should compute their estimated tax at the special rate for such taxpayers explained at ¶ 809. California has not adopted the federal provision that waives the underpayment penalty if the tax shown on the return is less than $500.

See ¶ 807 for a discussion of taxpayers required to submit estimated tax payments through electronic funds transfer. Such corporations do not submit a Form 100-ES.

● *Computation of estimated tax payments*

If the estimated tax is not over the minimum tax, the entire amount is payable on the 15th day of the 4th month of the corporation's income year. For S corporations, this includes the minimum tax for a QSSS incorporated in California, qualified to do business in California, or doing business in California. If the QSSS is acquired after the due date for the first installment, the minimum tax for the QSSS is due with the next required installment.

If the estimated tax is over the minimum tax, it is payable in equal installments on the 15th day of the 4th, 6th, 9th, and 12th months of the income year, respectively. However, the first installment generally may not be less than the minimum tax. The first installment may be less than the minimum tax if the taxpayer has been granted an exemption by the Franchise Tax Board or is subject to income tax only (rather than franchise tax) under California law.

If the requirements for making payments of estimated tax are first met after the 1st day of the 4th month, the payments are spread over the appropriate remaining quarters, depending on the quarter in which the requirements are first met, as in the case of the federal tax.

● *Estimated tax payments in first year*

A corporation that is incorporated or qualified to do business in California must file a voucher and pay estimated tax during its first year, even though it has already paid (at the time of incorporation or qualification) the minimum tax (see ¶ 809) for the privilege of doing business the first year. This initial minimum payment is the full tax for the first *taxable* year, regardless of the length of that year. The first *taxable* year also serves as the *income* year to measure the tax for the following year. The initial minimum payment is not related in any way to the tax that will be payable on the income of the first year, and it cannot be used as a credit or offset against the tax that is payable on that income. Estimated tax is payable during each income year, even though, as explained at ¶ 811, it is actually a tax for the privilege of doing business in the following year. If it is anticipated that there will be no income in the first year, the voucher will, of course, show an estimated tax of only the corporate minimum tax. (This discussion assumes that the corporation does not discontinue business during its first year; otherwise, see ¶ 812.)

For the 1999 income year, the minimum franchise tax for an eligible new corporation (see ¶ 809) is $300 for the corporation's first taxable year and $500 for the corporation's second taxable year. The minimum franchise tax for the second taxable year is paid during the corporation's first income year as its first estimated tax payment. However, a corporation that qualifies to do business in California after 1999 is exempt from paying the minimum franchise tax for the corporation's first and second taxable years.

● *Accounting periods less than 12 months*

Regulations provide that where the first accounting period is less than 12 months, the estimated tax payments should be made as follows (for calendar-year taxpayers; others should adjust dates accordingly):

Income Year Begins	Number of Installments	Percent to Be Paid	Due Date-15th
Jan. 1-Jan. 16	4	25%	Apr.-June-Sept.-Dec.
Jan. 17-Mar. 16	3	33⅓	June-Sept.-Dec.
Mar. 17-June 15	2	50	Sept.-Dec.
June 16-Sept. 15	1	100	Dec.
Sept. 16-Dec. 31	None		

¶ 806a

As discussed above, the amount of the first installment generally may not be less than the minimum tax.

● *Penalty for underpayment*

A penalty, in the form of an addition to the tax, is imposed when there has been an underpayment of estimated tax. The additional tax is computed as a percentage of the amount of the underpayment, for the period of underpayment.

The penalty rate is the same as the interest rate on deficiencies and refunds, which is established semi-annually (see ¶ 709 for rates). However, the penalty rate is not compounded.

An underpayment is defined as the excess of the amount that would be required to be paid on each installment of estimated tax if the estimated tax were equal to 100% of the tax shown on the return, over the amount actually paid on or before the due date of each installment. The tax shown on an amended return filed after the due date, or the tax as finally determined, is not to be used in computing underpayment penalties. If the tax due is the minimum tax and the corporation is not a "large corporation" (see discussion below), then the addition to the tax because of underpayment of any installment is calculated on the amount of the minimum tax.

The period of underpayment runs from the due date of each installment to the normal due date of the return, or to the date on which the underpayment was paid, if payment was made prior to the due date of the return.

● *Exceptions to underpayment penalty*

California shields a corporation from penalty if one of six exceptions applies. The first exception is related to the corporation's previous year's experience; that is, the total payments must equal or exceed the tax shown on the prior year's return, prorated to each installment. The exception to the underpayment penalty that is based on the preceding year's taxes has limited application to "large corporations" (see discussion below).

The second exception provides that there is no penalty if the installment meets the required percentage of the tax due, computed by placing the taxpayer's net income (or alternative minimum taxable income, if applicable) on an annualized basis as outlined by statute. A corporation may elect one of three different annualization methods.

The third exception relieves corporations of underpayment penalties if the required percentage of the tax for the income year was paid by withholding.

The fourth exception applies if the required percentage of the net income for the income year consisted of items subject to withholding and the amount of the first installment was at least equal to the minimum tax.

The fifth exception applies to corporations going through bankruptcy proceedings. The exception applies if (1) the tax was incurred by the estate and the failure to pay the tax occurred pursuant to a court finding of the probable insufficiency of funds of the estate to pay administrative expenses, or

(2) the tax was incurred by the debtor before a court order for relief or the appointment of a trustee, and the petition was filed before the date of the tax.

The sixth exception is for corporations earning seasonal income. This exception is generally the same as that contained in IRC Sec. 6655(e). Corporations qualify for this exception if they have seasonal income for any six consecutive months of the income year and if they had in the preceding three taxable years taxable income for the same six-month period that averaged 70% or more of the total income for the taxable year. They may annualize their income by assuming that the income is earned in the current year in the same pattern as in the preceding taxable years. Estimated income taxes would be required to be paid in the same seasonal pattern in which earned.

● *Special rules for large corporations*

For both California and federal purposes, a corporation that had taxable income of at least $1 million in any of its three immediately preceding income years is subject to an underpayment penalty if it fails to make estimated tax payments satisfying the required percentage of the current year's tax liability, even if the corporation's payments equal or exceed the amount of tax shown on its return for the prior year. A large corporation's tax liability for the prior year may, however, be used to determine the first installment of estimated tax for the current year, provided any difference is made up in the next installment.

● *Reporting of underpayment*

Where the figures on the return indicate that there has been an underpayment of estimated tax, FTB 5806 should be attached to show the computation of penalty or to explain why no penalty is due. (Federal forms should not be used with California returns.)

● *Penalty strictly applied*

In *Appeal of Bechtel Incorporated* (1978) (CCH CALIFORNIA TAX REPORTS ¶ 89-416.211), the taxpayer made estimated-tax payments in irregular amounts, totaling $495,000, against an ultimate liability of $1,059,849. The taxpayer claimed relief from penalty on the ground that the total payments exceeded the tax of $459,795 shown on its return for the preceding year. The State Board of Equalization (SBE) held that an underestimate penalty of $13,547 was properly imposed on the first two installments, since they did not meet the specific requirements for avoidance of penalty based on the preceding year's tax.

In *Appeal of Decoa, Inc.* (1976) (CCH CALIFORNIA TAX REPORTS ¶ 89-416.15), the taxpayer was a Florida corporation that began doing business in California in 1973. The corporation failed to pay estimated tax for its 1973 income year. The SBE held that the underpayment penalty was mandatory and could not be excused because of "extenuating circumstances." Relief was not available under the rules based on the preceding year's return, since such a return had not been filed and was not required to be filed. See also *Appeal of International Business Machines Corporation* (1979) (CCH CALIFORNIA TAX REPORTS ¶ 89-416.37) and *J.F. Shea Co., Inc.* (1979) (CCH CALIFORNIA TAX

¶ 806a

REPORTS ¶ 89-416.15); in the latter case an underpayment of $1,100 resulted in a penalty of $8,500.

In *Appeal of Uniroyal, Inc.* (1975) (CCH CALIFORNIA TAX REPORTS ¶ 89-416.42), the taxpayer could have avoided an underpayment penalty by timely payment of estimated tax of $100 (based on preceding year's tax, before the minimum was increased to $200). However, since the corporation was unable to prove it had filed or paid estimated tax, the penalty was based on the actual tax of $77,895, in accordance with the definition of "underpayment" set forth above. See also *Appeal of Lumbermans Mortgage Company* (1976) (CCH CALIFORNIA TAX REPORTS ¶ 89-416.21), to the same effect.

● *Refund of overpayment*

Where payments of estimated tax are made and the total amount of tax due on the completed return is subsequently determined to be less than the estimated tax payments, the balance will be refunded or will be credited against other taxes. No interest is payable on overpayments for the period prior to the due date of the return. Further, no interest will be payable if the refund or credit is made within 90 days after the due date or 90 days after the return is filed, whichever is later. (Note that the comparable federal grace period is 45 days.) See also ¶ 1417.

If any overpayment of tax is claimed as a credit against estimated tax for the succeeding income year, that amount shall be considered as payment of the tax for the succeeding income year (whether or not claimed as a credit in the return of estimated tax for the succeeding income year), and no claim for credit or refund of that overpayment will be allowed for the income year in which the overpayment occurred.

● *Combined reports*

In the case of corporations entitled or required to file a combined report, a combined payment of estimated taxes may be made for the group by the parent or other designated "key" corporation, under the procedure described at ¶ 1311. Alternatively, each member may make its own payments and have its payments applied against the ultimate tax liability of the combined group.

● *DISCs required to file*

California has nothing comparable to the special federal provisions for Domestic International Sales Corporations (DISCs). Accordingly, such corporations are subject to the regular California rules for payment of estimated tax. See *Appeal of Cerwin-Vega International* (1978) (CCH CALIFORNIA TAX REPORTS ¶ 89-410.3851, 89-416.15, 89-430.31), in which penalties were imposed on a DISC for underpayment of estimated tax and late payment of tax.

¶ 807 Payment of Tax

Law: Secs. 19001, 19004, 19005, 19011, 19021, 19022 (CCH CALIFORNIA TAX REPORTS ¶ 89-231, 89-235).

Comparable Federal: Secs. 6151, 6161, 6601 (CCH STANDARD FEDERAL TAX REPORTS ¶ 38,080, 38,100, 38,200, 40,310).

Taxpayers, including banks and financial corporations, must pay, on or before the due date of the return, the entire balance of tax due after applying the advance payments made under the estimated tax procedure outlined at ¶ 806a. Payment in the form of a check must be payable in United States funds. To expedite processing, it is suggested that payments for balance due and for estimated payments should not be combined in one check. The corporation number should be shown on each check.

● *Extension of time*

An extension of time for filing the return does not extend the time for payment of the tax (see ¶ 805).

● *Payment by mail*

Under Government Code Section 11002, a payment is deemed to be made on the date it is mailed, provided the envelope is properly addressed and the postage is prepaid. The federal rule is similar.

● *Payment by electronic funds transfer*

The Franchise Tax Board must allow payments to be made by electronic funds transfer (EFT). Such payments will generally be deemed complete on the date the transfer is initiated. A taxpayer whose estimated tax liability exceeds $20,000 or more with respect to any installment, or whose total tax liability exceeds $80,000 in any income year must remit payment by such electronic means. Once a taxpayer is required to make payments by EFT, all subsequent payments must be made by EFT regardless of the income year to which the payments apply. However, a taxpayer may elect to discontinue making payments in this manner if the threshold amounts set forth above were not met for the preceding income year.

A taxpayer required to remit estimated tax payments electronically may satisfy the requirement by means of an international funds transfer.

A penalty of 10% is imposed if mandated payments described above are made by other means, unless it is shown that failure to use EFT was for reasonable cause.

¶ 808 Tax Base

Law: Sec. 24341 (CCH CALIFORNIA TAX REPORTS ¶ 10-029, 10-318).

Comparable Federal: Secs. 63, 243 (CCH STANDARD FEDERAL TAX REPORTS ¶ 620, 13,051).

The California franchise tax and income tax are imposed generally upon net income. The California tax is imposed only on income from sources within the state, whether the taxpayer is a foreign or a domestic corporation.

"Net income" is defined as the gross income less the deductions allowed. For a discussion of "gross income," see Chapter 9; for "deductions," see Chapter 10.

¶ 809 Tax Rates

Law: Secs. 23114, 23151-54, 23181-88, 23802 (CCH CALIFORNIA TAX REPORTS ¶ 10-036, ¶ 10-105—10-123).

Comparable Federal: None.

The rate of franchise tax on corporations other than banks and financial corporations or S corporations is 8.84%. For calendar or fiscal years ending in 1987 to 1996, inclusive, and for any income year beginning before 1997, the rate was 9.3%.

The rate of the corporation income tax is the same as the franchise tax.

● *S corporation rate*

California subjects all S corporations, other than financial corporations, to franchise and income tax at a special 1.5% rate. Financial corporations that are S corporations are taxed at a higher rate of 3.5% .

● *Bank and financial corporation rate*

Financial institutions pay a higher rate, commonly called the "bank rate," designed to equalize the tax burden between financial institutions and other taxpayers. For income years ending after December 30, 1995, the bank rate is simply equal to the franchise tax rate on nonfinancial corporations plus 2%. For income years beginning after 1996, the rate is 10.84%.

The reason for the special bank rate is that banks and financial corporations are not subject to personal property taxes and license fees. The additional tax imposed by the bank rate is in lieu of the personal property taxes and license fees that are paid by nonfinancial corporations.

● *Constitutionality of bank rate upheld*

In *Security-First National Bank of Los Angeles, et al. v. Franchise Tax Board* (1961) (CCH CALIFORNIA TAX REPORTS ¶ 10-026.61), the California Supreme Court upheld the constitutional right of the state to tax banks at the special bank rate. The court held that, since the purpose of the special rate is to equalize tax burdens within the state, it is within the power of the legislature to authorize such taxing procedure and the tax is constitutional.

● *Minimum tax*

The amount of the minimum tax is $800, with some exceptions: the minimum tax is $25 for (1) corporations engaged in gold mining that have been inactive since 1950, and (2) corporations engaged in quicksilver mining that have been inactive since 1971 or have been inactive for a period of 24 consecutive months. In addition, credit unions and nonprofit cooperative associations that are certified by their local board of supervisors are exempt from any minimum tax. However, a credit union must prepay a tax of $25 when it incorporates under the laws of California or when it qualifies to transact business in California. A domestic bank or corporation that files a certificate of dissolution with the Secretary of State and does not thereafter do business is not subject to minimum tax for income years beginning on or after the date of the filing. A corporation is also not subject to the minimum tax if it did no business in the state during the income year and its income year was 15 days or less.

The $800 minimum tax must be prepaid when a corporation incorporates under the laws of California, when it qualifies to transact business in California, or when it is doing business in this state (whether or not incorporated or qualified). However, for income years commencing after 1998, for corporations that incorporate during 1999 the minimum tax for an eligible new, small corporation is $300 for the business's first year of operation and $500 for its second year of operation. Qualified new, small corporations were required to prepay $600 during the 1997 and 1998 income years. For income years beginning after 1998, an "eligible corporation" is a corporation that (1) incorporates after 1998 and before 2000 and begins business operations at or after the time of incorporation; (2) anticipates having gross receipts, less returns and allowances, of $1,000,000 or less; and (3) reasonably estimates that it will have a tax liability that does not exceed $800. The term does not encompass any corporation that began business operations as a sole proprietorship, partnership, or any other form of business entity prior to its incorporation, or any corporation that reorganizes solely for the purpose of reducing its minimum franchise tax. Consequently, all business entities other than corporations that are required to pay a minimum tax are ineligible for the reduced tax. If the new corporation's gross receipts exceed $1,000,000 in its first or second years in business, the corporation is liable for the difference between the reduced minimum tax and the regular minimum tax on the return due date for that year, without regard to extensions.

Corporations that incorporate or qualify to do business in California on or after January 1, 2000, are not subject to the minimum franchise tax for the corporations' first and second taxable years. This exemption does not apply to limited partnerships, limited liability companies, limited liability partnerships, regulated investment companies, real estate investment trusts, real estate mortgage investment conduits, financial asset securitization investment trusts, and qualified Subchapter S subsidiaries.

Also, the prepayment requirement is eliminated for all corporations, except credit unions, effective January 1, 2001.

The minimum tax should not be confused with the alternative minimum tax (¶ 810).

● *What is a "financial corporation"*

Franchise Tax Board (FTB) Regulation 23183 defines a "financial corporation" as one that deals predominantly in money or moneyed capital in substantial competition with the business of national banks. (The definition explicitly excludes corporations that are principally engaged in the business of leasing tangible personal property.) A corporation deals "predominantly" in money or moneyed capital if over 50% of its gross income is attributable to such dealings. However, a corporation's status does not change as a result of an occasional year in which its gross income from money dealings goes over or

¶ 809

under the 50% level. A corporation's classification as a financial (or nonfinancial) corporation changes only if there is a shift in the predominant character of its gross income for two consecutive years and the average of its gross income in the current and two immediately preceding years satisfies (or fails) the predominance test. Substantial amounts of gross income arising from incidental or occasional asset sales (such as the sale of a headquarters building) are excluded for these purposes.

In Legal Ruling 94-2 (CCH CALIFORNIA TAX REPORTS ¶ 10-036.67), the FTB stated its position that corporations whose principal business activity is the finance leasing of tangible personal property are properly classified as financial corporations because such corporations predominantly deal in money or moneyed capital in substantial competition with the business of national banks. A "finance lease" is a lease that is of the type permitted to be made by national banks and is the economic equivalent of an extension of credit.

Financial classification may result when only a portion of a corporation's income is derived from financial activities, but the financial corporation rate will nevertheless apply to its entire taxable income.

If, after operating in a nonfinancial field for a period of time, a corporation is classified as a financial corporation because of a change in the nature of its activities, the tax for the year of change is measured by the income of the preceding year, and computed at the financial rate, even though no financial income may have been earned in that preceding year. See *Appeal of First Investment Service Company* (1973) (CCH CALIFORNIA TAX REPORTS ¶ 10-036.23). On the other hand, when a financial corporation terminates its financial activities and continues in business in a nonfinancial field, the tax measured by the income of the year of change is computed at the general corporation rate, even though some of the income of that year is financial income.

● *Decisions of courts and State Board of Equalization*

For a discussion of the principal factors that have been considered by the courts and the State Board of Equalization (SBE) in determining financial-corporation status, see *Appeals of Delta Investment Co., Inc. and Delta Investment Research Corporation* (1978) (CCH CALIFORNIA TAX REPORTS ¶ 10-036.27). In that case the taxpayers were held to be taxable as financial corporations, although their loans were made primarily to affiliated corporations and they contended that their financial activities did not constitute the major aspect of their operations.

In *Appeal of Southern Securities Corporation* (1977) (CCH CALIFORNIA TAX REPORTS ¶ 10-036.25), the taxpayer was engaged in several activities, including use of surplus funds for real estate loans. The SBE held that the taxpayer was taxable as a "financial corporation."

In *Appeal of Cal-West Business Services, Inc.* (1970) (CCH CALIFORNIA TAX REPORTS ¶ 10-036.37), the SBE held that a corporation that purchased small retail customers' accounts and performed credit, billing, and bookkeeping services on the purchased accounts was taxable as a financial corporation. The SBE found that the taxpayer was in "substantial competition" with national banks in its locality, although testimony showed that the banks generally would not be interested in purchasing the same accounts. See also *Appeal of Atlas Acceptance Corporation* (1981) (CCH CALIFORNIA TAX RE-PORTS ¶ 10-036.65), to the same effect; this case involved the purchase and the collection of health spa membership contracts.

In *Appeal of the Diners' Club, Inc.* (1967) (CCH CALIFORNIA TAX RE-PORTS ¶ 10-036.51), the SBE held that a credit card company was taxable as a financial corporation because the corporate business was to deal in money and was in substantial competition with national banks.

In *Appeal of Stockholders Liquidating Corp.* (1963) (CCH CALIFORNIA TAX REPORTS ¶ 10-036.49), the SBE held that a mortgage loan correspondent, servicing mortgages it placed with an insurance company, was taxable as a financial corporation. It was determined that the taxpayer dealt in money and competed with national banks. To the same effect, see *Marble Mortgage Co. v. Franchise Tax Board* (1966) (CCH CALIFORNIA TAX REPORTS ¶ 10-036.15), decided by the California District Court of Appeal.

In *Appeal of Humphreys Finance Co., Inc.* (1960) (CCH CALIFORNIA TAX REPORTS ¶ 10-036.112), the SBE held that a corporation engaged solely in the purchase of conditional sales contracts arising out of the sale of personal property by a corporation affiliated with it through common control was properly classified as a financial corporation. It was determined that the taxpayer met the two tests for classification as a financial corporation: (1) it dealt primarily in money, as distinguished from other commodities; and (2) it was in substantial competition with national banks.

In *Appeal of Motion Picture Financial Corporation* (1958) (CCH CALI-FORNIA TAX REPORTS ¶ 10-036.59), the SBE held that a corporation organized to finance motion pictures was a "financial corporation," even though it made loans which a national bank would not make and such loans were made only to a controlling shareholder.

¶ 810 Alternative Minimum Tax

> *Law:* Secs. 23036, 23400, 23453, 23455, 23455.5, 23456, 23457, 23459 (CCH CALIFORNIA TAX REPORTS ¶ 10-125).
>
> *Comparable Federal:* Secs. 53, 55-59, 291 (CCH STANDARD FEDERAL TAX REPORTS ¶ 5100—5400, 15,190).
>
> *California Form:* Sch. P (100).

California imposes an alternative minimum tax (AMT) on corporations, except S corporations, in substantial conformity to the federal AMT.

The California AMT is calculated in the same manner as the federal AMT, except California requires modifications to the federal adjustments made in computing alternative minimum taxable income (AMTI) and items of tax preference. For California purposes, "regular tax," used in the calculation of the AMT, means either the California corporation franchise tax, the California corporate income tax, or the California tax on unrelated business income of an exempt organization or trust, before application of any credits. The tentative minimum tax, used for the calculation of the California AMT, is equal to 6.65% (the federal rate is 20%) of the amount by which AMTI for the taxable year exceeds the exemption amount.

California has not adopted the federal exemption from AMT available to small corporations that meet a $5 million gross receipts test. The federal exemption was adopted by the Taxpayer Relief Act of 1997, effective for tax years beginning after 1997. However, California has adopted an amendment made by the Taxpayer Relief Act of 1997 that provides that the recovery periods used for purposes of the AMT depreciation adjustment are the same as the recovery periods used for purposes of computing the regular tax with respect to property, including pollution control facilities, placed in service after 1998.

In computing AMTI California makes the following modifications:

(1) for purposes of the alternative net operating loss deduction, federal references to December 31, 1986, and January 1, 1987, are modified to refer to December 31, 1987, and January 1, 1988, respectively;

(2) adjustments for mining exploration/development costs are applicable only to years beginning after 1987 (after 1986 for federal purposes);

(3) the adjustment available for pollution control facilities may be made for California purposes only if the facility is located in California and certified by the State Air Resources Board or the State Water Resources Control Board; and

(4) California (but not federal) law requires that if a corporation elected to depreciate a grapevine that was replanted in a vineyard as a result of phylloxera or Pierce's Disease infestation over 5 years instead of 20 years for regular tax purposes (see ¶ 1008), it must depreciate the grapevine over 10 years for AMT purposes.

California adopts the federal adjustments on the basis of adjusted current earnings, as specified in IRC Sec. 56(g), with the modifications discussed below:

(1) although California adopts federal provisions enacted under the Revenue Reconciliation Act of 1993 that eliminate the depreciation adjustment to adjusted current earnings for corporate property placed in service after December 31, 1993, the adjustment is applicable for California purposes in income years beginning after 1997;

(2) depreciation allowed on non-ACRS property placed in service after 1980 and before 1987 is the amount that would have been allowable had the taxpayer depreciated the property under the straight-line method for each year of the useful life for which the property had been held; depreciation allowed on non-MACRS property placed in service after 1986 and before 1990 is the amount determined under the Alternate Depreciation System of IRC Sec. 168(g);

(3) California does not follow IRC Sec. 56(g)(4)(C)(ii), (iii), and (iv) relating to the federal dividend deduction; instead, California allows the deduction of the California dividends-received deduction;

(4) California follows IRC Sec. 56(g)(4)(D)(ii) in disallowing the current deduction of circulation expenditures and the amortization of organizational expenditures; however, such deduction or amortization could be different under federal and California law, and an appropriate modification must be made to reflect the difference;

¶810

(5) corporations subject to the income tax and, therefore, not subject to the minimum franchise tax, limit the interest income included in adjusted current earnings to the amount included for purposes of the regular tax;

(6) the interest expense deducted in determining adjusted current earnings is the same as the interest deduction for purposes of the regular California tax; a modification must be made to reflect any differences between the California and federal interest deductions in computing the regular taxes; and

(7) California law requires corporations whose income is subject to allocation and apportionment to calculate their adjustments based on adjusted current earnings by allocating and apportioning adjusted current earnings in the same manner as net income is allocated and apportioned for purposes of the regular tax.

California modifies federal items of tax preference as follows:

(1) federal treatment of tax-exempt interest as a tax preference item is inapplicable;

(2) the amount by which the deduction for contributions of charitable property would be reduced if capital gain property were taken into account at its adjusted basis is a tax preference item for California purposes (California has not conformed to the federal repeal by the Revenue Reconciliation Act of 1993 of the tax preference for such amounts);

(3) California (but not federal) law requires the addition of the amount by which the reserve deduction allowed exceeds the amount that would have been allowable on the basis of actual experience (a similar federal adjustment was repealed, effective for tax years beginning after 1995); and

(4) the excess of depreciation taken on IRC Sec. 1250 property (real property) placed in service before 1987 over the amount allowable under the straight-line method is an item of tax preference.

The AMT applies to commencing and dissolving corporations that are subject to special rules as discussed at ¶ 811 and ¶ 812.

● *Exemption amount*

For both federal and California purposes, the first $40,000 of alternative minimum taxable income is exempt from the AMT. However, the exemption amount is reduced (but not below zero) by an amount equal to 25% of the amount by which the taxpayer's alternative minimum taxable income exceeds $150,000.

● *Ten-year writeoff of certain tax preferences*

For both federal and California purposes, certain enumerated expenditures that would otherwise constitute tax preferences may be deducted ratably over a ten-year period (three years for circulation expenses) instead of being deducted in the income year of the expenditure. The expenditures covered include circulation expenses, research expenses, and intangible drilling costs.

¶ 810

● *Credits against AMT*

Under federal law as incorporated by California, the AMT is equal to the excess, if any, of the tentative minimum tax over the regular tax for the income year. If the regular tax exceeds the tentative minimum tax so that the AMT does not apply, the taxpayer may not then apply tax credits to reduce the regular tax below the tentative minimum tax. For California purposes, an exception is made so that credits for the following may reduce the regular tax below the tentative minimum tax: (1) solar energy, commercial solar energy, or commercial solar electric system (carryovers); (2) research and development expenditures; (3) clinical testing expenses (carryovers); (4) low-income housing; (5) sales and use tax paid or incurred in connection with the purchase of qualified property used in an enterprise zone, targeted tax area, local agency military base recovery area (LAMBRA), or the former Los Angeles Revitalization Zone (LARZ); (6) qualified hiring within an enterprise zone, targeted tax area, LAMBRA, or the former LARZ; and (7) manufacturing investment expenditures (see ¶ 810a).

● *Credit for prior year minimum tax*

California incorporates the federal credit provisions applicable to taxpayers who have incurred California AMT in prior years but not in the current tax year. See ¶ 810a for a discussion.

● *Short income year*

The AMT for a short income year is computed on an annual basis, in the same manner as under federal law.

¶ 810a Credits Against Tax

> **Law:** Secs. 23036, 23051.7, 23453, 23601.5, 23604, 23608-25, 23633, 23634, 23642-46, 23649, 23657, 23666, 24440. Former Secs. 23601, 23601.3, 23601.4, 23603, 23605, 23606, 23606.1, 23607, 23608, 23612.5, 23803 (CCH CALIFORNIA TAX REPORTS ¶ 10-151—10-298, 10-843, 10-853, 10-855, 10-873, 10-877, 10-884, 10-887, 10-892, 10-893, 10-897c—10-897d).
>
> **Comparable Federal:** Secs. 30, 38, 41, 42, 45C, 53, 280C (CCH STANDARD FEDERAL TAX REPORTS ¶ 4020, 4350, 4380, 4800).
>
> **California Forms:** FTB 3501, FTB 3507, FTB 3521, FTB 3523, FTB 3540, FTB 3546, FTB 3547, FTB 3548, FTB 3802, FTB 3805Z, FTB 3807, FTB 3808, FTB 3809, Sch. C (100S).

● *Tax credits—In general*

As in the personal income tax law (see ¶ 121), the corporation tax law provides rules for the order in which various tax credits are to be applied. The law provides that credits shall be allowed against "tax" (defined as the franchise or income tax, the tax on unrelated business taxable income, and the tax on S corporations) in the following order:

1. credits with no carryover;

2. credits with carryover;

3. the minimum tax credit; and

4. withholding tax credits.

As discussed at ¶ 810, only certain specified credits may reduce a taxpayer's regular tax below the tentative minimum tax.

Also, some credits may be limited because they arise from passive activities. The taxpayer must file FTB 3802 (Corporate Passive Activity Loss and Credit Limitations) if the taxpayer claims any of the following credits from passive activities: the orphan drug research credit carryover; the low-income housing credit; or the research and development credit.

● *S corporations*

An S corporation is limited to one-third of the amount of any credit against corporation franchise (income) tax, see ¶ 803.

● *Research and development credit*

California provides a credit for research and development expenditures that is generally the same as that provided by federal law (Sec. 41), with the exceptions discussed below.

(1) The applicable California percentage is 12% (11% for income years beginning before 1999) of the excess of qualified expenses over a specified percentage of the taxpayer's average annual gross receipts for the four preceding income years (the "base amount") and 24% (12% for income years beginning before 1997) of basic (university) research payments (the federal percentage is 20% of the excess of qualified expenses over a base amount and 20% of basic research payments). Also, under both California and federal law, taxpayers may elect to use an alternative method of computing the credit that uses reduced credit rates and fixed-base percentages. However, California limits the alternative credit percentages to 80% of the federal amounts.

(2) Research must be conducted in California (federal law requires that it be conducted within the United States).

(3) The California credit applies to expenses paid or incurred in income years beginning after 1986 and is available indefinitely thereafter. The federal credit does not apply to amounts paid or incurred after June 30, 1995, and before July 1, 1996, or after June 30, 1999.

(4) The California credit may be carried over (the federal credit is part of the general business credit subject to the limitations imposed by Sec. 38).

(5) The California credit for basic research payments includes payments for applied research. Also, for California purposes only, the credit is extended to payments that are made by taxpayers engaged in specified biopharmaceutical or biotechnology activities for university hospitals and special cancer research facilities.

(6) For purposes of determining the base amount under California law, only the gross receipts from the sale of property that is held primarily for sale to customers in the ordinary course of the taxpayer's trade or business and delivered or shipped to a purchaser within California, regardless of F.O.B. point or other conditions of sale, may be taken into account.

(7) California law, unlike federal law, prohibits a taxpayer from claiming the credit for expenses paid or incurred for property for which a sales and use

¶ 810a

tax exemption for teleproduction or other postproduction services may be claimed.

California has also adopted IRC Sec. 280C, which bars taxpayers from taking a business deduction for that portion of the research expenditures that is equal to the amount of the allowable credit (see ¶ 1017).

● *Credit for prior year minimum tax*

California allows a credit in the form of a carryover to corporate taxpayers who have incurred California alternative minimum tax in prior years but not in the current tax year.

The credit is computed in the same manner as the federal credit with the substitution of certain California figures in place of the federal. The credit is taken against the "regular tax" but may not reduce liability to less than the "tentative minimum tax." Both the federal and California credits are based on the amount of alternative minimum tax paid on "deferral preferences" (items that defer tax liability) as distinct from "exclusion items" (items that permanently reduce tax liability).

● *Low-income housing credit*

Corporations may qualify for a low-income housing credit, based upon federal law (IRC Sec. 42). The credit is the same as under personal income tax law and is discussed at ¶ 127.

A corporation that is entitled to the low-income housing credit may elect to assign any portion of the credit to one or more affiliated banks or corporations for each income year in which the credit is allowed.

● *Credits for establishing child care program or facilities*

In income years beginning before 2003, credits are available to employers for establishing child care programs or facilities, for contributing to child care information and referral services, and for contributions to qualified child care plans. The credits are the same as those available under the personal income tax law and are more fully discussed at ¶ 123.

● *Prison inmate job tax credit*

Employers may claim a credit equal to 10% of the wages paid to each prison inmate hired under a program established by the Director of Corrections. This credit is identical to the one provided under the personal income tax law (see ¶ 143).

● *Manufacturer's investment credit*

California allows qualified persons to claim a credit against net tax in an amount equal to 6% of the qualified cost incurred after 1993 for construction, reconstruction, or acquisition of qualified property that is placed in service in California. The credit is identical to the personal income tax credit discussed at ¶ 140.

¶ 810a

● *Tax-incentive credit—Sales tax equivalent*

The corporation tax law allows a tax credit for the amount of sales or use tax paid on the purchase of "qualified property" by businesses located in an enterprise zone, local agency military base recovery area (LAMBRA), or the targeted tax area. The conditions for allowance of the credit are the same as those for the personal income tax credit, as explained at ¶ 133, except that the corporate credit applies to purchases up to a value of $20 million.

● *Tax-incentive credit—Employers' hiring credit*

The corporation tax law allows a credit to employers for a portion of "qualified wages" paid to certain disadvantaged individuals who are hired to work in an enterprise zone, LAMBRA, targeted tax area, or a manufacturing enhancement area. The conditions for allowance of the credit are the same as those for the personal income tax, as explained at ¶ 134, ¶ 136, ¶ 137, and ¶ 138, respectively.

● *Salmon and steelhead trout habitat credit*

For income years beginning after 1996 and before 2000, California allows a credit against net tax for the lesser of (1) 10% of the qualified costs associated with certified salmon and steelhead trout habitat restoration and improvement projects, up to a maximum credit of $50,000 per taxpayer, or (2) a reduced amount certified by the Department of Fish and Game. Unused credit may be carried over until exhausted. The conditions for allowance of the credit are the same as those for the personal income tax, as explained at ¶ 124.

● *Disabled access expenditures credit*

California allows eligible small businesses a credit for 50% of up to $250 of the disabled access expenditures paid or incurred by those businesses to comply with the federal Americans with Disabilities Act. The conditions for allowance of the credit are the same as those for the personal income tax, as explained at ¶ 129.

● *Enhanced oil recovery credit*

California allows certain independent oil producers an enhanced oil recovery credit equal to ⅓ of the federal credit allowed under IRC Sec. 43, provided the costs for which the credit is claimed are attributable to projects located within California. The conditions for the allowance of the credit are the same as those for the personal income tax, as explained at ¶ 142.

● *Credit for costs of transporting donated agricultural products*

California allows a credit against net tax for 50% of the costs paid or incurred in connection with the transportation of agricultural products donated to nonprofit charitable organizations. The conditions for the allowance of the credit are the same as those for the personal income tax, as explained at ¶ 130.

¶ 810a

● *Farmworker housing credits*

California allows a credit for certain qualified costs associated with the construction or rehabilitation of farmworker housing located in California. The credit is substantially similar to the personal income tax credit discussed at ¶ 126.

In addition, banks and financial institutions may claim a credit for low-interest loans made to finance qualified expenditures associated with construction or rehabilitation of farmworker housing. The amount of the credit that may be claimed is 50% of the difference between the amount of interest income that could have been collected had the loan rate been one point above prime (or any other index used by the lender) and the lesser amount of interest income actually due for the term of the loan.

The credit may not be taken until the first income year in which construction or rehabilitation is completed and the housing is actually occupied by eligible farmworkers, and it must be taken in equal installment amounts over a 10-year period or for the term of the loan, whichever is less. Unused credit may not be carried over.

The credit may not be taken for (1) interest income on any loan with a term of less than three years, (2) interest income on any loan funded prior to 1997, (3) loan fees or other charges collected by the bank or financial institution with respect to a loan, or (4) interest income on any loan that did not receive prior certification by the California Tax Credit Allocation Committee.

● *Rice straw credit*

For income years beginning after 1996 and before 2008, California allows a credit equal to $15 for each ton of California-grown rice straw purchased during the income year. The conditions for the allowance of the credit are the same as those for the personal income tax, as explained at ¶ 144.

● *Community development investment credit*

For income years beginning after 1996 and before 2002, California allows a credit in an amount equal to 20% of each qualified deposit made into a community development financial institution. The conditions for the allowance of the credit are the same as those for the personal income tax, as explained at ¶ 145.

● *Joint Strike Fighter credits*

Effective for income years beginning after 2000 and before 2006, credits are allowed for qualified costs of qualified property placed in service in California and for qualified wages paid or incurred by a taxpayer under an initial contract or subcontract to manufacture property for ultimate use in a Joint Strike Fighter. The credits are identical to the personal income tax credits discussed at ¶ 131 and ¶ 132, respectively.

¶ 810a

● *Carryover credits*

Expired credits for which carryovers may be claimed (and the years for which the credits were available) include the following:

    1. solar pump credit (1981—1983);

    2. solar energy credit (1985—1988);

    3. energy conservation credit (1981—1986);

    4. ridesharing credits (1981—1986 and 1989—1995);

    5. credit for donation of computer or scientific equipment (1983—1986);

    6. credit for donation of computer software (1986—1987);

    7. commercial solar energy credit (1987—1988);

    8. credit for donation of agricultural products (1989—1991);

    9. orphan drug research credit (1987—1992);

    10. commercial solar electric system credit (1990—1993);

    11. recycling equipment credit (1989—1995);

    12. low-emission vehicles credit (1991—1995); and

    13. Los Angeles Revitalization Zone hiring and sales and use tax credits (1992—1997).

All of the above credit carryovers may be claimed on FTB 3540. See prior editions of the GUIDEBOOK for details about these credits.

¶ 811 Franchise Tax on Commencing Corporations

Law: Secs. 23151.1, 23181, 23183, 23221-26 (CCH CALIFORNIA TAX REPORTS ¶ 10-043, 10-045).

Comparable Federal: None.

Since the franchise tax is based on the income of the *preceding* year, it is necessary to have special rules for the first and last year in which a corporation is subject to tax.

As explained at ¶ 801a, every corporation that is incorporated or qualified in California prior to January 1, 2000, unless tax-exempt, is subject to the franchise tax from the time it is incorporated or qualified. Until such time as it commences to do business in California, the corporation pays only the minimum tax explained at ¶ 809. When a corporation commences to do business in California, it pays only the minimum tax for the year in which it commences to do business. The length of the year has no effect on the tax. The income for the first year of doing business ("income year") is used as the measure of tax for the following year. Thereafter, the income of each year is used as the measure of tax for the next year, until the final year at which time special rules come into play as explained at ¶ 812.

Prior to January 1, 2000, the franchise tax for the first year (minimum tax, as explained above) is payable at the time the corporation is incorporated or qualifies to do business in California. Thereafter, the corporation must estimate its income (if any) for the first year and pay during the first year its estimated tax for the privilege of doing business in the following year, as explained at ¶ 806a.

● *Change from income tax to franchise tax*

When a corporation that has been subject to the *income* tax starts to do business in California it does not pay a franchise tax for the year it commences to do business. Such a corporation pays income tax for the whole year in which it commences to do business, and thereafter it is taxed under the regular franchise tax rules. The franchise tax for the year following the year of change is the minimum tax, and the tax for each succeeding year is measured by the income of the preceding year under the regular franchise tax rules.

● *Commencing corporation in existence one-half month or less*

Franchise Tax Board Regulation 23222 provides that where a commencing corporation is in existence or is qualified in California for no more than one-half month prior to the end of its accounting period, such period may be disregarded provided the corporation was not doing business in and received no income from sources within the state during the period. The corporation is not required to file a return or pay a tax for such a period, but may be required to file affidavits to establish its right to come under this special rule. If a commencing corporation's incorporation or qualifying date is established so as to take advantage of this rule, it will, of course, save the minimum tax it would otherwise have had to pay for the short period. This rule does not apply to limited partnerships, which are also subject to the minimum franchise tax (see ¶ 612).

CCH **CCH Example: Corporation Not Required to File or Pay**

ABC Corporation files its articles of incorporation with the Secretary of State on December 17, and elects to files on a calendar year basis. However, ABC does no business in California and receives no income from California sources for the period from December 17 through December 31. In this case, no return would be required and no tax would be due for the period from December 17 through December 31. However, if ABC had filed its articles on December 10th, it would be required to file a return and pay at least the minimum tax, even if it remained inactive and received no income during the period from December 10 through December 31.

● *Cross references*

Special rules apply when a reorganization is involved—see ¶ 814.

¶ 812 Franchise Tax on Corporations Discontinuing Business

> *Law:* Secs. 23151.1, 23181, 23183, 23332, 23504 (CCH California Tax Reports ¶ 10-034, 10-050, 10-052).
>
> *Comparable Federal:* None.

The franchise tax for the privilege of doing business in the year in which a corporation ceases doing business is (a) a tax on the preceding year's income, plus (b) a tax on the income of the year during which the corporation ceases doing business. Thus, the tax for the final year is measured by the income of both the final year and the preceding year. It should be observed that the tax computation is not based on the combined income of the two years, but rather is computed separately on each year's income; this means that a loss of one year cannot be offset against income of the other year.

In any event, the tax on the year of discontinuing business may not be less than the minimum tax discussed at ¶ 809.

If a corporation commences to do business and ceases doing business in the same year, the tax is measured by the income for that year.

A corporation that commenced to do business before 1972 may be allowed a credit, in the year of dissolution or withdrawal, for tax paid during its commencing period—see ¶ 813.

If a corporation discontinues business but does not dissolve or withdraw until a later year, it is subject to the minimum franchise tax until it dissolves or withdraws. See ¶ 813.

If a corporation discontinues business and ceases to be subject to the franchise tax, but then becomes subject to the income tax, the franchise tax only is payable in the year of change and the income tax is payable for subsequent years.

¶ 813 Franchise Tax upon Dissolution or Withdrawal

> *Law:* Secs. 23151.2, 23201-04, 23281-82, 23331-35, 23561 (CCH California Tax Reports ¶ 10-054, 10-056, 10-058).
>
> *Comparable Federal:* None.

The franchise tax for the year of dissolution or withdrawal is based on the income of the year of discontinuing business, unless that income has previously been taxed. In the usual situation where dissolution or withdrawal occurs in the same year as discontinuance of business, there is of course no additional tax beyond that described at ¶ 812. In any event, the minimum tax is applicable unless certain conditions are satisfied (see below). Credit may be allowable for tax paid during the corporation's commencing years, as explained below.

● *Effective date of dissolution*

The effective date of dissolution is the date on which a "Certificate of Winding Up and Dissolution," or certified copy of a court order of dissolution, is filed with the Secretary of State. The effective date of withdrawal is the date on which a certificate of withdrawal is filed with the Secretary of State.

See *Appeal of Mount Shasta Milling Company* (1960) (CCH CALIFORNIA TAX REPORTS ¶ 10-058.15); also, *Appeal of Air Market Travel Corporation* (1978) (CCH CALIFORNIA TAX REPORTS ¶ 10-058.15).

In *Appeal of Rogers* (1950) (CCH CALIFORNIA TAX REPORTS ¶ 10-054.13), the State Board of Equalization (SBE) considered the question of the date on which a certificate of dissolution was "filed" for purposes of the rule described above. In that case the corporation offered a proper and adequate certificate to the Secretary of State on October 14, 1948, but the Secretary returned the certificate to the corporation for more information. The certificate was sent back to the Secretary, with the information requested, and was accepted for filing on November 1, 1948. The SBE held that the certificate was "filed" on October 14, the date it was first offered to the Secretary of State.

● *Tax clearance required*

A corporation is not permitted to dissolve until it obtains a clearance certificate from the Franchise Tax Board (FTB) to the effect that all tax liabilities have been paid or secured. A return that is filed by a corporation as its final return will be treated as a request for a tax clearance certificate from the FTB. Thereafter, the FTB must provide the corporation with information regarding all documents that are required to be filed with the FTB and the Secretary of State. The certificate is normally issued by the FTB within 30 days.

● *Minimum tax liability*

It is possible for a corporation that begins the process of dissolution or withdrawal near the close of its corporate accounting period to become liable for an additional minimum franchise tax when it enters a new fiscal year while its tax clearance is being processed by the FTB. The minimum franchise tax is not imposed on a prorated basis for the year of dissolution if a corporation (1) does no business in California during the taxable year and (2) files a certificate of dissolution with the Secretary of State prior to the beginning of that taxable year.

● *Shareholders' assumption of liability*

In *Appeal of B.&C. Motors, Inc.* (1962) (CCH CALIFORNIA TAX REPORTS ¶ 10-058.40), the SBE held that an assumption of liability executed by share-holders of a dissolving corporation imposes an obligation on the shareholders for all franchise taxes of the corporation, even though (1) the taxes apply to a period prior to the time the shareholders acquired their stock, and (2) the tax liability was not disclosed until after the assumption was executed.

● *Special rules*

When a corporation is suspended in one year and is not revived in the same year, but is revived in a later year, its tax for the year of revivor is computed as though it were a new corporation—see ¶ 811.

● *Credit for prepaid tax*

A corporation that commenced to do business before 1972 is allowed a credit in the year of dissolution or withdrawal for tax paid during the commencing period. The credit allowed is the excess of the tax paid over the minimum tax, for the first taxable year which constituted a full 12 months of doing business. The reason for this is that under the old commencing-corporation rules tax was paid twice on some income of the commencing years; this doubling up usually applied to the income of the first full year of doing business. (The doubling up was justified by the fact that under the old rules there was no tax on income of the corporation's final year.)

The law provides that the credit is allowable only upon submission by the taxpayer of evidence establishing the amount paid. If the taxpayer does not have a copy of the tax return or other competent evidence that shows the commencing-corporation tax it paid, the FTB will—upon request, and for a fee—supply the necessary information from its files if available.

Corporations that first became subject to the franchise tax before 1933 may encounter special problems in determining the credit; these are discussed in Legal Ruling No. 382 (1975) (CCH CALIFORNIA TAX REPORTS ¶ 10-056.70).

The credit may be allowed to a transferee corporation for tax paid by a transferor, where there is a "reorganization" as explained at ¶ 814. In this case the credit is not allowed to the transferor.

¶ 814 Franchise Tax on Reorganized Corporations

> *Law:* Secs. 23251-53 (CCH CALIFORNIA TAX REPORTS ¶ 10-050, 10-066, 10-069, 10-087).

> *Comparable Federal:* Secs. 368, 381(b) (CCH STANDARD FEDERAL TAX REPORTS ¶ 16,750, 17,004).

In cases involving certain types of reorganizations, the transferor and transferee corporations are treated in effect as one continuing corporation for franchise tax purposes. For this purpose the term "reorganization" is defined in IRC Sec. 368.

● *Procedure after reorganization*

In the case of a reorganization, IRC Sec. 381(b) shall apply in determining the close of the income year. This federal law provides that the taxable year of the transferor shall end on the date of the transfer.

● *Effect of insurance-company exemption*

In *First American Title Insurance and Trust Company v. Franchise Tax Board* (1971) (CCH CALIFORNIA TAX REPORTS ¶ 10-069.356), the transferee corporation took over four subsidiary corporations that were in the escrow business. The transaction was a "reorganization" as described in this paragraph. The transferee was exempt from franchise tax (see ¶ 804), except for its trust business. The court of appeal overruled the Franchise Tax Board and held that the transferee was not required to include the transferors' income for the preceding year in the measure of its tax, because the income came within the protection of the transferee's insurance-company exemption.

¶ 814

● *Transferee's credit for transferor's tax*

Under the system for taxing the income of a corporation's final year, as explained at ¶ 812 and ¶ 813, a transferee corporation may be allowed credit for tax paid by a transferor. Where there has been a "reorganization," as defined above, the transferee is allowed credit for tax that was paid by the transferor during the commencing period of the transferor. The credit is allowed in a later year when the transferee dissolves or withdraws, under the rules outlined at ¶ 813—it is not allowed in the year of the reorganization. This conforms to the idea of treating transferor and transferee as though they were one continuing corporation for franchise tax purposes. Thus, when the transferee corporation dissolves or withdraws, it gets the benefit of a credit for the transferor's commencing-corporation tax as well as for its own.

¶ 815 Tax on Corporations Having Income from Within and Without the State

Law: Secs. 25101, 25120-40 (CCH CALIFORNIA TAX REPORTS ¶ 12-405).

Comparable Federal: None.

Corporations having income from both within and without the state are taxed only on the income attributable to California. See Chapter 13 for full discussion of this subject.

Because income from sources outside the state is not subject to California tax, it is presumed that no income will be subject to tax by California and also by another state. Accordingly, California does not allow credit against the California tax for taxes paid to other states or countries. This is contrary to the treatment in the California personal income tax (see ¶ 115—¶ 119), and is also unlike the federal treatment of domestic corporations that have income from foreign sources.

¶ 816 Suspension and Revivor of Corporate Powers

Law: Secs. 23301-23305.5 (CCH CALIFORNIA TAX REPORTS ¶ 10-059).

Comparable Federal: None.

Except for the purpose of amending the articles of incorporation to change the corporate name or filing an application for exempt status, all of the powers, rights, and privileges of a corporation or limited liability company (LLC) may be suspended (or, in the case of a foreign corporation or LLC, forfeited) for failure to file a return or for nonpayment of taxes, penalties, or interest. Generally, these nonpayment provisions come into play if payment is not made within the following time limitations: (1) tax shown on return, by close of year following income year and (2) tax payable upon notice and demand, by close of 11th month after due date.

A corporation or LLC desiring to be relieved of the suspension described above may apply to the Franchise Tax Board (FTB) for a certificate of revivor. Such application must be accompanied by payment of all delinquent amounts, unless the FTB determines that prospects for collection will be improved by not imposing this requirement.

Corporations or LLCs may also be relieved of the contract voidability and penalty provisions imposed for failure to comply with reporting and payment requirements by entering into a voluntary disclosure agreement with the FTB (see ¶ 1420).

The FTB is authorized to provide letters of good standing verifying the status of a corporation or LLC for purposes of doing business in California and may charge a fee for the reasonable costs of responding to requests for such letters.

The law provides that even though a corporation may be suspended, it remains taxable on any income received during the period of suspension.

In *Appeal of Lomita Plaza, Inc.* (1961) (CCH CALIFORNIA TAX REPORTS ¶ 10-059.17, 10-059.305), the State Board of Equalization held that a corporation could not file a valid appeal against a proposed assessment of franchise tax at a time when the corporation was under suspension, even though the corporation was kept in existence for the sole purpose of defending against the proposed assessment and was subsequently revived.

Reference should be made to the law or regulations for detailed rules relating to this subject and the effect on the voidability of a contract of a corporation or LLC during suspension.

¶ 817 DISCs and FSCs

Law: Secs. 23051.5(b), 24272.3 (CCH CALIFORNIA TAX REPORTS ¶ 11-803, 11-836).

Comparable Federal: Sec. 865(b) (CCH STANDARD FEDERAL TAX REPORTS ¶ 27,040).

Except for the treatment of certain sales of unprocessed timber, California law specifically disallows any application of the IRC provisions on FSCs (Foreign Sales Corporations) or DISCs (Domestic International Sales Corporations). For California purposes, FSCs and DISCs are treated in the same manner as other corporations.

CHAPTER 9

TAXES ON CORPORATE INCOME
GROSS INCOME

¶ 901 Gross Income—In General

> *Law:* Secs. 24271, 24275 (CCH CALIFORNIA TAX REPORTS ¶ 10-301, 10-410, 10-446, 10-499).
>
> *Comparable Federal:* Secs. 61, 84, 88 (CCH STANDARD FEDERAL TAX REPORTS ¶ 5502, 6400, 7450).
>
> *California Form:* Form 100.

"Gross income" is generally the same as under federal law, except that California law specifically includes all interest on federal, state, and municipal bonds for franchise tax purposes (see ¶ 909). However, it may not be assumed from this that the items to be included are always the same under federal and California laws. For one thing, the exclusions are different in several respects,

¶ 901

as set forth in succeeding paragraphs. It is also possible for the law to be interpreted differently for California purposes than for federal. Any case involving a specific item of income should be checked against the exclusions listed in this chapter and, if there appears to be any question as to its status, should be checked further against the regulations or a more detailed reference work.

Federal law provides tax exemption for certain income of Foreign Sales Corporations. There is nothing comparable in the California law (see ¶ 817).

Gross income is reported on Form 100, unless otherwise indicated.

¶ 902 Life Insurance—Death Benefits

Law: Sec. 24305 (CCH CALIFORNIA TAX REPORTS ¶ 10-414).

Comparable Federal: Sec. 101 (CCH STANDARD FEDERAL TAX REPORTS ¶ 6502).

California law is the same as federal law.

Amounts received under life insurance and other contracts payable by reason of the death of the insured are not includible in income, except that when such amounts are held by the insurer under an agreement to pay interest, the interest is taxable.

¶ 903 Life Insurance—Other Than Death Benefits

Law: Sec. 24302 (CCH CALIFORNIA TAX REPORTS ¶ 10-342).

Comparable Federal: Sec. 72 (CCH STANDARD FEDERAL TAX REPORTS ¶ 6100).

Amounts received, other than death benefits, on life insurance, endowment, or annuity contracts are nontaxable until the amount received exceeds the aggregate premiums or other consideration paid. This is different from federal law. See also ¶ 214.

¶ 904 Life Insurance, Endowment, or Annuity Contract Transferred for Consideration—Other Than Death Benefits

Law: Secs. 24272.2, 24302 (CCH CALIFORNIA TAX REPORTS ¶ 10-342, 10-414).

Comparable Federal: Secs. 72, 101 (CCH STANDARD FEDERAL TAX REPORTS ¶ 6100, 6502).

California law is substantially the same as federal law. Generally, when amounts are received other than by reason of the death of the insured under a life insurance, endowment, or annuity contract that has been acquired for valuable consideration, they are includible in income to the extent that they exceed the consideration paid, plus any subsequent premiums. When the cost basis of such contracts carries over from the transferor to the transferee, or when the transferee is a corporation in which the insured is an officer or shareholder, the basis carried over, plus subsequent premiums, may be recovered tax-free. However, California incorporates a federal provision under which annuities held by corporations and other nonnatural persons are not entitled to the same preferential treatment as annuities held by individuals. Instead, a corporate annuity holder is taxed on the excess of (1) the sum of the net surrender value of the contract at the end of the tax or income year plus any amounts distributed under the contract to date over (2) the investment in the contract (the aggregate amount of premiums paid under the contract minus policyholder dividends or the aggregate amounts received under the contract that have not been included in income).

¶ 905 Lessee Improvements

Law: Sec. 24309 (CCH CALIFORNIA TAX REPORTS ¶ 10-454).

Comparable Federal: Sec. 109 (CCH STANDARD FEDERAL TAX REPORTS ¶ 7020).

Same as personal income tax—see ¶ 222.

¶ 905a Lessee Construction Allowances

Law: Sec. 24309.5 (CCH CALIFORNIA TAX REPORTS ¶ 10-456).

Comparable Federal: Sec. 110 (CCH STANDARD FEDERAL TAX REPORTS ¶ 7030).

Same as personal income tax—see ¶ 222a.

¶ 906 Recoveries of Bad Debts, Prior Taxes, etc.

Law: Sec. 24310 (CCH CALIFORNIA TAX REPORTS ¶ 10-470).

Comparable Federal: Sec. 111 (CCH STANDARD FEDERAL TAX REPORTS ¶ 7060).

Same as personal income tax—see ¶ 223.

¶ 907 Discharge of Indebtedness

Law: Secs. 24307, 24472 (CCH CALIFORNIA TAX REPORTS ¶ 10-446).

Comparable Federal: Sec. 108 (CCH STANDARD FEDERAL TAX REPORTS ¶ 7002).

Same as personal income tax—see ¶ 221.

¶ 908 Dividends and Other Corporate Distributions

Law: Secs. 23040, 23040.1, 24402, 24410, 24451-481, 24611, 25106 (CCH CALIFORNIA TAX REPORTS ¶ 10-720, 10-724, 10-907, 10-919, 11-033, 11-039, 11-051, 11-069, 11-115, 12-475).

Comparable Federal: Secs. 243-47, 301-46, 404, 951-52 (CCH STANDARD FEDERAL TAX REPORTS ¶ 13,051—13,300, 15,202—16,351, 18,330, 29,020—29,040).

Except for the provisions discussed below regarding deduction of dividends where the income has been subjected to tax in the hands of the payor, the corporation tax provisions regarding dividends and other corporate distributions are generally the same as in the personal income tax law as outlined at ¶ 225. As under the personal income tax law, federal law governing corporate distributions is generally incorporated by reference for corporate tax purposes.

● *Use of appreciated property to redeem stock*

California incorporates the federal provision under which, with some exceptions, a corporation is taxed on the appreciation of value of property used to redeem its own stock.

● *Distributions in kind*

When property is distributed in kind, it is valued in the hands of the recipient at its fair market value. California incorporates the federal rule in this area with minor modifications.

● *Deduction for dividends received*

California law (Sec. 24402) excludes from taxable income a portion of dividends received that are paid out of income that has been subject to either the franchise tax, the alternative minimum tax, or the corporation income tax in the hands of the paying corporation. The intent of this provision is to avoid double taxation of corporation income. The exemption is in the form of a *deduction* from gross income. In order for the recipient corporation to claim such a deduction, the paying corporation must have had income from sources in California that required the filing of a California income or franchise tax return.

One hundred percent of dividends received from a more than 50% owned corporation that is subject to California tax are excluded; also excluded are 80% of dividends from a 20% owned corporation, and 70% of dividends from a less than 20% owned corporation. The percentage owned refers to the percentage of stock owned by vote and value by the taxpayer. Preferred stock is not considered in determining the percentage of stock owned. California conforms to federal law tightening the rules regarding the holding period required to claim the dividends received deduction by requiring that the 46-day or 91-day holding period occur immediately before and/or after the taxpayer becomes entitled to receive the dividend. The limitation is effective for federal purposes for dividends paid or accrued after September 4, 1997, and for California purposes for dividends received or accrued after September 19, 1998. Special transitional provisions apply.

In *Rosemary Properties, Inc. v. McColgan* (1947) (CCH CALIFORNIA TAX REPORTS ¶ 10-720.20), the California Supreme Court held that dividends paid out of income that had been freed from tax to the paying corporation, by reason of that corporation's deduction for percentage depletion, were nevertheless exempt from tax to the recipient corporation; that is, the dividends were deductible under the predecessor to Section 24402, discussed above.

As to every corporation that has income from sources within and without California, the Franchise Tax Board (FTB) makes a computation each year, after the return is filed, to determine the percentage of the dividends paid during the year that is deductible by recipient corporations under Section 24402. In making this computation, a formula is used, apportioning within and without the state certain items, such as federal income tax, that affect earnings and profits but that do not affect the income taxable for California tax purposes. The office of the FTB will supply a copy of this formula, and also will give information regarding the latest known percentage of dividends deductible in individual cases, upon request.

In Legal Ruling No. 376 (1974) (CCH CALIFORNIA TAX REPORTS ¶ 12-475.41), the FTB discusses its treatment of dividend income in the computation mentioned above, in a case where the dividend received is deducted under Section 24402. The ruling holds that the dividend income is

¶ 908

"included in the measure of the taxes" for purposes of this computation, even though the income is actually relieved of tax by the Section 24402 deduction.

● *Intercompany dividends*

Intercompany dividends between members of a controlled group filing a combined report are excluded from income, to the extent such dividends are paid out of unitary income. Dividends received from noncontrolled affiliated corporations may be treated as "business" income, apportionable within and without the state as described in Chapter 13—see ¶ 1302.

● *Dividends from insurance subsidiary*

Corporations commercially domiciled in California are permitted to deduct dividends received from an insurance company subsidiary operating in California and subject to the gross premiums tax, provided at least 80% of each class of stock of the insurance company is owned by the parent corporation. The deduction is based on the portion of the dividend deemed to be attributable to California sources, determined by applying a special three-factor apportionment formula.

(CCH) **CCH Caution: Deduction Provision Unconstitutional**

In *Ceridian Corp. v. Franchise Tax Board* (1998) (CCH CALIFORNIA TAX REPORTS ¶ 10-724.20), a California superior court ruled that an out-of-state insurance company was also entitled to a deduction for dividends received from insurance company subsidiaries that were not domiciled in California but that received income from California sources. The court found that the statute limiting the deduction to California-domiciled insurance companies was unconstitutional because it (1) imposed a higher tax burden on out-of-state corporations than it imposed on similarly situated in-state corporations, (2) required the calculation of dividend deductions on the basis of a discriminatory three-factor formula, and (3) imposed a double tax on some premiums.

● *Expenses attributable to dividend income*

The FTB has taken the position in some cases that general and administrative expenses attributable to dividend income are not deductible. This is on the ground that expenses attributable to tax-exempt income are nondeductible. See ¶ 1015 and ¶ 1017.

● *Dividends from DISCs or FSCs*

California had nothing comparable to the special federal provisions for Domestic International Sales Corporations (DISCs) (see ¶ 817). Accordingly, a DISC was taxed under California law in the same manner as other corporations, and the special federal treatment of its dividends had no effect for California tax purposes. The DISC system was largely replaced in 1985 by a new system of Foreign Sales Corporations (FSCs). California has nothing comparable to the special federal provisions for certain distributions by FSCs.

● *Dividends paid to employee stock ownership plan*

California conforms to federal law allowing a deduction for specified dividends paid on stock held by an employee stock ownership plan. Effective for income years beginning after 1997, the deduction is unavailable to S corporations under both California and federal law.

● *Income from qualifying investment securities*

A corporation's distributive share of interest, dividends, and gains from qualifying investment securities that are sold or exchanged by an investment partnership in which the corporation is a partner is not income derived from sources within California and thus is not subject to the corporation income tax, provided (1) the income is the corporation's only income derived from sources within California, (2) the corporation does not participate in the management of the investment partnership's investment activities, and (3) the corporation is not engaged in a unitary business with another corporation or partnership that does not meet the requirements of (1) and (2) above.

● *Special rules for liquidations*

See ¶ 1213 for special rules regarding certain corporate liquidations.

¶ 909 Interest on Government Bonds

Law: Sec. 24272 (CCH California Tax Reports ¶ 10-430).

Comparable Federal: Secs. 103, 141-150 (CCH Standard Federal Tax Reports ¶ 6600, 7701).

Although federal law generally prohibits states from taxing obligations issued by the U.S. government, this prohibition does not apply to the imposition of a nondiscriminatory corporate franchise tax. Accordingly, corporations that are subject to the California franchise tax must include in gross income all interest received from federal obligations. Interest income from state, municipal, or other bonds must also be included in gross income for franchise tax purposes.

However, because the California corporate income tax is subject to the federal prohibition described above, corporations subject to the corporate income tax may exclude U.S. bond interest from gross income. Income from bonds issued by the state of California or by a local government within the state are similarly exempt from the corporate income tax.

The exemption of U.S. obligations does not extend to interest received on refunds of federal taxes (see ¶ 217). See ¶ 1206a for the treatment of gain or loss on the sale of government bonds.

Under federal law, interest on the obligations of a state or its political subdivisions and on obligations issued by the federal government are generally exempt from tax.

¶ 910 Income from Bond Discount, etc.

Law: Secs. 23051.5, 24344.5, 24991-94 (CCH California Tax Reports ¶ 11-980, 11-982—11-985).

Comparable Federal: Secs. 1271-88, 6706 (CCH Standard Federal Tax Reports 32,740—33,020, 40,875).

Same as personal income tax—see ¶ 236.

¶ 911 Commodity Credit Loans

Law: Sec. 24273 (CCH California Tax Reports ¶ 10-358).

Comparable Federal: Sec. 77 (CCH Standard Federal Tax Reports ¶ 6300).

As under federal law, a taxpayer may elect for California purposes to treat as income amounts received as loans from the Commodity Credit Corporation.

¶ 912 Contributions to Capital of a Corporation

Law: Secs. 24322, 24325 (CCH California Tax Reports ¶ 10-486).

Comparable Federal: Sec. 118, Former Sec. 597 (CCH Standard Federal Tax Reports ¶ 7200, 24,010).

The federal law contains a specific provision to the effect that a contribution to capital is not includible in the income of a corporate taxpayer. California specifically incorporates the federal provision.

Where property is contributed to capital by someone other than a shareholder, the corporation is required to reduce the basis of property by the amount of the contribution—see ¶ 1222.

¶ 913 Patronage Allocations from Cooperatives

Law: Sec. 24273.5 (CCH California Tax Reports ¶ 12-125).

Comparable Federal: Sec. 1385 (CCH Standard Federal Tax Reports ¶ 33,760).

Same as personal income tax—see ¶ 231.

¶ 914 Condominiums and Co-ops

Law: Sec. 23701t (CCH California Tax Reports ¶ 11-307, 89-139).

Comparable Federal: Sec. 528 (CCH Standard Federal Tax Reports ¶ 3299N).

Nonprofit homeowners' associations, such as condominium management associations and timeshare associations, are usually tax-exempt. However, any income from sources other than membership dues, fees, and assessments ("exempt-function income") is taxable if it exceeds $100 a year. Associations that have such taxable income should file a corporation income tax return, in addition to the usual information return or statement as explained at ¶ 805a. The California law conforms generally, but not completely, to the federal.

As one of the conditions required for exemption, California requires that any "exempt-function income" not expended for association purposes during the taxable year be "transferred to and held in trust" for proper use in the association's operations. There is nothing comparable in the federal law.

¶ 915 Income from Foreign Aircraft or Ships

Law: Secs. 24320-21 (CCH California Tax Reports ¶ 11-811).

Comparable Federal: Sec. 883 (CCH Standard Federal Tax Reports ¶ 28,220).

Income from the operation of foreign aircraft or ships is tax-exempt under certain conditions. The aircraft or ships must be registered or documented in a foreign country, and the income of the corporation must be exempt from national income taxes under a reciprocal agreement between the United States and the foreign country. The federal law contains a similar exemption.

In *Appeals of Learner Co. et al* (1980) (CCH California Tax Reports ¶ 12-500.65), the State Board of Equalization held that this exemption did not apply where the ship involved was documented in Liberia, because there was no reciprocal agreement between the United States and Liberia.

¶ 916 Merchant Marine Act Exemption

Law: Sec. 24272.5 (CCH California Tax Reports ¶ 10-490 .

Comparable Federal: Sec. 7518 (CCH Standard Federal Tax Reports ¶ 43,645).

Under Sec. 607 of the Federal Merchant Marine Act, commercial fishermen and carriers can enter into an agreement with the United States Department of Commerce to deposit part of their income in a fund to acquire or construct vessels, and can reduce their federal taxable income accordingly. Federal law provides detailed rules for treatment of deposits, withdrawals from the fund, etc. California conforms to the federal law for income years beginning after 1996.

¶ 917 Income from Investments in Depressed Areas

Law: Secs. 24384.5, 24385 (CCH California Tax Reports ¶ 10-864, 10-894).

Comparable Federal: None.

The corporation tax law allows a deduction for net interest received from loans made to a trade or business located in an enterprise zone (see ¶ 102b). It does not apply to any taxpayer that has an ownership interest in the debtor. A similar deduction was available for net interest received prior to December 1, 1998, from loans made after June 30, 1992, to a trade or business located in the Los Angeles Revitalization Zone.

¶ 918 Income from Recycled Beverage Containers

Law: Sec. 24315 (CCH California Tax Reports ¶ 10-498).

Comparable Federal: None.

Same as personal income tax—see ¶ 201.

¶ 919 Relocation Payments

Law: Sec. 7269, Government Code (CCH California Tax Reports ¶ 10-498a).

Comparable Federal: Public Law 91-646.

Same as personal income tax—see ¶ 235.

¶ 920 Rebates for Installation of Water Conservation Devices

Law: Sec. 24323 (CCH CALIFORNIA TAX REPORTS ¶ 10-474).

Comparable Federal: None.

Same as personal income tax (see ¶ 243), except that the corporation tax law does not provide special treatment for urinals using no more than one gallon per flush.

¶ 921 Energy Conservation Subsidies

Law: Sec. 24326 (CCH CALIFORNIA TAX REPORTS ¶ 10-480).

Comparable Federal: Sec. 136 (CCH STANDARD FEDERAL TAX REPORTS ¶ 7560).

Same as personal income tax—see ¶ 244.

¶ 922 Cost-Share Payments Received by Forest Landowners

Law: Sec. 24308.5 (CCH CALIFORNIA TAX REPORTS ¶ 10-494).

Comparable Federal: Sec. 126 (CCH STANDARD FEDERAL TAX REPORTS ¶ 7330).

California provides an exclusion from gross income for cost-share payments received by forest landowners from the Department of Forestry and Fire Protection pursuant to the California Forest Improvement Act of 1978 or from the United States Department of Agriculture, Forest Service, under the Forest Stewardship Program and the Stewardship Incentives Program, pursuant to the federal Cooperative Forestry Assistance Act. The amount of any excluded payment must not be considered when determining the basis of property acquired or improved or when computing any deduction to which the taxpayer may otherwise be entitled.

¶ 923 Earnings on Qualified State Tuition Programs

Law: Secs. 23711, 24306 (CCH CALIFORNIA TAX REPORTS ¶ 10-495).

Comparable Federal: Sec. 529 (CCH STANDARD FEDERAL TAX REPORTS ¶ 22,890).

California law follows federal law, which excludes from gross income any earnings under a qualified state tuition program. California has established a qualified state tuition program entitled the Golden State Scholarshare Trust. However, under California law, any distribution to a corporation as a result of a refund or credit on the Scholarshare Trust account is includible in a corporation's gross income to the extent that the distribution exceeds the amounts actually contributed.

CHAPTER 10

TAXES ON CORPORATE INCOME
DEDUCTIONS

¶ 1001 Trade or Business Expenses

> *Law:* Secs. 24343, 24343.7, 24383, 24415, 24443, 24602 (CCH CALIFORNIA TAX REPORTS ¶ 10-503, 10-505, 10-533, 10-537, 10-545, 10-549, 10-556a, 10-685, 10-812).

> *Comparable Federal:* Secs. 83, 162, 190, 274 (CCH STANDARD FEDERAL TAX REPORTS ¶ 6380, 8520, 12,260, 12,290, 32,640).

Same as personal income tax, as explained at ¶ 301 and ¶ 302, except for provisions that, by their terms, do not apply to corporations.

California has not adopted federal provisions enacted by the Revenue Reconciliation Act of 1993 that disallow a deduction for certain compensation above $1 million a year paid by a publicly held corporation to the corporation's chief executive officer or any of the corporation's four highest paid officers (other than the chief executive officer) for the tax year. The federal limit applies to compensation otherwise deductible in a tax year beginning after 1993.

Corporations are specifically precluded by California law from claiming business expense deductions for granting California qualified stock options (see ¶ 207 for a discussion of the favorable tax treatment afforded to California qualified stock options).

¶ 1001a Expenses of Soil Conservation, etc.

> *Law:* Secs. 24369, 24377 (CCH CALIFORNIA TAX REPORTS ¶ 10-633, 10-653).
>
> *Comparable Federal:* Secs. 175, 180 (CCH STANDARD FEDERAL TAX REPORTS ¶ 12,060, 12,140, 12,160).

Same as personal income tax—see ¶ 327.

¶ 1001b Circulation Expenditures of Periodicals

> *Law:* Sec. 24364 (CCH CALIFORNIA TAX REPORTS ¶ 10-627).
>
> *Comparable Federal:* Sec. 173 (CCH STANDARD FEDERAL TAX REPORTS ¶ 12,030).

Same as personal income tax—see ¶ 328.

¶ 1002 Interest

> *Law:* Secs. 24344, 24344.5, 24344.7, 24424, 24438-39, 24451 (CCH CALIFORNIA TAX REPORTS ¶ 10-557, 10-732, 10-748, 10-800, 12-475).
>
> *Comparable Federal:* Secs. 163, 249, 264, 265, 279, 385, 461(g) (CCH STANDARD FEDERAL TAX REPORTS ¶ 6360, 9102, 13,400, 14,050, 14,700, 17,340, 21,802).
>
> *California Form:* FTB 2424.

California incorporates by reference (see ¶ 801b) the federal rule generally providing a deduction for all interest paid or accrued on business debts. However, California restricts interest expense deductions of corporations subject to allocation and apportionment if their total interest expenses, less expenses deducted in arriving at net nonbusiness income, exceed business (apportionable) interest income. Deductible interest attributable to nonbusiness income includes federally deductible interest incurred for foreign investment, which may be offset against dividends deductible under Sec. 24411. The purpose of this "interest offset" provision is to limit interest expense deductions attributable to the production of nonbusiness income not included in the measure of the California tax.

The amount of interest expense subject to the foreign investment interest offset is generally equal to the amount of interest expense specifically assigned to foreign investment plus the amount of unassigned interest expense allocated to foreign investment. However, for income years beginning after 1996, the amount of foreign investment interest expense that may be offset against the foreign dividends deductible under Sec. 24411 must be computed by multiplying the amount of interest expense by the same percentage used to determine the taxpayer's foreign dividends deduction.

¶ 1001a

In *Hunt-Wesson, Inc. v. Franchise Tax Board* (1998) (CCH CALIFORNIA TAX REPORTS ¶ 10-557.35), a California court of appeal ruled that a foreign corporation's business interest expense deduction was properly disallowed on a dollar-for-dollar basis to the extent it received nontaxable dividend income received from its nonunitary subsidiaries, as California's interest offset provision was constitutional. The U.S. Supreme Court has granted the corporation's request to review this decision.

Also, in *Appeal of F.W. Woolworth Co. et al.* (1998) (CCH CALIFORNIA TAX REPORTS ¶ 12-475.20), a California court of appeal held that the interest expense deducted by a parent corporation and its wholly owned subsidiary was properly reduced by the amount of its nonunitary dividend income.

The exclusion of dividends deductible under Sec. 24402 applies to foreign domiciliary corporations as well as to California corporations—see Legal Ruling No. 379 (1975) (CCH CALIFORNIA TAX REPORTS ¶ 12-475.43).

Application of the rule limiting deductibility of interest expense was discussed in *Appeal of Kroehler Mfg. Co.* (1964) (CCH CALIFORNIA TAX REPORTS ¶ 12-475.59). The rule (as it stood prior to the 1967 amendment relating to intercompany dividends) was also discussed at length in the 1972 decision of the California Supreme Court, in *The Pacific Telephone and Telegraph Company v. Franchise Tax Board* (CCH CALIFORNIA TAX REPORTS ¶ 12-475.63).

In *Appeal of Sears, Roebuck and Co., et al.* (1970) (CCH CALIFORNIA TAX REPORTS ¶ 12-475.55), the State Board of Equalization (SBE) held that carrying charges on installment sales may not be treated as interest income in applying the rules set forth above. The SBE held that the special provisions permitting the buyer to treat a portion of carrying charges as interest (see ¶ 305) have no application to the seller.

The Franchise Tax Board ruled in Legal Ruling No. 59 (1958) (CCH CALIFORNIA TAX REPORTS ¶ 10-557.92) that interest on federal tax deficiencies is subject to the foregoing limitations.

● *Prepaid interest*

Both California and federal law require cash-basis taxpayers to deduct prepaid interest over the period to which it applies.

● *Interest on company-owned life insurance*

Under both California and federal law, an employer generally may not deduct interest expenses paid or accrued that are associated with debt incurred by the employer to purchase life insurance policies or endowment or annuity contracts for *any* individual for whom the employer has an insurable interest. However, an employer may still deduct interest paid or incurred on debt to purchase life insurance policies, annuities, and endowment contracts for a limited number of officers and 20% owners if (1) the aggregate amount of debt with respect to the policies and contracts does not exceed $50,000 per person and (2) the interest rate does not exceed a specified amount.

¶ 1002

● *California-federal differences*

Discussed below are the differences between California and federal rules regarding deduction of interest.

1. Federal law has nothing comparable to the special California rules for multistate corporations, discussed above.

2. Federal law disallows interest on indebtedness incurred or continued to carry tax-exempt obligations. California has no comparable provision regarding interest, although the same result presumably would be achieved under the California provision disallowing expenses allocable to tax-exempt income (see ¶ 1017). Such interest is deductible generally by financial institutions as a business expense. However, for years after 1982, federal deductions for such interest are reduced as a result of 1982 legislation reducing the benefits of certain tax preferences. For private activity bonds and certain other obligations not meeting federal qualifications issued after August 7, 1986, interest indebtedness expense is not deductible under federal law.

3. California has not conformed to special federal rules regarding bond registration requirements.

California conforms to the federal law regarding computation of deductions for original issue discount. However, California provides a special rule for obligations issued after June 9, 1984, and before January 1, 1987. This rule permits an adjustment in the year of disposition for the difference between federal and California deductions in intervening years (see ¶ 909a).

In *Appeal of Signal International* (1966) (CCH CALIFORNIA TAX REPORTS ¶ 12-475.61), the SBE held that interest on a loan was not deductible, where the loan proceeds were used to acquire property from which the income was allocable to sources outside California and therefore not subject to the California tax.

¶ 1002a Passive Activity Losses and Credits

Law: Sec. 24692 (CCH CALIFORNIA TAX REPORTS ¶ 11-258).

Comparable Federal: Sec. 469 (CCH STANDARD FEDERAL TAX REPORTS ¶ 21,960—21,966).

California Form: FTB 3802.

Same as personal income tax—see ¶ 326.

¶ 1003 Taxes

Law: Secs. 24345-46 (CCH CALIFORNIA TAX REPORTS ¶ 10-561).

Comparable Federal: Sec. 164 (CCH STANDARD FEDERAL TAX REPORTS ¶ 9500).

The California deduction for taxes is the same as the federal deduction, except for the following differences:

(1) unlike federal law, California does not permit deduction of the California franchise or income tax, or of any other tax based on income or profits and levied by any foreign country or by any state, territory, or taxing subdivision thereof; neither are such taxes allowed as a credit against the California tax—see ¶ 815;

¶ 1002a

(2) California law permits deduction of water or irrigation district general assessments levied on all lands within the district; there is nothing comparable under federal law; and

(3) California does not permit an increase in basis, as explained below, for sales tax for which a credit is claimed by enterprise zone, former Los Angeles Revitalization Zone, local agency military base recovery area, and targeted tax area taxpayers, as explained at ¶ 810a.

The prohibition against deduction of income taxes—item (1) above—is the same as under the personal income tax law. See the discussion at ¶ 306, including cases holding that the prohibition does not apply to some taxes based on *gross receipts*. However, the prohibition does apply to taxes based on *gross income*. See *MCA, Inc. v. Franchise Tax Board* (1981) (CCH CALIFORNIA TAX REPORTS ¶ 10-561.22), in which the Court of Appeal disallowed deductions for foreign taxes paid on film rentals and record royalties. The Court's opinion makes a careful distinction between "gross receipts" and "gross income."

In the *Appeal of Dayton Hudson* (1994) (CCH CALIFORNIA TAX REPORTS ¶ 10-561.311), the State Board of Equalization (SBE) allowed the taxpayer to deduct the total amounts paid under the Michigan Single Business Tax (MSBT) because the MSBT, a value added tax that included an element of return on capital (the labor portion of the costs of goods), was not a tax exclusively based on, or measured by, income.

In *Appeal of Occidental Petroleum Corporation* (1983) (CCH CALIFORNIA TAX REPORTS ¶ 12-430.69), the SBE held that a Libyan tax on oil exports was not based on income and therefore was deductible.

¶ 1004 Losses

Law: Secs. 24347-47.5, 24347.51 (CCH CALIFORNIA TAX REPORTS ¶ 10-569).

Comparable Federal: Sec. 165 (CCH STANDARD FEDERAL TAX REPORTS ¶ 1505).

California incorporates federal law allowing a deduction for losses sustained and not compensated for by insurance or otherwise.

The corporate provisions regarding the deduction and carryover of disaster losses are the same as the provisions for personal income (see ¶ 307).

See Chapter 12 of this GUIDEBOOK for a discussion of capital losses.

See ¶ 1214a for treatment of losses on redemption of United States Savings Bonds. See ¶ 1017 regarding disallowance of certain losses.

¶ 1005 Wash Sales

Law: Sec. 24998 (CCH CALIFORNIA TAX REPORTS ¶ 11-967).

Comparable Federal: Sec. 1091 (CCH STANDARD FEDERAL TAX REPORTS ¶ 4688).

Same as personal income tax—see ¶ 514a.

¶ 1006 Bad Debts

Law: Secs. 24347, 24348-48.5, 24434 (CCH CALIFORNIA TAX REPORTS ¶ 10-573, 10-772, 11-506).

Comparable Federal: Secs. 166, 271, 593, 595 (CCH STANDARD FEDERAL TAX REPORTS ¶ 10,502, 14,306, 23,802—23,862, 23,910, 23,970).

California law governing the deduction of bad debts is the same as federal law with the following modifications:

(1) California does not incorporate federal law as it applies to savings and loan associations, banks, and financial corporations, but has its own provisions that allow a deduction for a reasonable addition to a reserve for bad debts in lieu of any other bad debt deduction, in the discretion of the Franchise Tax Board (FTB);

(2) with respect to the partially worthless debts of savings and loan associations, banks, and financial corporations, if a portion of a debt is deducted in any year, no deduction is allowable in a subsequent year for any portion of the debt that was charged off in a prior year, whether claimed as a deduction in the prior year or not; and

(3) California incorporates federal law relating to bad debts with respect to securities held by financial institutions, but modifies a federal limitation on foreign corporations so that the limitation applies only to foreign corporations that have a water's-edge election in effect for the income year.

● *Bad debt v. capital contribution*

For a loan to qualify as a bad debt deduction, the taxpayer must have a reasonable expectation of repayment and a debtor-creditor relationship must exist. If a purported advance of funds is essentially a capital investment placed at the risk of the business, it does not qualify as a loan for a bad debt deduction.

● *Decisions of State Board of Equalization*

In *Appeal of Southwestern Development Company* (1985) (CCH CALIFOR-NIA TAX REPORTS ¶ 12-430.70), the State Board of Equalization (SBE) upheld the FTB's position that items deducted by the taxpayer as bad debts were actually capital contributions and, hence, not deductible. Funds placed at the risk of the business with no reasonable expectation of repayment were capital contributions. Advances made during the formation period of a business and later funds to protect the initial investment were also capital contributions. The SBE also held that losses from a business could not be claimed as totally worthless in a year when the business continued in operation beyond that particular year.

In *Appeal of San Fernando Valley Savings and Loan Association* (1975) (CCH CALIFORNIA TAX REPORTS ¶ 11-506.23), the taxpayer made inadequate additions to its bad-debt reserve in 1968 and 1969, resulting in a debit balance in the reserve. Adequate additions would have resulted in net operating losses for those years. In 1970 the taxpayer claimed a deduction for an addition to the reserve to reduce the debit balance built up in 1968 and 1969. The SBE upheld the FTB's disallowance of the 1970 deduction, pointing out that the taxpayer's accounting had the effect of a net operating loss carryover, which was not allowed under California law in effect at that time.

In *Appeal of Culver Federal Savings and Loan Association* (1966) (CCH CALIFORNIA TAX REPORTS ¶ 11-506.18), the SBE held that a reserve for bad debts entered on its books by the taxpayer and deducted for federal income tax purposes, but not for California, could nevertheless be claimed later to obtain a refund of California tax. The FTB applied the rationale of this case in Legal Ruling No. 417 (1981) (CCH CALIFORNIA TAX REPORTS ¶ 11-506.261), which provides that a savings and loan association may retroactively increase its bad debt deduction up to the amount of the year's addition to the reserve as shown on the association's books, but not beyond that amount.

¶ 1007 Worthless Securities

> *Law:* Sec. 24347 (CCH CALIFORNIA TAX REPORTS ¶ 10-569).
>
> *Comparable Federal:* Sec. 165 (CCH STANDARD FEDERAL TAX REPORTS ¶ 9802).

Same as personal income tax—see ¶ 307.

¶ 1008 Depreciation and Amortization

> *Law:* Secs. 24349-56.8, 24365, 24368.1, 24369.4, 24372.3-73, 24407-09, 24421-22, 24990 (CCH CALIFORNIA TAX REPORTS ¶ 10-575—10-613, 10-629, 10-649, 10-677, 10-701, 10-711, 10-711a, 10-728, 10-740, 10-875, 10-886, 10-895, 10-897e).
>
> *Comparable Federal:* Secs. 59, 167-69, 174, 178, 194, 197, 198, 248, 280F (CCH STANDARD FEDERAL TAX REPORTS ¶ 10-711a, 11,002—11,502, 12,100, 12,120, 12,190, 12,230, 12,280, 12,330, 13,350).
>
> *California Forms:* FTB 3805Z, FTB 3806, FTB 3807, FTB 3885, Sch. B (100S).

A corporate taxpayer is permitted a deduction for depreciation of real or personal property used in a trade or business or held for the production of income. The California depreciation provisions are generally the same as those contained in the pre-1987 personal income tax law (see "Assets Placed in Service Before 1987" at ¶ 310). Except as discussed below, the federal accelerated cost recovery system (ACRS) depreciation method for assets placed in service after 1980 and the federal modified accelerated cost recovery system (MACRS) depreciation method for assets placed in service after 1986 have not been adopted into the California corporation tax law.

Written agreements may be made between the taxpayer and the Franchise Tax Board as to the useful life and depreciation rate of a particular property.

● *ACRS depreciation allowed for S corporations*

An S corporation's deduction for depreciation and amortization is computed under the personal income tax law (see ¶ 310, ¶ 310a).

● *Residential rental property*

Although California does not incorporate MACRS or ACRS, California allows the use of these federal depreciation methods to determine a reasonable depreciation allowance for California purposes. Accordingly, under federal law as incorporated by California, corporate taxpayers are permitted to treat residential rental property on which construction began after 1986, and before July 1, 1988, as either 18-year real property, 27.5-year residential rental property, or asset depreciation range property.

● *Phylloxera infested vineyards*

The useful life for any grapevine replaced in a California vineyard is five-years if the grapevine was replaced as a direct result of (1) phylloxera infestation, or (2) effective for income years beginning after 1996, Pierce's Disease infestation. However, a taxpayer may elect to use the federal alternative depreciation system (see ¶ 310). If the taxpayer chooses to use this method and if the taxpayer elected not to capitalize the costs of replacing the infested vines, the replacement vines will have a class life of 10 years rather than the 20-year class life normally specified under federal law for fruit-bearing vines.

● *Luxury automobiles and listed property*

For corporate income tax purposes, California adopts a modified version of IRC Sec. 280F, which imposes a limitation on depreciation deductions for luxury automobiles and other listed property, including computers and peripheral equipment. The limitation is similar to that imposed under the personal income tax law (see ¶ 310), except that for corporate purposes, the terms "deduction" or "recovery deduction" relating to ACRS mean amounts allowable as a deduction under the bank and corporation tax law.

● *Property leased to tax-exempt entities*

California has adopted the IRC 168(h) limitation on deductions for property leased to tax-exempt entities for income years after 1986. For income years beginning after 1990, the amount of such deductions is limited to the amount determined under IRC Sec. 168(g), concerning the alternative depreciation system.

● *Salvage reduction*

The amount of salvage value to be taken into consideration in computing the amount subject to depreciation may be reduced by up to 10% of the depreciable basis of the property, except with respect to property for which California allows the use of the federal depreciation methods (as discussed above).

● *Additional first-year depreciation*

Except for S corporations, which take the deduction in the same manner as individuals (see ¶ 310a), California has not adopted the IRC Sec. 179 asset expense election for corporate purposes. However, California does allow a corporate taxpayer to take an additional 20% first-year (bonus) depreciation deduction on personal property (see ¶ 310b).

● *Clean fuel vehicles and refueling property*

Same as personal income tax (see ¶ 330).

¶ **1008**

The required basis reduction for clean-fuel vehicles or clean-fuel vehicle refueling property for which a deduction is claimed is discussed at ¶ 1235.

● *Pollution control facilities*

Same as personal income tax (see ¶ 310d).

● *Trademark, trade name, and franchise transfer payments*

Same as personal income tax (see ¶ 319a).

● *Films, video tapes, sound recordings, and similar property*

Same as personal income tax (see ¶ 310).

● *Indian reservation property*

Same as personal income tax (see ¶ 310).

● *Environmental remediation expenses*

Same as personal income tax (see ¶ 310g).

● *Reforestation expenses*

A corporate taxpayer may elect to write off certain "reforestation expenditures" over a seven-year period provided the expenses relate to qualified timber property located in California. This applies to direct costs of forestation or reforestation, including seeds, labor, equipment, etc. The amortization period begins on the first day of the second half of the income year of the expenditures. The deduction is taken from adjusted gross income and is limited to $10,000 per income year. For income years beginning before 1997, the amortization period was limited to 5 years rather than 7 years and there was no limitation as to where the timber property was located.

● *Child development facilities*

For income years before 1997, expenditures for certified child development facilities established by owners of places of employment for their employees could be amortized over a 60-month period. This amortization period was similar to that allowed for personal income tax purposes before 1987 and for federal purposes before 1982.

● *Research and experimental expenditures*

Same as personal income tax (see ¶ 319).

● *Amortization of cost of acquiring a lease*

Same as personal income tax (see ¶ 310c).

● *Organizational expenditures*

A corporate taxpayer may elect to amortize organizational expenses over a period of not less than 60 months, beginning with the month in which the corporation begins business.

¶ 1008

● *Term property interests*

California adopts federal law, under which no depreciation or amortization deduction is allowed for any term property interest (such as a life interest, an interest for a term of years, or an income interest in a trust) for any period during which the remainder interest is held, directly or indirectly, by a related person. The basis of such property for which a depreciation or amortization deduction has been allowed must be reduced by the amount of the disallowed deduction, and the basis of the remainder interest in such property must be increased by the same amount. For both federal and California purposes, the rule applies to interests created or acquired after July 27, 1989, in income years ending after that date.

● *Accelerated write-offs for depressed areas*

Same as personal income (see ¶ 310f), except that instead of disallowing the IRC Sec. 179 asset expense election if the write-offs are claimed by enterprise zone, local agency military base recovery area, targeted tax area, or former Los Angeles Revitalization Zone businesses, the additional first-year depreciation is disallowed.

● *Goodwill and other intangibles*

Same as personal income tax (see ¶ 319b).

¶ 1009 Depletion

Law: Secs. 24831-33 (CCH CALIFORNIA TAX REPORTS ¶ 11-551).

Comparable Federal: Secs. 611-38 (CCH STANDARD FEDERAL TAX REPORTS ¶ 24,520, 24,540, 24,560, 24,580, 24,720, 24,740).

Same as personal income tax—see ¶ 311.

¶ 1009a Development and Exploration Expenses of Mines, etc.

Law: Secs. 24423, 24831 (CCH CALIFORNIA TAX REPORTS ¶ 10-740, 11-558, 11-565).

Comparable Federal: Secs. 193, 263(c), 616-17 (CCH STANDARD FEDERAL TAX REPORTS ¶ 12,310, 13,700, 24,640, 24,660, 24,680).

Except for minor technical differences, the corporation tax law is the same as the personal income tax law, as explained at ¶ 311a. The corporation tax law also specifically provides for deduction of intangible drilling and development costs of oil and gas wells.

California has no provision comparable to the federal provision that provides a deduction for expenses incurred for tertiary injectants.

¶ 1010 Contributions

Law: Secs. 18648.5, 24357-59.1 (CCH CALIFORNIA TAX REPORTS ¶ 10-617).

Comparable Federal: Secs. 170, 6115 (CCH STANDARD FEDERAL TAX REPORTS ¶ 11,675, 22,680—22,700).

Corporations are allowed a California deduction for contributions paid to certain organizations, up to a limit of 10% of net income computed without the benefit of this deduction or certain other special deductions (dividends received, building and loan dividends paid, certain deductions of cooperatives, etc.). Contributions in excess of the 10% limit may be carried over to the next five succeeding income years.

● *California-federal differences*

(1) There are differences in the adjustments to income for purposes of computing the limitation. For federal purposes, income is adjusted for net operating loss carryovers and other special deductions not applicable to California. For California purposes, income is adjusted, as shown above, for special deductions not applicable to the federal computation.

(2) There are slight differences in the rules for contributions of appreciated property. California ordinarily reduces the contribution by the amount of the untaxed gain; in effect, the deduction is limited to the basis of the property. The federal law similarly limits the deduction to the donor's basis in the property. However, federal law retains an exception for donations of appreciated stock to certain private foundations made before 1995 or after June 30, 1996.

(3) Federal law allows a deduction for certain contributions of research property to a California college or university, the amount being the basis of the property plus one-half of the appreciation, limited to twice the basis. California allowed a similar, but not identical, deduction for contributions made between July 1, 1983, and December 31, 1993.

(4) California has no counterpart to the federal provision that denies deductions for charitable contributions to organizations that conduct certain lobbying activities for which a federal deduction is disallowed.

(5) California allows a deduction for charitable contributions only if the contributions are verified under regulations prescribed by the Franchise Tax Board. For federal purposes, charitable contributions may be deducted only if the contributions are verified under regulations prescribed by the Secretary of the Treasury.

In addition to differences resulting from the items outlined above, the California deduction may be different from the federal because of a difference in the amount of net income to which the 10% limitation is applied. The California limitation may also be affected by the apportionment of income within and without the state (see ¶ 1310).

¶ 1011 Amortization of Bond Premium

Law: Secs. 24360-63.5 (CCH CALIFORNIA TAX REPORTS ¶ 10-621).

Comparable Federal: Sec. 171 (CCH STANDARD FEDERAL TAX REPORTS ¶ 11,850).

Deduction is allowed, at the taxpayer's election, for amortization of premium on bonds owned. The general rule is the same as the federal, but there may be a difference in its application because of differences in taxability of government bond interest or because the taxpayer may elect to amortize for California purposes and not for federal, or vice versa. This may result in a difference in the adjusted cost basis, and consequently a difference in gain or loss, when bonds are sold. For California purposes, the premium of a taxable bond is allocated to the interest from the bond. In lieu of being deducted, the premium is applied against (and reduces) interest income from the bond.

No amortization is allowable on any portion of bond premium attributable to conversion features of the bond.

The federal law provides that the amortization period is to be determined with reference to the maturity date of the bonds, except that if use of an earlier call date results in a smaller amortization deduction, then the call date is to be used.

The California law contains nothing comparable to the federal provision that requires securities dealers to amortize premium paid on certain short-term municipal bonds. Because of the difference in treatment of interest on municipal bonds for franchise tax purposes, there would be no point in having such a provision in the California law.

¶ 1012 Payments to Pension or Profit-Sharing Plans

Law: Secs. 24601-12 (CCH CALIFORNIA TAX REPORTS ¶ 11-115).

Comparable Federal: Secs. 194A, 401-20, 4971-75 (CCH STANDARD FEDERAL TAX REPORTS ¶ 12,350, 17,733—19,200, 39,720—35,800).

Same as personal income tax, except that the corporation tax law incorporates by reference only those federal provisions that deal with employer deductions (see ¶ 318 and ¶ 606).

¶ 1012a Employee Stock Options

Law: Secs. 24379, 24601-12 (CCH CALIFORNIA TAX REPORTS ¶ 11-132).

Comparable Federal: Secs. 83, 421-24 (CCH STANDARD FEDERAL TAX REPORTS ¶ 6380, 19,602—20,100).

Except with respect to California qualified stock options, the California rules regarding an employer's treatment of employee stock options and other transfers of property for services are the same as federal.

An employer corporation is precluded by California law from claiming a business expense deduction for granting a California qualified stock option (see ¶ 207 for a discussion of the favorable tax treatment afforded California qualified stock options).

¶ 1012b Start-Up Expenditures

Law: Sec. 24414 (CCH CALIFORNIA TAX REPORTS ¶ 10-708).

Comparable Federal: Sec. 195 (CCH FEDERAL STANDARD TAX REPORTS ¶ 12,370).

Same as personal income tax—see ¶ 321.

¶ 1013 Subsidization of Employees' Ridesharing and Parking

Law: Sec. 24343.5 (CCH CALIFORNIA TAX REPORTS ¶ 10-509).

Comparable Federal: None.

The corporation tax law permits employers a business expense deduction for specific benefits paid or incurred relating to employee ridesharing and parking. These benefits are:

(1) subsidizing employees commuting in buspools, private commute buses, carpools, and subscription taxipools;

(2) subsidizing monthly transit passes to employees and their dependents;

(3) compensating employees who do not require free parking;

(4) providing free or preferential parking to carpools, vanpools, and any other vehicle used in a ridesharing arrangement;

(5) making facility improvements to encourage employees to participate in ridesharing arrangements, to use bicycles, or to walk; corporations are allowed a 36-month depreciation deduction for these improvements;

(6) providing company commuter van or bus service to employees for commuting to and from their homes; improvements (capital costs) to the vehicle are not allowed as a business expense deduction;

(7) providing employee transportation services that are required as part of the employer's business activities, if the employee is not reimbursed and there is no available ridesharing incentive program; and

(8) providing cash allowances to employees in amounts equal to the parking subsidies that the employer would otherwise pay to secure parking spaces for those employees.

¶ 1014 Deduction for Dividends Received

Law: Secs. 24402, 24410 (CCH CALIFORNIA TAX REPORTS ¶ 10-720, 10-724).

Comparable Federal: Secs. 243-47 (CCH STANDARD FEDERAL TAX REPORTS ¶ 13,051—13,300).

California law provides a deduction for dividends received when the income distributed has been subjected to tax in the hands of the paying corporation. This subject is discussed at ¶ 908.

¶ 1014

¶ 1015   Deductions Allowed to Special Classes of Organizations

Law: Secs. 24370, 24403-06.5, 24870-74 (CCH CALIFORNIA TAX REPORTS ¶ 11-516, 11-771, 12-101).

Comparable Federal: Secs. 521, 591, 851-60, 1381-83 (CCH STANDARD FEDERAL TAX REPORTS ¶ 22,830, 23,890—23,970, 26,700, 26,720, 26,740, 33,700-33,740).

The California law allows special deductions to certain classes of organizations, as follows:

(1) building and loan associations—dividends on shares allowed as a deduction;

(2) agricultural cooperative associations—income from nonprofit activities allowed as a deduction;

(3) other cooperative associations—income from certain non-profit activities allowed as a deduction (see below);

(4) retail cooperatives—certain allocated patronage refunds allowed as a deduction (see below);

(5) mutual savings banks—certain interest on deposits allowed as a deduction for franchise tax purposes;

(6) real estate investment trusts—income distributed during the year, or within a certain period after the year, is allowed as a deduction (see also ¶ 802a);

(7) regulated investment companies—exempt interest dividends distributed to shareholders allowed as a deduction (see also ¶ 802a);

(8) gas producers' cooperatives—patronage refunds paid to patrons allowed as a deduction; and

(9) credit unions—income from investments of surplus member savings capital allowed as a deduction.

Income allocations to members of agricultural cooperatives may be made within 8½ months after the close of the income year and still be considered as having been made on the last day of the income year, provided the members are advised of the dollar amount of such allocations.

Agricultural cooperatives are permitted to deduct all income, regardless of source, that is properly allocated to members. See Legal Ruling No. 389 (1975) (CCH CALIFORNIA TAX REPORTS ¶ 12-101.25) and Legal Ruling No. 418 (1981) (CCH CALIFORNIA TAX REPORTS ¶ 12-101.34).

Retail cooperatives are permitted to deduct patronage refunds allocated to their patrons, provided the refunds are made and allocated within specific restrictions set forth in the law.

In *Appeal of Certified Grocers of California, Ltd.* (1962) (CCH CALIFORNIA TAX REPORTS ¶ 12-101.35), the State Board of Equalization (SBE) held that a wholesale grocery cooperative could deduct patronage dividends and interest on members' accounts, following long-standing federal practice, irrespective of the fact that the California law did not provide specifically to this effect in the year involved.

● *Some expenses not deductible*

In *Security-First National Bank v. Franchise Tax Board* (1961) (CCH CALIFORNIA TAX REPORTS ¶ 10-113.251), it was held that a cooperative association could not deduct expenses allocable to income for which special deductions discussed above were allowable. To the same effect, see *Anaheim Union Water Company v. Franchise Tax Board* (1972) (CCH CALIFORNIA TAX REPORTS ¶ 12-101.393), involving the deductibility of operating losses of a nonprofit mutual water company against income from certain profit-making activities. The Court of Appeal held that the losses in question were nondeductible because they were allocable to exempt income. Also, to the same effect, see *Appeal of Los Angeles Area Dodge Dealers Association* (1978) (CCH CALIFORNIA TAX REPORTS ¶ 12-101.55), involving interest on short-term certificates of deposit. See also ¶ 1017.

In *Appeal of San Antonio Water Company* (1970) (CCH CALIFORNIA TAX REPORTS ¶ 12-101.39), the SBE held that gain on sale of land to a member of a cooperative was not deductible under item (3) above.

For a good discussion of the accounting rules applicable to organizations covered by item (3) above, see *Appeal of Redwood Mutual Water Company* (1980) (CCH CALIFORNIA TAX REPORTS ¶ 12-101.391).

In *Appeal of Imperial Hay Growers' Association* (1970) (CCH CALIFORNIA TAX REPORTS ¶ 12-101.27), the SBE held that a loss on plant abandonment was outside the scope of the special provisions described above and was deductible against income derived from nonmembers.

The federal law allows some special deductions somewhat comparable, in a general way, to the California deductions described above. In view of the many differences, no attempt is made here to compare the two laws.

¶ 1016 Tenant Expenses—Cooperative Apartment and Housing Corporations

Law: Sec. 24382 (CCH CALIFORNIA TAX REPORTS ¶ 10-712).

Comparable Federal: Sec. 216 (CCH STANDARD FEDERAL TAX REPORTS ¶ 12,600).

California law is the same as federal in allowing certain expenses of tenant-stockholders to be deducted.

¶ 1017 Items Not Deductible

Law: Secs. 24343.2, 24343.7, 24421-29, 24436-37, 24441-48, 24691 (CCH CALIFORNIA TAX REPORTS ¶ 10-521, 10-525, 10-529, 10-537, 10-545, 10-549, 10-553, 10-556a, 10-740, 10-752, 10-760, 10-764, 10-780, 10-788, 10-792, 10-804, 10-808, 10-809, 11-132).

Comparable Federal: Secs. 162, 261-68, 271, 274, 276-77, 280B, 280C, 280E, 280G (CCH STANDARD FEDERAL TAX REPORTS ¶ 13,502—14,200, 14,306, 14,402, 14,550—14,600, 14,900, 15,050, 15,150, 15,800).

Certain items are made expressly nondeductible, the principal items being:

(a) capital expenditures, certain life insurance premiums, interest on indebtedness incurred in connection with certain life insurance and annuity contracts, expenses allocable to tax-exempt income, carrying charges that the taxpayer elects to capitalize, etc.;

(b) losses on transactions between certain related interests;

(c) accrued expenses and interest payable to a person or corporation related to the payor, under certain circumstances (generally, the payor is required to report such items on the cash basis of accounting);

(d) expenses of certain illegal activities or of other activities that tend to promote or are otherwise related to such illegal activities, as explained at ¶ 322;

(e) illegal bribes, kickbacks, etc. and certain other expenses, as explained at ¶ 322;

(f) certain expenses attributable to substandard housing, as explained at ¶ 322;

(g) abandonment fees on open-space easements and timberland tax-recoupment fees, as explained at ¶ 322;

(h) certain expenses in connection with entertainment activities, business gifts, and foreign conventions, as explained at ¶ 302;

(i) deductions for remuneration of personal services that are not reported in required statements to employees (see ¶ 712a) or in required information returns (see ¶ 711) may be disallowed at the discretion of the Franchise Tax Board (FTB);

(j) deductions for interest, taxes, depreciation, and amortization are denied to property owners who fail to file proper information returns as explained at ¶ 711;

(k) business expenses incurred at a discriminatory club, as explained at ¶ 322; and

(l) expenses of advertising in political programs or for admission to political fundraising functions and similar events.

● *California-federal differences*

(a) There are no federal provisions comparable to items (d), (f), (g), (h), and (k) above, except for a federal provision that prohibits deductions and credits for illegal drug trafficking. Otherwise the California rules are generally similar to the federal rules, as they relate to corporations.

(b) The federal law provides that certain "golden parachute" payments are not deductible by the payor corporation. (An excise tax is imposed on the recipient.) California corporation tax law has not conformed to this provision.

(c) The federal law disallows deductions for certain compensation above $1 million a year paid by a publicly held corporation to the corporation's chief executive officer or any of the corporation's four highest paid officers (other than the chief executive officer) for the tax year. California has not conformed to this provision.

(d) Federal law contains a special provision disallowing expenses attributable to the production of an unharvested crop in certain cases when the land is sold after having been used in a trade or business. There is no necessity for a

¶ 1017

comparable California rule, because California has no special alternative method of computing the tax on capital gains.

(e) Federal law that generally prohibits a current deduction for capital expenditures does not apply for California purposes to expenditures for which a deduction is allowed under California law for enterprise zone, local agency military base recovery area, former Los Angeles Revitalization Zone, or targeted tax area property.

(f) Federal law disallows deductions for certain lobbying and political expenditures. California has not conformed to this provision.

(g) Federal law disallows deductions for club dues paid or incurred for membership in any business, pleasure, social, athletic, luncheon, sporting, airline, or hotel club. California has not conformed to this provision.

● *Entertainment and gifts*

Except with respect to the deductibility of club dues (as discussed above), California law is the same as federal law.

● *Shipping company and oil/gas drilling rig employee's meal expenses*

Both California and federal law allow a 100% deduction (rather than 50%) of meals to employees on offshore oil or gas rigs and to employees who are crew members of certain commercial vessels (see ¶ 302).

● *Expenses allocable to exempt income*

There may be a difference between federal and California treatment of expenses allocable to tax-exempt income, as referred to in item (a) above, in that certain items may be excludable or deductible from income for California purposes, but not for federal, such as interest earned by certain cooperative associations, dividends from income previously included in the measure of the California tax, etc. See ¶ 1015 for cases involving credit unions and cooperative associations, and ¶ 1002 regarding unallowable interest on indebtedness incurred to acquire property from which the income is allocable to sources outside California.

In *Appeal of Mission Equities Corporation* (1975) (CCH CALIFORNIA TAX REPORTS ¶ 10-752.332), the State Board of Equalization (SBE) followed the *Great Western Financial* case, below, in disallowing expenses allocable to dividends received from California subsidiaries. The SBE approved the FTB's allocation of indirect expenses between taxable and nontaxable income in proportion to the amount of each, the same formula having been approved by the Supreme Court in the *Great Western Financial* case.

In *Great Western Financial Corporation v. Franchise Tax Board* (1971) (CCH CALIFORNIA TAX REPORTS ¶ 10-752.33), the FTB disallowed deductions for interest and for general and administrative expenses of a parent corporation, on the ground that the deductions were allocable to income from dividends received from subsidiary California corporations and that such dividends were "exempt" income because they were deducted as explained in ¶ 908. The California Supreme Court held for the FTB, and concluded that "expenses incurred by a taxpayer in producing or receiving dividend income

¶ 1017

are properly deductible only when that taxpayer's dividend income is taxable."

According to the SBE, the FTB must follow IRS Revenue Procedure 72-18 in determining whether interest expense is allocable to taxable or nontaxable income. The FTB must focus on the taxpayer's purpose for incurring and continuing the subject indebtedness and must consider the actual use of the debt funds. In *Appeal of Zenith National Insurance Corporation* (1998) (CCH CALIFORNIA TAX REPORTS ¶ 10-752.20), the FTB determined that the income from the taxpayer's sale of debentures and purchase of preferred stock contributed to both the taxpayer's taxable and nontaxable activities and, therefore, utilized a general formula to allocate the interest expense in accordance with the ratio of the taxpayer's tax-exempt income to the taxpayer's gross income. However, the SBE found that the taxpayer incurred the expense for the purpose of producing taxable income for three of the four income years at issue and, thus, could claim the full deduction for those three years.

● *Expenses for which credits are allowable*

California incorporates the portion of IRC Sec. 280C that disallows a deduction for that portion of qualified research expenses or basic research expenses that is equal to the amount of the credit allowed for such expenses (see ¶ 810a). California does not incorporate the rest of IRC Sec. 280C, which disallows a deduction for expenses for which a federal work opportunity credit is allowed.

See ¶ 1002 regarding deduction of prepaid interest. See ¶ 1106 regarding certain deductions of farming corporations.

¶ 1018 Net Operating Loss Carryover

> *Law:* Secs. 24416, 24416.1-16.6, 25108, 25110 (CCH CALIFORNIA TAX REPORTS ¶ 10-625, 10-874, 10-888, 10-896, 10-897f).
>
> *Comparable Federal:* Sec. 172 (CCH STANDARD FEDERAL TAX REPORTS ¶ 12,002).
>
> *California Forms:* FTB 3805Q, FTB 3805Z, FTB 3806, FTB 3807, FTB 3809.

Same as personal income tax (see ¶ 309), except as follows:

● *Water's-edge corporations*

A multinational corporation that has made a water's-edge election for the current income year may not fully deduct a net operating loss (NOL) carryover from a prior income year in which it had no water's-edge election in effect. Rather, the deduction is denied to the extent that the NOL carryover reflects income and apportionment factors of affiliated entities that would not have been taken into account had a water's-edge election been in effect for the year of the loss.

In Legal Ruling 99-2 (1999) (CALIFORNIA TAX REPORTS ¶ 10-625.251), the Franchise Tax Board clarified that, despite a prior legal ruling stating the contrary, in determining whether a water's-edge taxpayer is an "eligible small business" or a "new business" for NOL purposes, the procedures for computing business assets and gross receipts do not deviate from the procedures used for other taxpayers.

¶ 1018

● *Corporations subject to allocation and apportionment*

California modifies federal law by providing that for multistate corporations subject to allocation and apportionment and corporations electing intrastate combined reporting, an NOL may be deducted from the sum of the net income or loss of a corporation apportionable or allocable to California. The effect of this modification is to limit the deduction to the amount specifically allocable to the company that generated the loss.

● *Combined reporting*

Corporations that are members of a unitary group filing a single return must use intrastate apportionment, separately computing the loss carryover for each corporation in the group using its individual apportionment factors and completing a separate FTB 3805Q for each taxpayer included in the combined report. Unlike the loss treatment for a federal consolidated return, a California loss carryover for one member in a combined report may not be applied to the income of another member included in the combined report.

● *Carryover for bankrupt or reorganized corporations*

A 10-year carryover period applies to NOLs attributable to income years beginning after 1986 and before 1994 that are incurred by a bank or corporation that was (1) under the jurisdiction of the court in a federal Title 11 (bankruptcy) or similar case at any time prior to 1994 or (2) in receipt of assets acquired in a transaction that qualifies as a tax-free reorganization under federal law.

Pre-1987 Tax Years

Prior law allowed NOLs to be carried forward only by "qualified taxpayers" engaged in a new small business, a business in an enterprise zone or program area, or in farming. These limited carryovers applied to losses for years 1984, 1985, and 1986. Although these provisions were repealed in 1987, carryover is permitted under the broader general net operating loss provision. For details of pre-1987 NOL carryovers, see prior editions of the GUIDEBOOK TO CALIFORNIA TAXES.

¶ 1019 "At Risk" Limitations

Law: Sec. 24691 (CCH CALIFORNIA TAX REPORTS ¶ 11-247).

Comparable Federal: Sec. 465 (CCH STANDARD FEDERAL TAX REPORTS ¶ 21,850).

California conforms to federal law (see ¶ 801b). A brief explanation of the federal provisions is covered at ¶ 325.

CHAPTER 11

TAXES ON CORPORATE INCOME
ACCOUNTING METHODS AND BASES, INVENTORIES

¶ 1100 Accounting Periods and Methods—In General

Law: Secs. 24631-726 (CCH CALIFORNIA TAX REPORTS ¶ 11-150—11-293).

Comparable Federal: Secs. 441-83 (CCH STANDARD FEDERAL TAX REPORTS ¶ 2701, 2720, 2731, 2754, 2761, 2775, 2785, 2823, 2885A, 2887, 2888, 2889, 2894, 2899, 2899I, 2899N, 2899V, 2901, 2917, 2921, 2924, 2926X, 2926Y, 2926Z, 2926ZL, 2926ZT, 2927A, 2951, 2966, 2969, 2972, 2990, 2994).

California generally conforms to, and in some cases incorporates, federal law governing accounting periods, accounting methods, year of inclusion and deduction, inventories, and adjustment. Differences are noted in the following paragraphs.

¶ 1101 Accounting Periods

Law: Secs. 24631, 24632 (CCH CALIFORNIA TAX REPORTS ¶ 11-157).

Comparable Federal: Sec. 441 (CCH STANDARD FEDERAL TAX REPORTS ¶ 20,302).

Same as personal income tax—see ¶ 401.

¶ 1102 Change of Accounting Period

Law: Secs. 24632, 24633, 24633.5 (CCH CALIFORNIA TAX REPORTS ¶ 11-157).

Comparable Federal: Sec. 442 (CCH STANDARD FEDERAL TAX REPORTS ¶ 20,400).

The income year of a corporation must be the same as the tax year used by the corporation for federal income tax purposes, unless a change in accounting period is initiated or approved by the Franchise Tax Board.

¶ 1103 Return for Short Period—Annualization of Income

Law: Secs. 24634-36 (CCH CALIFORNIA TAX REPORTS ¶ 11-163).

Comparable Federal: Sec. 443 (CCH STANDARD FEDERAL TAX REPORTS ¶ 20,500).

California law incorporates federal law, except that California still requires a short-period return when a taxpayer's year is terminated for jeopardy by the Franchise Tax Board.

¶ 1104 Change of Taxable Year—S Corporations

Law: Sec. 24637 (CCH CALIFORNIA TAX REPORTS ¶ 11-165).

Comparable Federal: Sec. 444 (CCH STANDARD FEDERAL TAX REPORTS ¶ 20,600).

California incorporates federal law by reference, (see ¶ 801b) with one modification relating to "required payments," noted further below.

Both federal and California law allow S corporations to elect to change to an income year with a three-month deferral period, or its previous income year deferral period, whichever is shorter.

Federal law requires that such an entity making the election federally must make certain "required payments" on April 15th of each calendar year following the calendar year in which the election begins (IRC Sec. 444(c)). California does not adopt the "required payments" requirement.

¶ 1105 Tax Rate Change During Taxable Year

Law: Secs. 23058, 24251 (CCH CALIFORNIA TAX REPORTS ¶ 89-030, 10-123).

Comparable Federal: Sec. 15 (CCH STANDARD FEDERAL TAX REPORTS ¶ 3285).

The general rule is the same as for personal income tax—see ¶ 406.

The corporation tax law also specifies that, except as otherwise provided, the tax of a fiscal year taxpayer in a year in which the law is changed equals the sum of:

(a) a portion of a tax computed under the law applicable to the first calendar year, based on the portion of the fiscal year falling in the first calendar year; and

(b) a portion of a tax computed under the law applicable to the second calendar year, based on the portion of the fiscal year falling in the second calendar year.

¶ 1102

¶ 1106 Accounting Methods—General

Law: Secs. 24651-54, 24661, 24673, 24673.2, 24675-79, 24681-82, 24685, 24688-90, 24692, 24721, 24725, 24726 (CCH CALIFORNIA TAX REPORTS ¶ 11-151, 11-169, 11-175, 11-181, 11-187, 11-208, 11-229, 11-293).

Comparable Federal: Secs. 186, 263A, 334, 336-38, 346, 361, 446-48, 451, 455-56, 458, 460-61, 464, 467-69, 481-83, 1341, 7701 (CCH STANDARD FEDERAL TAX REPORTS ¶ 6450, 12,210, 13,800, 16,150, 16,200—16,275, 16,351, 16,580, 20,606, 20,700, 20,800, 21,002, 21,510, 21,520, 21,540, 21,550, 21,802, 21,830, 21,840, 21,887, 21,900—21,960, 22,270, 22,280, 22,290, 33,380, 43,880).

California Form: FTB 3834.

With minor exceptions, California incorporates by reference (see ¶ 801b) federal accounting methods and definitions, including limitations on the cash method of accounting (IRC Sec. 448).

The corporation tax rules for accounting methods generally are the same as those for personal income tax (see ¶ 407) except for those provisions which, by their nature, are applicable only to individuals. The differences between California and federal laws discussed at ¶ 407 are applicable to corporation tax as well as to personal income tax. Provisions applicable only to corporations are discussed below.

● *Change of accounting method*

Although California has adopted the majority of federal accounting rules, California corporate tax law does not contain a provision permitting automatic acceptance of federal changes in method. However, the Franchise Tax Board (FTB) ordinarily deems a taxpayer that obtains federal approval for a change, or that is required or permitted to make a federal change without approval, to have made a proper change for California purposes. The change must be consistent with California law, the accounting must be consistent with published federal guidelines and procedures, and the change must be reflected in a timely California return. California will not accept the change if the FTB has publicly indicated in writing that the federal guideline or procedure will not be followed. Furthermore, California may modify the adjustments if, as a result of differences between California and federal law, the change produces a material distortion of California income.

California does not follow IRS Rev. Proc. 96-3 allowing an automatic consent procedure for a change of accounting method involving previously unclaimed allowable depreciation or amortization (see CCH CALIFORNIA TAX REPORTS ¶ 16-211.211).

● *"Spreadback" relief*

Special rules providing "spreadback" relief in certain cases for income attributable to several years, repealed for federal purposes in 1964 and replaced by the allowance of deductions (IRC Sec. 186), are still in effect for California purposes. These rules apply to:

1. income from patent infringement awards;

2. damages received for breach of contract, or breach of fiduciary relationship; and

3. lump sum antitrust awards under the Clayton Act.

● *Prepaid subscription income*

California has a special provision that treats prepaid subscription income, not previously reported when a corporation ceases to do business, as includible in the measure of tax in the last year the corporation is subject to tax.

● *Farm corporations*

Under California and federal law, corporations engaged in farming must use the accrual method of accounting and capitalize preproductive-period expenses. However, the following are exempt from the accrual method rule: S corporations; corporations operating nurseries or sod farms or raising or harvesting trees other than fruit and nut trees; family farm corporations with gross receipts of $25 million or less in each income year; and all other corporations with gross receipts of $1 million or less in each income year. Under both California and federal law, a corporation is required to change from the cash method to the accrual method of accounting in a year in which gross receipts exceed $1 million (or, in the case of a family farm corporation, $25 million). Previously, a family farm corporation that had gross receipts exceeding $25 million was allowed to establish a suspense account when it made the required change in its method of accounting. However, this provision allowing the establishment of suspense accounts was repealed for California purposes in income years beginning after 1997 and for federal purposes for tax years ending after June 8, 1997.

● *Long-term contracts*

California incorporates IRC Sec. 460, which generally requires use of the percentage-of-completion method of accounting for long-term contracts. A look-back rule is generally applied to correct errors in estimates of contract price or costs. A taxpayer may elect not to apply the look-back rule if, for each prior contract year, the cumulative taxable income or loss under the contract, as determined using estimated contract price and costs, is within 10% of the cumulative taxable income or loss, as determined using actual contract price and costs. The election may be made for contracts completed in income years beginning after 1997 for California purposes and for tax years ending after August 5, 1997, for federal purposes.

California has a special provision (Sec. 24673) authorizing the FTB to require that income from a contract be reported on the percentage-of-completion basis if the contract period exceeds one year, even if the corporation regularly uses the completed contract basis of accounting. The corporation may prevent such action by furnishing security guaranteeing the payment of a tax measured by the income received upon completion of the contract, *even though* the corporation is not doing business in California in the year subsequent to the year of completion. The principal purpose of this provision is to prevent avoidance of tax by foreign corporations that perform contracts in California.

¶ 1106

● *Inventory shrinkage*

Under both California and federal law, a business may determine its year-end closing inventory by taking a reasonable deduction for shrinkage, even if a year-end inventory has not been taken to measure the actual amount of shrinkage.

Shrinkage is generally inventory loss due to undetected theft, breakage, or bookkeeping errors. In order to claim the deduction for estimated shrinkage, a business must normally take a physical count of its inventories at each business location on a regular, consistent basis. It also must make proper adjustments to its inventories and to its estimating methods to the extent its estimates are more or less than the actual shrinkage.

● *Other California-federal differences*

There is no California statute comparable to IRC Sec. 1341, which permits adjustment of income in certain situations where income received under a "claim of right" is later refunded. However, it is clear from the case law that California does apply the claim-of-right doctrine. See *Appeal of J.H. McKnight Ranch, Inc.* (1986) (CCH California Tax Reports ¶ 12-028.10). See also ¶ 415.

● *Accrual basis required in final return*

In *Appeal of Williams & Glass Accountancy Corporation* (1982) (CCH California Tax Reports ¶ 11-181.86), a cash-basis taxpayer distributed in liquidation accounts receivable that represented earned income. The State Board of Equalization upheld the FTB in its use of the accrual method of accounting in the corporation's final return.

¶ 1107 Inventories

> *Law:* Secs. 24422.3, 24701 (CCH California Tax Reports ¶ 10-744, 11-259, 11-280).
>
> *Comparable Federal:* Secs. 263A, 471, 475 (CCH Standard Federal Tax Reports ¶ 13,800, 22,202, 22,265).

Same as personal income tax—see ¶ 409.

¶ 1108 Inventories—Last-In, First-Out Method

> *Law:* Secs. 24701, 24708 (CCH California Tax Reports ¶ 11-265—11-277).
>
> *Comparable Federal:* Secs. 472-74 (CCH Standard Federal Tax Reports ¶ 22,230—22,260).

California incorporates by reference IRC Sec. 472, authorizing the use of the last-in, first-out (LIFO) method of inventory identification, and IRC Sec. 474, permitting eligible small business to elect to use a simplified dollar-value LIFO method to account for their inventories. However, California has not incorporated IRC Sec. 473, which prescribes accounting procedures to be employed when qualified liquidations of LIFO inventories are made.

The Franchise Tax Board will allow automobile dealers that violate the LIFO inventory conformity requirement of IRC Sec. 472(c) or IRC Sec.

472(e)(2) to continue using the LIFO method for California purposes, provided that they qualify for relief granted under IRS Revenue Procedure 97-44 (see CCH CALIFORNIA TAX REPORTS ¶ 11-265.20). Taxpayers must send a copy of the memorandum submitted to the IRS as required under Rev. Proc. 97-44 with their California franchise or income tax returns for the accounting period that includes May 31, 1998. However, they will not be required to pay a settlement amount.

¶ 1109 Installment Sales

> *Law:* Secs. 24667-72 (CCH CALIFORNIA TAX REPORTS ¶ 11-193).
>
> *Comparable Federal:* Secs. 453, 453A, 453B, former Sec. 453C (CCH STANDARD FEDERAL TAX REPORTS ¶ 21,402, 21,450—21,480).

The same as under the personal income tax law (see ¶ 411).

● *Installment obligations in liquidation of subsidiary*

Both California and federal laws provide that no gain or loss will be recognized if installment obligations are distributed in a complete liquidation of a subsidiary into its parent corporation (see ¶ 1208); however, there is a difference between the two laws where the parent corporation is tax-exempt under California law. The State Board of Equalization held in *Appeal of C.M. Ranch Co.* (1976) (CCH CALIFORNIA TAX REPORTS ¶ 11-193.11) that a tax-exempt corporation technically is not a "corporation" under the corporation tax law; consequently it cannot qualify as a parent "corporation" so as to enable the distributing corporation to avoid recognition of gain or loss on distribution of installment obligations. This reasoning is not applicable under federal law, because the federal definition of "corporation" does not exclude a tax-exempt corporation.

● *Repossession of installment obligations*

See ¶ 505b regarding limitations on recognition of gain on installment sales of real property where repossession occurs in a subsequent year.

¶ 1110 Related Taxpayers, Acquisitions to Avoid Tax, etc.

> *Law:* Secs. 24431, 24725, 25102-03 (CCH CALIFORNIA TAX REPORTS ¶ 10-768, 11-287, 12-675).
>
> *Comparable Federal:* Secs. 269, 269A, 269B, 482 (CCH STANDARD FEDERAL TAX REPORTS ¶ 2258, 2267, 2267H, 2990).

California law, incorporating by reference IRC Sec. 482, gives the Franchise Tax Board (FTB) broad power to distribute or allocate income or deductions among related taxpayers if the FTB determines that it is necessary to do so in order to prevent evasion of taxes or clearly reflect income. In addition, the FTB may require combined or consolidated reports and adjust the income or tax of related taxpayers. See Chapter 13 for discussion of the apportionment formula as it relates to business done within and without the state.

In *Appeal of Baldwin and Howell* (1968) (CCH CALIFORNIA TAX REPORTS ¶ 11-287.36), the State Board of Equalization upheld an increase made by the FTB in the income of a parent corporation that was accomplished by transferring certain income from a subsidiary to the parent and by increasing the parent's charge to the subsidiary for the services of loaned employees.

California law is the same as federal law providing for the disallowance of tax benefits upon the acquisition of the stock or property of a corporation when the principal purpose of the acquisition is to evade or avoid tax.

California has not conformed to federal loophole-closing provisions regarding personal service corporations (IRC Sec. 269A) and "stapled interests" (IRC Sec. 269B).

¶ 1111 Election to Accrue Income on Noninterest-Bearing Obligations Issued at Discount

Law: Sec. 24674 (CCH CALIFORNIA TAX REPORTS ¶ 11-205).

Comparable Federal: Sec. 454 (CCH STANDARD FEDERAL TAX REPORTS ¶ 21,500).

A cash-basis taxpayer may elect to accrue the increment in value of noninterest-bearing bonds issued at a discount and redeemable for fixed amounts increasing at stated intervals. The election is binding for subsequent years. This rule is the same as the federal one, except that California law does not conform to a federal provision relating to the inclusion in income of the accrued increment in value of obligations owned at the beginning of the year in which the election is made.

See also ¶ 910, regarding special rules for discount bonds.

¶ 1112 Imputed Interest

Law: Secs. 24726, 24993 (CCH CALIFORNIA TAX REPORTS ¶ 11-291, 11-988).

Comparable Federal: Secs. 483, 7872 (CCH STANDARD FEDERAL TAX REPORTS ¶ 22,290, 44,856).

California law adopts by reference (see ¶ 801b) federal provisions concerning both imputed interest on certain deferred payment contracts and "foregone interest" on loans with below-market interest rates.

CHAPTER 12

TAXES ON CORPORATE INCOME
SALES AND EXCHANGES,
GAIN OR LOSS, BASIS

¶ 1201 Gain or Loss—General Rule

> *Law:* Secs. 24901-02, 24954, 24954.1 (CCH CALIFORNIA TAX REPORTS ¶ 11-855, 11-929).
>
> *Comparable Federal:* Secs. 1001, 1042, 1221-57 (CCH STANDARD FEDERAL TAX REPORTS ¶ 29,620, 31,720, 32,220—32,720).
>
> *California Form:* Form 100.

Gain or loss on the disposition of property is the difference between the property's adjusted basis and the amount realized. In general, California has adopted federal general and special rules for determining capital gains and losses. However, California has not adopted a federal amendment made by the Taxpayer Relief Act of 1997 under which the alternative tax rate of 35% applies to the lesser of the corporation's net capital gain or its taxable income (formerly, only to its net capital gain). The federal amendment applies in tax years in which the regular corporate tax exceeds 35% and that end after December 31, 1997.

Gains and losses are reported on Form 100 unless otherwise indicated.

¶ 1202 Involuntary Conversion

> *Law:* Secs. 24943-49.5 (CCH CALIFORNIA TAX REPORTS ¶ 11-907).
>
> *Comparable Federal:* Sec. 1033 (CCH STANDARD FEDERAL TAX REPORTS ¶ 31,540).

California has its own corporate tax provisions governing computation of gain and loss on involuntary conversions and does not generally incorporate the federal law in this area for corporate tax purposes, as it does for personal income tax purposes. However, the rules are generally the same—see ¶ 502.

¶ **1201**

¶ 1202a Gain from Sale of Assisted Housing

Law: Sec. 24955 (CCH CALIFORNIA TAX REPORTS ¶ 11-927).

Comparable Federal: Former Sec. 1039 (CCH STANDARD FEDERAL TAX REPORTS ¶ 31,660).

Same as personal income tax—see ¶ 502b.

¶ 1202b Foreign Currency Transactions

Law: Sec. 24905 (CCH CALIFORNIA TAX REPORTS (¶ 11-834).

Comparable Federal: Sec. 988 (CCH STANDARD FEDERAL TAX REPORTS ¶ 29,400).

Same as personal income tax—see ¶ 510a.

¶ 1203 Liquidation Under S.E.C. Order

Law: Sec. 24981 (CCH CALIFORNIA TAX REPORTS ¶ 11-963).

Comparable Federal: Sec. 1081 (CCH STANDARD FEDERAL TAX REPORTS ¶ 32,020).

Same as personal income tax—see ¶ 503.

¶ 1204 Exchange of Property for Like Property

Law: Sec. 24941 (CCH CALIFORNIA TAX REPORTS ¶ 11-899).

Comparable Federal: Sec. 1031 (CCH STANDARD FEDERAL TAX REPORTS ¶ 31,502).

Same as personal income tax—see ¶ 504.

¶ 1204a Exchange of Insurance Policies

Law: Sec. 24950 (CCH CALIFORNIA TAX REPORTS ¶ 11-910).

Comparable Federal: Sec. 1035 (CCH STANDARD FEDERAL TAX REPORTS ¶ 31,580).

Same as personal income tax (see ¶ 504a) except that the corporation tax law did not adopt for income years beginning before 1990 a 1986 Tax Reform Act amendment of the definition of "endowment contract."

¶ 1205 Exchange of Stock for Stock

Law: Sec. 24951 (CCH CALIFORNIA TAX REPORTS ¶ 11-915).

Comparable Federal: Sec. 1036 (CCH STANDARD FEDERAL TAX REPORTS ¶ 31,600).

Same as personal income tax—see ¶ 505.

¶ 1205a Exchange of Certain U.S. Obligations

Law: None (CCH CALIFORNIA TAX REPORTS ¶ 11-919).

Comparable Federal: Sec. 1037 (CCH STANDARD FEDERAL TAX REPORTS ¶ 31,620).

The California corporation tax law has nothing comparable to the federal provisions for the tax-free exchange of obligations of the United States issued under the Second Liberty Bond Act.

¶ 1205b Reacquisition of Property After Installment Sale

Law: Sec. 24952 (CCH CALIFORNIA TAX REPORTS ¶ 11-923).

Comparable Federal: Sec. 1038 (CCH STANDARD FEDERAL TAX REPORTS ¶ 31,640).

California has its own corporate tax provisions governing computation of gain and loss upon a seller's repossession of real property following an installment sale and does not incorporate the federal law in this area for corporate tax purposes, as it does for personal income tax purposes. However, the rules are generally the same—see ¶ 505b.

¶ 1206 Exchange of Property for Stock

Law: Sec. 24451 (CCH CALIFORNIA TAX REPORTS ¶ 11-021).

Comparable Federal: Sec. 351 (CCH STANDARD FEDERAL TAX REPORTS ¶ 16,402).

Same as personal income tax—see ¶ 506.

¶ 1206a Sale or Exchange of Tax-Exempt Bonds

Law: Sec. 24314 (CCH CALIFORNIA TAX REPORTS ¶ 10-430).

Comparable Federal: None.

The gain or loss from the sale or transfer of bonds yielding tax-exempt interest is not exempt. Federal policy is the same as to state and municipal obligations.

¶ 1206b Sale of Stock to ESOPs or Cooperatives

Law: Sec. 24954.1 (CCH CALIFORNIA TAX REPORTS ¶ 11-929).

Comparable Federal: Sec. 1042 (CCH STANDARD FEDERAL TAX REPORTS ¶ 31,720).

Same as personal income tax—see ¶ 506b.

¶ 1207 Exchange in Connection with Reorganization

Law: Sec. 24451 (CCH CALIFORNIA TAX REPORTS ¶ 11-027, 11-057, 11-075).

Comparable Federal: Secs. 354, 361, 368 (CCH STANDARD FEDERAL TAX REPORTS ¶ 16,431, 16,580, 16,750).

California incorporates federal law governing computation of gain and loss in connection with corporate reorganizations as of the current IRC tie-in date (see ¶ 801b).

No gain or loss is recognized if stock or securities in a corporation that is a party to a reorganization are exchanged solely for stock or securities in such corporation, or in another corporation that is a party to the reorganization. Also, no gain or loss is recognized if a corporation exchanges property solely for stock or securities in connection with a reorganization. "Reorganization" and other terms are specifically defined.

Nonqualified preferred stock received in exchange for stock other than nonqualified preferred stock is treated as "boot" rather than stock, and gain, but not loss, is recognized on such an exchange.

¶ 1207a "Spin-Off" Reorganization

Law: Sec. 24451 (CCH California Tax Reports ¶ 11-033).

Comparable Federal: Sec. 355 (CCH Standard Federal Tax Reports ¶ 16,460).

California incorporates federal law under which certain distributions of the stock or securities of a corporation controlled by the distributor in connection with a "spin-off," "split-up," or "split-off" reorganization may be received by distributees without recognition of gain or loss.

California also incorporates the federal rules governing the taxability of the distributing corporations, including a provision under which distributing corporations may be required to recognize gain on certain distributions resembling outright sales of subsidiaries.

¶ 1208 Complete Liquidation of Subsidiary

Law: Sec. 24451 (CCH California Tax Reports ¶ 10-979).

Comparable Federal: Sec. 332 (CCH Standard Federal Tax Reports ¶ 16,050).

No gain or loss is recognized upon the receipt by a corporation of property distributed in complete liquidation of a subsidiary corporation; 80% ownership is required and other conditions must be satisfied. California incorporates the IRC provisions (see ¶ 801b).

In *C.M. Ranch Co.,* discussed at ¶ 1109, it was held that the California provision for tax-free liquidation does not apply where the parent corporation is tax-exempt, since such a corporation is technically not a "corporation" under the corporation tax law.

¶ 1209 Exchanges of Stock in 10% Owned Foreign Corporations

Law: Sec. 24990.7 (CCH California Tax Reports ¶ 11-972).

Comparable Federal: Sec. 1248 (CCH Standard Federal Tax Reports ¶ 32,560).

California does not currently adopt the federal provision that taxes as a dividend the portion of gain on the sale or exchange of stock in a 10% owned foreign corporation attributable to earnings and profits of the corporation accumulated in taxable years beginning after 1962, and during the period or periods the stock was owned by the taxpayer.

¶ 1210 Exchanges Not Solely in Kind

Law: Sec. 24451 (CCH California Tax Reports ¶ 11-039, 11-045).

Comparable Federal: Sec. 356 (CCH Standard Federal Tax Reports ¶ 16,490).

Same as personal income tax—see ¶ 509.

¶ 1211 Exchanges Involving Foreign Corporations

Law: Sec. 24451 (CCH California Tax Reports ¶ 11-069).

Comparable Federal: Sec. 367 (CCH Standard Federal Tax Reports ¶ 16,640).

Same as personal income tax—see ¶ 510.

¶ 1212 Exchange of Property Under F.C.C. Order (Prior Law)

Law: Former Sec. 24971 (CCH CALIFORNIA TAX REPORTS ¶ 11-961).

Comparable Federal: Former Sec. 1071 (CCH STANDARD FEDERAL TAX REPORTS ¶ 32,000).

For income years beginning before 1997, California had its own corporate tax provisions governing computation of gain and loss in connection with an exchange of broadcast property pursuant to an FCC order and did not incorporate the federal law in this area for corporate tax purposes, as it did for personal income tax purposes. However, the rules were generally the same— see ¶ 511.

¶ 1213 Liquidation of Corporation

Law: Sec. 24451 (CCH CALIFORNIA TAX REPORTS ¶ 10-973, 10-997, 11-003).

Comparable Federal: Secs. 331, 334, 336-38 (CCH STANDARD FEDERAL TAX REPORTS ¶ 16,002—16,275).

Gain or loss is ordinarily recognized to a corporate stockholder upon liquidation of a corporation, the gain or loss being measured by the difference between the basis of the stock and the value of the property received. California incorporates the federal law (see ¶ 801b).

● *Liquidation of subsidiary*

See ¶ 1208 for special rules applying to the complete liquidation of a subsidiary.

● *California-federal differences*

Federal law contains special provisions for treatment of liquidating distributions by certain types of corporations, where corporate income has been taxed directly to shareholders. This applies particularly to Domestic International Sales Corporations and successor entities. Since such special corporations have no counterparts in the California law, their liquidating distributions are subject to the regular rules for California tax purposes.

¶ 1213a Carryovers in Corporate Acquisitions

Law: Secs. 24451, 24471, 24481 (CCH CALIFORNIA TAX REPORTS ¶ 11-087).

Comparable Federal: Secs. 381-84 (CCH STANDARD FEDERAL TAX REPORTS ¶ 17,002—17,200).

California incorporates federal provisions regarding carryover of certain corporate attributes in reorganizations and in liquidations of subsidiaries, with minor modifications substituting certain California credits for those enumerated in the federal law.

¶ 1214 Capital Gains and Losses

Law: Former Secs. 24904, 24905.5; Secs. 24956, 24990, 24990.5, 24995 (CCH CALIFORNIA TAX REPORTS ¶ 11-280, 11-930, 11-972).

Comparable Federal: Secs. 197, 475, 988, 1044, 1201-88 (CCH STANDARD FEDERAL TAX REPORTS ¶ 22, 265, 31,745, 32,151—32,901).

California law adopts by reference (see ¶ 801b) the federal treatment of capital gains and losses except for the following differences:

(1) the federal alternative tax on corporations is inapplicable;

(2) the limitation on capital losses does not apply to income years beginning before 1990;

(3) California allows a five-year carryover, but no carryback, of capital losses sustained in income years beginning after 1989; federal law provides for a three-year carryback in addition to a five-year carryover;

(4) the provisions dealing with the treatment of certain passive foreign investment companies do not apply for California purposes;

(5) provisions relating to gain from certain foreign stock sales or exchanges do not apply to transactions occurring after August 20, 1990, in income years beginning after 1989; and

(6) California incorporates the federal provision authorizing certain corporations to defer recognition of capital gain realized on sales of publicly traded securities if the proceeds are used within 60 days to purchase stock or a partnership interest in certain small business investment companies. However, the provision applies for federal purposes to sales occurring after August 9, 1993, in tax years ending on or after that date, while for California purposes the provision applies only for income years beginning after 1996.

● *"Small business" stock*

The limited exclusion for gain on the sale of small business stock that is available for personal income tax purposes (see ¶ 513) is not available for corporation franchise (income) tax purposes.

However, the corporation tax law previously provided for reduction of taxable gain from "small business stock" sold or exchanged before October 1, 1987.

¶ 1214a Retirement of Bonds, etc.

Law: Secs. 24439, 24990, 24994 (CCH CALIFORNIA TAX REPORTS ¶ 10-732).

Comparable Federal: Secs. 249, 1271-74A (CCH STANDARD FEDERAL TAX REPORTS ¶ 13,400, 32,740—32,800).

Except for United States Savings Bonds, gain on retirement of bonds is taxable income and loss is fully deductible. There is a difference between the franchise tax and the income tax in the treatment of gain or loss on redemption of savings bonds, resulting from the difference in the treatment of interest income as explained at ¶ 909.

Under the corporation income tax, a gain on redemption of Savings Bonds is not taxable and a loss is not deductible, as outlined at ¶ 518 for the personal income tax. Under the franchise tax, however, such a gain is fully taxable and such a loss is fully deductible, since interest on United States obligations is fully taxable for franchise tax purposes.

Where a corporation redeems bonds that were issued at a discount after May 27, 1969, a corporate holder's California gain may be different from the federal gain, since the federal gain will reflect the fact that the federal cost basis of the bonds has been increased by the amount of discount that has been reported as income as explained at ¶ 910. Although current California law provides for the same addition to basis, it did not become effective for income years before 1987. Differences in California and federal bases are to be accounted for in the year of disposition, or at the election of the taxpayer ratably in each of the first four income years beginning after 1986.

California law is the same as federal in restricting the amount of deduction for premium paid by a corporation on the repurchase of bonds convertible into stock. The deduction is limited to the amount of a normal call premium.

Original issue discount on bonds is discussed at ¶ 910.

¶ 1214b Corporation Dealing in Own Stock

Law: Sec. 24942 (CCH CALIFORNIA TAX REPORTS ¶ 11-903).

Comparable Federal: Sec. 1032 (CCH STANDARD FEDERAL TAX REPORTS ¶ 31,522).

No gain or loss is recognized to a corporation on the receipt of money or other property in exchange for stock, including treasury stock, of such corporation.

In *Federal Employees Distributing Company v. Franchise Tax Board* (1968) (CCH CALIFORNIA TAX REPORTS ¶ 11-903.21), the California District Court of Appeals held that fees collected for memberships by a nonprofit nonstock corporation were the corporation's sole source of equity capital and therefore were exempt under Sec. 24942 from franchise tax.

¶ 1215 Basis, General Rule

Law: Secs. 24912, 24966-66.2 (CCH CALIFORNIA TAX REPORTS ¶ 11-863, 11-957).

Comparable Federal: Secs. 1012, 1059, 1059A, 1060 (CCH STANDARD FEDERAL TAX REPORTS ¶ 29,680, 31,920, 31,940, 31,960).

Same as personal income tax—see ¶ 521. California law parallels and in some instances incorporates federal law in this area. The general rule is that the basis of an item of property is its cost. Exceptions are discussed in the following paragraphs.

¶ 1216 Basis, Inventoriable Property

Law: Secs. 24913, 24966.1 (CCH CALIFORNIA TAX REPORTS ¶ 11-867, 11-958).

Comparable Federal: Secs. 1013, 1059A (CCH STANDARD FEDERAL TAX REPORTS ¶ 29,700, 31,940).

Same as personal income tax—see ¶ 522.

¶ 1214b

¶ 1217 Basis of Property Acquired by Gift

Law: Secs. 24914-15 (CCH CALIFORNIA TAX REPORTS ¶ 11-871).

Comparable Federal: Sec. 1015 (CCH STANDARD FEDERAL TAX REPORTS ¶ 29,740).

Same as personal income tax—see ¶ 523—except that the corporation tax law does not provide for property acquired before 1921.

¶ 1218 Basis of Property Acquired by Transfer in Trust

Law: Sec. 24914 (CCH CALIFORNIA TAX REPORTS ¶ 11-871).

Comparable Federal: Sec. 1015 (CCH STANDARD FEDERAL TAX REPORTS ¶ 29,740).

Same as personal income tax—see ¶ 524—except that the corporation tax law does not provide for property acquired before 1921.

¶ 1219 Basis of Property Transmitted at Death

Law: None (CCH CALIFORNIA TAX REPORTS ¶ 11-869).

Comparable Federal: Sec. 1014 (CCH STANDARD FEDERAL TAX REPORTS ¶ 29,720, 29,860).

The California corporation tax law has no provision for basis of property transmitted at death.

¶ 1220 Basis of Property Acquired in Tax-Free Exchange

Law: Sec. 24451 (CCH CALIFORNIA TAX REPORTS ¶ 11-051).

Comparable Federal: Sec. 358 (CCH STANDARD FEDERAL TAX REPORTS ¶ 16,500).

Same as personal income tax—see ¶ 526.

¶ 1220a Basis of Stock After "Spin-Off" Reorganization

Law: Sec. 24451 (CCH CALIFORNIA TAX REPORTS ¶ 11-051).

Comparable Federal: Sec. 358 (CCH STANDARD FEDERAL TAX REPORTS ¶ 16,500).

Same as personal income tax—see ¶ 526b.

¶ 1221 Basis of Property Acquired in Reorganization

Law: Sec. 24451 (CCH CALIFORNIA TAX REPORTS ¶ 11-063).

Comparable Federal: Sec. 362 (CCH STANDARD FEDERAL TAX REPORTS ¶ 16,610).

In the case of property acquired by a corporation in a "reorganization," the property takes the transferor's basis, with adjustment for gain recognized upon the transfer.

¶ 1222 Basis of Property Acquired by Issuance of Stock or Contribution to Capital

Law: Sec. 24551 (CCH CALIFORNIA TAX REPORTS ¶ 11-063).

Comparable Federal: Sec. 362 (CCH STANDARD FEDERAL TAX REPORTS ¶ 16,610).

In the case of property acquired by a corporation by issuance of stock in a tax-free transaction under IRC Sec. 351 (see ¶ 506), or as a contribution to capital, the basis of the property is the transferor's basis, with adjustment for gain recognized on the transfer. However, if a contribution to capital is received from other than a shareholder, the corporation is required to reduce the basis of property by the amount of the contribution.

The California law is the same as the federal law.

¶ 1223 Basis of Property Acquired upon Involuntary Conversion

Law: Sec. 24947 (CCH CALIFORNIA TAX REPORTS ¶ 11-907).

Comparable Federal: Sec. 1033 (CCH STANDARD FEDERAL TAX REPORTS ¶ 31,540).

California has its own corporate tax provision regarding the basis of property acquired upon an involuntary conversion and does not generally incorporate the federal law in this area for corporate tax purposes, as it does for personal income tax purposes. However, the rules are generally the same—see ¶ 527.

¶ 1224 Basis of Securities Acquired in Wash Sale

Law: Sec. 24998 (CCH CALIFORNIA TAX REPORTS ¶ 11-967).

Comparable Federal: Sec. 1091 (CCH STANDARD FEDERAL TAX REPORTS ¶ 32,080).

Same as personal income tax—see ¶ 528.

¶ 1225 Basis of Property Acquired During Affiliation

Law: Sec. 24961 (CCH CALIFORNIA TAX REPORTS ¶ 11-931).

Comparable Federal: Sec. 1051 (CCH STANDARD FEDERAL TAX REPORTS ¶ 31,760).

In the case of property acquired by a corporation from an affiliated corporation during a period of affiliation, the basis of the property is determined under special rules, the general effect of which is to disregard the transfer from the affiliate. The California provision contains several references to federal law and is generally the same as the federal. There are some differences, however, and there may be important differences in the effect of the two laws because the periods of affiliation may be different under one law than under the other. Reference should be made to the law or regulations or to a more detailed reference work in case of any question involving this provision.

¶ 1226 Basis Prescribed by Revenue Acts of 1932 or 1934

Law: Sec. 24962 (CCH CALIFORNIA TAX REPORTS ¶ 11-935).

Comparable Federal: Sec. 1052 (CCH STANDARD FEDERAL TAX REPORTS ¶ 31,780).

The basis of property acquired after February 28, 1913, in an income year beginning prior to 1937, where the basis was prescribed by the federal Revenue Acts of 1932 or 1934, is as prescribed in those Acts. The California provision parallels the federal one, except that the federal provision applies only to transfers in tax years beginning prior to 1936.

¶ 1227 Basis of Property Acquired Before March 1, 1913

> *Law:* Sec. 24963 (CCH CALIFORNIA TAX REPORTS ¶ 11-939).
>
> *Comparable Federal:* Sec. 1053 (CCH STANDARD FEDERAL TAX REPORTS ¶ 31,800).

Same as personal income tax—see ¶ 531.

¶ 1228 Basis of FNMA Stock

> *Law:* Sec. 24965 (CCH CALIFORNIA TAX REPORTS ¶ 11-943).
>
> *Comparable Federal:* Sec. 1054 (CCH STANDARD FEDERAL TAX REPORTS ¶ 31,820).

The basis of stock issued by the Federal National Mortgage Association to an original holder is cost, reduced by the amount of any premium paid above face value. The premium may be deducted as an ordinary business expense in the year of purchase. The California provision parallels the federal one.

¶ 1229 Basis Under Redeemable Ground Rents

> *Law:* None (CCH CALIFORNIA TAX REPORTS ¶ 11-947).
>
> *Comparable Federal:* Sec. 1055 (CCH STANDARD FEDERAL TAX REPORTS ¶ 31,840).

The California corporate tax law contains nothing comparable to a federal provision that treats redeemable ground rents as being the equivalent of a mortgage.

¶ 1230 Basis of Property Acquired in Corporate Liquidation or Acquisition

> *Law:* Sec. 24451 (CCH CALIFORNIA TAX REPORTS ¶ 10-991, 11-005).
>
> *Comparable Federal:* Secs. 334, 338 (CCH STANDARD FEDERAL TAX REPORTS ¶ 16,150, 16,275).

In an ordinary corporate liquidation, the basis of property received by a corporate stockholder is the fair market value of the property at the date of liquidation. California incorporates federal law.

● *Liquidation in plan to purchase assets*

Upon the complete liquidation of a subsidiary under IRC Sec. 332 (see ¶ 1208) the property received by the parent corporation ordinarily takes the same basis it had in the hands of the subsidiary (transferor). However, a different result occurs if the corporation elects under IRC Sec. 338 to treat its acquisition of another business through purchase of a controlling interest (80%) in stock as the purchase of the assets of the acquired corporation. In this case, the buyer receives a fair market value basis in each asset and is entitled to claim depreciation and investment tax credit on a stepped-up basis. The tax attributes of the acquired (target) corporation disappear. In turn, the target corporation is subject to recapture tax liability.

Franchise Tax Board Regulation 24519 permits a California taxpayer to elect out of the federal election of IRC 338(g), which allows the purchasing corporation to have a stock purchase treated as an acquisition of assets.

¶ 1231 Basis of Property Acquired upon Transfers from Controlled Corporations

Law: Sec. 24964 (CCH California Tax Reports ¶ 11-895).

Comparable Federal: None.

Where a corporation subject to the franchise tax received property after January 1, 1928, from a controlled corporation, and where gain or loss was realized but was not taken into account for franchise tax purposes, the property takes the transferor's basis. There is no comparable federal provision.

¶ 1232 Basis of Rights to Acquire Stock

Law: Sec. 24451 (CCH California Tax Reports ¶ 10-937).

Comparable Federal: Sec. 307 (CCH Standard Federal Tax Reports ¶ 15,400).

Where the fair market value of stock rights is less than 15% of the value of the stock on which the rights are issued, the basis of the rights is zero unless the taxpayer elects to allocate to the rights a portion of the basis of the stock. This rule dates from 1954 in federal law and from 1955 in California law.

● *Allocation of basis*

As to the following rights, the basis of the stock is allocated between the stock and the rights according to their respective values at the time the rights are issued:

(a) all rights acquired in an income year beginning before January 1, 1937, *except* as to certain rights acquired before January 1, 1928 (see below); and

(b) nontaxable rights acquired in an income year beginning after December 31, 1936, where the value of the rights is more than 15% or the taxpayer elects to allocate as explained above.

If a stock right was acquired prior to January 1, 1928, and it constituted income under the Sixteenth Amendment to the Federal Constitution, the basis of the right is its fair market value when acquired.

● *Pre-1943 transactions*

Where stock rights were acquired and sold in an income year beginning prior to 1943 and the entire proceeds were reported as income, the basis of the stock is determined without any allocation to the rights.

● *California-federal differences*

California law now incorporates the federal law, but, as discussed below, there have been differences in effective dates in prior years.

(1) In item (a) above, the federal dates are January 1, 1936, in both cases instead of January 1, 1937, and January 1, 1928. As to both dates, the federal refers to *years beginning* before January 1, 1936, instead of to the *period prior* to the date specified.

(2) In item (b) above, the federal date is December 31, 1935, instead of December 31, 1936.

(3) In the rule stated above regarding rights acquired prior to January 1, 1928, the federal law refers to rights acquired in a taxable year beginning prior to January 1, 1936. Also, the federal rule is different in that it applies only if the value of the rights was included in gross income in the year acquired, whereas the prior California rule applies to all cases where the acquisition of the rights constituted income under the Sixteenth Amendment.

(4) In the rule stated above regarding rights acquired and sold prior to 1943, the federal law refers to rights acquired in any tax year beginning prior to 1939.

¶ 1233 Basis of Property Acquired Pursuant to S.E.C. Order

Law: Sec. 24988 (CCH CALIFORNIA TAX REPORTS ¶ 11-963).

Comparable Federal: Sec. 1082 (CCH STANDARD FEDERAL TAX REPORTS ¶ 32,040).

Special rules are provided for determination of basis in cases involving an order of the Securities and Exchange Commission under the Public Utility Holding Company Act. California incorporates the federal law.

¶ 1234 Basis of Property Acquired from Partnership

Law: None (CCH CALIFORNIA TAX REPORTS ¶ 11-651).

Comparable Federal: Sec. 732 (CCH STANDARD FEDERAL TAX REPORTS ¶ 25,640).

The corporation tax law contains no provision regarding basis of property distributed in kind by a partnership. However, California law provides that a corporation receiving *income* from an interest in a partnership is to treat that income in accordance with the provisions of the Personal Income Tax Law (see ¶ 530).

¶ 1235 Adjusted Basis

Law: Secs. 24911, 24916, 24916.2 (CCH CALIFORNIA TAX REPORTS ¶ 11-859, 11-875).

Comparable Federal: Secs. 1011, 1016-21 (CCH STANDARD FEDERAL TAX REPORTS ¶ 29,660, 29,760—29,840).

California law generally conforms to IRC Sec. 1016(a) concerning adjustments to basis. However, the following federal basis adjustments are inapplicable under California law:

(1) disallowed deductions on the disposal of coal or domestic iron ore;

(2) amounts related to a shareholder's stock in a controlled foreign corporation;

(3) the amount of "gas guzzler" tax on an automobile;

(4) certain federal investment tax credits;

(5) adjustments to the basis of a United States taxpayer's stock in a foreign personal holding company to reflect certain undistributed income of the company;

(6) amounts specified in a shareholder's consent;

(7) disallowed deductions on the sale of unharvested crops;

(8) amortization of premium and accrual of discount on bonds and notes held by a life insurance company;

(9) certain amounts deducted under IRC Sec. 59(e) that are not treated as tax preference items if so deducted;

(10) abandonment fees paid upon the termination of an open-space easement;

(11) tax recoupment fees on timberland;

(12) sales or use tax paid by the taxpayer in acquiring property, if the taxpayer claims the tax credit allowed for enterprise zone, local agency military base recovery area (LAMBRA), targeted tax area, or former Los Angeles Revitalization Zone (LARZ) businesses on certain "qualified property" (see ¶ 810a);

(13) farming soil and water conservation expenses; and

(14) amounts deducted for clean-fuel vehicle property (California no longer allows this deduction).

California law also requires that adjustments be made for certain deducted enterprise zone, LAMBRA, targeted tax area, or former LARZ business expenses (see ¶ 310f, ¶ 1008). No comparable basis adjustments are required under federal law.

Corporate taxpayers may be prohibited from making basis adjustments authorized by federal provisions that have not been adopted by California. For instance, in *Appeal of CRG Holdings, Inc.* (1997) (CCH CALIFORNIA TAX REPORTS ¶ 11-875.201), a taxpayer was not allowed to adjust its basis in the stock of its subsidiaries based on a consent dividend that was properly reported on the taxpayer's federal return, because California has never adopted the federal provision authorizing consent dividends. Similarly, in *Appeal of Rapid-American Corporation* (1997) (CCH CALIFORNIA TAX RE-PORTS ¶ 11-875.20), a taxpayer that sold its stock in its unitary subsidiaries was prohibited from increasing the basis of stock by the amount of earning and profits held in the subsidiaries that had previously been reported to California on the taxpayer's combined unitary report and that had not been distributed as dividends prior to the sales of stock. Although the disputed adjustment was authorized under federal law, California has never recognized earnings and profits as an appropriate basis adjustment.

¶ 1236 Substituted Basis

Law: Sec. 24917 (CCH CALIFORNIA TAX REPORTS ¶ 11-879).

Comparable Federal: Sec. 1016 (CCH STANDARD FEDERAL TAX REPORTS ¶ 29,760).

Same as personal income tax—see ¶ 535.

¶ 1237 Lessor's Basis for Lessee's Improvements

Law: Sec. 24919 (CCH CALIFORNIA TAX REPORTS ¶ 11-887).

Comparable Federal: Sec. 1019 (CCH STANDARD FEDERAL TAX REPORTS ¶ 29,820).

When the value of improvements by a lessee is excluded from income (see ¶ 905) there is no effect on the basis of the property to the lessor. When the value of such improvements was included in the lessor's gross income for any taxable year beginning before 1942, the basis of the lessor's property is adjusted accordingly. The California provision is the same as the federal one except for the effective date for California income tax purposes.

¶ 1238 Basis for Depreciation and Depletion

Law: Secs. 24353, 24831 (CCH CALIFORNIA TAX REPORTS ¶ 10-589, 11-551).

Comparable Federal: Secs. 167, 612-13 (CCH STANDARD FEDERAL TAX REPORTS ¶ 11,002, 24,540, 24,560).

Same as personal income tax—see ¶ 537.

For rules regarding percentage value depletion, see ¶ 311.

¶ 1239 Reduction of Basis—Income from Discharge of Indebtedness

Law: Secs. 24903, 24918 (CCH CALIFORNIA TAX REPORTS ¶ 11-883).

Comparable Federal: Sec. 1017 (CCH STANDARD FEDERAL TAX REPORTS ¶ 29,780).

When the taxpayer has elected to exclude from gross income gain from discharge of indebtedness, the amount excluded is applied to reduce the basis of property held by the taxpayer. Federal references to affiliated groups are applied to unitary members under California law. The California rules generally are the same as the federal.

California conforms to the federal requirement that the amount of income realized from the discharge of qualified real property business indebtedness that a taxpayer excludes from gross income must be applied to reduce the basis of business real property held by the taxpayer at the beginning of the income year following the income year in which the discharge occurs.

¶ 1240 Basis for Player Contracts

Law: Sec. 24989 (CCH CALIFORNIA TAX REPORTS ¶ 11-951).

Comparable Federal: Sec. 1056 (CCH STANDARD FEDERAL TAX REPORTS ¶ 31,860).

Same as personal income tax—see ¶ 538.

¶ 1241 Allocation of Transferred Business Assets

Law: Sec. 24966.2 (CCH CALIFORNIA TAX REPORTS ¶ 11-959).

Comparable Federal: Sec. 1060 (CCH STANDARD FEDERAL TAX REPORTS ¶ 31,960).

California has adopted the federal residual method for allocating purchases of assets that constitute a trade or business (see ¶ 801b). Generally, under the residual method, the purchase price is allocated first to the assets to the extent of their fair market value, and any excess is allocated to goodwill and going concern value. However, if a transferor and a transferee agree in writing concerning the allocation of consideration for transferred business assets, their agreement will generally be binding for tax purposes.

CHAPTER 13

TAXES ON CORPORATE INCOME
ALLOCATION AND APPORTIONMENT

¶ 1301 Scope of Chapter

The California taxes on corporate income are measured by income derived from or attributable to sources within California only. This applies both to corporations organized in California and to out-of-state ("foreign") corporations.

Where income is derived from sources both within and without the state, it is necessary to determine the income attributable to sources within the state. This chapter discusses the method of making this determination and points out some of the problems encountered. It covers not only situations where the income of only one corporation is involved, but also situations involving affiliated corporations. As pointed out in ¶ 1309, apportionment of all of the income of an affiliated group may be required even where only one of the affiliated corporations is engaged in any activity in California.

● *Uniform Division of Income for Tax Purposes Act*

California adopted the Uniform Division of Income for Tax Purposes Act (commonly referred to as UDITPA), effective in 1967; the Act has also been adopted by many other States. The California law deviates slightly from the original UDITPA draft, the principal differences being that (1) California does not exclude financial corporations and public utilities from the operation of the Act and (2) California's standard apportionment formula (see ¶ 1305) includes a double-weighted sales factor.

¶ 1301

In *Appeal of American Telephone and Telegraph Co.* (1982) (CCH CALIFORNIA TAX REPORTS ¶ 12-610.551), discussed at ¶ 1305 and ¶ 1306, the State Board of Equalization (SBE) stated that "UDITPA'S fundamental purpose is to assure that 100%, and no more and no less, of a multistate taxpayer's business income is taxed by the states having jurisdiction to tax it." The SBE cites decisions of courts of other states that have adopted UDITPA, and says that in each of those cases "the court sought to avoid an interpretation of UDITPA which would create a gap in the taxation of the taxpayer's income."

Franchise Tax Board Regulations 25121 through 25137 interpret UDITPA and provide detailed rules for application of the law. Regulation 25121 requires that the taxpayer be consistent in reporting to California and to other states to which the taxpayer reports under UDITPA; if the taxpayer is not consistent in its reporting, it must disclose in its California return the nature and extent of the inconsistency.

● *Multistate Tax Compact*

California has adopted the Multistate Tax Compact, which was developed by the Council of State Governments to promote uniformity among the States and to avoid duplicate taxation. The Compact includes the allocation and apportionment rules of UDITPA, discussed above. The constitutionality of the Compact was upheld by the U.S. Supreme Court in *United States Steel Corp. et al. v. Multistate Tax Commission et al.* (1978) (CCH CALIFORNIA TAX REPORTS ¶ 12-415.30).

¶ 1302 Apportionment of Business Income—General

Law: Secs. 25101, 25120-22 (CCH CALIFORNIA TAX REPORTS ¶ 12-405—12-430).

Comparable Federal: None.

California Forms: Form 100, Sch. R.

Subject to the limitations pointed out in ¶ 802 and ¶ 802a, any corporation deriving income from California sources is subject to California tax. If all of the income is from California, it is all subject to tax and there is, of course, no problem of apportioning a portion of the total net income to the state. However, the corporation may have income from sources outside California if (1) it is "doing business" outside of California, (2) it has property outside the state, or (3) it carries on some other activity outside the state.

● *When apportionment required*

The law provides that apportionment of income is required where business activities are *taxable* inside and outside California. For this purpose, a taxpayer is deemed to be taxable outside California if one of two specific qualifications is met:

    (a) the taxpayer is subject to a net income tax, a franchise tax measured by net income, a franchise tax for the privilege of doing business, or a corporate stock tax in another state, or

    (b) another state has jurisdiction to levy a net income tax on the taxpayer, *whether or not* the other state actually subjects the taxpayer to the tax.

¶ 1302

The other state is deemed to have jurisdiction to levy a net income tax if it would be permitted to levy a tax under the limitations imposed by the federal law (Public Law 86-272) pertaining to corporations engaged solely in interstate commerce. See ¶ 802a.

As used in these qualification tests, "another state" also means the District of Columbia, Puerto Rico, U.S. territories and possessions, and any foreign country or political subdivision.

Franchise Tax Board (FTB) Regulation 25122 provides rules for determining whether a taxpayer is taxable in another state, and gives several examples. The FTB may require proof that the taxpayer has filed a return and paid tax of the required type in another state.

● *Procedure to determine taxable income*

Where income is to be apportioned within and outside the state under the rule set forth above, the taxable income is determined by the following steps:

(1) eliminate from the total net income any "nonbusiness" income attributable to intangible assets or to other property not connected with the operation of the principal or unitary business (such items are considered allocable either wholly to California or wholly outside California, as explained in ¶ 1303);

(2) apportion the remaining net income, described as "business income," within and outside the state by means of a formula or otherwise, as explained in ¶ 1304 and 1305; and

(3) the income taxable is the amount of business income apportioned to California in step 2 plus the income (less the losses) determined in step 1 to be wholly attributable to California.

FTB Regulation 25120 provides that a single corporate entity may have more than one "trade or business." In this case the income of each business is separately apportioned inside and outside the state. Examples are provided to illustrate the determination of whether the taxpayer's activities constitute a single business or more than one. See ¶ 1304 for decisions of the State Board of Equalization (SBE) involving use of separate formulas.

● *Distinction between "business" and "nonbusiness" income*

FTB Regulation 25120 provides that income will be deemed to be "business" income, subject to apportionment, unless it is clearly classifiable as "nonbusiness" income. A series of examples is provided to illustrate the rules to be applied in determining whether income is "business" or "nonbusiness." In general, all income—including all of the types listed in ¶ 1303—is "business" income if it arises from the conduct of trade or business operations.

In Legal Ruling 98-5 (1998) (CCH CALIFORNIA TAX REPORTS ¶ 12-430.44), the FTB ruled that interest and dividend income generated from liquid assets in excess of current business needs and identified future business needs could not properly be characterized as business income. The fact that the excess income was available for business use did not make the income business income when neither the transactional nor functional test for business income was satisfied.

¶ 1302

In *Appeal of Bank of Tokyo, Limited, and Union Bank* (1995) (CCH CALIFORNIA TAX REPORTS ¶ 12-628.45), a California bank and a Japanese bank engaged in a unitary business were required to treat the Japanese bank's capital gains and dividends from investments in unrelated nonbanking companies as business income, even though a California bank could not have made the same type of investments, because the investment income was earned through a common practice in Japan in which banks own stock in companies to whom they lent funds.

In *Appeal of R.H. Macy & Co., Inc.* (1988) (CCH CALIFORNIA TAX REPORTS ¶ 12-430.701), the SBE held that interest from short-term marketable securities bought by a New York corporation engaged in retail operations in California was business income. The securities were bought with working capital awaiting use.

In the *Appeal of Inco Express, Inc.* (1987) (CCH CALIFORNIA TAX REPORTS ¶ 12-475.26), the interest earned on short-term working capital investments by a Washington-based trucking corporation was held to be business income by the SBE in the absence of a showing that the funds were earmarked for nonbusiness purposes.

In *Appeal of American Medical Buildings, Inc.* (1986) (CCH CALIFORNIA TAX REPORTS ¶ 12-475.23), the short-term investment income of a unitary construction business based in Wisconsin and engaged in business in California was held to be business income by the SBE. The income was intended to help finance the corporation's construction of medical buildings and was therefore integral to the company and apportionable to California.

In *Appeal of Louisiana-Pacific Corporation* (1986) (CCH CALIFORNIA TAX REPORTS ¶ 12-430.694), gain on the sale of a noncontrolling 50 percent stock interest in a raw materials supply affiliate was apportionable business income.

In *Appeal of Standard Oil Co. of California* (1983) (CCH CALIFORNIA TAX REPORTS ¶ 12-475.181), the taxpayer received substantial dividends from noncontrolled affiliated joint venture corporations. The joint venture corporations (Aramco and CPI) were major sources of supply for the taxpayer's worldwide activities. The SBE, in a lengthy and detailed opinion, held that the dividend income was integrally related to the taxpayer's business activities and was apportionable as part of the unitary income.

In *Appeal of Occidental Petroleum Corporation* (1983) (CCH CALIFORNIA TAX REPORTS ¶ 12-430.69), a California corporation contended that gains and losses on sale of stocks of five subsidiaries were business income, subject to apportionment. The SBE held that three of the subsidiaries were integrated parts of the unitary business, but that two of the subsidiaries were not; it followed that the gains on the latter two were nonbusiness income.

In *Appeal of Johns-Manville Sales Corporation* (1983) (CCH CALIFORNIA TAX REPORTS ¶ 12-430.691), the taxpayer contended that a loss suffered upon disposition of its 48% interest in a Belgian corporation was a business loss subject to apportionment. The SBE held that the taxpayer had not borne the burden of proving an integral relationship between its stockholding and its unitary business.

¶ 1302

In *Appeal of Joy World Corporation* (1982) (CCH CALIFORNIA TAX RE-PORTS ¶ 12-430.195), the taxpayer was one of a number of subsidiaries of a Japanese corporation. The taxpayer's principal activity was the purchase of raw cotton for sale to its parent. The business of the affiliated group was admittedly unitary. The FTB included in unitary income the gain realized by the affiliated group on the sale of certain of its securities and fixed assets; the taxpayer objected to this, using as one argument the assertion that the income involved was nonbusiness income under Japanese accounting principles. The SBE upheld the FTB.

In *The Times Mirror Co. v. Franchise Tax Board* (1980) (CCH CALIFOR-NIA TAX REPORTS ¶ 12-495.19), the parent corporation realized a capital gain on sale of stock of a subsidiary in 1969. The subsidiary was one of several that had been included in a combined return with the parent and had been treated for many years as parts of a unitary business for California tax purposes. The Court of Appeal held that the capital gain was "business" income, to be apportioned within and without the state along with other income of the unitary business.

Appeal of General Dynamics Corporation (1975) (CCH CALIFORNIA TAX REPORTS ¶ 12-495.191) involved gain on the sale of certain stock in 1967. The stock had been acquired in a complicated series of transactions that arose in the course of the unitary business. The SBE held that the gain was unitary "business income" rather than "nonbusiness income" attributable to its out-of-state situs. The SBE's opinion included this significant comment: "In deter-mining whether the income from intangibles constitutes business or nonbusi-ness income, the classifications normally given income, such as interest, dividends, or capital gains are of no assistance. The relevant inquiry is whether the income arises in the main course of the taxpayer's business operations." To the same effect, see *Appeal of Pacific Telephone and Tele-graph Co.* (1978) (CCH CALIFORNIA TAX REPORTS ¶ 12-495.49), involving business income gained on the sale of stock of an affiliated corporation that was received in a reorganization, and *Robert Half International, Inc. v. Franchise Tax Board* (1998) (CCH CALIFORNIA TAX REPORTS ¶ 12-430.43), involving a nonbusiness loss incurred on the acquisition of a warrant for stock.

● *Pertinent cases under prior law*

Under pre-1967 law, there were many decisions of the SBE and the courts dealing with the question of whether certain income was "unitary" income subject to "allocation" or was nonunitary income that was attributable en-tirely to a particular State. The reasoning of these cases should apply, generally, under present law, to the question of whether income is "business" or "nonbusiness." (However, as pointed out in the opinion in the *Times Mirror* case, discussed above, such prior-law cases cannot be used as *precedents* under the current law; also, as pointed out in the *Standard Oil* case, the pre-1967 law regarding dividends was different from current law.)

Appeal of Capital Southwest Corporation (1973) (CCH CALIFORNIA TAX REPORTS ¶ 12-495.39) involved a "small business investment company," with its head office outside California and a small office within the State. The SBE held that the taxpayer's income from dividends and capital gains was part of its unitary business income from long-term investments and was subject to apportionment.

In *Appeal of the Western Pacific Railroad Company* (1972) (CCH CALIFORNIA TAX REPORTS ¶ 12-575.26), the SBE held in 1972 that gains and losses on sales of land were not includible in unitary income subject to apportionment. The land was sold to prospective shippers to increase rail traffic, but it was never used in the unitary operations.

In *Appeal of W.J. Voit Rubber Company* (1964) (CCH CALIFORNIA TAX REPORTS ¶ 12-430.19), a California corporation sold an entire manufacturing plant located in another state. The out-of-state plant had previously been operated as part of a unitary business, and gain arising out of its sale was held to be unitary income subject to allocation within and without California. To the same effect, involving the out-of-state sale of motion pictures that had been produced in prior years in a unitary business, see *Appeal of Paramount Pictures Corp.* (1969) (CCH CALIFORNIA TAX REPORTS ¶ 12-495.69).

In *Appeal of the United States Shoe Corporation* (1959) (CCH CALIFORNIA TAX REPORTS ¶ 12-490.27), the SBE held that license fees received from licensees in foreign countries for technical information, services, advice, and manufacturing "know-how" were includible in unitary income, since the taxpayer's ability to furnish such advice and "know-how" arose out of its unitary business.

In *Appeal of Union Carbide & Carbon Corporation* (1957) (CCH CALIFORNIA TAX REPORTS ¶ 12-430.29), the SBE held that certain government project fees were part of unitary income to be allocated by formula. These fees were received for services of a managerial and technical nature, the services having been rendered at the Oak Ridge atomic energy plant and other locations outside of California. The SBE's decision was based on the reasoning that the fees were received for the use of skills developed in the taxpayer's regular business operations.

In *Appeal of International Business Machines Corp.* (1954) (CCH CALIFORNIA TAX REPORTS ¶ 12-490.27), the SBE held that royalty income of a foreign corporation was part of its unitary income and subject to allocation. In this case the corporation received large royalties for the use of its patents in foreign countries. The patents had been developed and were used in the corporation's regular business operations in this country. To the same effect, see *Appeal of National Cylinder Gas Company* (1957) (CCH CALIFORNIA TAX REPORTS ¶ 12-490.21) and *Appeal of Rockwell Manufacturing Company* (1958) (CCH CALIFORNIA TAX REPORTS ¶ 12-490.21).

● *Cases decided under UDITPA*

Later cases, involving the Uniform Division of Income for Tax Purposes Act that became effective in 1967, follow the pattern of the prior-law cases discussed above. In *Appeal of New York Football Giants, Inc.* (1977) (CCH CALIFORNIA TAX REPORTS ¶ 12-495.81), the SBE held that compensation to an out-of-state corporation for loss of a franchise was part of unitary "business income" to be allocated by formula. In *Appeal of Borden, Inc.* (1977) (CCH CALIFORNIA TAX REPORTS ¶ 12-495.45), the SBE held that losses on sale of a California plant and goodwill were "business income" subject to formula

¶ 1302

allocation. In *Appeal of Calavo Growers of California* (1984) (CCH CALIFORNIA TAX REPORTS ¶ 12-430.193), it was held that gain on the sale of Florida citrus groves was "business income"; the groves had been acquired in an earlier year upon default of a company to which the taxpayer had made loans. In *Appeal of Triangle Publications, Inc.* (1984) (CCH CALIFORNIA TAX REPORTS ¶ 12-430.192), the SBE cited and followed the *Borden* and *Calavo Growers* cases. In *Appeal of Kroehler Manufacturing Co.* (1977) (CCH CALIFORNIA TAX REPORTS ¶ 12-430.23), the SBE held that rebates received upon liquidation of the pension plan of a predecessor corporation were "business income" subject to formula apportionment. In *Appeal of Thor Power Tool Company* (1980) (CCH CALIFORNIA TAX REPORTS ¶ 12-495.42), the SBE held that gain on sale of land (former plant site) was "business income." In *Appeal of Fairchild Industries, Inc.* (1980) (CCH CALIFORNIA TAX REPORTS ¶ 12-490.35) the SBE held that gain on sale of patent rights was "business income."

The cases have held that the present law provides two alternative tests for determining what is "business income": the "transactional test" and the "functional test." For a discussion of these tests, see the decision of the SBE in *Appeal of DPF, Inc.* (1980) (CCH CALIFORNIA TAX REPORTS ¶ 12-430.25). In that case the SBE decided that gain on repurchase of debentures was "business income." On the other hand, in *Appeal of Beck Industries* (1982) (CCH CALIFORNIA TAX REPORTS ¶ 12-430.703) the SBE applied the two tests and found that interest received on certificates of deposit was nonbusiness income; in that case the deposited funds arose from selling discontinued business interests during a bankruptcy reorganization. However, interest income from short-term investment of excess funds was held to be business income in *Appeal of A. Epstein and Sons, Inc.* (1984) (CCH CALIFORNIA TAX REPORTS ¶ 12-500.604).

In two 1977 decisions involving UDITPA, the SBE held that real estate rentals were "business income" subject to formula allocation. See *Appeal of Isador Weinstein Investment Co.* (CCH CALIFORNIA TAX REPORTS ¶ 12-485.19) and *Appeal of O.K. Earl Corp.* (CCH CALIFORNIA TAX REPORTS ¶ 12-485.15).

¶ 1303 Allocation of Nonbusiness Income—General

Law: Secs. 25123-27 (CCH CALIFORNIA TAX REPORTS ¶ 12-475—12-495).

Comparable Federal: None.

As explained at ¶ 1302, most income is deemed to be "business" income—regardless of the form or type of income involved—but some is clearly classifiable as "nonbusiness." The law provides specific rules, discussed below, for the treatment of certain types of income, to the extent that they constitute "nonbusiness" income.

1. Net rents and royalties from real property, and gains and losses from the sale thereof, are allocable to the state in which the property is located.

2. Net rents and royalties from tangible personal property are allocable to the state in which the property is utilized. However, if the taxpayer was not organized in, or is not taxable in, the state in which the property is utilized, such income is taxable in the state of the owner's commercial domicile. If tangible personal property is utilized in more than one state, the income is allocated on the basis of the number of days

of physical location within and without California during the rental or royalty period of the income year. If the physical location during the period is unknown or unascertainable by the taxpayer, the property is deemed utilized in the state in which the property is located at the time the payer of the rent or royalty obtained possession.

3. Gains and losses from sale of tangible personal property are allocable to the state where the property is located at the time of sale. However, if the taxpayer is not taxable in the state in which the property is located at the time of sale, the gain or loss is allocable to the state of the taxpayer's commercial domicile.

4. Interest and dividends, as well as gains and losses from sale of intangible personal property, are allocable entirely to the state of the taxpayer's commercial domicile.

5. Patent and copyright royalties are allocable to the state in which the patent or copyright is utilized by the payer of the royalties. However, if the taxpayer is not taxable in the state in which the property is utilized, the royalty income is allocable to the state of commercial domicile. If a patent is utilized in more than one state in production, fabrication, manufacturing, etc., or if a patented product is produced in more than one state, the royalty income is allocable to the states of utilization on the basis of gross royalty receipts. However, if the taxpayer fails to maintain accounting records to reflect the states of utilization, the entire amount is allocable to the state of the taxpayer's commercial domicile. A copyright is deemed to be utilized in the state in which printing or other publication originates.

● *What is "commercial domicile"?*

The law defines "commercial domicile" as "the principal place from which the trade or business of the taxpayer is directed or managed." This is generally similar to the pre-1967 law, so the reasoning of the 1955 decision of the California District Court of Appeal in *Pacific Western Oil Corp. v. Franchise Tax Board* (CCH CALIFORNIA TAX REPORTS ¶ 12-475.171) presumably would be applicable under present law. In that case, the taxpayer was a Delaware corporation and received income from dividends, interest, and gains from sale of securities at its offices in New Jersey. However, it was held that the taxpayer's commercial domicile was in California and, therefore, the income from the intangibles was includible in the measure of the franchise tax. Important factors influencing the decision were: (1) revenue from sales of products was greater in California than in all other states combined, (2) the value of the fixed assets in California was several times greater than those located in other states, (3) over 90% of the employees were performing services in California, (4) the principal accounting records were kept in California, (5) the income from the intangibles had not been taxed by any other state, and (6) the federal income tax returns were filed in California.

In *Appeal of Vinnell Corporation* (1978) (CCH CALIFORNIA TAX REPORTS ¶ 12-480.30), the taxpayer (a predecessor corporation) was a wholly-owned subsidiary of a California corporation. The taxpayer was incorporated in Panama and was engaged in the construction business entirely outside the United States. The State Board of Equalization (SBE) held that the taxpayer's commercial domicile was not in California, although there were some contacts with California. The SBE dismissed the contacts as "artificial and lacking in substance" and commented that the concept of commercial domicile that has been developed by the courts is an "intensely practical" one.

In *Appeal of Norton Simon, Inc.* (1972) (CCH CALIFORNIA TAX REPORTS ¶ 12-480.15), the SBE held that the commercial domicile of a predecessor corporation (Harbor Plywood) was in California. The SBE held that "the essence of the concept of commercial domicile is that is the place where the corporate management functions, the place where real control exists . . ."

In *Appeal of Bristol-Myers Company* (1972) (CCH CALIFORNIA TAX REPORTS ¶ 12-495.53), a New York company suffered losses on its investment in a nonunitary subsidiary located in California. The corporation claimed deduction of the losses for franchise tax purposes, contending that it had commercial domiciles in both New York and California. The SBE held that the losses were attributable to New York, the state of the parent corporation's only domicile, and were not deductible.

● *Share of out-of-state partnership loss*

In *Appeal of The National Dollar Stores, Ltd.* (1986) (CCH CALIFORNIA TAX REPORTS ¶ 12-430.653), losses from an oil and gas drilling partnership in Colorado incurred by a California clothing retailer were nonbusiness income, unrelated to the retailer's unitary retail sales business. The losses were attributable to Colorado and not deductible.

In *Appeal of Custom Component Switches, Inc.* (1977) (CCH CALIFORNIA TAX REPORTS ¶ 12-480.32), a California corporation was a manufacturer of electrical equipment and was a member of a real estate partnership. The SBE held that partnership losses attributable to out-of-state property were from sources outside California and were not deductible.

● *Intercompany dividends*

Dividends received by one member from another member of a group of affiliated corporations filing a combined California report are excluded from income, to the extent such dividends are paid out of unitary income. In *Appeal of Louisiana-Pacific Corporation* (1987) (CCH CALIFORNIA TAX REPORTS ¶ 12-430.694), the exclusion for intercompany dividends paid from unitary income did not apply to distributions made prior to the time the payor corporation became a member of the unitary business.

● *Royalty income*

In the *Appeal of Masonite Corporation* (1987) (CCH CALIFORNIA TAX REPORTS ¶ 12-430.653), income derived from the production of oil and gas from reserves underlying taxpayer's Mississippi timberlands was nonbusiness income. The SBE held that income was unrelated to the taxpayer's unitary wood-products business because the oil production activities were, in fact, detrimental to the timberlands.

● *Allocation of gain or loss on sale of partnership interests*

An interstate or international corporation that sells a partnership interest must use an allocation formula to determine the portion of capital gain or loss realized from the sale that must be attributed to California taxable income. The allocation formula is based on the relationship that the original cost of the partnership's tangible property located in California bears to the original cost of all the partnership's tangible property. In the event that more than 50% of the partnership's assets consists of intangible property, the allocation to California income of the gain or loss realized must be determined by using the ratio of the partnership's California sales to the partnership's total sales during the first full tax period preceding the sale of the partnership interest.

¶ 1304 Methods of Apportioning Business Income

> *Law:* Secs. 25128, 25137 (CCH CALIFORNIA TAX REPORTS ¶ 12-500, 12-550—12-610).
>
> *Comparable Federal:* None.

The law provides detailed rules for apportionment of business income by formula. It also provides for use of separate accounting where apportionment by formula does not fairly reflect the extent of the taxpayer's business activity in the state, and permits the taxpayer to petition for use of separate accounting.

● *FTB policy on apportionment, separate accounting, and decombination*

Until recent years, it was the consistent policy of the Franchise Tax Board (FTB) to find business operations unitary (and thus require apportionment or, if separate affiliates were involved, combined reporting) if sufficient, minimum unitary criteria were met. For example, operations were generally considered unitary if there was any flow of goods or benefits between the part of the business within and the part outside the state, or where one part contributed directly or indirectly to the other. Examples of such relationships would be one division purchasing materials or merchandise from another; insurance or pension plans handled jointly; advertising done on a cooperative basis; centralized purchasing, selling, engineering accounting, financing, etc.

In August 1992, however, the FTB issued revised audit guidelines with respect to the unitary combination of diverse businesses (*FTB Notice No. 92-4*, CCH CALIFORNIA TAX REPORTS ¶ 12-500.63). According to the revised guidelines, there is no unique test for evaluating unity in diverse business cases. Unity may be established under any of the judicially acceptable tests (the three unities, contribution or dependency, and flow of value tests) and may not be denied merely because another of those tests does not simultaneously apply, i.e., the tests are not mutually exclusive. In addition, a lack of functional integration will not prevent a finding of unity. On the other hand, the fact that functionally integrated businesses may be found to be unitary does not mean that functional integration is a *requirement* for unity.

Also, presumptions of unity under Reg. 25120(b), which states that the activities of a taxpayer will be considered a single business if there is evidence to indicate that the segments under consideration are integrated with, depend on, or contribute to, each other and the operations of the taxpayer as a whole, although important considerations, are not conclusive in determining unity.

Finally, the guidelines state that *Mole-Richardson, Dental Insurance Consultants,* and *Tenneco West, Inc.* (all discussed below) are controlling of

¶ 1304

the diverse business issue and that State Board of Equalization (SBE) decisions that are not in accord with these cases should not be relied upon.

If the operations of a business are "unitary" in nature, it makes no difference whether there is only one corporation or an affiliated group. Consolidation and income-apportionment of a large group of corporations may be required even where only one of the corporations is subject to California tax. See *Edison California Stores* and other cases discussed below. See also ¶ 1309.

The FTB has issued a legal ruling containing guidelines for determining whether the "unity of ownership" requirement for unitary treatment is satisfied (see below) (*FTB Legal Ruling No.* 91-1, November 12, 1991, CCH CALIFORNIA TAX REPORTS ¶ 12-500.52).

● *Leading cases*

The courts have developed three general tests for determining whether a business is "unitary." These are (1) the three unities test, in the *Butler Brothers* case, (2) the contribution and dependency test, in the *Edison California Stores* case, and (3) the functional integration test, in the *Container* case. The existence of a unitary business is established if any of the three tests is met.

In *Butler Brothers v. McColgan* (1942) (CCH CALIFORNIA TAX REPORTS ¶ 12-500.15), the U.S. Supreme Court upheld use of the allocation formula (equivalent to the "apportionment" formula under present law) in preference to separate accounting. In that case the taxpayer corporation operated a number of stores throughout the country, one of which was in California. The unitary nature of the business was held to have been definitely established by the presence of the following factors:

    1. unity of ownership;

    2. unity of operation as evidenced by central purchasing, advertising, accounting, and management divisions; and

    3. unity of use in its centralized executive force and general system of operation.

Separate accounting showed a large loss for the California store, whereas application of the formula resulted in a substantial profit allocable to California. Nevertheless, the court upheld the use of the formula, since the taxpayer did not demonstrate convincingly that the formula produced a clearly unreasonable result and that separate accounting fairly and accurately reflected the income properly allocable to California.

In *Container Corporation of America v. Franchise Tax Board* (1983) (CCH CALIFORNIA TAX REPORTS ¶ 12-500.55), the U.S. Supreme Court upheld the application of the standard three-factor apportionment formula to a domestic corporation and several foreign subsidiaries. The court held that the parent and subsidiaries were unitary because they were linked by common managerial or operational resources that produced economies of scale and transfers of value. The court stated that whether businesses are unitary is determined by whether contributions to income result from functional integration, centralization of management, and economies of scale. Other issues in *Container Corporation of America* are discussed at ¶ 1309.

¶ 1304

In *Edison California Stores, Inc. v. McColgan* (1947) (CCH CALIFORNIA TAX REPORTS ¶ 12-500.17), the California Supreme Court held that the allocation formula (equivalent to the "apportionment" formula under present law) was properly applicable to the combined income of a California corporation and its foreign parent corporation and other subsidiaries. The taxpayer produced evidence to show that its separate accounting for the subsidiary was reasonable and proper, but the court held that the taxpayer had not met the burden of proving that the consolidation and the allocation formula produced an unreasonable result. The court stated clearly its test of whether or not a business is unitary: "If the operation of the portion of the business done within the state is dependent upon or contributes to the operation of the business without the state, the operations are unitary . . . ."

● *Other cases holding business to be unitary*

Over the years there have been many decisions of the courts and the SBE that have followed the lead of the *Butler Brothers* and *Edison* cases and have held that businesses were unitary. The following brief summaries of these cases will provide a "feel" for the trend of the decisions.

For a later case that followed *Butler Brothers* in a somewhat similar situation, see the SBE opinion in *Appeal of Ohrbach's, Inc.* (1961) (CCH CALIFORNIA TAX REPORTS ¶ 12-500.603). The taxpayer operated department stores in New York and California.

In *Appeal of PBS Building Systems, Inc., and PKH Building Systems* (1994) (CCH CALIFORNIA TAX REPORTS ¶ 12-500.831), the SBE held that a "passive" holding company was engaged in a unitary business with its operating subsidiary for combined reporting purposes, as evidenced by a complete overlap of officers and directors and extensive intercompany financing consisting of loans, loan guarantees, debt refinancing, debt reduction, and a covenant not to compete that was purchased by the holding company for the benefit of its subsidiary. Because "passive" holding companies are fully capable of providing and receiving a flow of value to or from an operating subsidiary, the factors to consider in determining whether a holding company is unitary with its operating subsidiaries are the same factors that must be considered with respect to any other business enterprise.

In *Dental Insurance Consultants, Inc. v. State Franchise Tax Board* (1991) (CCH CALIFORNIA TAX REPORTS ¶ 12-500.631), a court of appeal held that a dental insurance consulting corporation and its wholly owned farming subsidiary were engaged in a unitary enterprise. Although the FTB argued that the three unities test should be abandoned in favor of the functional integration test, the court determined that application of both tests was proper because they were not mutually exclusive. The court held that under both the three unities test and the functional integration test, the corporations were unitary. In addition, the court held that application of the dependency and contribution test was unnecessary because its use would result in the same conclusion yielded by the three unities test.

In *Mole-Richardson v. Franchise Tax Board* (1990) (CCH CALIFORNIA TAX REPORTS ¶ 12-500.633), a court of appeal held that a group of commonly owned and centrally managed corporations that did business both inside and outside of California constituted a unitary business even though the business they engaged in inside California was primarily the manufacture and sale of lighting equipment and the business they engaged in outside of California was primarily ranching. The court rejected the FTB's argument that the corporations constituted two distinct business groups because they were not "functionally integrated." In doing so, the court stated that "functional integration" was not a new concept by which business enterprises must be evaluated to justify unitary treatment. Moreover, the court held that the presence of strong centralized management and economies of scale was evidence that the corporations were functionally integrated.

In *Appeal of Capital Industries—EMI, Inc.* (1989) (CCH CALIFORNIA TAX REPORTS ¶ 12-500.551), a California corporation that produced and sold recorded music, sheet music, and blank audio tapes was engaged in a unitary business with its British parent, which conducted similar activities on a worldwide basis. Factors considered by the SBE as supporting unity were intercompany matrix agreements, intercompany sales, transfers of key personnel, common directors, joint use of key labels, intercompany financing, mutual international promotional activities, and exercise of parental control over the distribution of the music of the parent's artists.

In *Appeal of Trails End, Inc.* (1986) (CCH CALIFORNIA TAX REPORTS ¶ 12-500.605), the SBE denied rehearing an earlier decision that a California plastics manufacturer, a California vitamin manufacturer, and a Michigan corporation were in a unitary business relationship. The plastics manufacturer was a subsidiary of the vitamin manufacturer, which was itself a subsidiary of and engaged in a unitary business with the Michigan corporation. It is necessary in establishing unity only that the business within California is dependent upon or contributes to the business outside California, and it is the aggregate effect of one company on another that determines unity. The relationship between the plastics manufacturer and the Michigan corporation did not need to be direct to establish a unitary relationship; it was sufficient for franchise tax purposes if the unitary business relationship was indirect. Thus, because the plastics manufacturer was found to be engaged in a unitary business with the vitamin manufacturer, its operations could not justifiably be separated from the unitary operation of the Michigan corporation and the vitamin manufacturer.

In *Appeal of Atlas Hotels, Inc., et al.* (1985) (CCH CALIFORNIA TAX REPORTS ¶ 12-500.567), the taxpayer was in the hotel business and its subsidiary was in the restaurant business. The SBE found that the subsidiary became "instantly unitary" with the parent's unitary business from the date of its acquisition when there was evidence that many of the managerial and operational changes that demonstrated the subsidiary's integration with its parent not only were implemented immediately upon acquisition, but were planned or commenced well before the actual acquisition date.

In *Appeal of Allstate Enterprises, Inc., et al.* (1984) (CCH CALIFORNIA TAX REPORTS ¶ 12-500.567), the taxpayer and several affiliated corporations were engaged in providing vehicle financing and motor club services. Another subsidiary was engaged in the mortgage banking business, and the taxpayer contended that this corporation should not be included in the unitary group. The SBE held that the mortgage banking business was a part of a unitary operation.

¶ 1304

In *Appeal of Lancaster Colony Corporation and August Barr, Inc.* (1984) (CCH CALIFORNIA TAX REPORTS ¶ 12-500.569), there were seven divisions and fourteen subsidiaries engaged in a wide variety of industrial and consumer businesses. The SBE held that the operations constituted a single unitary business, based on flow of goods, supplying of administrative and technical services, interlocking officers and directors, and other indications of unity.

Appeal of Data General Corporation (1982) (CCH CALIFORNIA TAX REPORTS ¶ 12-500.321) involved a Delaware corporation that conducted a worldwide business in computers and related products with four domestic and twelve foreign subsidiaries. The SBE held that the group met both the "unity" and "dependency" tests for a unitary operation: the SBE referred to the taxpayer's public reports as one indication of the centralization and integration of management and operations.

In *Appeal of Kikkoman International, Inc.* (1982) (CCH CALIFORNIA TAX REPORTS ¶ 12-500.574), the taxpayer was a 70% owned California subsidiary of a prominent Japanese company. The taxpayer contended that the income attributable to California could be determined fairly only by separate accounting, because the property and payroll factors did not account for the disparity between California and Japan in property costs and wages. The SBE held that the companies were "a classic example of the type of vertically integrated enterprise to which the unitary concept has been applied," and required use of the standard apportionment formula.

See ¶ 1309 for discussion of other cases involving foreign operations, including the 1983 decision of the U.S. Supreme Court in the case of *Container Corporation of America.*

In *Appeal of Beck/Arnley Corporation of California* (1981) (CCH CALIFORNIA TAX REPORTS ¶ 12-500.32), the taxpayer was the wholly-owned subsidiary of a New York corporation. Both corporations were engaged in the sale of automobile parts and accessories. The SBE held that the operations were unitary under either the "unity" test or the "contribution and dependency" tests.

In *Appeal of Credit Bureau Central, Inc.* (1981) (CCH CALIFORNIA TAX REPORTS ¶ 12-500.58), a California corporation was one of 14 wholly owned subsidiaries of a Georgia corporation. All of the subsidiaries operated as collection agencies. The SBE held that the operations were unitary, based largely on centralized executive and management services.

In *Appeal of National Silver Co.* (1980) (CCH CALIFORNIA TAX REPORTS ¶ 12-500.555), the taxpayer was engaged in the marketing of houseware products. The corporation had various relationships with two affiliated out-of-state corporations and purchased ten percent of the output of one of the affiliates. The SBE held that the businesses of the three corporations were unitary.

In *Appeal of L&B Manufacturing Co.* (1980) (CCH CALIFORNIA TAX REPORTS ¶ 12-500.554), the taxpayer was a member of an affiliated group of seven corporations engaged in the restaurant and hotel furnishings business. The SBE held that the business was unitary, since the taxpayer did not carry the burden of proof to the contrary under either the "unity" or the "dependency" test.

¶ 1304

In *Appeal of Wynn Oil Company* (1980) (CCH CALIFORNIA TAX REPORTS ¶ 206-308), the taxpayer was engaged primarily in the manufacture and distribution of petrochemical products. The corporation supplied active management direction and services to a subsidiary that operated student dormitories on college campuses. The SBE held that, despite their diverse nature, the businesses of the parent and subsidiary were unitary. However, a 1990 decision of the SBE ruled that this decision has "no continuing validity as precedent" because the test following the U.S. Supreme Court decision in *Container Corporation v. FTB* requires an analysis on evidence of a functionally integrated enterprise (see *Appeal of Meadows Realty Co.* (1990), CCH CALIFORNIA TAX REPORTS ¶ 12-500.90).

In *Allright Cal., Inc.* (1979) (CCH CALIFORNIA TAX REPORTS ¶ 12-500.521), the taxpayer was one of 95 subsidiaries of a Texas corporation. The affiliated corporations operated a nationwide network of automobile parking lots. The SBE cited the *John Deere Plow Co.* case, discussed below (and others), and held that the operations were unitary and subject to formula apportionment. Principal unitary factors were ownership, interlocking officers and directors, centralized overhead functions, common pension plan, and parent-supplied financing and other services.

In *Appeals of Cascade Dental Laboratory, Inc., et al.* (1978) (CCH CALIFORNIA TAX REPORTS ¶ 12-500.581), the taxpayers were dental-laboratory subsidiaries of a health-service company that had its headquarters in Texas. The SBE held that the business was not unitary in the first year at issue, but that the character of the operation changed to the point that the business was unitary in later years.

In *Appeal of Parador Mining Co., Inc.* (1977) (CCH CALIFORNIA TAX REPORTS ¶ 12-500.585), the taxpayer was a closely held corporation engaged in mineral exploration. Most of its business was conducted in the home of the president and chief stockholder. The SBE held that the business was unitary and that its California income must be determined by formula rather than by separate accounting.

In *Appeal of Isador Weinstein Investment Co.* (1977) (CCH CALIFORNIA TAX REPORTS ¶ 12-485.19), the taxpayer's principal activity was real estate rentals. The SBE held that the operation was unitary and was subject to formula allocation. To the same effect, see *Appeal of O.K. Earl Corp.* (1977) (CCH CALIFORNIA TAX REPORTS ¶ 12-485.15), involving a variety of related activities in addition to real estate rentals.

Appeal of Beecham, Inc. (1977) (CCH CALIFORNIA TAX REPORTS ¶ 12-500.586) involved a large conglomerate with an English parent company. The SBE held that the business was unitary and that the income of the entire group was subject to allocation by formula. Although the propriety of including the foreign parent and its foreign subsidiaries was not a primary issue in the case, the SBE pointed out that in earlier cases the income of foreign subsidiaries has been held to be includible in a combined report and commented: "We are unable to discern any difference when the foreign corporation is the parent rather than the subsidiary."

In *Appeal of Putnam Fund Distributors, Inc., et al.* (1977) (CCH CALIFORNIA TAX REPORTS ¶ 12-500.5894), the SBE held that a Massachusetts mutual-fund-management company was engaged in a unitary operation with a 51% owned California corporation and other subsidiaries; the subsidiaries were engaged principally in sales activities.

In *Appeal of Automated Building Components, Inc.* (1976) (CCH CALIFORNIA TAX REPORTS ¶ 12-500.593), the taxpayer was a Florida corporation that had an operation in California and had foreign subsidiaries. The SBE held that the group was engaged in a unitary operation that required a combined report as discussed in ¶ 1309. The SBE's opinion discusses the general tests established in the *Butler Brothers* and *Edison California Stores* cases, and concludes that "a unitary business exists if *either* the three unities or the contribution or dependency tests are satisfied" (emphasis supplied).

In *Appeal of Grolier Society, Inc.* (1975) (CCH CALIFORNIA TAX REPORTS ¶ 12-500.5895), the SBE held that five Canadian subsidiaries and four Latin American subsidiaries were engaged in a unitary business with the taxpayer, its parent, and other subsidiaries.

In *Appeal of Harbison-Walker Refractories Company* (1972) (CCH CALIFORNIA TAX REPORTS ¶ 12-500.5896), the SBE decided that a Pennsylvania corporation and its Canadian subsidiary were engaged in a unitary business. The corporations had common officers and directors, common purchases, intercompany purchases and sales, and an intercompany management fee.

In *Appeal of Anchor Hocking Glass Corporation* (1967) (CCH CALIFORNIA TAX REPORTS ¶ 12-500.563), the SBE held that the use of common trademarks and patents and the interchange of "know-how" were significant factors in determining the existence of a unitary business between a U.S. parent and its foreign and domestic subsidiaries.

In *Appeal of Cutter Laboratories* (1964) (CCH CALIFORNIA TAX REPORTS ¶ 12-500.564), the SBE held that a parent corporation manufacturing and selling vaccines and pharmaceuticals for both human and animal consumption was engaged in a unitary business with its wholly owned subsidiary operating in another State in the manufacture and sale of veterinary instruments and animal vaccines. The taxpayer's contention that the corporations were engaged in different types of business was rejected when the two corporations were found to be closely related through common officers and directors, interstate flow of products, and joint participation in insurance, retirement, and automobile leasing plans.

In *Appeal of Youngstown Steel Products Company of California* (1952) (CCH CALIFORNIA TAX REPORTS ¶ 12-550.311), the SBE upheld the application of the allocation formula to the combined income of three corporations, only one of which operated in California, despite the fact that the California corporation operated under an "arm's-length" contractual arrangement similar to a previous arrangement with an unrelated corporation.

In *John Deere Plow Co. v. Franchise Tax Board* (1951) (CCH CALIFORNIA TAX REPORTS ¶ 12-500.560), the California Supreme Court upheld the FTB in applying the allocation formula to the combined income of a parent corporation and 84 subsidiaries, only one of which was doing business in California. The taxpayer contended unsuccessfully that use of the allocation formula was unreasonable because the income of the California branch was overstated rather than understated by the use of separate accounting. The taxpayer's

¶ 1304

argument was based partly on the fact that no charge had been made to the California branch for services rendered to it by the central office of the affiliated group.

● *Unity of ownership*

The FTB has issued detailed guidelines for determining whether ownership of a group of corporations satisfies the "unity of ownership" standard (*FTB Legal Ruling No. 91-1, supra*). Generally, unity of ownership is established only when the same interests directly or indirectly own or control more than 50% of the voting stock of all members of the purported unitary group. "Indirect ownership" may include direct ownership and control of more than half the voting stock of a corporation that in turn directly owns and controls the requisite amount of voting stock in another corporation. Likewise, "indirect control" includes control exercised through ownership or control of an intermediary corporation. "Direct control" of voting stock includes ownership of the voting rights alone, pursuant to a binding and permanent legal transfer of those rights.

The requisite control may also be exercised by a group of shareholders acting in concert. In *Rain Bird Sprinkler Mfg. Corp. v. FTB* (1991) (CCH California Tax Reports ¶ 12-500.524), seventeen corporations that were operated as a single business enterprise constituted a unitary business even though no *single* individual or entity held a majority interest in all of the corporations. The court held that "unity of ownership" existed because members of the same family held the majority of the voting stock in each of the corporations, and all of the stock of each corporation was subject to written stock purchase agreements prohibiting transfer to outsiders. According to the FTB, application of the "concerted ownership or control" principle of *Rain Bird* is not limited to members of the same family. Factors to be considered in determining whether a group of shareholders exercises concerted ownership or control of several corporations include the business relationships of the corporations involved, the relationships between the shareholders, the degree of common ownership, common voting patterns, and each shareholder's relative percentage of ownership or control. A similar conclusion was reached in *Appeal of AMP, Inc.* (1996) (CCH California Tax Reports, ¶ 12-500.529).

● *Cases holding business to be nonunitary*

In *Appeal of F.W. Woolworth Co. et al.* (1998) (CCH California Tax Reports ¶ 12-500.20), a California court of appeal held that a parent corporation was not engaged in a unitary business with its wholly owned subsidiary, because they were not in the same general line of business. The parent conducted a mass merchandising business in apparel and general merchandise and the subsidiary was engaged primarily in the manufacture and sale of shoes and there was not strong centralization of the management of the two corporations.

In *Appeal of Hearst Corporation* (1992) (CCH California Tax Reports ¶ 12-500.3291), a domestic corporation that was engaged in various business activities, including publication of newspapers, books, and magazines, was not engaged in a unitary business with its wholly owned foreign subsidiary, which published books and magazines in the United Kingdom. The taxpayer rebut-

¶ 1304

ted the presumption that the businesses were unitary by providing evidence that they had separate editorial, writing, and photographic staffs and that intercompany sales and use of material were extremely minimal. Additionally, the SBE found that no phase of the subsidiary's operations was actually integrated with the taxpayer's operations.

In *Tenneco West, Inc. v. Franchise Tax Board* (1991) (CCH CALIFORNIA TAX REPORTS ¶ 12-500.632), a court of appeal held that the taxpayer, which was in the oil and gas business, and its subsidiaries, which were in the business of shipbuilding, packaging, manufacturing automotive parts, manufacturing equipment used in construction, and farming, were not unitary. The court determined that there was no strong centralized management and that the subsidiaries were engaged in diverse activities unrelated to the parent's business and thus lacked integration.

In *Appeal of Meadows Realty Company et al.* (1990) (CCH CALIFORNIA TAX REPORTS ¶ 12-500.90), unity did not exist between a parent corporation's oil refining activities and its subsidiary's realty development activities even though the subsidiary received financial assistance and management services from the parent corporation. The SBE indicated that "functional integration" was required to establish the existence of a unitary business.

In *Appeal of Postal Press* (1987) (CCH CALIFORNIA TAX REPORTS ¶ 12-500.329), the SBE held that a 68.3% ownership of a subsidiary's stock by a taxpayer was insufficient to prove that it was engaged in a unitary business. The taxpayer specialized in commercial printing and its subsidiary specialized in instant printing. The SBE found that, despite the stock ownership and use of similar trademarks and names, other indications of unity, such as common management and operations, were absent.

In *Appeal of Nevis Industries, Inc.,* (1985) (CCH CALIFORNIA TAX REPORTS ¶ 12-500.31), ownership of a Nevada corporation and eight affiliated companies was shared equally (never exceeding 50 percent) by two brothers. The California Supreme Court held that the businesses were not unitary because no single entity owned more than 50 percent and had controlling interest in any of the involved companies. Stock owned directly or indirectly by family members is not attributed to other family members, for purposes of determining unity of ownership.

In *Appeal of Coachmen Industries of California* (1985) (CCH CALIFORNIA TAX REPORTS ¶ 12-500.567), the SBE found that a California company's evidence of independence from its Indiana parent was insufficient to prove it was not engaged in a unitary business. A number of factors, when taken in the aggregate, indicated that the two companies were involved in a single economic enterprise. The connections that indicated a unitary relationship included almost identical businesses, interlocking officers and directors, intercompany product flow, shared purchasing, exclusively intercompany financing, and shared group life and health insurance.

Appeal of The Grupe Company et al. (1985) (CCH CALIFORNIA TAX REPORTS ¶ 12-500.324) was another case in which the taxpayer contended that two businesses were unitary but was overruled by the SBE. In this case, land development operations were conducted in California and an alfalfa farm was operated on leased land in Nevada.

¶ **1304**

In *Appeal of Vidal Sassoon of New York, Inc.* (1984) (CCH CALIFORNIA TAX REPORTS ¶ 12-500.327), the taxpayer and 19 affiliated corporations operated hairdressing salons in the United States, Canada, and Europe under the common name "Sassoon." The SBE held that the operations in Europe were not unitary with those in the United States.

In *Appeals of Dynamic Speaker Corporation* and *Talone Packing Company* (1984) (CCH CALIFORNIA TAX REPORTS ¶ 12-500.327), the parent company of the taxpayers and six subsidiaries were engaged in a variety of diverse businesses. Although there were some unitary factors, the SBE held that the operations were not unitary. To the same effect, see also *Appeal of P and M Lumber Products, Inc.* (1984) (CCH CALIFORNIA TAX REPORTS ¶ 12-500.45) and *Appeal of Berry Enterprises, Inc.* (1986) (CCH CALIFORNIA TAX REPORTS ¶ 12-500.5672). In these cases, the taxpayers had contended that the businesses were unitary.

In *Appeals of Santa Anita Consolidated, Inc., et al.* (1984) (CCH CALIFORNIA TAX REPORTS ¶ 12-500.3294), the taxpayer and its four subsidiaries were engaged in a variety of activities including operation of a racetrack, transportation of automobiles, real estate development, etc. Although there were some unitary factors in management and operation, the SBE held that the business did not constitute a "functionally integrated enterprise" and was not unitary.

To the same effect, see *Appeal of Bredero California, Inc., Bredero Consulting, Inc., and Best Blocks, Inc.* (1986) (CCH CALIFORNIA TAX REPORTS ¶ 12-500.5673). Also to the same effect, see *Appeals of Andreini & Company and Ash Slough Vineyards, Inc.* (1986) (CCH CALIFORNIA TAX REPORTS ¶ 12-500.328), in which an agricultural insurance brokerage was found not to constitute a unitary business with its vineyard subsidiary.

In *Appeal of Holloway Investment Company* (1983) (CCH CALIFORNIA TAX REPORTS ¶ 12-500.431), the taxpayer held a variety of apparently unrelated property interests in California and Illinois. Citing some of the cases discussed below and also the U.S. Supreme Court decision in *Container Corporation* (see ¶ 1309), the SBE held that the business was not unitary.

In *Appeal of Unitco, Inc.* (1983) (CCH CALIFORNIA TAX REPORTS ¶ 12-500.36), the taxpayer was a closely held corporation that owned rental properties in California and three other states. The FTB contended that the operations were unitary, based largely on the similarity of activities in the four states and the personal participation of the three owner-officers in policy decisions. The SBE held that the business was not unitary, commenting that "at best, the suggested unitary connections are superficial and trivial."

In *Bay Alarm Company* (1982) (CCH CALIFORNIA TAX REPORTS ¶ 12-500.251), a California corporation had a burglar alarm business in California, an investment portfolio, and a cattle ranch in New Mexico. The SBE upheld the FTB in holding that the activities did not constitute a unitary business. To the same effect, see *Appeal of Myles Circuits, Inc.* (1982) (CCH CALIFORNIA TAX REPORTS ¶ 12-500.251), in which the taxpayer and its subsidiaries had a circuit breaker factory in California and a cattle ranch in Texas.

In *Appeal of Mohasco Corp.* (1982) (CCH CALIFORNIA TAX REPORTS ¶ 12-500.327), the taxpayer and its Mexican subsidiaries were engaged in the manufacture and sale of carpets and related products. Although there were some intercompany relationships and transactions, the SBE found that these were insignificant in the situation as a whole and held that the operations were not unitary.

In *Appeal of Hollywood Film Enterprises, Inc.* (1982) (CCH CALIFORNIA TAX REPORTS ¶ 12-500.322), the taxpayer operated wholly within California. It was a wholly owned subsidiary of a Delaware corporation with headquarters in New York and some operations in California. The two corporations were involved in diverse lines of business (although both involved motion picture films), but there were several intercompany activities of various kinds. In this case the taxpayer contended that the two businesses *should* be treated as unitary, while the FTB took the position that they should not. The SBE held that the taxpayer had not borne the required burden of proof that the businesses were unitary.

● *Use of separate accounting*

Despite the general preference for use of the allocation or apportionment formula, separate accounting may be permitted (or required) in some cases. The following are the principal situations where it may be used:

(a) businesses that by their nature permit accurate determination of results by separate accounting; and

(b) cases where a corporation is in entirely different businesses within and without the state, with no unitary factors present.

FTB Regulation 25137 provides that exceptions to the regular allocation formula will be permitted only where "unusual fact situations . . . produce incongruous results" under the regular rules. The regulation mentions specific industries that are subject to special treatment (see ¶ 1305a).

● *Cases upholding use of separate accounting*

In *Appeal of The National Dollar Stores, Ltd.* (1986) (CCH CALIFORNIA TAX REPORTS ¶ 12-500.327), a California clothing retail corporation was not unitary with a wholly owned subsidiary that imported and marketed Asian films. The SBE held that, though there was 100% unity of ownership, the unities of use and operation did not exist between the two. There was no evidence that either business contributed to or was dependent on the other.

In *Appeal of The Amwalt Group* (1983) (CCH CALIFORNIA TAX REPORTS ¶ 12-500.3294), a closely-held California architectural firm owned 100% of a leasing subsidiary and 80% of a heavy equipment dealership. Fiscal management was centralized and there were some intercompany transactions, and the corporations filed a combined report on a unitary basis. The FTB took the position that the operations were not unitary and required separate accounting for the three corporations; the SBE agreed.

In *Appeal of Carl M. Halvorson, Inc.* (1963) (CCH CALIFORNIA TAX REPORTS ¶ 11-287.10), the SBE held that separate accounting more clearly reflected income attributable to California by a heavy construction contractor engaged in construction projects located within and without the State. It was further held that overhead expenses were properly allocated to such projects on the basis of direct costs incurred. However, it is the policy of the FTB to require use of the apportionment formula in the construction business "where

¶ 1304

the usual tests of unitary business are met." The FTB has issued detailed regulations for apportionment of income from long-term contracts, and also detailed rules for corporate partners in joint ventures—see below and ¶ 1305a.

In *Appeal of Highland Corporation* (1959) (CCH CALIFORNIA TAX REPORTS ¶ 12-500.451), the SBE held that a business is not unitary when the only unitary factor is centralized management. The corporation operated a lumber business in Oregon, had oil interests in New Mexico, and was in the construction business and owned rental properties in California. All activities were controlled and supervised by executives who operated out of the corporation's head office, which was in California. In this case the FTB took the position that the business was not unitary and that separate accounting should be used, and the SBE agreed. To the same effect, see *Appeal of Allied Properties, Inc.* (1964) (CCH CALIFORNIA TAX REPORTS ¶ 12-500.45), involving a cattle ranch in Nevada and real estate investments in California.

● *Oil and gas operators*

The FTB for many years required oil and gas operators to use separate accounting in some situations, particularly where a profitable segment of an oil business was conducted in California while an extensive exploratory program was carried on in an out-of-state location of such magnitude as to produce deductions that offset or materially reduced the California income. However, the FTB was overruled by the SBE in a 1959 decision involving a situation of this type. In *Appeal of Holly Development Company* (CCH CALIFORNIA TAX REPORTS ¶ 12-500.602), it was held that a unitary business existed where the corporation was engaged in the acquisition and development of oil properties in both California and Texas, and the evidence showed centralized management, accounting, financing, and purchasing. To the same effect, see *Superior Oil Co. v. Franchise Tax Board* (CCH CALIFORNIA TAX REPORTS ¶ 12-500.25) and *Honolulu Oil Co. v. Franchise Tax Board* (CCH CALIFORNIA TAX REPORTS ¶ 12-500.25), both cases decided by the California Supreme Court in 1963.

Legal Ruling No. 366 (1973) (CCH CALIFORNIA TAX REPORTS ¶ 12-425.181) deals with allocation questions of unitary oil operations beyond the 3-mile continental limit. The ruling states that use of the standard allocation formula is appropriate, and provides that factors relating to offshore operations should be reflected only in the denominators of the formula; thus, no income from such operations is apportioned to California. Legal Ruling No. 396 (1976) (CCH CALIFORNIA TAX REPORTS ¶ 12-425.18) modifies the portion of Legal Ruling No. 366 pertaining to operations of drilling barges.

In the case of partnership interests in oil and gas properties that are deemed to be "tax shelters" and not part of the unitary business, income or loss has been held to be nonbusiness income allocated to the state where the oil or gas property is located. *Appeal of The National Dollar Stores, Ltd.* (1986) (CCH CALIFORNIA TAX REPORTS ¶ 12-430.653).

● *Combination of separate accounting and formula*

Where a taxpayer has more than one trade or business as discussed at ¶ 1302, it is possible to use a combination of separate accounting and the apportionment formula. One example under prior law may be found in *Appeal of Industrial Management Corporation* (1959) (CCH CALIFORNIA TAX REPORTS ¶ 12-500.451). In this case the corporation was engaged in the insecticide business both within and without California, and also was engaged in two businesses (sale of street improvement bonds and rental of real estate) solely within California. The principal office was in California. There was no unitary relationship between the insecticide business and the other two. The insecticide business showed a loss and the other two showed a profit. The SBE upheld the contention of the FTB that only the insecticide business was unitary and subject to allocation by formula; thus, the entire income of the two California businesses was taxed, with an offset for only an allocated portion of the loss on the unitary business.

In *Appeal of Hunt Foods & Industries, Inc.* (1965) (CCH CALIFORNIA TAX REPORTS ¶ 12-500.564), the FTB contended that, where the taxpayer operated a match manufacturing business and a food processing business, the income of each should be computed and allocated separately. However, the SBE held that a single allocation formula applied to the entire income of both businesses was proper, since there was common management, the products were sold in the same markets, they shared common warehouses, and other unitary factors were present.

In *Appeal of Simco, Incorporated* (1964) (CCH CALIFORNIA TAX REPORTS ¶ 12-500.43), the SBE permitted a combination of separate accounting and the allocation formula. The income of fruit orchards operated entirely in California was determined by separate accounting, and the allocation formula was applied to a farming and cattle business operated in both California and Nevada. The SBE held that centralization of management and of accounting, legal, and tax services did not mean that the entire business was unitary.

In *Appeal of Halliburton Oil Well Cementing Co.* (1955) (CCH CALIFORNIA TAX REPORTS ¶ 12-500.5897), the taxpayer was turned down in its attempt to use a combination of separate accounting and an allocation formula. The company used separate accounting for its income from service activities and from sale of purchased goods and used a (nonstandard) formula for income from sale of its own manufactured goods. The SBE upheld the FTB in requiring the use of the standard formula for both service and merchandising activities.

In *Appeal of American Writing Paper Corporation* (1952) (CCH CALIFORNIA TAX REPORTS ¶ 12-500.711), the SBE upheld the FTB in applying the allocation formula to the entire income of a foreign corporation that sold in California the products of some—but not all—of its plants. The taxpayer was unsuccessful in its contention that the income of the plants manufacturing the product sold in California should be determined by separate accounting and the allocation formula applied only to that income instead of to the entire income from operations of all plants.

● *Use of separate formulas*

As explained at ¶ 1302, separate apportionment formulas may sometimes be used for different portions of a taxpayer's business. In *Appeal of Lear Siegler, Inc.* (1967) (CCH CALIFORNIA TAX REPORTS ¶ 12-500.37), a single corporation had six separate manufacturing divisions, each operating within

¶ 1304

and without California. The SBE permitted the taxpayer to apply six separate apportionment formulas to the various divisions.

In *Appeal of United Parcel Service* (1986) (CCH CALIFORNIA TAX RE-PORTS ¶ 12-635.35), the taxpayer was a unitary business with package delivery cars that ordinarily operated within the state and tractor-trailer rigs that operated both within and without the state. The SBE, in reversing the FTB's application of separate apportionment formulas to the two classes of equipment, held that the special interim formula developed by the FTB for truckers applied to all the taxpayer's trucks whether in interstate or intrastate commerce.

● *Treatment of partnership interests*

FTB Regulation 25137-1 outlines the appropriate method for apportionment and allocation of partnership income in unitary situations where a corporation has an interest in a partnership and one or both have income from sources within and without the State. The corporation is not required to own any particular percentage of the partnership for this regulation to apply. The partnership income and apportionment factors are included in determining unitary income only to the extent of the corporation's percentage of ownership interest.

In *Appeal of Powerine Oil Company* (1985) (CCH CALIFORNIA TAX REPORTS ¶ 12-500.951), the taxpayer was engaged in oil refining and distribution and also had a 50% interest in a joint venture engaged in copper mining in California. The SBE cited the *Pittsburgh-Des Moines Steel Company* case, above, and held that the taxpayer's share of joint-venture losses could be included in determining the unitary income allocable to California.

In *Appeal of A. Epstein and Sons, Inc.* (1984) (CCH CALIFORNIA TAX REPORTS ¶ 12-500.604), the taxpayer was a member of a group of closely-held affiliated corporations under common control of two brothers. The brothers also owned a New York partnership that had been formed (because of legal requirements) to render architectural services at cost to the corporations. The SBE held that the affiliated group of corporations was engaged in a unitary business, subject to formula allocation, but denied inclusion of the partnership in the computation. See also *The National Dollar Stores, Ltd.*, under Oil and Gas Operators above.

In *Appeal of Pittsburgh-Des Moines Steel Company* (1983) (CCH CALIFORNIA TAX REPORTS ¶ 12-500.95), the taxpayer corporation was engaged in a unitary business involving various aspects of the steel business. The corporation had a 50% interest in a joint venture with a real-estate operator; the joint venture was formed to build and lease two office buildings in California. The SBE held that the corporation's share of the income and apportionment factors of the joint venture should be included in the corporation's combined report. To the same effect, see *Appeal of Willamette Industries, Inc.* (1987) (CCH CALIFORNIA TAX REPORTS ¶ 12-430.711).

In *Appeal of Saga Corp.* (1982) (CCH CALIFORNIA TAX REPORTS ¶ 12-500.570), the taxpayer corporation and subsidiaries supplied food service to colleges, hospitals, and other organizations throughout the United States. The corporation owned 50.51% of another corporation that developed and managed off-campus student dining and housing facilities in California and elsewhere; the subsidiary employed the taxpayer (or other subsidiaries) to provide food services in these facilities. The corporation also owned 50% of a partnership that owned and constructed a dormitory complex for which the two corporations provided management and food services. The SBE held that the subsidiary and the partnership were both parts of a unitary operation with the taxpayer, and that the partnership's income and apportionment factors should be taken into account to the extent of the taxpayer's 50% interest.

In *Appeal of Albertson's, Inc.* (1982) (CCH CALIFORNIA TAX REPORTS ¶ 12-500.85), the taxpayer corporation operated a multistate chain of supermarkets selling principally food items. The corporation owned 50% of a partnership that operated a chain of supermarkets selling both food items and general merchandise. The corporation shared, with the other 50% owner, the overall control and direction of the partnership's management policies and also provided some financial and management assistance. The SBE held that the partnership was engaged in a unitary business with the taxpayer, and that the partnership factors should be taken into account to the extent of the taxpayer's 50% ownership interest.

In *Appeal of Pup 'n' Taco Drive Up* (1977) (CCH CALIFORNIA TAX REPORTS ¶ 12-500.5893), the taxpayer was a California fast-food corporation with a majority interest in two out-of-state partnerships. The SBE held that the corporation and the partnerships were engaged in a unitary business and were subject to formula allocation.

¶ 1305 Apportionment Formula

> *Law:* Secs. 25128, 25137 (CCH CALIFORNIA TAX REPORTS ¶ 12-405, 12-550, 12-575, 12-605, 12-625—12-632).
>
> *Comparable Federal:* None.
>
> *California Form:* Sch. R.

The apportionment formula is used only to compute a percentage, which is then applied to the total "business" income to determine the portion taxable in California. It should be kept in mind throughout the discussion of the formula that the items attributed to California in computing the various factors are not taxed directly, but are only used in the computation of a percentage to be applied to the net income. This point was illustrated in *Appeal of North American Aviation, Inc.* (1952) (CCH CALIFORNIA TAX REPORTS ¶ 12-585.27). Under the peculiar facts in that case title to certain goods sold had passed twice and technically there were two "sales." The State Board of Equalization (SBE) sustained the Franchise Tax Board (FTB) in eliminating the duplication in computing the sales factor in the allocation formula. The SBE's opinion pointed out that to include both sales would be unreasonable, in view of the purpose of the sales factor as a measure of the taxpayer's activity within and without California.

● *Standard apportionment formula*

The standard apportionment formula applied in California is a double-weighted sales factor formula consisting of the following factors: (1) property, both real and tangible personal property, owned or rented by the taxpayer (see ¶ 1306); (2) payroll, including all forms of compensation paid to employees (see

¶ 1307); and (3) sales, meaning all gross receipts of the taxpayer from the sale of tangible and intangible property (see ¶ 1308).

The double-weighted sales factor formula is applied by determining the ratios of the property, payroll, and two times the sales factors within California to the property, payroll, and sales factors everywhere. The sum of the ratios is divided by four and the resulting factor is applied to the total income of the taxpayer to arrive at California taxable income. The California double-weighted sales factor formula may be depicted graphically as:

$$\frac{\text{Calif. Prop.}}{\text{Total Property}} + \frac{\text{Calif. Payroll}}{\text{Total Payroll}} + \frac{2 \times \text{Calif. Sales}}{\text{Total Sales}} \; / \; 4 \; = \; \text{Calif. factor}$$

However, an equally-weighted apportionment formula applies in California to taxpayers that derive more than 50% of their "gross business receipts" from (1) extractive or agricultural business activity, (2) savings and loan activity, or (3) for income years beginning after 1995, banking or financial business activity. The equally weighted apportionment formula is the same as the above formula except that the California sales factor is not multiplied by two and the sum of the ratios is divided by three instead of four.

If the income and apportionment factors of two or more affiliated banks or corporations must be included in a combined report (see ¶ 1309), the above apportionment formulas apply to the combined income of those banks or corporations.

● *Deviations from standard formula*

The Uniform Act provides for deviation from the standard formula, where necessary to fairly reflect the extent of the taxpayer's business activity in California. This may be accomplished by excluding, adding, or modifying one or more factors, or by other means, as indicated in the cases discussed below. (Some of these cases were decided under pre-1967 law, but their reasoning is applicable generally under the present law.) The FTB may require such special treatment or the taxpayer may petition for it, in which case the FTB may grant a hearing.

In *Appeal of Evergreen Marine Corporation (Calif.), Ltd.* (1986) (CCH CALIFORNIA TAX REPORTS ¶ 12-550.193), the taxpayer, its parent corporation, and affiliates were engaged in various aspects of the ocean freighter business. In upholding the FTB's application of the standard formula to the unitary income of the corporate group, the SBE held that methods other than the standard formula may be used only in exceptional circumstances where UDITPA's provisions do not fairly represent the extent of the taxpayer's business activity in the state. The challenge to the formula must attack each element of the formula equation, and show that the formula as a whole unfairly apportions net income to California. Furthermore, deviations from the formula are not permitted simply because there is a better approach. If the standard formula fairly represents the extent of in-state activity it must be used.

In *American Telephone and Telegraph Co.* (1982) (CCH CALIFORNIA TAX REPORTS ¶ 12-610.551), discussed at ¶ 1306, the FTB adjusted the California property factor by including property located in outer space and on the high seas. The SBE upheld the FTB, and expressed the belief that the law autho-

¶ 1305

rizes the FTB to deviate from UDITPA's standard provisions "in order to prevent some . . . business income from escaping taxation entirely."

Appeal of Universal C.I.T. Credit Corporation (1972) (CCH CALIFORNIA TAX REPORTS ¶ 12-575.89) involved a large finance company with a Delaware parent corporation and more than fifty subsidiaries. The taxpayer agreed to the three-factor formula used in the finance company cases cited above, but contended that receivables originating in California had a business situs outside the State and therefore could not properly be attributed to California in computing the "property" factor (loans outstanding). The SBE held that the loans were a proper measure of the portion of the business emanating from California, citing as support a court decision dealing with tangible property in the property factor and expressing the belief that the same principles apply to intangible property.

In *Appeal of Public Finance Company, et al.* (1958) (CCH CALIFORNIA TAX REPORTS ¶ 12-500.60), the corporations involved were engaged in the small loan business. The FTB used an allocation formula consisting of the factors of (1) average loans outstanding, (2) payroll, and (3) interest earned. The taxpayers contended that their income should be determined by separate accounting. The SBE held that the business was unitary and approved the formula used. See also *Appeal of Beneficial Finance Co. of Alameda and Affiliates* (1961) (CCH CALIFORNIA TAX REPORTS ¶ 12-550.231). A similar result was reached in *Appeal of Tri-State Livestock Credit Corporation* (1960) (CCH CALIFORNIA TAX REPORTS ¶ 12-575.85). In this case the taxpayer's only office was in California, but many loans were made outside the State. The SBE apportioned the factor of average loans outstanding entirely to California, on the theory that a loan has a business situs where it is serviced. The interest-earned factor, being somewhat comparable to the sales factor in the usual formula, was developed by assigning interest income to the places where employees solicited the loans.

● *Omission of one or more factors*

Where property is a negligible factor in the business, as in the case of some service corporations, the property factor might be omitted; the computation would then be made by averaging only the other two factors. The same procedure may occasionally be applied also to the wages or sales factor, in special cases where use of the factor would be meaningless or impracticable or would result in distortion. For example, in the case of a gold mining operation the sales factor might be omitted, since all gold must be sold to the U.S. Government and there is no sales activity in the usual sense.

In *Appeal of Twentieth Century-Fox Film Corporation* (1962) (CCH CALIFORNIA TAX REPORTS ¶ 12-550.27), the SBE held that a taxpayer could not use a single factor formula (gross receipts) to determine the California portion of one segment of its income—i.e., distribution of films for unrelated producers—and another formula (the usual 3-factor formula) to determine California income from distribution of its self-produced films.

In *Appeal of Farmers Underwriters Association* (1953) (CCH CALIFORNIA TAX REPORTS ¶ 12-575.83), the taxpayer was a service corporation and contended that the property factor should be omitted from the allocation formula. The SBE sustained the FTB in requiring inclusion of the property factor,

¶ 1305

because the taxpayer used a substantial amount of property (land, buildings, furniture, office equipment, supplies, and motor vehicles) in its business. However, in *Appeal of Woodward, Baldwin & Co., Inc.* (1963) (CCH CALIFORNIA TAX REPORTS ¶ 12-575.21), it was held that where a manufacturer's sales agent employed a relatively small amount of owned property in its business, the property factor should be ignored, and income allocated according to the remaining two factors of payroll and sales.

● *Cases involving professional sports*

Two 1977 decisions of the SBE involved questions of deviating from the standard formula in special situations. *Appeal of Danny Thomas Productions* (CCH CALIFORNIA TAX REPORTS ¶ 12-610.55) involved production of television shows; *Appeal of New York Football Giants* (CCH CALIFORNIA TAX REPORTS ¶ 12-585.51) involved a professional football team. The SBE allowed some deviations (too complicated for discussion here) and commented that the party desiring to deviate from the standard formula must bear the burden of proving that it does not produce a fair result. See also *Appeal of Milwaukee Professional Sports and Services, Inc.* (1979) (CCH CALIFORNIA TAX REPORTS ¶ 12-585.782), involving a professional basketball team, and *Appeal of Boston Professional Hockey Association, Inc.* (1979) (CCH CALIFORNIA TAX REPORTS ¶ 12-585.78), involving a professional hockey team. See ¶ 1305a for discussion of special statutory rules for professional sports teams.

¶ 1305a Apportionment Rules for Specialized Industries

Law: Secs. 25137, 25141 (CCH CALIFORNIA TAX REPORTS ¶ 12-610—12-635).

Comparable Federal: None.

Over the years the Franchise Tax Board (FTB) has provided modified apportionment rules for a number of specialized industries, and for specialized types of business such as foreign operations and partnerships. Some of these rules have been issued as official regulations. In addition, FTB Regulation 25137 sets forth the circumstances under which it will permit a taxpayer to use an apportionment method other than that prescribed by law. Following is a listing of special industries and other groups (in alphabetical order) for which modified apportionment rules apply, with a brief summary for each category.

● *Airlines*

The law (Sec. 25101.3) provides a special formula for the property factor, as explained at ¶ 1306. FTB Regulation 25137-7 provides detailed rules for computation of all three of the standard factors.

● *Banks and financial corporations*

FTB Regulation 25137-4.2 provides detailed rules for computation of the property and sales factors. Loans, receivables, and other intangible assets are included in the property factor. The regulation is substantially similar to a Multistate Tax Commission model regulation, under which banks and financial corporations apportion their income using a three-factor formula consisting of equally-weighted sales, property, and payroll factors.

¶ 1305a

FTB Regulation 25137-10 details the rules regarding the computation of income of a unitary business consisting of a bank or financial corporation and a general corporation.

See ¶ 1305 for a discussion of *Appeal of Universal C.I.T. Credit Corporation* and other cases involving apportionment of income of financial corporations.

● *Commercial fishing*

FTB Regulation 25137-5 provides special rules for computation of the three standard-formula factors. Allocations are based largely on the ratio of California port days to total port days. Port days represent time spent either in port or at sea while a ship is "in operation."

● *Construction contractors*

FTB Regulation 25137-2 provides detailed rules and examples for apportioning income from long-term contracts under the completed-contract method and the percentage-of-completion method of accounting. The three standard-formula factors are used, but special rules apply to the computation of each factor. The regulation also covers the application of the special rules for corporations that discontinue doing business in California (see ¶ 811).

FTB Regulation 25137-1, regarding partnerships (see below), provides special rules for apportionment where a corporation is a member of a construction-contractor partnership. See also *Appeal of Donald M. Drake Company* (1977) (CCH CALIFORNIA TAX REPORTS ¶ 12-615.41), involving a construction contractor reporting income on the completed-contract basis. The State Board of Equalization (SBE) held that the taxpayer's share of joint ventures' property, payroll, and sales should be included in the allocation formula in the years the project is in progress rather than in the year the contract is completed.

In *Appeal of Robert E. McKee, Inc.* (1983) (CCH CALIFORNIA TAX REPORTS ¶ 12-615.341), the taxpayer was engaged in numerous construction projects in California and other States. The SBE applied the methodology specified in the regulations, and cited, with approval, the *Drake* case.

● *Franchisors*

FTB Regulation 25137-3 provides rules for corporations engaged in the business of franchising. Special rules are provided for the payroll and sales factors.

● *Motion picture and television producers and broadcasters*

FTB Regulation 25137-8 provides rules for the apportionment of income of motion picture and television producers and television network broadcasters. Topical film properties are included in the denominator of the property factor at full value for one year and other film properties are included at full value for twelve years. All other film properties are included at eight times the receipts generated in an amount not to exceed the original cost of such properties. Special rules are also provided for other situations peculiar to the industry.

¶ 1305a

● *Offshore drilling companies*

Legal Ruling No. 366 (1973) (CCH CALIFORNIA TAX REPORTS ¶ 12-550.37) deals with allocation questions of unitary oil operations beyond the 3-mile continental limit. The ruling states that use of the standard allocation formula is appropriate, and provides that factors relating to offshore operations should be reflected only in the denominators of the formula; thus, no income from such operations is apportioned to California. Legal Ruling No. 396 (1976) (CCH CALIFORNIA TAX REPORTS ¶ 12-425.18) modifies the portion of Legal Ruling No. 366 pertaining to operations of drilling barges.

● *Partnerships*

FTB Regulation 25137-1 provides detailed rules for apportionment where a corporation is a partner. Special rules are provided for long-term contracts, intercompany transactions, etc. See also ¶ 1304.

● *Personal service companies*

See *Appeal of Farmers Underwriters Association* and *Appeal of Woodward, Baldwin & Co., Inc.,* discussed at ¶ 1305, involving questions of which factors should be used in apportioning income of service corporations.

● *Professional sports teams*

The law (Sec. 25141) provides rules for calculating the apportionment formula for all professional sports teams.

Section 25141 applies to any "professional athletic team" that:

    1. has at least five participating members;

    2. is a member of a league of at least five teams;

    3. has paid attendance of at least 40,000 for the year; and

    4. has gross income of at least $100,000 for the year.

Section 25141 provides rules for computation of each of the three standard factors in the allocation formula. The basic approach is that *all* property, payroll, and sales are to be allocated to the state or country in which the team's operations are based. The base of operations is in the state in which the team derives its territorial rights under the league's rules. Special rules are provided for cases where the team is subject to an apportioned tax in another state or country.

Entities that operate a professional sports organization are treated as corporations for purposes of the minimum franchise tax on corporations. The liability of any corporation owning a sports organization is satisfied by the minimum tax if that corporation is not otherwise doing business in the state.

See cases discussed at ¶ 1305 that involve question of deviating from the standard allocation formula by sports organizations.

● *Publishers of print media*

FTB Regulation 25137-12 provides rules for the apportionment of income of taxpayers in the business of publishing, selling, licensing, or distributing newspapers, magazines, periodicals, trade journals, or other printed material.

¶ 1305a

A special circulation factor is used to determine the amount of the taxpayer's gross receipts from advertising and the sale, rental, or use of customer lists that must be included in the numerator of the sales factor.

● *Trains*

FTB Regulation 25137-9 provides special rules for computation of income from railroad operations. Generally the three standard-formula factors are used, but special rules apply to the computation of each factor.

● *Trucking companies*

FTB Regulation 25137-11 provides special rules for computation of income from trucking companies. Special rules are provided for the property and sales factor.

¶ 1306 Property Factor in Apportionment Formula

Law: Secs. 25101.3, 25107, 25129-31 (CCH CALIFORNIA TAX REPORTS ¶ 10-007, 12-430, 12-575, 12-580).

Comparable Federal: None.

California Form: Sch. R.

In computing the property factor, all real estate and tangible personal property owned or rented by the corporation and used in the business is included. Property used to produce "nonbusiness" income is excluded from the factor, but property used to produce both "nonbusiness" and "business" income is included to the extent it is used to produce "business" income. Property owned by the corporation that is in transit between states is generally considered to be located at its destination. Franchise Tax Board (FTB) Regulation 25129 gives examples that show what to include in the property factor in unusual situations such as a plant under construction, closing of a plant, etc., and provides specific rules for property in transit, movable property, etc.

● *Closing of plant*

In *Appeal of Ethyl Corporation* (1975) (CCH CALIFORNIA TAX REPORTS ¶ 12-575.96), the taxpayer closed its California plant and started to sell its equipment in 1963 and contended that the property was permanently removed from the unitary business in that year. The State Board of Equalization (SBE) held that the plant was includible in the property factor until it was dismantled in 1965.

● *Property under construction*

In *Appeal of O.K. Earl Corp.* (1977) (CCH CALIFORNIA TAX REPORTS ¶ 12-575.361), the taxpayer questioned the regulations regarding inclusion of costs of construction in progress in the property factor of construction contractors. The SBE upheld the provision that such costs are to be included only to the extent they exceed progress billings.

¶ 1306

● *In-transit inventory*

In *Appeal of Craig Corporation* (1987) (CCH CALIFORNIA TAX REPORTS ¶ 12-575.661), goods ceased to be "in transit" and entered the taxpayer's unitary business when received from Japan at the taxpayer's California facility for customs inspection, repackaging, and shipment to the taxpayer's regional warehouses in other states. The SBE held that within the context of a multistate unitary business it was too restrictive to interpret "destination" as the goods' ultimate storage place prior to sale. The imported goods were properly included in the California property factor numerator.

● *Property in outer space*

In *Appeal of American Telephone and Telegraph Co.* (1982) (CCH CALIFORNIA TAX REPORTS ¶ 12-610.551), the FTB revised the California property factor by including the following property not physically located in the State: (1) the high-seas portion of certain jointly-owned California-Hawaii cables, and (2) a portion of certain leased satellite circuits in outer space. The FTB first contended that the property was "used" in California within the intent of the law, but the SBE rejected this argument. However, the SBE permitted the same result to be achieved by applying the provision of the law (discussed at ¶ 1305) that provides for deviation from the standard formula to fairly reflect the extent of California business activity. To the same effect, see the Court of Appeal decision in *Communications Satellite Corporation v. Franchise Tax Board* (1984) (CCH CALIFORNIA TAX REPORTS ¶ 12-610.53); this case applied the same reasoning to the sales factor.

● *Property neither owned nor rented*

In *Appeal of Union Carbide Corporation* (1984) (CCH CALIFORNIA TAX REPORTS ¶ 12-580.11), the taxpayer operated rent-free a government-owned nuclear gas-separation plant outside California. The SBE held that, under FTB Regulation 25137 regarding deviations from the standard formula for exceptional circumstances, the property in question was properly includible in the denominator of the property factor.

● *Transportation companies*

Transportation companies present unusual problems in the property factor, and special procedures have been developed for them. The law provides a statutory formula for airlines and air taxis, based on time in California, number of arrivals and departures, etc.

Although the law does not provide specific formulas for other transportation companies, the FTB has developed a special formula for railroads and trucking companies based on "revenue miles" and a formula for sea transportation companies based on "voyage days" within and without California.

● *Use of original federal cost basis*

Property owned by the taxpayer is included in the property factor at its original cost ("basis") for *federal* income tax purposes. This means that depreciation is ignored. However, certain adjustments are allowed, including adjustments for any subsequent capital additions or improvements, special

¶ 1306

deductions, and partial deductions because of sale, exchange, abandonment. Inventory is included in accordance with the method of valuation for *federal* income tax purposes. FTB Regulation 25130 provides specific rules and examples for determining "original cost" in unusual situations such as corporate reorganizations, inherited property, etc.; in each case, the determination relates to the *federal* cost basis of the property. Leasehold improvements are included at their original cost. In the case of property acquired as a result of involuntary conversion or exchange, the original federal cost is carried over to the replacement property—see Legal Ruling No. 409 (1977) (CCH CALIFORNIA Tax Reports ¶ 12-575.97).

In *Appeal of Pauley Petroleum, Inc.* (1982) (CCH CALIFORNIA TAX REPORTS ¶ 12-575.561), the taxpayer had elected to expense intangible drilling and development costs for federal income tax purposes, but included them as costs in the property factor of the State apportionment formula. The SBE held that the costs could not be included in the property factor, since they were not included in the federal tax basis of the property.

● *Rental property and royalties*

Rental property is included in the property factor at eight times the net annual rental rate. Any subrentals received—provided they constitute "non-business" income—are ordinarily deducted from rentals paid to determine the net annual rate; however, FTB Regulation 25137 provides for special treatment in exceptional cases where deduction of subrentals would produce a distorted result. FTB Regulations 25130 and 25137 give examples to illustrate treatment of this and other unusual situations, and also provide rules and examples for determining the "net annual rental" in cases of short-term leases, reorganizations, payments in lieu of rent, nominal rental rates, etc.

In FTB Legal Ruling 97-2 (1997) (see CCH CALIFORNIA TAX REPORTS ¶ 12-575.32) the FTB announced its position that royalty payments made by a corporation with respect to the corporation's oil and gas and/or timber rights are treated as equivalents to rental payments to the extent that the property for which the royalty payments are made is actually used.

● *Averaging for year*

The amount to be included in the property factor is the average value for the year. This is usually determined by averaging the values at the beginning and end of the year. However, the FTB may require or allow averaging by monthly values, where substantial fluctuations occur during the year or large amounts of property are acquired or disposed of during the year or where membership in the unitary group changes during the year. The FTB was sustained in this position by the SBE in *Appeal of Craig Corporation* (1987) (CCH CALIFORNIA TAX REPORTS ¶ 12-575.661).

● *International banking facility*

An international banking facility maintained by a bank within California is to be treated for purposes of the apportionment formula as though it were doing business outside the state.

¶ 1306

¶ 1307 Payroll Factor in Apportionment Formula

Law: Secs. 25107, 25132-33 (CCH CALIFORNIA TAX REPORTS ¶ 10-007, 12-430, 12-605).

Comparable Federal: None.

California Form: Sch. R.

The payroll factor includes all salaries, wages, commissions, and other compensation to employees. The test of whether a person is an employee is the way the person is treated for payroll tax purposes; if the person is not considered to be an employee for payroll taxes the person's compensation is not included. Compensation is attributable to California where:

(a) the employee performs services entirely within California;

(b) the employee performs services both within and without the state, but the services performed outside the state are merely incidental to those performed within the state;

(c) the employee performs some services within the state, and the base of operations is in the state, or if there is no base of operations, the place from which services are directed or controlled is in California; or

(d) the employee performs some services within the state and the base of operations, or the place from which services are directed or controlled, is not in any state in which some part of the services are performed, but the employee's residence is in California.

In *Appeal of Photo-Marker Corporation of California* (1986) (CCH CALIFORNIA TAX REPORTS ¶ 12-605.60), wages paid principal corporate officers residing in California were includible in the California numerator because the base of operations for the officers was in California even though the corporation was headquartered in New York.

Compensation attributable to "nonbusiness" income (see ¶ 1303) should be excluded from the payroll factor. Capitalized payroll costs (e.g., plant construction) should be included in the payroll factor, even though they also become part of the property factor.

Special rules have been developed over the years for determining the payroll factor in unusual industry situations. For example, in the case of transportation companies, payroll of traveling personnel may be apportioned according to "revenue miles" or "voyage days" as discussed in ¶ 1306.

The California payroll of an international banking facility, is to be treated for purposes of the apportionment formula as payroll outside the state.

¶ 1308 Sales Factor in Apportionment Formula

Law: Secs. 25107, 25134-36 (CCH CALIFORNIA TAX REPORTS ¶ 10-007, 12-430, 12-585, 12-590).

Comparable Federal: None.

California Form: Sch. R.

For purposes of the sales factor, the term "sales" generally means gross receipts from operations that produce "business" income, less returns and allowances. Franchise Tax Board (FTB) Regulations 25134 through 25136 provide specific rules for determining what should be included. FTB Regulation 25137 provides that gross receipts from an incidental or occasional sale of a fixed asset, such as sale of a factory or plant, should be excluded. Gross receipts from an incidental or occasional sale of intangible property is also excluded (Legal Ruling 97-1, CCH CALIFORNIA TAX REPORTS ¶ 12-600.30).

In *Appeal of Triangle Publications, Inc.* (1984) (CCH CALIFORNIA TAX REPORTS ¶ 12-500.472), the State Board of Equalization (SBE) held that FTB Regulation 25137 regarding occasional sales contradicted statutory language and could not be applied in that case. However, the ruling in *Triangle Publications* was disavowed in *Appeal of Fluor Corporation* (1996) (CCH CALIFORNIA TAX REPORTS ¶ 12-600.25), in which the SBE held that, based on FTB Regulation 25137, the FTB improperly included in the sales factor income received from the sale of the taxpayer's headquarters. The SBE went on to say that *any* party wishing to deviate from the method prescribed by regulation, when found to be applicable, must first establish by clear and convincing evidence that the prescribed method does not fairly represent the extent of the taxpayer's activities in the state.

The law provides specific rules for determining which sales are attributable to California. Sales of tangible personal property are deemed to be California sales if the property is delivered or shipped to a purchaser, other than the United States government, located in California; this applies regardless of the f.o.b. point or other conditions of sale. Such sales are also attributable to California if shipped from an office, warehouse, store, factory, or other storage facility in California, where the purchaser is the U.S. government or where the seller is not taxable in the state or country where the purchaser is located. See *Appeal of Chromalloy American Corporation* (1977) (CCH CALIFORNIA TAX REPORTS ¶ 12-585.53), in which the SBE approved this rule as it applies to sales to the U.S. government. If a seller transfers possession of goods to a purchaser at the purchaser's place of business in California, the sale is a California sale. However, if goods are transferred to the purchaser's employee or agent at some other location in California and the purchaser immediately transports the goods to another state, the sale is not a California sale.

Until December 1, 2000, sales of unprocessed timber are attributable to California if the timber was cut from an area within California and delivered or shipped to a purchaser outside the United States.

● *Sales to U.S. government*

Sales to the U.S. government include only sales for which the government makes direct payment to the seller under a contract with the seller; in other words, only prime contracts are included and subcontract sales are excluded.

● *Effect of Public Law 86-272*

If the other state, territory, or country could tax the seller but does not actually do so, the seller is nevertheless deemed to be "taxable" there and sales shipped there from California are not attributable to California. On the other hand, when Public Law 86-272 (see ¶ 802a) would preclude taxing of the seller by the other state, sales shipped from California are attributable ("thrown back") to California.

¶ 1308

In Legal Ruling 99-1 (1999) (CCH CALIFORNIA TAX REPORTS ¶ 12-415.23), the FTB ruled that a corporation's sales of tangible personal property shipped from California into Puerto Rico should be included in the corporation's sales factor for apportionment purposes because Puerto Rico had no authority to impose a tax on the corporation. The corporation was protected from Puerto Rico taxation under Public Law 86-272 because its activity there was limited to the solicitation of orders. Although a commonwealth, Puerto Rico was a destination state for purposes of Public Law 86-272.

In *McDonnell Douglas Corporation v. Franchise Tax Board* (1994) (CCH CALIFORNIA TAX REPORTS ¶ 12-585.45), a California court of appeal held that an aircraft manufacturer was permitted to exclude from the California sales factor numerator of the apportionment formula its sales of aircraft that were destined for use outside California but that were delivered to purchasers in California.

However, in *Appeal of Mazda Motors of America, Inc.* (1994) (CCH CALIFORNIA TAX REPORTS ¶ 12-585.451), the SBE held that an automobile importer's sales receipts for vehicles that the importer stored, assembled, serviced, repaired, and subsequently shipped to the purchaser in Texas were properly included in the numerator of the apportionment formula's sales factor for purposes of calculating the taxpayer's California taxable income. Unlike the situation in *McDonnell Douglas Corp.*, where the purchaser merely picked up the goods in this state for shipment to an out-of-state destination, the taxpayer exercised sufficient possession and control over the vehicles while they were in California to subject the goods to taxation by the state.

In *Appeal of Schwinn Sales West, Inc.* (1988) (CCH CALIFORNIA TAX REPORTS ¶ 12-550.60), the nonsolicitation activities in California of a regional sales manager of an Illinois bicycle manufacturer, along with the company's conducting of service schools for its California dealers, indicated that the company's activities were regular and systematic, exceeding protected solicitation.

In *Appeals of Foothill Publishing Co. and the Record Ledger, Inc.* (1986) (CCH CALIFORNIA TAX REPORTS ¶ 12-585.814), the income derived by two California publishers for printing Nevada and Arizona publications was "thrown back" to California because under Public Law 86-272 neither Nevada nor Arizona could tax the publishers. The only business activity in those states was the solicitation of orders that were sent outside the state for approval and then delivered from California.

In *Appeal of Union Carbide Corporation* (1984) (CCH CALIFORNIA TAX REPORTS ¶ 12-585.812), the taxpayer's subsidiaries sold its products in various foreign countries. The taxpayer contended that it would have been taxable in those countries except for certain tax treaties; however, it did not offer any evidence that the foreign activities were extensive enough to subject it to the tax jurisdiction of the foreign countries. The SBE held that the foreign sales were properly "thrown back" to California.

In *Appeal of The Olga Company* (1984) (CCH CALIFORNIA TAX REPORTS ¶ 12-585.817), the taxpayer shipped its products from California to more than 30 other states. Although the taxpayer did not pay income taxes in the other states, it contended that the other states had jurisdiction to tax because of the taxpayer's extensive sales activities. The SBE held that the sales in other states should be "thrown back" to California.

In *Appeal of Dresser Industries* (1982) (CCH CALIFORNIA TAX REPORTS ¶ 12-585.813), the taxpayer sold its products in Japan through several subsidiaries. The SBE held that these sales could not be attributed ("thrown back") to California, because the FTB did not show that Japan lacked jurisdiction to tax the parent corporation. The SBE held that the criteria of Public Law 86-272 could not be applied, because P.L. 86-272 does not apply to foreign commerce. See also the opinion on rehearing in this case.

In *Appeals of Learner Co. et al.* (1980) (CCH CALIFORNIA TAX REPORTS ¶ 12-500.65), the taxpayer shipped scrap metal to customers in Japan. The taxpayer contended that it would have been taxable by Japan if the standards of Public Law 86-272 had been applicable there. The SBE held that the taxpayer would not have been taxable by Japan, and that the sales to Japan were properly assigned to California for purposes of the allocation formula.

In *Hoffmann-La Roche, Inc. v. Franchise Tax Board* (1980) (CCH CALIFORNIA TAX REPORTS ¶ 12-585.57), the taxpayer questioned the constitutionality of the rule involving Public Law 86-272 discussed above. The FTB attributed to California sales that were shipped from California to certain other states, in which states the taxpayer (seller) was not taxable. A federal appellate court upheld the constitutionality of the rule.

● *Throwback rule in context of combined unitary group*

See ¶ 1309 for a discussion of the throwback rule in connection with unitary group apportionment when some group members are exempted from California taxation under P.L. 86-272.

● *Sales other than of tangible personal property; sales of services*

Sales of other than tangible personal property are attributable to California if the activity that produced the sale is performed in California. If the income-producing activity is performed both within and without the state, then the sale is attributed to California only if a greater portion of the income-producing activity is performed in California than in any other state, based on costs of performance. These rules apply to income from personal services and any income from property that does not come within the category of "sales of tangible personal property." FTB Regulation 25136 provides specific rules and examples for treatment of income of these types. The regulation provides that income from personal services is to be attributed to California to the extent the services are performed in California.

In *Appeal of Mark IV Metal Products, Inc.* (1982) (CCH CALIFORNIA TAX REPORTS ¶ 12-585.531), the taxpayer fabricated metal products in California for a customer in Texas. The SBE held that the taxpayer was selling services, and sales to the Texas customer were attributable to California for purposes of the sales factor.

In *Appeal of The Babcock and Wilcox Company* (1978) (CCH CALIFORNIA TAX REPORTS ¶ 12-585.58), the taxpayer was engaged in the design, manufacture, and sale of steam generating systems. The taxpayer contended that sales of these systems were sales of "other than tangible personal property" and

¶ 1308

therefore were subject to the rules for such property rather than to the rules for tangible personal property. The SBE held that the sales in question were of tangible personal property, attributable entirely to California; the SBE pointed out that the property and payroll factors fairly reflected the out-of-state activity in planning, engineering, etc.

● *Installment sales*

In Legal Ruling No. 413 (1979) (CCH CALIFORNIA TAX REPORTS ¶ 12-585.35), the FTB ruled that an apportioning corporation reporting a sale on the installment basis should include the total sales price in the sales factor in the year of sale, and should apportion the installment income each year according to the apportionment percentage of the year of sale.

● *Cost-plus contracts*

In *Appeal of Bechtel Power Corporation, et al.* (1997) (CCH CALIFORNIA TAX REPORTS ¶ 12-585.711), the SBE ruled that in order to accurately reflect the taxpayer's economic activities in California, client-furnished materials used to fulfill a "cost-plus" contract were required to be included in the taxpayer's sales factor for apportionment purposes.

● *Special rules and decisions*

The FTB has developed special rules for the sales factor in some unusual industry situations. In the case of sea transportation companies, income from carrying cargo is attributed to California under a formula based on "voyage days" (see also ¶ 1306).

In *Appeals of Pacific Telephone and Telegraph Co.* (1978) (CCH CALIFORNIA TAX REPORTS ¶ 12-585.80), the taxpayer contended that the sales factor should include gross receipts from sale or redemption of certain securities in the operation of large "pools" of working capital. The SBE ruled against the taxpayer, holding that the sales factor would be distorted by inclusion of the amounts in question.

In *Appeal of Royal Crown Cola Co.* (1974) (CCH CALIFORNIA TAX REPORTS ¶ 12-585.54), the taxpayer argued for a novel computation of the sales factor. The taxpayer contended that, to avoid a distorted result, the sales of certain subsidiaries should be excluded from the sales factor and intercompany sales of the parent to the subsidiaries (normally eliminated) should be included instead. The SBE held against the taxpayer, citing several of the cases discussed above at ¶ 1304 and emphasizing the broad discretion vested in the FTB in apportionment matters.

● *International banking facility*

The California sales of an international banking facility are to be attributed outside the state for purposes of the apportionment formula.

¶ 1308

¶ 1309 Affiliated Corporations—Combined Reporting

Law: Secs. 23801, 25101.15, 25102, 25104-05, 25106.5 (CCH CALIFORNIA TAX REPORTS ¶ 12-675, 89-130, 89-137).

Comparable Federal: None.

California Forms: FTB Pub. 1061, Form 100.

As explained at ¶ 806, the California law specifically provides for the filing of consolidated franchise tax returns only by certain railroad corporations. However, when a group of corporations conducts a unitary business (discussed at ¶ 1304), members of the group are generally required to file a combined report if the unitary activities are carried on within and without California. The combined report shows the manner in which the unitary business apportions and allocates its income to California and to other states in which it does business, but should not be equated with a combined group return (discussed at ¶ 1311). Members of a unitary group deriving income solely from California sources may elect to file a combined report, but are not required to do so; such an election must be made annually. When computing the elements of sales, property, and payroll for a combined report, some intercompany transactions must be eliminated (see discussion below).

While Franchise Tax Board (FTB) Publication 1061 indicates that combined reporting is required whenever a unitary business conducts unitary activities both within and without the state, the applicable statutes state that combined reporting is generally required only if the corporations are members of a "commonly controlled group." A "commonly controlled group" is any of the following: (1) a group of corporations connected through stock ownership (or constructive ownership) if the parent corporation owns stock possessing more than 50% of the voting power of at least one corporation and, if applicable, the parent or one or more of the other corporations own stock cumulatively representing more than 50% of the voting power of each of the corporations (other than the parent); (2) any two or more corporations if stock representing more than 50% of the voting power of the corporations is owned (or constructively owned) by one person; (3) any two or more corporations if more than 50% of the ownership or beneficial ownership of the stock possessing voting power in each corporation consists of stapled interests; or (4) any two or more corporations if stock representing more than 50% of the voting power of the corporations is cumulatively owned (without regard to constructive ownership) by, or for the benefit of, members of the same family. A corporation eligible to be a member of more than one commonly controlled group must elect to be a member of a single group. Such membership will be terminated when stock of the corporation is sold, exchanged, or otherwise disposed of, unless the corporation meets the requirements for being a member of the same commonly controlled group within a two-year period.

When a corporation is a partner in a partnership that is part of a unitary business, the corporation is not required to own more than 50% of the partnership before the partnership may be included in a combined report. Since the partnership is not a separate taxable entity, its income and apportionment factors are included only to the extent of the corporate partner's percentage of ownership interest. See cases cited at ¶ 1304.

¶ 1309

S corporations are generally prohibited from being included in a combined report. However, in some cases, the FTB may use combined reporting methods to clearly reflect income of an S corporation.

Under California's water's-edge law, taxpayers may elect to exclude certain foreign affiliates from a combined report. For further details, see ¶ 1309a.

● *Combination of general and financial corporations*

FTB Regulation 25137-10 sets forth in detail how a unitary business that consists of at least one bank or financial corporation and at least one general corporation whose predominant activity is not financial, allocates and apportions income in a combined report.

● *Insurance affiliate excluded*

In Legal Ruling No. 385 (1975) (CCH CALIFORNIA TAX REPORTS ¶ 12-670.39), the FTB ruled that a California corporate insurer engaged in a unitary business must be excluded from a combined report for apportionment of unitary income, because the state constitution exempts such organizations from franchise and income taxes.

● *Parent company excluded*

Legal Ruling No. 410 (1979) (CCH CALIFORNIA TAX REPORTS ¶ 12-670.35) involved a situation where three subsidiaries were engaged in a unitary business but their parent was not involved. The ruling concluded that the subsidiaries must be included in a combined report but the parent corporation should be excluded.

● *FTB policy*

The FTB requires combined reporting of multistate operations wherever a "unitary" business is operated within and without California. As discussed more fully at ¶ 1304, there are three judicially acceptable tests for determining whether a business is unitary. These are (1) the three unities test, (2) the contribution and dependency test, and (3) the flow of value test.

In August 1992, the FTB issued revised audit guidelines with respect to the unitary combination of diverse businesses (*FTB Notice No. 92-4*, CCH CALIFORNIA TAX REPORTS ¶ 12-500.63). According to the revised guidelines, there is no unique test for evaluating unity in diverse business cases. Unity may be established under any of the judicially acceptable tests and may not be denied merely because another of those tests does not simultaneously apply, i.e., the tests are not mutually exclusive. In addition, a lack of functional integration will not prevent a finding of unity. On the other hand, the fact that functionally integrated businesses may be found to be unitary does not mean that functional integration is a *requirement* for unity.

Also, presumptions of unity under Reg. 25120(b), which states that the activities of a taxpayer will be considered a single business if there is evidence to indicate that the segments under consideration are integrated with, depend upon, or contribute to, each other and the operations of the taxpayer as a whole, although important considerations, are not conclusive in determining unity.

Finally, the guidelines state that *Mole-Richardson, Dental Insurance Consultants,* and *Tenneco West, Inc.* (each discussed at ¶ 1304), are controlling of the diverse business issue and that State Board of Equalization (SBE) decisions that are not in accord with these cases should not be relied upon.

● *Corporations under common control*

In *Rain Bird Sprinkler Mfg. Corp. v. Franchise Tax Board* (1991) (CCH CALIFORNIA TAX REPORTS ¶ 12-500.524), a California court of appeal allowed seventeen corporations to file a combined report even though no single individual or entity held a majority interest in all of the corporations. The court, rejecting what it called "a host" of SBE decisions requiring ownership by a single individual or entity, held that "unity of ownership" existed because members of the same family held the majority of the voting stock in each of the corporations, and all of the stock of each corporation was subject to written stock purchase agreements prohibiting transfer to outsiders.

● *Other cases involving questions of control*

In *Appeal of Armco Steel Corp.* (1984) (CCH CALIFORNIA TAX REPORTS ¶ 12-500.311), the taxpayer owned exactly 50% of the stock of a "captive mining corporation" that supplied iron ore to the taxpayer at cost. The captive corporation was treated as a partnership for federal tax purposes. The SBE followed the *Revere Copper and Brass* case (below) in holding that the taxpayer could not include the captive corporation's factors in its computation of unitary income, even though the factors could have been included if the captive corporation had been a partnership (see also ¶ 1304).

In *Appeal of Revere Copper and Brass Inc.* (1977) (CCH CALIFORNIA TAX REPORTS ¶ 12-500), the taxpayer was admittedly engaged in a unitary business. The taxpayer bought a substantial portion of its raw material requirements from a subsidiary that was 50% owned by the taxpayer. The SBE held that the subsidiary was not includible in a combined return, since the taxpayer's ownership in the subsidiary was not more than 50%. To the same effect, see *Appeal of Standard Brands, Inc.* (1977) (CCH CALIFORNIA TAX REPORTS ¶ 12-500.31). However, in *Appeal of Signal Oil and Gas Co.* (1970), the SBE held that a 50% owned German subsidiary of a Swiss subsidiary of a California parent should be included in the computation of unitary income, since the 50% stock ownership carried with it decisive control over the subsidiary's operations.

● *Apportionment of tax within group*

Where income of an affiliated group is combined and there are two or more corporations having activity in California, there may be a question of how the total tax on the combined income taxed by California should be divided between the corporations having income from California sources. Legal Ruling No. 234 (1959) (CCH CALIFORNIA TAX REPORTS ¶ 12-550.15) prescribes the method of apportionment to be used. The apportionment is based upon the California income attributable to each member of the affiliated group, such income being assigned to each corporation on the basis of the

¶ 1309

average ratio of the California factors of each corporation to the total factors of the group. This method is illustrated in the ruling as follows:

	Corp. A	Corp. B	Corp. C	Total
Totals within and without the State:				
Property	$ 500,000	$ 64,000	$ 36,000	$ 600,000
Payroll	300,000	74,000	26,000	400,000
Sales	4,000,000	600,000	400,000	5,000,000
Totals within the State:				
Property	24,000	—0—	36,000	60,000
Payroll	14,000	—0—	26,000	40,000
Sales	150,000	450,000	400,000	1,000,000
Allocating fractions:				
Property	4.0%	—0—	6.0%	10.0%
Payroll	3.5	—0—	6.5	10.0
Sales	3.0	9.0%	8.0	20.0
Total	10.5%	9.0%	20.5%	40.0%
Average	3.5%	3.0%	6.83⅓%	13⅓%

Applying the foregoing fractions to a combined business income of $1,000,000 would result in $133,333 being attributed to California sources. This amount would then be allocated to each corporation, and the tax computed at the appropriate rate, as follows:

Corp. A (3.5% of $1,000,000)	$ 35,000
Corp. B (3% of $1,000,000).	30,000
Corp. C (6.83⅓% of $1,000,000)	68,333
Total	$133,333

● *Significance of apportionment within group*

Apportionment of California income (determined by application of the apportionment formula) to the various corporations included in a combined report may be a significant computation when used in connection with the determination of the dividends received deduction under Sec. 24402 (see ¶ 908).

It was also determined to be important in *Appeal of Joyce, Inc.* (1966) (CCH CALIFORNIA TAX REPORTS ¶ 12-425.211). In this case, one of the corporations included in the combined report had so little activity in California that California was precluded by federal law (Public Law 86-272, see ¶ 803a) from taxing its income. However, it did have some payroll and sales factors in California. To the extent that these factors resulted in apportionment to it of a part of the entire unitary income, it was determined that such portion of the unitary income could not be taxed in California. The decision points out that this result could not have been reached had the out-of-state affiliate been incorporated in California. *Joyce* was overruled by *Appeal of Finnigan Corporation* (1990) (CCH CALIFORNIA TAX REPORTS ¶ 12-425.212), in which the SBE held that the part of the sales factor attributable to a member of a unitary group that was excluded from taxation under Public Law 86-272 could be assigned to California under the throwback rule if at least one unitary group member was taxable in California. In *Appeal of Huffy Corp.* (1999) (CCH CALIFORNIA TAX REPORTS ¶ 12-425.21), the SBE abandoned the position it established in *Finnigan* and prospectively readopted the rule it established in

Joyce. Thus, a unitary group member's California destination sales are once again excluded from the California sales factor numerator of the group's combined report if the individual member that made the sales is not itself subject to tax in California. The *Joyce* rule applies to income years beginning after April 21, 1999. However, if a unitary group has members whose income years begin on different dates and who are required to fiscalize their income to a commmon accounting period in order to apportion the group's business income, the *Joyce* rule applies prospectively to those common accounting periods that begin after August 31, 1999.

⊂CH̄ CCH Comment: Readoption of the *Joyce* Rule

The readoption of the *Joyce* rule has given unitary business groups new opportunities to achieve favorable tax consequences through careful planning. By limiting activities that could give rise to taxable nexus in California (such as servicing and installing products or collecting accounts) to certain affiliates, other members of the unitary group may be able to exclude their California destination sales from the sales factor numerator of the group's combined report, thus reducing the unitary group's income subject to taxation in California. Of course, these sales may be "thrown back" to the state from which the products were shipped. Conversely, with the prospective abandonment of the *Finnigan* rule, taxpayers shipping products from California can no longer rely on the activities of unitary affiliates in other states to avoid throwback of those sales to California. When conducting tax planning, taxpayers need to bear in mind that there are many other issues to be considered when trying to manage nexus by using multiple entity structures, including attributional nexus based on an agency relationship.

● *Minimum tax applies to each corporation*

The minimum tax (discussed at ¶ 809) is imposed on *each* corporation in the combined group that is incorporated or qualified to do business in California, even though the combined report shows a net loss or shows taxable income that would produce a lower tax.

● *Allocation of credits and capital gains and losses*

Unless otherwise provided by statute, specific credit(s) are only available to the taxpayer corporation that incurred the expense that generated the credit(s). Reg. 25106.5-2 allows capital gains attributable to one member of a unitary group to be offset by capital losses incurred by another member.

● *Adjustments for intercompany transactions*

FTB Pub. 1061 dicusses the adjustments necessary to properly reflect intercompany transactions among unitary affiliates included in the combined report. The adjustments concern inventories, intangible assets, fixed assets and capitalized items, dividends, and other factor adjustments. In FTB Notice 97-2 (1997) (CCH CALIFORNIA TAX REPORTS ¶ 12-675.25), the FTB announced a new policy allowing for the deferral of income from a nondividend distribu-

¶ 1309

585

tion between members of a combined group when the distribution exceeds the basis of the stock. A taxpayer may claim the deferral retroactively to any open tax year by executing a closing agreement with the FTB (see ¶1418 for a discussion of closing agreements).

● *Accounting methods and periods*

Regs. 25106.5 et seq. provide detailed rules concerning the accounting methods and periods to be used by a unitary group and its individual members. Under these rules, each member of a combined reporting group has its own accounting methods and elections. However, the unitary group is authorized to make an election on behalf of an individual member if that member has not otherwise made an election on a California or federal return. The principal member's accounting period is used as a reference period for all members of the combined reporting group to aggregate and apportion combined report business income of the group. The regulations also address fiscalization issues and clarify how to incorporate/exclude a business's income that joins/leaves the unitary group mid-year.

Pre-1988 Tax Years (Pre-Water's Edge)

● *Inclusion of foreign operations—Constitutionality*

The apportionment of income within and without California on the basis of the business income or unitary theory may apply even though one or more of the corporations in the affiliated group operates in a foreign country. See, for example, *Appeal of American Can Company, Inc.* (1959) (CCH CALIFORNIA TAX REPORTS ¶ 12-500.563), and *Appeal of Anchor Hocking Glass Corporation* (1967) (CCH CALIFORNIA TAX REPORTS ¶ 12-500.563).

In *Barclays Bank PLC v. Franchise Tax Board of California* and *Colgate-Palmolive Company v. Franchise Tax Board of California* (1994) (CCH CALIFORNIA TAX REPORTS ¶ 12-415.25), the U.S. Supreme Court held that California's use of the worldwide combined reporting (WWCR) method to determine the corporation franchise (income) tax owed by members of a foreign-based multinational unitary group and by the parent of a domestic-based multinational unitary group did not violate the Commerce Clause or the Due Process Clause of the U.S. Constitution. The Court determined that the taxing scheme did not prevent the federal government from speaking with "one voice" when regulating commercial relations with foreign governments, because Congress has implicitly permitted the use of the WWCR method by the states. In addition, the Court determined that the taxing scheme did not enhance the risk of multiple taxation or impose an inordinate compliance burden on foreign-based multinationals.

In *Container Corporation of America v. Franchise Tax Board* (1983) (CCH CALIFORNIA TAX REPORTS ¶ 12-550.12), the U.S. Supreme Court considered in detail the constitutional questions involved when foreign operations are included in the unitary return of a combined group. The court held, in a 5-3 decision, that a domestic corporation and its 20 foreign subsidiaries constituted a unitary business and that the use of the three-factor apportionment formula was proper; further, that the California tax did not violate federal law or policy. (The dissenting opinion held that the California tax was unconstitutional, and pointed out that the majority opinion did not deal with the more

¶1309

difficult question that arises where the parent is a foreign corporation. See below for discussion of lower-court decisions that have approved the inclusion of a foreign parent.)

● *Some foreign operations excluded*

Chase Brass and Copper Co. v. Franchise Tax Board (1970) (CCH CALIFORNIA TAX REPORTS ¶ 12-500.564), decided by the California Court of Appeal, involved the Kennecott group of copper companies. The court held that operations of some of the affiliated corporations were unitary and must be included in the computation of income allocable to California; however, it did not require inclusion of the affiliated corporation that mined copper in Chile, because the relationship of that corporation to the one doing business in California was insufficient to justify application of the unitary theory.

● *Foreign subsidiaries included*

In *Appeal of The Stanwick Corporation* (1984) (CCH CALIFORNIA TAX REPORTS ¶ 12-500.568), the taxpayer and its international subsidiary provided professional services to the U.S. Navy and to other domestic and foreign clients. The SBE held that the foreign subsidiary must be included in the unitary business.

In *Appeal of Pfizer, Inc.* (1984) (CCH CALIFORNIA TAX REPORTS ¶ 12-500.5671), the taxpayer and its subsidiaries were engaged in a worldwide business in pharmaceuticals and other products. The SBE held that the foreign subsidiaries must be included with the domestic operations in applying the allocation formula.

In *Appeal of Texaco, Inc.* (1978) (CCH CALIFORNIA TAX REPORTS ¶ 12-500.583), the SBE held that a wholly-owned Iranian subsidiary must be included in the unitary group. The subsidiary had no employees or property; its sole purpose and activity was to purchase and resell oil to another subsidiary.

In *Appeal of Regal of California, Inc.* (1977) (CCH CALIFORNIA TAX REPORTS ¶ 12-500.588), a California corporation was a subsidiary of an out-of-state corporation which also had another subsidiary that operated solely in the Orient. Although it appeared that the Orient corporation had no direct relationship with the California corporation, the SBE held that there was a unitary operation requiring all three corporations to be included in a combined return.

In *Appeals of the Anaconda Company, et al.* (1972) (CCH CALIFORNIA TAX REPORTS ¶ 12-500.65), the SBE decided that several Chilean and Mexican mining subsidiaries were includible in the unitary group of 36 companies for franchise tax purposes. The SBE considered the precedent of the *Chase Brass and Copper* case discussed above, which involved a generally similar situation, but decided that it could not be relied upon for guidance in this case. The same conclusion was reached by the California Court of Appeal in a case involving the same years (1955-1958), in *Anaconda Company v. Franchise Tax Board* (1982) (CCH CALIFORNIA TAX REPORTS ¶ 12-430.25).

In *Appeal of F.W. Woolworth Co.* (1972) the SBE held that the taxpayer must include its Canadian subsidiary in the unitary group, despite the fact

¶ 1309

that there was practically no unity of operation. The decision was based principally on such factors as interlocking directors and officers, exchange of information and know-how, common trademarks and goodwill, etc. However, in *F.W. Woolworth Co. v. Franchise Tax Board* (1984) (CCH CALIFORNIA TAX REPORTS ¶ 12-500.327), a California court of appeal overruled the SBE and held that the taxpayer could *not* be required to include its Canadian subsidiary in the unitary group; the court held that the degree of centralization was not sufficient to show that the two corporations operated as a unitary enterprise.

● *Foreign subsidiaries excluded*

In *Appeal of Scholl, Inc., et al.* (1978) (CCH CALIFORNIA TAX REPORTS ¶ 12-500.327), an affiliated group of 5 domestic and 18 foreign corporations was engaged in the manufacture and distribution of foot and leg care products. The SBE held that the parent and its domestic subsidiaries constituted a unitary business; however, the SBE held that the foreign subsidiaries were not a part of the unitary group, despite the unity of ownership and the common use of patents and trademarks. (See also the Court of Appeal decision in *F.W. Woolworth Co.*, cited above.)

● *Unusual groups combined*

Appeal of Cox Hobbies, Inc. (1980) (CCH CALIFORNIA TAX REPORTS ¶ 12-500.651) involved an affiliated group that included a parent corporation, five domestic subsidiaries, three foreign subsidiaries, and a domestic international sales corporation. The SBE held that all of the corporations were parts of a unitary business group and were required to be included in a combined return.

In *Appeal of Arkla Industries, Inc.* (1977) (CCH California Tax Reports ¶ 12-500.587), the taxpayer was a member of a group of corporations consisting of a parent corporation and five subsidiaries. Two of the subsidiaries, including the taxpayer, were qualified to do business in California, although none of the corporations in the group had its principal place of business in California. The parent corporation was a regulated company that produced and sold natural gas in five states, not including California. The SBE held that the entire group constituted a unitary operation required to file a combined return.

● *One or more subsidiaries excluded*

In *Appeal of C.H. Stuart, Inc.* (1984) (CCH CALIFORNIA TAX REPORTS ¶ 12-500.324), the taxpayer and several subsidiaries were engaged in an admittedly unitary business of manufacturing and selling jewelry and china. The taxpayer also owned four other subsidiaries that were engaged in diverse lines of business, and contended that all of the subsidiaries should be included in the unitary group because of intercompany financing, interlocking directors, and centralized administrative functions. The SBE held that the taxpayer had not shown that the intercompany relationships were of sufficient substance to justify unitary treatment.

In *Appeal of Daniel Industries, Inc.* (1980) (CCH CALIFORNIA TAX REPORTS ¶ 12-500.322), the taxpayer was admittedly engaged in a unitary business with four of its five subsidiaries. The SBE held that the fifth subsidiary was not a part of the unitary group; the SBE concluded that the unitary factors involving the subsidiary were insubstantial and had little effect on the income of the combined operations. To the same effect, see *Appeal of Triangle Publications, Inc.* (1984) (CCH CALIFORNIA TAX REPORTS ¶ 12-500.472).

● *New subsidiaries included*

In *Appeal of Household Finance Corp.* (1968) (CCH CALIFORNIA TAX REPORTS ¶ 12-500.564), the taxpayer was operating an admittedly unitary business through 485 subsidiaries. The SBE held that new subsidiaries started during the taxable year were includible in the unitary computation from the time they commenced business, and were also subject separately to the commencing-corporation provisions of prior law.

● *Foreign parent corporation*

There has been widespread public discussion of the propriety of including in a combined report a parent corporation in a foreign country. Although this was not the primary issue in the case, the question was considered and commented upon by the SBE in *Appeal of Beecham, Inc.* (1977) (CCH CALIFORNIA TAX REPORTS ¶ 12-500.586). As explained at ¶ 1304, the SBE approved the inclusion of the foreign parent.

In *Appeal of Nippondenso of Los Angeles, Inc.* (1984) (CCH CALIFORNIA TAX REPORTS ¶ 12-500.574), the taxpayer was a 75%-owned subsidiary of a Japanese parent. Both corporations were engaged in the business of automobile parts and accessories. Approximately 80% of the taxpayer's sales were to Toyota, U.S.A., its 25% owner. The SBE held that the business of the taxpayer and its parent was unitary, citing flow of goods, interlocking directors and officers, common trade name, and other indications of unity.

Appeal of Aimor Corp. (1983) (CCH CALIFORNIA TAX REPORTS ¶ 12-500.657) involved a Japanese parent corporation, a Japanese subsidiary, and a California subsidiary. There was an admittedly unitary relationship between the parent and its California subsidiary and also between the parent and its Japanese subsidiary, but none between the two subsidiaries. The SBE required inclusion of all three corporations in a combined return.

Another case involving a Japanese parent was *Appeal of Ito Cariani Sausage Co., Inc.* (1983) (CCH CALIFORNIA TAX REPORTS ¶ 12-500.572), in which the SBE cited and followed the *Shachitata*, discussed below, and the *Container Corporation* case, discussed above. In the *Ito Cariani* case, the California subsidiary, formed by the Japanese parent in 1974, continued a business that had been operating independently since 1898.

In *Appeal of Shachihata, Inc., U.S.A.* (1979) (CCH CALIFORNIA TAX REPORTS ¶ 12-500.652), the taxpayer was a wholly-owned subsidiary of a Japanese parent corporation. The operations of the two corporations appeared clearly to be unitary under the tests discussed at ¶ 1304, but the taxpayer advanced several constitutional arguments based on the fact that the parent was a foreign corporation. The SBE followed its long-standing policy of not ruling on constitutional questions and upheld the requirement of a combined return. See also, to the same effect, *Appeal of Kikkoman International, Inc.,* discussed at ¶ 1304; in that case, the SBE rejected the argument that a combined report would impose hardships because of language difficulties, different accounting standards, currency exchange rates, etc. Some of the same arguments were also rejected by the SBE in *Appeal of New Home Sewing Machine Company* (1982) (CCH CALIFORNIA TAX REPORTS ¶ 12-500.573); this case also involved a unitary group of corporations with a Japanese parent. See also companion cases *Appeal of California First Bank* and *Appeal of The Bank of Tokyo, Ltd.* (1985) (CCH CALIFORNIA TAX REPORTS ¶ 12-500.97), involving a Japanese bank and its 52%-owned California subsidiary. The latter cases were cited as authority in the *Appeals of Sumitomo Bank of California* and the *Sumitomo Bank, Ltd. of Osaka, Japan* (1987) (CCH CALIFORNIA TAX REPORTS ¶ 12-500.971), involving a finding of unity between a Japanese parent bank and its 55%-owned California subsidiary.

Some foreign corporations have sued and lost in Federal courts, in an effort to prevent California from taxing their unitary operations. See *EMI Limited* (1982) (CCH CALIFORNIA TAX REPORTS ¶ 12-500.14), *Alcan Aluminum Limited v. Franchise Tax Board* (1983) (CCH CALIFORNIA TAX REPORTS ¶ 12-500.141), and *Shell Petroleum, N.V. v. Mary Ann Graves et al.* (1983) (CCH CALIFORNIA TAX REPORTS ¶ 12-500.142); in all of these cases the U.S. Supreme Court declined to review the lower court's decision.

¶ 1309a Water's-Edge Election for Multinational Unitary Businesses

Law: Secs. 24344, 24411, 25110-14 (CCH CALIFORNIA TAX REPORTS ¶ 12-650).

Comparable Federal: None.

California Forms: FTB 2424, Form 100, Form 100-WE.

Multinational taxpayers have an option to compute their California tax base on a water's-edge basis. Taxpayers that make such an election are taxed on income from sources solely within the U.S.

The following are the major water's-edge provisions:

(1) *Qualifying entities:* Under the water's-edge election, California taxable income is computed based on the income and apportionment factors of only the following entities: (a) any corporation (other than a bank) the average of whose U.S. property, payroll, and sales is 20% or more; (b) U.S.-incorporated entities (excluding those incorporated in U.S. territories or possessions) not eligible to file a consolidated federal return, provided that more than 50% of their stock is controlled by the same interest; (c) DISCs, FSCs, and Export Trade Corporations; (d) any affiliated bank or corporation that is a "controlled foreign corporation" (CFC) as defined in IRC Sec. 957 and has "Subpart F income" as defined in IRC Sec. 952 (the income and apportionment factors of a CFC are multiplied by a fraction representing the ratio of Subpart F income to earnings and profits. A CFC is treated as having no Subpart F income if such income is less than $1 million and represents less than 5% of the CFC's earnings and profits); and (e) any entity not described above, to the extent that its income is derived from or attributable to U.S. sources.

Prior to 1996, taxpayers were also required to take into account the income and apportionment factors of affiliated banks or corporations that were eligible to file a consolidated return (excluding those electing "possession treatment" under IRC Sec. 936).

No entity may be included in the group unless it would have been a part of the taxpayer's unitary business had the water's-edge election not been made.

(2) *Deduction of dividends:* A qualifying water's-edge group may deduct up to 75% of dividends received from a 50% owned corporation if the average of the payor's U.S. property, payroll, and sales is less than 20%. Effective for income years beginning after 1997, dividends received from banks that meet this criteria also qualify for the deduction. The dividend deduction is computed on Schedule H of Form 100.

To qualify for water's-edge treatment, the taxpayer must agree that dividends received by *other* unitary group members from (1) an entity that is engaged in the same general business and that is more than 50% owned by members of the group, and (2) an entity that is a purchaser of 15% or more of either input or output from or source of supply to the unitary business are business income. Dividends received from any other entity will be classified as business or nonbusiness income under existing provisions.

A special provision permits a 100% deduction of dividends from foreign construction projects whose locations are not subject to the groups' control, provided certain other water's-edge conditions are met.

The deductible amount of qualifying foreign dividends is reduced by the amount of any interest expense incurred for puposes of foreign investment.

(3) *Water's-edge contract:* A water's-edge election is to be made by contract with the Franchise Tax Board (FTB) in the original tax return for the year, and is effective only if every water's-edge member who is required to file a California franchise or income tax return consents to the election. FTB Regulation 25111-1 indicates that an election contract will be considered valid as long as there has been substantial performance of the requirements for entering into the contract. "Substantial performance" means that despite noncompliance with one or more statutory or procedural requirements for making the election, there exists additional objective evidence that the election was intended. In the absence of a common parent election, the determination of whether there has been substantial performance will be made with reference to the actions of the entire water's-edge group. It is not necessary for every member of the group to substantially perform for an election to be valid.

For purposes of making an election, an "original return" is the last return filed on or before the due date (taking into account extensions) or, if no return is filed by that date, the first return filed after that date. An election cannot be made on an amended return filed after the due date (taking into account extensions) of the original return. However, timely filings that only supplement a previously filed return and are consistent with the previous filing will be treated as part of the original return, provided they contain objective evidence of substantial performance of the requirements for entering into an election contract.

An election (or notice of nonrenewal) by the common parent of a commonly controlled group constitutes an election (or nonrenewal) by all members

¶ 1309a

of the commonly controlled group that are members of the water's-edge group. A common parent may make such an election even if the common parent is not a taxpayer required to file a California return or will not be a member of the water's-edge group for which the election is being made. In such a case, the election must be made on an original return filed by a member of the water's-edge group required to file a California return. A taxpayer or group of affiliated taxpayers engaged in more than one unitary business may make the election with respect to one or more of the businesses, but need not make the election for all of its businesses.

The original contract is for 84 months, and is automatically renewed each year for an additional one-year period unless the taxpayer gives written notice of nonrenewal. The contract is in effect for 84 months from the beginning of the income year covered by the most recent anniversary date. If the members of a water's-edge group are on different fiscal years, each member must make the election on its original return for the income year for which the election is being made. The election will then be effective for each member of the water's-edge group from the beginning of the income year of the last member of the water's-edge group to file its return and election. The election may be terminated by a taxpayer prior to the end of the initial 84-month period under certain conditions.

A taxpayer electing water's-edge treatment must retain and make available upon request by the FTB various kinds of information and documents relating to, among other things, pricing policy, methods of allocating income and expense, apportionment factors, assignment of income to the U.S. or to foreign jurisdictions, information filed with the IRS, and tax returns from other states. The FTB is given broad auditing powers with respect to a water's-edge group.

¶ 1310 Deductions for Interest and Contributions

> *Law:* Secs. 24344, 24357 (CCH California Tax Reports ¶ 10-557, 10-617, 12-475, 12-570).

> *Comparable Federal:* Secs. 163, 170 (CCH Standard Federal Tax Reports ¶ 9102, 11,675).

Adjustment of deductions for interest and contributions may be required where income is allocated within and without the State.

The deduction for interest expense is limited where income from interest or dividends is allocated outside California—see ¶ 1002 for details.

● *Limit on deduction for contributions*

As explained at ¶ 1010, the deduction for contributions is limited to 10% of the net income; this deduction may require adjustment in some cases where a portion of the total net income is allocated outside of California. The usual practice is to treat contributions as one of the deductions entering into the computation of the net income from unitary operations that is subject to allocation within and without the state. If this is done where the total contributions exceed 10% of total net income (and the total deduction has been limited accordingly) and where all the income and deductions relate to the unitary operations, the adjustment of the effective contributions deduction to

10% of the net income used as the measure of the tax is automatic. On the other hand, in a case where the total contributions amount to less than 10% of the net income allocated to California, there is no problem of limitation of the deduction. Under some other circumstances, however, the contributions deduction may require special treatment to limit the deduction to 10% of the net income that is used as the measure of the tax after allocation.

¶ 1311 Allocation and Apportionment—Administration

Law: Sec. 25101 (CCH CALIFORNIA TAX REPORTS ¶ 12-670, 12-675, 12-690).

Comparable Federal: None.

California Forms: Sch. R, FTB Pub. 1061.

The return form contains a separate schedule (Schedule R) for allocation of income, with instructions for its use. The schedule provides for the use of the allocation formula described above.

● *Information required from affiliated group*

Where an affiliated group of corporations is involved, the taxpayer is required by the Franchise Tax Board (FTB) to submit information regarding income and business of the group. The information submitted should include, in columnar form, profit and loss statements, a combined apportionment formula disclosing for each corporation the total amount of property, payroll, and sales and the amount of California property, payroll, and sales, and schedules disclosing for each corporation: (1) the various adjustments necessary to convert the combined profit and loss statement to the combined income subject to apportionment; (2) any items of nonbusiness income or expense allocated to California; (3) computations of the amount of the interest offset and the charitable contributions adjustment; (4) the alternative minimum tax calculation; (5) information required by Form 100; and (6) the computation of income apportionable and allocable to California and the computation of each member's tax credits and tax liability.

The combined apportionment schedule must reflect the elimination of intercompany sales and other intercompany revenue items, intercompany rent charges, intercompany dividends, and intercompany profits in inventories, if any.

● *Corporations separate entities for some purposes*

Despite the combined reporting approach discussed above, members of the combined group are treated as separate entities for some purposes. Thus, elections to report sales on the installment basis or to use the completed-contract method of accounting should be made individually for each corporation involved. Use of accelerated depreciation methods is based upon the experience of individual group members.

● *Instruction booklet available*

A booklet entitled "Guidelines for Corporations Filing a Combined Report" (FTB Pub. 1061) is available from the FTB. It outlines the rules and schedule format to be followed in preparing such reports.

¶ 1311

● *Filing of single combined return*

The FTB permits taxpayers to elect to file one combined return for all the corporations in a unitary group, in lieu of separate returns for each corporation. The parent, or other designated "key" corporation, files the return and pays the entire tax. If the parent corporation is not a California taxpayer, the key corporation should be the taxpayer with the largest value of assets in California. The election is made on Schedule R-7. Each corporation included in the group return must (1) be a taxpayer required to file a return in this state, (2) be a member of a single unitary group for the entire income year, (3) have the same income year as the key corporation or an income year that is wholly included within the income year of the key corporation, and (4) have the same statutory filing date as the key corporation for the income year.

● *Separate returns for group members*

If a unitary group does not elect the combined-return procedure, a separate return must be filed for each subject corporation. Each such return should carry a notation stating that a combined report has been filed and referring to the inclusion of the necessary supporting schedules in the return of the appropriate corporation. The return of each corporation should reflect the tax on the income allocated to that corporation in the supporting schedules; or, alternatively, the minimum tax may be assessed on all returns except one, and the balance of the entire tax of the affiliated group assessed on the return of one of the group.

● *Reporting should be consistent*

Once a determination has been made as to whether the income should be reported on a combined basis or by separate accounting, the returns should thereafter be prepared on the agreed basis until conditions change so that the method is no longer proper.

¶ 1311

CHAPTER 14

TAXES ON CORPORATE INCOME
ADMINISTRATION, DEFICIENCIES, REFUNDS

¶ 1401 Administration of Tax—General

Law: Secs. 18624-25, 19376, 19501-04.7, 19801-02, 19525, 19530, 19717, 21001-26 (CCH CALIFORNIA TAX REPORTS ¶ 10-017, 89-300, 89-315, 89-345, 89-410, 89-416, 89-430, 89-510).

Comparable Federal: Secs. 6107, 6109, 7430, 7811 (CCH STANDARD FEDERAL TAX REPORTS ¶ 37,920, 37,960, 42,340).

Same as personal income tax—see ¶ 701.

¶ 1401

¶ 1401a Taxpayers' Bill of Rights

Law: Secs. 19225, 21001-27 (CCH CALIFORNIA TAX REPORTS ¶ 89-510).

Comparable Federal: Sec. 7811.

Taxpayers dealing with the Franchise Tax Board (FTB) are given a wide range of protections under the "Katz-Harris Taxpayers' Bill of Rights." The provisions contained in the "Bill of Rights" govern the FTB's administration of both the personal income and corporation franchise (income) taxes.

● *Suspension of corporate powers*

The FTB may not suspend a taxpayer's corporate powers for failure to pay taxes, penalties, or interest, or for failure to file required returns or statements, without mailing the taxpayer a written notice of the suspension at least 60 days in advance. The notice must indicate the date on which the suspension will occur and the statute under which the action is being taken.

● *Hearing and appeal procedures*

Protest hearings before the FTB's audit or legal staff must be held at times and places that are reasonable and convenient to the taxpayer. Prior to the hearing, the taxpayer must be informed of the right to have an attorney, accountant, or other agent present. Hearings may be recorded only with prior notice, and the taxpayer is entitled to receive a copy of any such recording. Further information on protest hearings is at ¶ 1402.

Taxpayers who appeal to the State Board of Equalization (SBE) and who are successful may be awarded reimbursement for reasonable fees and expenses related to the appeal that were incurred after the appeal was filed. The decision to make such an award is discretionary with the SBE, which must determine, in ruling upon a reimbursement claim filed with the SBE, whether action taken by the FTB's staff was unreasonable and, in particular, whether the FTB has established that its position in the appeal was substantially justified. Effective for fees and expenses incurred after April 7, 2000, (1) the starting point after which reasonable fees and expenses may be awarded is the date of the notice of proposed deficiency assessment rather than the date the appeal was filed and (2) fees may be awarded in excess of the fees paid or incurred if the fees paid or incurred are less than reasonable fees.

For appeals to the SBE from an action of the FTB on a deficiency assessment protest or refund claim, the burden of proving the correctness of certain items of income reported by third parties on information returns filed with the FTB also shifts to the FTB if the taxpayer asserts a reasonable dispute with respect to the reported amounts and fully cooperates with the FTB. The items of income to which the shift applies are the same as under federal law.

Further information on appeals to the SBE is at ¶ 1403 and ¶ 1414.

● *Tax levy protections*

Applicable to tax collection actions initiated after June 29, 2000, the FTB is generally required to send a notice of levy to a taxpayer at least 30 days prior to issuing a levy for unpaid tax. Also, if the FTB holds the collection of

¶ 1401a

unpaid tax in abeyance for more than six months, the FTB must mail the taxpayer an additional notice prior to issuing a levy. If a taxpayer requests an independent administrative review within the 30-day period, the levy action will be suspended until 15 days after there is a final determination in the review.

Except in the case of property seized as a result of a jeopardy assessment, a previously issued tax levy must be released whenever (1) the state's expenses in selling the property levied upon would exceed the taxpayer's liability, (2) the proceeds of the sale would not result in a reasonable reduction of the taxpayer's debt, (3) the levy was not issued in accordance with administrative procedures, (4) the release of the levy will facilitate the collection of the tax liability or will be in the best interest of the taxpayer and the State, or (5) the FTB otherwise deems the release of the levy appropriate. Certain goods are exempt from levy under California's Code of Civil Procedure; the taxpayer must be notified in writing of these exemptions prior to the sale of any seized property. A taxpayer may be reimbursed for bank charges incurred as a result of an erroneous levy.

● *Civil actions against the FTB; litigation costs*

Taxpayers aggrieved by the reckless disregard of the FTB's published procedures on the part of an officer or employee of the FTB may bring a Superior Court action against the State for actual damages. In determining damages, the court must take into consideration any contributing negligence on the taxpayer's part. A taxpayer prevailing in such an action is entitled to reasonable litigation costs, but there is a penalty of up to $10,000 for filing frivolous claims.

A taxpayer may also file a civil action against the State for direct economic damages and costs totaling up to $50,000 if an officer or employee of the FTB intentionally entices an attorney, certified public accountant, or tax preparer representing the taxpayer into disclosing taxpayer information in exchange for a compromise or settlement of the representative's tax liability. However, the action is not allowed if the information was conveyed by the taxpayer to the representative for the purpose of perpetuating a fraud or crime. The action must be brought within two years after the date the activities creating the liability were discoverable by the exercise of reasonable care.

● *Reliance on FTB written opinions; taxpayers' remedies*

Under certain circumstances, taxpayers may be relieved of penalties, interest, or tax liability itself when the taxpayers relied to their detriment on written rulings from the FTB.

The discussion at ¶701b generally applies to corporate taxpayers, with some differences regarding requests for advance rulings. The FTB will not issue advance rulings to corporate taxpayers under the following circumstances (FTB Notice No. 89-277, CCH CALIFORNIA TAX REPORTS ¶89-050.25):

> (1) the question is of a type that the IRS has announced it will not rule on in advance (e.g., hypothetical questions, alternative plans of proposed transactions);

(2) the taxpayer's name or identifying number is omitted from the request;

(3) the requester is a professional preparer or taxpayer representative who has not provided the FTB with his or her own legal analysis and conclusion;

(4) the law is already clear or is the same as federal law;

(5) the question is primarily one of fact (e.g., whether a business is unitary);

(6) the issue arises in an ongoing audit, appeal, or protest involving the requesting taxpayer; or

(7) the issue is currently pending in an appeal or court decision.

● *Tax liens*

A taxpayer is entitled to preliminary notice of the proposed filing or recording of a tax lien, mailed at least 30 days beforehand; in the interim, the taxpayer may prevent the filing or recording by presenting substantial evidence that the lien would be in error. Also, applicable to tax collection actions initiated after June 29, 2000, the FTB must notify taxpayers in writing of the filing or recording of a notice of state tax lien at least five business days after the date the notice of lien is filed. If the FTB holds the collection of unpaid tax in abeyance for more than six months, the FTB must mail the taxpayer an additional notice prior to filing or recording a notice of state tax lien. An independent administrative review with the FTB is available if the taxpayer makes a request within the 15-day period beginning on the day after the five-day period described above.

If the FTB finds that its action was in error, it must mail a release to the taxpayer and the lien recorder within seven working days. The FTB may also release a lien if it determines that the release will facilitate the collection of tax or will be in the best interest of the taxpayer and the State.

● *Unassociated payments*

If the FTB receives a payment from a taxpayer that the FTB cannot associate with the taxpayer's account, the FTB must make reasonable efforts to notify the taxpayer of this situation within 60 days after receipt of the payment.

● *Annual notice of tax delinquencies*

The FTB must mail an annual notice to each taxpayer who has a delinquent tax account, indicating the amount of the delinquency as of the date of the notice, unless a previously mailed notice has been returned to the FTB as undeliverable or the account has been discharged from accountability.

● *Other provisions*

The Taxpayers' Bill of Rights also requires the FTB to undertake extensive taxpayer education and information programs; report annually to the legislature concerning areas of noncompliance with the tax laws; develop simplified written statements of taxpayer rights and FTB procedures; develop and implement an employee and officer evaluation program; and draw up plans to reduce the time required to resolve amended return claims for refunds, protests, and appeals. As under the personal income tax law (see ¶ 719), the FTB is authorized to settle certain civil tax disputes. FTB officers and employees are prohibited from authorizing, requiring, or conducting the investigation or surveillance of taxpayers for reasons unrelated to tax administration.

¶ 1402 Deficiencies—Procedure, Protests

Law: Secs. 19031-34, 19036-51, 19054, 19057-58, 19064-67, 19087 (CCH CALIFORNIA TAX REPORTS ¶ 89-302, 89-523).

Comparable Federal: Secs. 6211—6213, 6501, 7609 (CCH STANDARD FEDERAL TAX REPORTS ¶ 38,535, 38,540, 39,910, 43,790).

Same as personal income tax—see ¶ 702.

¶ 1403 Deficiencies—Appeal to State Board of Equalization

Law: Secs. 19045-48 (CCH CALIFORNIA TAX REPORTS ¶ 10-017, 89-523).

Comparable Federal: Secs. 6211-13 (CCH STANDARD FEDERAL TAX REPORTS ¶ 38,535—38,555).

Same as personal income tax—see ¶ 703.

¶ 1404 Final Assessment of Deficiency

Law: Secs. 19042, 19049 (CCH CALIFORNIA TAX REPORTS ¶ 89-302, 89-523).

Comparable Federal: Secs. 6155, 6213 (CCH STANDARD FEDERAL TAX REPORTS ¶ 38,140, 38,545).

Same as personal income tax—see ¶ 704.

¶ 1405 Jeopardy Assessments

Law: Secs. 19081-86 (CCH CALIFORNIA TAX REPORTS ¶ 89-306).

Comparable Federal: Secs. 6861, 6863 (CCH STANDARD FEDERAL TAX REPORTS ¶ 41,260, 41,320).

Same as personal income tax—see ¶ 705.

¶ 1406 Bankruptcy and Receiverships

Law: Sec. 19088 (CCH CALIFORNIA TAX REPORTS ¶ 89-308).

Comparable Federal: Secs. 6871-73 (CCH STANDARD FEDERAL TAX REPORTS ¶ 41,410, 41,440, 41,450).

Same as personal income tax—see ¶ 706.

¶ 1407 Transferee Liability

Law: Secs. 19071-74 (CCH CALIFORNIA TAX REPORTS ¶ 89-310).

Comparable Federal: Secs. 6901-4 (CCH STANDARD FEDERAL TAX REPORTS ¶ 41,500, 41,580, 41,605, 41,640).

The law contains provisions permitting assessment and collection of tax from persons secondarily liable. The period of limitations is extended for assessments against transferees and fiduciaries. California law is the same as federal law.

Both California and federal laws provide for suspension of the running of the period of limitations against the transferee while the taxpayer is exercising an administrative remedy.

¶ 1408 Statute of Limitations on Assessments

Law: Secs. 19057-67 (CCH CALIFORNIA TAX REPORTS ¶ 89-139, 89-161, 89-181, 89-302, 89-304).

Comparable Federal: Secs. 1311-14, 6501-4, 7609 (CCH STANDARD FEDERAL TAX REPORTS ¶ 33,300—33,360, 39,910—40,000, 43,790).

Same as personal income tax, as explained at ¶ 708, except that the corporation tax law extends the limitation period under certain circumstances as to transferees and fiduciaries whereas the personal income tax law does not. The running of the statute of limitations is also suspended until a taxpayer reports required information to the FTB concerning foreign corporations or transfers to foreign persons (see ¶ 1412a for a discussion of the reporting requirements).

California has no provision for a shortened period of limitations for dissolving corporations; federal law does.

¶ 1409 Interest on Deficiencies

Law: Secs. 19101-04, 19106, 19108, 19111-15, 19521 (CCH CALIFORNIA TAX REPORTS ¶ 89-430, 89-436).

Comparable Federal: Secs. 6404, 6601, 6621 (CCH STANDARD FEDERAL TAX REPORTS ¶ 39,520, 40,310).

Interest is charged on deficiencies, other delinquent payments of tax, and on extensions of payment of tax and penalties. The rules are generally the same as for the personal income tax, as outlined at ¶ 709. However, there is a special higher interest rate applicable to large corporate underpayments (see below) and the abatement available to disaster victims is inapplicable to corporate taxpayers.

Interest rates are as follows:

January 1, 1996—June 30, 1996	9%
July 1, 1996—December 31, 1996	9%
January 1, 1997—June 30, 1997	9%
July 1, 1997—December 31, 1997	9%
January 1, 1998—June 30, 1998	9%
July 1, 1998—December 31, 1998	9%
January 1, 1999—June 30, 1999	8%
July 1, 1999—December 31, 1999	7%
January 1, 2000—June 30, 2000	8%

The rate is determined semiannually and compounded daily, as explained at ¶ 709.

Both federal and California law allow the abatement of all or any portion of interest that results from errors or delays in the performance of ministerial acts by the respective taxing agencies, as explained at ¶ 709.

There is a special rule that applies to certain cases involving related items where overpayments are offset against deficiencies. In such cases, no interest is charged on the portion of the deficiency extinguished by the credit for overpayment for the period subsequent to the date the overpayment was made.

● *Interest on large corporate underpayments*

Both California and federal law require all corporations except S corporations to pay interest on large underpayments at 2% above the regular rate. A large underpayment is one that exceeds $100,000 for any taxable period. Under federal law, the 2% interest rate increase generally applies to periods after the 30th day following the date the IRS sends either a "30-day letter" or a deficiency notice, whichever is earlier. California modifies this provision so that the increased interest rate applies to periods after the 30th day following either the date on which a proposed assessment is issued or the date when the notice and demand is sent, whichever is earlier. Under both California and federal law, interest does not begin to accrue until after the mailing of a letter or notice of deficiency, proposed deficiency, assessment, or proposed assessment shows an amount exceeding $100,000. For income years beginning before 1999 for California purposes and for tax years beginning before 1998 for federal purposes, interest began to accrue whenever a notice was sent, even if the initial amount listed was $100,000 or less. FTB Notice 98-6 (1998) addresses the calculation of the additional interest imposed against unitary corporate members filing a group return (see CCH CALIFORNIA TAX REPORTS ¶ 89-430.821).

¶ 1410 Penalties

Law: Secs. 19131-36, 19141-41.6, 19164, 19166-69, 19176-81, 19183, 19187, 19254, 19262, 19442, 19701-715, 19719-21, 21015, 23186 (CCH CALIFORNIA TAX REPORTS ¶ 10-059, 89-139, 89-181, 89-330, 89-410—89-420).

Comparable Federal: Secs. 6050I, 6651-53, 6657-58, 6662-65, 6673, 6694, 6700-03, 6706, 6721-24, 7201-06 (CCH STANDARD FEDERAL TAX REPORTS ¶ 40,370—40,400, 40,500, 40,520, 40,540, 40,585, 40,755, 40,825—40,845, 40,875, 40,965—40,995, 40,010—42,030).

[*NOTE:* See ¶ 1401a for possible relief after detrimental reliance on advice from the Franchise Tax Board (FTB).]

Same as personal income tax, as explained at ¶710, except as noted below.

The corporation tax law does not include provisions for the penalties listed at items (1), (2), (7), (15), (16), (17), (23), (25), (26), (27), (28), (33), (43), or (44) in ¶710.

The corporation tax law contains provisions similar to those described at items (34), (35), (36), (37), and (38) in ¶710, but the possible fines are higher, reaching a maximum of $200,000.

The corporation tax law provides the following penalties in addition to those described at ¶710:

(1) failing without reasonable cause to file return if corporation is doing business in the state without being qualified—$2,000 per income year;

(2) failing to file corporate organization statement—$250 ($50 for nonprofit corporation);

(3) failing to furnish information concerning foreign-controlled corporation—$10,000 per year of failure;

(4) failing to furnish information concerning transfers to foreign persons—25% of gain on transaction;

(5) failing to report transactions between foreign corporations and foreign investors—$10,000 per year of failure;

(6) failing to keep water's edge records—$10,000 per year; if 90 days after notice by the FTB, $10,000 per 30-day period, not to exceed $50,000;

(7) failing to file copy of federal information return concerning large cash transactions—$50 per return, up to $100,000 maximum per year; if intentional disregard, $100 per return, or, if greater, 5% of the aggregate amount of items required to be reported;

(8) failing to provide information that is required to determine rate of bank and franchise tax—$5,000 and disallowance of specified deductions; and

(9) exercising the powers of a corporation suspended for nonpayment of taxes or transacting interstate business of a forfeited foreign corporation—misdemeanor; $250 to $1,000 and/or up to one year in jail (however, the penalty does not apply to any insurer, or counsel retained by an insurer, who provides a defense for a suspended or forfeited corporation in a civil action for personal injury, property damage, or economic losses, and who prosecutes, in conjunction with that defense, any subrogation, contribution, or indemnity rights against other persons or entities in the name of the suspended or forfeited corporation).

See ¶805a for penalties imposed for late filing of returns of exempt organizations.

A penalty for the failure to file a federal cash transaction return is imposed in accordance with federal law.

¶1410

● *Penalties imposed under Corporations Code*

The corporation tax law imposes a penalty of $250 for failure to file with the Secretary of State an annual statement required by California Corporations Code Sec. 1502—see ¶ 805. The tax law also imposes a penalty of $50 for failure of a nonprofit corporation to file with the Secretary of State a statement required by Corporations Code Sec. 6210 or 8210—see ¶ 805a.

● *Collection and filing enforcement fees*

Collection and filing enforcement fees similar to those discussed at ¶ 710 are imposed under the corporation tax law, but the applicable fees for the state's 1999-2000 fiscal year are $141 and $206, respectively. The fees do not apply to exempt organizations.

● *Relief from penalties*

Relief from the penalties listed in items (3), (4), and (5), above, may be granted, provided that the taxpayer's failure to furnish the required information neither jeopardized the best interests of the state nor resulted from the taxpayer's willful neglect or an intent not to comply.

● *Cases and rulings*

Appeal of BSR USA, Ltd., and BSR North America, Ltd. (1996) (CCH CALIFORNIA TAX REPORTS ¶ 89-410.2891) involved the imposition of the 25% penalty for failure to furnish information on notice and demand by the FTB. The corporate taxpayers failed to respond to repeated requests by the FTB for information concerning the income and apportionment factors of the taxpayers' foreign affiliates. The penalty was not subject to abatement, because the taxpayers' conduct indicated a pattern of delay and misdirection that belied their contention that the requested information was either not available or too costly to obtain.

In *Appeal of Vidal Sassoon, Inc.* (1986) (CCH CALIFORNIA TAX REPORTS ¶ 89-410.59), the reasonable cause exception was not applicable to late extension requests and the State Board of Equalization (SBE) upheld the late-filing penalty.

In *Appeal of Krofft Entertainment, Inc.* (1984) (CCH CALIFORNIA TAX REPORTS ¶ 89-410.37), the taxpayer claimed that its failure to file a timely franchise tax return was due to reasonable cause. The SBE upheld the imposition of a $17,436 penalty, despite the fact that the Internal Revenue Service had removed a similar federal penalty upon a finding of reasonable cause.

In *Appeal of Avco Financial Services, Inc.* (1979) (CCH CALIFORNIA TAX REPORTS ¶ 89-410.385), a late payment penalty was imposed in a case where 84% of the tax was paid by the regular due date. The SBE upheld the penalty, noting that the difficulty of estimating the tax on worldwide income did not constitute reasonable cause for the underpayment. To the same effect, see *Appeal of Diebold, Incorporated* (1983) (CCH CALIFORNIA TAX REPORTS ¶ 89-410.851); in this case, the taxpayer's extensive operations required the filing of approximately 350 state and local tax returns.

¶ 1410

¶ 1411 Information at Source

> *Law:* Secs. 18631, 18636-45, 18647-49 (CCH CALIFORNIA TAX REPORTS ¶ 89-171).
>
> *Comparable Federal:* Secs. 6041, 6041A, 6042, 6050I, 6050L (CCH STANDARD FEDERAL TAX REPORTS ¶ 36,920, 36,940, 36,960, 37,300, 37,360).

Same as personal income tax—see ¶ 711.

¶ 1412 Withholding of Tax at Source

> *Law:* Secs. 18661-62, 18665, 18667-77, 19009 (CCH CALIFORNIA TAX REPORTS ¶ 89-335, 89-440).
>
> *Comparable Federal:* Secs. 1441, 1445 (CCH STANDARD FEDERAL TAX REPORTS ¶ 33,902, 33,980).

The corporation tax law gives the Franchise Tax Board broad power to require the withholding of tax on payments to payees subject to either franchise or income tax. Withholding of tax is required on income paid to corporations that do not have a permanent place of business in this state. A corporation has a permanent place of business in this state if it is organized under the laws of this state or if it is a foreign corporation qualified to transact business in this state.

Corporations, among others, are required to withhold tax on certain payments to nonresidents, to withhold amounts due from delinquent taxpayers, to withhold tax on dispositions of California real estate, and to withhold tax from wages—see ¶ 712 and ¶ 712a.

¶ 1412a Reports on Foreign and Foreign-Owned Corporations, Transfers to Foreign Persons

> *Law:* Secs. 19141.2, 19141.5, 21015 (CCH CALIFORNIA TAX REPORTS ¶ 89-171, 89-179, 89-410).
>
> *Comparable Federal:* Secs. 6038, 6038A, 6038B, 6038C (CCH STANDARD FEDERAL TAX REPORTS ¶ 50,068M).

Corporations that are incorporated in California or doing business in the state and that are more than 25% foreign owned must file a copy of the information return required by IRC Sec. 6038A with respect to transactions with related parties. Special record-keeping requirements are also imposed. Failure to comply subjects a corporation to a $10,000 penalty.

In addition, California has adopted the information reporting requirements of IRC Secs. 6038B and 6038C. However, California does not incorporate the penalty imposed under IRC Sec. 6038B against a person that fails to notify the Franchise Tax Board (FTB) regarding a transfer of property to a foreign partnership in exchange for a partnership interest. IRC Sec. 6038B requires the filing of information returns with respect to certain transfers of property to foreign corporations and other foreign persons and, in cases of failure to report, imposes a penalty equal to 25% of the amount of gain realized on the exchange. IRC Sec. 6038C requires foreign corporations engaged in U.S. business to file information returns and imposes a $10,000 penalty for noncompliance.

Relief from these penalties may be granted, provided that the taxpayer's failure to furnish the required information neither jeopardized the best interests of the state nor resulted from the taxpayer's willful neglect or an intent not to comply.

Domestic corporations subject to California corporation franchise (income) tax that own more than 50% of the combined voting power, or the value, of all classes of stock of a foreign corporation are required to file with the FTB a copy of the information return required by IRC Sec. 6038 with respect to interests in a foreign corporation (federal Form 5471). Effective for income years beginning after 1997, if a taxpayer fails to comply without reasonable cause and not due to willful neglect, the taxpayer will be subject to the same penalty imposed under federal law prior to its amendment by the Taxpayer Relief Act of 1997. The California penalty is $1,000 for each annual accounting period in which the information is not supplied and an additional $1,000 for each 30-day period (or fraction thereof) beyond the first 90 days, up to a maximum penalty of $24,000. The penalty may be waived if (1) a copy of the information return is filed with the FTB within 90 days after notification and the taxpayer agrees to attach a copy of the information to the taxpayer's original return for subsequent income years or (2) the taxpayer enters into a voluntary disclosure agreement with the FTB (see ¶ 1420).

¶ 1413 Overpayments and Refunds—Procedure

> *Law:* Secs. 19301-24, 19331-35 (CCH California Tax Reports ¶ 89-237, 89-248, 89-526, 89-532).
>
> *Comparable Federal:* Secs. 6401-08 (CCH Standard Federal Tax Reports ¶ 39,430—39,610).
>
> *California Form:* Form 100X.

Same as personal income tax, as explained at ¶ 713, except that refund claims should be filed on Form 100X (Amended Corporation Franchise or Income Tax Return).

A corporation that overpays its tax under the estimated-tax procedure may obtain a refund before the return is filed—see ¶ 806a.

¶ 1414 Refund Claims—Appeal to State Board of Equalization

> *Law:* Secs. 19332-34 (CCH California Tax Reports ¶ 89-532, 89-541).
>
> *Comparable Federal:* Secs. 6401-7 (CCH Standard Federal Tax Reports ¶ 39,430—39,610).

Same as personal income tax—see ¶ 714.

¶ 1415 Statute of Limitations on Refund Claims

> *Law:* Secs. 19041.5, 19306-14 (CCH California Tax Reports ¶ 89-526).
>
> *Comparable Federal:* Sec. 6511 (CCH Standard Federal Tax Reports ¶ 40,010).

Same as personal income tax, as explained at ¶ 715, except that the special 7-year rule (item (c)) does not apply to worthless securities losses.

The law permits a barred refund of one taxpayer to be offset against a deficiency of an affiliated taxpayer in cases where the tax is determined on a combined basis as discussed at ¶ 1309. This provision also permits a similar offset where items of income or deductions have been transferred from one year to another. However, an offset will not be allowed in either case where more than seven years have elapsed from the due date of the return on which the overpayment is determined.

¶ 1416 Suits for Refund

Law: Secs. 19041.5, 19381-92 (CCH CALIFORNIA TAX REPORTS ¶ 89-505, 89-559).

Comparable Federal: Sec. 6532 (CCH STANDARD FEDERAL TAX REPORTS ¶ 40,220).

Same as personal income tax—see ¶ 716.

¶ 1417 Interest on Overpayments

Law: Secs. 19325, 19340-51, 19363 (CCH CALIFORNIA TAX REPORTS ¶ 89-433, 89-436).

Comparable Federal: Sec. 6611 (CCH STANDARD FEDERAL TAX REPORTS ¶ 40,330).

The corporation tax rules for interest on overpayments are generally the same as for personal income tax, as explained at ¶ 718. The interest rate is the same as the rate for deficiencies, as explained at ¶ 1409.

In *Appeal of MCA, Inc.* (1967) (CCH CALIFORNIA TAX REPORTS ¶ 89-433.25), the State Board of Equalization allowed interest on an overpayment of franchise tax although the Franchise Tax Board had contended that such interest was not payable because the overpayment was not made "incident to a bona fide and orderly discharge of an actual liability."

¶ 1418 Closing Agreements

Law: Secs. 19441-42 (CCH CALIFORNIA TAX REPORTS ¶ 89-360).

Comparable Federal: Sec. 7121 (CCH STANDARD FEDERAL TAX REPORTS ¶ 41,880).

Same as personal income tax—see ¶ 719.

¶ 1419 Compromise of Tax Liability

Law: Sec. 19443 (CCH CALIFORNIA TAX REPORTS ¶ 89-360).

Comparable Federal: Sec. 7122 (CCH STANDARD FEDERAL TAX REPORTS ¶ 41,910).

California Form: 4905BCT.

Same as personal income tax—see ¶ 720.

¶ 1420 Voluntary Disclosure Agreements

Laws: Secs. 19191-94 (CCH CALIFORNIA TAX REPORTS ¶ 89-360).

Comparable Federal: None.

Same as personal income tax—see ¶ 721.

¶ 1421 Recovery of Erroneous Refunds

Law: Secs. 19054, 19411-13 (CCH CALIFORNIA TAX REPORTS ¶ 89-350).

Comparable Federal: Secs. 6532, 6602, 7405 (CCH STANDARD FEDERAL TAX REPORTS ¶ 40,220, 40,320, 42,255).

Same as personal income tax—see ¶ 722.

PART V
SALES AND USE TAX

CHAPTER 15

SALES AND USE TAXES

¶ 1501 Overview of Sales and Use Taxes

Law: Secs. 6051-51.4, 6201-01.4, 7200-12 (CCH CALIFORNIA TAX REPORTS ¶ 60-110, 60-120).

The California sales tax was first imposed in 1933; the use tax in 1935. These taxes, which are administered by the State Board of Equalization, have become a major source of the state's revenue.

The sales tax is imposed upon retailers for the privilege of selling tangible personal property at retail. Although the tax is not levied directly on the consumer, it is ordinarily passed on to the consumer. The use tax, enacted as a complement to the sales tax, is imposed upon the storage, use, or other consumption in California of tangible personal property purchased from a retailer without being subjected to the sales tax.

The sales or use tax payable in connection with any given transaction is the sum of three components: (1) the basic state sales and use tax, (2) the Bradley-Burns local tax, and (3) additional local "transactions and use" taxes, if any.

The basic state sales and use tax rate, which applies to all taxable transactions, is 6%.

The Bradley-Burns Uniform Local Sales and Use Tax Law authorizes counties to impose an additional $1\frac{1}{4}$% tax on all transactions that are subject to state sales and use tax, and every California county does so. Accordingly, if a transaction is taxable at all, it is subject to a combined rate of at least $7\frac{1}{4}$%—the basic 6% state rate plus the $1\frac{1}{4}$% Bradley-Burns rate.

State law also authorizes counties, cities, and certain special taxing districts to impose local "transactions and use" taxes for various purposes. The per-county cap on combined transactions and use taxes is 1½%, except in the City and County of San Francisco, where such taxes may be imposed at a maximum rate of 1¾%, and in San Mateo County, where such taxes may be imposed at a maximum rate of 2% under certain circumstances.

For purposes of determining which local taxes apply to a transaction, all retail sales are deemed to occur at the place of business of the seller. This rule applies regardless of the physical location of the property sold and regardless of where title to the property passes to the buyer. Special rules apply to determine the place of use of leased vehicles for purposes of reporting and transmitting local use tax.

¶ 1502 Imposition of Tax—Constitutional Limitations

> **Law:** Secs. 2-4, Art. XIIIA, Cal. Constitution; Secs. 23027, 50075 et seq., Government Code; Sec. 99550, Public Utility Code (CCH CALIFORNIA TAX REPORTS ¶ 61-710).

Counties, cities, and special districts are prohibited from imposing "special taxes" (those levied to fund a specific governmental project or program) unless two-thirds of the local electorate approves. In *Richard J. Rider et al. v. County of San Diego et al.* (1991) (CCH CALIFORNIA TAX REPORTS ¶ 61-710.46), the California Supreme Court invalidated a transactions and use tax imposed by the San Diego County Regional Justice Facility Financing Agency with the approval of a bare majority of the district's voters, because the agency was a "special district" and the tax it imposed was a "special tax." The *Rider* court determined that the term "special district" includes any taxing agency created to raise funds for city or county purposes to replace revenues lost because of Proposition 13's restrictions on property taxation (see ¶ 1702 for a discussion of Proposition 13). Approval by a two-thirds vote was similarly required in *Howard Jarvis Taxpayers' Association et al. v. State Board of Equalization* (1993) (CCH CALIFORNIA TAX REPORTS ¶ 61-710.464) for any local sales and use tax imposed by a county justice facilities financing agency in Orange, Humboldt, Los Angeles, Riverside, San Bernardino, Stanislaus, or Ventura county.

In *Hoogasian Flowers, Inc., et al. v. State Board of Equalization* (1994) (CCH CALIFORNIA TAX REPORTS ¶ 61-730.39) a California court of appeal held that a local sales and use tax imposed by the San Francisco Educational Financing Authority for the general purpose of providing financial assistance to schools was invalid because it was not approved by two-thirds of the electorate voting on the measure, as required under *Rider.*

State law prohibits retroactive application of the *Rider* decision to any tax imposed by a transportation agency with the approval of a simple majority of the district's voters prior to December 19, 1991 (the date of the *Rider* decision).

In *Santa Clara County Local Transportation Authority v. Carl Guardino et al.* (1995) (CCH CALIFORNIA TAX REPORTS ¶ 61-710.465), the California Supreme Court upheld a majority vote approval requirement for "general taxes" proposed by local governments. At the November 5, 1996, general election, California voters approved a measure that specifically prohibits *all* local governments, including charter cities, from imposing, extending, or increasing any general tax after November 5, 1996, without the approval of a majority of the local electorate. In addition, all general taxes imposed, extended, or increased by local governments without voter approval after 1994 and before November 6, 1996, must be submitted to local voters for approval by November 6, 1998, and be approved by a majority of the voters in order to continue to be imposed.

¶ 1503 Transactions Subject to Sales Tax

Law: Secs. 6001-6294 (CCH California Tax Reports ¶ 60-210—60-760).

The sales tax applies to the gross receipts of retailers from the sale of tangible personal property, with the exceptions listed in ¶ 1504 below. A "retail sale" is defined as a sale of tangible personal property for any purpose other than for resale in the regular course of business. The tax applies to certain rental transactions, and to many occasional and non-recurring sales by persons who ordinarily would not be thought of as "retailers" (see ¶ 1503c, ¶ 1504a). Sales tax also applies to certain fabrication services and to certain services that are a part of the sale or lease of tangible personal property.

Anyone who makes more than two retail sales within a 12-month period is a "retailer" and therefore subject to tax. This rule has been held applicable to liquidating sales made by the executor or administrator of an estate—see *Audra Second v. State Board of Equalization* (1954) (CCH California Tax Reports ¶ 60-210.36). Where the customer furnishes the material, the tax applies to charges for fabrication labor (but not for installation, repairs, or alterations).

The sale of tangible personal property at auction is deemed to be a taxable transaction, irrespective of the fact that the sale is made with the understanding (1) that the property will not be delivered to the successful bidder, or (2) that any amount paid for the property by the successful bidder will be returned to the bidder. The tax is applied to the amount of the successful bid.

The "true object" test determines whether a transaction involves a taxable sale of tangible personal property or the transfer of property incidental to the performance of a nontaxable service. If the true object sought by the purchaser is a service, tax does not apply to the transaction, even if some property is transferred.

In *Navistar International Transportation Corp. et al. v. State Board of Equalization et al.* (1994) (CCH California Tax Reports ¶ 60-310.111), a library of custom computer programs produced in-house for use by a taxpayer was subject to sales tax when sold as part of the taxpayer's business because the true object of the transaction was to sell the computer programs as tangible personal property and not to provide a service. Although the service of developing or designing custom computer programs is exempt from sales tax, once the computer programs were designed for the taxpayer's in-house use, the service had been completed, and the subsequent sale involved only the transfer of tangible personal property.

In *State Board of Equalization v. Los Angeles International Airport Hotel Associates* (1996) (CCH California Tax Reports ¶ 60-210.25), a U.S.

¶ 1503

bankruptcy appellate court held that a hotel owner was required to pay sales tax on complimentary beverages and breakfasts provided to guests because the money paid by guests for their rooms was consideration for the hotel's duty to provide not only rooms but also beverages and breakfasts. The complimentary beverages and breakfasts had been offered to induce travelers to rent a room at the hotel. However, in *Petitions of Embassy Suites Inc., et al.* (1996) (CCH CALIFORNIA TAX REPORTS ¶ 60-210.251), the State Board of Equalization (SBE) took the opposite position, ruling that complimentary beverages and breakfasts provided by hotels to their guests were not subject to sales tax, because the retail value of the beverages and breakfasts was *de minimis*, equaling 10% or less of the average daily rate charged for rooms. In 1999, the SBE incorporated its ruling in *Embassy Suites, Inc.* into its regulation governing taxable sales of food products.

Special rules are provided for various nonprofit organizations, to the effect that under certain conditions they are not considered to be "retailers." Special rules are provided for vending machine operators, flea market or swap meet operators, and special event operators. Special rules are also provided for sales of mobile homes and manufactured homes.

Sale and leaseback transactions are not subject to sales tax if (1) the tax was paid by the person selling (and leasing back) the property, and (2) the acquisition sale and leaseback is consummated within 90 days of that person's first functional use of the property.

Amounts charged for nontaxable intangible personal property that is transferred with taxable tangible personal property pursuant to a technology transfer agreement are specifically exempted from sales and use tax.

¶ 1503a Transactions Subject to Use Tax

Law: Secs. 6201-94 (CCH CALIFORNIA TAX REPORTS ¶ 60-210, 61-450).

The use tax is imposed on the storage, use, or other consumption in California of property purchased from a retailer for such storage, use, or other consumption. It applies to certain rental transactions and to out-of-state fabrication of customer-furnished materials. Because the use tax does not apply to cases where the sale of the property is subject to the sales tax (except when the purchase is in a district with a lower rate than the district in which the property is purchased to be used and is actually used, and in certain lease transactions—see ¶ 1503c), the application of the use tax generally is to purchases made outside of California for use within the state. Although this tax is imposed upon the purchaser, any retailer engaged in business in the state is required to collect the tax and remit it to the state.

A "retailer" that has any kind of an establishment in California or representatives conducting any kind of sales activity in the state is deemed to be "engaged in business" in the state. The law applies whether the retailer is involved directly or through a subsidiary or agent.

A regulation provides that an out-of-state retailer whose only contact with California is the use of a computer server on the Internet to create or maintain a World Wide Web page or site is not "engaged in business" in the state for use tax purposes and, consequently, is not required to collect or remit tax. The regulation also excludes from use tax collection requirements any out-of-state retailer whose contact with California is limited to use of an in-state independent contractor to perform warranty or repair services on tangible personal property that the retailer sells.

Among others, retailers soliciting orders by mail are considered to be engaged in business in California and, thus, are obligated to collect and remit use tax if the solicitations are substantial and recurring and the retailer benefits from various in-state services (i.e., banking, financing, debt collection, authorized installation services). However, this provision becomes operative only upon the enactment of a congressional act that authorizes states to compel out-of-state retailers to collect state sales and use taxes.

Prior to January 1, 2000, a retailer was also engaged in business in California and required to collect and remit use tax if the retailer (1) solicited orders through telecommunication or television shopping systems through cable television to California consumers, or (2) had a franchisee or licensee conducting business in California under the retailer's trade name.

In *Direct Marketing Association, Inc. v. William M. Bennett* (1991) (CCH CALIFORNIA TAX REPORTS ¶ 60-075.343), a federal district court held that out-of-state retailers could not be required to collect and remit California use tax solely because of their substantial and recurring solicitation of sales to California customers and acceptance of credit cards issued by California financial institutions. Because the out-of-state retailers did not have outlets, representatives, or property in California, they lacked a nexus with the state sufficient to render them liable for the collection of California use tax. Accordingly, the state was enjoined from requiring such out-of-state retailers to collect and remit use tax on sales to California customers, and the court denied a request by members of the State Board of Equalization to allow the continued enforcement of the use tax laws against such retailers pending an appeal.

The *Direct Marketing* decision was based on the 1967 U.S. Supreme Court decision in *National Bellas Hess, Inc. v. Department of Revenue* (CCH CALIFORNIA TAX REPORTS ¶ 60-075.34), which held that a foreign mail order company was not required to collect and remit use tax on sales made to Illinois consumers when the company's only activity in the state was solicitation of sales by catalogs and fliers followed by delivery of the goods by mail or common carrier.

Although the U.S. Supreme Court, in *Quill Corporation v. North Dakota* (1992) (CCH CALIFORNIA TAX REPORTS ¶ 60-075.341), upheld the test of physical presence established in *National Bellas Hess, Inc.*, stating that physical presence is still required by the Commerce Clause of the U.S. Constitution to bring out-of-state retailers within the jurisdiction of a state's sales and use tax laws, such physical presence is not required to satisfy the Due Process Clause. The court held that the Due Process Clause by itself would permit a state's enforcement of its use tax against an out-of-state retailer who had an "economic presence" within the state (i.e., continuous and widespread solicitation of business in the state).

¶ 1503a

● *Computer telecommunications networks*

A retailer who takes orders from customers in California through a computer telecommunications network located in the state is not required to collect and remit use tax, provided that (1) the telecommunications network is not owned by the retailer when orders are taken, (2) the orders result from the electronic display of products on the network, and (3) the network consists substantially of on-line communications services other than displaying and taking orders for products.

● *Convention or trade show participation*

A retailer whose sole physical presence in California is to engage in convention or trade show activities is not generally required to collect sales and use tax provided that the retailer and its representatives do not engage in California convention and trade show activities for more than seven days during any 12-month period and did not derive more than $10,000 of gross income from those activities in California during the prior calendar year. However, the retailer is required to collect use tax with respect to any sale occurring during or at California convention or trade show activities, including orders taken during such activities.

● *Interstate transactions*

In *Montgomery Ward & Co., Inc. v. State Board of Equalization* (1969) 272 CA2d 728, 78 CRptr 373, cert. den. 396 US 1040, 90 SCt 688, the state attempted to force out-of-state stores to collect use tax on over-the-counter sales in Oregon and Nevada that were billed to California residents. The Court of Appeal held that the stores could not be required to collect use tax where the goods were delivered outside the state.

In *National Geographic Society v. California State Board of Equalization* (1977) (CCH CALIFORNIA TAX REPORTS ¶ 60-075.35, 60-210.147) the U.S. Supreme Court held that the Society could be required to collect use tax on out-of-state mail order sales to California residents. The Society had two small offices in California.

The law provides that the terms "storage" and "use" do not apply to cases where property is brought into the state to be transported outside the state, or to be processed or fabricated into property which is to be transported outside the state, for use outside the state, or to the rental of certain cargo containers for use in interstate or foreign commerce.

● *Commerce Clause requirements*

In *National Railroad Passenger Corporation v. State Board of Equalization* (1986) (CCH CALIFORNIA TAX REPORTS ¶ 60-450.62), the state attempted to impose a tax on railroad passenger cars that was not imposed on other passenger vehicles used by common carriers. A federal district court held that such imposition was discriminatory and, therefore, prohibited.

● *Purchases of automobiles, boats, or airplanes*

A purchaser acquiring an automobile without the payment of sales or use tax is required to pay use tax to the Department of Motor Vehicles when

¶ 1503a

applying for transfer of registration, unless the seller is a close relative (parent, grandparent, child, grandchild, spouse, or minor brothers or sisters) of the purchaser and is not in the automobile business. A similar rule applies to the purchase of a boat or airplane.

The law presumes that any automobile brought into California within 90 days from the date of its purchase is subject to the tax. An exception is provided for military service personnel or any one else who can prove that the automobile was originally purchased for use outside the state.

● *Insurance companies*

Although insurance companies are exempt under the California Constitution from all taxes other than the gross receipts tax, the California Supreme Court ruled in *Occidental Life Insurance Company v. State Board of Equalization* (1982) (CCH CALIFORNIA TAX REPORTS ¶ 60-440.17), that retail sales of personal property to insurance companies are subject to the California sales tax because the incidence of the tax is on the retailer, not the purchaser. Insurance companies are also liable for the collection of the use tax from their customers as held in *Beneficial Standard Life Insurance Company v. State Board of Equalization* (1962) (CCH CALIFORNIA TAX REPORTS ¶ 60-440.15, 61-210.11), decided by the California District Court of Appeal. In that case, an insurance company was required to pay use tax on purchases of automobiles and furniture from (or through) the company by its employees.

¶ 1503b Sales for Resale

Law: Secs. 6012, 6051, 6091-95, 6201, 6241-45 (CCH CALIFORNIA TAX REPORTS ¶ 61-020).

A sale for resale is exempt from tax. However, it is presumed that all gross receipts are subject to tax until the contrary is established. To be relieved from liability, a seller must obtain a "resale certificate" from the purchaser. To be effective, the resale certificate must be taken in good faith from a person who holds a seller's permit and is engaged in the business of selling tangible personal property. If a resale certificate is not obtained, the seller may still be able to prove by other evidence that the sale was for resale.

If tax is paid on a purchase of property that is resold prior to any use, the amount of the purchase may be deducted on the purchaser's sales tax return. On the other hand a taxpayer who buys property tax free with the intention of reselling it but uses it instead (other than for demonstration, display, etc.) must report and pay a tax on the purchase price. Even if the property is later resold, the tax on self-consumption must be paid if the property is used for anything except demonstration or display at any time before it is resold. However, if the use is limited to an accommodation loan to a customer while awaiting property purchased or leased, the tax is imposed only on the fair rental value for the duration of the loan. Also, the tax on property used for demonstration or display or for loans during repairs is measured by the rental value.

¶ 1503c Rental Transactions

Law: Secs. 6006-18.8, 6094.1, 6368.7, 6381, 6390, 6406 (CCH CALIFORNIA TAX REPORTS ¶ 60-460).

The tax is applicable to a lease of tangible personal property, except:

(a) motion picture films and tapes, other than video cassettes, videotapes, and videodiscs for private use;

(b) linen supplies under a continuing laundry or service contract;

(c) household furniture included in a lease of living quarters;

(d) mobile transportation equipment for use in for-hire transportation of persons or property, except one-way rental trucks;

(e) other tangible personal property leased in substantially the same form as acquired by the lessor, where the lessor has paid the sales or use tax on the purchase price of the property; and

(f) certain leases involving the U.S. Government or its agencies.

Special rules apply to mobile home leases. If a mobile home was originally purchased by a retailer without payment of sales or use tax and first leased before July 1, 1980, its lease is taxable unless the mobile home becomes subject to local property taxation, in which case it is exempt from sales and use tax. The lease of a *used* mobile home that was first sold new in California after July 1, 1980, is not subject to sales or use tax. The lease of a mobile home that was originally purchased by a retailer without payment of sales or use tax and first leased on or after July 1, 1980, is not subject to sales tax, but the lessor's use of the property is subject to use tax.

"Lease" is defined to exclude the use of tangible personal property for less than one day for a charge of less than $20, where the use of the property is restricted to the business location of the seller.

A "lease" is defined as a sale under a security agreement if the lessee is bound for a fixed term and obtains title after making the required payments or has the option to purchase the property for a nominal amount.

A lease of tangible personal property is deemed to be a continuing sale by the lessor and a continuing purchase by the lessee for the entire period that the leased property is located in California.

Where a lease of tangible personal property covers property that is in substantially the same form as when it was acquired by the lessor, and the lessor has paid the sales or use tax on its acquisition, the rental receipts are not subject to tax; however, this rule does not apply to chemical toilets, and their rentals are therefore taxable. As indicated above, the tax does apply where the leased property is *not* in substantially the same form as when acquired by the lessor, or where the property was acquired by the lessor in a transaction not subject to sales or use tax; e.g., in an "occasional sale" transaction.

¶ 1503c

¶ 1504 Exempt Transactions

Law: Secs. 6351-6423 (CCH California Tax Reports ¶ 61-010—61-020).

California law allows full or partial sales and use tax exemptions for a very large number of items, transactions, and organizations. The main sales and use tax exemption categories are the following:

admission charges
aircraft gasoline and certain aircraft sales
animal life, feed, and medication
carbon dioxide packing
cash discounts (excluded from the measure of tax)
charitable organizations, goods made, goods donated
common carriers, certain sales
custom computer programs
food products and containers
food stamp purchases
ground control stations, limited
installation charges (excluded from the measure of tax)
insurers, sales by (sales tax exemption only)
interstate and foreign commerce
leases, various items (see ¶ 1503c)
lodging
lottery tickets
meals delivered to homebound elderly or disabled persons
meals served by religious organizations or social clubs
meals served in health care and residential facilities or boarding
  houses
meals served to low-income elderly persons or students
medical devices and equipment
mobile homes, used
newspapers and periodicals (see below)
occasional sales (see below)
prescription medicines
realty
resales
research and manufacturing equipment, start-up entities (partial,
  see below)
returned merchandise
"safe harbor" sale and leaseback arrangements
seeds, plants, and fertilizer
space flight property
stocks, bonds, and securities
telegraph and telephone lines
teleproduction and postproduction property
United States, purchases, sales
utilities' charges
vehicles purchased by family members or foreigners
vessels and watercraft, limited

● *Internet Tax Freedom Act*

Effective January 1, 1999, a three-year moratorium bans the imposition of new sales and use taxes by cities and counties on Internet access and online computer services and on the use of such access and services. The tax moratorium also applies to per transaction taxes and taxes measured by the electronic transmission of digital information. Moreover, local taxation of technological or operating characteristics of the Internet is likewise prohibited. The moratorium does not apply to a tax that is imposed or assessed in a uniform and nondiscriminatory manner without regard to whether the activities or transactions taxed are conducted through the use of the Internet, Internet access, or online computer services.

● *Newspapers and periodicals*

Only newspapers and periodicals issued at regular intervals that are (1) distributed free of charge, (2) distributed by nonprofit organizations to their members, (3) published or purchased by organizations qualifying for tax exempt status under IRC Sec. 501(c)(3), or (4) sold by subscription and delivered by mail qualify for the exemption. In each instance, the exemption covers the sale, storage, use, or consumption of the newspaper or periodical, as well as the sale, storage, use, or consumption of tangible personal property that becomes an ingredient or component of the newspaper or periodical. A nonprofit organization's membership publication qualifies for exemption only if it is distributed to members at least partly in return for membership fees and the costs of printing it are less than 10% of membership fees for the distribution period. An IRC Sec. 501(c)(3) organization's publication qualifies for exemption only if it either (1) accepts no commercial advertising or (2) is distributed to contributors or to members in return for payment of membership fees.

All other newspapers and periodicals are subject to sales and use tax. For purposes of the tax on newspapers, a newspaper's publisher or distributor, rather than the newspaper carrier, is considered the retailer of the newspaper. Accordingly, the publisher or distributor is responsible for payment of the tax, which is measured by the price charged to the customer by the newspaper carrier.

● *Occasional sales*

So-called "occasional sales" are exempt; however, this does not apply to boats or airplanes, or to automobiles required to be registered under the Motor Vehicle Code. This exemption is strictly applied in practice. It may or may not apply to the sale of a going business (see ¶ 1504a).

● *Manufacturing and research property*

The partial start-up entity exemption for manufacturing, research, and recycling property is available only to certain new businesses that are organized or formed and first commence business activity in the state after 1993, and that have been in existence less than three years. The business must be one described in the manufacturing division of the Standard Industrial Classification Manual, 1987 edition. The exemption is from all except 1% of state

¶ 1504

sales and use taxes. However, the exemption does not apply to local sales and use taxes.

Additionally, if sales and use tax is due on a purchase of manufacturing and research property, a refund of a portion of the sales and use tax paid may be claimed if the purchase is eligible for the manufacturer's investment credit against personal or corporate income taxes but the credit is not claimed (see ¶ 140 and ¶ 810a). The amount of the available refund is the same as the income tax credit.

Leases of tangible personal property that are classified as "continuing sales" and "continuing purchases" of tangible personal property may qualify for the exemption if the property is leased to a qualified start-up business and used for one of the purposes required for the exemption. Lessors may claim the exemption for a period of six years from the date the lease commences.

Also, certain lessors of manufacturing and research property may make an irrevocable election to pay use tax measured by the lessor's cost price in lieu of reporting tax measured by rentals payable pursuant to a lease. The election is available with respect to leases of property to taxpayers who qualify for the income tax credit for manufacturing and research property (see ¶ 140 and ¶ 810a).

● *Federal defense contractors*

There has been controversy over the years on the question of whether the U.S. Constitution provides sales-tax immunity to some sellers and lessors in United States defense contract situations. See the 1993 United States Supreme Court decision in *United States of America v. California State Board of Equalization* (CCH CALIFORNIA TAX REPORTS ¶ 60-420.14). Also, see the 1981, 1982, and 1983 decisions of the United States Court of Appeals in *United States of America v. California State Board of Equalization* (CCH CALIFORNIA TAX REPORTS ¶ 60-420.12, ¶ 60-420.27, ¶ 60-420.60), the 1984 decision in the case of *Edward W.W. Howell, d.b.a. Howell Electric Co. v. State Board of Equalization* (CCH CALIFORNIA TAX REPORTS ¶ 60-420.48), and the 1990 decision in the case of *Aerospace Corporation v. California State Board of Equalization* (CCH CALIFORNIA TAX REPORTS ¶ 60-420.51).

¶ 1504a Sale of a Business

Law: Secs. 6006.5, 6281, 6292, 6367 (CCH CALIFORNIA TAX REPORTS ¶ 60-590).

The sale of an entire business and other sales of machinery, equipment, etc., used in a business is usually subject to the sales tax. The "occasional sales" exemption ordinarily does not apply to such transactions. The tax may even apply to cases where the principal activity of the business does not involve the sale of tangible personal property and where the seller does not hold a sales tax permit.

The tax would not ordinarily apply to merchandise inventory included in the sale of a business, since the inventory is sold for resale. Neither would it apply to any property that is attached to a building in such a way that it is classified as "real property" rather than "personal property"; the tax may apply to machinery, equipment, etc., in some cases.

● *Exemption where no real change of ownership*

The tax does not apply to the sale of a business where the "real or ultimate ownership" of the business is substantially the same after the sale as it was before. Unusual problems may arise in "reorganization" transactions that are tax-free under the income tax laws. The State Board of Equalization (SBE) has ruled that statutory mergers (qualifying under Sec. 368(a)(1)(A) of the Internal Revenue Code) are not subject to the sales tax, whereas the same transaction accomplished in an "assets for stock" exchange (under IRC Sec. 368(a)(1)(C)) would be taxable, at least as to those assets deemed to be "tangible personal property sold at retail."

In *Simplicity Pattern Co. v. State Board of Equalization* (1980) (CCH CALIFORNIA TAX REPORTS ¶ 60-210.105, 60-590.33), the taxpayer sold its subsidiary's business to another company in exchange for common stock. The California Supreme Court held that the transaction was not exempt from sales tax, even though it presumably would have been exempt if cast in the form of a statutory merger.

An example where the "real or ultimate ownership" test applies to exempt the transaction from sales tax is the incorporation of an existing business by the transfer of assets from a predecessor partnership or proprietorship to the new corporation in exchange for its stock. In *Pacific Pipeline Construction Co. v. State Board of Equalization* (1958) (CCH CALIFORNIA TAX REPORTS ¶ 60-590.14), the California Supreme Court held that a transfer of certain machinery and equipment in a corporate reorganization was not exempt under the "occasional sale" rule, even though the seller was not engaged in an activity normally requiring the holding of a seller's permit.

● *Other cases involving sale of business*

In *Beatrice Company v. State Board of Equalization* (1993) (CCH CALIFORNIA TAX REPORTS ¶ 60-590.112), the California Supreme Court held that a parent corporation's transfer of all of the assets of one of its divisions to a commencing subsidiary corporation in exchange for stock in the subsidiary and an assumption by the subsidiary of the division's liabilities was a taxable retail sale.

In *Ontario Community Foundation, Inc. v. California State Board of Equalization* (1984) (CCH CALIFORNIA TAX REPORTS ¶ 60-590.34) the California Supreme Court held that the sale of hospital equipment as part of the sale of an entire hospital was exempt as an "occasional sale," since the equipment sold had not been used in operations subject to sales tax.

In *Davis Wire Corporation v. State Board of Equalization* (1976) (CCH CALIFORNIA TAX REPORTS ¶ 60-210.39, 60-590.18), the California Supreme Court cited the *U. S. Industries* case, among others, and held that the sale of the entire business of certain manufacturing businesses was subject to sales tax. The sellers had made no retail sales in the ordinary course of their business. The Court distinguished the *Glass-Tite* case, cited below, on the ground that in *Glass-Tite* the seller's products were component parts of a type that could not have been sold at retail, whereas in *Davis Wire* the seller's products were finished products suitable for sale at retail. To the same effect, see the decision of the District Court of Appeal in *Santa Fe Energy Co. v. The*

¶ 1504a

Board of Equalization of California (1984) (CCH CALIFORNIA TAX REPORTS ¶ 60-590.20).

In *Hotel Del Coronado Corporation v. State Board of Equalization* (1971) (CCH CALIFORNIA TAX REPORTS ¶ 60-590.10), a California District Court of Appeal held that the sale of hotel equipment, as part of a sale of the entire property, was subject to the sales tax.

In *Glass-Tite Industries, Inc. v. State Board of Equalization* (1968) (CCH CALIFORNIA TAX REPORTS ¶ 60-590.16), the seller was a manufacturer of electronic components. The District Court of Appeal held that the sale of the business was exempt from sales tax as an "occasional sale", because it was an isolated transaction and the taxpayer was not really required to have a seller's permit even though it actually had one.

In *U.S. Industries, Inc., et al. v. State Board of Equalization* (1962) (CCH CALIFORNIA TAX REPORTS ¶ 60-590.15), a California District Court of Appeal held that the sales tax was applicable to the sale of all the tangible assets used in operating a business, in conjunction with the sale of the business. Consideration for the sale included stock and debentures, as well as cash.

● *Liability of purchaser and seller*

The purchaser of a business is personally liable for any sales or use tax liability of the seller, unless the purchaser withholds enough of the purchase price to cover the liability or obtains from the seller evidence from the SBE to the effect that any liability has been paid or that no amount is due. For a discussion of this provision, see *Knudsen Dairy Products Co. v. State Board of Equalization* (1970) (CCH CALIFORNIA TAX REPORTS ¶ 61-470.18), in which the provision was held applicable to the acquisition of a business in return for cancellation of indebtedness.

The seller of a business who fails to surrender a sales tax permit to the SBE upon transfer of the business is liable for any sales tax liability incurred by the purchaser if the seller has knowledge that the purchaser is using the permit. The seller's liability is generally limited to the quarter in which the business is transferred, plus the three subsequent quarters.

¶ 1505 Permits, Returns, and Payment

Law: Secs. 6066-74, 6451-80.23, 6591, 7053-54 (CCH CALIFORNIA TAX REPORTS ¶ 61-210—61-260, 61-805—61-810).

Anyone in the business of selling tangible personal property of the type subject to tax, other than certain sellers of animal feed, must obtain a sales tax permit.

● *Direct payment permits*

A qualified big business may obtain a sales tax direct payment permit that allows the business to give a seller an exemption certificate when making a purchase, thereby shifting the duty to pay sales tax from the seller to the business holding the permit. A business may obtain a sales tax direct payment permit only if it had gross receipts from sales of tangible personal property of at least $75 million and purchases of taxable tangible personal property of at least $75 million in each calendar quarter during the 12 months preceding the application. Use tax direct payment permits, which allow taxpayers to self-assess and pay state and local use tax directly to the State Board of Equalization (SBE), may be issued to (1) businesses that purchase or lease tangible personal property valuing $500,000 or more in the aggregate during the calendar year immediately preceding the application for the permit and (2) county and/or city governments and redevelopment agencies.

● *Prepayments of tax*

Generally, returns must be filed and the tax paid quarterly. However, if the SBE determines that the taxpayer's taxable transactions average $17,000 or more per month, quarterly prepayments of tax must be made.

In the first, third, and fourth calendar quarters, the taxpayer must prepay no less than 90% of the state and local tax liability for each of the first two months of each quarter. In the second calendar quarter, the taxpayer must make a first prepayment of 90% of the state and local tax liability for the first month of the quarter and a second prepayment of either (1) 90% of the state and local tax liability for the second month of the quarter plus 90% of the state and local tax liability for the first 15 days of the third month of the quarter, or (2) 135% of the state and local tax liability for the second month of the quarter.

In the first, third, and fourth quarters, prepayments and reports are due by the 24th day following the end of the first two months of the quarter. In the second quarter, the first prepayment and report are due by the 24th day of the second month of the quarter; the second prepayment is due by the 24th day of the third month.

● *Prepayment of tax on motor vehicle fuel*

Distributors and brokers of motor vehicle fuel, after being notified by the SBE, must collect prepayment of the retail sales tax from anyone to whom they distribute or transfer any fuel subject to the motor vehicle fuel license tax, except aviation gasoline and fuel sold to bonded distributors. From April 1, 1999, through March 31, 2000, the rate of prepayment is 7¢ per gallon. Provision is made for annual adjustment or re-adjustment of the rate. Returns and payments must be filed and paid on or before the 25th day of the calendar month following the prepayment.

The SBE is also authorized to require fuel producers, importers, and jobbers to collect retail sales tax prepayments at a rate 1.5¢ per gallon below the rate applicable to distributors and brokers. However, effective January 1, 2000, the SBE is required to use a new method to compute the tax prepayment rate for fuel producers, importers, and jobbers.

● *Installment payments*

A taxpayer may enter into a written installment payment agreement with the SBE for the payment of any taxes, penalties, and interest. The SBE may terminate the agreement if the taxpayer fails to comply with the terms of the agreement.

¶ **1505**

● *Penalty for failure to pay*

If prepayments are not made when required, a penalty is imposed. If the prepayment is actually made after its due date (but no later than the due date of the quarterly return), the penalty is 6% of the prepayment. If the prepayment is not made, but the quarterly return and payment are timely, the penalty is 6% of the amount (either 90% or 95%) of the actual tax liability for each month for which a prepayment should have been made. If failure to prepay is due to negligence or intentional disregard of the rules, the penalty is 10% instead of 6%. The penalty for failure to prepay on time may be waived if a showing of reasonable cause is made.

Interest is imposed on any person who is granted relief from the penalties for late prepayments. The interest rate is the same as that charged on sales and use tax deficiencies (see ¶ 1506). The SBE may relieve a person from such interest if the person's failure to make timely prepayments was due to a disaster rather than negligence or willful neglect.

● *Time for filing returns; penalty for late filing*

Returns must be filed quarterly, on or before the last day of the month following the quarterly period. The law authorizes the requirement of more frequent returns if deemed necessary to insure payment or facilitate collection; in practice this has resulted in monthly returns being required in some cases. The tax is payable in full with the return, to the extent not previously paid under the prepayment procedure. The due date for returns or payments may be extended for not more than one month, upon the filing of a request showing good cause. An extension of more than one month may be granted if the taxpayer requesting the extension is a creditor of the state who has not been paid because the legislature failed to adopt a budget for the State by July 1 of the tax year in question. Such an extension expires on the last day of the month in which the budget is adopted or one month from the due date of the return or payment, whichever is later.

A 10% penalty is imposed against taxpayers that fail to file a sales and use tax return in a timely fashion.

● *Bad debts*

Accounts that have been determined to be worthless and charged off for income tax purposes (or, in the case of organizations exempt from income tax, charged off in accordance with generally accepted accounting principles) may be excluded from the measure of the sales or use tax. If the tax has previously been paid, the worthless accounts may be deducted from other taxable sales in the quarter in which they are determined to be worthless and charged off, or a refund may be claimed. If there is a subsequent recovery on such accounts, the amount collected must be included in the first return filed after such collection and tax paid accordingly.

● *Form for return*

The sales tax return and the use tax return are combined in one form. A return showing information relating only to one tax is deemed to be a return also for the tax for which no information is shown. The California Supreme

¶ 1505

Court held to this effect in *People v. Universal Film Exchanges, Inc.* (1950) (CCH CALIFORNIA TAX REPORTS ¶ 61-520.15); the case involved the question of whether the "return" sufficed to start the running of the limitation period on a deficiency assessment of use tax.

● *Other provisions*

A credit against the California use tax is allowed for sales or use tax paid to another state on property purchased in another state prior to its use in California.

Where retailers collect sales and use taxes from customers in excess of amounts legally due, such excess amounts must be returned to the customers; otherwise, the excess collections become obligations due to the state and the customers may then recover such amounts directly from the state.

Retailers who engage in business without a permit or after a permit has been revoked are guilty of a misdemeanor.

● *Payment by credit card*

Taxpayers may make sales and use tax payments using credit cards issued by NOVUS (e.g., NOVUS/Discover card), American Express, and MasterCard. Payments by credit card are authorized only for taxes that are due with the taxpayer's sales and use tax return, including prepayment forms. Delinquent taxes or taxes required to be paid by electronic funds transfer may not be charged to a credit card. The SBE has established a special phone number for taxpayers desiring to make payments by credit card. The phone number is 1-800-477-4141.

● *Electronic funds transfer payment requirement*

Anyone whose estimated sales and use tax liability averages $20,000 or more per month must remit amounts due by electronic funds transfer. In addition, with the SBE's approval, those whose estimated sales and use tax liability averages do not meet this threshold amount may voluntarily remit payments electronically. The electronic funds transfer payment requirement will not apply to taxpayers who collect use taxes voluntarily.

¶ 1506 Administration, Deficiencies, Refunds

Law: Secs. 6481-88, 6511-96, 6901-63, 7051-99 (CCH CALIFORNIA TAX REPORTS ¶ 61-410, 61-420, 61-440, 61-520, 61-530, 61-610—61-640).

The tax is administered by the State Board of Equalization (SBE). The SBE maintains a staff of field auditors who examine the books of taxpayers.

● *Auditing procedures*

The SBE's auditors have commonly used a procedure known as the "test-check." For example, one or more supposedly typical periods are checked to determine the extent to which sales are improperly reported as being for resale; the percentage of error found in the test period is then assumed to run through the entire period under audit, the same percentage of error is applied to the sales of the whole period and a tax deficiency is assessed accordingly.

¶ 1506

Another type of test-check is used where the sales appear to be too low in relation to the cost of goods sold. In such cases the auditor may test the gross profit percentage by computing the mark-up on typical items of merchandise; the percentage of mark-up computed on these items may then be applied to the total costs for the period under audit to determine the taxable sales. This procedure was approved in 1950 by the California District Court of Appeal in the case of *Maganini v. Quinn* (CCH CALIFORNIA TAX REPORTS ¶ 61-410.05).

Auditors will frequently rely on SBE sales and use tax annotations when examining a particular transaction. These annotations consist of a compilation of replies by the SBE's legal staff to questions posed by auditors and taxpayers concerning the taxability of particular transactions. In *Yamaha Corporation of America v. State Board of Equalization* (1999) (CCH CALIFORNIA TAX REPORTS ¶ 60-410.20), the California Supreme Court reversed an appellate court's decision in which the appellate court relied on an SBE annotation. The Supreme Court determined that because the annotation was merely an agency's statutory interpretation it could not be equated with an agency rule to which the courts must give judicial deference. However, on remand, and consistent with the California Supreme Court's instructions, a California court of appeal assigned "great weight" to two SBE annotations in support of its opinion because of the SBE's consistency and expertise and evidence of legislative concurrence.

● *Managed audit program*

If selected by the SBE, taxpayers may participate in a managed audit program, in which taxpayers self-audit their books and records under the SBE's guidance. To be eligible to participate in the program, a taxpayer must: (1) have not received written notice requiring tax prepayments (see ¶ 1505); (2) have a business that has few or no statutory exemptions and has a small number of clearly identified tax issues; (3) agree to participate; and (4) have the resources to comply with SBE instructions. Taxpayers who participate in the program are entitled to a reduced interest rate of $1/2$ the regular rate on liabilities covered by the audit period. Participation in the managed audit program does not limit the SBE's authority to otherwise audit a taxpayer.

● *Procedure for deficiencies*

If the SBE determines a deficiency, it must give written notice of its determination. A petition for redetermination may be filed within 30 days of service of such notice, and an oral hearing will be granted if requested. If no petition is filed, the determination becomes final at the expiration of the 30-day period. If a petition is filed, the SBE's order or decision on the petition becomes final 30 days after service of notice of such order or decision. Provision is also made for jeopardy assessments when collection of the tax will be jeopardized by delay.

The limitation period for assessing deficiencies, generally, is three years. The period is eight years when no return is filed. There is no limitation in case of fraud. The limitation period may be extended by waiver agreement and also may be extended for a redetermination of tax under certain conditions.

¶ 1506

● *Deficiency procedures for out-of-state retailers*

The limitation period for assessing deficiencies for "qualifying" out-of-state retailers that failed to file a return or report is three years. A "qualifying" out-of-state retailer is a retailer doing business in California that, never having previously registered with the SBE, voluntarily registers prior to being contacted by the SBE. In addition, if the SBE determines that the retailer's failure to file is due to reasonable cause, the SBE may waive any corresponding penalties.

● *Interest and penalties*

In connection with deficiencies, a penalty of 10% is imposed for negligence or intentional disregard of the rules, and a penalty of 25% is imposed where fraud is involved. A taxpayer that is required to make payments by electronic transfer funds, who is issued a deficiency determination after failing to remit the tax in a timely fashion, will be assessed an additional 10% penalty of the amount of tax due. This penalty is exclusive of other penalties that might be imposed for delinquencies applicable to other payment methods.

Interest is charged on deficiencies at a rate established semiannually. The following chart indicates the rates of interest in effect for the designated periods:

From	To	Modified Adjusted Annual Rate
January 1, 1996	June 30, 1996	12%
July 1, 1996	December 31, 1996	12%
January 1, 1997	June 30, 1997	12%
July 1, 1997	December 31, 1997	12%
January 1, 1998	June 30, 1998	12%
July 1, 1998	December 31, 1998	12%
January 1, 1999	June 30, 1999	11%
July 1, 1999	December 31, 1999	10%
January 1, 2000	June 30, 2000	11%

For tax liabilities that arise during taxable periods commencing after June 30, 1999, the SBE may abate all or part of the interest imposed on tax liabilities resulting from (1) an SBE employee's unreasonable error or delay or (2) the Department of Motor Vehicle's error in calculating the use tax on a vehicle or vessel. In addition, for actions for recovery of an erroneous refund made after June 30, 1999, if the SBE finds that neither the person liable for payment of tax nor any person related to that person caused the erroneous refund, no interest will be imposed on the amount of the erroneous refund until 30 days after the date on which the SBE mails a notice of determination for repayment of the erroneous refund. The act of filing a claim for refund will not be considered as causing the erroneous refund.

Criminal penalties are imposed upon anyone who gives a resale certificate with knowledge that the property is not to be resold, and criminal penalties for other offenses are increased. A penalty of 50% of the tax is imposed upon anyone who registers a vehicle, vessel, or aircraft outside California for the purpose of tax evasion. The state is empowered to employ out-of-state collec-

¶ 1506

tion agencies and to add their compensation to the amount of tax due. The state may establish a reward program for information leading to the collection of underreported taxes.

A $50 penalty is imposed on paid preparers of sales and use tax returns for each failure to enter their name, social security number, and business name and address on a return.

● *Taxpayer's bill of rights*

A "bill of rights" has been enacted to protect a taxpayer's privacy and property rights during the sales and use tax collection process. It is substantially identical to the one described briefly at ¶701a, relating to taxpayer rights in connection with personal income and corporate tax collections, except that the agency involved is the SBE rather than the Franchise Tax Board.

● *Refunds*

The limitation period for filing refund claims, generally, is three years from the due date of the return or in the case of a deficiency or jeopardy determination or nonfiling of a return, the later of six months from the date a deficiency determination becomes final or within six months of the overpayment. However, a taxpayer has three years from the date of overpayment to file a refund claim if the overpayment was collected as a result of the SBE's collection of an outstanding tax liability through issuance of a levy, lien, or other enforcement procedure. In *Dan J. Agnew v. California State Board of Equalization* (1999) (CCH CALIFORNIA TAX REPORTS ¶61-620.25), the California Supreme Court held that a taxpayer is *not* required to pay the accrued interest on a tax deficiency in addition to the tax claimed to be due and owing as a prerequisite to administrative review of a claim for refund of an alleged overpayment of sales and use tax.

Effective January 1, 2000, the limitations period for filing a refund claim is suspended during any period that a person is unable to manage his or her financial affairs because of a physical or mental impairment that is life threatening or that is expected to last for at least 12 months. This waiver does not apply to individuals who are represented in their financial matters by their spouses or by other persons.

If the SBE disallows a claim, the claimant may bring suit within 90 days after the mailing of notice of the SBE's action. If the SBE fails to act on the claim within six months after the claim is filed, the claimant may consider the claim disallowed and proceed to bring suit.

Interest is payable by the State on refunds at the modified adjusted rate per month, which is the modified adjusted rate per annum divided by 12. Interest is payable on refunds from the first day of the calendar month following the month during which the overpayment was made to (1) the last day of the calendar month in which the taxpayer is notified that the claim may be filed or (2) the date the claim is approved by the SBE, whichever is earlier. Interest may be waived for a period, in cases where the taxpayer requests deferred action on a refund claim.

The following chart indicates the rates of interest for the designated periods.

From	To	Applicable Period Interest Rate
January 1, 1996	June 30, 1996	6%
July 1, 1996	December 31, 1996	5%
January 1, 1997	June 30, 1997	5%
July 1, 1997	December 31, 1997	5%
January 1, 1998	June 30, 1998	5%
July 1, 1998	December 31, 1998	5%
January 1, 1999	June 30, 1999	4%
July 1, 1999	December 31, 1999	4%
January 1, 2000	June 30, 2000	5%

● *Special refund procedure for invalid local taxes*

Retailers who reside or conduct business in a taxing district in which an invalid tax was imposed must report sales and use tax at the currently effective combined state and local rate but may claim a 0.75% credit against the total amount of taxes reported. A corresponding 0.75% reduction must be made in the amount of sales or use taxes that retailers collect from purchasers. The 0.75% credit may be claimed for taxes due on the first day of the first calendar quarter beginning at least 120 days after a final court determination that a local sales and use tax is invalid.

A nonretailer who pays a local sales and use tax that is subsequently held invalid may file a claim for refund of the invalid tax, provided the claim states in writing the specific ground upon which it is made and is accompanied by proof of payment. However, only claims for a single purchase or aggregate purchases of $5,000 or more will be eligible for refund, and any such claim must be filed within one year of the first day of the first calendar quarter after a local sales and use tax has been held invalid.

A California court of appeal held in *Kuykendall v. State Board of Equalization et al.* (1994) (CCH CALIFORNIA TAX REPORTS ¶ 61-610.353) that the statutory scheme of reimbursing consumers for the local sales and use tax declared unconstitutional in *Rider* (see ¶ 1502) through a sales tax rollback and through direct refunds for claims involving documented purchases of $5,000 or more did not violate constitutional guarantees of due process and equal protection.

● *Liability upon termination of business*

Upon termination or dissolution of a corporation or limited liability company, certain officers, members, managers, or other persons may be held personally liable for unpaid sales and use taxes.

● *Relief for innocent spouse*

If two spouses' names appear on an application for a seller's permit and a sales and use tax liability is understated by one spouse, the innocent spouse may be relieved of liability for tax, including interest, penalties, and other amounts attributable to the understatement, if he or she did not know of or

¶ 1506

have reason to know of the understatement and if, under the circumstances, it would be inequitable to hold him or her liable for the deficiency.

An innocent spouse will be granted relief for underpayment and nonpayment of tax (including interest and penalties) if (1) the underpayment or nonpayment is attributable to the other spouse, (2) the innocent spouse can establish a lack of knowledge that was reasonable, and (3) relief from liability is deemed to be equitable under the circumstances.

Relief is not available for either underreporting or nonpayment in any calendar quarter that is (1) more than five years from the final date on an SBE determination, (2) more than five years from the return due date for nonpayment on a return, (3) more than one year from the first contact with the innocent spouse claiming relief, or (4) closed by *res judicata,* whichever is later.

● *Settlement of civil tax disputes*

The Executive Officer of the SBE, or his or her designee, may settle any civil tax dispute involving amounts of $5,000 or less. For civil tax disputes involving amounts in excess of $5,000, the SBE may approve the settlement recommendations made by its Executive Officer (or Chief Counsel if authorized by the Executive Officer) and reviewed by the Attorney General.

PART VI
Death Taxes

CHAPTER 16

DEATH TAXES AFTER JUNE 8, 1982

¶ 1601 Scope of Chapter

The California inheritance tax, in effect since 1893, was repealed on June 8, 1982. However, California still imposes two death taxes, which are discussed in this chapter: (1) the estate "pick-up" tax, and (2) the generation skipping transfer tax. Neither of these taxes imposes any tax burden, because both are so-called "pick-up" taxes that simply collect a tax that would otherwise go to the federal government. The California taxes obtain for the State the maximum benefit for the federal credits that are allowed for State taxes.

The generation skipping transfer tax has been in effect since 1977, and was not affected by the repeal of the inheritance tax law. It constitutes Part 9.5 of Division 2 of the Revenue and Taxation Code.

California also imposed a gift tax, first imposed in 1939. The gift tax was also repealed on June 8, 1982.

For details of the repealed taxes, see 1984 or prior editions of the GUIDEBOOK.

¶ 1602 Estate Tax—Application

> *Law:* Secs. 13302-411 (CCH INHERITANCE, ESTATE AND GIFT TAX REPORTS, California ¶ 1300 et seq.).

The California estate tax is the portion of the allowable federal credit for state taxes that is attributable to property located in California; that is, to property having a "situs" in California. The residence of the decedent is

¶ 1602

immaterial, except insofar as it might have an effect on the "situs" of property.

If the decedent leaves property in California and also in another state, the California tax is a proportionate part of the total federal credit. The apportionment of the credit is determined on the basis of the property's gross value as finally determined for federal estate tax purposes.

Corporate stock owned by a deceased nonresident of the United States is considered to have a California situs if the corporation (1) is organized in California, (2) has its principal place of business in California, or (3) does the major part of its business in California.

¶ 1603 Estate Tax—Returns and Payment

Law: Secs. 13501-04, 13530-33 (CCH Inheritance, Estate and Gift Tax Reports, California, ¶ 2000, 2210).

The California estate tax is due and payable at the date of the decedent's death, and becomes delinquent nine months after death. The tax is payable to the Controller, through the Treasurer.

When an estate is subject to the California tax, a California return must be filed together with a copy of the federal return. The California return must be filed by the due date (including any extension of time) for the federal return. Return forms can be obtained from the State Controller, Sacramento, California 95814.

If an amended federal return is filed, an amended California return must be filed "immediately," with a copy of the federal return. Upon final determination of the federal tax, written notice must be given to the State Controller within 60 days.

¶ 1604 Estate Tax—Interest and Penalties

Law: Secs. 13510, 13550-51 (CCH Inheritance, Estate and Gift Tax Reports, California ¶ 2005, 2225).

Until January 1, 1999, interest on late payments is charged at 12% per annum from the date the tax becomes delinquent. Effective for delinquent amounts unpaid on or after January 1, 1999, the rate of interest levied against tax underpayments is the same as the adjusted quarterly rate set under Internal Revenue Code Sec. 6621(a)(2).

If the return is not filed on time, a penalty may be added at the rate of 5% per month up to a total of 25% of the tax. The penalty may be waived for reasonable cause.

¶ 1605 Estate Tax—Administration, Deficiencies, Collection

Law: Secs. 13516-20, 13555-57, 13601-14302 (CCH Inheritance, Estate and Gift Tax Reports, California ¶ 2040, 2200, 2205).

The law is administered by the State Controller. The Controller may determine a deficiency in tax at any time up to four years after the return is filed, or later if so provided by mutual agreement in writing. In case of an erroneous determination, the limitation date for correction is three years after the date of the erroneous determination. In case of a false or fraudulent return or failure to file, there is no limitation period on a deficiency determination.

The Controller has broad powers to bring suit and take other measures to collect the tax, and to compromise regarding the amount of tax. The law includes the "Uniform Act on Interstate Arbitration of Death Taxes," which enables the Controller to make compromises and arbitration agreements with other states in cases of multiple jurisdiction.

¶ 1606 Estate Tax—Refunds

> *Law:* Secs. 13560-63 (CCH INHERITANCE, ESTATE AND GIFT TAX REPORTS, California ¶ 2050).

A refund may be made if the Controller determines that the tax has been overpaid. Application for refund must be made to the Controller within one year after final determination of the federal estate tax.

Interest is payable on refunds at a rate each year equal to the "Federal Reserve Rate" on January 1, not to exceed 7% per annum.

¶ 1607 Generation Skipping Transfer Tax—Application

> *Law:* Sec. 16710 (CCH INHERITANCE, ESTATE AND GIFT TAX REPORTS, California ¶ 5000, 5020).

The California generation skipping transfer tax is imposed where death occurred after September 26, 1977. It applies where the original transferor was a California resident at the date of the original transfer, or where the property transferred is real or personal property in California. This is a "pick-up" tax, similar in effect to the California estate tax, designed to obtain for the state the benefit of the credit allowed against the federal tax of the same name.

If the federal tax involves property in California and also in another state, the California tax is a proportionate part of the total federal credit.

¶ 1608 Generation Skipping Transfer Tax—Returns and Payment

> *Law:* Secs. 16720-22, 16750-61 (CCH INHERITANCE, ESTATE AND GIFT TAX REPORTS, California ¶ 5070).

The California return is due at the same time as the federal return, with a copy of the federal return attached. If the federal credit is revised after the original return is filed, an amended California return must be filed. Return forms can be obtained from the State Controller, Sacramento, California 95814.

The California tax is due at the same time as is the federal tax, and becomes delinquent after the last day allowed for filing a return. The tax is payable to the State Treasurer, through the Controller. Interest is charged at 12% per annum from the date the tax becomes delinquent.

¶ 1609 Generation Skipping Transfer Tax—Administration, Deficiencies, Collection

Law: Secs. 16730-34, 16800-30, 16880-950 (CCH INHERITANCE, ESTATE AND GIFT TAX REPORTS, California ¶ 5070, 5080).

The law is administered by the State Controller. The Controller may determine a deficiency at any time up to four years after the return is filed or one year after a federal tax increase becomes final. In case of a false or fraudulent return or failure to file, there is no limitation period on a deficiency determination.

The Controller has broad powers to bring suit and take other measures to collect the tax.

¶ 1610 Generation Skipping Transfer Tax—Refunds

Law: Secs. 16850-71 (CCH INHERITANCE, ESTATE AND GIFT TAX REPORTS, California ¶ 5070).

A refund may be made if the Controller determines that the tax has been overpaid. Application for refund must be made to the Controller within four years after the due date of the return or within one year from the date of overpayment. The taxpayer may file suit for refund in the superior court.

Interest is payable on refunds at 12% per annum, provided the overpayment was not due to the taxpayer's error.

PART VII
Miscellaneous Taxes

CHAPTER 17

PROPERTY TAXES

¶ 1701 Scope of Chapter

California does not impose a general ad valorem tax on real and personal property. However, local governmental units throughout the state do impose such a tax. Because of the statewide character of this tax and the fact that its provisions are included in the state Revenue and Taxation Code, this chapter is included for the sake of completeness, despite the fact that the tax is not, strictly speaking, a "state tax."

The purpose of this chapter is to give a very general picture of the nature and application of the property tax and the manner of its administration. It is not intended to provide detailed coverage. It covers, generally, the questions of what property is subject to tax, the base and rate of tax, and the requirements for filing returns and making payment.

¶ 1702 Imposition of Tax

Law: Secs. 1-2, Art. XIIIA, Sec. 2, Art. XIIIC, Cal. Constitution; Secs. 51, 61-75.80, 110.1, 170, 401-405, Revenue and Taxation Code (CCH CALIFORNIA TAX REPORTS ¶ 20-055, 20-083, 20-087, 20-700—20-730).

The impact of property taxes in California was drastically reduced by the passage of Proposition 13 on June 6, 1978, adding Article XIIIA to the State Constitution. Following is a brief overview of the provisions of Article XIIIA.

1. The overall rate of property taxation is limited to 1% of "full cash value" as specifically defined for this purpose (see ¶ 1705 for discussion of prior rates and of permissible additions to the 1% limit) and also a potential adjustment for a decline in value.

2. Valuations of real property are frozen at the value of the property in March 1975, with an allowable adjustment of up to 2% per year for inflation. However, property is assessed at its current value when it is purchased or newly constructed or a "change of ownership" occurs, with subsequent annual adjustment (up to 2%) for inflation. Valuations of personal property are not frozen; they are determined annually as of January 1.

3. No new property, sales, or transaction taxes may be imposed on real property.

4. A 2/3 vote of the legislature is required for any increases in other state taxes.

5. A 2/3 vote of qualified electors is required for the imposition of special taxes by local governments. A majority vote of qualified electors is required for the imposition of any new or higher general taxes by local government.

A measure approved by California voters at the November 5, 1996, general election, clarifies the voter approval requirement for general taxes by specifically prohibiting *all* local governments, including charter cities, from imposing, extending, or increasing any general tax after November 5, 1996, without the approval of a majority of the local electorate. In addition, all general taxes imposed, extended, or increased by local governments without voter approval after 1994 and before November 6, 1996, must be submitted to local voters for approval by November 6, 1998, and be approved by a majority of the voters in order to continue to be imposed.

● *Transfers of base-year value for seniors and disabled persons*

Homeowners who are over the age of 55 or who are severely and permanently disabled may transfer the adjusted base-year value of their original residence to a replacement dwelling of equal or lesser fair market value in the same county, provided the purchase of the replacement principal residence is within two years of the sale of the original home. The same property tax relief is given for moves between counties if the county where the replacement home is located has adopted an ordinance permitting the valuation transfer. As of May 1999, the counties that authorize the transfer of base-year value are Alameda, Kern, Los Angeles, Modoc, Monterey, Orange, San Diego, San Mateo, Santa Clara, and Ventura. Generally, the carryover of a residence's base-year value by a person over the age of 55 or a severely and permanently disabled person is available one-time only. However, a person over the age of 55 who previously transferred the base-year value of a former residence to a replacement residence may utilize the base-year value transfer provisions a second time if the person subsequently becomes severely and permanently disabled.

Taxpayers who transfer their adjusted base-year value from an original residence to a replacement home are not reassessed for subsequent improvements to the replacement residence, so long as the sum of the fair market value of the replacement property and any improvements to the replacement property does not exceed the fair market value of the original home. This applies to improvements completed within two years of (before or after) the sale of the original property and only for replacement dwellings purchased or

¶ 1702

newly constructed after 1990. Businesses are not eligible to transfer original base-year values.

The base-year value of property damaged or destroyed in a declared disaster area may be transferred to replacement property within the same county or, under certain circumstances, to replacement property in a different county. (See the discussion of "Damaged property," below.)

● Contaminated property

An owner of qualified contaminated property may transfer the base year value of that property to replacement property located within the same county or within a different county if the other county authorizes such transfers. Alternatively, an owner of qualified property may rebuild a structure destroyed or damaged by environmental remediation on qualified contaminated property without incurring a property tax reassessment for new construction (discussed below). To qualify for the base-year value transfer or the exemption from new construction reassessment, the fair market value of the replacement property must be equal to or less than the fair market value of the qualified contaminated property if the property were not contaminated, and the replacement property must be acquired or newly constructed within five years after ownership of the qualified contaminated property is sold or otherwise transferred.

● New construction

New construction requiring revaluation includes site development of land, improvements erected on land, additions to existing improvements, and new fixtures (e.g., store fixtures, machinery) that relate directly to the function of the structure. The construction of or addition to an "active solar energy system" requires a reassessment and adjustment to the property's base-year value.

The value of new construction, including construction in progress, is added to the base-year value. See below for temporary exemption for new construction under certain conditions.

The law provides relief for certain cases where reconstruction or improvement is required to comply with local ordinances on seismic safety. In these cases, revaluation is deferred for 15 years.

New construction, for purposes of reassessment, does not include certain (1) earthquake safety improvements, (2) fire protection improvements, (3) access improvements for the disabled, (4) for the 1999-2000 through 2004-2005 fiscal years, active solar energy system improvements, and (5) underground storage tank upgrades.

● Change of ownership

The law provides detailed definitions of what constitutes a change of ownership that will trigger a revaluation of real property. Discussed below is a very brief summary of transactions that are not considered to be changes of ownership.

¶ 1702

1. Interspousal transfers, including those made in divorce settlements. Sale of an undivided interest results in a revaluation of the portion transferred; however, there is no revaluation if the interest transferred is less than 5% and its value is under $10,000.

2. Transfers of partnership interests, or addition or deletion of partners, unless a controlling interest is acquired.

3. Transfers of property among members of an affiliated group of corporations, as specifically defined.

4. A transfer into a trust, if the transferor is the beneficiary or the trust is revocable.

5. Transfers of joint tenancies that do not result in changes of beneficial ownership.

6. An acquisition of property as a replacement for property that was condemned. However, where the value of the property acquired exceeds the value of the property replaced by more than 20%, the excess is revalued and added to the base-year value of the replaced property.

7. Certain transfers of residences to children or wards upon death of parents or guardians. To qualify, the children or wards must have (1) been disabled for at least five years prior to the transfer, (2) lived in the property at least five years, and (3) family income of $20,000 or less.

8. Transfers of the principal residence and up to $1 million in other property between parents and their children or between grandparents and their grandchildren when the parents of the children are deceased.

9. Certain transfers of mobilehome parks to nonprofit entities. This also applies to transfers of rental spaces to tenants under certain conditions.

10. The acquisition by an employee benefit plan of indirect or direct control of the employer corporation.

New owners are required to notify the assessor of a change of ownership and may be penalized for failure to do so. As a part of the effort to enforce the change-of-ownership rules, corporation and partnership income-tax return forms require reporting of changes in property ownership.

● *Constitutionality of acquisition value assessment*

In *Nordlinger v. Hahn* (1992) (CCH CALIFORNIA TAX REPORTS ¶ 21-930.203), the U.S. Supreme Court concluded that the acquisition value assessment method mandated by Proposition 13 does not violate the principles of the Equal Protection Clause of the Fourteenth Amendment, even though the method may result in significant assessment disparities between similar properties acquired at different times. The same conclusion was reached by a California court of appeal in *R.H. Macy v. Contra Costa County* (1990) (CCH CALIFORNIA TAX REPORTS ¶ 21-930.202), which involved commercial property. The taxpayer's commercial premises, which were acquired before Proposition 13 was adopted, were held to have been properly assessed at full value (i.e., market price) for the 1987 tax year, when the taxpayer underwent a corporate reorganization that constituted a change of ownership triggering reassessment under Proposition 13.

¶ 1702

● *Damaged property*

Where property is damaged or destroyed by a "misfortune or calamity," detailed rules are provided for reduction in the assessed valuation.

The base-year value of property damaged or destroyed in an area declared a disaster by the Governor may be transferred to comparable replacement property acquired or constructed within the same county or to comparable replacement property in a *different* county, provided the replacement property is located in a county whose board of supervisors has authorized such a transfer prior to the taxpayer's relocation.

The time period during which a base-year value transfer may be made for property damaged or destroyed by a disaster is (1) three years from the date of the disaster for intracounty transfers (except for property damaged or destroyed by the January 1994 Northridge earthquake, for which the base-year value transfer period is five years from the date of the disaster) and (2) the later of January 1, 1996, or three years from the date the replacement property is purchased or constructed for intercounty transfers.

Damaged or destroyed property is reassessed at current market value but retains its old base-year value if that value is lower than the reassessed value, notwithstanding the transfer of the base-year value to replacement property. Restoration or repair of the property is considered to be new construction, triggering a reassessment at that time.

● *Purchase price as value*

State Board of Equalization Rule No. 2 (CCH CALIFORNIA TAX REPORTS ¶ 28-003) provides that the value of property for revaluation purposes in the case of a change of ownership is the purchase price paid unless there is substantial and convincing evidence that the property would not have transferred for such price in an open market transaction.

● *Effective date of revaluation*

The annual lien date and valuation date for locally assessed property taxes is January 1; this date applies to taxes for the fiscal year beginning on the following July 1.

The law provides that new construction or change of ownership will result in revaluation in the following month and a consequent increase in tax liability. Thus, new construction or change of ownership in July increases taxes for the fiscal year beginning in July, by $11/12$ths of a full year's tax attributable to the increased valuation. A change in August increases the current tax by $10/12$ths of the tax for a full year, and so on through the fiscal year.

New construction or a change of ownership occurring on or after the lien date but on or before May 31 results in an increase in taxes both for the current fiscal year and for the following fiscal year. If new construction or a change of ownership occurs on or after June 1 and on or before the next lien date, the assessor will need to determine only one supplemental assessment.

New construction is exempt from the supplemental assessment explained above until certain events occur (sale, rental, occupancy), provided the owner

¶ 1702

gives the assessor prescribed notice and requests exemption within specified time limits.

¶ 1703 Property Subject to Tax

Law: Secs. 201, 229, 1150-54, 5801-15 (CCH CALIFORNIA TAX REPORTS ¶ 20-103 et seq., 20-275, 20-375).

All real and tangible personal property in the state is subject to tax unless specifically exempt. There is no tax on intangible property. "Possessory interests" of lessees in tax-exempt public property are subject to tax if they are independent, durable, and exclusive of rights held by others in the property. Examples of possessory interests are leases of oil and gas properties, homesites, and boat berths.

In *United States v. County of San Diego et al.* (1995) (CCH CALIFORNIA TAX REPORTS ¶ 20-330.303), a federal court of appeals held that the taxpayer, a private research firm that conducted nuclear fusion research for the United States Department of Energy, had a taxable possessory interest in a nuclear device belonging to the Department of Energy because the taxpayer was entitled to exclusive and independent use of the device. Moreover, the property tax assessment was properly calculated using the value of the nuclear device because tax was assessed on the possessory interest of the taxpayer rather than on the ownership interest of the United States.

Certain types of property are subject to special taxes "in lieu" of property taxes and therefore are not subject to the general property tax. This applies to motor vehicles and private cars, as explained at ¶ 1903 and ¶ 1905.

Airplanes used by domestic airlines and air taxis operated in scheduled air taxi operations are assessed in proportion to the time they are in California. Aircraft owned by foreign airlines are exempt. Special rules apply to the valuation of certificated aircraft and airline possessory interests.

Special rules are provided for mobilehomes and manufactured homes. Those on a permanent foundation are taxed as real property. Others are subject either to vehicle license fees or to property taxes, depending on date of purchase and other factors.

Floating homes are taxed as real property, with 1979 (rather than 1975) used as the valuation base for purposes of Proposition 13 (see ¶ 1702). A floating home does not include a vessel.

¶ 1704 Exemptions

Law: Secs. 201-61 (CCH CALIFORNIA TAX REPORTS ¶ 20-505—20-520).

Many categories of property and property owners are partially or fully exempt under the property tax law. There have been numerous changes in the exemptions over the years. Detailed listing and discussion is beyond the scope of this book.

Property tax is not imposed on the following categories of property: business inventories (including livestock held for sale), household goods and personal effects not held or used in a trade or business, employee-owned hand tools (up to $20,000), intangible property, nonprofit cemetery property, cargo

¶ 1703

containers, and certain vessels and aircraft. In *Hahn v. State Board of Equalization* (1999) (CCH CALIFORNIA TAX REPORTS ¶ 20-150.80), a California court of appeal upheld a State Board of Equalization rule that basic operational computer programs (although intangible property) are not exempt from property tax when sold bundled with computer hardware but are exempt when sold separately.

A property tax exemption is provided for $7,000 of the value of a homeowner's dwelling. Partial exemptions are also allowed for certain agricultural products, immature timber, fruit and nut trees, and grapevines. These exemptions are in addition to constitutional exemptions for property in interstate and international commerce.

In addition, California's property tax law provides full or partial exemptions for qualified property held by religious institutions and organizations, governments and their agencies, Native American tribes, educational institutions, charitable, scientific, and hospital organizations, certain veterans and their surviving spouses, veterans organizations, banks and insurance companies (personal property only), and volunteer fire departments.

Some exemptions require the filing of an annual return or affidavit. In case of any question about exemptions or filing requirements, the assessor's office should be consulted.

¶ 1704a Senior Citizens and Disabled Persons Property Tax Assistance

Law: Secs. 20501-641 (CCH CALIFORNIA TAX REPORTS ¶ 20-358).

Some property tax relief is provided for "senior citizens" in the form of "property tax assistance" payments made by the Franchise Tax Board (FTB) to reimburse qualified homeowners for property taxes paid on their primary residence. This program includes mobilehomes and floating homes, and also applies to renters, based upon a property tax equivalent presumed to be paid by renters. To qualify, a homeowner or renter must be age 62 or older or blind or disabled and must have "household income" within specified limits. "Household income" consists of taxable income plus nontaxable income such as social security, public assistance payments, etc. A regulation addresses specific eligibility and application requirements for resident aliens.

The amount of relief to a homeowner is a portion of the tax on the first $34,000 of the full value of the home, the percentage varying in inverse ratio to the household income. The percentage is 96% where the income is $8,283 or less, decreasing by steps to 4% where the income is more than $31,572 but not more than $33,132. All these figures are adjusted for inflation for calendar years after 1999.

The amount of relief to a renter is a portion of $250, which is the statutory property tax equivalent, the percentage varying in inverse ratio to the household income. The percentage is 96% where the income is $8,283 or less, decreasing by steps to 4% where the income is more than $31,572 but not more than $33,132. Again, these figures are adjusted for inflation for calendar years after 1999. The claimant must pay rent of at least $50 per month to qualify for assistance.

¶ 1704a

The blank forms necessary to claim assistance are distributed by the FTB. Claims should be filed with the Property Tax Assistance Division annually after May 15 of the fiscal year for which assistance is claimed but before August 31 of the next succeeding fiscal year.

● *Property tax postponement*

Persons age 62 or over and disabled and blind persons may postpone payment of property taxes on their home under certain conditions. The claimant must own (including possessory interests) and occupy the property involved, which may be a mobilehome, houseboat, or floating home, and may be in cooperative housing or in a multipurpose or multiunit structure. The claimant must have at least a 20% equity, based on property-tax valuation.

To be eligible, the claimant must have "household income" of no more than $24,000.

"Household income" consists of taxable income plus nontaxable income such as social security, public assistance payments, etc.

The postponed taxes are covered by a lien on the property. They become payable, generally, if the claimant disposes of the property or dies without leaving a spouse living in the home.

Application for postponement should be filed with the State Controller, who will supply forms and information upon request.

¶ 1705 Basis and Rate of Tax

Law: Sec. 3, Art. XIII, Sec. 1, Art. XIIIA, Cal. Constitution; Secs. 93, 109, 208-12, Revenue and Taxation Code (CCH CALIFORNIA TAX REPORTS ¶ 20-080—20-087, 20-252, 20-615, 20-735).

As explained at ¶ 1702, the overall rate of property tax is now 1% of "full cash value." This may be increased by any amount necessary to pay interest and redemption charges on any indebtedness approved by the voters before July 1, 1978, or bonded indebtedness for the acquisition or improvement of real property approved on or after July 1, 1978, by two-thirds of those voting in a local election.

The value of intangible assets and rights relating to the going concern value of a business or the exclusive nature of a concession, franchise, or similar agreement must not enhance or be reflected in the value of taxable property. However, taxable property may be assessed and valued by assuming the presence of intangible assets or rights necessary to put the taxable property to beneficial or productive use. Intangible attributes of real property such as zoning, location, and other such attributes that relate directly to the real property must be reflected in the value of the real property.

Additionally, in any case in which the cost approach method of valuation is used to value special use property, a component for entrepreneurial profit may not be added unless there is market-derived evidence that such profit exists and has not been fully offset by physical deterioration or economic obsolescence.

The "assessed value" of property, generally, is the full cash value as modified by Proposition 13 (see ¶ 1702). The assessed value may be retroactively reduced when a disaster occurs after the assessment date (see ¶ 1706). The base-year value of certain property damaged by a disaster may be transferred to replacement property (see ¶ 1702).

Special rules are provided for reduced valuation of several categories of property, including certain vessels engaged in fishing or research, "enforceably restricted" open-space land, motion pictures, computer software programs, and business or professional records.

Although Article XIIIA of the Constitution (Proposition 13) refers only to real property, the 1% rate limitation also applies to personal property.

The law provides that personal property shall be treated as "secured" only if located upon real property of the same owner at the lien date. Personal property not so located may be treated as "secured" under certain conditions. In order for such property to be treated as "secured" where it is not located upon real property of the same owner, the property must be located in the same county and the taxpayer must record a certificate from the assessor to the effect that the real property is sufficient to secure the payment of the tax.

¶ 1706 Assessment Procedure and Equalization

Law: Secs. 108, 170, 401-05, 441-60, 721-59, 1601-45.5 (CCH CALIFORNIA TAX REPORTS ¶ 20-605 et seq.).

Property is assessed annually as of 12:01 A.M. on the first day of January. Each taxpayer must file a personal property statement with the county assessor during any year the aggregate cost of his or her taxable personal property is $100,000 or more. Others must file a statement if requested by the assessor. The statement must include a description of all taxable property owned, claimed, possessed, controlled or managed by the individual, firm, or corporation involved.

The board of supervisors of each county acts as a board of equalization to equalize valuations of the county assessor. Boards of supervisors of certain counties may create assessment appeals boards to handle their equalization duties. With the exception of state-assessed property, property owners may appear before the county board of equalization or assessment appeals board to protest their assessments. The State Board of Equalization (SBE) reviews the valuation of a public utility's state-assessed property where a petition for reassessment has been made.

The law authorizes the board of supervisors of any county to provide by ordinance for the reassessment of property damaged or destroyed by a "misfortune or calamity" such as earthquake, fire, flood, or landslide.

The SBE assesses property, as of 12:01 A.M. on the first day of January, of certain classes of public utilities and other inter-county property, even though the property is taxed by local jurisdictions. However, land and rights-of-way through which intercounty pipelines run are subject to assessment by county assessors.

¶ 1707 Returns and Payment

> *Law:* Secs. 194-4.9, 441-60, 2605-19, 2701-05.5 (CCH California Tax Reports ¶ 20-740, 20-820, 21-011—21-017).

As explained above at ¶ 1706, taxpayers may be required to file annually with the county assessor a written statement of property owned, claimed, possessed, or controlled. The statement must be filed between January 1 and April 1. In cases where the cities do their own assessing, a separate statement should be filed with the city.

As noted at ¶ 1704, owners of certain classes of exempt property must file an annual return or affidavit claiming the exemption.

A county tax collector must consolidate all of a requesting taxpayer's property tax obligations into a single tax bill. Consolidated property tax bills may be obtained only in counties in which an authorizing memorandum is recorded with the county recorder and only with respect to property listed on the secured property tax roll.

Except in a few cities (see below), property taxes are payable:

(a) on real property: first installment (1/2) due and payable November 1 and delinquent after December 10; second installment due and payable February 1 and delinquent after April 10;

(b) on personal property:

(1) if secured by real estate, payable (in full) with the *first* installment of real estate tax, by December 10;

(2) if unsecured, due on first day of March and delinquent after August 31.

If the delinquency date falls on Saturday, Sunday, or a holiday, the taxes do not become delinquent until 5 p.m. or the close of business, whichever is later, on the next business day. If a county board of supervisors, by adoption of an ordinance or resolution, closes the county's offices for business prior to the time of delinquency on the "next business day" or for a whole day, that day will be considered a legal holiday for purposes of establishing the delinquency date.

A few cities that do their own assessing do not use the payment dates shown above; there is no uniformity in the dates used in such cases.

An owner of property that has sustained substantial damage as the result of a disaster in a county declared by the Governor to be in a state of disaster may apply for deferral of the first postdisaster installment of regular secured property taxes. A claim for reassessment of the disaster-damaged property must be filed, or the property must have been otherwise reassessed, in conjunction with any such application for deferral. Taxpayers that were participating in an installment payment agreement prior to the disaster may qualify to defer tax payments for one year.

● *Payment on supplemental assessments*

Where supplemental assessments are made in cases of new construction or changes of ownership, as explained at ¶ 1702, a supplemental tax bill is mailed by the tax collector. The additional tax is due on the date the bill is mailed,

¶ 1707

but may be paid in two installments that become delinquent according to the month in which the bill is mailed. If the bill is mailed in the period July-October, the delinquency dates are as follows:

(a) first installment, December 10;

(b) second installment, April 10.

If the bill is mailed in the period November-June, the delinquency dates are as follows:

(a) first installment, last day of month following the month the bill is mailed;

(b) second installment, last day of the fourth calendar month following the date the first installment is delinquent.

¶ 1708 Administration—Penalties, Refunds

Law: Secs. 461-82, 501-33, 2617, 3691, 4833.1, 4985.3, 5096-97.2, 5367, 5901-09 (CCH CALIFORNIA TAX REPORTS ¶ 21-185, 21-405—21-420, 21-500, 21-855).

Severe penalties may be imposed for failing to supply required information or giving false information. A taxpayer may be fined up to $1,000 and may be imprisoned for not more than six months; a corporate taxpayer is subject to an additional fine of $200 a day, up to a maximum of $20,000. In addition, civil penalties may be imposed.

A taxpayer who fails to file a required property statement (see ¶ 1706) is subject to a 10% penalty assessment on the unreported property. A taxpayer who willfully fails to supply information or conceals property is subject to a 25% penalty assessment. These penalties may be abated upon a showing of reasonable cause. For cases involving a fraudulent act, omission, or concealment of property, the taxpayer is subject to a 75% penalty assessment. New owners who fail to file the required notification of change of ownership (see ¶ 1702) are subject to a penalty of $100 or 10% of the current year's tax. Life insurance companies that own real property in a separate account and fail to file the required property statement (see ¶ 1706) or fail to file a required statement of transfer (see ¶ 1702) are subject to a penalty of $1,000 in addition to any other penalty prescribed by law.

If property taxes are not paid until delinquent, a penalty is added: the rate is 10%. An additional penalty is added for continued delinquency: the rate is 1½% per month. See ¶ 1707 for delinquency dates. Delinquency penalties may be canceled under certain conditions.

In the case of assessment corrections and cancellations, a taxpayer will be relieved of only those penalties for failure to pay tax that apply to the difference between the county board of equalization's final determination of value and the assessed value that was appealed, unless the taxpayer has paid at least 80% of the final assessed value.

Property may be sold to satisfy liens for delinquent taxes. The law provides detailed rules for such sales, redemptions, etc.

The state law provides for refunds of property taxes, on order of the board of supervisors, under certain conditions. Generally, a claim for refund must be filed within four years from the date of payment or within one year from the date of mailing of the assessor's notice of overpayment. (Refunds of city property taxes may be subject to different limitations, since they are subject to the law of the city involved.)

● *Taxpayer's bill of rights*

A "bill of rights" for property taxpayers permits county assessors to respond to taxpayer requests for written rulings on certain property tax issues and may relieve a taxpayer from penalties and interest assessed or accrued as a direct result of the taxpayer's reasonable reliance on such a written ruling.

Additional protections extended to property taxpayers (1) require notice of proposed escape assessments, hearings before a county board of equalization, or judgment liens on taxpayers' unsecured property; (2) extend the limitations period for certain escape assessment refund claims; (3) authorize taxpayers to inspect and copy assessors' market data and assessment information; and (4) provide a procedure for making stipulations with respect to property tax refund claims.

CHAPTER 18

UNEMPLOYMENT INSURANCE TAX

¶ 1801 Scope of Chapter

This chapter discusses briefly the California unemployment insurance tax. Its purpose is to give a general idea of the impact of the tax law. It is not intended to provide detailed coverage.

¶ 1802 History and Imposition of Tax

The unemployment insurance tax was first imposed in 1936. It is tied in with the Federal unemployment tax, as are the similar taxes in other states.

As explained in subsequent paragraphs, the tax is levied upon employers and is, generally speaking, based upon wages paid for employment in California. California is one of the few states which also levies a tax upon employees. The employees' tax goes into a special fund for disability rather than unemployment benefits. Payment of the employees' tax may be avoided entirely where there is a private plan for disability benefits which meets the requirements of the law; however, because of the difficulty of complying with the standards that have been set up, there are very few private plans in operation.

The tax is administered by the Employment Development Department.

¶ 1803 Employers Subject to Tax

(CCH Unemployment Insurance Reports, California ¶ 4081—4089B, 4122—4122M).

The tax applies to employers of one or more employees in covered employment during either the current or preceding calendar year. Generally, it applies to employers who pay wages of more than $100 in a calendar quarter. However, there are special rules for household employers, as explained at ¶ 1808a. Some employers not otherwise subject may become subject by election under certain conditions. Individual employers may also elect to be

¶ 1803

covered as *employees* under certain conditions. In addition, self-employed individuals may elect disability benefits coverage for themselves. Special rules are provided for cases where the employee performs services both within and without the State. Along with other States, California has adopted the uniform definition of "employment" to avoid interstate conflicts and overlapping.

¶ 1804 Exempt Employers and Employment

(CCH UNEMPLOYMENT INSURANCE REPORTS, California ¶ 4095-4121B).

Some employers and employment are exempt. The exemptions include, among others, some service not in the course of the employer's business, some services of corporate directors, certain family employment, some governmental organizations, some services by students, student nurses, most newspaper or magazine carriers under age 18, golf caddies, court reporters, consultants performing professional services as independent contractors, service for a political candidate, certain brokers and direct sellers, etc. There have been numerous changes in the exemptions over the years; any questions about current exemptions should be checked with the Employment Development Department.

¶ 1805 Employers' Tax—Base and Rates

(CCH UNEMPLOYMENT INSURANCE REPORTS, California ¶ 4134I—4162, 4176—4200).

The California employer's tax is imposed upon the first $7,000 of taxable wages paid by each employer to each employee.

Wages paid to an individual on which the employer paid tax to another state may be included in determining when the limit on taxable wages is reached.

The standard tax rate is 3.4% and this rate plus the 0.1% employment and training tax, applies to new employers until their accounts have been subject to changes during 12 consecutive completed calendar months ending on June 30 unless a new employer opts to acquire a previous owner's adjustable rate. After the first three years, an employer's rate is adjusted on the basis of the employer's "experience rating," as explained below. Rates for 1999 range from 0.7% to 4.2% for positive-balance employers (including zero reserve ratio), and from 4.4% to 5.4% for negative-balance employers. There is also a 0.1% extra tax for positive-balance employers in 1999, to be deposited in the Employment and Training Fund.

● *Experience rating*

The tax rates of most employers are determined under a system of "experience rating"—sometimes referred to as "merit rating." Under this system the rate depends upon two factors: (1) the balance in the State's unemployment fund, and (2) the employer's reserve ratio, which is the ratio of the balance in the employer's individual reserve account, to its average annual taxable payroll for the preceding 3 years. The computation of the employer's reserve ratio is made on June 30 for purposes of determining the rate for the following calendar year. The employer's reserve account is credited with employer contributions and, generally, charged with unemployment benefits

¶ 1804

paid to the employer's former employees (except extended benefits). The employer receives notice of claims made by its former employees, and a protest may be filed if the employer thinks an employee is not entitled to the benefits claimed. If the protest is upheld, the employer is relieved of a direct charge to its reserve account for the disputed benefits.

Individual reserve accounts are charged and credited proportionately for some items of expense and income of the unemployment fund that are not related to particular employers. This applies, for example, to charges for disputed benefits and to credits for interest earned by the fund.

After an employer has qualified for "experience rating," its contribution rate is established by the Employment Development Department from one of seven schedules as summarized below, depending on the percentage relationship between the balance in the Unemployment Trust Fund and total taxable wages paid. The rate schedule that applies in 1999 is Schedule C. Rates for 1999 under Schedule C (not including the 0.1% special contribution to the Employment and Training Fund by certain employers) may be determined from the following schedule:

Employer's Reserve Ratio	*1999 Rate (%)*
Less than −20%	5.4
−20% to −18%	5.4
−18% to −16%	5.4
−16% to −14%	5.4
−14% to −12%	5.4
−12% to −11%	5.4
−11% to −10%	5.3
−10% to − 9%	5.3
− 9% to − 8%	5.2
− 8% to − 7%	5.1
− 7% to − 6%	5.0
− 6% to − 5%	4.9
− 5% to − 4%	4.8
− 4% to − 3%	4.7
− 3% to − 2%	4.6
− 2% to − 1%	4.5
− 1% to zero	4.4
zero to 1%	4.2
1% to 2%	4.0
2% to 3%	3.8
3% to 4%	3.6
4% to 5%	3.4
5% to 6%	3.2
6% to 7%	3.0
7% to 8%	2.8
8% to 9%	2.6
9% to 10%	2.4
10% to 11%	2.2
11% to 12%	2.0
12% to 13%	1.8
13% to 14%	1.6
14% to 15%	1.4
15% to 16%	1.2
16% to 17%	1.1
17% to 18%	1.1
18% to 19%	0.9
19% to 20%	0.8
20% or more	0.7

¶ 1805

Ratio of Trust Fund to taxable wages	Schedule	Contribution Rates	
		Positive-balance employers	Negative-balance employers
Over 1.8%	AA	0.1%-3.4%	3.7%-5.4%
1.6%-1.8%	A	0.3%-3.6%	3.8%-5.4%
1.4%-1.6%	B	0.5%-3.9%	4.1%-5.4%
1.2%-1.4%	C	0.7%-4.2%	4.4%-5.4%
1.0%-1.2%	D	0.9%-4.5%	4.7%-5.4%
0.8%-1.0%	E	1.1%-4.8%	5.0%-5.4%
0.6%-0.8%	F	1.3%-5.1%	All-5.4%

If the Trust Fund balance falls below 0.6% an emergency solvency surtax is added, computed at 1.15 times the Schedule F rate.

Contributing employers, except for new employers, negative-balance employers, and delinquent employers, will be allowed to make voluntary contributions. No voluntary contribution may reduce an employer's rate by more than three rates in the applicable rate schedule, and no voluntary contribution will be allowed for any year in which Schedule E or F is in effect or any year in which the emergency surcharge is in effect.

● *Employment training tax*

Generally, any contributing employer other than a negative-balance employer, and certain agricultural and domestic employers, are required to pay a 0.1% employment and training tax for calendar years 1983 through 2001, based on the amount of benefits paid that are charged to their accounts.

● *"Reimbursement-financing" method*

Certain California State and nonprofit organizations are permitted or required to use the "reimbursement financing" method of paying for employee benefits, in lieu of paying taxes under the regular rules discussed above. Detailed rules are provided for use of this method. Two or more reimbursing employers may establish a joint account and share the costs of benefits paid.

¶ 1806 Employees' Tax

(CCH UNEMPLOYMENT INSURANCE REPORTS, California ¶ 4145A, 4164—4167B, 4241, 4587—4589, 4655—4677).

The annual taxable limitation on employees' wages for disability benefit purposes is determined as an amount equal to 4 times the maximum weekly benefit amount for each calendar year, multiplied by 13 and divided by 55%. This amount is $31,767 for 1998 and 1999. The employees' tax rate for disability purposes is adjusted annually on the basis of the balance in the disability fund and the level of employee benefits; it may range from 0.1% to

1.3%, but may not decrease from the previous year's rate by more than 0.2%. The employee tax for 1998 and 1999 is 0.5%.

Employers and self-employed individuals may elect disability insurance coverage under certain conditions, generally paying a somewhat higher rate in lieu of the regular rate. This special rate is redetermined annually. The rate for 1999 is 2.15%.

The employees' tax is applicable to the same wages as those subject to the employers' unemployment tax, except for the difference in wage limitations and except for provisions that limit disability benefits coverage and employees' tax to certain categories covered under the employers' tax.

If an employee works for more than one employer during the year he or she may obtain a refund of amounts withheld in excess of the tax on the maximum wage limits referred to above, plus interest. The excess tax withheld is allowed as a credit on the income tax return of the year involved, as explained at ¶ 120. Credit will not be allowed unless a claim is made on a return filed within three years of the last day prescribed to file the return. If the individual is not required to file an income tax return, he or she may file a refund claim on Form DE 1964, explaining and certifying his or her exemption from income tax; such claim must be filed within three years after the close of the calendar year involved.

The employees' tax does not go into the unemployment fund, but into a separate fund for the payment of disability benefits. An employer may have a private, or "voluntary," plan for disability benefits. If such private plan meets the requirements and is approved by the state, employees covered under the plan are not required to pay tax to the state. Approval of a voluntary plan may be denied, if the approval would result in a "substantial selection of risks adverse to the Disability Fund." The employer may require its employees to contribute to the cost of the private plan, up to the amount they would otherwise have to pay to the state.

Voluntary plans are assessed for state administrative costs and also for the unemployed disabled account. The rate of these assessments is 14% of the product obtained by multiplying the rate of worker contributions for the year by the amount of taxable wages paid to employees covered by the voluntary plan.

See ¶ 1808a regarding special rules for household employers.

¶ 1807 Employees' Benefits

(CCH UNEMPLOYMENT INSURANCE REPORTS, California ¶ 4251—4269N, 4515—4533B, 4696).

Normal unemployment benefits range from a low of $40 to a high of $230 per week, for a maximum of 26 weeks during one "benefit year." The maximum amount of benefits for a benefit year is the lesser of 26 times the weekly benefit or one-half the total wages during the qualifying base period. Additional extended benefits may be available during periods of widespread unemployment. The amount of regular benefits depends upon the employee's wages during the quarter of his base period in which the employee's wages were highest and in some cases, on his total base-period wages. Numerous conditions (waiting period, availability for work, etc.) are imposed upon the receipt of benefits.

Disability benefits range from $50 to $336 per week, for a maximum of 52 weeks during one "disability benefit period," but in no case may be more than the total wages paid to the employee during the disability period.

¶ 1808 Registration, Returns, Reports, and Payment

(CCH UNEMPLOYMENT INSURANCE REPORTS, California ¶ 4203—4205, 4217, 4218).

An employer must register with the Employment Development Department (EDD) within 15 days after becoming subject to the tax. Registration is handled at state sales tax offices (along with issuance of sales tax permits) as well as at offices of the EDD. Returns of tax payable must be made quarterly, on or before the last day of the month following the close of the calendar quarter. Reports are timely filed if postmarked on or before the due date. The employer's tax is payable in full with the return.

Reimbursement payments are due within 30 days of the date of mailing of the notice of determination of the amount due unless an extension is granted.

Employers must furnish information regarding each newly hired employee on a W-4 form or its equivalent, which may be transmitted electronically or magnetically by the employer. Reports are due no later than 20 days after the hire date.

Reporting and payment of employees' disability insurance contributions are administered by the EDD, along with administration of income tax withholding. Semiweekly deposits of such taxes are required if income tax withholding exceeds certain amounts. Any amounts withheld for disability insurance are due and payable at the same time as the payments for income tax withholding, regardless of the amounts involved.

Extension of time for filing returns and paying tax may be granted for a period up to 60 days.

¶ 1808a Household Employers ("Nanny Taxes")

(CCH UNEMPLOYMENT INSURANCE REPORTS, California ¶ 4122G, 4122M, 4205, 4218B)

Special rules apply to employers of domestic help. Such employers must register with the Employment Development Department (EDD) within 15 days after paying cash wages of $750 or more in a calendar quarter, and must withhold and transmit to the EDD the "employee's tax" (state disability insurance) described at ¶ 1806.

Household employers who pay cash wages of $1,000 or more in a calendar quarter must also pay the "employer's tax" (unemployment insurance) described at ¶ 1805.

After becoming subject to tax, as explained above, at the $750 or $1,000 per quarter level, if wages paid drop below those levels the employer must continue to pay taxes through the following year.

¶ 1808

Household employers who pay $20,000 or more a year in wages (cash and non-cash) must file reports and pay both unemployment insurance and state disability insurance taxes quarterly. Household employers who pay less than $20,000 a year may elect to submit wage information quarterly and pay annually. Domestic employers may file their reports with the EDD by telephone.

Agencies that refer domestic workers must meet statutory requirements in order to not be deemed the employer of the workers they refer.

¶ 1809 Administration, Deficiencies, Refunds

(CCH UNEMPLOYMENT INSURANCE REPORTS, California ¶ 4031—4072A, 4221, 4224—4240-A2, 4243, 4245-4246, 4250-4250L).

If a tax deficiency is assessed, the Employment Development Department (EDD) gives the employer written notice of such assessment and the employer has 30 days within which to petition for reassessment. Such petition is reviewable by an Administrative Law Judge, and the Administrative Law Judge's decision may be appealed to the Appeals Board.

If any part of a deficiency is due to negligence or intentional disregard of the law or regulations, a penalty of 10% is added to the tax. If due to fraud, the penalty is 50%. Penalties may also be imposed for failure to file wage information. Interest is charged on deficiencies at the rate established annually for income tax purposes, as explained at ¶ 709.

The employer may file a claim for refund of tax overpaid. No refund shall be made or credit allowed unless a claim therefor is filed with the director within three years from the last day of the calendar month following the close of the calendar quarter for which the overpayment was made or within six months of an assessment becoming final or within 60 days from the date of overpayment, whichever period expires later. If a claim is disallowed, the employer receives notice and has 30 days within which to file a petition for review by an Administrative Law Judge and the Administrative Law Judge's decision may be appealed to the Appeals Board. Interest is allowable on refunds under certain conditions.

Employees may obtain refund of excess withholding of disability insurance tax—see ¶ 120.

● *EDD settlement authority*

The Unemployment Insurance Appeals Board is authorized to approve the settlement of any civil tax matter dispute of $7,500 or more recommended by the Director of the EDD provided that the recommendation has been reviewed by the Attorney General. Settlements of matters involving lesser amounts may be approved by the director or an administrative law judge, whichever may be reviewing the claim.

¶ 1809

CHAPTER 19

OTHER STATE TAXES

¶ 1901 Scope of Chapter

Law: Secs. 7080-99 (CCH CALIFORNIA TAX REPORTS ¶ 61-620).

This chapter outlines generally and very briefly certain California state taxes and fees that have not already been covered in the text. No effort is made to explain these taxes and fees in detail or to discuss the detailed rules applicable to them. The purpose is merely to indicate in general terms the basis of each tax or fee, by whom it is administered, and where further information may be obtained if desired.

● *Enactment of taxes and fees*

Regulatory fees, such as certain environmental fees, may be enacted by a majority vote of the legislature, unlike taxes which require a two-thirds vote of either the legislature or the electorate (see *Sinclair Paint Co. v. State Board of Equalization* (1997) (CCH CALIFORNIA TAX REPORTS ¶ 33-050.30)).

● *Taxpayer's bill of rights*

A "bill of rights" has been enacted to protect the privacy and property rights of taxpayers who are subject to the following State Board of Equalization (SBE) administered taxes and fees: motor vehicle fuel license tax, use fuel tax, underground storage tank maintenance fees, hazardous substances tax, solid waste disposal site cleanup and maintenance fees, alcoholic beverages tax, and cigarette and tobacco products taxes. A similar "bill of rights" has been enacted for taxpayers who are subject to various state and local excise taxes and fees. Both are substantially similar to the "bill of rights" described at ¶ 701a, relating to personal income and corporate tax collections, except that the agency involved is the SBE rather than the Franchise Tax Board.

¶ 1901

¶ 1902 Insurance Taxes

Law: Secs.12201-84 (CCH CALIFORNIA TAX REPORTS ¶ 88-100—88-600).

A gross premiums tax is imposed upon insurance companies (other than ocean marine insurers). This tax is in lieu of all other state and local taxes and licenses, with the exception of real estate taxes and motor vehicle license fees. The rate of tax on insurers in general is 2.35% of gross premium income. The rate is 1/2% on premiums received under pension and profit-sharing plans that are qualified under the income tax provisions of the Internal Revenue Code. Ocean marine insurers are taxed at the rate of 5% on their underwriting income. Surplus line brokers and nonadmitted insurers, with some exceptions, are taxed at the rate of 3% of gross premiums, less return premiums.

The administration of the gross premiums tax is divided among the Insurance Commissioner, the State Board of Equalization (SBE), the State Controller, and the Franchise Tax Board (FTB). Insurance companies other than nonadmitted insurers must file an annual tax return with the Commissioner, as shown below. A copy is transmitted to the SBE, which assesses the taxes imposed on insurers for the preceding calendar year, and notifies them of any excess or deficiency. Examination of the return by the Commissioner may result in a deficiency assessment.

Returns and annual payments are due as follows:

	Returns	Payments
Insurance companies generally	April 1	April 1
Ocean marine insurance	June 15	June 15
Retaliatory taxes	April 1	April 1
Surplus line brokers	March 1	March 1

Nonadmitted insurers must file a return with the FTB by the first day of the third month following the close of the calendar quarter during which a taxable insurance contract took effect or was renewed.

Insurance companies and surplus line brokers, with some exceptions, whose tax liability for the preceding year was $5,000 or more, are required to make monthly installment payments. In addition, any insurer whose annual insurance tax exceeds $20,000 must remit all tax payments by electronic funds transfer. A penalty of 10% of the taxes due will be imposed for failure to comply with the electronic funds transfer requirement.

Insurance companies may qualify for a low-income housing credit or, effective for tax years beginning after 1998 and before 2002, a credit for qualified deposits made into a community development financial institution. These credits are the same as those allowed under the personal income tax law and are discussed at ¶ 127 and ¶ 145, respectively. Effective January 1, 2000, an insurer may also claim a credit equal to the amount of the gross premiums tax due from the insurer on account of pilot project insurance issued to provide low-cost insurance to qualified low-income residents of San Francisco and Los Angeles.

¶ 1902

¶ 1903 Motor Vehicle Taxes

Law: Sec. 8880.68, Government Code; Secs. 5003.1-03.2., 5136, 5328, Public Utility Code; Secs. 7232-36, 10752-58, Revenue and Taxation Code; Secs. 4601-02, 6262, 9400, Vehicle Code (CCH California Tax Reports ¶ 50-050, 50-150, 50-210, 50-270, 50-290).

The following motor vehicle taxes are imposed:

(a) *Registration and weight fees.* Motor vehicles are required to be registered annually. The general annual state registration fee is $28, but miscellaneous additional fees may be imposed by the state and certain local jurisdictions. In addition, there are annual weight fees for the operation of certain commercial vehicles, the amount depending on the weight of the vehicle and other factors. Trailer coaches are also subject to registration and licensing. The administrative agency is the Department of Motor Vehicles.

A $300 smog impact fee is also required at the time of registration of certain model year motor vehicles that were previously registered outside the state. However, this fee was ruled unconstitutional by a California court of appeal in *Jordan et al. v. California Department of Motor Vehicles et al.* (1999) (CCH California Tax Reports ¶ 403-050).

(ссн)   **CCH Tip: Individuals Should Apply for Refunds**

Pending a legislative decision on whether to reimburse individuals‛ for all previously paid smog impact fees, individuals who have paid the fees should protect their rights by applying for refunds through the Department of Motor Vehicles.

(b) *Automobile "in lieu" tax.* The "in lieu" tax, so called because it is a form of property tax that is imposed in lieu of local property taxation of automobiles, including automobiles awarded in a state lottery, is in effect a license fee in addition to the registration fee discussed above. The tax is imposed at 2% of the "market value" of the make and model involved, computed under a formula provided by law. The amount of the fee computed under the above procedures is reduced by 25% for fees with a final due date during the 1999 calendar year, and an additional 10% (for an overall reduction of 35%) for fees due during the 2000 calendar year. Further reductions are authorized for fees with a final due date after 2000, the exact percentage of the reduction being dependent on the realization of targeted revenue amounts. The license fee is paid at the same time as the registration fee. The above information regarding administration of registration and weight fees is equally applicable to this tax.

(c) *Motor carrier fees.* For-hire motor carriers other than household goods carriers or motor carriers of property engaged in interstate or foreign transportation of property must pay an annual permit fee consisting of the following amounts: a safety fee (ranging from $60 to $1,030), a cargo theft interdiction fee (ranging from $10 to $260), and a uniform business license tax fee (ranging from $60 to $2,000).

(d) *Household goods carriers.* Household goods carriers must pay an annual permit fee of $500. A regulatory fee is also imposed on household goods carriers owning or operating motor vehicles and transporting property for hire on the public highways. The fee is $15 plus 1/3 of 1% of gross operating revenue, payable quarterly to the Public Utilities Commission, if the carrier is under the regulatory jurisdiction of the Commission. However, if the carrier is not under the regulatory jurisdiction of the Commission or is transporting used office, store, and/or institution furniture or fixtures, the fee is $15 plus 1/10 of 1% of gross operating revenue. In addition, household goods carriers are subject to a license fee of 1/10 of 1% of gross operating revenue, payable quarterly to the Commission.

Copies of pertinent laws and regulations may be obtained from the State Board of Equalization.

¶ 1904 Alcoholic Beverage Taxes

Law: Secs. 23954.5, 23396.3, Business and Professions Code; Secs. 32151, 32201, Revenue and Taxation Code (CCH CALIFORNIA TAX REPORTS ¶ 35-100—35-300).

All those engaged in the production, distribution, or handling of alcoholic beverages in California must be licensed by the Department of Alcoholic Beverage Control. Licenses are issued for a period of one year, and license fees are payable annually. There is a long schedule of annual license fees for various classifications and additional fees and surcharges apply.

The application fee for an original on-sale or off-sale general license is $12,000.

An excise tax is imposed upon the sale of alcoholic beverages within the State. The rates are as follows:

Beverage	Rate
Beer	20¢ per gallon
Still wines	20¢ per gallon
Champagne, sparkling wine	30¢ per gallon
Sparkling hard cider	20¢ per gallon
Distilled spirits (proof strength or less)	$3.30 per gallon
Nonliquid distilled spirits containing 50% or less alcohol by weight	2¢ per ounce

Distilled spirits in excess of proof strength and nonliquid distilled spirits containing more than 50% alcohol by weight are taxed at double the above rate.

Generally, returns of excise tax must be filed and the tax paid monthly to the State Board of Equalization (SBE). However, the SBE may require returns and payments for quarterly or annual periods.

¶ 1905 Special Taxes in Lieu of Property Tax

Law: Secs. 5701-22, 11251-406 (CCH CALIFORNIA TAX REPORTS ¶ 20-336, 20-341).

A form of property tax is levied by the state upon the value of racehorses and upon the value of private cars operated on railroads within California. The railroad car tax is in lieu of local taxation of such property, and is imposed at the average rate of general property taxation for the preceding year as determined by the State Board of Equalization (SBE). Persons owning private railroad cars must make an annual report to the SBE. The tax is payable annually on or before December 10.

Racehorses are taxed annually by the head in three classes, stallions (the rate is based on the stud fees), brood mares, and racehorses (the rate is based on the amount of winnings).

¶ 1906 Cigarette and Tobacco Products Tax

Law: Secs. 30008-123 (CCH California Tax Reports ¶ 55-100—55-400).

A state tax is imposed on cigarettes. The tax rate applied to cigarettes is 87¢ per pack. Tobacco products are taxed at an equivalent rate, determined annually by the State Board of Equalization (SBE). Monthly reports must be filed by distributors and others by the 25th of the month for the preceding calendar month. Distributors are allowed a stamping or metering cost allowance of .85% of the tax. Sales to members of the armed forces in exchanges and commissaries, to state veterans' homes, and to law enforcement agencies for authorized use in a criminal investigation are exempt.

The tax is administered by the SBE.

¶ 1907 Other Taxes and Fees

Law: Secs. 13430-34, Business and Professions Code; Secs. 13244.5, 25299.41-99.43, Health and Safety Code; Secs. 3402, 48650-71, Public Resources Code; Sec. 4458, Public Utility Code; Secs. 7306-56, 7380-81, 8604-55, 38115, 40016, 41020, Revenue and Taxation Code (CCH California Tax Reports ¶ 33-100, 40-110—40-730, 45-110, 45-210, 80-110—80-140).

Following is a very brief statement of other taxes imposed by the state:

(a) *Motor vehicle fuel taxes.* A tax is imposed upon the privilege of distributing motor fuel, and a complementary use tax applies to gasoline and other fuels. The state rate on gasoline is 18¢ per gallon. If the federal license or use tax is reduced below specified levels, then the state rate will be increased by the amount of the federal reduction. Returns by persons distributing motor vehicle fuel must be made monthly to the State Board of Equalization (SBE), and returns by vendors and users must generally be made quarterly to the SBE.

A separate tax is imposed for the privilege of storage, removal, entry, or use of diesel fuel. The state rate is 18¢ per gallon of diesel fuel, subject to adjustment should the federal fuel tax rate be reduced. An additional surcharge is imposed on interstate users of diesel fuel purchased outside California and used in California. Returns and payments are generally made on a quarterly basis.

Some local jurisdictions are also authorized to impose a limited per gallon tax on the sale, storage, or use of motor vehicle fuel, if approved by the voters.

(b) *Aircraft jet fuel tax.* A license tax is imposed on aircraft jet fuel dealers at the rate of 2¢ per gallon. Monthly returns are required.

(c) *Public utilities.* "Public utilities" are not specially taxed as such. However, some companies so classified are subject to special license taxes or fees. These include certain transportation companies (see also ¶ 1903), and operators of toll bridges, toll roads, toll ferries, street railroads, and private wharves. Information may be obtained from the Public Utilities Commission.

(d) *Oil and gas severance tax.* A small regulatory tax is imposed on the production of oil and sale of gas. Information may be obtained from the state Department of Conservation.

(e) *Business license taxes.* License fees are imposed on many businesses, occupations, and professions. The fees range from nominal amounts to very large amounts (e. g., in the case of horse racing). Since there are over 100 categories of license taxes, a listing of them is beyond the scope of this book. Information may be obtained from the various state boards, commissions, etc., involved, or from the Department of Consumer Affairs in Sacramento.

(f) *Energy resources surcharge.* A nominal surcharge is imposed on electrical energy purchased from an electric utility.

(g) *Timber yield tax.* Forest trees on privately and publicly-owned land are subject to a severance tax at the time of harvest, at rates to be determined from time to time. Information may be obtained from the SBE.

(h) *Emergency telephone users' surcharge.* A nominal surcharge is imposed on intrastate telephone services, to finance the state's emergency telephone system.

(i) *Motor oil fee.* A fee is imposed on certain producers and dealers for the purchase or sale of motor oil. The maximum rate is 2¢ per gallon.

(j) *Lubricating oil tax.* Manufacturers of lubricating oil sold or transferred in California must pay a tax at the rate of 4¢ per quart.

(k) *Underground storage tank fee.* Certain underground storage tank owners must pay a fee in the amount of 12 mills for each gallon of petroleum placed in the tank. Quarterly returns are required.

(*l*) *Propane fees.* A nominal surcharge is imposed on sales of propane by operators of propane distribution systems. Also, a fee not to exceed $250 is imposed on owners of propane storage systems.

¶ 1908 Realty Transfer Tax

Law: Sec. 11911 (CCH California Tax Reports ¶ 34-701).

Cities and counties are authorized to impose a tax on transfers of interests in real estate with a value of more than $100. The county tax is at the rate of 55¢ for each $500, and the noncharter city rate is one-half of the county rate. The tax is payable to the County Recorder at the time the instrument transferring the property is recorded.

¶ 1909 Environmental Taxes and Fees

Law: Secs. 25205.1-05.12, Health and Safety Code; Secs. 43053-152.15, Revenue and Taxation Code (CCH California Tax Reports ¶ 34-450).

California imposes a variety of fees in connection with the generation, storage, treatment, disposal, and cleanup of waste, including hazardous waste disposal fees; facility, generator, permit, and hauler fees; fees imposed on solid waste landfill operators; tire disposal fees; various oil spill and medical waste fees; and a general "environmental fee" payable by virtually all corporations employing 50 or more persons (see below).

● *Environmental fee imposed on corporations*

All corporations with an SIC (Standard Industrial Classification) code for industries that use, generate, or store hazardous materials or conduct activities in California related to hazardous materials are subject to an annual environmental "fee," whether or not they are actually conducting activities related to hazardous materials. Only corporations doing business as private households are excluded. The fee is based on the number of employees in California during the previous calendar year:

Number of employees	Fee
1-49	$ 0
50-74	200
75-99	350
100-249	700
250-499	1,500
500-999	2,800
1000 or more	9,500

¶ 1909

PART VIII
DIRECTORY/RESOURCES

CHAPTER 20

CALIFORNIA RESOURCES

Franchise Tax Board—
General Information & Forms
PO Box 942840 Sacramento CA 94240 800-852-5711
Tax Practitioner Hotline
PO Box 942840 Sacramento CA 94240 916-858-0571
Internet Address
http://www.ftb.ca.gov

Trade & Commerce Agency—
Main Office
Ste 1700 801 K St. Sacramento CA 95814 916-322-1394
Business Development
Ste 1700 801 K St. Sacramento CA 95814 916-322-1398
Small Business
Ste 1700 801 K St. Sacramento CA 95814 916-324-1295
International Trade & Investment
Ste 1700 801 K St. Sacramento CA 95814 916-324-5511

Office of Small & Minority Business Development—
Department of General Services
Rm 100 1808 14th St. Sacramento CA 95814 916-322-5060

PART IX
DOING BUSINESS IN CALIFORNIA

CHAPTER 21

FEES AND TAXES

¶ 2101 Domestic Corporation Costs

Law: Secs. 12184-86, 12196, 12199, 12200-02, 12203.7, 12205-08, 12210-10.5, 26850-51, Government Code; Sec. 23221, Revenue and Taxation Code (CCH CALIFORNIA STATE TAX REPORTS, ¶ 1-121).

● *Initial fees and taxes*

The following fees are charged by the Secretary of State:

SERVICE PERFORMED	FEE
Accepting service of process	$ 50.00
Biennial statement of information	$ 20.00
Articles of incorporation (no shares authorized)	$ 30.00
Articles of incorporation (shares authorized)	$ 100.00
Certificate of dissolution	No fee
Certificate of official character	$ 20.00
Certificate of surrender	No fee
Change of address	No fee
Miscellaneous filing fee	$ 30.00
Registration of corporate name	$ 50.00
Reservation of corporate name	$ 10.00
Certification of a document	$ 5.00
Issuing certificate of status or filing	$ 5.00

The filing fee for a certificate of merger is ordinarily $100; if the merger involves corporations with one or more other types of business entities, the filing fee is $150.

For filing a certificate of amendment converting a nonprofit corporation to a business corporation, the fee is $70.

A fee of $2.25 is charged by a county clerk for the filing of any document or the issuance of any certificate relating to a corporation.

● *Minimum franchise tax*

The minimum franchise tax must be paid to the Secretary of State when the articles of incorporation are filed. However, corporations that incorporate in California on or after January 1, 2000, are exempt from the minimum

¶ 2101

franchise tax for their first two taxable years. Also, the requirement to prepay minimum franchise tax at the time of incorporation is eliminated for all corporations, other than credit unions, effective January 1, 2001.

Fees pertaining to foreign corporations are discussed below at ¶ 2102.

¶ 2102 Foreign Corporation Costs

Law: Secs. 12186, 12199, 12204, 12210-10.5, 12212, Government Code; Sec. 23221, Revenue and Taxation Code (CCH CALIFORNIA STATE TAX REPORTS, ¶ 2-30).

● *Initial fees and taxes*

The following fees are imposed on foreign corporations by the Secretary of State:

(1) Biennial statement by foreign corporation, $20;

(2) Registration of a corporate name, $50;

(3) Reservation of a corporate name, $10; and

(4) Statement of address by nonqualified foreign lending institution, $50.

Miscellaneous fees applicable to domestic corporations also apply to foreign corporations (see above at ¶ 2101).

● *Minimum franchise tax*

A foreign corporation that qualifies to transact business in this state must prepay the minimum franchise tax to the Secretary of State when the statement and designation by a foreign corporation is filed. However, corporations that qualify to do business in California on or after January 1, 2000, are exempt from the minimum franchise tax for their first two taxable years. Also, the requirement to prepay minimum franchise tax at the time of the incorporation is eliminated for all corporations, other than credit unions, effective January 1, 2001.

Table of Cases Cited

Paragraph | Paragraph

Paragraph

Paragraph

Paragraph | Paragraph

Table of Franchise Tax Board

Legal Rulings

Table of Franchise Tax Board

Notices

State of California — Franchise Tax Board   FTB Pub. 1006
CALIFORNIA TAX FORMS AND RELATED FEDERAL FORMS

CALIFORNIA FORM NUMBER	TITLE OR DESCRIPTION OF CALIFORNIA FORMS	COMPARABLE FEDERAL FORM	FED. FORM MAY BE USED See *Explanation of Notes
DE 1	Registration Form	SS-4	No**
DE 4	Employee's Withholding Allowance Certificate	W-4	Yes
DE 4P	Withholding Certificate for Pension or Annuity Payments	W-4P	Yes
DE 4S	Request for State Income Tax Withholding From Sick Pay	W-4S	Yes
DE 6	Quarterly Wage and Withholding Report	941	No
DE 7	Annual Reconciliation Statement	W-3	No
DE 166	Magnetic Media — Transmittal Sheet Quarterly and Withholding Information	4804	No
100	California Corporation Franchise or Income Tax Return	1120, 1120A, 1120F, 1120-FSC, 1120-H, 1120-POL, 1120-RIC, 1120-REIT, 990-C, Sch D (1120)	No No No No No
Sch H (100)	Dividend Income Deduction	None	N/A
Sch P (100)	Alternative Minimum Tax and Credit Limitations— Corporations	4626	No
Sch R	Apportionment and Allocation of Income	None	N/A
Sch R-7	Election to File a Taxpayers' Group Return and List of Affiliated Corporations	851	No
100-ES	Corporation Estimated Tax	1120-W	No
100S	California S Corporation Franchise or Income Tax Return	1120S	No
Sch B (100S)	S Corporation Depreciation and Amortization	None	N/A
Sch C (100S)	S Corporation Tax Credits	None	N/A
Sch D (100S)	S Corporation Capital Gains and Losses and Built-In Gains	Sch D (1120S)	No
Sch H (100S)	S Corporation Dividend Income	None	N/A
Sch K-1 (100S)	Shareholder's Share of Income, Deductions, Credits, etc.	Sch K-1 (1120S)	No
100X	Amended Corporation Franchise or Income Tax Return	1120X	No
100-WE	Water's-Edge Contract	None	N/A
FTB 1116	Notice of Nonrenewal of Water's-Edge Contract	None	N/A
FTB 1117	Request to Terminate Water's-Edge Election	None	N/A
FTB 2416	Retained Earnings of Controlled Foreign Corporations	None	N/A
FTB 2424	Water's-Edge Foreign Investment Interest Offset	None	N/A
FTB 2426	Water's-Edge Cover Sheet	None	N/A

CALIFORNIA FORM NUMBER	TITLE OR DESCRIPTION OF CALIFORNIA FORMS	COMPARABLE FEDERAL FORM	FED. FORM MAY BE USED See *Explanation of Notes
FTB 3560	S Corporation Election or Termination/Revocation	2553	No
FTB 3565	Small Business Stock Questionnaire	None	N/A
FTB 3830	S Corporation's List of Shareholders and Consents	None	N/A
FTB 3885	Corporation Depreciation and Amortization	4562	No
109	California Exempt Organization Business Income Tax Return	990-T	No
199	California Exempt Organization Annual Information Return	990, 990EZ, 990-PF, Sch A (990)	No No
540	California Resident Income Tax Return—Individuals	1040	No
540 "Scannable"	California Resident Income Tax Return—Individuals	1040PC	No
Sch CA (540)	California Adjustments— Residents	None	N/A
Sch D (540)	California Capital Gain or Loss Adjustment	Sch D (1040)	No
Sch D-1	Sales of Business Property	4797	No
Sch G-1	Tax on Lump-Sum Distributions	4972	No
Sch P (540)	Alternative Minimum Tax and Credit Limitations—Residents	6251	No
Sch S	Other State Tax Credit	None	N/A
FTB 3885A	Depreciation and Amortization Adjustments—Individuals	4562	No
540A	California Resident Income Tax Return—Individuals	1040A	No
540A "Scannable"	California Resident Income Tax Return—Individuals	None	N/A
540-ES	Estimated Tax for Individuals	1040-ES	No
540-ES "Scannable"	Estimated Tax for Individuals	None	N/A
540EZ	California Resident Income Tax Return For Single and Joint Filers With No Dependents	1040EZ	No
540 2EZ	California Resident Income Tax Return	None	N/A
540NR	California Nonresident or Part-Year Resident Income Tax Return—Individuals	1040, 1040A, 1040NR, 1040NR-EZ	No
540TEL	California TeleFile Tax Record	TeleFile Tax Record	No
Sch CA (540NR)	California Adjustments— Nonresidents or Part-Year Residents	None	N/A
Sch P (540NR)	Alternative Minimum Tax and Credit Limitations— Nonresidents or Part-Year Residents	6251	No
540X	Amended Individual Income Tax Return	1040X	No
541	California Fiduciary Income Tax Return	1041	No
Sch D (541)	Capital Gain and Loss	Sch D (1041)	No

CALIFORNIA FORM NUMBER	TITLE OR DESCRIPTION OF CALIFORNIA FORMS	COMPARABLE FEDERAL FORM	FED. FORM MAY BE USED See *Explanation of Notes
Sch J (541)	Trust Allocation of an Accumulation Distribution	Sch J (1041)	No
Sch K-1 (541)	Beneficiary's Share of Income, Deductions, Credits, etc.	Sch K-1 (1041)	No
Sch P (541)	Alternative Minimum Tax and Credit Limitations—Fiduciaries	Sch I (1041)	No
541-A	Trust Accumulation of Charitable Amounts	1041-A	No
541-B	Charitable Remainder and Pooled Income Trusts	5227	No
FTB 3885F	Depreciation and Amortization—Fiduciairies	4562	No
541-ES	Estimated Tax for Fiduciaries	1041-ES	No
541-ES "Scannable"	Estimated Tax for Fiduciaries	None	N/A
541-QFT	California Income Tax Return for Qualified Funeral Trusts	1041-QFT	No
541-T	California Allocation of Estimated Tax Payments to Beneficiaries	1041-T	No
565	Partnership Return of Income	1065	No
Sch D (565)	Capital Gain or Loss	Sch D (1065)	No
Sch K-1 (565)	Partner's Share of Income, Deductions, Credits, etc.	Sch K-1 (1065)	No
FTB 3885P	Depreciation and Amortization—Partnerships	4562	No
568	Limited Liability Company Return of Income	None	N/A
Sch D (568)	Capital Gain or Loss	1065	No
Sch K-1 (568)	Member's Share of Income, Deductions, Credits, etc.	Sch K-1 (1065)	No
FTB 3832	Limited Liability Company's List of Members and Consents	None	N/A
FTB 3885L	Depreciation and Amortization—Limited Liability Companies	4562	No
570	Nonadmitted Insurance Tax Return	None	N/A
587	Nonresident Withholding Allocation Worksheet	None	N/A
588	Nonresident Withholding Waiver Request	None	N/A
590	Withholding Exemption Certificate	1078	No
590-P	Nonresident Withholding Exemption Certificate for Previously Reported Income of Partners and Members	None	N/A
592	Nonresident Withholding Annual Return	1042, 8804	No
592-A	Nonresident Withholding Remittance Statement	8813	No
592-B	Nonresident Withholding Tax Statement	1042S, 8805	No

CALIFORNIA FORM NUMBER	TITLE OR DESCRIPTION OF CALIFORNIA FORMS	COMPARABLE FEDERAL FORM	FED. FORM MAY BE USED See *Explanation of Notes
597	Nonresident Withholding Tax Statement for Real Estate Sales	8288, 8288-A	No
597-E	Nonresident Withholding Exchange Affidavit	None	N/A
597-I	Nonresident Withholding Installment Sale Agreement	None	N/A
597-W	Withholding Exemption Certificate and Nonresident Waiver Request for Real Estate Sales	8288-B	No
FTB 3500	Exemption Application	1023, 1024	No
FTB 3501	Employer Child Care Program/ Contribution Credit	None	N/A
FTB 3507	Prison Inmate Labor Credit	None	N/A
FTB 3509	Political or Legislative Activities by Section 23701d Organizations	None	N/A
FTB 3510	Credit for Prior Year Alternative Minimum Tax— Individuals or Fiduciaries	8801	No
FTB 3516 (Side 1)	Request for Copy of Personal Income Tax or Fiduciary Return	4506	No
FTB 3516 (Side 2)	Request for Copy of Bank & Corporation or Partnership Return	4506	No
FTB 3519	Payment Voucher for Automatic Extension for Individuals	None	N/A
FTB 3519 "Scannable"	Payment Voucher for Automatic Extension for Individuals	None	N/A
FTB 3520	Power of Attorney	2848	No
FTB 3521	Low-Income Housing Credit	8586	No
FTB 3522	Limited Liability Company Tax Voucher	None	N/A
FTB 3523	Research Credit	6765	No
FTB 3525	Substitute for Form W-2, Wage and Tax Statement, or Form 1099-R, Distributions From Pensions, Annuities, Retirement, or Profit-Sharing Plans, IRAs, Insurance Contracts, Etc.	4852	No
FTB 3526	Investment Interest Expense Deduction	4952	No
FTB 3533	Change of Address	8822	No
FTB 3535	Manufacturers' Investment Credit	None	N/A
FTB 3537	Payment Voucher for Automatic Extension for Limited Liability Companies	None	N/A

CALIFORNIA FORM NUMBER	TITLE OR DESCRIPTION OF CALIFORNIA FORMS	COMPARABLE FEDERAL FORM	FED. FORM MAY BE USED See *Explanation of Notes
FTB 3538	Payment Voucher for Automatic Extension for Limited Partnerships, LLPs, and REMICs	None	N/A
FTB 3539	Payment Voucher for Automatic Extension for Corporations and Exempt Organizations	None	N/A
FTB 3540	Credit Carryover Summary	None	N/A
FTB 3546	Enhanced Oil Recovery Credit	8830	No
FTB 3547	Donated Agricultural Products Transportation Credit	None	N/A
FTB 3548	Disabled Access Credit for Eligible Small Businesses	8826	No
FTB 3553	Enterprise Zone Employee Credit	None	N/A
FTB 3555	Request for Tax Clearance Certificate—Corporations	None	N/A
3555A	Request for Tax Clearance Certificate—Exempt Organizations	None	N/A
FTB 3555L	Request for Tax Clearance Certificate—Limited Liability Company	None	N/A
FTB 3555W	Request for Corporation Dissolution and Waiver Certificate	None	N/A
FTB 3557	Application for Certificate of Revivor	None	N/A
FTB 3561	Financial Statement— Individuals	433-D	No
FTB 3563	Payment Voucher for Automatic Extension for Fiduciaries	None	N/A
FTB 3563 "Scannable"	Payment Voucher for Automatic Extension for Fiduciaries	None	N/A
FTB 3567	Installment Agreement Request	9465	No
FTB 3570	Waiver Extending Statute of Limitations	872	No
FTB 3571	Request for Estate Income Tax Certificate	None	N/A
FTB 3574	Special Election for Business Trusts and Certain Foreign Single Member LLCs	None	N/A
FTB 3580	Application to Amortize Certified Pollution Control Facility	None	N/A
FTB 3582	Payment Voucher for Electronically Transmitted Returns	None	N/A
FTB 3582 "Scannable"	Payment Voucher for Electronically Transmitted Returns	None	N/A
FTB 3583	California TeleFile Payment Voucher	None	N/A

CALIFORNIA FORM NUMBER	TITLE OR DESCRIPTION OF CALIFORNIA FORMS	COMPARABLE FEDERAL FORM	FED. FORM MAY BE USED See *Explanation of Notes
FTB 3595	Special Handling Required	None	N/A
FTB 3601	Transmittal of Information Returns Reported on Magnetic Media	4804	No
FTB 3602	Transmittal of Annual 1099-MISC, Information for Tax Year _____	4804	No
FTB 3800	Tax Computation for Children Under Age 14 with Investment Income	8615	No
FTB 3801	Passive Activity Loss Limitations	8582	No
FTB 3801-CR	Passive Activity Credit Limitations	8582-CR	No
FTB 3802	Corporate Passive Activity Loss and Credit Limitations	8810	No
FTB 3803	Parent's Election to Report Child's Interest and Dividends	8814	No
FTB 3805A	Information to Support Exemption Claimed for Dependent	None	N/A
FTB 3805E	Installment Sale Income	6252	No
FTB 3805P	Additional Taxes Attributable to IRAs, Qualified Retirement Plans, Annuities, Modified Endowment Contracts, and MSAs	5329	No
FTB 3805Q	Net Operating Loss (NOL) Computation and NOL and Disaster Loss Limitations— Corporations	3621	No
FTB 3805V	Net Operating Loss (NOL) Computation and NOL and Disaster Loss Limitations— Individuals, Estates, and Trusts	Sch A (1045)	No
FTB 3805Z	Enterprise Zone Deduction and Credit Summary	None	N/A
FTB 3806	Los Angeles Revitalization Zone Deduction and Credit Summary	None	N/A
FTB 3807	Local Agency Military Base Recovery Area Deduction and Credit Summary	None	N/A
FTB 3808	Manufacturing Enhancement Area Credit Summary	None	N/A
FTB 3809	Targeted Tax Area Deduction and Credit Summary	None	N/A
FTB 3834	Interest Computation Under the Look-Back Method for Completed Long-Term Contracts	8697	No
FTB 3860	Financial Condition Statement—Individuals	None	N/A
FTB 3861	Financial Condition Statement—Corporations	None	N/A

CALIFORNIA FORM NUMBER	TITLE OR DESCRIPTION OF CALIFORNIA FORMS	COMPARABLE FEDERAL FORM	FED. FORM MAY BE USED See *Explanation of Notes
FTB 4012	Publications Price List	None	N/A
FTB 4092	Magnetic Tape Filing Application—1099 Information	4419	Yes
FTB 5805	Underpayment of Estimated Tax by Individuals and Fiduciaries	2210	No
FTB 5805F	Underpayment of Estimated Tax by Farmers and Fishermen	2210F	No
FTB 5806	Underpayment of Estimated Tax by Corporations	2220	No
FTB 5870A	Tax on Accumulation Distribution of Trusts	4970	No
8453	California Individual Income Tax Declaration for Electronic Filing	8453	No
FTB 8633	California Application to Participate in the e-File Program	8633	No
9000	Homeowner Assistance Claim	None	N/A
9000R	Renter Assistance Claim	None	N/A
9110	Rental Income	None	N/A

State of California — Franchise Tax Board   FTB Pub. 1006
FEDERAL TAX FORMS AND RELATED CALIFORNIA FORMS

FEDERAL FORM NUMBER	TITLE OR DESCRIPTION OF FEDERAL FORMS	COMPARABLE CALIFORNIA FORM	FED. FORM MAY BE USED See *Explanation of Notes
SS-4	Application for Employer Identification Number	DE 1	No**
T (Timber)	Forest Industries Schedules	None	Yes
W-2	Wage and Tax Statement	None	Yes
W-3	Transmittal of Wage and Tax Statements	DE 7	No
W-4	Employee's Withholding Allowance Certificate	DE 4	Yes
W-4P	Withholding Certificate for Pension or Annuity Payments	DE 4P	Yes
W-4S	Request for Federal Income Tax Withholding From Sick Pay	DE 4S	Yes
W-9	Request for Taxpayer Identification Number and Certification	None	Yes
56	Notice Concerning Fiduciary Relationship	None	Yes
433-D	Installment Agreement	FTB 3561	No
851	Affiliations Schedule	Sch R-7 (100)	No
872	Consent to Extend the Time to Assess Tax	FTB 3570	No
875	Acceptance of Examiner's Findings By a Partnership, Fiduciary, S Corporation, or Interest Charge Domestic International Sales Corporation	None	Yes
907	Agreement to Extend the Time to Bring Suit	None	Yes
926	Return by a U.S. Transferor of Property to a Foreign Corporation, Foreign Estate or Trust, or Foreign Partnership	None	Yes
941	Employer's Quarterly Federal Tax Return	DE 6	No
966	Corporate Dissolution or Liquidation	None	Yes
970	Application to Use LIFO Inventory Method	None	Yes
982	Reduction of Tax Attributes Due to Discharge of Indebtedness (and Section 1082 Basis Adjustment)	None	Yes
990	Return of Organization Exempt from Income Tax	199	No
990 (Sch A)	Organization Exempt Under (Section 501(c)(3))	199	No
990-C	Farmers' Cooperative Association Income Tax Return	100	No
990EZ	Short Form Return of Organization Exempt From Income Tax	199	No

FEDERAL FORM NUMBER	TITLE OR DESCRIPTION OF FEDERAL FORMS	COMPARABLE CALIFORNIA FORM	FED. FORM MAY BE USED See *Explanation of Notes
900-PF	Return of Private Foundation or Section 4947(a)(1) Nonexempt Charitable Trust Treated As a Private Foundation	199	No
990-T	Exempt Organization Business Income Tax Return	109	No
1023	Application for Recognition of Exemption Under Section 501(c)(3) of the Internal Revenue Code	FTB 3500	No
1024	Application for Recognition of Exemption Under Section 501(a) of the Internal Revenue Code	FTB 3500	No
1040	U.S. Individual Income Tax Return	540	No
Sch A (1040)	Itemized Deductions	None	Yes
Sch B (1040)	Interest and Dividend Income	None	Yes
Sch C (1040)	Profit or Loss From Business	None	Yes
Sch C-EZ (1040)	Net Profit From Business	None	Yes
Sch D (1040)	Capital Gains and Losses	Sch D (540)	No
Sch E (1040)	Supplemental Income and Loss	None	Yes
Sch F (1040)	Profit or Loss From Farming	None	Yes
Sch R (1040)	Credit for the Elderly or the Disabled	N/A	N/A
1040A	U.S. Individual Income Tax Return	540A	No
1040-ES	Estimated Tax for Individuals	540-ES	No
1040EZ	Income Tax Return for Single and Joint Filers With No Dependents	540EZ	No
None	TeleFile Tax Record	540 TEL	No
1040NR	U.S. Nonresident Alien Income Tax Return	540NR	No
1040NR-EZ	U.S. Income Tax Return for Certain Nonresident Aliens With No Dependents	540NR	No
1040-V	Return Payment Voucher for Individuals	None	N/A
1040X	Amended U.S. Individual Income Tax Return	540X	No
1041	U.S. Income Tax Return for Estates and Trusts	541	No
Sch D (1041)	Capital Gains and Losses	Sch D (541)	No
Sch I (1041)	Alternative Minimum Tax— Fiduciaries	Sch P (541)	No
Sch J (1041)	Accumulation Distribution for a Complex Trust	Sch J (541)	No
Sch K-1 (1041)	Beneficiary's Share of Income, Deductions, Credits, etc.	Sch K-1 (541)	No
1041-ES	Estimated Income Tax For Estates and Trusts	541-ES	No
1041-A	U.S. Information Return on Trust Accumulation of Charitable Amounts	541-A	No
1041-T	Allocation of Estimated Tax Payments to Beneficiaries	541-T	No

FEDERAL FORM NUMBER	TITLE OR DESCRIPTION OF FEDERAL FORMS	COMPARABLE CALIFORNIA FORM	FED. FORM MAY BE USED See *Explanation of Notes
1041-QFT	U.S. Income Tax Return for Qualified Funeral Trusts	541-QFT	No
1042	Annual Withholding Tax Return for U.S. Source Income of Foreign Persons	592	No
1042S	Foreign Person's U.S. Source Income Subject to Withholding	592-B	No
1065	U.S. Partnership Return of Income	565	No
Sch D (1065)	Capital Gains and Losses	Sch D (565)	No
Sch K-1 (1065)	Partner's Share of Income, Credits, Deductions, etc.	Sch K-1 (565)	No
1078	Certificate of Alien Claiming Residence in the United States	590	No
1096	Annual Summary and Transmittal of U.S. Information Returns	None	Yes 1
1098	Mortgage Interest Statement	None	Yes
1099-A	Acquisition of Abandonment of Secured Property	None	Yes
1099-B	Proceeds From Broker and Barter Exchange Transactions	None	Yes
1099-C	Cancellation of Debt	None	Yes
1099-DIV	Dividends and Distributions	None	Yes
1099-G	Certain Government Payments	None	Yes
1099-INT	Interest Income	None	Yes
1099-LTC	Long-Term Care and Accelerated Death Benefits	None	Yes
1099-MISC	Miscellaneous Income	None	Yes
1099-MSA	Distribution From Medical Savings Account	None	Yes
1099-OID	Original Issue Discount	None	Yes
1099-PATR	Taxable Distributions Received From Cooperatives	None	Yes
1099-R	Distributions From Pensions, Annuities, Retirement or Profit-Sharing Plans, IRAs, Insurance Contracts, etc.	None	Yes
1120	U.S. Corporation Income Tax Return	100	No
Sch D (1020)	Capital Gains and Losses	100	No
1120-A	U.S. Corporation Short-Form Income Tax Return	100	No
1120F	U.S. Income Tax Return of Foreign Corporation	100	No
1120-FSC	U.S. Income Tax Return of Foreign Sales Corporation	100	No
1120-H	U.S. Income Tax Return for Homeowners Associations	100	No
1120-POL	U.S. Income Tax Return for Certain Political Organizations	100	No
1120-REIT	U.S. Income Tax Return for Real Estate Investment Trusts	100	No
1120-RIC	U.S. Income Tax Return for Regulated Investment Companies	100	No

FEDERAL FORM NUMBER	TITLE OR DESCRIPTION OF FEDERAL FORMS	COMPARABLE CALIFORNIA FORM	FED. FORM MAY BE USED See *Explanation of Notes
1120S	U.S. Income Tax Return for an S Corporation	100S	No
Sch D (1120S)	Capital Gains and Losses and Built-In Gains	Sch D (100S)	No
Sch K-1 (1120S)	Shareholder's Share of Income, Credits, Deductions, etc.	Sch K-1 (100S)	No
1120-W	Estimated Income Tax for Corporations	100-ES	No
1120X	Amended U.S. Corporation Income Tax Return	100X	No
1128	Application to Adopt, Change, or Retain a Tax Year	None	Yes
1310	Statement of Person Claiming Refund Due a Deceased Taxpayer	None	Yes
2106	Employee Business Expense	None	Yes
2106-EZ	Unreimbursed Employee Business Expenses	None	Yes
2120	Multiple Support Declaration	None	Yes
2210	Underpayment of Estimated Tax by Individuals, Estates and Trusts	FTB 5805	No
2210F	Underpayment of Estimated Tax by Farmers and Fishermen	FTB 5805F	No
2220	Underpayment of Estimated Tax by Corporations	FTB 5806	No
2350	Application for Extension of Time to File U.S. Income Tax Return	N/A	N/A
2441	Child and Dependent Care Expenses	None	No
2553	Election By a Small Business Corporation	FTB 3560	Yes
2678	Employer Appointment of Agent	None	Yes
2688	Application for Additional Extension of Time to File U.S. Individual Income Tax Return	N/A	N/A
2758	Application for Extension of Time to File Certain Excise, Income, Information, and Other Returns	N/A	N/A
2848	Power of Attorney and Declaration of Representative	FTB 3520	No
3115	Application for Change in Accounting Method	None	Yes
3468	Investment Credit	N/A	N/A
3621	Net Operating Loss Computation—Individuals, Corporations, and Estates and Trusts	FTB 3805Q, FTB 3805V	No
3903	Moving Expenses	None	Yes
4070	Employee's Report of Tips to Employer	None	Yes
4137	Social Security and Medicare Tax on Unreported Tip Income	N/A	N/A
4255	Recapture of Investment Credit	N/A	N/A
4419	Application for Filing Information Returns Magnetically/ Electronically	FTB 4092	Yes

FEDERAL FORM NUMBER	TITLE OR DESCRIPTION OF FEDERAL FORMS	COMPARABLE CALIFORNIA FORM	FED. FORM MAY BE USED See *Explanation of Notes
4461	Application for Approval of Master or Prototype and Regional Prototype Contribution Plan	None	Yes
4466	Corporation Application for Quick Refund of Overpayment of Estimated Tax	N/A	N/A
4506	Request for Copy of Tax Form	FTB 3516	No
4562	Depreciation and Amortization	FTB 3885, FTB 3885A, FTB 3885F, FTB 3885L, FTB 3885P	No No No No No
4571	Explanation for Filing Return Late or Paying Tax Late	None	N/A
4626	Alternative Minimum Tax—Corporations	Sch P (100)	No
4669	Employee Wage Statement	None	Yes
4670	Request for Relief from Payment of Income Tax Withholding	None	Yes
4684	Casualties and Thefts	None	Yes
4797	Sales of Business Property	Sch D-1	No
4804	Transmittal of Information Returns Reported Magnetically/Electronically	FTB 3601, FTB 3602, DE 166	No
4835	Farm Rental Income and Expenses	None	Yes
4852	Substitute for Form W-2, Wage and Tax Statement or Form W-2P, Statement for Recipients of Annuities, Pensions, Retired Pay or IRA Payments	FTB 3525	No
4868	Application for Automatic Extension of Time to File U.S. Individual Income Tax Return	N/A	N/A
4952	Investment Interest Expense Deduction	FTB 3526	No
4970	Tax on Accumulation Distribution of Trusts	FTB 5870A	No
4972	Tax on Lump-Sum Distributions	Sch G-1	No
5227	Split-Interest Trust Information Return	541-B	No
5329	Additional Taxes Attributable to IRAs, Other Qualified Retirement Plans, Annuities, Modified Endowment Contracts and MSAs	FTB 3805P	No
5471	Information Return of U.S. Persons With Respect to Certain Foreign Corporations	None	Yes
5472	Information Return of a 25% Foreign-Owned U.S. Corporation or a Foreign Corporation Engaged in a U.S. Trade or Business	None	Yes
5498	Individual Retirement Arrangement Information	None	Yes

FEDERAL FORM NUMBER	TITLE OR DESCRIPTION OF FEDERAL FORMS	COMPARABLE CALIFORNIA FORM	FED. FORM MAY BE USED See *Explanation of Notes
5500-C/R	Return/Report of Employee Benefit Plan	N/A	N/A
5754	Statement by Person(s) Receiving Gambling Winnings	None	Yes
5884	Jobs Credit	None	No
6198	At-Risk Limitations	None	Yes
6251	Alternative Minimum Tax— Individuals	Sch P (540), Sch P (540NR)	No No
6252	Installment Sale Income	FTB 3805E	No
6765	Credit for Increasing Research Activities	FTB 3523	No
7004	Application for Automatic Extension of Time to File Corporation Income Tax Return	N/A	N/A
8023	Elections Under Sec. 338 for Corporations Making Qualified Stock Purchases	None	Yes
8275	Disclosure Statement	None	Yes
8275-R	Regulation Disclosure Statement	None	Yes
8288	U.S. Withholding Tax Return for Dispositions by Foreign Persons of U.S. Real Property Interests	597	No
8288-A	Statement of Withholding on Dispositions by Foreign Persons of U.S. Real Property Interests	597	No
8288-B	Application for Withholding Certificate for Dispositions by Foreign Persons of U.S. Real Property Interests	597-W	No
8300	Report of Cash Payments Over $10,000 Received in a Trade or Business	None	Yes
8453	U.S. Individual Income Tax Declaration for Electronic Filing	FTB 8453	No
8582	Passive Activity Loss Limitations	FTB 3801	No
8582-CR	Passive Activity Credit Limitations	FTB 3801-CR	No
8586	Low-Income Housing Credit	FTB 3521	No
8615	Tax for Children Under Age 14 Who Have Investment Income of More than $1,300	FTB 3800	No
8697	Interest Computation Under the Look-Back Method for Completed Long-Term Contracts	FTB 3834	No
8736	Application for Automatic Extension of Time to File Return for a U.S. Partnership, REMIC, or for Certain Trusts	N/A	N/A
8801	Credit for Prior Year Minimum Tax—Individuals, Estates and Trusts	FTB 3510	No
8804	Annual Return for Partnership Withholding Tax (Section 1446)	592	No
8805	Foreign Partner's Information Statement of Section 1446 Withholding Tax	592-B	No

FEDERAL FORM NUMBER	TITLE OR DESCRIPTION OF FEDERAL FORMS	COMPARABLE CALIFORNIA FORM	FED. FORM MAY BE USED See *Explanation of Notes
8810	Corporate Passive Activity Loss and Credit Limitations	FTB 3802	No
8813	Partnership Withholding Tax Payment (Section 1446)	592-A	No
8814	Parent's Election To Report Child's Interest and Dividends	FTB 3803	No
8822	Change of Address	FTB 3533	No
8824	Like-Kind Exchanges	None	Yes
8826	Disabled Access Credit	FTB 3548	No
8827	Credit for Prior Year Minimum Tax—Corporations	Sch P (100), Part III	No
8830	Enhanced Oil Recovery Credit	FTB 3546	No
8842	Election to Use Different Annualization Periods for Corporate Estimated Tax	None	Yes
9465	Installment Agreement Request	FTB 3567	No

*Explanation of Notes

No   Comparable California form must be used.

****   Form number may vary based on industry specific registration.

Yes   If there is no difference between California and federal amounts, you may use a copy of the federal form. If there is a difference between California and federal amounts, use the related California form. If there is no related California form, complete the federal form using California amounts and attach it to your California tax return.

N/A   Federal form is not applicable to California tax or California form is not applicable for federal tax.

Yes[1]   Copies of paper information returns (1099 series, 1098, and 5498) filed with the Internal Revenue Service are not required to be filed with the Franchise Tax Board (FTB). However, if federal and California amounts differ, information returns may be attached to Form 1096 and filed with FTB.

When to attach a copy of a complete federal return to the California return.

Form 540A, Form 540EZ and Form 540 2EZ: Do not attach the federal tax return.

Form 540: Attach a copy of the complete federal return when federal forms and schedules other than Schedule A or Schedule B are attached to the federal return.

Form 540NR: Always attach a copy of the complete federal return. (The FTB will accept Form 1040PC as the federal return attachment.)

INDEX

References are to paragraph (¶) numbers.

700